Human Behavior in the Macro Social Environment

An Empowerment Approach to Understanding
Communities, Organizations, and Groups

THIRD EDITION

Karen K. Kirst-Ashman
University of Wisconsin – Whitewater

BROOKS/COLE
CENGAGE Learning

Australia • Brazil • Canada • Mexico • Singapore • Spain
United Kingdom • United States

BROOKS/COLE
CENGAGE Learning™

Human Behavior in the Macro Social Environment: An Empowerment Approach to Understanding Communities, Organizations, and Groups
Third Edition
Karen K. Kirst-Ashman

Executive Editor: Schreiber-Ganster

Acquisitions Editor: Seth Dobrin

Developmental Editor: Robert Jucha

Assistant Editor: Arwen Petty

Editorial Assistant: Rachel McDonald

Media Editor: Dennis Fitzgerald

Marketing Manager: Trent Whatcott

Marketing Assistant: Darlene Macanan

Marketing Communications
    Manager: Tami Strang

Content Project Manager: Michelle Cole

Creative Director: Rob Hugel

Art Director: Caryl Gorska

Print Buyer: Linda Hsu

Rights Acquisitions Account
    Manager, Text: Roberta Broyer

Rights Acquisitions Account Manager,
    Image: Leitha Etheridge-Sims

Production Service: Christian Holdener,
    S4Carlisle Publishing Services

Photo Researcher: Bill Smith Group

Copy Editor: Kristen Balyati

Cover Designer: Lisa Langhoff

Cover Image: Bruce Dale

Compositor: S4Carlisle Publishing Services

For product information and technology assistance, contact us
at **Cengage Learning Customer & Sales Support,
1-800-354-9706.**

For permission to use material from this text or product, submit
all requests online at **www.cengage.com/permissions.**
Further permissions questions can be e-mailed to
permissionrequest@cengage.com.

Library of Congress Control Number: 2009943345
ISBN-13: 978-0-495-81365-1
ISBN-10: 0-495-81365-6

Brooks/Cole
20 Davis Drive
Belmont, CA 94002-3098
USA

Cengage Learning is a leading provider of customized learning solutions with office locations around the globe, including Singapore, the United Kingdom, Australia, Mexico, Brazil, and Japan. Locate your local office at **www.cengage.com/global.**

Cengage Learning products are represented in Canada by Nelson Education, Ltd.

To learn more about Brooks/Cole, visit
www.cengage.com/brookscole

Purchase any of our products at your local college store or at our preferred online store **www.CengageBrain.com.**

Printed in the United States of America
1 2 3 4 5 6 7 14 13 12 11 10

To Mabel F. Scholtka, my beloved aunt who provides incredible inspiration for everyone around her.

Brief Contents

Contents

CHAPTER 8 **Human Behavior, Management, and Empowerment in Organizations   224**

CHAPTER 10 **Assessment of Geographic Communities and Empowerment   301**

CHAPTER 12   **Diversity, Populations-at-Risk, and Empowerment
in the Macro Social Environment   366**

Preface

Focusing on empowerment and stressing critical thinking, this book explores human behavior in task groups, organizations, and communities. The intent is to provide a sound knowledge base for understanding how the macro social environment works and make it easier for students to apply theory in subsequent practice courses. Theories and major concepts concerning communities, organizations, and groups are explained. A strengths perspective, empowerment, and resiliency are underlying themes throughout the book. Applications of how macro systems operate and impact human behavior are examined. Critical thinking questions are posed throughout to stimulate students' understanding of content and exploration of issues. Professional ethics are emphasized throughout in new *Focus on Ethics* segments. A new chapter on values and principles that guide generalist practice in the macro social environment has been added. Human diversity is consistently emphasized and highlighted. Note that the title has been modified to reflect more accurately the book's subject matter and target audience. Content reflects the Council on Social Work Education's (CSWE) 2008 Educational Policy and Accreditation Standards (EPAS) requirements. A chapter on social justice and the global community stresses the need to advocate for social and economic justice and human rights at the international level.

Numerous case examples are presented of how communities, organizations, and groups can enhance people's optimal health, well-being, and quality of life. These include how macro systems affect the lives and behavior of people of color, women, lesbian and gay people, people in spiritual communities, older adults, and people with developmental disabilities.

A major concern in social work education today is the strong tendency for students to veer away from thinking about how communities and organizations affect human behavior. Instead, students are frequently drawn to the perceived psychological drama and intensity of more clinically oriented practice with individuals, families, and treatment groups. This book relates content about the macro social environment directly to generalist social work practice. Applications of content to practice settings are integrated throughout. Students should clearly understand why a macro focus is a necessity in practice, in addition to their acquisition of micro and mezzo skills.

This book is especially written for undergraduate and graduate courses in human behavior and the social environment (HBSE) that incorporate content on communities, organizations, and task groups. It can be used independently to teach human behavior in the social environment content (HBSE) from a macro perspective, or in conjunction with other textbooks such as *Understanding Human Behavior and the Social Environment* (Zastrow & Kirst-Ashman, 2010) that include content on biological, social, cultural, psychological, and spiritual development throughout the life course. The intent here is to emphasize the dynamic interaction among systems in the macro social environment and provide breadth and depth of insight into the functioning of communities, organizations, and task groups.

As already noted, the book is written to comply with CSWE's 2008 EPAS, which requires that the following content be covered (CSWE, 2008):

- The range of social systems in which individuals live (community, organizational, group, family, and individual) (EP 2.1.7)
- Ways social systems promote or deter people in maintaining or achieving optimal health and well-being (Purpose, EP 2.1.7)
- Empirically based theories and knowledge that focus on the interactions between and among individuals, groups, societies, and economic systems as a foundation for understanding "person and environment" (EP 2.1.7)
- The assessment of client system "strengths and limitations" (EP 2.1.10[b]), the interpretation of relevant data (EP 2.1.7), and the appraisal of "emerging societal trends" (EP 2.1.9)
- Emphasis on the respect for all people, recognition of personal values, and the application of professional ethics (EP 1.1, 2.1.2)
- Use of critical thinking to analyze and assess a wide range of issues (EP 2.1.3)
- Promotion of respect for diversity by emphasizing the intersectionality of a broad range of diverse human groups and attributes (EP 2.1.4)
- The advancement of and advocacy for human rights, and social and economic justice (EP 2.1.5, B2.2)
- A global perspective (Purpose, EP 2.1.5) exploring "the forms and mechanisms of oppression and discrimination" (EP 2.1.5) and the resulting need for advocacy to "enhance the quality of life for all persons" (Purpose)

A major thrust of this text is to present the material in a readable, interesting fashion. It uses numerous case applications and jargon-free language so that the reader can readily grasp theory and concepts. The three adjectives the author hopes best describe this text are *relevant*, *practical*, and *readable*. The macro social environment and the social forces acting upon it are clearly defined. Theory and major concepts are presented in a straightforward and thought-provoking manner. Applications to actual macro practice situations are emphasized throughout, as is the importance of client system empowerment. Concepts that students can readily understand, such as power, leadership, and interpersonal dynamics in macro settings, are stressed to enhance students' ability to grasp their relevance and practical significance.

In summary, the overall intent is to provide a dynamic, interesting, and relevant social work perspective on human behavior in the macro social environment. The author strives to enhance students' understanding of social work values, develop their ability to empathize with people's situations and conditions in the macro environment, critically think about issues, and help them focus on the need for macro change in local, organizational, neighborhood, community, and global contexts. Students should be able to relate these values and this knowledge to how social workers make assessments in real practice situations. They should have a glimpse into the vivid and fascinating macro environment in which social workers practice.

New Additions

New to this edition are the addition and elaboration of critical thinking questions. A new chapter on values and principles that guide generalist practice in the macro social environment has been added. New *Focus on Ethics* segments that explore various aspects of how professional ethics apply to issues in the macro social environment are integrated throughout. Concept summaries have been included to elucidate theory and other complicated topics. New content, including the new Chapter 2 concerning values and principles, complies with the 2008 Educational Policy and Accreditation Standards (EPAS). Specific content has been added in the following respective chapters:

Chapter 1

- Expansion of the concepts involved in understanding the meaning of *macro social environment*
- Expansion of the definition of *generalist practice* in compliance with 2008 educational policy
- New content on research-informed practice
- The ecological concepts of habitat and niche
- Update on macro practice approaches versus traditional community organization

Chapter 2

- The importance of identification with the social work profession
- New content on professional values and ethics, human diversity, and advocacy for human rights and the pursuit of social and economic justice
- Discussion of new concepts including: the intersectionality of factors involved in human diversity; human rights; power, privilege, and acclaim; and marginalization and alienation
- Ethical topics including discussion of the National Association of Social Workers *Code of Ethics*, ethical dilemmas occurring in the macro social environment, and the support of human rights in the United States

Chapter 3

- Updated content on feminist theories
- Leader-centered versus group-centered leadership
- The ethical issue of confidentiality in groups in the macro social environment

Chapter 4

- Staff development groups
- Functions of an effective board of directors
- The ethical issue of how to handle negative feelings in task groups

Chapter 5

- The dynamics of gender-based power in organizations
- Expansion of recommendations to organizations regarding the application of feminist principles
- Political-economy theory and the institutional perspective

Chapter 6

- Faith-based social services
- Managed care's means of controlling costs, the future of managed care, and problems with access to adequate health care

Chapter 7

- Supervision and consultation in organizational settings
- Focus on the ethics of political behavior in organizations

Chapter 8

- Updated content on total quality management, including the concept of continuous improvement

Chapter 9

- Focus on the ethical issues concerning the functionalist perspective on homelessness, corporate accountability for production, and dual relationships in rural communities

Chapter 10

- President Barack Obama's experience in community organizing and community building
- Examples of community building in rural areas, including a grant-funded comprehensive community initiative, approaches to enhancing rural youths' interest in higher education, community-supported agriculture, agritourism, and producer cooperatives
- Focus on the ethical issues of informed consent and community action, and the relationship between community building and professional ethics

Chapter 11

- Focus on the ethical issue of the dynamics involved in neighborhood segregation

Chapter 12

- The significance of the Deaf community and Deaf culture
- Empowerment of older adults
- Focus on the ethical issues of discrimination against a person with a disability and the meaning of disability

Chapter 13

- Exploration of the concept of human rights
- Immigration status
- A case example in international social work
- Revision of the definitions and concepts involved in community and social development
- The International Federation of Social Workers (IFSW) and the International Association of Schools of Social Work (IASSW) *Ethics in Social Work, Statement of Principles*
- Focus on the ethical issues of vast discrepancies in wealth and the crisis of global poverty

Supplement Package

Note that the supplements include a student workbook including dozens of classroom exercises related to the book's content. These exercises are intended to enhance students' knowledge base of human behavior in the macro social environment. This should prepare them "to guide the processes of assessment, intervention, and evaluation"; it should also provide them with opportunities to "critique and apply knowledge to understand person and environment" (Council on Social Work Education [CSWE], 2008, Educational Policy [EP] 2.1.7 ["Apply knowledge of human behavior and the social environment"]).[1] Most of the exercise objectives are intended to comply with required competencies cited in the CSWE Educational Policy and Accreditation Standards (2008). (Please note that in no way do these exercises claim to *verify* compliance with EPAS standards. Only the Council on Social Work Education Commission on Accreditation can make those determinations.) Rather, the exercises are designed to help provide potential means of measuring various competencies related to human behavior and the social environment.

Electronic Instructor's Manual: This electronic, downloadable manual contains course outlines, class discussion questions, suggested lecture topics, sample syllabi and other valuable resources for professors.

---

[1] Council on Social Work Education (CSWE). (2008). *Educational policy and accreditation standards (EPAS)*. Alexandria, VA: Author.

Electronic Test Bank: This electronic, downloadable gallery of exam questions makes compiling in-class or take-home exams simple. The Test Bank offers questions in varying formats, including True & False, Multiple Choice, and essay questions for your convenience.

Companion Website: A full website dedicated to the text. Here you can find assignable practice exam questions that you won't find in the Test Bank, as well as PowerPoint slides to accompany your lectures. Additionally, you will find a glossary of key terms, web resources, and many other learning materials to assist students and professors alike.

Chapter Learning Objectives

Also note that each chapter in the book begins with learning objectives. These are reiterated at the end of each chapter with a summary of relevant content. Exam questions available in the supplementary resources are linked to the attainment of specific chapter learning objectives. The intent is to assist in demonstrating and articulating the acquisition of knowledge and attainment of competencies identified in accreditation standards.

Acknowledgements

The author wishes to express her heartfelt appreciation to Nick Ashman, who cooked for and supported her throughout the writing process. The author also expresses indebtedness to Seth Dobrin, Acquisitions Editor, Robert Jucha, Senior Development Editor, Arwen Petty, Assistant Editor, Rachel McDonald, Editorial Assistant, and the other staff at Brooks/Cole, a part of Cengage Learning, who enthusiastically encouraged her to pursue this endeavor and provided ongoing help and support. Many thanks to Christian Holdener, Project Editor, who moved the publication process along conscientiously, efficiently, and effectively, and to Michelle Cole, Brooks/Cole Content Project Manager for her careful oversight.

The author would also like to thank the following reviewers of the second edition of this book for their help and input.

Monica M. Alzate
University of Oklahoma

Scott Bloom, LCSW
New York University

Kim Boland-Prom
Governors State University

Dr. Luther Brown
Castleton State College

Pam Clary
Missouri Western State University

Robin Cleeland
Dalton State College

Jeana Culbert
Lubbock Christian University

Carol Edwards
Florida State University

Judi Egbert
Ball State University

Mark Kaufman
Washburn University

Dr. C. G. Kledaras
Campbell University

Frances Bernard Kominkiewicz
Saint Mary's College

Jo-Ann G. Lauderdale
Siena Heights University

Faith Lucas
University of Texas, El Paso

Murali Nair
Cleveland State University

Alzena Robinson
Denmark Technical College

Marge Shirilla
Dalton State College

Introduction to Human Behavior in the Macro Social Environment

Social workers can address important social issues in the macro social environment.

CHAPTER CONTENTS

- *A social worker employed by a large public social services department hears increasing numbers of complaints from clients about drug houses popping up in their residential neighborhoods. The worker identifies clients and other concerned citizens in the communities and organizes a community meeting. She then assists community residents in formulating a plan to band together, identify drug house locations, and establish a procedure to report such houses to the authorities.*

- *The main tasks of a Foster Care Unit are to assess potential foster parent applicants, monitor placement and manage cases as they move in and out of foster care, and train foster parents in parenting and behavior management skills. The unit social workers hold bi-weekly meetings where they discuss how to improve agency service provision. The workers take turns organizing the meetings and running the discussions.*

- *A social worker employed by a neighborhood center determines that the range of workers and other professionals working with various adolescent clients within the community are not communicating with each other. For example, school social workers have no established procedure for conveying information to protective services workers who, in turn, do not communicate readily with probation and parole workers. This is despite the fact that most of these professionals are working with many of the same clients. The neighborhood-center social worker decided to pull together representatives from the various involved agencies and establish more clearly defined communication channels.*

- *A social worker employed by a large private family-services agency specializes in international adoptions, especially those involving the states in the former Soviet Union. He discovers that many of the adoptive children are experiencing health problems resulting from early nutritional deprivation. The worker feels that the problem goes beyond one or two cases, and reflects a serious pattern. No referral process is in place to automatically assess adoptive children and refer them to needed resources, including designated medical specialists. The worker begins to establish a systematic process for assessment and referral.*

- *Agency administration asks one of three social workers in a large residential health care complex for older adults to assess the effectiveness of its social services program.*

- *A social worker at a public assistance agency is terribly troubled by the conditions of the agency's waiting room for clients and by the tedious process required for clients' intakes. She explores the issue, develops a proposed plan for improvement, and makes an appointment to speak with the agency's executive director about it.*

- *A local charitable funding organization decides to cut off its funding contribution to a Planned Parenthood agency that has three satellite clinics in addition to its larger, centrally located main clinic.[1] The result would be a severe cutback in services including the closure of at least two of its satellite clinics.*

---

[1] *Planned Parenthood* agencies assist people in making decisions about pregnancy and promote birth control and contraception.

A huge number of clients would find it difficult if not impossible to receive adequate services. A social work counselor at one of the clinics, with the support of her supervisor, gathers facts to support her argument that funding is necessary and arranges a meeting with the funding organization's leaders to discuss the cuts and try to persuade these leaders to change their minds.

- *A juvenile probation officer is distressed by a proposed legislative action to delete a vocational training program for juvenile offenders because of its expense. He talks to other workers and administrators in his state agency, and gathers facts and statistics that support the program's cost-effectiveness. He then begins calling and writing involved legislators and sets up a meeting with the chairperson of the legislative committee that recommended the program's deletion. Additionally, he contacts other concerned social workers and encourages them to participate in similar activities.*

- *A group of community residents approach a social worker about starting a Neighborhood Watch program.[2] The worker provides them with both encouragement and some information about how to go about it.*

None of the vignettes just described involves direct service to clients. Yet, all are examples of social workers undertaking necessary activities as part of their daily role in providing effective service. Each scenario describes how social workers can help people within the context of larger macro environments, namely, organizations and communities. Generalist social work is much more than working with individual clients and families. It also is working in and with larger systems.

People do not function in a void. They interact dynamically on many levels, assuming structured behavior patterns and having active involvement in various interpersonal relationships. Mary Beth is a sister, a mother, an aunt, a member of Mothers Against Drunk Driving (MADD), a Republican, a member of St. Mary and St. Antonious Coptic Orthodox Church, and a dentist, all at the same time. Understanding everything about human behavior, with all its complexity, is a vast task.

The Council on Social Work Education (CSWE) that accredits social work programs requires that students "apply knowledge of human behavior and the social environment"; this includes knowledge about "the range of social systems in which people live . . . and the ways social systems promote or deter people in maintaining or achieving health and well-being" (CSWE, 2008, p. 6). The intent is to provide a foundation so that social workers can "utilize conceptual frameworks to guide the processes of assessment, intervention, and evaluation; and critique and apply knowledge to understand person and environment" (CSWE, 2008, p. 6).

Social workers practice *in agency organizational settings* to help clients *who live in communities.* The work environments of social work practitioners provide

---

[2] *Neighborhood Watch* programs involve neighborhood residents coming together and making a commitment to prevent crime in their neighborhood. They devise a system for observing any suspicious behavior, especially on the part of strangers, and for alerting the proper authorities in order to deter crime. Members also usually educate new people moving into the neighborhood about the program and publicize that the program exists via window decals and signs.

the structure and resources allowing them to help clients. A healthy organizational work environment permits social workers to function effectively and get things done for clients. An unhealthy work environment (for example, one with few resources, poor morale, or policies not supportive of clients) interferes with social workers' performance and their potential to assist clients. Clients, in turn, live in communities that enjoy various degrees of prosperity and offer their citizens diverse levels of resources, support, and safety. Social workers must understand and negotiate the mazes of these macro environments in order to do their jobs effectively.

This book focuses on understanding human behavior in the *macro* social environment. How do communities, organizations, and groups serve as the background for human behavior? How do individuals and macro systems reciprocally influence each other? How do these organizations and communities operate to keep themselves and society going? What are the internal environment of communities, organizations, and the groups within them like? Exactly how and why do the answers to these questions affect how social workers can do their jobs?

Several terms reflect the meaning of *macro*, including: large scale; affecting many people; emphasis on social, political, and economic forces; and a focus on community. It is social workers' responsibility to seek changes in the macro social environment that improve services, increase resources for clients and citizens, and change policies to implement improvements. This contrasts with a *micro* perspective, which emphasizes the actions and personal issues of individual clients. Micro practice skills focus on treatment of individuals that helps them solve their problems.

Communities, organizations, and the task groups functioning within them are important in understanding human behavior because they consist of individuals. Comprehending the nuances of behavior involves not only the psychological makeup of individuals and the interpersonal dynamics of intimate relationships but also the interaction of these individuals with all the macro systems with which they're in contact.

Learning Objectives

A. Define and explore the macro social environment.
B. Introduce material addressed by the remainder of the book.
C. Define *generalist practice* and explain the relationship between some of its major concepts and the macro social environment. These concepts include: working within an organization structure; using a seven-step planned change process; targeting any size system for change; adopting a wide range of professional roles; applying critical thinking skills; and incorporating research-informed practice.
D. Examine ecosystems theory and explain the concepts involved that are derived from systems theories and the ecological perspective.
E. Discuss people's involvement with multiple systems in the macro social environment.
F. Provide a brief history of social work practice in the macro social environment and describe contemporary macro practice.
G. Define *critical thinking* and discuss its use in generalist practice.
H. Introduce critical thinking questions that will be raised throughout the book.

What is the Macro Social Environment?

The *social environment* is the sum total of social and cultural conditions, circumstances, and human interactions that encompass human beings. The *macro* social environment, for our purposes, is the configuration of communities, organizations, and groups within the latter that are products of social, economic, and political forces and social institutions. The following breaks down the definition of the macro social environment into various facets and explains what each means.

Communities

The macro social environment involves communities, organizations, and groups and how these systems affect people. A *community* is "a number of people who have something in common that connects them in some way and that distinguishes them from others" (Homan, 2008, p. 8). The concept of community with which you're probably most familiar involves geographic areas. People in geographic communities, of course, share the common variable of location. A geographic community has a huge impact on its residents' quality of life, accessible resources, available role models, and life opportunities. For example, consider the geographic community you come from. How has that community affected you and how your life has progressed? How would you describe that community? Critical Thinking Questions 1.1 encourages you to think about the types of variables that characterize and differentiate geographical communities. (A subsequent section of this chapter will discuss the concept of critical thinking more thoroughly.)

In addition to geographic areas based on location, communities may also involve groups of people who have similar interests or who identify with each other. For example, people with degrees in social work who practice in the field are part of the professional social work community. There are communities involving scuba divers, hikers, bikers, Corvette clubs, Christmas ornament collectors, community theater groups, and any number of other groups of people who share something in common. Some communities are based on sexual orientation. Spiritual or religious communities include people who believe in the same doctrine and/or belong to the same religious denomination. Ethnic, racial, and cultural communities include people who have a similar background based on those variables. Later chapters discuss various aspects of communities, including theories, community empowerment, and neighborhood empowerment.

Organizations

Another facet of the macro social environment concerns organizations. Various organizations exist within the community context. *Organizations* are "(1) social entities that (2) are goal directed, (3) are designed as deliberately structured and coordinated activity systems, and (4) are linked to the external environment" (Daft, 2007, p. 10). In other words, organizations are structured groups of people who come together to work toward some mutual goal and perform established work activities that are divided among various units. Organizations have a clearly defined membership in terms of knowing who is in and who is out.

Critical Thinking Questions 1.1

How would you describe the geographic community you come from? Think about the following aspects (that represent only some of the variables characterizing such communities) (Kirst-Ashman & Hull, 2009a):

- *Rural or urban setting.* Would you characterize your home community as being in the country, a small town, a medium-sized city, a major metropolis, or a suburb of a bigger city?
- *Population density.* How many people live in your community of origin? Would you describe the area as being spread out, crowded, or something between the two?
- *General standard of living.* How would you describe the social class of people living in the community? Poor? Middle-class? Fairly well-to-do? Wealthy?
- *Housing.* What are the residents' homes like? Do most residents own their own property, or do they rent houses or apartments? How would you describe the quality of the homes? Older? Newer? Run-down? Well-kept? Are dwellings bunched together and cramped, or do homes have spacious yards? Does adequate affordable housing exist to meet community residents' needs?
- *Available resources.* To what extent are hospitals, parks, police and fire protection, garbage collection, and shopping readily available? Are there services and resources accessible for people in need, including shelters for battered women, crisis intervention hotlines, food pantries, counseling, and other social services?
- *Spiritual opportunities.* Are there churches and religious organizations in the community? How many? To what extent do community residents pursue spiritual involvement?
- *Education.* How would you characterize the educational system in your home community? Is it generally considered "good," "effective," "poor," or "substandard"? How does it compare with educational systems in neighboring communities? How would you describe the education you received there?
- *Other factors.* What other aspects of your home community are important to you and why?
- *Summary impression.* When you think of your home community, what words first come to mind? How would you describe it to a complete stranger? What would you emphasize? Was it a generally happy, pleasant place? Or was it hostile, dangerous, and impoverished?

Think of the organizations around you. They all are clearly defined entities made up of people with structured roles that pursue designated purposes or goals. There are many examples of organizations. Businesses are organizations that have goals of production or sales and profit. Each person working for the business has a structured role[3] and responsibilities (e.g., as employee, supervisor, or manager). The schools you attended are a type of organization aimed at providing young people with education. Students, teachers, and administrators all had defined roles and expectations. Churches, mosques, and synagogues are organizations aimed at

---

[3] A *role* is a culturally expected behavior pattern for a person having a specified status or being involved in a designated social relationship.

serving their members' spiritual needs. Your college or university is also a type of organization with the ultimate goal of providing you with an advanced education. Later chapters explore different facets of organizations and how they can operate to benefit or detract from clients', citizens', and employees' best interests, health, and well-being.

Organizations Providing Social Services   Especially relevant to social work are organizations that provide social services. *Social services* include the work that social work practitioners and other helping professionals perform in organizations for the benefit of clients.

Goals include improving people's health, enhancing their quality of life, increasing autonomy and independence, supporting families, and helping people and larger systems improve their functioning in the macro social environment (Barker, 2003). That is quite a mouthful. In essence, social services include the wide range of activities that social workers perform in their goal of helping people solve problems and improve their personal well-being. Social services can be provided both to people who are poor and those who are not; they include resources and activities that may involve counseling, child protection, residential treatment for emotional and behavioral problems, provision of financial resources, sheltered employment and assistance for people with disabilities, daycare, and employment coaching, among many other services (Popple, 2008).

A *social agency*, or *social services agency*, is an organization providing social services that typically employs a range of helping professionals including social workers in addition to office staff, paraprofessionals (persons trained to assist professionals), and sometimes volunteers (Barker, 2003). Social agencies generally serve some designated client population experiencing some defined need. Services are provided according to a prescribed set of policies regarding how the agency staff should accomplish their service provision goals.

Groups

A *group* is at least two individuals gathered together because of some common bond, to meet members' social and emotional needs, or to fulfill some mutual purpose. Our concern with groups involves their significance in the context of communities and organizations. Communities and organizations are made up of groups, which in turn are composed of individuals. Chapter 3 and Chapter 4 will describe various types of groups and focus on the operation of task groups in the macro social environment.

Figure 1.1 depicts the complexity of the macro social environment. Groups, organizations, and communities are made up of individuals like you. The large outer circle reflects the geographic community in which someone like you might live. You are portrayed in the bolded circle near the center of the large community circle. Also depicted are numerous organizations within the community. Each organization is also made up of various groups (e.g., task groups, departments, units, or levels of management). The macro environment also has numerous other groups of people who are not necessarily members of organizations. These might include friendship groups, recreational groups, study groups, neighborhood groups, and any other type of group configuration you might think of. In any community, you,

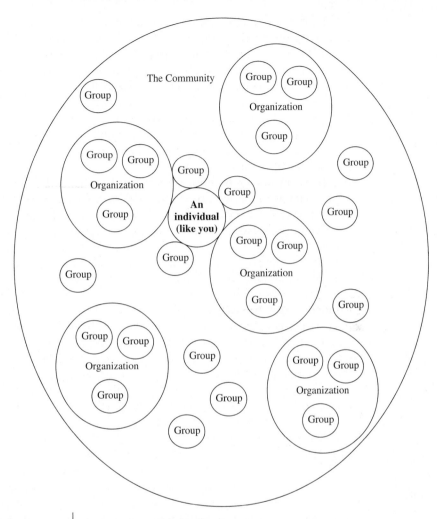

Figure 1.1 | The Macro Social Environment

obviously, will not be involved with all groups and organizations. You probably won't even be aware of some of them. The groups and organization circles that touch the bolded circle representing you reflect those groups and organizations with which you are involved—perhaps including organizations like the college you attend and groups like your closest circle of friends. The point is that the macro social environment is a complex matrix of these various components. People don't function in a vacuum. They are integrally involved with others around them.

Social, Economic, and Political Forces

Social forces are values and beliefs held by people in the social environment that are strong enough to influence people's activities, including how government is structured or restricted. Key words here are "values" and "beliefs." For example, social forces fire the debate between anti-abortion and right-to-choice factions over the abortion issue.

Economic forces are the resources that are available, how they are distributed, and how they are spent. The key word here is "resources." They involve how taxes are spent at the national level and how salaries are distributed to an agency's workers.

Political forces are the current governmental structures, the laws to which people are subject, and the overall distribution of power among the population. Political forces are reflected in laws and public policies. Here the key word is "government." Elected politicians make decisions about what rules should govern public behavior and how to distribute resources. Consider the public welfare grant program Temporary Assistance to Needy Families (TANF) established by political forces. The program, discussed more thoroughly in a later chapter, structures how needy children and their families are treated.

Often, issues, programs, or situations reflect a blend of forces. For instance, the complicated issue of national health insurance, making health care available to all citizens, has been debated for decades. Social forces reflect values on health and good medical care. However, another value is the ability to choose. Many people fear that a national health care policy will cause them to lose their ability to select a health care provider. Economic forces are also involved, as making national health care available for all would be very expensive. Currently, people who hold "good" jobs usually have health insurance provided primarily, and sometimes totally, by their employers. Some people fear that a national policy would cause them to lose resources in the form of health care benefits. Health care resources would have to be shared by more people, and therefore easy access would be more difficult for some. Political forces clearly are involved in the national health care arena as political debate continues.

Social Institutions

Social forces converge over time to form social institutions. A *social institution* is an established and valued practice or means of operation in a society resulting in the development of a formalized system to carry out its purpose. Examples of social institutions are "religion, the family, military structure, government, and the social welfare system" (Barker, 2003, p. 404). See Figure 1.2.

Social institutions establish expectations and requirements for expected behavior, and govern these through policies and laws. Communities provide the macro environments for social institutions to be upheld. Organizations carry out policies and distribute services social institutions deem necessary. Decision-making groups and administrators in organizations and communities implement policies and distribute services based on social institutions.

For example, consider public education in the United States. The right of all U.S. citizens to receive public education until age eighteen is a social institution. Individual schools are organizations that comply with this concept. Individual communities make decisions regarding how schools will accomplish their educational goals. Community residents determine whether new schools will be built or old ones will suffice. They decide what content will be taught to students in family life education courses and whether or not to offer music or art.

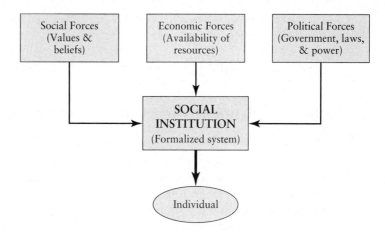

Figure 1.2 | Social, Economic, and Political Forces Result in Formalized Social Institutions That Affect Individuals

Intricate interconnections exist among social forces, social institutions, communities, organizations, and groups carrying out public directives. Sometimes, forces and institutions are not clearly distinguishable from each other. All are collectively intertwined to make up the macro social environment.

Concept Summary 1.1 | **Important Aspects of the Macro Social Environment**

Community: "A number of people who have something in common that connects them in some way and that distinguishes them from others" (Homan, 2008, p. 8).

Organization: A "(1) social entity that (2) is goal-directed, (3) is designed as a deliberately structured and coordinated activity system, and (4) is linked to the external environment" (Daft, 2007, p. 10).

Social services: The work that social work practitioners and other helping professionals perform in organizations for the benefit of clients.

Social (or social services) agency: An organization providing social services that typically employs a range of helping professionals including social workers in addition to office staff, paraprofessionals (persons trained to assist professionals), and sometimes volunteers (Barker, 2003).

Group: At least two individuals gathered together because of some common bond, to meet members' social and emotional needs, or to fulfill some mutual purpose.

Social forces: Values and beliefs held by people in the social environment that are strong enough to influence people's activities, including how government is structured or restricted.

Economic forces: Resources that are available, how they are distributed, and how they are spent.

Political forces: Current governmental structures, the laws to which people are subject, and the overall distribution of power among the population.

Social institution: An established and valued practice or means of operation in a society resulting in the development of a formalized system to carry out its purpose.

Note that the macro social environment may include macro systems of various dimensions depending on your focus of attention. It may include small groups in organizations, neighborhoods, towns, cities, large metropolitan areas, counties, states, nations, and the global macro social environment.

The Macro Social Environment and Generalist Social Work Practice

Social workers help people in need using a wide range of methods. They counsel individuals, work with families, run various types of groups, help clients in their communities, and strive to improve the organizations in which they practice. It is the ethical responsibility of professional social workers to address problems and issues in the macro social environment and to initiate and implement positive change (National Association of Social Workers [NASW], 2008). To do all this requires acquisition of a wide range of skills. Regardless of who their clients are or what their goals might be, social workers must follow an orderly process to get things done that stresses professional core values. This perspective is referred to as generalist practice.

Generalist practice is conducted in the context of the macro social environment. To understand the significance of this environment, it is necessary to know what social workers actually do in it. Therefore, we will spend some time here defining and examining generalist practice.

The Definition of Generalist Practice

Generalist practice, occurring *within an organizational structure*, is the application of an extensive and diverse knowledge base, professional values, and a wide range of skills by using a *seven-step planned change process* to *target any size system for change* within the context of seven equally essential dimensions. (Note that this definition's major concepts are emphasized by italics.)[4] The first three involve the process of generalist practice and the last four the values and principles that guide generalist practice.

First, generalist practice requires the assumption of *a wide range of professional roles*. Second, it involves the *application of critical thinking skills* to the planned change process. Third, it *incorporates research-informed practice* to determine the most effective ways to help people and serve clients. Fourth, it necessitates the *adherence to professional values and the application of professional ethics*. Fifth, it stresses the importance of *understanding human diversity* and how diverse factors affect people's quality of life. Sixth, it emphasizes *client empowerment, strengths, and resiliency*. Seventh, it incorporates *advocacy for human rights, and the pursuit of social and economic justice*.

---

[4] Most of these concepts and ideas are taken directly from the *Educational Policy and Accreditation Standards*, developed by the Council on Social Work Education (CSWE) (CSWE, 2008).

Concept Summary 1.2	**Major Concepts Inherent in the Definition of Generalist Practice**

- Practice within an organizational structure
- Use of a seven-step planned change process
- Targeting of any size system for change

The Process of Practice:
- Assumption of a wide range of professional roles
- Application of critical thinking skills
- Incorporation of research-informed practice

Values and Principles That Guide Practice (Addressed in Chapter 2):
- Adherence to professional values and the application of professional ethics
- Understanding of human diversity
- Emphasis on client empowerment, strengths, and resiliency
- Advocacy for human rights, and the pursuit of social and economic justice

Subsequent sections of this chapter will address major principles in the definition of generalist practice through those involving the process of practice. Chapter 2 will continue by defining and explaining the remaining dimensions—the values and principles that guide practice.

Note that the terms *generalist social worker, worker, generalist practitioner,* and *practitioner* will be used interchangeably throughout this book to refer to professionals undertaking generalist social work practice.

Defining Generalist Practice:
Work within an Organizational Structure

One important concept in the definition of generalist practice is that practitioners *work within an organizational structure. Organizational structure* is "the manner in which an organization divides its labor into specific tasks and achieves coordination among these tasks" (Johns, 1996, p. 490). Social workers are employed by social service agencies. Each such organization has its own organizational structure involving job descriptions and responsibilities, departments addressing various aspects of agency functioning, communication systems, and management hierarchy (Daft, 2007). (Later chapters will discuss these variables and many others characterizing organizations in greater depth.)

Agencies are integral parts of larger communities in the macro social environment. Workers, thus, must understand how social service organizations and communities function both together and independently. Practitioners must know how organizational and community systems work in order to improve how they provide resources and services.

Defining Generalist Practice:
Using a Seven-Step Planned Change Process

A second basic concept in the definition of generalist practice involves the structured change process. *Planned change* and *problem-solving* are often used interchangeably in social work. Some feel the term "change" has more positive

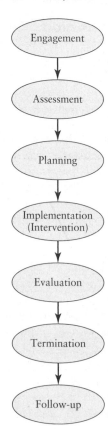

Figure 1.3
The Planned
Change
Process in
Generalist
Practice

connotations than the term "problem." Regardless of whether social workers are working with individual clients, families, large communities, or any other client systems, they follow the basic seven-step process portrayed in Figure 1.3 to solve a problem or pursue a positive change (Kirst-Ashman & Hull, 2009a, b):

Step 1. *Engagement* is the process of establishing a positive professional relationship between the worker and the client. It may include greeting the client, portraying appropriate verbal and nonverbal behavior, listening to the client's issues, discussing agency services, and identifying client expectations (Kirst-Ashman & Hull, 2009b).

An example of engagement in an organization is a worker approaching the administration with a new idea about how to distribute information to clients about the agency's services. A community example is a social worker attending a meeting at a senior citizen's center, introducing herself, and presenting some ideas about developing recreational activities.

Step 2. *Assessment* is the identification of the "nature and extent of client needs and concerns, as well as critical information about client resources and supports and other environment factors" so that a helping plan can be devised and implemented (Blythe & Reithoffer, 2000, p. 551). From the perspective of this book, assessment is the most significant step in the planned change process. This book's purpose is to provide information so that you, as a social worker, can understand what's going on in the organization where you work, other organizations with which you have contact, and the community in which all the organizations function. It should provide information for how you should think about proceeding to make and undertake effective plans.

Step 3. *Planning* is the process of identifying goals, rationally considering various ways to implement them, and establishing specific steps to achieve them. Since this and the following steps involve learning skills that are taught in practice courses, they will only be briefly mentioned here.

Step 4. *Intervention* is the actual doing or implementation of the plan. It concerns applying the skills you will learn in practice classes to achieve goals.

Step 5. *Evaluation* is the appraisal of the effectiveness of the plan and its implementation. How well did the plan work? To what extent were goals achieved?

Step 6. *Termination* is the ending of the social worker–client relationship. Virtually all relationships come to an end. Clients move. Workers get different jobs. Goals are attained and there's no longer any need for worker–client contact.

Step 7. *Follow-up* is the retrieval of information about a client's functioning after the intervention has been terminated. Follow-up may provide information about the intervention's effectiveness after the fact or it may be useful to determine if the client has new needs.

Defining Generalist Practice: Targeting any Size System for Change

The third relevant concept in the definition of generalist practice involves *targeting any size system for change*. The important thing is that generalist practitioners work with and on the behalf of systems of all sizes, including individuals, families, groups, organizations, and communities. At the community macro level, a worker might help a group of neighborhood residents develop a plan for identifying and getting rid of drug houses or start a summer recreation program for youth. At the organizational macro level, a social worker might advocate on clients' behalf with administrators to change a restrictive policy. Similarly, an agency worker might lead a task group to develop a training program for teaching workers new skills to work with involuntary or angry clients.

Theoretical or conceptual perspectives provide symbolic representations or pictures for how to view the world—in this case, the macro world of communities, organizations, and groups. Because the environment is so important in the analysis and understanding of human behavior, conceptual perspectives must be clearly defined. Social work focuses on the interactions between individuals and various systems in the environment. Because of the importance of both systems terminology and the terminology used to refer to the social environment (based in the ecological approach), the following section will explore the foundation theory upon which this book is based, namely, ecosystems theory.

Ecosystems Theory and the Macro Social Environment

Ecosystems theory provides one significant means of conceptualizing and understanding human behavior (Beckett & Johnson, 1995; Compton, Galaway, & Counoyer, 2005; Kondrat, 2008; Poulin, 2005). It often serves as an "organizing framework" to help social workers comprehend people's interaction with various systems in the macro social environment (p. 1394); "according to ecosystems theory, psychological processes are manifestations of complex biological, interpersonal, cultural, legal, economic, organizational, and political forces" that "work together to influence human behavior throughout the life span" (Beckett & Johnson, 1995, p. 1391).

Social systems theory can serve as a "way of thinking" or "a theory about theories" (Anderson & Carter, 1999, p. xix). Ecosystems theory is "systems theory used to describe and analyze people and other living systems and their transactions" (Beckett & Johnson, 1995, p. 1391; Zastrow & Kirst-Ashman, 2010). In other words, terms proposed by ecosystems theory can be used to characterize and explain the behavior of individuals, groups, organizations, or communities even when discussing the application of other theories. Ecosystems theory provides a general perspective and vocabulary for describing systems' functioning in the macro social environment. In essence, ecosystems theory serves as an umbrella encompassing other theories.

This book will define and explore both systems and ecological concepts that relate to understanding human behavior within the macro social environment. Later chapters will introduce additional theories relating to groups, organizations, and communities. These are included to help you gain a variety of perspectives for understanding macro systems.

Ecosystems Theory: Basic Terms Taken from Social Systems Theories

A number of terms based in social systems theories are extremely important in understanding ecosystems theory and its relationship to social work practice.

They include *system, boundaries, subsystem, homeostasis, role, relationship, input, output, feedback, interface, differentiation, entropy, negative entropy,* and *equifinality.*

System   A *system* is a set of elements that are orderly, interrelated, and a functional whole. An individual person is a system with biological, psychological, and social qualities and characteristics. Examples of systems are Slab City, WI; a large urban department of social services; a tiny two-person, part-time counseling center in a town of 2,356 residents; Washington, DC; Buzzard, Saskatchewan; and a local chapter of Gamblers Anonymous.

Boundaries   *Boundaries* are borders or margins that separate one entity (for example, a system) from another. For instance, your skin provides a boundary between you as an independent, living system and the external environment. Boundaries determine who is a member of a system and who is not. If you haven't paid your dues to the National Association of Bungee Jumpers, the National Rifle Association, or your social work student club, you are not a member of that system. You are not within that particular system's boundaries. You are either in it or not.

Subsystem   A *subsystem* is a secondary or subordinate system. It may be thought of as a smaller system within a larger system. The social work program, for example, is a subsystem of your college or university. Similarly, each member of the Denver Broncos is a subsystem of the team system.

Homeostasis   *Homeostasis* is the tendency for a system to maintain a relatively stable, constant state of balance. If something disturbs the homeostatic system, that system will strive to return to its prior stable state. Members of the group Neighborhood Warriors on Trash maintain homeostasis as long as they can relate well enough to stay together and pick up garbage, their designated purpose. The system, in this case, the group, must maintain some kind of homeostasis to function.

Homeostasis, however, does not mean that all group members will like each other or even talk to each other. Harry, for example, can't stand Izod, whom he feels bullies other group members by telling them the best way to organize trash collection. However, Harry feels the group and its purpose are important enough to continue his support and involvement. He simply ignores Izod. Homeostasis merely means maintaining the status quo. Sometimes, that status quo can be ineffective, inefficient, or seriously problematic.

Another example is a community that strives to maintain its homeostasis despite having corrupt political leaders. Community members may hesitate to depose their leaders because potential replacements scare residents even more. At least the residents already know about the leaders they have. The unknown is scary even though it might be better. It also might be worse.

Roles   A *role* is a culturally expected behavior pattern for a person having a specified status or being involved in a designated social relationship. In other words, each individual involved in a system assumes a role within that system. For instance, you assume the role of student in class. Expectations include performing required work, receiving grades the instructor assigns, and working toward your degree. If you hold a job, you assume the role of employee with whatever work expectations that job role involves. In a community, the mayor assumes a role with the decision-making responsibilities required in such a position.

Relationships   A *relationship* is the dynamic interpersonal connection between two or more persons or systems that involves how they think about, feel about, and behave toward each other. For example, a social worker may have a professional relationship with her agency supervisor. Ideally, their communication and interaction maximizes the worker's effectiveness.

Relationships may exist between systems of any size. Workers within an agency have relationships with each other. Likewise, one agency or organization has a relationship with another. A local church may establish a relationship with a community Boys' Club. Together they could recruit and train volunteers, share activity space, and cosponsor community activities for the community's male youth.

Input   *Input* is the energy, information, or communication flow received from other systems. You receive input from instructors regarding class assignments. Elected officials receive input from constituents when they vote on whether or not to support a referendum that allows building a nuclear plant. As an employee, you receive input in the form of a paycheck, not necessarily a big enough paycheck, but it is still input. Other examples include a person who breaks both arms after falling with her new 800-pound hog motorcycle who will require substantial input by others to help her take care of daily personal tasks. Still another example of input is information received from the Atlanta Centers for Disease Control about new annual flu epidemic mutations.

Output   *Output*, on the other hand, is what happens to *input* after it's gone through and been processed by some system. It is a form of energy going out of a person's life or taking something away from it. For instance, a Moose Lodge may "adopt a highway" and take responsibility for cleaning up two miles of a local road. Another form of output is paying money to purchase a 2001 Honda Civic coupe. Yet another form of output is the progress made with a client. Pablo, a worker, can expend time and energy, use his knowledge and skills, and work with a client, Astrid, to achieve the goal of finding employment. The intervention's output is Astrid's employment and her level of satisfaction with it.

At times these terms are confusing. For example, in the case above, Pablo provides Astrid with his input (time, energy, knowledge, skill, and expertise). Astrid then, hopefully, has output (attaining her goal of finding a job). However, if we focus on Pablo instead of Astrid, we can apply the terms differently. Pablo's *input* includes his salary, ongoing skill development, and help from supervisors. Pablo's *output*, on the other hand, is the time, energy, knowledge, skill, and expertise he exercises to achieve intervention goals. How terms are applied and used depend on which individual, subsystem, or element of the systems involved is the focus of attention. One person's input is another's output.

A related issue critically significant in social work practice is whether the output is worth all the input. Are treatment results worth how much the treatment costs? Does a community program to fight crime (that requires significant financial input) have adequate results (output) to justify how much it costs? If ten officers are hired to implement the program, how successful must the program be? Is it successful if crime is cut by 10 percent? Or 30 percent? What about 2 percent?

Many times it's difficult to measure input and output in equal units. If money is the only measurement of inputs and outputs, it makes it easier. If a stockbroker invests more (input) than he earns (output), he is losing money and better change his investment strategy. In social services, it is often difficult to measure the value of a service or the extent it adds to peoples' quality of life. For example, is a hospice program geared to enhancing the comfort of terminally ill people worth the expense? The input in terms of financial resources for treatment, care, housing, and medicine can be substantial. However, the value of such care to a dying person (the output) may be priceless.

The bottom line concerns whether the community or agency is using its resources efficiently and effectively. Or, can those resources be put to a better use by providing some other more effective and efficient service?

Negative and Positive Feedback   *Feedback* is a special form of input where a system receives information about that system's own performance. As a result of *negative feedback*, the system can choose to correct any deviations or mistakes and return to a more homeostatic state.

For example, Natasha, a community resident, might give negative feedback to Boris, another, about how Boris' small children regularly run out into a busy street while playing and riding bikes. As Natasha feels it is very dangerous for Boris' children, she gives Boris feedback about the problem. Hopefully, Boris will use this negative feedback to correct it.

Positive feedback, also valuable, is the informational input a system receives about what it is doing correctly in order to maintain itself and thrive. Receiving a significant pay raise resulting from an excellent job-performance review provides positive feedback to a worker that she is doing a good job. Likewise, an agency receiving a specific federal grant gets positive feedback that it has developed a plan worthy of such funding.

Interface   An *interface* is the point where two systems (including individuals, families, groups, organizations, or communities) come into contact with each other, interact, or communicate. An interface may be the interaction and communication between an agency supervisor and her supervisee. It may also be your communication with an instructor regarding expectations for some class assignment. A board of directors may be the interface between a community and a residential treatment center for adolescents with serious emotional and behavioral problems. Such a board is usually composed of volunteers who are influential in the community and serve to oversee agency policies, goals, and how the agency is generally run.

During an assessment of a client system's strengths, needs, and problems, the interface must be clearly in focus in order to target the appropriate interactions for change. For example, a young single mother of three is homeless and desperately needs services. The interface between her and the macro systems providing human services includes those services for which she might be eligible. The interface also involves her interactions with social workers helping to provide those services.

Differentiation *Differentiation* is a system's tendency to move from a simpler to a more complex existence. As you grow older, get wiser, have more varied experiences, meet increasing numbers of people, and assume more responsibilities in general, your life gets more complicated. You experience differentiation. Likewise, as a social agency grows over time, it will likely develop more detailed policies and programs. A women's center might start out with one support group for battered women run by one volunteer. If that support group is a success, years later it may expand and differentiate into an entire program where eight groups addressing other issues commonly experienced by women are run by paid program staff and supervised by a director. Similarly, as laws and clarifications to laws proliferate in the legal system, that system differentiates and becomes more complex.

Entropy *Entropy* is the natural tendency of a system to progress toward disorganization, depletion, and death. The idea is that nothing lasts forever. People age and eventually die. After early periods of growth and differentiation, agencies grow old, often obsolete, and disappear. As history moves on, older agencies and systems are eventually replaced by new ones.

Negative Entropy *Negative entropy* is the process of a system toward growth and development. In effect, it is the opposite of entropy. Individuals develop physically, intellectually, and emotionally as they grow. Social service agencies grow and develop new programs and clientele. A sheltered workshop that provides supervised training and vocational guidance for people with cognitive disabilities begins in one small building with twenty clients. Negative entropy characterizes the agency as it grows to serve over one hundred clients and adds new programs. These include an information and referral helpline, a volunteer program called Special Friends that is similar to Big Brothers/Big Sisters programs, and a wide range of supervised recreational activities.

Equifinality *Equifinality* refers to the fact that there are many different means to achieve the same end. It is important not to get locked into only one way of thinking. In any particular situation, alternatives do exist. Some may be better than others, but, nonetheless, there are alternatives. For example, a community may need funding to start up a new community center for holding community meetings and housing social and recreational events. The end goal is establishment of a place to conduct community activities. However, there are many ways to attain this goal. A citizen group may apply for grants from public and private sources, the community may undertake a massive fundraising campaign on the center's behalf, or residents might work with county and state leaders to solicit support.

| Concept Summary 1.3 | Major Concepts in Systems Theories |

System: A set of elements that are orderly, interrelated, and a functional whole.

Boundaries: Borders or margins that separate one entity from another.

Subsystem: A secondary or subordinate system.

Homeostasis: The tendency for a system to maintain a relatively stable, constant state of balance.

Role: A culturally expected behavior pattern for a person having a specified status or being involved in a designated social relationship.

Relationship: The dynamic connection between two or more persons or systems that involves how they think about, feel about, and behave toward each other.

Input: The energy, information, or communication flow received from other systems.

Output: What happens to input after it's gone through and been processed by some system.

Negative feedback: A special form of input where a system receives information about that system's own performance.

Positive feedback: The informational input a system receives about what it is doing correctly in order to maintain itself and thrive.

Interface: The point where two systems (including individuals, families, groups, organizations, or communities) come into contact with each other, interact, or communicate.

Differentiation: A system's tendency to move from a simpler to a more complex existence.

Entropy: The natural tendency of a system to progress toward disorganization, depletion, and death.

Negative entropy: The process of a system toward growth and development.

Equifinality: The fact that there are many different means to achieve the same end.

Ecosystems Theory: Basic Terms Taken from the Ecological Perspective

Ecosystems theory incorporates basic ecological concepts in addition to those proposed by systems theories. The ecological perspective emphasizes the dynamic interactions between people and their environment. Gitterman and Germain (2008b) explain:

> Human beings act within physical, social, and cultural environments. Physical environments include the natural world; structures built by people; the space that supports, contains, or arranges these structures; and the rhythms of environmental and human biology. Social environments include family, friends, and social networks of two or more significant people; larger groups such as organizations, institutions, and the community (which are also physical settings); and society itself, including its political, economic, and social structures and the law. Culture is part of the environment and part of the person, and is expressed through each person's values, norms, beliefs, and language. (p. 52)

We have established that concepts from both systems theories and the ecological perspective provide useful means for social workers to view the world. Both approaches focus on systems within the environment and how these systems interact with and affect people, resulting in ecosystems theory.

Some would say that subtle differences exist between the approaches and the terms inherent in each. Schriver (2004) explains: "The ecological perspective . . . explicitly defines the environment as including physical (nonhuman) elements. Social systems [theories] . . . are less explicit about the place and role of nonhuman elements in the environment. Some would also argue that social systems and ecological approaches differ in their conceptualizations of boundaries and exchange across boundaries. Recognizing these areas of disagreement, we will consider these two perspectives similar enough to be treated together here" (p. 124). Hence, we will conceptualize this as ecosystems theory.

The following concepts derived from the ecological perspective are important facets of ecosystems theory: *social environment; transactions; energy; input; output; interface; adaptation; person-in-environment fit; stress, stressors, and coping; relatedness; habitat; niche;* and *personal characteristics including competence, self-esteem, and self-direction.* As noted, input, output, and interface are terms used in both approaches. See Highlight 1.1 for brief comparison of terms. To avoid redundancy, please refer to the earlier descriptions of these terms within the context of social systems theories.

Highlight 1.1	Comparison of Some of the Major Concepts in Systems Theory and the Ecological Perspective

Some Major Concepts in Systems Theory	Similar Concepts in Both	Some Major Concepts in the Ecological Perspective
System	Input	Social Environment
Boundaries	Output	Energy
Subsystem	Interface	Adaptation
Homeostasis		Person-in-Environment Fit
Roles		Stress, Stressors, & Coping
Relationships		Relatedness
Negative Feedback		Habitat
Positive Feedback		Niche
Differentiation		Personal Characteristics
Entropy		Competence
Negative Entropy		Self-Esteem
Equifinality		Self-Direction

The Social Environment   The *social environment* involves the conditions, circumstances, and human interactions that encompass human beings. Persons are dependent upon effective interactions with this environment in order to survive and thrive. The social environment includes the actual physical setting that society provides. This involves the type of home a person lives in, the type of work that's done, the amount of money that's available, and the laws and social rules by which people live. The social environment also includes all the individuals, groups, organizations, and systems with which a person comes into contact. Families, friends, work groups, organizations, communities, and governments are all involved.

The *macro social environment* extends beyond the individual's interaction with immediate friends, relatives, and other individuals. We have established that it is the configuration of communities, organizations, and groups within the latter that are products of social, economic, and political forces and social institutions.

People communicate and interact with others in their environments. Each of these interactions or types of interactions are referred to as *transactions*. Transactions are active and dynamic. That is, something is communicated or exchanged. They may be positive or negative. A positive transaction may be the revelation that you won the lottery. Another positive transaction might be that you are named state social worker of the year. A negative transaction, on the other hand, might be receiving news your house burnt down or was ruined in an earthquake, destroying almost all of your personal possessions. Another negative transaction is a huge fight with your significant other in which you discover your partner is having an affair.

Energy   *Energy* is the natural power of active involvement between people and their environments. Energy can take the form of **input** or **output**. Use of these latter terms in the ecological perspective resembles that in systems theories.

Interface   The *interface* is also similar to the same term in systems theory. Namely, it is the exact point where the interaction between an individual and the environment takes place.

Adaptation   *Adaptation* is the capacity to adjust to surrounding environmental conditions. It implies an ongoing process of change. A person must adapt to new conditions and circumstances in order to continue functioning effectively. An individual diagnosed with severe rheumatoid arthritis must adapt to new, less difficult levels of physical activity. The individual must also adapt to the process of taking required medications and performing the appropriate exercises to maximize comfort, endurance, and agility. Another example is a family whose primary breadwinner is laid off from a high-paying management job after a serious dip in the economy. Family members must adapt to a less costly lifestyle until input returns to its former level when the breadwinner gets a new job.

Environments also adapt and react to people. Consider the destruction of Brazil's rainforest to supply lumber and provide farmland. Many questions have been raised concerning the potential effects of this damage and the extinction of plant and animal life. Questions even have been asked about the impacts on global weather as oxygen-producing plants are destroyed. Plants, animals, and humans must all adapt to new conditions, positive or not, if they are to survive.

Person-in-Environment Fit   *Person-in-environment fit* is the extent to which "the needs, capacities, behavioral styles, and goals of people" or groups of people fit or match "the characteristics of the environment" (Gitterman & Germain, 2008b, p. 55). Such "fit" involves the degree to which physical, social, and cultural needs are met. Sometimes, person-in-environment fit is amazingly good. Other times, it is exceedingly poor. Many variables are involved in how an environment meets individual and groups needs.

The person-in-environment fit would likely be poor for a person using a wheelchair whose home is a third-story apartment without elevators or ramps. Likewise, Nassir is a Muslim person of color who is just beginning to learn English and lives in a neighborhood composed almost exclusively of Roman Catholic white people. The extent to which Nassir suffers neighbors' discrimination and rejection because of his differences negatively affects his person-in-environment fit. On the other hand, the extent to which neighbors accept and appreciate his differences enhances that fit.

Stress, Stressors, and Coping   Because they are so interrelated, stress, stressors, and coping will be addressed here together. A *stressor* is "a demand, situation, or circumstance" that results in physiological and/or emotional tension, in other words, stress (Zastrow & Kirst-Ashman, 2010, p. 605). *Stress*, then, is the resulting physiological and/or emotional tension produced by a stressor that affects a person's internal balance. Stressors include any of a wide range of variables and circumstances: traumatic events such as sudden deaths or discovery of fatal disease; potentially troublesome life transitions such as adolescence or old age; and other changes in living patterns such as divorce. Even positive events such as getting a job, moving to a new home, or falling in love can be stressors. Adapting to new circumstances, regardless of what they are, can cause stress.

Coping is a form of adaptation where people respond to stress by expending effort to change (1) their own behavioral, cognitive, or emotional reactions; (2) the environmental conditions contributing to the stress; (3) the interaction between their own reactions and the environment; or (4) some combination of these responses (Gitterman & Germain, 2008a, 2008b). For example, a parent must cope with the worry and distress caused by a sick child. Either that parent must decrease the extent of distress by curbing his or her worry (targeting personal reactions), make certain the child immediately gets the necessary treatment available in the medical environment (targeting the environment), or advocate with medical personnel and the insurance company to provide needed medical services (targeting the interaction between the family and the environment). That parent may also cope by pursuing a combination of these goals at the same time.

From a macro perspective, an example concerns an agency that must cope with new strict government regulations about service provision. Agency administration might work to accept and adjust to these regulations (targeting agency staff's own reactions), persuade government officials that these regulations really don't apply (targeting the environment), or establish a compromise with government officials to relax regulations so they aren't as stringent (targeting the agency's interaction with the governmental environment). Agency administration may also pursue all three of these tactics.

One other macro example involves a community that must cope with state and federal funding cuts. Either community administrators and residents must learn to live with the cuts (targeting their own reactions), fight with state and federal government to abolish the funding cuts (targeting the environment), or work toward some compromise to decrease the cuts (targeting interaction with the state and national environment). As in the earlier illustrations portraying a parent and an agency, the community may also pursue a number of coping strategies.

Social workers help people cope with problems and issues. Assessing both people's coping skills (whether they are part of a group, organization, or community) and the potential for change in the macro environment is a critical aspect of preparing for generalist intervention.

Relatedness   *"Relatedness"* is "the capacity to form attachments" (Payne, 2005, p. 151). People need to feel they belong and have support from others. Attachments may be made both to formal and informal resources and networks. *Formal service networks* include "public and private agencies and institutions" (e.g., the college or university you attend); *informal networks* include "friends, neighbors, workmates," and people having the same spiritual beliefs (Gitterman & Germain, 2008b, p. 62).

Think of your first day of class as a first-year student and all the unknowns you had to face. To what extent did you feel a sense of relatedness to the college environment? To what extent has your sense of relatedness changed from then until now? How many more people do you know now? How many friends have you made? With how many instructors' expectations have you learned to cope? To what extent do you feel a relatedness with the college or university?

Similarly, residents may experience various degrees of relatedness with their community. They may know most of the neighbors, be a member of a neighborhood association, and participate regularly in community events. On the other hand, residents may know no neighbors, lack involvement in any community activities, and feel isolated and alone. Whether an individual is a member of a group, an employee in an organization, or a neighborhood resident, that person must experience a positive sense of relatedness in order to achieve good person-in-environment fit. Assessing people's relatedness in their immediate social environment provides social workers with important clues for how to help clients get their needs met. A client's relatedness can pose many strengths upon which to draw in solving problems. Supportive people in the environment can be called upon to provide emotional, financial, housing, babysitting, and daycare support. If they have substantial support systems, how can these systems be used to the best advantage? If social support is sadly lacking, how can it be improved? Later, we will discuss further how groups, organizations, and communities can serve to enhance or detract from people's sense of relatedness and their overall well-being.

Habitat and Niche   *Habitats* are "the physical and social settings" of people (Payne, 2005, p. 151). Related terms are *home ranges* and *territory*; Gitterman and Germain (2008b) explain the significance of a habitat:

> For humans, physical habitat may be rural or urban, and include residential dwellings, transportation systems, workplaces, schools, religious structures, social agencies, hospitals, and amenities such as parks, recreation facilities, entertainment centers, libraries, and museums. Habitats that do not support the growth, health, and social functioning of individuals and families, and do not provide community amenities to an optimum degree, are likely to produce isolation, disorientation, and helplessness. Thus habitats may interfere with basic functions of family and community life. (pp. 55–56)

A *niche* is "the particular social position held" by a person within the social structure of the habitat (Payne, 2005, p. 151). An individual's niche can be positive and supportive, or negative and isolating. Gitterman and Germain (2008b) remark:

> What constitutes a growth-supporting, health-promoting human niche is defined differently in various societies and in different historical eras. In the United States, a set of rights, including the right to equal opportunity, generally shapes a niche. Yet millions of children and adults occupy niches that do not support human needs, rights, and aspirations—often because of some personal or cultural characteristic devalued by society. (p. 56)

In other words, for example, an extremely poor person of a race discriminated against by the ruling majority might experience a niche that is characterized by deprivation and suffering. Conceptualizing the social environment in this manner helps generalist practitioners identify people in need and look carefully at the social conditions contributing to these needs.

All of the terms discussed thus far that are taken from the ecological perspective involve the essence of dynamic interactions between and among people. Highlight 1.2 cites three personal characteristics that also affect human interaction in the social environment.

People's Involvement with Multiple Systems in the Social Environment

We have established that people are constantly and dynamically involved in interactions with other systems in the social environment. There is constant activity, communication, and change. Understanding human behavior seeks to answer the question, "What is it in any particular situation that causes a problem or creates a need?" Ecosystems theory provides a perspective for social workers to assess and understand many aspects of a situation by looking at the various systems involved. A number of useful terms for conceptualizing interaction include *target of change, micro system, mezzo system, macro system, client system, and macro client system.*

Generalist social work practitioners work on the behalf of individuals, families, groups, organizations, and communities. Any of these systems may be a *target of change*, the system that social workers need to change or influence in order to accomplish goals. It is helpful to think of different systems as micro, mezzo, or macro systems.

| Highlight 1.2 | **Personal Characteristics Affecting Human Interaction in the Social Environment** |

At least three basic concepts inherent in the ecological approach reflect personal characteristics (Germain & Gitterman, 1995, p. 818; Payne, 2005, p. 151). *Competence* involves people's "sense that they have relevant skills, or can get help from others" (Payne, 2005, p. 151). An inherent assumption is that people are naturally "motivated to affect their environment in order to survive" (Germain & Gitterman, 1995, p. 181). People should have opportunities throughout life to effectively manipulate, improve, and thrive in their environment. The implication is that social workers should nurture people's natural tendency to work and succeed in their environment. This applies to people from all walks of life. For example, impoverished people living in a border shantytown require opportunities to improve their living conditions. In addition to food and clothing, needs include financial resources for building materials, skilled help regarding how to improve dwellings, and education to establish a higher standard of living.

Self-esteem involves "the extent to which [people] feel significant and worthy" (Payne, 2005, p. 151). Each individual must feel important. In the university setting, I always try to demonstrate respect and consideration for janitors and administrative assistants. Their jobs are necessary to keep the university running. They deserve to feel important and to have self-esteem, even though their job positions and salaries fall low on the status ladder of higher education.

Self-direction involves people's "sense of having control over their lives, alongside taking responsibility for their actions while respecting others' rights" (Payne, 2005, p. 151). This concept is almost synonymous with self-determination, a core concept in social work values. People have the right to make their own decisions and control their own behavior within their environment as long as their actions don't harm others. Thus, practitioners must vigilantly assess the extent to which people's involvement in groups, organizations, and communities allows them to demonstrate self-direction.

A *micro system* is an individual. We have established that a system is a set of elements that are orderly, interrelated, and a functional whole. In a broad sense, this definition applies to individual persons. Hence, a person is also a type of system, for our purposes, a *micro system*. Individual systems entail all the many aspects of personality, emotion, beliefs, behavior, interests, goals, strengths, and weaknesses that make a person unique. Targeting a micro system for change involves working with an individual, identifying issues and strengths, and enhancing that person's functioning. Figure 1.4 illustrates the complexity of any individual micro system.

A *mezzo system* refers to any small group. Figure 1.5 reflects how individuals make up mezzo systems. In the macro environment, groups include those involved with organizations or communities.

A *macro system* is any system larger than a small group. This book, of course, focuses on organizations and communities.

Macro settings are made up of individuals and groups of individuals. Thus, workers must use their skills in developing relationships, interviewing, and problem-solving with individuals and groups who are responsible for making decisions about communities' and organizations' policies and activities. Workers can undertake projects, seek policy changes, and develop programs within the macro context. (Note that the explanation of specific skills for effecting macro-level change is beyond the scope of this book and is saved for future practice classes.) Figure 1.6 depicts an organizational macro system that is made up of

| **Concept Summary 1.4** | **Major Concepts in the Ecological Perspective** |

Social environment: The conditions, circumstances, and human interactions that encompass human beings.

Energy: The natural power of active involvement between people and their environments.

Input: The energy, information, or communication flow received from other systems.

Output: What happens to input after it's gone through and been processed by some system.

Interface: The exact point where the interaction between an individual and the environment takes place.

Adaptation: The capacity to adjust to surrounding environmental conditions.

"Person-in-environment fit": The extent to which "the needs, capacities, behavioral styles, and goals of people" fit or match "the characteristics of the environment" (Gitterman & Germain, 2008b, p. 55).

Stressor: "A demand, situation, or circumstance" that results in physiological and/or emotional tension (i.e., stress) (Zastrow & Kirst-Ashman, 2010, p. 605).

Stress: The resulting physiological and/or emotional tension produced by a stressor that affects a person's internal balance.

Coping: A form of adaptation where people respond to stress by expending effort to change (1) their own behavioral, cognitive, or emotional reactions; (2) the environmental conditions contributing to the stress; (3) the interaction between their own reactions and the environment; or (4) some combination of these responses (Gitterman & Germain, 2008a, 2008b).

"Relatedness": "The capacity to form attachments" (Payne, 2005, p. 151).

Habitat: "The physical and social settings of people" (Payne, 2005, p. 151).

Niche: "The particular social position held" by a person within the social structure of the habitat (Payne, 2005, p. 151).

Competence: People's "sense that they have relevant skills, or can get help from others" (Payne, 2005, p. 151).

Self-esteem: "The extent to which [people] feel significant and worthy" (Payne, 2005, p. 151).

Self-direction: People's "sense of having control over their lives, alongside taking responsibility for their actions while respecting others' rights" (Payne, 2005, p. 151).

Personality
Emotion   Strengths
Beliefs   Weaknesses
Behavior   Goals
Interests
MICRO SYSTEM
(An Individual)

Figure 1.4 | An Individual Micro System

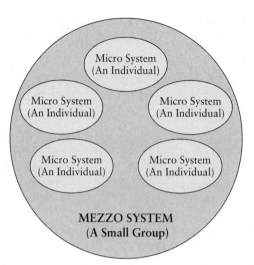

Figure 1.5 | Micro Systems Make Up Mezzo Systems

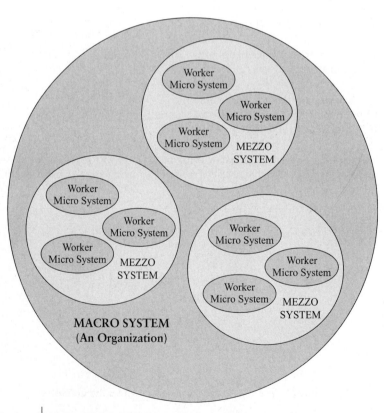

Figure 1.6 | Organizations Are Macro Systems

various groups and units (mezzo systems) that in turn are made up of individual workers (micro systems). Figure 1.7 illustrates a community macro system that is a complex, interconnected array of various smaller macro systems and groups (for example, neighborhoods, businesses, social service agencies, schools, and churches).

The *client system* is any individual, family, group, organization, or community who will ultimately benefit from social work intervention. Figure 1.8 portrays how social workers, client systems, and macro systems operate within the social environment. A client system may be micro, mezzo, or macro. The client system and the social worker work together for change, reflected by their close contact or interface. Arrows leading from the social worker/client system to the organization and community macro systems depict how social workers and clients work together with these macro systems in the social environment on the behalf of clients. The two-way arrow between the organization and community macro systems reflects how organizations and communities are integrally involved with each other.

Macro client systems include communities, organizations, and larger groups of clientele who have similar issues and problems and are potential beneficiaries of positive change. The concept of macro intervention concerns agency or social change that affects larger numbers of people than an individual client or family. For example, a social worker might work with a community to establish a *food bank* (a program where surplus food is collected from restaurants, cafeterias,

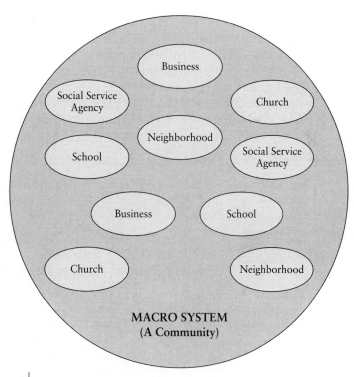

Figure 1.7 | Communities Are Macro Systems

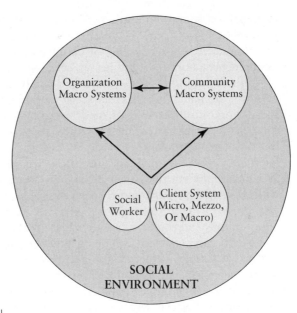

Figure 1.8 | Social Workers Help Clients Negotiate the Social Environment

grocery stores, individuals, and anywhere else it might be available, and redistributed to places such as soup kitchens serving people in need). A practitioner might also work with a social services organization to create a new position for an interpreter to serve as translator for a large population of Hmong clients who recently immigrated from Southeast Asia. The next section describes a history of generalist practice with and within communities serving various macro client systems.

The History of Generalist Practice with and within Communities

Macro practice is generalist social work practice intending to affect change in large systems, including communities and organizations. Historically, *community*

Concept Summary 1.5 | **Concepts Concerning Social Work Practice with Multiple Systems in the Macro Social Environment**

Target of change: The system that social workers need to change or influence in order to accomplish goals.

Micro system: An individual.

Mezzo system: A small group.

Macro system: Any system larger than a small group.

Client system: Any individual, family, group, organization, or community who will ultimately benefit from social work intervention.

Macro client system: Communities, organizations, and larger groups of clientele who have similar issues and problems and are potential beneficiaries of positive change.

organization has been the term used to refer to macro practice in social work. The methods and directions of social work practice have changed and evolved, just as the economic and social realities of the times have drastically changed. However, reviewing the historical perspective on community practice helps us to understand the significance of community assessment and work today.

Past major methods of community organization engaged in by social workers have included social action, social planning, and locality development (Rothman, 2001). *Social action* is coordinated effort to advocate for change in a social institution to benefit a specific population (for example, homeless people), solve a social problem, enhance people's well-being, or correct unfairness (for example, racism) (Kirst-Ashman & Hull, 2009a, b). (*Racism* is the belief that people of different races are inherently different and that some races are superior to others.) Social action applies macro-practice skills to advocate for people in local, state, national, and global communities. Frequently, social action can be used to remedy imbalances of power.

Social planning involves "a technical process of problem-solving with regard to substantive social problems, such as delinquency, housing, and mental health" (Rothman, 2001, p. 31). The emphasis here is to call in experts or consultants to work, usually with designated community leaders, to solve specific problems. People in the general community would have little, if any, participation or input into the problem-solving process. For example, a city might call in an urban renewal expert to recommend what should be done with a deteriorating area in the community.

Locality development emphasizes "community change . . . pursued optimally through broad participation of a wide spectrum of people at the local community level in determining goals and taking . . . action" (Rothman, 2001, p. 29). The idea is to involve as many people as possible within the community in a democratic manner to define their goals and help themselves. Locality development fits extremely well with social work values. Individual dignity, participation, and free choice are emphasized.

Highlight 1.3 describes more contemporary approaches to macro practice.

Defining Generalist Practice: A Wide Range of Professional Roles

Another concept important in the definition of generalist practice involves the assumption of a wide range of professional roles. Such roles when working with macro systems include the following (Kirst-Ashman & Hull, 2009a, pp. 22–26; Yessian & Broskowsky, 1983, pp. 183–184):

- *Advocate:* One who steps forward on the behalf of the client system in order to promote fair and equitable treatment or gain needed resources.
- *Mediator*: One who resolves arguments or disagreements among micro, mezzo, or macro systems by assuming a neutral role.
- *Integrator/Coordinator:* One who oversees the process of assembling different elements to form a cohesive whole, product, or process (for example, a new agency policy) and subsequently watches over its functioning to make sure it's effective.

Today, macro practice is still a major thrust of generalist social work. The basic concept of community is just as important as ever. However, Rothman (2007) proposes a new outlook more appropriate to current macro practice that calls for "multi modes of intervention" (p. 11). Two new ideas predominate.

One major initiative is that the traditional three community organization methods should be brought up to date to reflect a modification in focus. First, "social advocacy" should replace social action (p. 12). "*Social advocacy* deems the application of pressure as the best course of action to take against people or institutions that may have [brought about] . . . the problem or that stand in the way of its solution—which frequently involves promoting equity or social justice. When interests clash in this way, conflict is a given" (p. 12). Advocacy becomes the focus of attention.

"*Planning and policy practice*" then replace the traditional social planning approach (p. 12). Planning continues to involve "proposing and enacting particular solutions" (p. 12). *Policy practice* entails "efforts to change policies in legislative, agency, and community settings, whether by establishing new policies, improving existing ones, or defeating the policy initiatives of other people" (Jansson, 2008, p. 14). Changing policy often becomes an objective.

"Community capacity development" is substituted for community development (Rothman, 2007, p. 12). "*Community capacity development* assumes that change is best accomplished when the people affected by problems are empowered with the knowledge and skills needed to understand their problems, and then work cooperatively together to overcome them. Thus there is a premium on consensus as a tactic and on social solidarity [unity including diverse community groups that is based on mutual interests, support, and goals] as [a means] . . . and outcome" (Rothman, 2007, p. 12). Here community *capacity* (the potential use of the community's inherent strengths, resources, citizen participation, and leadership) is stressed.

The second primary initiative posed for contemporary macro practice involves the flexibility of mixing various aspects of these three approaches to get things done. Rothman (2007) reflects that macro practice is often a complex process that requires emphasizing various aspects of these three approaches depending on the situation. For example, planning and policy practice may require varying degrees of social advocacy. *Advocacy*, of course, involves stepping forward on the behalf of the client system in order to promote fair and equitable treatment or gain needed resources. *Policy advocacy* is "policy practice that aims to help powerless groups, such as women, children, poor people, persons of color, gay men and lesbians, and people with disabilities to improve their resources and opportunities" (Jansson, 2009, p. 563).

Rothman (2007) provides several examples of people undertaking policy advocacy to improve policies that affect groups at risk of harm; these policy advocates include:

> Dr. David Kessler, who as head of the Federal Drug Administration clashed with the pharmaceutical companies on behalf of safe and affordable medications for patients; Dr. Everettt Koop, who as Surgeon General, stood up to the cigarette companies in the first major effort to warn the public about the serious health dangers in smoking: and Peter Edelman, who faced off with the Clinton administration over sizable service cuts affecting welfare recipients. (p. 21)

Another example of a more flexible combination of methods involves community capacity development with an emphasis on planning. Rothman (2007) explains:

> Classic [community] capacity development typically has the practitioner starting with a blank page and encouraging residents to decide what situations within their community bother them the most and then what changes they want to initiate. . . .
>
> Community economic [capacity] development [that emphasizes planning], on the other hand, starts with a concrete agenda and organizing mechanisms. It believes that what distressed communities need most is an upgrade of economic conditions. Residents are called on to mount programs and actions that will accomplish that. According to Soifer (2002), this means concentrating on housing development, land development, job creation, and setting up more relevant financial institutions—primarily banks. (p. 25)

- *Manager:* One who assumes some level of administrative responsibility for a social services agency or other organizational system.
- *Educator:* One who gives information and teaches skills to other systems.
- *Analyst/Evaluator:* One who determines the effectiveness of a program or agency for an organization or community.
- *Broker:* One who links any size system (individuals, families, groups, organizations, or communities) with community resources and services.
- *Facilitator:* One who guides a group experience.
- *Initiator:* One who calls attention to an issue or problem.
- *Negotiator:* One who acts to settle disputes and/or resolve disagreements, acting on the behalf of one of the parties involved.
- *Mobilizer:* One who identifies and convenes community people and resources and makes them responsive to unmet community needs.

Defining Generalist Practice: Application of Critical Thinking Skills

Critical thinking is yet another important concept in the definition of generalist practice. *Critical thinking* is (1) the careful scrutiny of what is stated as true or what appears to be true and the resulting expression of an opinion or conclusion based on that scrutiny, and (2) the creative formulation of an opinion or conclusion when presented with a question, problem, or issue. Critical thinking concentrates on "the process of reasoning" (Gibbs & Gambrill, 1999, p. 3). It stresses *how* individuals think about the truth inherent in a statement or *how* they analyze an issue to formulate their own conclusions. As Gibbs and Gambrill (1999) so aptly state, "Critical thinkers question what others take for granted" (p. 13). This is an essential concept when trying to understand what's going on in the macro environment in which you work as a social worker.

Two dimensions included in the definition of critical thinking are significant. First, critical thinking focuses on the questioning of beliefs, statements, assumptions, lines of reasoning, actions, and experiences. You read a "fact" in a book or hear about it from a friend or an instructor. Critical thinking focuses on *not* taking this "fact" at face value. Rather, it entails assuming the following Triple A approach to seriously examine and evaluate its validity:

1. *Ask* questions.
2. *Assess* the established facts and issues involved.
3. *Assert* a concluding opinion. (Kirst-Ashman, 2010)

For example, a friend and fellow student might tell you, "Gasoline prices will never go down again." To what extent is this statement really true? To find out, first you could *ask* questions about what the statement is really saying. What does "never" mean? Does it include differences in price from day to day, or between one gas station and another or one area of the country and another? What future economic factors might influence the cost of gas? Is it possible to predict the future accurately as if looking into a crystal ball? What experiences has your friend had to come to such a conclusion?

Second, *assess* the established facts and issues involved by seeking out information to answer the questions. What is the track record of the average daily gas price in your area? To what extent has it fluctuated over time? What variables might affect the cost and potentially decrease its cost—discovery of new oil fields, drilling in Alaska, development of alternative fuels, increased use of public transportation, regulation of gas costs by the government?

Third, *assert* a concluding opinion. To what extent do you agree with your friend's statement? Or, would you prefer to assume a more optimistic stance and wait and see?

Critical thinking can be applied to virtually any belief, statement, assumption, line of reasoning, action, or experience proposed as being true. Consider the following statements that someone might maintain as "facts":

- Rich people are arrogant.
- Politicians are crooks.
- It is physically impossible for pigs to look up into the sky.
- Rats and horses can't vomit.
- A duck's quack doesn't echo, and no one knows why.[5]

These statements are silly (although some may be true), but the point is that critical thinking can be applied to an infinite array of thoughts and ideas. For each of the statements above: (1) what questions would you *ask;* (2) how would you *assess* the established facts and issues involved; and (3) what concluding opinion would you finally *assert?*

The second facet of the definition of critical thinking is the creative formulation of an opinion or conclusion when presented with a question, problem, or issue. Instead of being presented with a proposed "fact" to be scrutinized for its validity, you are asked your opinion about an issue, assumption, or action. Examples include:

- Should murderers receive the death penalty?
- Should national health care be made available to all citizens who need it and be paid for by the government?
- What is the best way to eliminate poverty in this nation?

Consider answering the last question. It could be posed as a term paper question in one of your courses. First, what questions about it would you *ask?* What are the reasons for poverty in a relatively rich industrialized country? What social welfare programs are currently available to address poverty? What innovative new ideas for programs might be tried? Where might funding for such programs be found? How much money would it take to eliminate poverty, and who would pay for it?

Second, what facts and issues would you seek to address and *assess?* You probably would first seek to define poverty—what makes a person or family considered "poor"? What income level or lack of income is involved? You then might research statistics, costs, and studies concerning the effectiveness of various

---

[5] The last three statements were received in an email from Keith McClory on January 12, 2002.

programs intended to reduce poverty. You might also investigate innovative ideas. Perhaps there are proposals for programs that you feel look promising. You might explore what various programs cost and how they are funded. Note that these suggestions only scratch the surface of how you might examine the issue.

Third, *assert* your opinion or conclusion. To what extent do you think it is possible to eliminate poverty? What kinds of resources and programs do you think it would take? What do you feel citizens and their government should do about poverty?

Critical thinking enhances self-awareness and the ability to detect various modes of distorted thinking that can trick people into assuming truth (Gibbs & Gambrill, 1999). The following are among the many traps to avoid by using critical thinking (Ruscio, 2006, pp. 6–10):

- *Outward appearance of science.* A supposed "fact" may superficially be cited in the context of scientific proof. How many times have you seen some well-groomed man wearing a doctor's lab coat appear in a television commercial and state that this weight-loss supplement's effectiveness has been scientifically proven many times over? What questions might you ask about this? What tests were run to prove this effectiveness? Was the supplement taken by people who also were implementing other weight-loss approaches, including exercise and diet restrictions? Is the professional-looking person on TV telling the truth or being paid to read from a script? A related issue involves dietary supplements of all kinds that are supposed to do miraculous things for your health. Current federal standards allow "for anyone to sell almost any drug to the public, as long as he or she refers to the drug as a dietary supplement and does not make specific health claims about its effects. . . . Unproven remedies . . . are now officially tolerated under the guise of dietary supplements. . . . Vague wording and the sheer number of people who routinely violate . . . [legislative] provisions . . . have resulted in insufficient enforcement of even these weak standards" (Ruscio, 2006, p. 65). Hence, we really don't know the extent to which various supplements are helpful or harmful.
- *Absence of skeptical peer review.* Has the fact been evaluated by credible professionals who support its validity? There is an almost infinite number of websites on the Internet addressing almost any topic you could think of and claiming almost any "fact" to be true. A scary thing is that it's almost impossible to tell which sites have well-established validity and credibility and which do not. Usually, websites ending in *.edu* or *.gov* enhance credibility potential because they're supposed to be initiated by formal educational or governmental organizations. But, how do you know for sure?
- *Reliance on personal experience and testimonials.* A woman enthusiastically proclaims, "This exercise equipment gave me awesome abs and made me look twenty years younger!" Because an approach worked for one person doesn't mean it will work for all. Perhaps that woman worked out with the equipment three hours a day for the past year. How has diet and stress management contributed to her youthful appearance? How old is she anyway, and can she prove it? Is she telling the truth? What scientific evidence is available to document the effectiveness of the equipment?

- *Wishful thinking* (p. 43). Hoping that something is so can provide a powerful incentive to believe in it. For example, consider the idea, "Putting magnets on your head can cure headaches." It would be nice to find an automatic cure for headaches that did not involve imbibing some substance. However, Ruscio (2006) explains:

> What about the alleged healing power of magnets as they interact with our bodies? The suggestion for how a magnetic field might be useful in curing disease is that it increases the flow of blood (which contains iron) to a targeted area, thereby bringing extra nutrients and carrying away the waste products of our metabolism. This theory, too, is directly contradicted by known facts. Blood, as with other bodily tissue and fluids, consists primarily of water. Thus, the fact that water is slightly repelled by a magnetic field is especially relevant. Why? Because the primary constituent of the human body—including not only our blood but also, as in most forms of life, all of our tissues and fluids—is water. We are therefore weakly repelled by magnetic fields. In principle, a strong enough magnet could be used to levitate a person, as has been done with drops of water, flowers, grasshoppers, and frogs. The small amounts of iron in our blood's hemoglobin do not exist in sufficiently dense quantities to offset the repulsive effect of the much larger amount of water. Therefore, to the extent that magnets have *any* influence on our blood—and this influence is minimal—they will drive blood *away* from the targeted areas. (pp. 82–83)

- *The "ancient wisdom" fallacy* (p. 59). "That must be the right way to do it because we've always done it that way." Ruscio (2006) points out that this type of argument can have dangerous consequences, because "if beliefs are granted truth owing merely to their age, this would provide justification for sexism, racism, anti-Semitism, and a host of other repellent notions that have been widely held throughout human history" (p. 59).
- *The popularity fallacy* (p. 59). "Everybody else is doing it, so it must be right." I once had a classmate, age twenty-six no less, who said in an election year that he was going to vote for the current president because that president had already been elected, and all those people who voted for him surely couldn't be wrong. I stared at him in total disbelief. How could he be so naïve? How could he not think for himself? And, at his age? He obviously believed in the popularity fallacy.

Because of the importance of critical thinking in social work and in generalist practice, as well as in understanding macro systems and the social environment, a wide range of critical thinking questions will be posed throughout this book.

 Critical Thinking Questions 1.2

What do you think about critical thinking? Do you use it often? If so, to what extent have you found it useful?

Defining Generalist Practice: Incorporation of Research-Informed Practice

One final important dimension of generalist practice involves the use of research. Social work students must demonstrate competency in *research-informed practice*. This means social workers should use the approaches and interventions in their practice that research has determined are effective. Social workers should employ "research findings to improve practice, policy, and social service delivery" (CSWE, 2008, p. 5). Social workers might also have opportunities to participate in *practice-based research*. This research, which closely involves the everyday work of practitioners, focuses on collecting data and providing results directly related to the processes of social work practice (Tripodi & Lalayants, 2008, p. 518). Highlight 1.4 introduces a concept related to research-informed practice—evidence-based practice.

Why Research Is Important

Knowledge of social work research is important for two basic reasons. First, it can help social workers become more effective in their direct practice by choosing interventions that have been proven successful, thereby getting better and clearer results. Framing social work interventions so they can be evaluated through research provides information about which specific techniques work best with which problems. Evaluation of practice throughout the intervention process can help determine whether a worker is really helping a client.

Second, accumulated research helps build a foundation for planning effective interventions. Knowledge of what has worked best in the past provides guidelines for approaches and techniques to be used in the present and in the future. Research establishes the basis for the development of programs and policies that affect many people. Such knowledge can also be used to generate new theories and ideas to further enhance the effectiveness of social work practice.

Highlight 1.4	Evidence-Based Practice

Another term frequently used in social work, which has a meaning similar to research-informed practice, is *evidence-based practice*. This is "the conscientious, explicit, and judicious use of current best evidence in making decisions about the care of clients" (Gambrill, 2000, p. 46; Race, 2008; Rubin, 2008). Gambrill (2000) explains:

It involves integrating individual practice expertise with the best available external evidence from systematic research as well as considering the values and expectations of clients. External research findings related to problems are drawn on if they are available and they apply to a particular client. Involving clients as informed participants in a collaborative helping relationship is a hallmark of evidence-based practice. Clients are fully informed about the risks and benefits of recommended services as well as alternatives (including the alternative of doing nothing). . . . The term *evidence-based practice* is preferable to the term *empirical practice*. The latter term now seems to be applied to material that has been published, whether or not it is evidence-based. Such use represents an appeal to authority (not evidence). (pp. 46–47)

Chapter Summary

The following summarizes this chapter's content as it relates to the learning objectives presented at the beginning of the chapter. Objectives include the following:

A. Define and explore the macro social environment.

The macro social environment is the configuration of communities, organizations, and groups within the latter that are products of social, economic, and political forces and institutions. A community is "a number of people who have something in common that connects them in some way and that distinguishes them from others" (Homan, 2008, p. 8). Organizations are "(1) social entities that (2) are goal directed, (3) are designed as deliberately structured and coordinated activity systems, and (4) are linked to the external environment" (Daft, 2007, p. 10). Some organizations provide social services. A group is at least two individuals gathered together because of some common bond, to meet members' social and emotional needs, or to fulfill some mutual purpose. Social, economic, and political forces operate within and affect the macro social environment.

B. Introduce material addressed by the remainder of the book.

The Council on Social Work Education (CSWE) that accredits social work programs requires that students "apply knowledge of human behavior and the social environment"; this includes knowledge about "the range of social system in which people live . . . and the ways social systems promote or deter people in maintaining or achieving health and well-being" (CSWE, 2008, p. 6). The intent is to provide a foundation so that social workers can "utilize conceptual frameworks to guide the processes of assessment, intervention, and evaluation; and critique and apply knowledge to understand person and environment" (CSWE, 2008, p. 6). This book focuses on how social workers practice in agency organizational settings to help clients who live in communities. To accomplish this, generalist practitioners often work in organizational and community groups.

C. Define *generalist practice* and explain the relationship between some of its major concepts and the macro social environment.

Generalist practice, occurring within an organizational structure, is the application of an extensive and diverse knowledge base and a wide range of skills by using a seven-step planned change process to target any size system for change within the context of seven equally essential dimensions. These dimensions include: the assumption of a wide range of professional roles, the application of critical thinking skills, and the incorporation of research-informed practice to determine the most effective ways to help people and serve clients. Social workers conduct generalist practice in the context of the macro social environment. They follow a planned change process that includes engagement, assessment, planning, implementation, evaluation, termination, and follow-up.

D. Examine ecosystems theory and explain the concepts involved that are derived from systems theories and the ecological perspective.

Ecosystems theory provides one significant means of conceptualizing and understanding human behavior. Concepts taken from systems theory include system, boundaries, subsystem, homeostasis, role, relationship, input, output, negative and positive feedback, interface, differentiation, entropy, negative entropy, and equifinality. Terms taken from the ecological perspective include: the social environment; energy; input; output; interface; adaptation; person-in-environment fit; stress, stressors, and coping; relatedness; habitat; and niche.

E. Discuss people's involvement with multiple systems in the macro social environment.

A target of change is the system that social workers need to change or influence in order to accomplish goals. A micro system is an individual. A mezzo system refers to any small group. A macro system is any system larger than a small group, including organizations and communities. A client system is any individual, family, group, organization, or community who will ultimately benefit from social work intervention. Macro client systems include communities, organizations, and larger groups of clientele who have similar issues and problems and are potential beneficiaries of positive change.

F. Provide a brief history of social work practice in the macro social environment and describe contemporary macro practice.

Traditional methods of macro practice include social action, social planning, and locality development. In contemporary macro practice, social advocacy replaces social action, planning and policy practice replace social planning, and community capacity development replaces locality development.

G. Define *critical thinking* and discuss its use in generalist practice.

Critical thinking is (1) the careful scrutiny of what is stated as true or what appears to be true and the resulting expression of an opinion or conclusion based on that scrutiny, and (2) the creative formulation of an opinion or conclusion when presented with a question, problem, or issue. Generalist practitioners can use a Triple A approach to assess information and situations: (1) Ask questions; (2) assess the established facts and issues involves; and (3) assert a concluding opinion.

H. Introduce critical thinking questions that will be raised throughout the book.

Critical thinking questions addressed evaluation of one's geographic community and the frequency of using critical thinking.

Looking Ahead

This chapter described the macro social environment as the context for generalist social work practice. Some of the major concepts in the definition of generalist practice were defined and discussed. The next chapter will continue the explanation of generalist practice by examining the values and principles that guide such practice in the macro social environment.

For Further Exploration on the Internet

See this text's website at **www.cengage.com/social_work/kirst-ashman** for learning tools such as tutorial quizzing, Web links, glossary, flashcards, and PowerPoint® slides.

2 CHAPTER | Values and Principles that Guide Generalist Practice in the Macro Social Environment

Values and principles concerning human rights guide generalist social work practice.

© Viviane Moos/Corbis

CHAPTER CONTENTS

What values are most important to you? Caring for others? Self-preservation? Charity? Fairness? Equality? Material possessions? Financial stability? Honesty? Loyalty? Freedom of speech?

How do you make decisions about what is right and what is wrong? Do you have a personal code of ethics that guides your behavior? Do you consider yourself more of an independent thinker? Or do you tend to go along with the crowd and usually do what you're told?

What are your thoughts about the value of human diversity? Is it some vague concept that is difficult to relate to? Do you think of specific groups of people? Are there any groups about whom you harbor some negative feelings—for example, people with physical or cognitive disabilities, older adults, religious organizations or sects, certain racial groups, migrants and people who immigrate illegally, or people with a sexual orientation different from yours? If so, what are these negative perceptions?

Do you have thoughts about the status of human rights in the world today? Are there oppressed populations? If so, who are they? What do you think are the causes of oppression? Should it and can it be stopped? If so, how should it be stopped? Who should stop it?

We all have values and opinions about what is good and bad, right and wrong. We each have an individualized view of how the world goes round and how it ideally should go round.

Social work as a profession also promotes professional values. Additionally, the profession requires ethical conduct on the part of practitioners. Social work also views the world from a perspective that values human diversity, and seeks social and economic justice for oppressed populations. Therefore, to understand the dynamics involved in the macro social environment, it's crucial to understand the values and principles that guide generalist practitioners in their work.

This chapter will continue to discuss and explain the definition of generalist practice, which is undertaken in the context of the macro social environment. Chapter 1 defined generalist practice as follows: *generalist practice, occurring within an organizational structure,* is the application of an extensive and diverse knowledge base, professional values, and a wide range of skills by using a *seven-step planned change process* to *target any size system for change* within the context of seven equally essential dimensions. (Note again that this definition's major concepts are emphasized by italics.)

First, generalist practice requires the assumption of *a wide range of professional roles.* Second, it involves the *application of critical thinking skills* to the planned change process. Third, it *incorporates research-informed practice* to determine the most effective ways to help people and serve clients. Fourth, it necessitates the *adherence to professional values and the application of professional ethics.* Fifth, it stresses the importance of *understanding human diversity* and how diverse factors affect people's quality of life. Sixth, it emphasizes *client empowerment, strengths, and resiliency.* Seventh, it incorporates *advocacy for human rights, and the pursuit of social and economic justice.*

The first three of these seven dimensions involve the process of generalist practice and were discussed in Chapter 1. The last four dimensions involve the values and principles that guide generalist practice, which this chapter will explore.

Learning Objectives

A. Complete the discussion of the definition of generalist practice and explain the relationship between the remaining major concepts and the macro social environment. These concepts include: adhering to professional values and applying professional ethics; understanding human diversity; emphasizing client empowerment, strengths, and resiliency; and advocating for human rights and the pursuit of social and economic justice.

B. Review the National Association of Social Workers *Code of Ethics*, summarize professional ethical responsibilities, and examine ethical dilemmas.

C. Introduce the importance of identifying with the social work profession.

D. Describe human diversity with its multiple, overlapping factors (CSWE, 2008).

E. Examine diversity with respect to gender and sex, in addition to culture.

F. Define *cultural competence* and address four competencies involved.

G. Review the significance of client empowerment, strengths, and resiliency.

H. Explore the importance of advocacy for human rights and social and economic justice.

I. Examine some of the dynamics involved in oppression.

J. Introduce various critical thinking questions.

K. Focus on ethical topics.

Defining Generalist Practice: Adherence to Professional Values and the Application of Professional Ethics

Professional values and ethics are at the heart of social work. Thus, these characterize the next significant dimension in the definition of generalist practice. *Values* involve what you do and do not consider important. They concern what is and is not considered to have worth. They also involve judgments and decisions about relative worth—that is, about what is more valuable and what is less valuable.

Ethics concern principles that specify what is good and what is bad. They clarify what should and should not be done. The National Association of Social Workers (NASW) *Code of Ethics* (2008) is based on professional values and provides guidelines for what practitioners should do when confronting a range of difficult situations.

Ethics and values are clearly related although they are not synonymous. Dolgoff, Loewenberg, and Harrington (2009) explain, "Ethics are deduced from values and must be in consonance with them. The difference between them is that values are concerned with what is *good* and *desirable*, while ethics deal with what is *right* and *correct*" (p. 22). Values determine what beliefs are appropriate. Ethics address what to *do* with, or how to *apply,* those beliefs.

Cournoyer (2005) clearly summarizes the momentous importance of social work ethics as he directs his comments to generalist practitioners working in the macro social environment:

> You must consider every aspect of practice, every decision, every assessment, every intervention, and virtually every action you undertake as a social worker must be considered from the perspective of your professional ethics and obligations. This dimension supersedes all others. Ethical responsibilities take precedence over theoretical

Highlight 2.1 | The Importance of Identification with the Social Work Profession

While working within an organization, a generalist practitioner should maintain and demonstrate a professional identity. *Identification with the social work profession* means that "social workers [should] serve as representatives of the profession, its mission, and its core values" (CSWE, 2008, p. 3). Such identification includes a commitment to "the profession's enhancement and to their own professional conduct and growth" in addition to knowledge of the profession's history (CSWE, 2008, p. 3). Identification, then, involves adherence to professional ethics, demonstration of professional roles (discussed in Chapter 1), and participation in lifelong learning to enhance knowledge and skills (CSWE, 2008).

knowledge, research findings, practice wisdom, agency policies, and, of course, the social worker's own personal values, preferences, and beliefs. (p. 90)

Because of the core significance of professional values and ethics for social workers, their identification with the social work profession is a basic necessity (CSWE, 2008). Highlight 2.1 underscores the importance of this identification as generalist practitioners work in groups, organizations, and communities in the macro social environment.

The NASW *Code of Ethics*

Simply put, ethics guides professional behavior. The *Code's* mission "is to enhance human well-being and help meet the basic human needs of all people, with particular attention to the needs and empowerment of people who are vulnerable, oppressed, and living in poverty" (NASW, 2008). The six core values include

1. *Service:* Providing help, resources, and benefits so that people may achieve their maximum potential.
2. *Social justice:* Upholding the condition that in a perfect world, all citizens would have identical "rights, protection, opportunities, obligations, and social benefits" regardless of their backgrounds and membership in diverse groups (Barker, 2003, pp. 404–405).
3. *Dignity and worth of the person:* Holding in high esteem and appreciating individual value.
4. *Importance of human relationships:* Valuing the dynamic reciprocal interactions between social workers and clients, including how they communicate, think and feel about each other, and behave toward each other.
5. *Integrity:* Maintaining trustworthiness and sound adherence to moral ideals.
6. *Competence:* Having the necessary skills and abilities to perform work with clients effectively.

The most extensive portion of the *Code* is devoted to specific "Ethical Standards." It encompasses 155 specific principles clustered under six major categories. These include social workers' ethical responsibilities to clients, to colleagues, in practice settings, as professionals, to the social work profession, and to the broader society. Focus on Ethics 2.1 summarizes the major concepts involved in each of the six broad areas. Note that the entire *Code* is available from NASW online at www.naswdc.org/pubs/code/default.asp.

| **Focus on Ethics 2.1** | **A Summary of Ethical Standards in the NASW *Code of Ethics*** |

1. Social Workers' Ethical Responsibilities to Clients

    1.01 Commitment to Clients
    1.02 Self-Determination
    1.03 Informed Consent
    1.04 Competence
    1.05 Cultural Competence and Social Diversity
    1.06 Conflicts of Interest
    1.07 Privacy and Confidentiality
    1.08 Access to Records
    1.09 Sexual Relationships
    1.10 Physical Contact
    1.11 Sexual Harassment
    1.12 Derogatory Language
    1.13 Payment for Services
    1.14 Clients Who Lack Decision-Making Capacity
    1.15 Interruption of Services
    1.16 Termination of Services

2. Social Workers' Ethical Responsibilities to Colleagues

    2.01 Respect
    2.02 Confidentiality
    2.03 Interdisciplinary Collaboration
    2.04 Disputes Involving Colleagues
    2.05 Consultation
    2.06 Referral for Services
    2.07 Sexual Relationships
    2.08 Sexual Harassment
    2.09 Impairment of Colleagues
    2.10 Incompetence of Colleagues
    2.11 Unethical Conduct of Colleagues

3. Social Workers' Ethical Responsibilities in Practice Settings

    3.01 Supervision and Consultation
    3.02 Education and Training
    3.03 Performance Evaluation
    3.04 Client Records
    3.05 Billing
    3.06 Client Transfer
    3.07 Administration
    3.08 Continuing Education and Staff Development
    3.09 Commitments to Employers
    3.10 Labor–Management Disputes

4. Social Workers' Ethical Responsibilities as Professionals

    4.01 Competence
    4.02 Discrimination
    4.03 Private Conduct
    4.04 Dishonesty, Fraud, and Deception
    4.05 Impairment
    4.06 Misrepresentation
    4.07 Solicitations
    4.08 Acknowledging Credit

5. Social Workers' Ethical Responsibilities to the Social Work Profession

    5.01 Integrity of the Profession
    5.02 Evaluation and Research

6. Social Workers' Ethical Responsibilities to the Broader Society

    6.01 Social Welfare
    6.02 Public Participation
    6.03 Public Emergencies
    6.04 Social and Political Action

Social Workers' Ethical Responsibilities to Clients The first category of ethical standards identifies social workers' sixteen ethical responsibilities to clients. How should practitioners behave with respect to clients? What aspects of worker/client interaction are most significant within an ethical context? The standards range from supporting client *self-determination* (each individual's right to make his or her own decisions) to maintaining the highest possible level of *confidentiality* (the principle that workers should not share information provided by or about a client unless they have the client's explicit permission to do so) to avoiding sexual relationships with clients.

Social Workers' Ethical Responsibilities to Colleagues The *Code* specifies eleven areas in which practitioners have ethical responsibilities to colleagues. These focus on having respect for colleagues, even when differences of opinion arise. The areas also address working cooperatively for clients' benefit. Social workers should make referrals to professionals with other areas of expertise when necessary. Finally, social workers should address situations when colleagues are functioning ineffectively due to personal problems or unethical conduct.

Social Workers' Ethical Responsibilities in Practice Settings This section of the *Code* focuses on ten standards for appropriate behavior in practice settings. Social workers who supervise others should be competent and evaluate supervisees fairly. Any information or data any social worker records should be accurate. Social workers should advocate for increased funding both inside and outside their agencies when resources are needed for clients. Social workers should "act to prevent and eliminate discrimination in the employing organization's work assignments and in its employment policies and practices" (NASW, 2008, 3.9e). Finally, practitioners should make sure their employers are aware of unethical practices.

Social Workers' Ethical Responsibilities as Professionals Social workers' ethical responsibilities as professionals include eight broad dimensions by which they should judge their behavior and responsibility. First and foremost, they should be competent to do their jobs. If they are not, they should either seek out the education and learn the skills needed to become competent, or get another job. Social workers should not "practice, condone, facilitate, or collaborate with any form of discrimination on the basis of race, ethnicity, national origin, color, sex, sexual orientation, gender identity or expression, age marital status, political belief, religion, immigration status, or mental or physical disability" (NASW, 2008, 4.02). They should be honest, avoid fraud, and seek help when personal problems begin to interfere with their professional effectiveness. They should represent themselves and their qualifications accurately, and never take credit for someone else's work.

Social Workers' Ethical Responsibilities to the Social Work Profession Ethical responsibilities to the social work profession focus on two dimensions: integrity, and evaluation and research. *Integrity* refers to social workers' promotion of high practice standards. Social workers should strive to maintain and enhance professional knowledge, values, and ethics. Social workers should participate in activities aimed at professional contributions, such as "teaching, research, consultation, service, legislative testimony, presentations in the community, and participation in their professional organizations" (NASW, 2008, 5.01c), and contribute to the social work knowledge base.

Social Workers' Ethical Responsibilities to the Broader Society Ethical responsibilities to the broader society include four areas that reflect the basic core of social work, namely, to advocate and work for people's general welfare. This responsibility surpasses those merely listed in most job descriptions. Social workers should promote people's general welfare on all levels from the local to the global.

They should become actively involved in the formulation of public policy, flock to provide help during emergencies (e.g., floods, tornadoes, or earthquakes), and actively participate in social and political action.

It is beyond the scope of this book to elaborate on each specific ethical standard here. However, a number of designated standards and ethical issues will be discussed through various Focus on Ethics perspectives periodically portrayed throughout the book. Focus on Ethics 2.2 introduces the concept of ethical dilemmas.

Focus on Ethics 2.2 | ## Ethical Dilemmas

Note that from a superficial perspective, professional judgments may look like a simple matter of common sense. Just do the right thing, right? However, in real-life decisions, values and ethical principles constantly conflict. This can result in *ethical dilemmas*, namely, problematic situations where one must make a difficult choice among two or more alternatives where ethical standards conflict. No one perfect answer can conform to all the ethical standards involved. Sometimes, there is substantial personal or professional risk for the practitioner who raises unpopular questions.

Consider the following two examples occurring in the macro social environment:

• One practitioner, Bruce, reflects on his predicament, "I work in an agency that is not providing the services agreed to in exchange for grant money. Its brochures advertise the services as available and the agency documentation shows the services as provided, so the grantor believes the services are in place. The staff doesn't have the necessary resources, so those directly responsible for the care of the individuals who should be receiving the services are under a lot of stress. The consumers were promised something and are not getting it" (Kenyon, 1999, p. 213).

Answer the following questions:

1. What major issues are involved here?
2. What alternatives are available to Bruce?
3. What are the pros and cons of each alternative?
4. What do you think is the "right thing" to do?
5. What would you do if you were Bruce?

• "Adriana works in a community mental health clinic, and most of her time is devoted to dealing with immediate crises. The more she works with people in crisis, the more she is convinced that the focus of her work should be on preventive programs designed to educate the public. Adriana comes to believe strongly that there would be far fewer clients in distress if people were effectively contacted and motivated to participate in growth-oriented educational programs. She develops detailed, logical, and convincing proposals for programs she would like to implement in the community, but they are consistently rejected by the director of her center. Because the clinic is partially funded by the government for the express purpose of crisis intervention, the director feels uneasy about approving any program that does not relate directly to this objective" (Corey, Corey, & Callanan, 2007, p. 506).

Answer the following questions:

1. What major issues are involved here?
2. What alternatives are available to Adriana?
3. What are the pros and cons of each alternative?
4. What do you think is the "right thing" to do?
5. What would you do if you were Adriana?

This brief discussion simply introduces the concept of ethical dilemmas.

Professional ethical standards always stand at the forefront of effective generalist practice. To understand the dynamics and issues characterizing the macro social environment, it is necessary to identify and assess various potential ethical pitfalls. Later chapters will continue to discuss the importance of values and ethics.

Defining Generalist Practice: Understanding and Appreciating Human Diversity

The next dimension important for defining generalist practice is the appreciation and engagement of human diversity (CSWE, 2008). *Human diversity* refers to "the range of differences between people in terms of race, ethnicity, age, geography, religion, values, culture, orientations, physical and mental health, and other distinguishing characteristics" (Barker, 2003, p. 203). Lum (2004) reflects:

> *Diversity* emphasizes *the similarities and differences among ethnic and cultural persons and groups.* The diversity of the United States is comprised of ethnic, gender, sexual orientation, and age groups. In speaking of diversity, we recognize *the similarities that bind us together and respect the differences among cultures* in our country. (p. 5)

Social work by nature addresses virtually any type of problem posed by any type of person from any type of background. To help people, practitioners must be open-minded, nonjudgmental, knowledgeable, and skilled to work with any client. Social work education is charged with teaching knowledge, skills, and values concerning "the intersectionality of factors including age, class, color, culture, disability, ethnicity, gender, gender identity and expression, immigration status, political ideology, race, religion, sex, and sexual orientation" (CSWE, 2008, p. 5).

Intersectionality of Diverse Factors

The concept of *intersectionality* involves the idea that people are complex and can belong to multiple, overlapping diverse groups. "The intersectional perspective acknowledges the breadth of human experiences, instead of conceptualizing social relations and identities separately in terms of either race *or* class *or* gender *or* age *or* sexual orientation"; rather, an intersectional approach focuses on the "interactional affects" of belonging to multiple groups (Murphy, Hunt, Zajicek, Norris, & Hamilton, 2009, p. 2). People may experience injustice from a combination of reasons. The concept of intersectionality "underscores the complex nature of cultural and personal identities and human experiences that cannot be defined simply by one dimension of inequality or difference—either race or gender or sexual orientation or ability. The social worker, who is involved in working with individuals, families, groups, and communities belonging to diverse groups, must develop the cultural competence to work with people at the intersections of the multiple dimensions of diversity" (Murphy et al., 2009, p. 42).

Murphy and her colleagues (2009) provide the following case example demonstrating the complexity of intersectionality:

> The Vue family emigrated from Laos six months ago. They were happy to find a small apartment that is convenient to a grocery store and meat-packing plant where Mr. Vue works long hours. They have three daughters, aged five years, four years, and six months. Shortly after they moved in, a neighbor called the local Department of Human Services (DHS). The neighbor, Mrs. Smith, had spotted one of the girls sitting alone in

front of the apartment door one afternoon. Mrs. Smith was surprised to see the front door open, the younger girl on the couch, and the infant sleeping. The police arrived on the scene about the same time Mrs. Vue returned home, carrying grocery bags. She was taken aback to see the police in her apartment. Mrs. Vue said she had left the children for thirty minutes to buy milk. The children were taken into DHS custody, and Mr. And Mrs. Vue were told that they would have to appear in court three days later.

The Vue family will be assigned a case worker who is responsible for understanding how race, ethnicity, and class affect this family. Moving from a small village in Laos, could this family have understood the new dangers and expectations that come with parenting in the United States? How does their economic position affect their ability to find appropriate child care? What other factors affect their needs as a family? (p. 42)

Types of Human Diversity

We will arbitrarily spend some time here discussing selected aspects of human diversity, namely concepts related to gender and sex, in addition to culture. It is beyond the scope of this chapter to discuss each aspect of human diversity. Highlight 2.2 does offer definitions for each concept. Chapter 11 explores and discusses various diverse facets in greater detail. Additionally, a range of issues concerning human diversity is addressed throughout the book.

Human Diversity: The Complexity of Gender and Sex

Gender is an aspect of diversity that is really much more complex than it may initially seem. "*Gender* refers to the social and psychological characteristics associated with being female or male. Characteristics typically associated with the female gender include being gentle, emotional, and cooperative; characteristics typically associated with the male gender include being aggressive, rational, and competitive. In popular usage, gender is dichotomized as an either/or concept (feminine or masculine), but gender may also be viewed as existing along a continuum of femininity and masculinity" (McCammon & Knox, 2007, p. 112).

Other important concepts related to gender are gender identity, gender expression, gender roles, and gender role socialization. *Gender identity* is a person's internal psychological self-concept of being either a male or a female, or, possibly, some combination of both (Gilbert, 2008). *Gender expression* concerns how we express ourselves to others in ways related to gender that include both behavior and personality. *Gender roles* are the "attitudes, behaviors, rights, and responsibilities that society associates with" being male or being female (Strong, Yarber, Sayad, & De Vault, 2008, p. 130). *Gender role socialization* is the process of conveying what is considered appropriate behavior and perspectives for males and females in a particular culture.

We will differentiate the concepts of gender and sex. *Sex* "refers to the biological distinction between being female and being male, usually categorized on the basis of the reproductive organs and genetic makeup" (McCammon & Knox,

Highlight 2.2 | Definitions for Aspects of Human Diversity

Age: Some period of time during a person's lifespan. Age is often considered an important aspect of human diversity for older adults, as they experience *ageism,* discrimination based preconceived notions about older people, regardless of their individual qualities and capabilities.

Class (or social class): People's status or ranking in society with respect to such standards as "relative wealth, power, prestige, educational level, or family background" (Barker, 2003, p. 402).

Race: The category of people who share a common descent and genetic origin that may be distinguished by "certain physical traits," or "interests, habits, or characteristics" (Mish, 2008, p. 1024).

Ethnicity: The affiliation with a large group of people who have "common racial, national, tribal, religious, linguistic, or cultural origin or background" (Mish, 1995, p. 398).

(People of) Color: "A collective term that refers to the major groups of African, Latino and Asian Americans, and First Nations People [Native Americans] who have been distinguished from the dominant society by color" (Lum, 2007, p. 117).

Culture: "A way of life including widespread values (about what is good and bad), beliefs (about what is true), and behavior (what people do every day)" (italics deleted) (Macionis, 2008, p. 2).

Disability: "Any physical or mental impairment [or ongoing health or mental health condition] that substantially limits one or more major life activities"; these activities include "seeing, hearing, speaking, walking, breathing, performing manual tasks, learning, caring for oneself, and working"

(Equal Employment Opportunity Commission, 1997, p. 1).

Gender: "The social and psychological characteristics associated with being female or male" (McCammon & Knox, 2007, p. 112).

Gender identity: A person's internal psychological self-concept of being either a male or a female, or, possibly, some combination of both (Gilbert, 2008).

Gender expression: The manner in which we express ourselves to others in ways related to gender that include both behavior and personality.

Sex: "The biological distinction between being female and being male, usually categorized on the basis of the reproductive organs and genetic makeup" (McCammon & Knox, 2007, p. 606).

Sexual orientation: Sexual and romantic attraction to persons of one or both genders.

Immigration status: A person's position in terms of legal rights and residency when entering and residing in a country that is not that person's legal country of origin.

Political ideology: The "relatively coherent system of ideas (beliefs, traditions, principles, and myths) about human nature, institutional arrangements, and social processes" that indicate how a government should be run and what principles that government should support (Abramovitz, 2007, p. 126).

Religion: People's spiritual beliefs concerning the origin, character, and reason for being, usually based on the existence of some higher power or powers, that often involves designated rituals and provides direction for what is considered moral or right.

2007, p. 606). Gender, then, emphasizes social and psychological aspects of femaleness or maleness; sex, on the other hand, focuses on the biological qualities of being male or female. Subsequent sections address sexual orientation, intersex, and transgenderism.

Sexual Orientation   *Sexual orientation,* a significant aspect of diversity in some ways related to gender, is sexual and romantic attraction to persons of one or both genders. Terms concerning sexual orientation are important to understand. Puglia and House (2006) explain:

> Language is important for what it communicates as well as what it implies. Throughout their lives, gays, lesbians, and bisexuals hear biased and offensive street language such as "queer," "faggot," "homo," "dyke," and "queen." This language affects the self esteem of gays, lesbians, and bisexuals, stigmatizes them, and is just as offensive to these populations as ethnic slurs are to various ethnic populations. (p. 516)

People having a sexual orientation toward the same gender are generally referred to as *gay* if they are male and *lesbian* if they are female. However, many people use the term *gay* to refer both to lesbians and gay men. The older term referring to same-gender sexual orientation is *homosexual*. People having a sexual orientation toward persons of the opposite gender are *heterosexual,* also referred to as *straight*. People sexually oriented toward either gender are referred to as *bisexual*.

It's difficult if not impossible to state exactly how many people are lesbian or gay. Many lesbian and gay organizations maintain that they make up 10 percent of the population. One lesbian and gay organization is called "The Ten Percent Society." Carroll (2010) reflects:

> Although there is much work to be done in determining the prevalence of homosexuality, scholars generally agree that between 3% and 4% of males are predominantly gay, 1.5% to 2% of women are predominantly lesbian, and about 2% to 5% are bisexual. (p. 282)

Variations in the Expression of Gender: Intersex and Transgender People   In an overly simplistic, naïve view of the world, one might think, "You're either a male or you're a female. Period." However, in reality neither gender nor sexual orientation are such simple concepts. Money (1987) proposes eight factors of gender that more fully portray some of the complexity of gender. The first six are physical variables that include: chromosomal predisposition to gender; the presence of either ovaries or testes; exposure to male or female hormones prior to birth; brain differentiation resulting from hormones prior to birth; the presence of female or male internal reproductive organs; exterior genital appearance; and the production of either male or female hormones during puberty. The two psychological variables are the gender assigned at birth ("It's a boy" or "It's a girl") and the person's *gender identity* (one's perception of oneself as being either "female" or "male").

It is estimated that 1 out of every 1,500 to 2,000 babies born has some combination of physical characteristics demonstrated by both sexes (Crooks & Baur, 2008; Intersex Society of North America [ISNA], 2006). Such a person is referred to as *pseudohermaphrodite* or *intersex*. A true *hermaphrodite* is a person "born with fully formed ovaries and fully formed testes, which is exceptionally rare" (Carroll, 2010, p. 89).

Another variation in the expression of gender involves *transgenderism,* including "people whose appearance and/or behaviors do not conform to traditional gender roles" (Crooks & Baur, 2008, p. 62). These people "live full- or part-time in the other gender's role" (that is, their nonbiological gender) (Carroll, 2010, p. 101). Among these people are *transsexuals,* people who feel they are imprisoned in the physical body of the wrong gender. Since their gender identity and sense of self are at odds with their biological inclination, they often seek to adjust their physical appearance closer to that of their gender identity through surgery and hormonal treatment. Many transsexual people prefer to be referred to as *transgender* people. The word *transsexual* emphasizes "sexual," whereas *transgender* emphasizes "gender" identity, which they say is the real issue.

Because lesbian, gay, bisexual, and transgender people face some of the same problems, when referring to them as a group, we will use the term LGBT (i.e., lesbian, gay, bisexual, and transgender) (Morrow, 2006). Highlight 2.3 discusses homophobia, which is often experienced by many LGBT people.

Human Diversity: Culture

Another crucial aspect of human diversity involves culture, a term often used with respect to the macro social environment. *Culture* is "a way of life including widespread values (about what is good and bad), beliefs (about what is true), and behavior (what people do every day)" (italics deleted) (Macionis, 2008, p. 2). It involves "the sum total of life patterns passed on from generation to generation within a group of people and includes institutions, language, religious ideals, habits

---

Highlight 2.3	Homophobia

A major problem LGBT people face is *homophobia,* the irrational "fear and hatred" of gay, lesbian, bisexual, and transgender people (Morrow, 2008, p. 79). Although not all LGBT people suffer from homophobia in all its forms everyday, all LGBT people must endure some forms at some times (Morrow, 2008; Tully, 2001). In order to help LGBT people cope with the results of homophobia, social workers must understand their life situations and environmental issues.

LGBT people may suffer from homophobia in at least three ways, one of which is *overt victimization* (Miller, 2008). Dworkin (2000) remarks:

> Anti-LGB[T] violence is more common than most people realize. . . . All the symptoms commonly associated with posttraumatic stress [a condition in which a person continues to reexperience some traumatic event like a bloody battle or a sexual assault] are likely to follow a physical or verbal attack, in varying degrees of intensity, depending on the circumstances of the attack and the vulnerability of the victim. In a 4-year study of hate crimes against LGB[T] people, Herek et al. (1997) found that stress, depression, and

anger lingered for as long as 5 years after the attack. In addition to posttraumatic symptoms, an LGB[T] client can experience anxiety about his or her sexual identification (Bridgewater, 1992). (p. 170)

A second way LGBT people encounter homophobia involves *covert victimization,* where discrimination occurs that is not obvious. For instance, Erik, a twenty-one-year-old gay man and college student, applies for a part-time job at Bubba's Big Burgers, a local fast-food restaurant. Bruce, the manager, somehow found out that Erik is gay. He chooses to hire another applicant for the position who is heterosexual (or so Bruce thinks) because that applicant is more "appropriate."

A third way LGBT people suffer from homophobia involves internalizing it (Miller, 2008; Tully, 2001). If the majority of those around them are homophobic, making fun of and severely criticizing LGBT people, it's fairly easy for LGBT people to start believing it themselves. Results may include "low self-esteem, depression, suicidal ideation, substance abuse, isolation, self-loathing, . . . or acting out" (Tully, 2001, p. 610).

of thinking, artistic expressions, and patterns of social and interpersonal relationships" (Hodge, Struckmann, & Trost, 1975; Lum, 2007, pp. 4–5). Aspects of culture are often related to people's ethnic, racial, and spiritual heritage.

Culture is evident in both communities and organizations. For example, a geographic community's culture may be based on Hispanic, Jewish, African-American, or white Anglo customs and expectations. Or, it may reflect a mixture of cultural traditions and heritages.

Organizations also have culture. On one level organizational culture involves the diversity and backgrounds of its staff. On another level, *organizational culture* is defined as "the set of key values, beliefs, understandings, and norms shared by members of an organization" (Daft, 2008, pp. 85–86). Later chapters further discuss organizational culture.

Cultural Competence   *Cultural competence* is "the mastery of a particular set of knowledge, skills, policies, and programs used by the social worker that address the cultural needs of individuals, families, groups, and communities" (Lum, 2005, p. 4). Social workers must develop cultural competence in order to work effectively with clients from various cultural, ethnic, and racial backgrounds.

Cultural competence, strongly supported by the NASW *Code of Ethics,* involves several dimensions (Lum, 2005; NASW, 2008, 1.05). Workers should strive to develop an awareness of personal values, assumptions, and biases. They should establish a positive approach toward and an appreciation of other cultures. They should work to understand how their own cultural heritage and belief system differ from and may influence interaction with clients who have a different cultural background. Workers should recognize the existence of stereotypes, discrimination, and oppression for various diverse groups. They should develop a nonjudgmental attitude and learn about the cultures of their clients. Finally, practitioners should develop attitudes that respect differences and effective skills for working with people from other cultures. Cultural competence is strongly supported by the NASW *Code of Ethics* (NASW, 2008, 1.05). Highlight 2.4 describes how a generalist practitioner might strive for cultural competence.

Highlight 2.4	**Competencies for Cultural Competence**

Sue (2006) suggests that social workers should have four competencies (that is, appropriate skills, knowledge, ability, and understanding) in the area of cultural competence.

Competency One: Becoming Aware of One's Own Assumptions, Values, and Biases about Human Behavior

What biases, stereotypes, and beliefs do you hold about various diverse groups? Everyone has them. Social workers must take care not to make auto-matic assumptions about diverse groups in the social environment. They must strive to appreciate human differences, yet view each client system as an individual. It's an ongoing, endless process to identify, clarify, and evaluate your own values.

Competency Two: Understanding the Worldview of Culturally Diverse Clients

Before social workers can work objectively and effectively with clients, they must strive to become aware of the lens through which they view the

continued

Highlight 2.4 | *continued*

  | ### Critical Thinking Questions 2.1

Do you automatically make assumptions about any particular group based on their race, culture, gender, sexual orientation, religion, economic status, or ability level? If so, what are these assumptions? To what extent are they fair or accurate?

world. *Worldview* concerns "one's perceptions of oneself in relation to other people, objects, institutions, and nature. It relates to one's view of the world and one's role and place in it" (Leashore, 1995, p. 112). Slattery (2004) explains:

> Our worldview influences whether we see the glass as half full or half empty or even whether it contains fluid at all. . . . [It] is a way of organizing and distilling huge amounts of complex material into simple and understandable forms, which allows us to respond to the world more rapidly and efficiently. Imagine the feeling of having to pay attention to every piece of information that was received every minute of the day. The sound of the rain on the window, the temperature of the room, the feel of a book, the sound of pages being turned, and one leg on the opposite knee with one foot on the floor. The amount of information sensed at any moment is overwhelming. So, we perceive only part of it and use a still smaller portion. . . . Our worldview serves as a filter, accepting information that makes sense and discarding information that does not fit. (pp. 88–89)

Social workers must be aware of their own values and biases so that they don't impose their

  | ### Critical Thinking Questions 2.2

How would you describe your own worldview? What are the major values and beliefs that support this worldview?

ideas on clients. They must also explore carefully with clients the clients' own worldviews. It is a practitioner's job to try to view the social environment from the client's perspective in order to help that client make the most effective decisions.

Competency Three: Developing Appropriate Intervention Strategies and Techniques

Sue (2006) explains:

> Social work and social workers must begin the process of developing appropriate and effective helping, teaching, communication, and intervention strategies in working with culturally diverse groups and individuals. This competency means . . . systems intervention as well as traditional one-to-one relationships. Additionally, it is important that the social worker have the ability to make use of indigenous helping/healing approaches and structures that may already exist in the minority community . . . The concept here is to build on the strengths of a community and to empower [its residents] . . . in their ability to help themselves . . . Effectiveness in helping clients is most likely enhanced when the social worker uses intervention modalities and defines goals that are consistent with the life experiences and cultural values of clients. (p. 27)

Competency Four: Understanding Organizational and Institutional Forces That Enhance or Negate Cultural Competence

Communities may not be tolerant or supportive of various diverse groups. "In many cases, organizational customs do not value or allow the use of cultural knowledge or skills. Some social service organizations may even actively discourage, negate, or punish multicultural expressions. Or client problems may be the result of institutions that oppress them. Thus, it is imperative to view cultural competence for organizations as well. . . . Developing new rules, regulations, policies, practices, and structures within organizations that enhance multiculturalism is important" (Sue, 2006, p. 28).

Defining Generalist Practice:
Focus on Empowerment, Strengths, and Resiliency

Another vital concept in the definition of generalist practice and an ongoing theme throughout social work is *empowerment*, the "process of increasing personal, inter-personal, or political power so that individuals can take action to improve their life situations" (Gutierrez, 2001, p. 210). The empowerment approach is a perspective on practice that provides "ways of thinking about and doing practice" (Lee, 2001, p. 32). Throughout the assessment process and our quest to understand human behavior in macro systems, it's critical to emphasize, develop, and nurture strengths and positive attributes in systems of all sizes to empower people. Empowerment aims at enhancing individuals', groups', families', and communities' power and control over their destinies. Empowerment involves social workers striving to improve people's:

- *Positive sense of self-worth and competence* ("I am important." "I am capable of getting things done.")
- *Ability to influence the course of one's life* ("I have control over what I do." "I can make and follow plans to accomplish my goals.")
- *Capacity to work with others to control aspects of public life* ("I am an important part of my community and other larger systems, and can work with others to improve our quality of life." "In collaboration with others, I can make improvements in my community, in the organization where I work, and in other groups to which I belong.")
- *Ability to access the mechanisms of public decision making* ("I can influence community and organizational decision makers." "My vote counts.") (Walsh, 2006, p. 21; Lee, 2001)

Walsh (2006) explains:

Many clients do not, or perceive that they do not, have power, either over themselves, their significant others, or the agencies and communities in which they reside. This sense of powerlessness underlies many problems in living. It can be internalized and lead to learned helplessness and alienation from one's community. An empowerment orientation to practice represents the social worker's efforts to combat the alienation, isolation, and poverty . . . in clients' lives by positively influencing their sense of worth, sense of membership in a community, and ability to create change in their surroundings. (p. 21)

Empowerment in generalist practice involves critical thinking about how macro systems affect people (Lee, 2001). To what extent are people getting the resources and support they need from their communities and organizations within their communities? Why or why not?

The Strengths Perspective

Focusing on strengths can provide a sound basis for empowerment. Sometimes referred to as the *strengths perspective*, this orientation focuses on client resources, capabilities, knowledge, abilities, motivations, experience, intelligence, and other positive qualities that can be put to use to solve problems and pursue positive changes (Sheafor & Horejsi, 2009).

Assessment of human behavior establishes the basis for understanding people's problems and issues, and subsequently helping them improve their lives. Social workers address people's problems every day, but it's the identification of people's strengths that provides clues for how to solve these problems and improve their life situations. Saleebey (2006) cites the following principles involved in the strengths perspective:

- *Every individual, group, family, and community has strengths.* Even during people's darkest times, it's important to identify and emphasize strengths. Strengths include intelligence, good character, close family, good friends, spiritual faith, a job, a place to live, talent, personality, and any other positive thing you can think of.
- *Trauma and abuse, illness, and struggle may be injurious, but they may also be sources of challenge and opportunity.* Think of one of the worst experiences you've ever had. Regardless of how terrible it was at the time, were you able to turn it around and learn something from it? To some extent, did it make you a stronger or wiser person?
- *Assume that you do not know the upper limits of the capacity to grow and change and take individual, group, and community aspirations seriously.* It's impossible to foresee the future and know all the opportunities you will encounter and the barriers you will face. A strengths perspective emphasizes that it's important to set goals and to eagerly pursue opportunities when they occur.
- *We best serve clients by collaborating with them.* Saleebey (2006), a social worker, reflects about a client he knows:

  > Mrs. Johnson knows more about thriving in a public housing project than anyone I can think of. Over the course of 35 years, she successfully raised 11 children. She maintained a demeanor of poise, and she demonstrated intelligence and vigor, even as her community underwent dramatic, often frightening changes. Her contributions to the community are, simply put, amazing. She has much to teach us and other residents of her community. I certainly would not presume to work *on* Ms. Johnson but would be privileged to work *with* her. (p. 18)

- *Every environment is full of resources.* Resources can provide great strengths. One of social workers' major roles is to link clients with the resources they need to empower them to improve their lives.
- *Caring, caretaking, and context are key.* Social workers care about others. They are concerned about the environment or context in which people live. They recognize that communities and social service organizations should, respectively, take care of their citizens and the people they serve (pp. 16–19).

Individuals, families, groups, organizations, and communities all have strengths. It's a goal of generalist practice to identify these strengths and use them to solve problems and make effective plans to enhance people's well-being.

Critical Thinking Questions 2.3: What Are Your Strengths?

Individual Strengths

- What do you see as your most significant personal strengths?
- What challenges have you overcome about which you're especially proud?

Family Strengths

- What strengths do you see in your own family?
- In what ways does your family put these strengths to use?
- In times of trouble, how does your family contribute to your own personal sense of strength?

Group Strengths

- To what social, work, and other types of groups do you belong?
- Do you have special people upon whom you can rely? If so, who are they and in what ways do they support you?
- What are the strengths inherent in these groups?
- How do these group strengths contribute to your own personal sense of strength?

Organizational Strengths

- To what organizations do you belong (for example, clubs, work settings, churches, recreational groups, sports groups, volunteer groups)?
- What are the strengths in these organizations?
- How do these organizational strengths contribute to your own personal sense of strength?

Community Strengths

- What are the strengths in the community where you live?
- How do these strengths contribute to your own quality of life?

Resiliency: Using Strengths to Combat Difficulty

A concept related to the strengths perspective and empowerment is resiliency. *Resiliency* is the ability of an individual, family, group, community, or organization to recover from adversity and resume functioning, even when suffering serious trouble, confusion, or hardship. Whereas the "strengths perspective focuses on capabilities, assets, and positive attributes rather than problems and pathologies," resiliency emphasizes the use of strengths to cope with adversity and survive, despite difficulties (Gutheil & Congress, 2002, p. 41).

Norman (2000) provides an illustration of the concept of resiliency:

When a pitched baseball hits a window, the glass usually shatters. When that same ball meets a baseball bat, the bat is rarely damaged. When a hammer strikes a ceramic vase, it too usually shatters. But when that same hammer hits a rubber automobile tire, the tire quickly returns to its original shape. The baseball bat and the automobile tire both demonstrate resiliency. (p. 3)

Resiliency involves two dimensions—risk and protection (Norman, 2000). In this context, *risk* involves "stressful life events or adverse environmental conditions that increase the *vulnerability* [defenselessness or helplessness] of individuals" or other systems (p. 3). *Protection*, on the other hand, concerns those factors that "buffer, moderate, and protect against those vulnerabilities" (p. 3).

Perez-Koenig (2000) describes an example of an organization in a community that builds on the strengths and resiliency of Hispanic youth. The Unitas Extended Family Circle (UEFC) conducts outreach to Hispanic youth in the South Bronx of New York City. UEFC "recognizes the devastating effects of urban ghettos on people, particularly children and youth, and firmly believes in the healing power of all people, in their strengths, capacities, aspirations, and the availability of internal and external resources" (Perez-Koenig, 2000, pp. 143–144). It builds on

strengths that emanate from the Hispanic culture's core values of "personalismo" [that is, "valuing and building interpersonal relationships" (Santiago-Rivera, Arredondo, & Gallardo-Cooper, 2002, p. 44)] and respect, familism [that is, "a preference for maintaining a close connection to family" (Santiago-Rivera et al., 2002, p. 42)] and spirituality. Each individual is respected and valued, regardless of status. Respect emphasizes "being" and "who," rather than competition and "what." There is a substantial reverence for life, and for living in the moment. Familism locates the family, rather than the individual, as the most important social system. The family is a source of identity and support. Familism for most Hispanics includes the entire extended family. This extendedness emphasizes strong feelings of identification, loyalty, and solidarity. Extended family refers not only to the traditional kin, related by blood or marriage, such as aunts, uncles, and cousins, but also includes non-blood, non-marriage related persons who are considered family—compadres and comadres (godfathers and godmothers) and hijos de crianza (children who are raised as members of the family). The extended family provides an indispensable source of instrumental and expressive support. . . .
. . . UEFC invites children and adolescents to become members of make-believe small families and of the large, agencywide, extended family. . . . Through corrective make-believe family relationships (in small groups as well as in the larger group of the community) participants develop better adaptive or coping mechanisms. . . . The large family circle is decentralized into small symbolic families, to permit an individual sense of belonging without anonymity. . . . UEFC meetings reinforce in each participant their identity as a member of this extended family (a make-believe extended kinship network), as well as their membership in their small symbolic families. The use of rituals, stories, group discussions, and clear norms and rules maintain a milieu necessary for healing relationships to be experienced in an emotional climate of mutual trust and peaceful, nonviolent transactions. (Perez-Koenig, 2000, pp. 145–149)

The importance of spirituality, which "lies at the core of the Hispanic culture," is stressed (Perez-Koenig, 2000, p. 146). In addition,

The make-believe parents, aunts, and uncles (caretakers) participate in an ongoing weekly training program led by a professional social worker. The goal of these sessions is to enable "helpers of children" to learn interpersonal skills which will encourage children to be effective, happy, and cooperative. In the training program they learn skills to raise children's self-esteem and feelings of competency; skills to communicate effectively with children; skills to help children resolve conflicts and solve problems. (Perez-Koenig, 2000, p. 149)

The formulated families meet weekly. Children are encouraged to share their feelings and ideas. Caregivers work to meet children's and adolescents' needs by nurturing them, teaching them communication and problem-solving skills, and providing an environment where they feel important and safe. The basic idea is to enhance children's natural resiliency by stressing and developing their strengths.

Defining Generalist Practice: Advocacy for Human Rights and Social and Economic Justice

Advocacy for human rights and social and economic justice represents the final dimension in the definition of generalist practice. The pursuit of these goals should characterize generalist practice in the macro social environment. Several important concepts are involved.

Advocacy

The first concept is that of *advocacy,* which has been defined as the act of stepping forward on the behalf of the client system in order to promote fair and equitable treatment or gain needed resources. NASW policy states that:

Advocacy has always been the cornerstone of the social work profession. All social workers in their specialized fields of practice must commit to advocacy. The social worker is a key part of the advocacy process that will shape the social and economic conditions of the years ahead. . . . The social worker is called on to be involved at the micro, mezzo, and macro levels of practice. Social workers advocate for social justice, alleviating social ills and oppression at all levels of society. (NASW, 2009, p. 325)

Human Rights

Generalist practitioners have the responsibility of advocating for human rights. *Human rights* involves the premise that all people, regardless of race, culture, or national origin, are entitled to basic rights and treatment.

Reichert (2006) cites three facets of human rights. The first set of rights includes "political and human freedoms that are similar to what U.S. citizens view as human rights. Political and civil human rights include the right to a fair trial, freedom of speech and religion, freedom of movement and assembly, and guarantees against discrimination, slavery, and torture" (p. 3).

The second set of rights involves "attempts to ensure each resident of a country an adequate standard of living based on the resources of that country. Under this second set, everyone 'has the right to a standard of living adequate for the health and well-being of himself and of his family, including food, clothing, housing and medical care and necessary social services.' In addition, 'motherhood and childhood are entitled to special care and assistance,' and everyone has the right to a free education at the elementary level (United Nations, 1948, arts. 16–27)" (p. 3). Focus on Ethics 2.3 addresses human rights and health care in the United States.

Focus on Ethics 2.3 | **The United States and Human Rights**

In the United States, 15.8 percent of the total population and 11.7 percent of children are not covered by health insurance (U.S. Census Bureau, 2008). To what extent does the United States "fulfill its obligation to promote positive human rights" by providing adequate health care to all citizens (Reichert, 2006, p. 3)? To what extent does the United States provide adequate food, clothing, and housing to all of its citizens? What are the reasons for your answers? What, if anything, should be done?

The third set of human rights involves "rights among nations" on a global basis where "everyone is entitled to a social and international order in which human rights can be fully realized" (Reichert, 2006, pp. 3–4). This includes international cooperation for "environmental protection and economic development," and avoidance of exploitation of some countries by others (Reichert, p. 4). Chapter 13 further explores these concepts in addition to social and economic justice on a global basis.

Social and Economic Justice

Generalist practitioners also have the responsibility to advocate for social and economic justice (CSWE, 2008; NASW, 2009). *Social justice* entails upholding the condition that in a perfect world, all citizens would have identical "rights, protection, opportunities, obligations, and social benefits" regardless of their backgrounds and membership in diverse groups (Barker, 2003, pp. 404–405). *Economic justice* concerns the distribution of resources in a fair and equitable manner.

In real life, social and economic justice is a hard goal to attain. Rarely are rights and resources fairly and equitably distributed. Even the definition of *fair* and *equitable* are widely debated. What does "fair" mean? Does it mean that all people should receive the same income regardless of what they do, or even whether or not they have jobs at all? The point is that social workers must be vigilantly aware of the existence of injustice. It is our ethical responsibility to combat injustice whenever it is necessary and possible to do so.

We have already indicated that the NASW *Code of Ethics* stresses that workers' ethical responsibility to the broader society is to advocate and work for people's general welfare. This responsibility reflects the basic core of social work, although most job descriptions do not specifically reflect this. The *Code* reads, "Social workers should promote the general welfare of society, from local to global levels, and the development of people, their communities, and their environments. Social workers should advocate for living conditions conducive to the fulfillment of basic human needs and should promote social, economic, political, and cultural values and institutions that are compatible with the realization of social justice" (NASW, 2008, 6.01).

The *Code* continues that as part of their professional responsibility, social workers should pursue social and political action seeking fair and equal access to resources and opportunities. They should actively support policies to improve the human condition and promote social justice for all. Practitioners should especially work to enhance opportunities for "vulnerable, disadvantaged, oppressed, and exploited people and groups" (NASW, 2008, 6.04b). Social workers should support conditions and policies that respect cultural diversity. Similarly, they should work to prevent and eliminate conditions and policies discriminating against or exploiting people, especially vulnerable populations.

Oppression

When talking about issues involving fairness, justice, and human rights, many other concepts come into play. Advocacy for people who need to be empowered implies that people belonging to some groups experience a significant lack of power. In other words, people belonging to some groups are oppressed. *Oppression* entails "putting extreme limitations and constraints on some person, group, or larger system" (Kirst-Ashman, 2010, p. 53). Essentially, oppression involves conditions where "one segment of the population acts to prevent another segment from attaining access to resources"; often the dominating group tries to inhibit the other group's freedom or look for ways to "devalue them" (van Soest & Garcia, 2003, p. 35).

Power, Privilege, and Acclaim   Such dominating groups are often characterized by power, privilege, and acclaim. *Power* is the ability to move people on a chosen course to produce an effect or achieve some goal (Homan, 2008). *Privilege* entails special rights or benefits enjoyed because of elevated social, political, or economic status. *Acclaim* is enthusiastic public praise or approval (Lindberg, 2007). People who experience acclaim, such as high-level politicians, well-known professionals, and famous entertainers, maintain broad influence over what other people think. Subsequently, people with much privilege and acclaim have greater power to influence and control their destinies and those of others.

Marginalization, Alienation, and Poverty   People with lesser power, usually falling into some category of distinguishable characteristics (e.g., race, ethnicity, religion, political party, age, or disability), may be denied rights, treated unfairly, or put down by a group holding greater power. People in downtrodden groups often suffer marginalization and alienation. *Marginalization* is the condition of having less power and being viewed as less important than others in the society because of belonging to some group or having some characteristic (e.g., being poor) (Barker, 2003). *Alienation,* related to marginalization, is the feeling that you don't fit in or aren't treated as well as others in the mainstream of society (Barker, 2003). Often, victims of oppression also suffer *poverty,* the condition "of not having enough money to buy things that are considered necessary and desirable" (Kornblum & Julian, 2007, p. 195).

Populations-at-Risk, Stereotypes, and Discrimination   *Populations-at-risk* are populations or groups of people who share some identifiable characteristic that places them at greater risk of social and economic deprivation and oppression than the general mainstream of society. Often those in power harbor stereotypes about oppressed groups that result in discrimination against them. A *stereotype* is "a fixed mental picture of a member of some specified group based on some attribute or attributes that reflect an overly simplified view of that group, without consideration or appreciation of individual differences" (Kirst-Ashman, 2010, p. 53). Stereotypes may relate to any of the factors indicating types of diversity. We have established that these include "age, class, color, culture, disability, ethnicity, gender, gender identity and expression, immigration status, political ideology, race, religion, sex, and sexual orientation" (CSWE, 2008, p. 5). *Discrimination*, a concept closely related to that of oppression, is "the act of treating people differently based on the fact they belong to some group" rather than on their individual merit (Kirst-Ashman, 2010, p. 53).

For example, harboring the false stereotype that people with physical disabilities also have cognitive disabilities might result in job discrimination against people with physical disabilities. Similarly, maintaining the false stereotype that women are too emotional to be effective leaders might result in discrimination against a woman in her pursuit of a powerful political position.

Common Elements in Oppression   Van Soest and Garcia (2003) introduce at least three elements that are common to all oppression:

> First, oppression always bestows power and advantage on certain people who are regarded as the norm and denied to others based on status as the "other" or different. The defined norm (i.e., White, male, heterosexual) is the standard of *rightness* against which all others are judged; the "other" (i.e., not White, not male, not heterosexual) is not only different from the norm, but is also believed and perceived to be inferior and deviant, which then justifies conferring advantage on those who fit the norm and disadvantaging the other. . . .
>
> A second element common to all oppressions is that they are held in place by ideology [i.e., a systematic manner of thinking, in this case, about people and their behavior] and violence or the threat of violence. The ideology on which racial oppression is based is that of superiority based on race (i.e., White supremacy). Likewise, the ideology on which sexual oppression is based is that of superiority based on gender (i.e., male) and the basis for homosexual oppression is an ideology of superiority based on sexual orientation (i.e., heterosexual). Violence is used to enforce and maintain all oppressions. Violence comes in many forms and may be physical and direct (e.g., lynching, rape, battering, gay bashing), or personal and psychological (e.g., name-calling based on dominant ideology and negative stereotypes). Violence may be indirect and/or institutionalized. For example, it may be associated with high poverty rates, the predominance of men of color in the criminal justice system and on death row, and the reality of police brutality.
>
> A third common element of all oppressions is that they are institutionalized. This means that racism, sexism, and heterosexism are built into the norms, traditions, laws, and policies of a society so that even those who have non-racist, non-sexist, and non-heterosexist beliefs are compelled to act in accordance with institutional interest. (pp. 35–36)

A major thrust of social work is to combat oppression and advocate on the behalf of oppressed groups. It has been stressed that advocacy is the act of speaking up, pushing for change, or pleading clients' causes. It is workers' responsibility to actively thwart any cruelty, unfairness, or discrimination they observe. This

Critical Thinking Questions 2.4

When you think of the word *oppression*, what groups come to mind? What are the reasons that you feel these people are oppressed?

Concept Summary 2.1	**Concepts Related to Social and Economic Justice**

Advocacy: The act of stepping forward on the behalf of the client system in order to promote fair and equitable treatment or gain needed resources.

Human rights: The premise that all people, regardless of race, culture, or national origin, are entitled to basic rights and treatment.

Social justice: Upholding the condition that in a perfect world, all citizens would have identical "rights, protection, opportunities, obligations, and social benefits" regardless of their backgrounds and membership in diverse groups (Barker, 2003, pp. 404–405).

Economic justice: The distribution of resources in a fair and equitable manner.

Oppression: Putting extreme limitations and constraints on some person, group, or larger system.

Power: The ability to move people on a chosen course to produce an effect or achieve some goal (Homan, 2008).

Privilege: Special rights or benefits enjoyed because of elevated social, political, or economic status.

Acclaim: Enthusiastic public praise or approval (Lindberg, 2007).

Marginalization: The condition of having less power and being viewed as less important than others in the society because of belonging to some group or having some characteristic (e.g., being poor) (Barker, 2003).

Alienation: The feeling that you don't fit in or aren't treated as well as others in the mainstream of society (Barker, 2003).

Poverty: The condition "of not having enough money to buy things that are considered necessary and desirable" (Kornblum & Julian, 2007, p. 195).

Populations-at-risk: Populations or groups of people who share some identifiable characteristic that places them at greater risk of social and economic deprivation and oppression than the general mainstream of society.

Stereotype: A fixed mental picture of a member of some specified group based on some attribute or attributes that reflect an overly simplified view of that group, without consideration or appreciation of individual differences.

Discrimination: The act of treating people differently based on the fact they belong to some group rather than on their individual merit.

---

standard places the ultimate responsibility upon the individual worker to make certain that service is provided fairly and people are treated justly. This doesn't relinquish the responsibility of agency administrators. However, individual professional social workers also have responsibility to advocate for and pursue positive change.

Chapter Summary

The following summarizes this chapter's content as it relates to the learning objectives presented at the beginning of the chapter. Objectives include the following:

A. Complete the discussion of the definition of generalist practice and explain the relationship between the remaining major concepts and the macro social environment.

Generalist practice, occurring within an organizational structure, is the application of an extensive and diverse knowledge base and a wide range of skills by using a seven-step planned change process to target any size system for change within the context of several equally essential dimensions. The dimensions discussed include the adherence to professional values and the application of professional ethics; the understanding of human diversity and how diverse factors affect people's quality of life; an emphasis on client empowerment, strengths, and resiliency; and advocacy for human rights and the pursuit of social and economic justice. Social workers conduct generalist practice with an emphasis on these dimensions in the context of the macro social environment.

B. Review the National Association of Social Workers (NASW) Code of Ethics, summarize professional ethical responsibilities, and examine ethical dilemmas.

The NASW Code of Ethics has six core values: service, social justice, dignity and worth of the person, importance of human relationships, integrity, and competence (NASW, 2008). Social workers' ethical responsibilities include those to clients, to colleagues, in practice settings, as professionals, to the social work profession, and to the broader society. Ethical dilemmas are problematic situations where one must make a difficult choice among two or more alternatives where ethical standards conflict.

C. Introduce the importance of identifying with the social work profession.

Identification with the social work profession means that "social workers [should] serve as representative of the profession, its mission, and its core values" (CSWE, 2008, p. 3).

D. Describe human diversity with its multiple, overlapping factors.

Human diversity refers to "the range of differences between people" (Barker, 2003, p. 203). Aspects characterizing human diversity include "age, class, color, culture, disability, ethnicity, gender, gender identity and expression, immigration status, political ideology, race, religion, sex, and sexual orientation" (CSWE, 2008, p. 5).

E. Examine diversity with respect to gender and sex, in addition to culture.

Gender and sexuality are aspects of diversity that are really much more complex than they may initially seem. Inherent concepts include gender, gender identity, gender expression, gender roles, gender role socialization, sex, sexual orientation, intersex, and transgender people. Homophobia is the irrational "fear and hatred" of gay, lesbian, bisexual, and transgender people (Morrow, 2008, p. 79).

Culture is "a way of life including widespread values (about what is good and bad), beliefs (about what is true), and behavior (what people do every day)" (Macionis, 2008, p. 2). Culture is evident in both communities and organizations.

F. Define cultural competence and address four competencies involved.

Cultural competence is "the mastery of a particular set of knowledge, skills, policies, and programs used by the social worker that address the cultural needs of individuals, families, groups, and communities" (Lum, 2005, p. 4). Competencies involved in cultural competence include self-awareness, understanding the worldview of culturally diverse clients, developing appropriate intervention strategies, and understanding organizational and institutional forces that enhance or negate cultural competence.

G. Review the significance of client empowerment, strengths, and resiliency.

Empowerment is the "process of increasing personal, interpersonal, or political power so that individuals can take action to improve their life situations" (Gutierrez, 2001, p. 210). The strengths perspective focuses on client resources, capabilities, knowledge, abilities, motivations, experience, intelligence, and other positive qualities that can be put to use to solve problems and pursue positive changes (Sheafor & Horejsi, 2009). Resiliency is the ability of an individual, family, group, community, or organization to recover from adversity and resume functioning, even when suffering serious trouble, confusion, or hardship. Empowerment, strengths, and resiliency can be used to help clients combat difficulty.

H. Explore the importance of advocacy for human rights and social and economic justice.

Advocacy is the act of stepping forward on the behalf of the client system in order to promote fair and equitable treatment or gain needed resources. Human rights involves the premise that all people, regardless of race, culture, or national origin, are entitled to basic rights and treatment. Social justice entails upholding the condition that in a perfect world, all citizens would have identical "rights, protection, opportunities, obligations, and social benefits" regardless of their backgrounds and membership in diverse groups (Barker, 2003, pp. 404–405). Economic justice

concerns the distribution of resources in a fair and equitable manner. Generalist practitioners should advocate for human rights and social and economic justice (CSWE, 2008; NASW, 2009).

I. Examine some of the dynamics involved in oppression.

Oppression entails putting extreme limitations and constraints on some person, group, or larger system. Dominating groups often are characterized by power, privilege, and acclaim. People with lesser power often suffer marginalization and alienation. Stereotypes and resulting discrimination often affect populations-at-risk. Common elements in oppression include assuming standards of "rightness," an established ideology, and institutionalization of beliefs.

J. Introduce various critical thinking questions.

Critical thinking questions addressed the use of critical thinking, personal assumptions about human diversity, personal worldview, personal and related strengths, and oppressed groups.

K. Focus on ethical topics.

Ethical topics included the National Association of Social Workers *Code of Ethics*, ethical dilemmas occurring in the macro social environment, and the support of human rights in the United States.

Looking Ahead

This chapter completed discussion of the definition of generalist practice. It focused on values and principles that guide generalist practice in the macro social environment. The next chapter will discuss the theories and dynamics of how generalist practitioners function in small groups in the macro social environment.

For Further Exploration on the Internet

See this text's website at **www.cengage.com/ social_work/krist-ashman** for learning tools such as tutorial quizzing, Web links, glossary, flashcards, and PowerPoint® slides.

3 CHAPTER | Human Behavior in Groups: Theories and Dynamics

Communication, cooperation, and conflict may be part of the dynamic group process.

© Caryn Becker/Alamy

CHAPTER CONTENTS

*LaTonya, the university's Social Work Club (SWC) president, called the full mem-
bership meeting to order. SWC had much to accomplish tonight. The goal was to
identify a range of volunteer activities in which members could participate. At the
last meeting, the club passed the requirement that all members participate in at
least thirty hours of volunteer activities. Now it was up to the club to identify volunteer possibilities in the university's small town and help members get involved.*

*The SWC board consisted of LaTonya, Bert (vice-president), Ernie (secretary),
Sallie (treasurer), and Morticia (activities director). Board meetings were held every
other Tuesday night, with full membership meetings on alternate Tuesdays.*

*LaTonya felt the SWC board generally got along well except for periodic
minor conflicts between herself and Bert. Bert liked to vie for power and control
of both board and membership meetings. LaTonya felt Bert somewhat resented
that she had been elected SWC president.*

*LaTonya, however, had assessed their interpersonal dynamics the first time the
newly elected board met. From the second board meeting on, whenever Bert got on
a control kick, LaTonya tactfully cut him off, regained control, and got the meeting back on track. After all, interpersonal feuding just consumed unnecessary
energy and ate away at SWC's process and effectiveness. LaTonya took her role
as president very seriously. She and the SWC membership had a lot to do tonight
to get the volunteer program on its feet and running.*

The above scenario highlights how groups consist of people having unique personalities, issues, and concerns. On the one hand, a group must accomplish its purpose
as a unified entity. On the other, individual members come to a group with their
own desires and needs. As in organizations and communities, human behavior in
groups is complex.

A *group* is at least two individuals gathered together because of some common
bond, to meet members' social and emotional needs, or to fulfill some mutual purpose. Social work practitioners must understand human behavior in groups for
many reasons. Working with others to get something done is a core component of
generalist social work practice in organizations and communities.

There are four main reasons why groups are relevant in social work (Garvin &
Galinsky, 2008, pp. 288–289). First, sharing *common interests and pursuits* provides a group of individuals with support, information, and motivation. It is also
likely that a group of people can exert greater influence on the social environment
than a single individual.

Second, groups enhance *creative and problem-solving potential*. They "provide
an arena in which members can exchange ideas and opinions, review the problems
they face, engage in new experiences, and develop new approaches" (Garvin &
Galinsky, 2008, p. 288). Exposure to perspectives different than one's own can initiate ideas and enhance creativity.

A third reason groups are important involves *small-group forces*. Working
together in a group, members exert social pressure and influence on each other.
A group member is accountable to other members for assuming responsibility and
getting things done. In this way members can empower each other to make progress and achieve goals.

The fourth reason groups are important to social work is *convenience*. When a number of individuals are involved in decision making, planning, advocating, or intervening, groups often provide the most efficient way of communicating, solving problems, and making decisions.

Chapter 3 will describe the types of groups relevant to generalist social work practice. A number of theoretical perspectives can conceptualize any group's functioning regardless of type. Theory provides a framework for understanding how groups work. Additionally, some concepts characterize interpersonal group dynamics such that you can use them in conjunction with any theoretical perspective. The greater your comprehension of group functioning, the more effectively you will lead or participate in groups.

Learning Objectives

A. Explain major theoretical perspectives on groups, including field, social exchange, learning, psychoanalytic, systems, empowerment, and feminist theories.
B. Examine basic concepts inherent in interpersonal group dynamics, including communication, interpersonal interaction, norms, roles, group cohesion, power and status, and leadership.
C. Focus on the ethical issue of confidentiality in groups.
D. Describe the phases of task group development.
E. Introduce various critical thinking questions.

Theoretical Perspectives on Groups

Theoretical perspectives provide avenues for understanding how communities, organizations, or groups function. Theories about groups discussed here include field, social exchange, learning, psychoanalytic, systems empowerment, and feminist theories.

Field Theory

According to *field theory*, initially developed by Kurt Lewin (1951), a group should be viewed as an entity moving through its immediate environment in pursuit of its goals. A major strength of field theory is that it stresses the importance of examining the relationship of the group to its environment (Martin, 2003; Toseland & Rivas, 2009). Picture a bowling ball rolling down an alley or a soccer ball speeding down a field. Each rolls or reacts within its own context or field. Movement involves the force and direction with which it was hit and the ruts, gutters, or impediments encountered along the way. This is overly simplistic, however, as field theory sees groups as dynamic entities whose members constantly adapt to their environments. Observing bowling or soccer balls when not moving is about as dynamic as watching rocks.

Field theory emphasizes how groups function in order to achieve designated goals. It views groups as progressing or failing to progress because of positive and negative forces acting on them both internally and externally in the environment.

These forces can either help or hinder the group's advancement. Field theory predicts that groups experiencing numerous positive forces, rewards, and encouragements will continue functioning. Groups encountering primarily negative forces will probably fail if positive forces don't counterbalance the negative. Such forces that push toward or pull one away from group involvement and participation are called *valences* (Martin, 2003).

An important concept in field theory in *cohesion*, the collective sum of forces affecting individuals that encourage them to remain group members (Garvin, 1987; Toseland & Rivas, 2009). Examples of positive forces might be how much group members like each other and enjoy each others' company, or members' commitment to the group's purpose. Negative forces might include inconvenient meeting times or other pressures on members' time external to the group.

Field theory views leadership within a group as being democratic, authoritarian, or laissez-faire (Lewin, Lippitt & White, 1939; Toseland & Rivas, 2009). Leadership, discussed more thoroughly later on, significantly impacts how the group functions and moves along toward accomplishing goals. *Authoritarian* leaders take control of group functioning and make decisions with little or no input from other group members. Needless to say, group members may seriously resent this approach. They may balk at group goals, behave in ways that obstruct group progress, or quit the group altogether. On the other hand, some groups may require such strong leadership when members lack necessary knowledge, skill, or direction.

In contrast, *democratic* leaders maximize member input and participation. They emphasize open discussion of issues, even uncomfortable ones such as disagreements among group members or hostility toward the group leader. Advantages of a democratic approach are equal input for all and open knowledge of the issues. Disadvantages include the fact that members may not really be equal in terms of motivation, competence, skills, or participation.

Finally, *laissez-faire* leaders assume a laid-back, nondirectional approach where the group is left to function or struggle on its own. This approach usually doesn't work unless group members are highly knowledgeable, competent, and independent, requiring little guidance to accomplish tasks.

Field theory also introduced a number of concepts regarding the importance of internal group interaction. In the context of a small group, *roles* are expected behavior patterns based on individuals' status or position within the group. *Norms* are collective rules and expectations held by group members concerning what is appropriate behavior within the group. *Power* is the ability to move people on a chosen course to produce an effect or achieve some goal (Homan, 2008). *Consensus* is the extent to which group members concur about group goals and other aspects of group interaction.

Social Exchange Theory

Field theory views a group as a single entity, stressing its functioning as a unit. Although some attention is given to interpersonal dynamics within the group, the focus remains on how the group functions as a unit. *Social exchange theory*, on the other hand, stresses the importance of the individual within the group context.

Concept Summary 3.1 | **Field Theory**

Valences: Forces that push toward or pull one away from involvement and participation.

Cohesion: The collective sum of forces affecting individuals that encourages them to remain group members.

Authoritarian leadership: Taking control of group functioning and making decisions with little or no input from other group members.

Democratic leadership: Maximizing member input and participation.

Laissez-faire leadership: Assuming a laid-back, nondirectional approach where the group is left to function or struggle on its own.

Role: Expected behavior patterns based on individuals' status or position within the group.

Norms: Collective rules and expectations held by group members concerning what is appropriate behavior within the group.

Power: The ability to move people on a chosen course to produce an effect or achieve some goal.

Consensus: The extent to which group members concur about group goals and other aspects of group interaction.

It views the group as the place where social exchange takes place. *Social exchange* at its most basic level is interpersonal interaction, which involves both rewards and costs. *Rewards* are the pleasures, fulfillment, enjoyment, and other positive emotions a person experiences when involved in a relationship. Individual group members continue in the group because they receive social rewards for group membership. This membership is based on receiving more rewards than experiencing costs. *Costs* include negative experiences, the expenditure of time and energy required to maintain a relationship, or the loss of rewards because of making ineffective choices (for example, spending time talking with a group member you don't like much instead of one you do).

Garvin (1987) explains:

> People enter into social interactions with the expectation of rewards. Because each person in the interaction has the same motivation, it logically follows that each must offer something of value to the other in the exchange. . . . What an individual offers another in an exchange—whether energy, time, or resources—is referred to as a "cost."

Social exchange theory focuses on interactions between and among individuals. Each interaction can be broken down into a series of behaviors and responses. Each behavior or response is evaluated in terms of how rewarding or punishing it is to the other member of any pair of members in the group. When group members experience more rewards and fewer costs, the social exchange is likely to be positive and to reinforce group participation.

Several assumptions are inherent in exchange theory. First, relationships have an interdependent dimension. That is, the ability of each participant to receive rewards is dependent on that person's ability to bestow rewards. If you can't give rewards to others, they probably won't give any to you. Second, the process of

| **Concept Summary 3.2** | **Social Exchange Theory** |

Rewards: The pleasures, fulfillment, enjoyment, and other positive emotions a person experiences when involved in a relationship.

Costs: Negative experiences, the expenditure of time and energy required to maintain a relationship, or the loss of rewards because of making ineffective choices.

Social exchange: Interpersonal interaction, which involves both rewards and costs.

social exchange is governed by values and expectations such as fairness and the importance of a mutual sense of give and take. It follows, then, that giving rewards should result in eventually receiving rewards. Third, "trust and commitment" develop as more social exchanges occur over time, which tends to "stabilize" relationships. As people get to know each other and expectations become established, relationships become more predictable. Highlight 3.1 analyzes a conversation according to social exchange theory.

| **Highlight 3.1** | **Analysis of a Conversation According to Social Exchange Theory** |

Francine and Horace, members of a volunteer community group whose goal is to maintain cleanliness on four city block sidewalks, have the following conversation. Each response is followed by a brief analysis according to social exchange theory.

Francine says to Horace, "Did you finish your assigned block yet?" *(Neutral question, although a minor cost to Francine in terms of effort expended)*

Horace responds, "Heck, yes. I appreciate your suggestions about removing the dog dirt. I just don't know why people keep big dogs in the city." *(Reward for Francine; minor cost for Horace for effort expended)*

Francine states, "Yeah, that Super Duper Pooper Scooper really works. Will you be cleaning your assigned sidewalks on a weekly basis?" *(Minor cost to Francine for effort expended)*

Horace replies, "Nah, once a month is plenty. Don't want to wear myself out." *(Cost to Francine because it's not what she wants to hear; minor cost to Horace for effort expended)*

Francine vehemently states, "What! This neighborhood will be a pig sty if you don't assume your responsibility and do it every week." *(Cost to Horace because Francine criticized his behavior; cost to Francine because of her anger and for effort expended)*

Horace huffily retorts, "You can't tell me what to do. This is a voluntary neighborhood group. One more crack like that and I quit." *(Cost to Horace because of his anger; cost to Francine because she doesn't want Horace to quit, as she would probably have to do his work)*

"I'm sorry," Francine humbly replies. "I just get so upset when people mess up the neighborhood so." *(Reward for Horace because he appreciates Francine's apology; cost to Francine because of the effort it took to apologize)*

"Oh, don't worry about it," Horace says. "We're all in this together. You're probably right. I'll do my part and clean up at least every two weeks. The Super Duper Pooper Scooper does make it easier." *(Reward to Francine because she appreciates Horace's effort; cost to Horace for effort expended)*

Learning Theory

Learning theory is a theoretical orientation that conceptualizes the social environment in terms of behavior, its preceding events, and its subsequent consequences (Zastrow & Kirst-Ashman, 2010). It posits that behavior can be learned, and therefore, that maladaptive behavior can be unlearned. Learning theory provides a framework for understanding how behavior develops. Like social exchange theory, learning theory focuses on individual group members rather than the entire group's process and functioning. It is usually applied to treatment groups, specifically therapy, for individual clients rather than task groups in macro settings. However, because of learning theory's significance in understanding human behavior and the increasing body of research documenting its effectiveness in many settings, it merits brief discussion here (Kazdin, 2001; Miltenberger, 2008; Sundel & Sundel, 2005).

Learning theory proposes three primary means of affecting people's behavior within groups. First, *respondent conditioning* refers to the elicitation of behavior in response to a specific stimulus. If a group member suddenly screams, "FIRE!" (a stimulus), other group members will probably run for their lives out of the room (response). Another example is a group of social workers receiving in-service training on solving ethical dilemmas. When the group leader gets up and goes to the chalkboard (stimulus), other group members dig out notebooks from their briefcases to take notes (response).

A second type of learning is *modeling*, the learning of behavior by observing another individual engaging in that behavior. For example, a social worker leads an educational group of community residents interested in writing their legislators about some hot political issue. The worker can serve as a model by writing to designated legislators herself. She can model what to write and how to say it.

A third type of learning is *operant conditioning*, "a type of learning in which behaviors are altered primarily by regulating the consequences which follow them" (Kazdin, 2001, p. 458). One type of behavioral consequence is *reinforcement*, a procedure or consequence that increases the frequency of the behavior immediately preceding it. *Positive reinforcement* is the positive event or consequences that follow a behavior and act to strengthen or increase the likelihood that the behavior will occur again. Consider an agency task group working to establish a new recording format for monitoring clients' progress. Karl, one group member, states to Max, another, "Thanks so much for sharing your ideas. They're great." Max likes the compliment, which is positive by nature. If Karl's response increases Max's future sharing of ideas, it is positive reinforcement.

Negative reinforcement is the removal of a negative event or consequence that serves to increase the frequency of a particular behavior. First, something must be removed from the situation. Second, the frequency of a particular behavior is increased. In this manner, positive and negative reinforcement resemble each other. Both function as reinforcement that, by definition, serves to increase or maintain the frequency of a behavior. Highlight 3.2 provides an example of negative reinforcement in a macro setting.

Learning theory describes another type of consequence, *punishment*, which is the presentation of an aversive event or the removal of a positive reinforcer that results in the decrease infrequency or elimination of a particular behavior. In a

Highlight 3.2 | **An Example of Negative Reinforcement in a Macro Setting**

An example of negative reinforcement in a macro setting involves a group of community leaders. An ancient tradition for the group is to read both the meeting's minutes and any new reports at the beginning of the meeting. Because this is so excruciatingly dull, most group members come about 45 minutes late, or don't show up at all. Matt Tress, the group's chairperson, decides that reading all that boring material is a waste of time and is really turning people off. Matt sent a written announcement to all group members stating that minutes and new reports will no longer be read during meetings because it wastes precious time. Rather, members are expected to read the material in advance of meetings so that it can be addressed. It was amazing how group members started showing up on time after only a meeting or two when the meetings dealt with business items instead of boring reading. Halting readings (removing a negative event) reinforced group members' punctuality and attendance (increased frequency of behavior).

way, punishment is the opposite of reinforcement in that it weakens or decreases the frequency of behavior instead of increasing it. Highlight 3.3 provides an example of punishment in a macro setting.

Cognitive-Behavioral Theory   Cognitive-behavioral theory combines components of learning theory and cognitive theory. Behavioral theory (also known as behavioral therapy) involves the practical application of learning theory principles to changing behavior. Cognitive theory emphasizes people's ability to make rational decisions and alter their behavior.

Concept Summary 3.3 | **Learning Theory**

Respondent conditioning: The elicitation of behavior in response to a specific stimulus.

Modeling: The learning of behavior by observing another individual engaging in that behavior.

Operant conditioning: "A type of learning in which behaviors are altered primarily by regulating the consequences which follow them" (Kazdin, 2001, p. 458).

Reinforcement: A procedure or consequence that increases the frequency of the behavior immediately preceding it.

Positive reinforcement: The positive event or consequences that follow a behavior and act to strengthen or increase the likelihood that the behavior will occur again.

Negative reinforcement: The removal of a negative event or consequence that serves to increase the frequency of a particular behavior.

Punishment: The presentation of an aversive event or the removal of a positive reinforcer that results in the decrease in frequency or elimination of a particular behavior.

| **Highlight 3.3** | **An Example of Punishment in a Macro Setting** |

Punishment can occur in groups. Consider Yaakov, a social services supervisor, who's holding a group supervisory meeting with his financial assistance workers. Yaakov often tends to drone on when trying to make a point. Akuba, one of the workers, interrupts, tactfully in her perception, and asks a question for clarification before discussion moves on and the question becomes irrelevant. Obviously annoyed, Yaakov sharply retorts, "Never, never interrupt me again in the middle of a thought!"

Akuba learns. She never, ever interrupts Yaakov again. In fact, she hesitates to speak to him at all unless she has to. Yaakov's sharp rebuttal is punishment because Akuba's interrupting behavior never occurs again (decreased frequency or, in this case, elimination of behavior).

Four basic assumptions are involved in cognitive-behavioral theory (Vourlekis, 1999). First, it's relatively optimistic. It asserts that people are capable of making positive changes if obstacles in the environment don't prevent them from doing so.

Second, people are not considered dry sponges that automatically soak up any bit of information and knowledge with which they come into contact. Rather, people continuously process information, make choices about beliefs, and construct their own worldview.

Third, the act of thinking (*cognition*) mediates or affects people's behavior. Mental processes like selective attention, coming to conclusions, and judgment "influence one's motivation to act, shape the nature of one's action, and color one's feeling about the action after the fact" (p. 179). Note that cognition's role in influencing behavior is "not a one-way street" (p. 179). Other variables including "behavioral consequences, adequacy of performance, [and] physiological states . . . also influence thinking" (p. 179).

Fourth, "the three subsystems" of cognition, emotion, and behavior "provide feedback to each other; all may contribute to a given outcome or state, and change in one may lead to change in the others" (p. 180). If you feel depressed (emotion), you might think very negative thoughts about yourself (for example, "I'm such a rotten person") (cognition), and may avoid friends to isolate yourself (behavior). Similarly, if you studied very hard and received 98% after taking a recent exam (behavior), you might think very positive thoughts about yourself (for example, "I'm so smart") (cognition), and feel extremely happy (emotion). Hence, the three subsystems can affect each other.

Cognitive-behavioral theory has been used extensively in treatment groups. As with learning theory, it has rarely been applied to task groups and other groups operating in macro settings.

Cognitive-behavioral theory can be applied in group therapy with troubled youth (Rose, 1998). Great emphasis is placed on *modeling* positive behavior such as coping strategies to deal "with problematic situations, inducing anger, stress, or other strong emotions, that young people confront every day" (p. 10). *Positive reinforcement* is used to reinforce positive behaviors. Such reinforcers might include "tokens, points, goods, small objects, activities," and whatever else might be both manageable and valued by group members (p. 22). *Social (positive) reinforcement*

Concept Summary 3.4 | ## Cognitive-Behavioral Theory

Cognition: The act of thinking.

Modeling: The learning of behavior by observing another individual engaging in that behavior (e.g., coping strategies).

Positive reinforcement: The positive event or consequences that follow a behavior and act to strengthen or increase the likelihood that the behavior will occur again (e.g., "praise, tokens, points, good, small objects, activities" [Rose, 1998, p. 22]).

Social (positive) reinforcement: "Praise, approval, support, and attention" (Corey, 2008, p. 345).

Cognitive restructuring: "the process of identifying and evaluating one's cognitions, understanding the negative behavioral impact of certain thoughts, and learning to replace these cognitions with more realistic and appropriate thoughts" (Corey, 2008, p. 348).

in the form of "praise, approval, support, and attention" can also be powerful in changing cognition and behavior (Corey, 2008, p. 345). Finally, *cognitive restructuring* "is the process of identifying and evaluating one's cognitions, understanding the negative behavioral impact of certain thoughts, and learning to replace these cognitions with more realistic and appropriate thoughts" (Corey, 2008, p. 348). An assumption is that thought can affect behavior. "These cognitions include how one values oneself and one's action and how one specifically thinks or responds covertly in a given situation. Youth are trained to identify their thoughts in stress- or anger-inducing situations. They later help each other to change thoughts that are self-defeating, illogical, or damaging to self-enhancing or coping thoughts" (Rose 1998, p. 23). Many other techniques are also applied, but these are beyond this book's scope. Our focus is on groups in macro versus treatment contexts.

Psychoanalytic Theory

Psychoanalytic theory emphasizes the impact of early life experiences on current feelings and behavior. It has been applied to individual and group situations, although it is primarily used in treatment instead of macro contexts. Because of its significance in the conceptualization of group work, however, it merits some attention here.

Psychoanalytic theory focuses on three major aspects of group functioning (Garvin, 1987). The first is how group members act out in the group context unsettled issues encountered early in life, usually within their own families (Corey, 2008). Yalom (1985) comments, "Without exception, patients enter group therapy with the history of a highly unsatisfactory experience in their first and most important group—the primary family" (p. 15). For example, a group member may have had difficulties communicating with his father, who ruled the family with an iron fist. That group member might then view "the group leader as the all-powerful father figure who reigns supreme over group members" (Toseland & Rivas, 2009, p. 59).

A second aspect of group functioning emphasized by psychoanalytic theory is the attention given to the emotional reactions "by group members both to each other and the leader" (Garvin, 1987, p. 688). These may include "helpless dependence" on the leader(s) who group members see as being very powerful; "blind defiance of the leaders" who members may see as threatening their rights and autonomy; "bitter competition" among group members vying for attention from the leader(s) and other group members; the quest for forming subgroups of allies gaining power against the group leader(s) or other members; and extreme selflessness when trying to meet other group members' needs at the expense of their own (Yalom, 1985, p. 15).

Psychoanalytic theory's third focus on groups involves "the distorted perceptions members may have of each other and of group events because of forces in the personality" (Garvin, 1987, p. 688). Psychoanalytic theory poses a number of concepts used to explain such personality forces. For instance, it views people as experiencing frequent conflict among three levels of consciousness—the id, the ego, and the superego. The *id* is the primitive force hidden in the unconscious arena of the brain that represents basic primitive drives such as hunger, sex, and self-preservation. The *ego* is the rational component of the mind that evaluates consequences and determines courses of action in a logical manner. The *superego* is the conscience which decides what actions and behaviors are right and wrong. Highlight 3.4 presents a case example illustrating these concepts.

Another concept important in understanding a psychoanalytic perspective on group functioning is the *defense mechanism*, any unconscious attempt to adjust to conditions such as anxiety, frustration, or guilt that are painful to experience. For example, without realizing it, in order to cope with her anxiety about group involvement, a group member is excessively quiet and withdrawn (a defense mechanism).

Psychoanalytic theory emphasizes careful scrutiny of individual members' feelings, behaviors, and interactions. These are then closely examined while the group leader and other members give feedback. The intent is for group members to attain *insight*, an understanding of their motivations, emotions, behaviors, and issues, a primary goal of the group process.

Highlight 3.4 | **Case Example—Id, Ego, and Superego**

Pearl, a member of a community action group to prevent drug abuse, provides an example of how these three mental dimensions might conflict. She attends a planning meeting to designate responsibilities for implementing a drug-prevention program. Unfortunately, she was so busy she skipped both breakfast and lunch, so she is ravenously hungry at the 1:30 P.M. meeting. Her *id* tells her to leave the meeting and get something to eat immediately.

However, her *ego* tells her it isn't socially appropriate to leave the meeting abruptly and get something to eat. She should have thought ahead rationally and brought a sandwich. Finally, her *superego* says she must stay and participate to the best of her ability because of her strong belief in controlling illegal drug use. The right thing to do is to help the community's children and, although almost starving, remain at the meeting.

| **Concept Summary 3.5** | **Psychoanalytic Theory** |

Id: The primitive force hidden in the unconscious arena of the brain that represents basic primitive drives such as hunger, sex, and self-preservation.

Ego: The rational component of the mind that evaluates consequences and determines courses of action in a logical manner.

Superego: The conscience, which decides what actions and behaviors are right and wrong.

Defense mechanism: Any unconscious attempt to adjust to conditions such as anxiety, frustration, or guilt that are painful to experience.

Insight: An understanding of one's motivations, emotions, behaviors, and issues, a primary goal of the group process.

Systems Theory

"Social work practice with groups is guided by a view of groups as social systems" (Garvin & Galinsky, 2008, p. 289). "In a sense all small-group theories may be thought of as systems oriented inasmuch as they portray the small group as an organic entity with boundaries, purposes, and mechanisms for attaining change while maintaining stability" (Garvin, 1987, p. 687). We have established that systems theories provide an exceptionally useful means for understanding human behavior in many contexts, including the interactions of individuals, groups, families, organizations, and communities in the macro social environment.

A group is a *system*, a set of related elements that are orderly and interrelated and a functional whole. The group is distinguished by *boundaries*, repeatedly occurring patterns that characterize relationships within the group system and give that system its particular identity. Think of the group as a living cell having a membrane or boundary around it. This boundary determines who is a group member and who is not.

Subsystems are subordinate or secondary systems within the group system. For example, two group members may form a special friendship that distinguishes their relationship from that of others in the group. They then become a subsystem.

Group systems strive to maintain a state of *homeostasis*, the tendency for a system to maintain a relatively stable, constant state of balance. Groups must maintain some homeostasis—or status quo—in order to survive and thrive.

Group members assume roles within the group. We have established that *roles* are expected behavior patterns based on individuals' position or status within the group. Group members may assume roles such as leader, emotional supporter, idea person, task director, and so on.

Group members have relationships with each other. A *relationship* is the dynamic interpersonal connection between two or more persons or systems that involves how they think about, feel about, and behave toward each other. Relationships among various group members may be cooperative, friendly, helpful, hostile, or strained, depending on group members' patterns of interactions.

Objectives of Groups in Systems Theory Group systems strive to attain four primary objectives (Bales, 1950; Garvin, 1987; Parsons, Bales & Shils, 1953; Toseland & Rivas, 2009). First, they seek *integration*, the means whereby group members fit and work together. Group members must get along and communicate well enough to get things done.

Second, group systems pursue *pattern maintenance*, the means by which the group adheres to its basic processes and procedures. Group members establish procedures and expectations for ongoing interaction, such as how members should relate to each other, how decisions are made, or how members are given opportunities to voice opinions.

Third, group systems strive for *goal attainment*, achievement of their ultimate tasks and goals. Group systems exist for a purpose. To be worthwhile, the group must achieve its goals.

Fourth, group systems seek *adaptation*, the group's capacity to adjust to surrounding environmental conditions through an ongoing process of change. For example, if the building in which the group meets is condemned to be torn down, the group must adapt by finding another meeting location.

Balance between Task and Socio-Emotional Functions in Systems Theory
Bales (1950) sees group systems as striving to maintain a balance between two basic functions: task functions and socio-emotional functions. This is true both for task and treatment groups. Task functions, which pursue goal attainment and adaptation, include exchanging information, establishing plans, and evaluating progress toward goals. They concern work and responsibility in groups. Socio-emotional functions, on the other hand, represent the feeling and emotional needs of group members. Such functions, geared to maintaining the group system's integration and pattern maintenance, are positive when they "reduce tensions, seek agreement, or show solidarity" (Garvin, 1987, p. 687). Negative socio-emotional functions, on the other hand, increase conflict, tension, and disagreement.

Group Functioning in Systems Theory Homans (1950) stressed that the following four concepts are critical in understanding a group system's functioning:

1. *Activities* are the happenings and actions conducted in a group.
2. *Interactions* are the reciprocal behaviors and communications engaged in by group members.
3. *Sentiments* are the emotional feelings and reactions manifested by group members.
4. *Norms* are the expectations held by group members regarding how they should behave in the group.

Homans maintained that these four dimensions are critical to a group system's ongoing health and well-being. Furthermore, he developed an ecosystems approach to viewing these dimensions. He stressed how a group system functions along these dimensions in reaction to its internal and external environments. Group system activities, interactions, sentiments, and norms are oriented to and affect the internal group environment when they relate to group members' adaptation to each other.

These same variables are oriented to and affect the external environment when group members must adapt to pressures posed by that environment.

For example, consider a group planning a soup and sandwich supper fundraising project to raise money for a community's homeless population. Group activities, interactions, sentiments, and norms may focus on the internal group relationships and process when two members are fighting about which one has the best chunky chicken soup recipe. The internal group environment is the focus of attention. However, when the planning group finds out that its treasurer has absconded with its funds (to pay for the food) and run off to Mexico, it must turn its attention to the external environment. Its activities, interactions, sentiments, and norms now must focus on obtaining new funding to do the supper.

 Critical Thinking Questions 3.1

Picture some formal group with which you've been involved (for example, a student organization, religious group, class group project, recreational group, or sports team).

- In what kind of specific *activities* did the group participate?
- How would you explain the *interactions* of group members?
- How would you describe the *sentiments* experienced by yourself and other group members?
- What *norms* did the group assume for how you should behave?

Concept Summary 3.6 | # Systems Theory

System: A set of related elements that are orderly and interrelated and a functional whole.

Boundaries: Repeated patterns characterizing a group system.

Subsystem: Subordinate or secondary systems within the group system.

Homeostasis: The tendency for a system to maintain a relatively stable, constant state of balance.

Role: A culturally expected behavior pattern for a person having a specified status or being involved in a designated social relationship.

Relationship: The dynamic interpersonal connection between group members.

Integration: The means whereby group members fit and work together.

Pattern maintenance: The means by which the group adheres to its basic processes and procedures.

Goal attainment: Achievement of a group's ultimate tasks and goals.

Adaptation: The group's capacity to adjust to surrounding environmental conditions through an ongoing process of change.

Group activities: The happenings and actions conducted in a group.

Interactions: The reciprocal behaviors and communications engaged in by group members.

Sentiments: The emotional feelings and reactions manifested by group members.

Norms: The expectations held by group members regarding how they should behave in the group.

Empowerment Theory

We have defined *empowerment* as the "process of increasing personal, interpersonal, or political power so that individuals can take action to improve their life situations" (Gutierrez, 2001, p. 210). Groups provide "the optimum medium for empowerment on all levels" (Lee, 2001, p. 291). "An empowering perspective on group work also involves linking group techniques to women's social, historical, and political environments to affect change" (Gutierrez & Lewis, 1999, p. 69). Groups using an empowerment approach can strive "to change oppressive cognitive, behavioral, social, and political structures or conditions that thwart the control people have over their lives, that prevent them from accessing needed resources, and that keep them from participating in the life of their community" (Breton, 2004, p. 59). We will discuss five dimensions regarding how empowerment theory applies to groups. These include social justice, consciousness raising, mutual aid, power, and multicultural socialization (Breton, 2004; Finn & Jacobson, 2008; Gutierrez & Lewis, 1999; Lee, 2001).

Social Justice   *Social justice* involves the idea that in a perfect world, all citizens would have identical "rights, protection, opportunities, obligations, and social benefits" (Barker, 2003, pp. 404–405). An underlying theme of empowerment theory is that society is structured so that some groups are oppressed and denied their right to resources, free choice, and equal opportunity. Action groups can be formed to address these issues and advocate for positive change. (Of course, treatment groups also can and should assume an empowerment approach, but here we're focusing on macro settings.)

Consciousness Raising   *Consciousness raising* is the process of enhancing people's awareness of themselves, of others, or of issues in the social environment. It occurs when they either have not thought of these ideas before or have made superficial assumptions about them, not having used critical thinking to evaluate the ideas' validity. People often have a tendency to blame oppressed groups for their oppression. People may think that it's the group members' fault that they are subject to social injustice. People feel group members should've worked harder. Or that they're too stupid to do better. Or that they're immoral. Because the oppressed group members are part of the macro social environment, they may also fall into the trap of blaming themselves (Breton, 2004; van Wormer, 2004).

Consciousness raising helps people ask themselves questions about their personal predicament. Facts and ideas are brought to their attention regarding why they, in addition to numerous others, are experiencing social injustice. This process helps people link issues like poverty and racism to the social, political, and economic configurations in which they live. Essentially, consciousness raising empowers people to view themselves more positively and realistically. Through consciousness raising they identify their strengths and see their capabilities for action. They become stronger, both personally and politically. Consciousness raising "provides group members opportunities to begin to see themselves as members of a community and eventually to fully participate in the life of that community"; they "begin to identify themselves as citizens—political beings—who, in a democracy, have the right and responsibility to participate on the sociopolitical scene, to be heard, and to influence policies so that they can access the resources they need" (Breton, 2004, pp. 60, 63).

Mutual Aid Empowerment stresses how group members can help and empower each other through *mutual aid*, the act of providing support, feedback, and information within a group context (Breton, 2004; Lee, 2001; Parsons, 2008). Group members may see themselves as "a group of peers perceived as equal partners striving and helping each other to gain control over their lives" (Breton, 2004, p. 67). They view each other "as active and having power to make a difference in the group, as social beings who need to belong and as social learners who help each other in learning. They establish bonds, empathy, and identification. Differences are supported and a balance is sought between the needs of the individual and the needs of the group" (Lee, 2001, p. 293).

Power We have established that *power* is the ability to move people on a chosen course to produce an effect or achieve some goal. Potential power discrepancies exist within any group (Gutierrez & Lewis, 1999). Some members may be more assertive, knowledgeable, skilled, or have greater status for any variety of reasons. If a leader has been designated in a group or if a leader emerges, there is a natural power discrepancy that may work against mutual aid and empowerment.

Five styles of communication in groups affect the potential for empowerment through mutual aid in a group (Lee, 2001, pp. 294–295; Wood & Middleman, 1989). First, the *Maypole* demonstrates a communication pattern where the leader (for example, a social worker) remains at the center of the group, controlling the members and paying attention to each individual separately. Group interaction among members is discouraged. The second communication pattern involves the *Round Robin*, where the leader maintains control but each group member takes turns speaking. A third type, the *Hot Seat*, involves the leader maintaining control by directing all attention to one group member (in the hot seat) while the other members watch. The fourth communication style is the *Agenda-Controlled*, where the leader maintains strict order by using Robert's Rules of order or some other structured form of running a meeting. The final communication style is the *Free Form*, where no leader emerges and group members feel free to contribute at will.

The most empowering communication style is the *Free Form*, where members empower themselves and are free to support each other (Lee, 2001; Wood & Middleman, 1989). A disadvantage of this style might be a lack of structured order. It's possible that group members can get off track, thus interfering with the achievement of group goals. Gutierrez and Lewis (1999) propose two solutions. First, co-leadership may be established where two group members take turns leading the group. This may prevent a dominant and controlling leader from emerging. A second suggestion is for all group members to rotate the leadership role. Group members can learn from others who can model leadership approaches, and power is distributed more equally among members. Greater empowerment of each member should result.

Multicultural Socialization   Empowerment in any group also involves multicultural understanding and socialization. Group leaders and members should strive to identify, be sensitive to, and appreciate any differences that might exist among members in terms of "ethnicity, race, gender, sexual orientation, class, and ability" (Gutierrez & Lewis, 1999, p. 69). Heterogeneous groups can empower all members only if leaders and members "are willing to explicitly and repeatedly identify (1) the sources of diversity within the group, (2) the different approaches that can be used to resolve target problems, (3) the different resources brought to the group setting of both leaders and members and, in particular, (4) the potential for bicultural or multicultural socialization of group members" (Gutierrez & Lewis, 1999, p. 71). (*Socialization* is the process by which a group or society conveys its knowledge, values, beliefs, and expectations to its members.)

Use of false assumptions and stereotypes can hastily serve to "turn off" group members, disrupting group cohesion and empowerment. (*Group cohesion* is the extent to which group members feel that they belong in a group and desire to continue being members.) "For example, irreparable damage could result from conduct as blatant as a group facilitator asking a Puerto Rican group member if she would prepare tacos for the last group meeting (tacos are not even a staple dish in Puerto Rico)" (Gutierrez & Lewis, 1999, p. 70).

Another example of insensitivity concerns sexual orientation (Gutierrez & Lewis, 1999, p. 74) (*Sexual orientation* is the "pattern of sexual and emotional attraction based on the gender of one's partner" [Strong, et al., 2008, p. 6–11].):

> Jiwan and Imani, the two lesbian women in Liz and Anna's group, sat together during the first group meeting. No mention of it was made. As the second group convened, however, these same two women moved to occupy adjacent seats. Jean . . . [another group member], said aloud to Anna, "Why is it that the lesbians always sit together?" Liz overheard the remark and responded, "Probably for the same reasons that all the heterosexual women have sat together." Somewhat perplexed, Jean then looked around the room at how others had chosen to arrange themselves and found that group members had indeed organized themselves in this fashion. She responded, "I never thought of it that way before?" Liz and Anna then began the group with a discussion of choices and their multiple interpretations, using the seating experience as an illustration. As all members of the group began to understand their collective lack of comfort in this new situation, they also began to gain additional information about choices others made that they had previously misunderstood. Seating options in later group sessions began to vary from the pattern exhibited during the first two weeks. [In other words, after addressing and thinking about this aspect of diversity, sexual orientation no longer dictated who sat together and who did not.] (Gutierrez & Lewis, 1999, pp. 74–75).

 Critical Thinking Questions 3.2

To what extent do you feel you have multicultural knowledge and awareness? In what group situations involving people from diverse backgrounds, if any, might you feel uncomfortable and why? What things might you do to enhance your own multicultural knowledge, awareness, and sensitivity?

| Concept Summary 3.7 | Empowerment Theory |

Empowerment: The "process of increasing personal, interpersonal, or political power so that individuals can take action to improve their life situations" (Gutierrez, 2001, p. 210).

Social justice: The idea that in a perfect world, all citizens would have identical "rights, protection, opportunities, obligations, and social benefits" (Barker, 2003, pp. 404–405).

Consciousness raising: The process of enhancing people's awareness of themselves, or others, or of issues in the social environment.

Mutual aid: The act of providing support, feedback, and information within a group context.

Power: The ability to move people on a chosen course to produce an effect or achieve some goal.

Socialization: The process by which a group or society conveys its knowledge, values, beliefs, and expectations to its members.

Group cohesion: The extent to which group members feel that they belong in a group and desire to continue being members.

Feminist Theories

Feminist theories involve "the liberation of women and girls from discrimination based on gender. The goal of feminist theory and practice is women's self-determination. [*Self-determination* is each individual's right to make his or her own decisions.] For some feminists this means securing equal rights for women within existing institutions—from marriage and the family to government policy and law. For others it means fundamentally changing these institutions" (Kirk & Okazawa-Rey, 2007, p. 6). Many feminist theories "were developed in the context of women's organizing for change—for the abolition of slavery, for women's suffrage, for labor rights, the civil rights of people of color, women's rights, and gay/lesbian/bisexual/transgender rights. Feminist theories have been concerned with fundamental questions: Why are women in a subordinate position in our society and, indeed, worldwide? What are the origins of this subordination, and how is it perpetuated? How can it be changed?" (Kirk & Okazawa-Rey, 2007, pp. 14–15).

Note that various feminist theories exist that emphasize different concepts (Kirk & Okazawa-Rey, 2007, pp. 15–17). The following are a few examples. *Liberal feminism* "grew out of one of the most significant strands of U.S. political thought, liberalism, a theory about individual rights, freedom, choice, and privacy" (p. 15). *Socialist feminism* "grew out of Marxist theories of the economy" and is "particularly concerned with the economic-class aspect of women's lives" (pp. 15–16). *Radical feminism* emphasizes how "male domination manifests itself in women's sexuality, gender roles, and family relationships, and it is carried over into the male-dominated world of work, government, religion, and law" (p. 16). *Postmodern feminism* stresses "the particularity of women's experiences in specific cultural and historical contexts" (for example, racial and class contexts) (p. 17).

For our purposes, we will arbitrarily select some of the major themes characterizing most feminist theories and apply them to organizational functioning. These include using a gender filter, assuming a pro-woman perspective, empowerment, consciousness raising, viewing personal issues as political concerns, stressing the importance of process, seeing "unity in diversity," and "validation" (Bricker-Jenkins & Lockett, 1995, p. 2531; Gutierrez & Lewis, 1998; Hyde, 2008; Lee, 2001). Often these themes have common characteristics.

Using a Gender Filter   Using a gender filter to view the plight of women in the macro social environment establishes a new way of looking at the world, with women and their issues becoming the focus of attention (Hyde, 2008). Such a filter emphasizes that women are not only part of the larger community, but themselves make up a community of women within that larger community.

Assuming a Pro-Woman Perspective   Bricker-Jenkins and Netting (2009) reflect that "feminist practice is pro-woman but not anti-man; women's diverse histories, conditions, developmental patterns, and strengths are shaped and subjugated under conditions of oppression but can be reshaped through collective work" to achieve justice in relationships (p. 279). Feminist theories maintain that women should have equal rights, responsibility, and opportunity, and call for a "fundamentally transformed, nonexploitive social order" (Lee, 2001, p. 175).

Empowerment   Feminist empowerment involves women coming together concerning a common cause and promoting "human liberation" (Lee, 2001, p. 175). The emphasis here, of course, is the empowerment of women by focusing on their strengths. Use of collaboration and consensus building is emphasized; democratic processes and procedures are stressed (Hyde, 2008).

Consciousness Raising   Consciousness raising, an important principle in empowerment theory, is just as significant from a feminist perspective. In this context, *consciousness raising* is the development of "critical awareness of the cultural and political factors that shape identity, personal and social realities, and relationships" and of one's position and opinions with respect to these issues (Bricker-Jenkins & Lockett, 1995, p. 2533). It involves undertaking a serious examination of a woman's self and her feelings about a range of issues involving women. Women must become aware of the issues engulfing them in their environment before they can take steps to address them. Bricker-Jenkins and Lockett (1995) suggest that a basic approach for consciousness raising entails asking oneself a series of questions and considering potential answers. Questions include:

- "Who am I?" What are my needs, my desires, my visions of a life that is safe, healthy, and fulfilling?
- "Who says?" What is the source of my self-definition and that of my reality? Does it conform to my experience of self and the world?
- "Who benefits from this definition?" Does it conform to my needs, my "truths"? Is it possible for me to live by these definitions? If not . . .
- "What must change, and how?" (p. 2535)

Answers to these questions should focus on defining a woman's self-worth, what she values, and how fairly the world is treating her. If she determines that her treatment is unfair or inadequate because she is a woman, how can she make changes in her macro environment to receive better or more fair treatment? Consciousness raising thus can become a foundation of empowerment. First, a woman explores herself. Next, she examines issues and appraises her status. Finally, she proposes plans to improve her life and her environment.

For example, LaShondra is a single mother of two children, ages two and a half and four. She can support her children well enough by working as an optometrist's assistant. However, she must work some evenings in addition to 9:00–5:00 on most weekdays. One of her problems is finding adequate and flexible daycare. Another problem is receiving court-mandated child support payments from her ex-husband. He just can't seem to hold down a job for very long. Still another problem is her high rent for a tiny apartment due to lack of adequate affordable housing. Other problems are lack of a social life and difficulties in obtaining credit to buy a sorely needed new car. Her "ex" ruined her credit rating while they were married.

Alone LaShondra feels stuck. She views her problems as personal and individual. She tends to blame herself after the fact for making the "wrong decisions." However, talking to other women, getting information, and discussing issues can help to raise LaShondra's consciousness. She can become aware of how she is not alone, but shares her plight with many other women in similar situations. She can come to realize that many things in her world are not her fault. Rather, they result from basic social conditions working against her.

The final facet of consciousness raising involves proposing and working toward positive changes in the macro environment. With others, LaShondra can confront community leaders and politicians about the lack of adequate child care. Can community funds be directed to help subsidize centers? Can she and other local women establish their own center, together paying for staff and volunteering their free time to help cut costs?

How can LaShondra and other women not receiving child support from itinerant ex-husbands or partners seek their fair share? Is there some community agency available to help them search for missing fathers and require payment? If not, why not? Can such a service be developed?

LaShondra discovers that other community women share similar concerns regarding the lack of adequate reasonable housing. How can the community address this problem? Can community leaders help? Can private developers be encouraged or subsidized to build housing community mothers need?

Together, LaShondra and other women can address their social issues. Can they organize and sponsor community events to fulfill social needs and decrease isolation? Can they form clubs or groups to help them "get out" regularly?

Finally, can LaShondra and other community women work together to find ways to establish credit? Can they as a group approach local banks and businesses to discuss the issues? Can processes be established to determine when credit problems are not their fault, but rather the fault of ex-spouses?

The Personal as Political   Viewing *the personal as political* is a major aspect of consciousness raising from a feminist perspective; "individual and collective pain and problems of living always have a cultural and/or political dimension" (Bricker-Jenkins & Netting, 2009, p. 279; Fisher & Burghardt, 2008). GlennMaye (1998) defines the personal and political facets of consciousness raising:

> The personal dimension of consciousness raising involves (1) identifying one's own feelings, perceptions, and needs from the vantage point of one's own experiences, (2) naming or defining one's experiences in one's own language, and (3) telling one's own life story. . . . The political dimension of consciousness raising involves (1) linking one's personal experiences to one's position as a woman in a male-dominated society, (2) identifying oneself as a woman who shares a common fate with all women, and (3) taking action to change oneself and the social structures that oppress women.
>
> The personal and the political aspects of consciousness raising cannot really be separated. They exist as [an intellectual, logical process of reasoning] . . . in which personal experience and social reality are discovered, tested, and recreated. The full meaning of feminist consciousness resides in apprehending the complex reality of one's situation as a woman with the faith in one's ability and right to a fully human existence. (p. 37)

Thus, a feminist perspective proposes that all women are "connected," that "there are no personal private solutions," and that "personal growth" can only be attained "through political action" (Bricker-Jenkins & Lockett, 1995, p. 2531).

The Importance of Process   Feminist theories emphasize that the process of *how* things get done is just as important as *what* gets done (Bricker-Jenkins & Lockett, 1995; Butler & Wintram, 1992; Hyde, 2008). A traditional patriarchal perspective that stresses male dominance focuses on the significance of end results and goal achievement. For example, consider a wealthy male politician who readily gets elected to the position of state senator after spending a huge amount of money on his political campaign. A patriarchal perspective emphasizes the importance of having won the election. It does not focus on how the election was won. Attention centers neither on the amount of money that was spent nor what contributions the senator received from large corporations expecting to receive privileged treatment.

Feminist theories stress that decision making is based on equality and the participation of all. All group members' input is important. No one should have power over another. Feminist theories focus on aspects of process such as making certain all participants have the chance to speak and be heard, adhering to principles of ethical behavior, working toward agreement and consensus, and considering personal issues as important.

Unity in Diversity: "Diversity Is Strength"   Feminist theories stress unity and harmony, on the one hand, and appreciation of diverse characteristics on the other (Bricker-Jenkins & Netting, 2009; Hyde, 2008). Gutierrez and Lewis (1999) explain that "efforts are made to bridge differences between women based on such factors as race, class, physical ability, and sexual orientation with the principle that *diversity is strength*" (p. 105). Women working together can achieve a better quality of life for all. In order to remain unified, women must appreciate each other's differences. Diverse characteristics are sought out and welcomed. New ideas to improve old ways of doing things are encouraged.

Validation   *Validation* is the process of accepting a person and a person's actions as justifiable and relevant. A feminist perspective does not exclude the importance of "rationality, analytical skills, order, and efficiency" (Lee, 2001, p. 175). However, it also includes validation of the nonrational, that is, aspects of life and human interaction that go beyond structured scientific reasoning (Bricker-Jenkins & Lockett, 1995). Feelings, emotions, and intuition are taken into account (Lee, 2001). Spirituality is another dimension given precedence. *Spirituality* "includes one's values, beliefs, mission, awareness, subjectivity, experience, sense of purpose and direction, and a kind of striving toward something greater than oneself" (Frame, 2003, p. 3)

Parsons, Gutierrez, and Cox (1998) comment on the importance of "validation through collective [or group] experience":

> In collective experience, the self and others recognize shared experience; i.e., that some of one's perceptions about oneself and the surrounding world are indeed valid and therefore legitimate to voice. This recognition contributes to a collective view that reduces self-blame, increases the tendency to look beyond personal failure as the cause of the problem at hand, brings about a sense of shared fate, and raises consciousness. Collective experience can motivate one to seek change beyond the individual level toward other systems, such as the family or community." (pp. 4–5)

Critical Thinking Questions 3.3

To what extent do you agree with the concepts inherent in feminist theories? To what extent do you feel you are or are not a feminist and why?

Critical Thinking Questions 3.4

Of all the theories discussed here (field, social exchange, learning, psychoanalytic, systems, empowerment, and feminist), which concepts do you think are most relevant in understanding how groups work? Explain why.

Concept Summary 3.8	Feminist Theories

Using a gender filter: Viewing the world with women and their issues becoming the focus of attention.

Assuming a pro-woman perspective: The perspective that "women's diverse histories, conditions, developmental patterns, and strengths are shaped and subjugated under conditions of oppression but can be reshaped through collective work" to achieve justice in relationships" (Bricker-Jenkins & Netting, 2009, p. 279).

Empowerment: The process where women come together concerning a common cause and promote "human liberation" (Lee, 2001, p. 175).

Consciousness raising: The development of "critical awareness of the cultural and political factors that shape identity, personal and social realities, and relationships" and of one's position and opinions with respect to these issues (Bricker-Jenkins & Lockett, 1995, p. 2533).

The "personal as political": The view that "individual and collective pain and problems of living always have a cultural and/or political dimension" (Bricker-Jenkins & Netting, 2009, p. 279).

The importance of process: The perspective that *how* things get done is just as important as *what* gets done.

Unity in diversity: "Diversity is strength": The view that aspects of diversity should be appreciated as strengths and used to establish unity (Gutierrez & Lewis, 1999, p. 105).

Validation: The process of accepting a person and a person's actions as justifiable and relevant.

Understanding Groups in the Macro Social Environment: Group Dynamics

What goes on in task groups? What do you need to know about groups to understand how groups work so you can be an effective group member or leader? At least seven concepts tend to characterize groups—communication, interpersonal interaction, norms, roles, group cohesiveness, power and status, and leadership.

Communication

Communication, the exchange of information, is the heart of a group. Communication may be *verbal*, using spoken or written words, or nonverbal. *Nonverbal behavior* includes any means by which information is conveyed not using spoken or written words. Group members must communicate effectively in order to get things done.

Wheelan (1999) explains:

You would be surprised at the number of groups . . . encountered whose members receive feedback about group performance but do not use that feedback to implement constructive changes. In most cases, this is due to a simple flaw in the group's internal processes. Groups that do not utilize feedback constructively usually do not have a mechanism [or procedure] in place to evaluate the validity of the feedback and to make decisions about what changes they should make based on that feedback. An example of such a mechanism might be that internal and external feedback is sought on a regular basis and that the feedback is discussed and evaluated at the beginning of the next meeting. If the feedback is judged to be valid and helpful, members discuss ways to improve team performance, decide what changes to make, and implement those changes.

This may seem like an elaborate process, but in reality it usually takes 10 minutes or less. The trick is to collect the feedback from internal members at the end of one session and discuss it at the beginning of the next. Feedback from external sources should be collected between meetings. (p. 43)

Positive Verbal Communication in Effective Task Groups   Four aspects tend to characterize verbal behavior in effective task groups functioning in macro settings (Wheelan, 1999). First, they should "have an *open communication structure* that . . . [encourages] all members to participate. Individuals are listened to regardless of their age, title, sex, race, ethnicity, profession, or other status characteristics. This enhances productivity since all ideas and suggestions get heard" (p. 42).

Second, effective groups regularly seek out feedback about the efficiency and success of their process and output. In successful groups, members accurately can evaluate themselves, their interaction, and their results. They ask for feedback both from each other and from outside sources with whom the group is involved.

Third, in effective task groups, members provide each other with feedback that is practical and useful. Useful feedback satisfies one of two criteria. First, it can help the group achieve its goals. Second, it can provide information to members about improving their individual performance within the group.

Fourth, effective task groups actually put to use both the internal and external feedback they receive. Group members not only seek out and obtain information about group functioning, but they implement recommendations to improve the group's performance.

Nonverbal Communication in Task Groups   We've established that nonverbal behavior includes any means by which information is conveyed not using spoken or written words. Eye contact, facial expressions, body positioning (for example, relaxed or extremely tense), and posture all can convey vital information among group members. Nonverbal communication can give important clues about what's really going on in group members' heads. Sometimes a group member will say one thing but mean another and provide nonverbal evidence for the latter. For example, a task group member might say while grimacing and looking desperately at her watch, "That's a great idea, but we should really save our discussion for when we have more time." The nonverbal cues may indicate that the member really means that she's quite annoyed that the other group member introduced the topic so late in the meeting. She really doesn't think it's a "great idea" at all.

Carroll, Bates, and Johnson (2004) discuss the importance of nonverbal communication, particularly from the perspective of group leaders. (This information is just as important for group members who are not leaders to comprehend what's really going on in a group.) They write:

Nonverbal behavior is a particularly important source of information for group leaders. Alertness and sensitivity to nonverbal data can provide group leaders with a rich source of interactive material. The thumb tucked tightly inside a fist, a flexing jaw muscle, arms folded tightly across the chest, the drumming of an index finger . . . all represent important messages to group leaders. Although leaders may not always respond immediately to verbal or silent signals such as tight fists, drumming fingers, excessive yawns, inappropriate smiles, or a flushed neck, leaders observe and draw tentative meaning from them. When verbal and nonverbal cues . . . [do not coincide], when the tone of voice insinuates one thing while the words say another, when lips are smiling but hands are clenched, the leader is watchful. The language of nonverbal communication in a group is rich with silent signals that can be received by a leader's [and other group members'] sensitive antennae. The leader "hears" as many of these signals as possible, then responds selectively and in a responsible manner.

Group leaders [and other group members] also may note changes of posture, rates of speech, direction of gaze, length of messages and silences, and changes in facial expression" to provide indications of what members are thinking. (p. 68)

Cross-Cultural Differences in Communication   Note that it's important to be sensitive to cultural differences concerning the meaning of specific nonverbal and verbal behaviors in task group settings. Corey, Corey, and Callanan (2007) explain:

Many cultural expressions are subject to misinterpretation, including appropriate personal space, eye contact, handshaking, dress, formality of greeting, perspective on time, and so forth. Mainstream Americans frequently feel uncomfortable with periods of silence and tend to talk to ease their tension. In some cultures silence may be a sign of respect and politeness rather than a lack of a desire to continue to speak. Silence may be a reflection of fear or confusion, or it may be a cautious expression and reluctance [to participate further in discussion.] (pp. 125–126)

Eye contact provides an example of diverse cultural expectations for this type of nonverbal behavior. Cormier and Hackney (2008) explain:

In some cultures . . . eye contact is appropriate when listening. In other cultures, an individual may look away as a sign of respect or may demonstrate more eye contact when talking and less eye contact while listening. Good eye contact [in mainstream American culture]—eye contact that reinforces [attentiveness and makes] . . . communication easier—lies somewhere between the fixed gaze and 'shifty eyes,' or frequent breaks of eye contact. (p. 45)

For instance, Chinese people speaking together "use much less eye contact, especially when it is with the opposite sex"; thus, a male group participant's direct eye contact with a Chinese woman might be "considered rude or seductive in Chinese culture" (Ivey, Ivey & Zalaquett, 2010; Zhang, 2010, p. 76).

Barriers to Communication   A number of barriers can interfere with communication and group progress. Sometimes, the communication sender is unclear, vague, or evasive in terms of what she's saying. For example, a group member says, "That idea is interesting." What does "interesting" mean? What do you mean when you say you got an "interesting" birthday gift? Is it good or bad? Are you happy or unhappy?

Other times, communication barriers are due to the communication's receiver. The receiver may be biased against the sender, more interested in other concerns, or floating off somewhere in Never Never Land. For example, a group member sends the following communication to another group member, "Time is short. We must come to a decision quickly. How do you vote, yes or no?" The receiving group member responds, "Huh?" The receiver had been thinking about how his parking meter was probably overdue and how he hoped he wouldn't get a parking ticket. The last one he got was for $85.

Still other times, communication barriers exist in the group environment, either internally or externally. Examples are noise and distractions in the hallway, phones ringing, or outbursts, interruptions, and whispering by other group members. A screaming child outside might distract group members who wonder what's happening to him. A communication receiver might be unable to clearly hear a sender's message because other group members are rudely talking about their social plans for Friday night. A fire alarm might disrupt the group altogether.

Communication is effective in groups when senders' intents, that is, what they wish to convey match their impacts, that is, what the receiver understands. Groups work most effectively when members pay attention and strive to clarify and understand what each other means.

Self-Disclosure One other aspect of communication worthy of note is *self-disclosure*, the sharing of personal feelings and information. Self-disclosure can enhance group members' feelings of belonging and acceptance in a group. It forms the basis for members getting to know and trust each other.

Corey, Corey, and Corey (2010) urge that group members use care when self-disclosing. For example, going into intimate detail of some former experience not really related to the group or the group's purpose may detract from the group's effectiveness and annoy other members. These authors make some suggestions for using self-disclosure. Group members should only self-disclose when the information has direct bearing on the group's purpose. Members should use careful discretion regarding what they really want to share with others and what is too private or irrelevant to reveal. Finally, self-disclosure is often more appropriate after a group has been meeting for a while instead of during its initial sessions. Highlight 3.5 provides a case example of self-disclosure.

Highlight 3.5 | **Case Example—Self-Disclosure**

Mindy and Mort are members of a community group in the small town of Big Littlehorn that is, trying to raise community residents' awareness about the need for a new elementary school. Big Littlehorn has begun to serve as a bedroom community for a nearby metropolitan area. Mindy self-discloses to Mort, "Thanks for volunteering to talk to the town board chairperson. It's always so difficult for me to talk to community leaders." Here she takes a personal risk of possible criticism by confessing to Mort a weakness of hers. Mort responds "Oh, no problem. I like talking to that guy and pushing him a little. He always thinks he knows everything." Mort's response to Mindy is pleasant implies warmth, and avoids criticism. As a result Mindy's and Mort's relationship is enhanced just a little bit by providing mutual support that increases trust.

| Highlight 3.6 | Case Examples—Interpersonal Interaction |

One group, a foster care unit, provides an example of contrasting interpersonal interaction by various members. The unit is made up of a social work supervisor, Ada, and her five supervisees, Tom, Dick, Harry, Mary, and Herman. Tom, Dick, Harry, and Mary almost worship Ada. They respect her expertise, appreciate her support, and genuinely like her. Herman, on the other hand, harbors bitter resentment toward Ada because she had been chosen unit supervisor over him. Herman typically pouts during group meetings, interspersing occasional negative or critical comments. The other group members simply ignore him.

Another example of how interpersonal interaction affects group process is a group of community residents on a search committee for the neighborhood's youth recreational center. Applicants include both community residents and candidates from other parts of the city. In order to maintain fairness, avoid hurt feelings, and fulfill legal responsibilities, group members agree that all comments made within the group will go no further.

One group member, Cathy, makes a few comments to Ludwig, one of the applicants from the community who happens to be a good friend of hers. Cathy informs Ludwig of the criticisms made by other group members, implying he shouldn't get his hopes up too high about getting the job. Ludwig irately calls the group members who had criticized him, tells them of Cathy's communication, and angrily complains.

Thereafter, Cathy's credibility within the group is totally blown. When confronted, Cathy refuses to acknowledge that she is the one who blew the whistle to Ludwig. She won't admit to doing it, but she won't admit to not doing it either. Ludwig told group members she was the one who informed him. Worse yet, group members no longer trust that group discussion will be kept confidential. Productive conversation about the pros and cons of each candidate is severely inhibited. Eventually, the position is filled, for better or worse. However, the other group members swear they will never again serve on another committee with Chatty Cathy.

Interpersonal Interaction

Interpersonal interaction is the result of verbal and nonverbal communication, expressed emotions and attitudes, and behavior between or among persons. It is much more complicated than communication because emotions, attitudes, and behaviors in addition to reciprocal responses are integrally involved. Interpersonal interaction can reflect mutual respect, liking, dislike, resentment, admiration, encouragement, discouragement, approval, disapproval, or mistrust. Through interaction, group members express ideas, emotions, and attitudes to each other. Highlight 3.6 provides a case example involving interpersonal interaction in a group.

Norms

Norms are unwritten, collective rules and expectations held by group members concerning what is appropriate behavior within the group. In essence, norms are "codes of conduct" about what is and is not supposed to be done within the group's interaction (Aldag & Kuzuhara, 2005; Johns, 1996, p. 241). An example of a group norm is a shared expectation that only one group member speaks at a time. Members should not interrupt each other. Another norm may be that all issues discussed within the group are confidential and therefore should not be shared outside of the group. Cathy's breaking of this norm was described in High-light 3.6, an illustration of interpersonal interaction in the group context.

Norms are communicated to group members in at least three basic ways (Dumler & Skinner, 2008). First, a group leader may simply and explicitly state the unwritten rules. Second, group members may discuss among themselves and verbally identify norms. Third, incidents occurring in the group's history may shape norms. Dumler and Skinner (2008) propose the following four examples of how events happening in and to a group can mold group norms, (p. 328):

1. *Leadership "rotation."* One example involves an early point in a group's history where a group member aggressively tries to establish control and become the group's forceful leader. Other group members resent this tack and seek to prevent such an occurrence in the future. Thus, they establish a group norm that leadership will be formally rotated every time the group meets. Such rotation, of course, could also be specified for every month, every other group meeting, or some other designated rotation.

2. *The importance of "timeliness" and punctuality.* Consider a group that misses the important deadline of submitting a report to the agency's executive director (the person highest in the agency's power structure). As a result, the agency director chews out the group mercilessly about how the agency's funding depends on getting information to funding sources in a timely manner and that this should NEVER happen again. The group then may establish the norm that deadlines absolutely must be met and excuses for lateness will not be tolerated.

    A similar issue involves being late for meetings. If one or two group members typically saunter into meetings five or ten minutes late, the rest of group is forced to wait, collectively wasting a significant amount of their time. As a result, the group may establish the norm that meetings will start on time. Period. Anyone coming in late will just have to miss anything transpiring during the beginning of the meeting.

3. *Expectations for "loyalty."* In the Highlight 3.6 case example where confidentiality was broken, the group might have openly discussed, changed, and established a new norm requiring loyalty to the group in the form of confidentiality. *Confidentiality* is the ethical principle that workers should not share information provided by or about a client unless that worker has the client's explicit permission to do so. Within the macro social environment, confidentiality can also be applied to group participation in organizations and communities. Focus on Ethics 3.1 addresses the importance of confidentiality in groups.

4. *The pursuit of "fairness."* Consider a social work unit in a public welfare department. Historically, the first person putting in a request for vacation days automatically gets the days requested. Only a limited number of workers can be on vacation at any one time because enough staff must remain to serve clients adequately. Some of the unit workers who had children in elementary school were unable to put in requests very early because of their children's as-yet-unscheduled sports and other activities. The social work unit group determined that the norm governing the vacation request process was unfair and instituted a new one. The new norm established a process where names were rotated on a list. The worker having first choice for vacation this year would

| Focus on Ethics 3.1 | Confidentiality in Groups |

Confidentiality is very important in groups (Corey et al., 2010). Depending on the group's purpose, information might involve job applicants being discussed and considered (as demonstrated in Highlight 3.6), other administrative decisions and issues that concern people's performance or personal lives, or clients (such as during treatment conferences where staff get together to review clients' progress and goals). Some information shared within a group setting should be kept confidential; that is, it should be entrusted in confidence among group members only. Sharing some types of information outside of a group has the potential of invading people's privacy, harming people's reputation, and causing mistrust among group members and nonmembers. An example in an academic setting might be a group of senior faculty reviewing the performance of a newer faculty member to determine whether or not to renew her teaching contract. Group members may not "gossip maliciously about others in their group" or those people being discussed in the group; however, "they may talk more than is appropriate outside the group" about matters that are confidential to those being discussed or about the group's internal functioning (Corey et al., 2010, p. 79). Perhaps, you've been involved in a study group, religious group, volunteer organization, student organization, or department at work where you found out that another group member had been "talking behind your back." Perhaps it involved criticizing your performance in the group. Or it may have concerned some personal information you shared in the group that you did not want shared outside of the group.

Corey and her colleagues (2010) make the following suggestions regarding confidentiality in groups:

- Confidentiality is crucial to the success of a group, but the leader can do little to guarantee that the policy on confidentiality will be respected by all members. Leaders can only ensure confidentiality on their part, not on the part of others in the group. . . .
- Group leaders describe at the outset the roles and responsibilities of all parties and the limits of confidentiality . . .
- Members be informed that absolute confidentiality in groups is not possible (Lasky & Riva, 2006); they should be told about the limits of confidentiality so they can determine what (and how much) personal information [or opinions about others] they will reveal in group sessions.
- Leaders need to help members understand the importance of maintaining confidentiality as a way of demonstrating respect for protecting the personal disclosures of other members (Lasky & Riva, 2006). (pp. 83–84)

be rotated to having last choice next year, thereby giving all workers a chance at getting the vacation days they wanted.

Note that norms, even once established, are not necessarily static; they often change over time as group purpose, membership, and needs change. Consider an agency work group formed to discuss fundraising mechanisms. Initially, the group maintains a formal dress code norm, the expectation that members wear three-piece suits or their equivalent during meetings. As group members get to know each other better and become more comfortable, they start attending group meetings in more comfortable informal attire. The dress code norm changes from formal suits to sweatshirts and jeans.

Roles

Roles are expected behavior patterns based on individuals' position or status within the group. Two types of roles are necessary in order to achieve group goals effectively on an ongoing basis (Aldag & Kuzuhara, 2005). First, *task-oriented roles* are those with the purpose of conducting tasks to achieve goals. Group members "who initiate tasks, gather information for use by the . . . [group], offer suggestions, and help motivate others" are performing task-oriented roles (p. 446). *Relations-oriented roles* are those with the purpose of keeping group members happy and satisfied with group progress and interaction. Group members "who keep the group harmonious, assist in helping members resolve disputes, and encourage members as they face barriers are engaging in relations-oriented roles" (p. 446). Sometimes, group members also assume *self-oriented roles*, where these members seek their own satisfaction and control, often without concern for other group members' well-being (Aldag & Kuzuhara, 2005, p. 446). For example, a group member might try to bully other group members into accepting him as group leader. People assuming self-oriented roles often disrupt the group's ability to work together and get things done.

Roles may be formal or informal. A formal role is that of a committee chairperson assigned by the agency's executive director. Another formal group role is that of a secretary elected by a group majority vote.

Informal roles vary widely. A group member with established expertise might serve as the group expert on certain matters. A member with a well-developed sense of humor might become the group clown, helping the group dissipate anxiety and interact more comfortably. Group leaders might also develop informally. On a court jury, for example, a task-oriented person with good listening, communication, and organizational skills might emerge as leader by group consent.

Group Cohesiveness

Group cohesiveness is the extent to which group members feel close to each other or connected as group members. It makes sense that in most groups, cohesiveness doesn't occur immediately but rather develops over time (Corey et al., 2010). Indicators of cohesiveness include good attendance and punctuality, efforts by group members to maintain confidentiality and make each other feel safe, use of good listening skills and support among group members, and a willingness to provide feedback and share perceptions about other members' issues (Corey et al., 2010).

Group cohesiveness obviously facilitates a group's ability to function effectively. Effects include members' increased willingness to participate in group activities and functions, encouragement of nonconforming members to get with the program and cooperate, and increased success at achieving goals (Dumler & Skinner, 2008; Johns, 1996).

Power and Status

Related concepts to interpersonal interaction and cohesiveness in groups are power and status. *Power* is the potential ability to move people on a chosen course to produce an effect or achieve some goal (Homan, 2008). *Status*, a concept closely related to power, is the relative rank assigned to members within the group. People with higher status usually have more power, and those with lower status lesser power. People with more power and higher status can exert greater influence on what a group does.

Aldag and Kuzuhara (2005) describe the three ways that power can be used in groups:

- **Power over.** This is power used to make another person act in a certain way; it maybe called *dominance.*
- **Power to.** This is power that gives others the means to act more freely themselves; it is sometimes . . . [referred to as a type of *empowerment*] . . .
- **Power from.** This is power that protects us from the power of others; it may be called *resistance.* (p. 366)

They indicate that "these uses of power suggest that power is more than just a way to change others' behaviors (although that function is certainly important). It may also be used to help others act more freely or to prevent others from forcing us to do things we don't want to do" (p. 366).

Possible Sources of Power in Groups   There are five possible sources of power in groups: legitimate, reward, coercive, referent, and expert (Capuzzi & Gross, 2006; Dubrin, 2009; Dumler & Skinner, 2008; French & Raven, 1968). Each can contribute to a group member's potential to influence the group.

Legitimate power is that attained because of one's position and vested authority. Police officers, judges, and state governors have some degree of legitimate power because of their positions.

Reward power is that held because of the ability to provide positive reinforcement or rewards to others. Examples of rewards are raises, "A's" on papers, allowances, promotions, days off, awards, and social praise.

Coercive power is that based on the capability of dispensing punishments or negative reinforcement in order to influence other members' behavior. Bosses wield coercive power over their employees by reprimanding them or by imposing limitations on what they're allowed to do. In addition to legitimate power, police officers have coercive power over speeders by giving expensive speeding tickets. The head nurse on a mental institution's ward can exert coercive power over uncooperative patients by restricting privileges.

Referent power is that held as a result of other group members' respect and high esteem. A military hero might have referent power in his platoon because of great acts of bravery. Famous actors and actresses, some high-level politicians, famous authors, and well-known playwrights have referent power to the extent that they are admired and command respect.

Finally, *expert power* is that based on established authority or expertise in a particular domain. A famous family therapist and author of many books on family therapy may have expert power among a group of social work practitioners who work with families. Likewise, a successful investment counselor volunteering to assist a group of urban residents in getting their financial affairs in order has expert power within that group.

Leadership

Leadership is the act of exerting influence on other group members to direct their behavior, activities, attitudes, or interaction. Leadership may be formally assigned or informally established. The new executive director of a community mental health center has power based on her formal status, that is, legitimate power. Depending on her qualifications and the parameters of her job description, she may also possess reward, coercive, referent, or expert power.

Informal leaders who gradually develop within a group context might establish their status through referent and expert power. Group members might discover over time that a particular member is exceptionally responsible, conscientious, considerate of others' feelings, and organized. Such a person might emerge as a group leader by consensus or majority agreement.

Types of Leadership   One way of looking at leadership within a group involves "leader-directed" versus "group-directed" approaches (Jacobs, Masson, & Harvill, 2009, p.22). *Leader-directed* approaches involve greater structure and control imposed by the leader. *Group-directed* methods, on the other hand, allow group members to have greater control over what happens in the group. Jacobs and his colleagues (2009) discuss the differences:

> Effective leaders who follow the leader-directed model never demand that the members follow them as if they were gurus; rather, they lead in a manner that is valuable for the members. The leader-directed style of leadership does not mean that the leader is on an ego trip or that the group has to serve the personality of the leader. It simply means that the leader has an understanding of the members' needs and structures the group to meet those needs.
>
> Leaders using the group-directed approach often turn the group over to the members and have the members determine the direction and content. This can be quite valuable for some groups. However, there are times when this approach wastes much time, especially for a group that is meeting only once or for only a few sessions. Often members don't know what they need. . . .
>
> Even though the leader is responsible, the amount of leading will depend on the kind of group and the composition of its members. For certain groups, the leader may primarily want the members to direct the group; for other groups, the leader will want to assume much of the directing. (pp. 22–23)

In conclusion, they suggest that *"people don't mind being led when they are led well"* (p. 22).

Leadership Skills   In addition to power base, effective leaders require three skills: promoting group functioning; collecting and assessing information; and taking action (Toseland & Rivas, 2009). Promoting group functioning centers on involving and motivating group members. Attending and responding skills are essential. Basic communication skills such as simple encouragement are important. For example, sometimes a simple one-word response or nonverbal head nod while maintaining eye contact is enough to encourage a group member to continue. Another effective communication skill is *rephrasing*, stating what another person says, but by using different words than those used by that person. One other useful communication skill is *clarification*, making certain that what a group member says is understood. This is often done by asking a question about a statement. The group leader must make group members feel they are important group participants. Highlight 3.7 discusses ways that group leaders can empower group members.

The second skill in successful group leadership is collecting and assessing information. This involves soliciting necessary information from group members, synthesizing its meaning, and analyzing its importance. For example, an agency group is established to develop an *in-service training program*. This is a program provided by an employing agency, usually conducted by a supervisor or an outside expert, designed to help agency staff improve their effectiveness (e.g., providing education about specific treatment techniques) or better understand agency functioning (e.g., educating staff about new legal issues or policy changes). An effective group leader

---

| Highlight 3.7 | **Empowerment by Group Leaders** |

Toseland and Rivas (2009) emphasize that it's critical for group leaders to share power and encourage member participation beginning at the very first meeting. They cite at least five ways that leaders can empower members to become involved, take responsibility for group activities, and feel that they are important contributors to the group:

1. A group leader should promote communication *among group members* instead of structuring communication primarily *between him- or herself and a member*. Members directing attention only to the group leader gives that leader great power and control over what happens in the group. When group members communicate with each other, it decreases the leader's power in a positive way. Relationships may then develop among members, they may feel freer to share ideas with each other, and they may be more willing to work productively together.

2. A group leader should seek "members' input into the agenda for the meeting and the direction the group should take in future meetings" (p. 95). Asking for input implies that the leader respects what group members have to say. A leader who responds to group members' suggestions by incorporating their input can empower group members and make them feel that their participation in the group really matters.

3. A group leader should support group members who have natural leadership potential when they "make their first, tentative attempts at exerting their own influence in the group" (p. 95). A leader should not hoard power and abruptly halt other group members' access to it. Rather, a leader should appreciate group members' strengths and energy, encouraging the use of these qualities to further fulfill group goals.

4. A group leader should support "attempts at mutual sharing and mutual aid among members" (p. 95). We've discussed *mutual aid*—the act of providing support, feedback, and information within a group context—as a process of empowering groups and group members. Spending group time in this way can enhance development of relationships, trust, and competence in working together.

5. A group leader should "model and teach members selected leadership skills early in the life of the group" (p. 95). A good group leader can use the group context to teach group members effective leadership skills by utilizing such skills during the group process.

asks members "the right questions" to elicit the necessary information. The group leader should help the group address what types of training agency staff require, how the group should solicit this information from staff, who could provide training, and what scheduling would be most convenient. The leader should help the group summarize information and prioritize tasks. Such action includes "pointing out patterns in the data, identifying gaps in the data, and establishing mechanisms or plans for obtaining data to complete the assessment" (Toseland & Rivas, 2009, p. 111).

The third type of skill necessary for effective leadership is taking action, that is, those skills that are those geared to developing plans and assisting group members in plan implementation. An effective leader should encourage members' input, assist them in communication with each other (both of which are discussed in Highlight 3.7), provide direction when necessary, keep the group on task, and resolve conflicts as they arise.

Concept Summary 3.9 | **Group Dynamics**

Communication: The exchange of information.

Nonverbal behavior: Any means by which information is conveyed not using spoken or written words.

Self-disclosure: The sharing of personal feelings and information.

Interpersonal interaction: The result of verbal and nonverbal communication, expressed emotions and attitudes, and behavior between or among persons.

Norms: Unwritten, collective rules and expectations held by group members concerning what is appropriate behavior within the group.

Roles: Expected behavior patterns based on individuals' position or status within the group.

Group cohesiveness: The extent to which group members feel close to each other or connected as group members.

Power: The potential ability to move people on a chosen course to produce an effect or achieve some goal.

Legitimate power: That attained because of one's position and vested authority.

Reward power: That granted because of the ability to provide positive reinforcement or rewards to others.

Coercive power: That based on the capability of dispensing punishments or negative reinforcement in order to influence other members' behavior.

Referent power: That held as a result of other group members' respect and high esteem.

Expert power: That based on established authority or expertise in a particular domain.

Status: The relative rank assigned to members within the group.

Leadership: The act of exerting influence on other group members to direct their behavior, activities, attitudes, and interaction.

Critical Thinking Questions 3.5

Once again, picture some group with which you've been involved. What kind of group was it? Who was the leader of that group? What kinds of power (legitimate, reward, coercive, referent, and/or expert) did that leader bring to the group? How would you describe the leader's style—more leader-directed or group-directed? To what extent did the leader empower group members? What specific techniques did the leader use to facilitate empowerment?

Stages of Task Group Development

Groups usually proceed through a number of stages as they develop through time. These include composition, beginnings, assessment, stabilization and working, and endings stages (Corey et al., 2010; Toseland & Rivas, 2009).

Stage 1: Task Group Composition

Whether individuals are appropriate for membership in any particular group depends on that group's purpose. There must be a reason for participants to become group members. Therefore, they must share some common purpose or motivation. In treatment groups, it makes sense to select members who are working on common problems or addressing similar issues. For example, a support group for people with multiple sclerosis might focus on experiences commonly encountered by persons with the disease and how such experiences might best be dealt with. (*Multiple sclerosis* is a disease where the central nervous system slowly deteriorates resulting in paralysis, numbness, muscle tremors and weakness, visual impairments, and speech problems [Barker, 2003; Mish, 2008].) Likewise, a treatment group for people with schizophrenia would focus on their common issues and problems. (*Schizophrenia* is a mental disorder where people experience a range of cognitive and emotional problems, including "delusions," "hallucinations," "disorganized speech," "grossly disorganized or catatonic behavior," and "other negative symptoms" [American Psychiatric Association, 2000, p. 297].) The disorder, lasting at least six months, interferes with people's ability to function in occupational or interpersonal settings.

Composing task groups in the macro environment requires different considerations. Task groups may be either formal or informal. Formal groups requiring structured representation in membership include *delegate councils* (groups of representatives from a series of agencies or units within a single agency), committees composed of elected representatives, and task forces appointed by administration. Because informal groups are "groups that emerge naturally in response to the common interests of organizational members," there may be great diversity in membership (Johns, 1996, p. 233).

Definition of the Group's Purpose   A major consideration in task group composition is a definition of the group's purpose to determine who will be the most useful group members. (Aldag & Kuzuhara, 2005; Garvin & Galinsky, 2008;

Toseland & Rivas, 2009). For example, two social workers bring a group of community members together to address the community issue of sexual assault. Who would logically support or be interested in addressing this issue? Who might have expertise to help define the problems involved and develop plans? Who has potential resources to contribute for plan implementation? The workers identified a number of potential group members, including the local physician who examines sexual assault survivors; a police officer who has access to legal statistics and is often the first one called to the crime scene; upstanding community leaders, such as the bank president, who lend credibility to the issue and have significant access to resources; and women's studies faculty from the local university, who have natural interest in this women's issue.

The Group's "Social Context"   Another factor to consider regarding group composition is the "social context" of the group (Fatout & Rose, 1995, p. 33). One aspect is location and sponsorship (Toseland & Rivas, 1999). Is an agency sponsoring the meeting? If so, what agency representation is required? What resources will the agency provide? If no agency is technically sponsoring the meeting, where in the community will group meetings be held?

The perceptions held by others in the external environment about the issue and the group's purpose is another aspect of social context. With respect to the community group formed to address sexual assault identified earlier, is public sentiment sympathetic to or blaming of assault survivors? Will the community likely support or resent the group and its purpose?

Group Size   Group size is still another element of group composition (Jacobs et al., 2009; Toseland & Rivas, 2009). There appears to be no magical answer regarding the best size of a group (Corey et al., 2009). The trick is to include enough people to generate ideas and get work done, but not so many that the group process becomes unmanageable. Group membership should reflect a broad enough range of abilities and behavior "to ensure a breadth of perspective and capability for solving problems" (Schopler & Galinsky, 1995, p. 1135). A group should be "big enough to give ample opportunity for interaction and small enough for everyone to be involved and to feel a sense of 'group'" (Corey et al., 2010 p. 119).

As groups increase in size, they tend to become more formal and develop structures resembling those in larger organizations (Fatout & Rose, 1995). For example, a social work student club may have very informal interactions when there are only five members. However, when the group expands to thirty-five, the membership elects officers and follows more formal procedures for running meetings such as *parliamentary procedure* (a highly structured technique designed to make decisions and conduct business).[1]

---

[1] It should be noted that parliamentary procedure can be and often is used with any size group. Major concepts include "motion" (a proposal submitted to the group that requires action), "second" (an indication of approval of a proposed motion), "amend" (to add, delete, or substitute words or portions of a motion), "majority vote" (greater than one-half of the total of persons voting or ballots cast), and "table" (a motion to postpone action indefinitely on a motion already on the floor) (Kirst-Ashman & Hull, 2009a, pp. 102–106).

Stage 2: Beginnings

During the beginnings stage, group members get to know each other and begin establishing the group's interpersonal dynamics. Initially, introductions are in order. Members begin addressing trust issues so that group cohesion is enhanced. They discuss the group's purpose and goals to establish the group's ongoing direction. A group usually seeks a consensus regarding goals so that it may begin identifying the tasks necessary to achieve those goals. Contracting involves establishing agreements about individual and group responsibilities. Goals, procedures, roles, and basic arrangements such as regularity of meetings and meeting place are established.

The beginnings period allows the group to structure itself in terms of leadership and division of responsibility (Corey et al., 2010). In some groups, one strong authoritarian leader will emerge. Other groups will assume a much more democratic perspective, more evenly distributing responsibility for maintenance and tasks.

Stage 3: Assessment

We have established that effective group leaders conduct ongoing assessment of group dynamics and functioning. Assessment is cited as stage 3 because it should begin when the group is formed.

Assessment involves all of the concepts described earlier in the discussion of group dynamics. Leading a group requires focusing attention on communication, interpersonal interaction, norms, roles, cohesion, power, and status. As group interaction is ongoing, so is assessment. A leader's role involves making certain the group gets along well and remains on task. Assessment of group functioning is important both during initial group involvement and as an ongoing maintenance task.

Conflict, referred to as *storming*, often characterizes both this phase and the beginnings phase of the group (Johnson & Johnson, 2009, p. 28). Members may experience disagreement regarding where they think the group should go or how it should be run. It is important for leadership to address such conflicts in order for the group to continue and accomplish its goals.

Stage 4: Stabilization and Working

Stabilization and working is the task group's productive period. Order must be established for the group to function and progress. Sometimes, the stabilization process is referred to as *norming*, where "the group establishes some consensus regarding a role structure and group norms for appropriate behavior" (Johnson & Johnson, 2009, p. 28). Group members must come to a consensus about how disagreements will be handled so that they may proceed with their assigned tasks.

During the working phase, group leadership must pay special attention to meeting preparation, clear designation regarding how and when tasks will be performed, empowering participants, enhancing motivation, minimizing conflict, keeping members on track, and evaluating the progress of both individuals and the entire group (Toseland & Rivas, 2009). Sometimes, this is referred as the *performing* phase of the group, where the focus is on completing tasks (Johnson & Johnson, 2009, p. 28).

Stage 5: Endings and Evaluation

Not all groups terminate. Some are ongoing, such as a city council or a civic association like the Jaycees. Even with ongoing groups, membership usually changes. People move away, lose interest, or must attend to other priorities. Endings for individual group members and full groups happen inevitably, just like death.

Some approaches help to facilitate endings in groups. First, leadership can help prepare group members by talking about the group's termination ahead of time. This dulls the surprise factor when a group abruptly ends. It also gives members time to think about the group's end ahead of time, deal with their feelings, and think of alternative ways for spending their time.

Another suggestion for helping groups end is to encourage the sharing of ending feelings (Anderson, 1997). Group members can get negative feelings such as regret and loss out in the open, in addition to receiving emotional support from other group members.

Finally, evaluating and summarizing the group's accomplishments is helpful (Anderson, 1997; Schopler & Galinsky, 1995). Especially with a successful group that accomplished many or most of its goals, giving the group and members credit for their achievement can be very rewarding. In the event that goals were not achieved, the group might discuss reasons why and suggest alternative methods to achieve goals in the future.

Chapter Summary

The following summarizes this chapter's content as it relates to the learning objectives presented at the beginning of the chapter. Objectives include the following:

A. **Explain major theoretical perspectives on groups, including field, social exchange, learning, psychoanalytic, systems, empowerment, and feminist theories.**

Important concepts in field theory include: valence; cohesion; authoritarian, democratic, and laissez-faire leadership; role; norms; power; and consensus. Significant concepts in social exchange theory include rewards, costs, and social exchange. Learning theory concepts include respondent conditioning, modeling, operant conditioning, positive and negative reinforcement, and punishment. Cognitive-behavioral theory constructs include cognition, modeling, positive reinforcement, social (positive) reinforcement, and cognitive restructuring. Concepts significant in psychoanalytic theory include id, ego, superego, defense mechanism, and insight. Systems theory concepts include system, subsystem, homeostasis, role, integration, pattern maintenance, goal attainment, adaptation, group activities, interactions, sentiments, and norms. Important concepts in empowerment theory are empowerment, social justice, consciousness raising, mutual aid, power, socialization, and group cohesion. Constructs underlying feminist theories include using a gender filter, assuming a pro-woman perspective, empowerment, consciousness raising, the "personal as political" (Bricker-Jenkins & Netting, 2009, p. 279), the importance of process, unity in diversity ("diversity is strength") (Gutierrez & Lewis, 1999, p. 105), and validation.

B. **Examine basic concepts inherent in interpersonal group dynamics, including communication, interpersonal interaction, norms, roles, group cohesion, power and status, and leadership.**

Communication is the exchange of information. Nonverbal behavior involves any means by which information is conveyed not using spoken or written words. Self-disclosure is the sharing of personal feelings and information. Interpersonal interaction is the result of verbal and nonverbal communication, expressed emotions and attitudes, and behavior between or among persons. Norms are unwritten, collective rules and expectations held by group members concerning what is appropriate behavior within the group. Roles are the expected behavior patterns based on individuals' position or status within the group. Group cohesiveness is the extent to which group members feel close to each other or connected as group members. Power is the potential ability to move people on a chosen course to produce an effect or achieve some goal. Power can be in the form of legitimate, reward, coercive, referent, or expert. Status is the relative rank assigned to members within the group.

Leadership is the act of exerting influence on other group members to direct their behavior, activities, attitudes, and interaction. Leadership can be "leader-directed" or "group-directed" (Jacobs et al., 2009, p. 22). Leadership skills include promoting group functioning, collecting and assessing information, and taking action. Leaders can empower group members by sharing power and encouraging member participation.

C. **Focus on the ethical issue of confidentiality in groups.**

Confidentiality is the ethical principle that workers should not share information provided by or about a client unless that worker has the client's explicit permission to do so. Within the macro social environment, confidentiality can also be applied to group participation in organizations and communities. Group leaders should stress both the importance and the limitations of confidentiality in groups.

D. **Describe the phases of task group development.**

Stages of task group development include (1) task group composition, (2) beginnings, (3) assessment, (4) stabilization and working, and (5) endings and evaluation.

E. **Introduce various critical thinking questions.**

Critical thinking questions addressed personal formal group involvement, multicultural knowledge and awareness, agreement with feminist theories, the relevance of various group theories, and group leadership.

Looking Ahead

This chapter discussed the theories and dynamics of how generalist practitioners function in small groups in the macro social environment.

The next chapter will discuss the types of groups functioning in the macro social environment.

For Further Exploration on the Internet

See this text's website at **www.cengage.com/ social_work/kirst-ashman** for learning tools such as tutorial quizzing, Web links, glossary, flashcards, and PowerPoint® slides.

4

CHAPTER

Types of Groups in the Macro Social Environment

Many types of organizational and community groups function in the macro social environment.

CHAPTER CONTENTS

Sunshine is the social worker on a homeless shelter's assessment team. Other team members are a physician, nurse, psychologist, in-house living supervisor, and vocational counselor. Together, the team works with incoming homeless families, conducting individual and family assessments. Their initial plans involve meeting families' immediate health and survival needs. Long-term planning focuses on permanent housing, access to health care, vocational planning, and counseling needs. Sunshine's been working with the group for almost six years now. She thinks they function together pretty well, as they're used to each other's little personality quirks.

Aaron, a social worker at a group home for adults with chronic mental illness,[1] is leading a treatment conference on behalf of Harry, one of the group home's residents. Aaron is responsible for calling together the home care supervisor, psychiatrist, and daytime care counselors to discuss Harry's case. Aaron will formulate an agenda for the meeting, lead the discussion, solicit feedback from participants, assist the group in establishing intervention plans, and write up the final report including recommendations.

Giovanna, the supervisor of a hospital social work unit, is a member of an administrative group comprised of the hospital director, the head nursing supervisor, and the physical therapy supervisor. Their purpose is to evaluate the hospital's policies regarding job expectations for members of each professional group and make recommendations for changes.

Javier, a school social worker, was elected by the other workers in his school district to serve as a delegate to the state's School Social Work Advocacy Association. This group meets in the state capitol four times each year to identify common issues, discuss concerns, and make recommendations to state legislators that advocate for school policy improvements.

Ginny, a school worker at a large residential facility for people with cognitive disabilities, is a member of the agency's Facilities Improvement Committee. The group includes representatives from various other agency units such as adult care counselors and educational specialists. The group's task is to evaluate the adequacy of living conditions for residents. Plans include assessment of various institutional facets including: furniture and paint conditions throughout the institution; food preparation and quality; transportation availability for residents (for example, to meet health care and recreational needs); regularity of treatment plan updates; and general staff conduct toward residents. Ultimately, the group will make recommendations to the agency's administration for improvements.

Jude, a social worker at a county social services department, organized a group of neighborhood center residents to advocate for a summer sports and recreation program for community youth. The social action group's goal is to persuade elected county officials to divert some funds to the center so that volunteers might develop and run the program.

---

[1] *Mental illness* or *mental disorder* is any of a wide range of psychological, emotional, or cognitive disorders that impair a person's ability to function effectively. Causes may be "biological, chemical, physiological, genetic, psychological, or social" (Barker, 2003, p. 269). *Chronic* mental illness means that it is ongoing or long lasting.

Each of the chapter-opening scenarios illustrates how social workers can be involved in task groups. Social workers, of course, also run treatment groups. For example, a worker might run a group for adult survivors of sexual abuse, adult children dealing with their parents' deteriorating health, or children struggling with their parents' divorce. Or, a worker might lead a group to educate teens about HIV transmission, new parents about the behavioral management of their children, or unemployed adults about job possibilities in their community.

Because groups vary so radically in size, purpose, and process, there are many ways to categorize them. Most of the ensuing discussion will address task groups because of their significance in the macro social environment.

Learning Objectives

A. Define *task groups* and explain their relevance within generalist practice in the macro social environment.

B. Describe task groups formed to meet client needs (teams, treatment conferences and staff development groups), organizational needs (administrative groups, committees, and boards of directors), and community needs (delegate councils and social action groups).

C. Focus on the ethical issue of how to handle your own negative feelings in task groups.

D. Discuss barriers to successful teamwork and team empowerment.

E. Address empowerment through good committee leadership.

F. Define *treatment groups*, including therapy, support, educational, growth, and socialization groups.

G. Address the differences between treatment conferences and treatment groups.

H. Examine how social action groups can empower their members to alter the external social environment.

I. Raise critical thinking questions concerning task groups.

Task Groups

Task or *work groups* are those applying the principles of group dynamics to solve problems, develop innovative ideas, formulate plans, and achieve goals. Task groups in the macro social environment are formed to meet the needs of individuals, families, groups, organizations, or communities. For example, an agency task group might focus on developing treatment strategies to meet the needs of Eastern European immigrants seeking agency resources. This targets helping individuals and families. Another task group might include social services personnel and representatives from community neighborhoods to coordinate a neighborhood watch program aimed at preventing crime. This task group works on behalf of various neighborhood groups and the entire community. Still another organizational task group consists of representatives from various departments to review the agency's policy manual and recommend changes. This task group serves the organization.

Eight main types of task groups will be discussed in the following sections. They include groups formed to meet client, organizational, and community needs (Toseland & Horton, 2008, pp. 299–300; Toseland & Rivas, 2009, pp. 30–32).

Groups to Meet Client Needs

Social services organizations structure various types of groups to meet clients' needs. These groups include teams, treatment conferences, and staff development groups (Toseland & Horton, 2008, pp. 299–300; Toseland & Rivas, 2009, pp. 30–32).

Teams

A *team* is a group of two or more people gathered together to work collaboratively and interdependently to pursue a designated purpose. Within the macro environment of social service provision, team members function together to improve client treatment and service provision. Note that not just any old work group is a team. A team consists of committed members working in unison on the behalf of clients (Johnson & Johnson, 2009).

Teams, then, differ from other types of work groups in two major ways (Johnson & Johnson, 2009; Katzenbach & Smith, 2003). First, members depend on each other and clearly acknowledge that fact, whereas other work groups often consist of members working more independently of each other. Second, teams emphasize achievement of team goals, whereas other work groups tend to focus on achievement of individual tasks and goals within the group context. A good way for conceptualizing an effective team is to think of a successful sports team; "such teams are small groups made up of highly skilled individuals who are able to meld these skills into a cohesive effort" (Johns, 1996, p. 256). Team members have a unified identity and see themselves as a unit working together to achieve mutual goals.

Teams may be formed either internally within an agency environment or they may include representatives from other systems in the macro environment external to the agency. Six types emerge (Compton, Galanay, & Cournoyer, 2005).

First, a team may consist solely of social work practitioners from the same agency. An example is a team of social workers in a Veteran's Administration hospital where social workers assigned to the temporary housing unit for homeless vets, a substance abuse counseling unit, and the hospital surgical unit work together on the behalf of a homeless vet who is an alcoholic and has serious kidney malfunctioning.

A second type of team is also one composed solely of social workers, but they come from a variety of agencies within the community. An example involves social workers from various agencies including a community recreational center, the school, protective services, and a shelter for victims of domestic abuse. These workers come together as a team to establish a service plan for a family with children ages seven, nine, and eleven and a physically abusive father.

A third type of team involves professionals from a variety of disciplines within the same agency. An example is a social worker, psychiatrist, nursing supervisor, and an occupational therapist[2] working in a nursing home. Together, they function as a team to develop residents' plans involving medication, exercise, activities, and counseling.

A fourth type of team also includes a variety of professionals, but they come from different agencies. Consider a young man with a cognitive disability who lives in a group home and needs to establish a vocational plan for his future. The group home social worker forms a team with an independent psychologist who does ability and achievement testing along with a vocational rehabilitation counselor from a sheltered workshop to establish a plan.

A fifth type of team involves social work practitioners working together with indigenous helpers or paraprofessionals within the parameters of the same agency. An *indigenous worker* is a community member who either volunteers or is employed to assist professionals. Tasks may include conducting basic problem assessments, providing necessary information about available services, or connecting people with services (Barker, 2003). A *paraprofessional* is a person with specialized skills and training who assists a professional in conducting his or her work. Examples include paralegals and physicians' assistants (Barker, 2003). This type of team might include an agency social worker and a foster parent working together to establish a service plan for a child in foster care (Compton et al., 2005).

The final type of team also involves social work practitioners working with indigenous workers or paraprofessionals, but who come from outside the agency's parameters. An example is a social worker employed by a homeless shelter who forms a team with volunteer community residents to raise funds for area homeless people. Highlight 4.1 discusses barriers to successful teamwork and team empowerment.

Focus on Ethics 4.1 addresses how negative feelings might surface in task groups including teams, and what to do about them.

Even professionals from the same discipline—including social work—might have very different perspectives on how to do things. One social worker might be very behaviorally oriented and feel that all goals and means to achieve them should be clearly defined and started immediately. Another social worker might assume that it's much more important to spend time talking about things and examining goals carefully before proceeding. Have you ever worked on a group project for some class where you and some of the other group members had totally different ideas about how the project should proceed? It is suggested that team members "should recognize the inevitability . . . of diverse perspectives and opinions, and learn to negotiate them, in the best interests" of whomever the team is trying to help or whatever goals it's trying to accomplish (Compton et al., 2005, p. 294).

---

[2] *Occupational therapy* is "therapy based on engagement of meaningful activities of daily life (such as self-care skills, education, work, and social interaction)," often to enhance functioning despite physical or mental impairment (Mish, 2008, p. 858). It often focuses on enhancing fine motor coordination (such as eye/hand coordination) and sensory integration (the ability to take in, sort out, and connect sensory information gathered from the external environment).

Barriers to Successful Teamwork and Team Empowerment

Sometimes a social worker may be hesitant to participate on a team. Compton and her colleagues (2005) propose a scenario that might be used to describe such unwillingness:

> A man crossing the street was hit by a truck. When passers-by rushed over to help, they saw the man crawling away as fast as he could, on hands and one knee, dragging one leg helplessly. They said, "Where are you going? Don't you realize you've just been hit by a truck? You need help." The man replied, "Please leave me alone. I don't want to get involved." (p. 293)

The following four dynamics can become obstacles to team participation (Compton et al., 2005, pp. 293–294):

1. *The Myth of Good Intentions.* "Social workers sometimes assume that good intentions and a cooperative attitude are sufficient to ensure effective teamwork. If we are friendly, respectful, and considerate of others, surely good interdisciplinary collaboration must follow? This rests on the assumptions that getting along with others is a relatively simple and natural ability, that teamwork depends primarily on personal characteristics, and that specific knowledge and skills are nonessential" (p. 293). Instead, a team effort should be conducted carefully as it is a complex process "that involves a great deal more than good intentions and desirable personal qualities. . . . [K]nowledge and skills for effective teamwork must be learned and refined" (p. 293).

2. *Helplessness in the Face of Authority.* Some social workers practice in settings dominated by other professions. For example, primary and secondary schools are governed by educators, and health care personnel preside over hospital or other health care settings. Being in the minority might discourage a social worker from speaking up and actively contributing on a team. Social workers should be encouraged to develop confidence in their knowledge and skills, and to assertively contribute to the team's process of goal achievement.

3. *Professional Boundaries.* "Professionals who serve on helping teams tend to have both distinct and common areas of expertise. Indeed, some tasks can be completed by team members from several professions or disciplines. Because of the overlapping responsibilities associated with these common tasks, specific negotiation is required to avoid misunderstanding, conflict, and duplication of effort. Some professionals, including certain social workers, view their turf as large and expansive. They may consign other team members from other professions and disciplines to peripheral roles. Some other professionals may eschew specialization and insist that all members of the team—regardless of discipline—can deal effectively with any problem. Neither extreme seems especially productive. Teams reflect diverse talents and abilities. Effective service often requires a combination of specialized and general expertise. Teams benefit from recognition and use of members with special competence and clarification about who should do what within those common areas that overlap" (p. 293). Therefore, it's important to discuss and specify who will assume what role in getting things done.

4. *Professional Differences.* Professionals from different disciplines may assume different perspectives on the "right" way to accomplish goals. For example, consider a doctor and a social worker who are dealing with an older adult who broke her hip and now must find an alternative supportive living environment. The doctor and other health care personnel might stress her physical needs, her physical limitations, and her medication. A social worker, on the other hand, would probably focus more keenly on the patient's ability to fit into and be comfortable in whatever environment she enters (person-in-environment fit). For instance, who might serve as her support system? How will she get around to conduct her daily living affairs, such as grocery shopping and washing clothes? Who could she call upon to help her in the event of an emergency?

| **Focus on Ethics 4.1** | **No One Is Immune from Being Human and Having Human Emotions** |

There is a difference between having normal human feelings and how you choose to behave. Ephross and Vassil (2004) discuss some ethical aspects of working in task groups:

> Working effectively with working [task] groups requires some sense of one's own and of others' dignity, but certainly not immunity from human failings. Like other people, social workers who work in working groups get tired, get annoyed, do not appreciate being the targets of blame, and are entitled to their hang-ups and feelings. All feelings are acceptable for professionals in groups. All behaviors certainly are not. Understanding and guarding strictly the boundary between feelings and behaviors is called professional skill. It is also called observing professional ethics. Two examples may make this point clearer. It is quite normal for professional staff to feel attracted to certain group members. It is not acceptable to act on these feelings, neither to favor some group members over others nor to undertake intimate relationships with a group member while one carries responsibility for maintaining a professional relationship. Conversely, it is normal for a professional to like some group members less than others, even not to like some group members. Again, the principle is that the feeling is acceptable, perhaps to be worked through by introspections, perhaps not. Hostile behavior toward such group members is not acceptable and flies in the face of professional ethics. (p. 408)

Team Empowerment

Hellriegel and Slocum (2009) emphasize that effective teams are empowered by having high degrees of at least three variables. First, teams are empowered by members who actually feel the team is *effective*. Members are motivated when they feel their work is worth it. To what extent are team members confident in their ability and power to achieve goals? A second variable empowering teams is the extent to which members feel their work and *goals are valuable*. To what extent do they feel they can really make an impact? To what extent is what they're doing important to others? A third empowering variable involves the extent to which team members feel they have *adequate autonomy* and can exercise their own judgment, even though the team must function as a unit. Team members should not feel ignored, bullied, or overly pressured. They should feel their voices are heard as they work with others to compromise and get things done.

  Critical Thinking Questions 4.1

Have you ever been a member of a team or task group? If so, what were the circumstances? What variables acted as barriers to effective teamwork? What factors helped to empower the group to achieve its goals?

Treatment Conferences

Treatment conferences are groups who meet to establish, monitor, and coordinate service plans on the behalf of a client system (Summers, 2009; Toseland & Rivas, 2009; Woodside & McClam, 2006). They may also be called case conferences, case staffings, treatment staffings, or, simply, staffings. A treatment conference may be conducted by a team, if the group meets the definition of a team, namely, that members are interdependent and work together toward a unified goal.

However, treatment conferences often differ from teams in at least three ways (Toseland & Rivas, 2009). First, group members might not have established a working relationship as a unit. Second, treatment conferences might be held infrequently, such as at six-month or one-year intervals, preventing the bonding necessary to establish a team. Third, treatment conferences might involve a different configuration of participants at each meeting since long periods of time pass, clients' needs change, and staff come and go.

Treatment conferences may involve internal agency professionals and staff, or they may include professionals and staff from other agencies. It depends on which agencies and staff are involved in service provision. Usually, the involvement of all service providers, regardless of their agency affiliation, is encouraged.

Sometimes, clients and their families are invited to attend treatment conferences. Other times, clients are invited to attend only a portion of the conference. Some agencies indicate that having clients and other outsiders present interferes with the frank presentation of information about clients and their families. Other agencies feel that content may be too emotionally stressful for clients and their families to hear.

Case Example of a Treatment Conference   The following is an example of a treatment conference in a diagnostic and treatment center for children with multiple physical and psychological disabilities. The client Timmy, age three, has severe *cerebral palsy*, a disability resulting from damage to the brain before, during, or shortly after birth that results in problems with muscular coordination and speech (Mish, 2008). Timmy has very little control of his extremities, torso, face, and mouth. He has some limited control of his eyes.

After Timmy is referred for assessment, extensive testing is performed by speech, occupational, and physical therapists. A physician conducts a thorough physical examination and orders relevant tests. Sometimes, a geneticist is involved to establish the etiology of the disorder. However, Timmy experienced oxygen deprivation at birth due to the umbilical cord being wrapped around his neck. Since the etiology of the disability has been established, the program director, a physician, determines that a genetic assessment is unnecessary. A psychologist conducts perceptual and ability testing. Finally, a social worker carries out a family assessment.

All evaluators subsequently attend the treatment conference. This particular group cannot be considered a team, because it does not work together on a regular basis. For example, there are five occupational therapists and three social workers. The configuration of participants for any particular client varies drastically as only one professional per discipline is involved with each case. During the treatment

The following are five examples of goals such a group might establish for its members (Stauffer et al., 2006). First, participants might learn to carefully examine their own behavior for symptoms of depression and replace old behavior patterns with new, more functional ones. Second, members might work on decreasing negative thinking about themselves and substituting more positive, objective thinking about their strengths. Third, these women might learn relaxation and stress-reduction techniques. Fourth, participants might provide a supportive environment where they feel free to express their concerns. Fifth, members may use the group as a forum for practicing "positive and assertive communication" that they then could apply to other settings in their lives (p. 362).

Case Example: Support Groups for GLBT People

Examples of support groups include those benefiting GLBT (gay, lesbian, bisexual, and transsexual) people. "Lesbians and gay men are often traumatized by the emotional, and sometimes physical, abuse visited on them by a virulently homophobic culture" (Finnegan & McNally, 1996, p. 117; Martin, 2008; Messinger & Brooks, 2008). Such oppression may contribute to "conditions such as depression, substance abuse, suicide, homelessness, and injury or death from perpetrators of hate crimes" (DeLois, 1998, p. 65; Miller, 2008; Morrow, 2008).

Communities and agencies can establish support groups to address any number of issues, depending on needs. Several themes often emerge in gay men's support groups, including the following (Ball & Lipton, 1997; Puglia & House, 2006):

- Dealing with the stigma and shame associated with being gay that is imposed by the encompassing society
- Coming out, the "ongoing developmental process of gay identity formation organized around revealing and accepting one's sexual orientation" (Ball & Lipton, p. 265)

- AIDS/HIV
- Family issues such as acceptance or lack thereof by their family of origin
- Relationships and intimacy in a society that doesn't foster gay relationships
- The resolution of ethnic and cultural identities with the many issues involved

Similarly, Engelhardt (1997) describes common themes addressed in lesbian women's support groups:

- "Management of oppression, stigma, and difference."
- The "invisibility of the lesbian woman's experience."
- "Safety and vigilance issues . . . ranging from verbal harassment to physical assault."
- "Lesbian relationships and sexual expression."
- "Living with dignity as a declared lesbian woman" (pp. 281–283).

Educational Groups

Educational groups provide information to participants. Information may be of virtually any kind. Examples of educational groups include an infomational meeting of parents of children having a rare genetic disorder characterized by extremely frail bones that are easily broken (osteogenesis imperfecta); teens receiving sex education; a presentation by an employment counselor to a group of adults interested in finding jobs; and a group of older adults in a nursing home requesting information about their prescribed drugs.

Toseland and Rivas (2009) explain the functioning of educational groups:

> All educational groups are aimed at increasing
> members' information or skills. Most groups routinely
> involve presentations of information and knowledge
> by experts. They also often include opportunities for
> group discussion to foster learning. When leading
> educational groups, workers concentrate on both the

continued

Highlight 4.2 | *continued*

individual learner and the group as a whole as vehicles for learning, reinforcement, and discussion.

Members of educational groups are bonded by a common interest in the material to be learned and by common characteristics, such as being an adolescent, a prospective foster parent, a union worker, or a board member. In composing educational groups, workers consider each member's knowledge of the subject matter and level of skills and experience so that all members can derive the most benefit from the learning process. (p. 24)

Growth Groups

Growth groups are those aimed at expanding self-awareness, increasing potential, and maximizing optimal health and well-being. Growth groups often emphasize exploring hidden thoughts and emotions in addition to disclosing these to other group members for feedback. Examples include a group of heterosexual singles exploring their attitudes about the opposite gender; "a values clarification group for adolescents"; and a group of gay men focusing on gay pride issues (Toseland & Rivas, 2009, p. 24).

Case Example: Growth Groups for African-American Juvenile Offenders

Harvey (2005) describes the development and implementation of growth groups for African-American juvenile offenders that use an Afrocentric approach. *Afrocentricity* is a worldview that emphasizes the history, culture, and experiences of people who have black African ancestry as a basis for understanding how the world functions and how people are treated (Barker, 2003). These growth groups provide a good example of how a macro system can develop a program to enhance the well-being of a population-at-risk. Here, a type of "treatment group" can also address broader needs (that is, fighting oppression, increasing social awareness, and enhancing self-confidence) in a macro context.

African Americans have endured a turbulent and oppressive history. "Amid inhumane assaults and

against great odds it is remarkable that they have made substantial improvements in advancing the quality of their lives, as well as the lives of Americans in general" (Leashore, 1995, p. 107). Sue and Sue (2008) emphasize:

> [T]he great diversity that exists among African Americans, who may vary greatly from one another on factors such as socioeconomic status, educational level, cultural identity, family structure, and reaction to racism. Many middle- and upper-class African Americans are receptive to the dominant society, believe that advances can be made through hard work, feel that race has a relative rather than a pervasive influence in their lives, and embrace their heritage. . . . However, even among . . . successful Black men earning $75,000 a year or more, 6 in 10 reported being victims of racism, and that someone close to them was murdered or had been in jail. (p. 332)

Davis, Wallace, and Shanks (2008) report:

> When reviewing the important indicators that document quality of life and economic resources, African Americans often fall woefully short of national averages. Whether the measure is family stability, employment, income, wealth, education, incarceration rates, or health, persistent disparities exist for African Americans [compared to whites]. (p. 72)

African Americans make up over 12.8 percent of the U.S. population (or 13.5 percent when considered in combination with one or more other races); African-American people continue to suffer the following injustices when compared with whites (U.S. Census Bureau, 2008):

- Children are much more likely to live in poor families.
- Infant mortality is almost two and a half times that of whites.
- African Americans are over 40 percent less likely to graduate from college.
- Income levels are significantly less.

- African Americans are much more likely to be incarcerated in the criminal justice system. African Americans make up almost 39 percent of people in correctional facilities and almost 42 percent of people on death row.

The purposes of forming Afrocentric growth groups of African-American juvenile offenders include enhancing members' self-respect; establishing a stronger identity with African heritage and culture; developing ties with a positive peer group; widening vocational aspirations; and strengthening the ability to make socially responsible decisions (Harvey, 2005). In addition to providing a treatment context where they work on developing personal strengths, these groups address and help members cope with broader social issues.

Young African-American offenders are viewed within their macro context. Poverty, marital and family dissolution, white oppression and discrimination, the strong social pressure of negative street-corner peer groups and gangs, and lack of career hopes all contribute to an environment where crime becomes a logical means of survival. These young men typically express a number of themes (Harvey, 2005):

- Adults around here do it, so why shouldn't I?
- Violence is a way of life. If you don't stand up for yourself, you're history.
- How can I be moral and still survive the horrendous peer pressure to be bad?
- You have to be strong and not express emotion to get any respect and protect yourself (p. 166).
- Shouldn't women be treated as inferior and be handled with violent behavior?
- Police are the bad guys.
- How can I deal with whites' racist treatment?
- I don't know that much about African culture.

An Afrocentric approach emphasizes both spirituality and connectedness with others in the environment, including individuals, family, and community. Its goal is to engender self-understanding, self-respect, and "a strong sense of responsibility for the well-being and harmonious interconnection between self and others" (Harvey, 2005, p. 241; Nobles, 1976). The Afrocentric approach rests on seven basic principles, called the Nguzo Saba (Harvey, 2005, Karenga, 1965, 2000). These include (1) "unity" with "the family, community, nation, and race," (2) "self-determination," (3) "collective work and responsibility," (4) "cooperative economics" (to own and operate business for profit), (5) "purpose" (to develop a positive and great community), (6) "creativity," and (7) "faith" ("to believe in our parents, our teachers, our leaders, our people, and ourselves, and in the righteousness and victory of our struggle") (Harvey, 2005, pp. 241–242).

Growth groups, then, are designed to provide members with "a positive perspective on African and African-American culture, assist them in developing their own African-American group identity, and provide them with tools to deal with the oppressiveness of white supremacy" (Harvey, 2005, pp. 242–243). Groups consist of fifteen boys ages fourteen through eighteen who are on probation. Offenses include dope dealing, sexual assault, car theft, armed robbery, burglary, and numerous other criminal acts.

Group co-leaders include social workers or people with other types of expertise such as that in African studies, music, or theater. Group process involves the acquisition of skills such as positive interpersonal interaction, relationship building, communication, and introspection. Groups stress enhancing members' self-concepts, developing "constructive lifestyles and positive solutions to life problems," and appreciating their cultural heritage and personal strengths (Harvey, 2005, p. 245).

During the initial eight-week group phase, co-leaders teach members about group process, the Afro-centric perspective, and the important formalized rites of passage involved in group membership. Group members then participate in a weekend retreat where co-leaders and a group of older adult men decide which fifteen young men will be included in the group. Chosen members then undergo an initiation ritual where they pledge to

continued

Highlight 4.2 | *continued*

uphold the principles of Nguzo Saba, are given an African name, and are presented a "special identifying symbol" they are expected to wear at all group meetings. No new members are admitted after this point (Harvey, 2005, p. 246).

Groups then meet weekly for ninety minutes, as members develop their group identity, learn, and develop skills. Group activities may include videos and music, depending on the topics addressed. Guests are invited to speak on various topics, called "modules," that stress the importance of African and African-American culture (Harvey, 2005, p. 246). Modules, which last from four to six group sessions, address any number of topics ranging from African-American culture to relationships between men and women to dealing with racism.

Upon completion of all modules, group members participate in another weekend experience, where they demonstrate their newly learned skills and prepare for the final special recognition ceremony. This ceremony becomes the culmination of the group experience, where members demonstrate before their families and community what they have achieved. They proclaim their sacred name and "receive a symbol and a certificate of sacred transformation" (Harvey, 2005, p. 247).

We have established that this process intends to enhance group members' self-respect, sense of African-American identity, and sense of responsibility for and belonging to the African-American community. It is hoped that other anticipated effects will include crime reduction, improved school attendance, better grades, and increased employment. Initial results were promising (Harvey, 2005). Family members reported improved behavior at home, and group members expressed enhanced self-respect and appreciation of African heritage.

Socialization Groups

Socialization groups help participants improve interpersonal behavior, communication, and social skills so that they might better fit into their social environment. Social activities and role plays are often used for group members to practice new social skills. Examples of such groups include an urban neighborhood's youth activities group, a school-based group of shy teens working to improve interpersonal skills, and a Parents Without Partners group sponsoring various social activities, such as parties and outings (Toseland & Rivas, 2009).

Corey (2008) explains the process involved in leading socialization groups (Rose, 1986):

> Before beginning the social skills training process, the group leader discusses with the members the general purposes of the group and the main procedures that are likely to be used. The members are given a variety of examples and are encouraged to ask questions. The group leader attempts to draw on the experiences of those members who have used these procedures themselves. If the members have had no prior experience with role playing, the leader generally provides them with some training. Then situations are given to the group, and experienced members from previous groups are asked to demonstrate how to role play. Once members learn role-playing skills, they are then trained to develop situations that lend themselves to social skills training. After the group is trained in the development of problem situations, the members are asked to keep a diary of situations as they occur during the course of the week. Each week at least one situation of each member is handled by the group.
>
> Either the therapist or some group member models the desired verbal and nonverbal behaviors in a brief demonstration. Clients then practice their roles in the situation by using the agreed-on behaviors. If clients have trouble using a strategy during the rehearsal, they can be coached by the group leader or other members. When coaching is used, it is generally eliminated in later rehearsals. After each rehearsal, clients receive feedback from the group pertaining to their strengths and weaknesses. Clients assign themselves homework to carry out in the real world. As they complete these assignments, they are

asked to observe themselves in new situations and to keep a diary of problems. (p. 352)

Groups Serving More Than One Purpose

Sometimes, a treatment group will serve more than one function and not fit neatly into a designated category. For example, consider a group of young adults

with cognitive disabilities formed to improve group members' assertiveness skills. The group serves as a growth group because it expands members' self-awareness, a socialization group to improve social skills, an educational group to provide members with assertiveness training, and a support group for members to help and encourage each other.

agency's programs and services. The scope and breadth of such programs will depend on the agency's size and resources. Smaller agencies may collaborate with other human service organizations to conduct training in areas of mutual interest and in response to similar staff needs. Again, the focus is on the relatedness of the training content to the specifics of the job. . . . [S]taff development may focus on promoting awareness of and sensitivity to the particular characteristics, cultures, and needs of the clients, as well as the practice technologies and methodologies relevant to effective service provision and positive service outcomes. (p. 102)

Examples of staff development groups include:

- "A group of professionals who attend a series of seminars about pharmacology offered by a regional psychiatric center
- An in-service development seminar on codependency for the staff of an alcoholism treatment agency
- Group supervision offered by an experienced social worker for social workers who work in school districts in which there are no supervisors
- A program director who conducts a weekly supervisory group for paraprofessionals who work in a community outreach program" for older adults. (Toseland & Rivas, 2009, p. 36) (*Community "outreach* involves systematically contacting isolated people in their homes or wherever they reside [institutions, streets], or in the neighborhoods where they congregated, and linking them to services and financial programs" [Hardcastle & Powers, 2004, p. 194].)

Leaders of staff development groups generally have an expertise in the topic addressed. Various learning formats are used, including "lectures, discussions," electronic presentations, DVDs, outside speakers, role plays, and modeling of techniques by leaders (Toseland & Rivas, 2009, p. 36). Group members can confer about content, practice skills via simulations, and get feedback about their performance from other group members.

Staff development groups may involve an agency unit of staff (for example, a social work department, or all helping professionals who work with a particular client population). This might become part of the supervisory process for the group where ongoing staff development is provided (Hopkins, 2009; Sheafor & Horejsi, 2009). Staff development groups may also be composed of new staff who receive "orientation and training" about job requirements, expectations, and policies (Sheafor & Horejsi, 2009, p. 61). Another aspect of staff development concerns groups that include most of an agency's staff who attend an in-service training session or series of sessions.

Groups to Serve Organizational Purposes

A social service organization's administration is expected to maintain effective agency functioning, hire staff competent to do their jobs effectively, plan for the future, provide supervision for employees, manage financial resources, monitor agency functioning, and evaluate the effectiveness of service provision (Lewis, Packard, & Lewis, 2007). At least three types of groups often characterize agency environments. These include administrative groups, committees, and boards of directors.

Administrative Groups

Various clusters of supervisors and managers may be organized to maintain and improve agency functioning (Ephross & Vassil, 2004; Fatout & Rose, 1995). Usually, agency lines of authority are described in a hierarchical fashion, as illustrated by an organizational chart described in Chapter 7. Most often, decision makers are clustered into groups so they can communicate about what's happening in the organization, make decisions, and coordinate their leadership. Such groups often include various levels of administrative staff such as supervisors, directors, managers, and department heads. Such an administrative group usually meets on a regular basis to discuss issues and develop plans for running various aspects of the organization. An example of an administrative group in a residential treatment center for girls with serious behavioral and emotional problems is the assistant director, social work director, home care staff director, and on-grounds school principal. An example in a sheltered workshop serving people with cognitive disabilities is the activities director, vocational director, social work supervisor, and transportation manager.

Committees

A *committee* is a group of persons "delegated to consider, investigate, take action on, or report on some matter" (Mish, 2008, p. 250). Committees are common entities in organizations that operate to meet various organizational needs (Toseland & Rivas, 2009). They consist of volunteers, appointees, or elected representatives who meet to address any significant issue concerning the organization's functioning. Sometimes committees are ongoing; other times, they are temporary or ad hoc.

Examples of committees include a group of staff representatives appointed to investigate, assess, and make recommendations about the quality of food served to residents in a nursing home. Another example is a large county department of social services that establishes a committee of unit representatives to develop a plan for coordinating and scheduling scarce meeting space within the facility. As the agency was housed in an old Grumbles department store building built many decades earlier, adequate meeting rooms were rare.

Highlight 4.3 discusses how a good leader can empower a committee and enhance its functioning.

| Highlight 4.3 | **Empowerment through Good Committee Leadership** |

Brody (2005) stresses how good leadership can help committees and other task groups function more effectively. When a social worker has been designated, appointed, or elected as a committee leader, six tactics facilitate successful meetings:

1. The leader should clearly state the purpose of the meeting immediately at the beginning. All committee members should be on track and know generally what to expect.
2. An agenda for the meeting should be prepared in advance of the meeting and distributed ahead of time to all committee members. An *agenda* is an ordered list of topics to be covered at the meeting (Kirst-Ashman & Hull, 2009b, p. 102). Agenda items are usually one to a few words that alert committee members to discussion topics. This allows them to think about the issues ahead of time and possibly bring information that they feel applies to the topic.
3. Ground rules should be clearly explained right at the outset of a committee meeting. The leader (or chairperson) "identifies expectations on how members are to interact with each other and how the business of the meeting would be conducted. This includes clarifying the process for decision making" (Brody, 2005, p. 359). For example, *Robert's Rules of Order* (Robert, 1971) illustrate one method of running meetings with highly structured techniques such as *formal motions* ("proposed actions that the group is asked to support") and voting procedures (Kirst-Ashman & Hull, 2009b, p. 102).
4. Committee members should get specific assignments so that their understanding of

what they need to do by the next meeting is perfectly clear. Sometimes, a leader will ask for volunteers to complete assignments or volunteers will suggest their own assignments. Other times, a leader may make assignments. But a leader should be very careful that committee members are really willing to carry them out, or they probably won't get done.

5. An effective leader should deal with any conflict emerging in the group. Conflicts may arise because of interpersonal or emotional issues occurring among members, differences of opinion regarding how the group should proceed, or competition for control of the group. A good leader will address the conflict and seek a compromise without taking sides.

    Wheelan (1999) remarks, "Some groups navigate their conflicts well, and others disband or become dysfunctional by dealing with their differences ineffectively. What do successful teams do to promote positive conflict resolution? Members of successful teams communicate their views clearly and explicitly. They avoid generalizations and are specific in their communication. They talk about trust and cooperation during the discussion" (p. 65). They also will argue their points straightforwardly so that the group may come to some resolution. A good leader will facilitate this process.
6. Finally, an effective leader will periodically summarize the discussion throughout the committee's meeting. This helps to establish a consensus regarding where the group is going and keep the group on track.

Boards of Directors

A *board of directors* is another type of administrative group (Toseland & Rivas, 2009). It is a group of people authorized to formulate the organization's mission, objectives, and policies, in addition to overseeing the organization's ongoing activities. A board of directors also has ultimate control over the agency's higher administration, including its executive director or chief executive officer. Boards are usually made up of respected volunteers recruited from the community on the basis of "their power, status, and influence in the community; their expertise; and their representation of particular interest groups and constituencies" (Toseland & Rivas, 2009, p. 39). Examples of boards of directors include one overseeing a large private substance abuse treatment center and another governing an organization running seven hospices. (A *hospice* is a nonhospital facility where people having terminal illnesses can die as comfortably as possible with the best quality of life possible.)

An effective board of directors can serve a number of positive functions for an agency. It can:

- Serve as an ambassador to communicate the organization's mission, policies, programs, and services [to clients, community residents, staff, governmental units, and other social services agencies] . . . ;
- Interpret and communicate to the organization the needs of the communities served by the organization;
- Define the organization's position on public policies and serve as advocates;
- Protect the organization from inappropriate intrusions by government and special interests;
- Promote the organization to [financial] donors and potential donors. (Axelrod, 2005, p. 137; Lewis et al., 2007, p. 36)

Groups to Serve Community Needs

At least two types of groups also can be formed to meet community needs. These include delegate councils and social action groups (Toseland & Rivas, 2009, p. 32).

Delegate Councils

A *delegate council* is a group of representatives from a series of agencies or units within a single agency. Representatives may be elected by their constituencies or appointed by agency decision makers. Typical goals include enhancing cooperation and communication among professionals in different units or agencies, reviewing issues relevant to service provision, enhancing management approaches, and pursuing social action goals (Toseland & Rivas, 2009).

An example of a delegate council is a group of representatives from four private social service agencies in three states. Each agency provides a range of services, including mental health counseling, substance abuse counseling, group homes for people with various disabilities, residential treatment centers for troubled youth, recreational programs for families, and foreign adoptions. In two agencies, administrators appointed five representatives each. In the other two agencies, representatives were elected by staff in their respective six service divisions. One recent delegate council conference focused on integrating new management principles throughout the agencies' administrative structures.

Another example of a delegate council is a group of professionals working in rape crisis centers throughout the state. Each agency designates a representative to meet in the council to discuss education and treatment issues in addition to inter-agency cooperation.

Social Action Groups

Social action groups are formed to engage in some planned change effort to shift power and resources in order to modify or improve aspects of the macro social or physical environment (Netting, Kettner, & McMurtry, 2008; Toseland & Rivas, 2009). They may consist of professionals, clients, community residents, or some combination of these groups. Social workers can use social action groups to con-nect people with necessary services and resources, address and solve problematic situations, and alter conditions in the macro social environment to enhance living conditions and quality of life.

Social action groups in communities often involve one of three dimensions—"geographic, issue, or identity" (Staples, 2004, p. 344). First, a group from a *geograph-ical area* (for example, a neighborhood, a town, a county, a state, or even a whole region) might band together and address issues of concern to them all. Such problems might include "housing, education, recreation, employment, environmental issues, transportation, or health care" (p. 345). One example is a group of agency workers and community residents collaborating to raise funds to establish a neighborhood park. Another example is the Coalition for a Better Acre, a group of primarily Central American and Cambodian residents who live in one of the poorest neighborhoods of Lowell, Massachusetts (Staples, 2004, p. 345). Their goal is social action for neighbor-hood improvement through cleanup, increasing inexpensive housing availability, and development of programs serving young people.

A second dimension often fueling community social action groups concerns specific social *issues,* regardless of particular geographic residence. Such issues might include "clean elections, tax reform, women's rights, environmental justice, or elderly issues" (p. 345). One example of such a social action group is a coalition of social work practitioners working to improve professional social work licensing standards in their state. Another example is the Massachusetts Senior Action Coun-cil (MSAC), which involves members throughout the state. Its goal is social action for improved living conditions for older adults, improved and better-maintained senior housing, improved prescription drug coverage, and "a managed-care patients' bill of rights" (p. 346). (*Managed care* is "a generic label for a broad and constantly changing mix of health insurance, assistance, and payment programs that seek to retain quality and access while controlling the cost of physical and mental health services" [Lohmann, 1997, p. 200].)

The third focus involving community social action groups is "*identity*, for instance, ethnicity, religion, sexual orientation, or physical or mental disability. The Latino Immigrant Committee in Chelsea, Massachusetts, is composed primar-ily of recent immigrants from El Salvador, Honduras, Guatemala, Colombia, Chile, and Nicaragua. A core group of 30 people is most active and has engaged in social action focused on discriminatory treatment at the local branch of the post office, on worker safety at a local meat processing plant, on gang violence, on immigrant rights, and on increased participation in the political process" (Staples, 2004, p. 346).

Note that sometimes the distinctions among these three dimensions are not that clear. The MSAC example that addresses the concerns of older people might also be considered an issue of identity. However, the point is that social action groups are formed to improve social and economic policies, as well as to enhance people's overall well-being.

Social Action Groups and Empowerment

Social action often means pushing a macro system to change, moving against the mainstream, or making demands on scarce resources. To do this requires substantial effort. Expenditure of output or effort requires adequate energy or strength. Social action groups can be used to empower group members internally, and thus enhance their strength for altering the external environment in several ways (Carr, 2004; Cox, 1991; Fisher, 2001; Staples, 2004).

Increasing Understanding

First, communicating with other group members about their perceptions of problems and issues can greatly expand group members' understanding of these issues (Carr, 2004). The depth of understanding and insight increases as group members share personal insights about how relatives and friends view these issues.

For example, consider a group of neighborhood residents and agency social workers formed to evaluate the adequacy of neighborhood housing and the extent to which it complies with established building codes. Horace, one group member, lives with his family in a rented home with horribly drafty windows. He understands that problem from personal experience. However, as other group members share their perceptions, Horace's understanding of such problems significantly deepens.

Quanisha, another group member, talks of how her seven-year-old son, paraplegic from an accidental bullet to the spinal cord during a neighborhood gang battle, can't get into their rented home without being carried. Ramps are nonexistent. Quanisha indicates that she can cope with the situation now while the boy is small. However, the bigger he gets, the harder it is to move him.

Robert, still another group member, tells how his aging parents, who live in a rented home next door to him, have broken windows whose cracks are plastered with masking tape, making it almost impossible for his parents to see outside. Additionally, their two outside doors don't close properly, so that in winter the place is like a wind tunnel. Robert's parents are afraid to tell the landlord, as they fear he will get mad and evict them. In similar cases, neighborhood landlords found reasons to evict tenants or simply shut the properties down, saying that the upkeep wasn't worth the meager rent they received.

Horace's understanding of the neighborhood housing problems and issues is greatly expanded by hearing about other residents' issues and experiences. His individual view is multiplied many times so that he now better understands the nuances and complexities of the housing problem.

Inspiring Others

A second way that social action groups can empower group members is how "members who have survived or overcome aspects of powerlessness can inspire and motivate others" (Carr, 2004; Cox, 1991, p. 82). This can include serving as a role model, providing emotional support, and sharing relevant skills and knowledge.

For example, Thelma is part of a social action group aimed at increasing voter registration and education about issues in her community. She shares with the group how she was once totally apathetic regarding voting. At the time, she thought no matter how she felt or what she did, it really didn't matter. She felt like a tiny goldfish in Lake Ontario. Thelma then told of how her neighbor Louise got her involved in the social action process. Louise recruited Thelma to get out, pound the pavement, and encourage community residents to vote. Louise also helped Thelma dispense brochures about issues affecting the community. At first Louise accompanied Thelma to visit community residents. As Thelma gained experience and confidence, she soon went out by herself.

Thelma now helps other action group members become empowered to carry out the group's tasks. She gives them tips about how to handle crabby and irascible residents. She often accompanies new members when they start out. In essence, Thelma provides a significant role model of empowerment for other group members.

Consciousness Raising

A third way social action groups can empower members is through consciousness raising, a concept introduced and discussed in Chapter 3 (Carr, 2004; Cox, 1991). Social workers can encourage group members to relate their personal problems and issues to what's happening around them in the macro social environment (Carr, 2004). For example, Chapter 3 established that group members, like many people in American culture, may feel that poverty is the result of personal failure rather than an institutionalized socioeconomic condition of unfairness and lack of equal opportunity. A social worker might assist group members in looking beyond their own circumstances by asking questions. "Why does poverty, then, affect, so many people?" "Why are so many poor people working, yet still can't make it?" "Why are so many children and older adults poor?" In this way, group members might begin to view poverty as a structural problem that the political and economic system needs to address.

■ | **Critical Thinking Questions 4.3**

Consider a social action group working to improve state laws regarding how sexual assault perpetrators and survivors are treated. The group discusses the history, legalities, and oppressive issues involved. In this way, action group members enhance their awareness of issues they never considered before. For example, how fair is it that wives cannot legally prosecute their husbands for sexually assaulting them? When prosecuting an assault case, how rational is it to explore the survivor's detailed sexual history with the perpetrator and with other sexual partners? How significant is the amount of force the perpetrator used against the survivor (for example, use of a weapon or gang rape)? How relevant is the amount of resistance offered by the survivor to protect herself?

Providing Mutual Support

Provision of mutual aid or support among action group members is a fourth means of group empowerment. Chapter 3 also introduced and discussed this important concept involved in empowerment. The group context "provides a medium of mutual social-emotional support for members in their struggle to cope with and bring about change in both the personal and political aspect of the problem" (Carr, 2004; Cox, 1991, p. 82). Consider an action group working on getting signatures for a petition to improve the quality of health care provided by a managed care organization. When the group experiences extreme resistance on the part of that organization's administration to its recommendations, group members can turn to each other for support, encouragement, and the generation of new ideas.

Another example is an action group of single mothers receiving public assistance whose purpose is to improve benefits, educate recipients regarding their rights, and inform members and others of community resources. Group members become increasingly supportive of each other in addressing related personal problems such as difficulties with men, dealing with substance abuse, "sharing economic resources, providing small loans or child care," and participating in recreational activities with each other (Cox, 1991, p. 85).

Using Cooperation

A fifth means of empowerment within social action groups is ongoing communication and cooperation concerning the macro change process (Carr, 2004; Staples, 2004). It's often easier to work with others toward a designated goal than to pursue it in isolation. The planned change effort is usually uneven, having ups and downs in terms of making progress. New impediments can emerge in the political environment. Action group members can work together to adjust to changes in the environment, alter plans accordingly, and continue monitoring progress toward goals.

For example, school social workers from secondary schools in a large metropolitan area form a social action group to seek increased funding for students' extracurricular activities. With shrinking budgets, one special activity after another has been eradicated. These include band, drama club, play productions, debate, golf, and tennis. The workers feel young people require positive activities to experience healthy growth and development. Without such activities, the teachers feel teens are much more likely to turn to gangs, drugs, and crime.

Parents form a similar social action group with the same concerns about their children's school activities. The social workers' group invites the parents' group to merge with it, thereby enhancing both groups' mutual power and influence. Both groups must adjust to the new changes in membership. For example, parents provide a different perspective concerning expectations and needs. The social workers' group will need to learn to encompass this new perspective. Together, social workers and parents develop new cooperative goals.

When the state legislators abruptly decrease property taxes, and, hence, the amount of resources available to schools, the social action group must respond accordingly. With continuously shrinking state funding, the group starts exploring new alternatives. One idea is to form a fundraising Booster Club that sponsors pancake breakfasts and charity concerts, in addition to sending members door-to-door to solicit funds.

The point is that conditions often are in flux for social action groups. A strength of a group context is that members can help each other work out new alternatives and plans of action for accomplishing goals. The group can monitor its progress in a coordinated fashion without full responsibility falling on an individual member.

Chapter Summary

The following summarizes this chapter's content as it relates to the learning objectives presented at the beginning of the chapter. Objectives include the following:

A. Define *task groups* and explain their relevance within generalist practice in the macro social environment.

Task or work groups are those applying the principles of group dynamics to solve problems, develop innovative ideas, formulate plans, and achieve goals. Task groups in the macro social environment are formed to meet the needs of individuals, families, groups, organizations, or communities.

B. Describe task groups formed to meet client needs (teams, treatment conferences, and staff development groups), organizational needs (administrative groups, committees, and

boards of directors), and community needs (delegate councils and social action groups).

A team is a group of two or more people gathered together to work collaboratively and interdependently to pursue a designated purpose. There are six types of teams. Treatment conferences are groups who meet to establish, monitor, and coordinate service plans on the behalf of a client system. Staff development groups strive to improve, update, and refine workers' skills, the ultimate goal being to improve service to clients (Toseland & Rivas, 2009). A board of directors is a group of people authorized to formulate the organization's mission, objectives, and policies, in addition to overseeing the organization's ongoing activities.

A delegate council is a group of representatives from a series of agencies or units within a single agency with typical goals of enhancing cooperation and communication among professionals in different units or agencies, reviewing issues relevant to service provision, enhancing management approaches, and pursuing social action goals (Toseland & Rivas, 2009). Social action groups are formed to engage in some planned change effort to shift power and resources in order to modify or improve aspects of their macro social or physical environment.

Administrative groups involve various clusters of administrative staff, such as supervisors, directors, managers, and department heads, organized to maintain and improve agency functioning. A committee is a group of persons "delegated to consider, investigate, take action on, or report on some matter" (Mish, 2008, p. 250).

C. Focus on the ethical issue of how to handle your own negative feelings in task groups.

It's normal for negative feelings to surface sometimes while participating in task groups. However, negative feelings should not be manifested in the form of hostile behavior.

D. Discuss barriers to successful teamwork and team empowerment.

Barriers to successful teamwork include "the myth of good intentions," "helplessness in the face of authority," "professional boundaries," and "professional differences" (Compton et al., 2005, pp. 293–294). In empowered teams, members feel effective, goals are deemed valuable, and members experience adequate autonomy (Hellriegel & Slocum, 2009).

E. Address empowerment through good committee leadership.

A good leader clearly and initially states a meeting's purpose, establishes an agenda, explains ground rules, clarifies specific group member assignments, deals with conflict, and periodically summarizes the ongoing discussion.

F. Define *treatment groups*, including therapy, support, educational, growth, and socialization groups.

Treatment groups help individuals solve personal problems, change unwanted behaviors, cope with stress, and improve group members' quality of life. Therapy groups help members with serious psychological and emotional problems change their behavior. Support groups consist of participants who share common issues or problems and meet on an ongoing basis to cope with stress, give each other suggestions, convey information, and furnish emotional support (Barker, 2003). Educational groups provide information to participants. Growth groups are those aimed at expanding self-awareness, increasing potential, and maximizing optimal health and well-being. Socialization groups help participants improve interpersonal behavior, communication, and social skills so that they might better fit into their social environment.

G. Address the differences between treatment conferences and treatment groups.

Treatment groups offer counseling to a group of people gathered together at the same time with goals of achieving positive change for members in the internal group environment. Treatment conferences, on the other hand, are task groups with goals of achieving change in the group's external environment.

H. Examine how social action groups can empower their members to alter the external social environment.

Social action groups can increase members' understanding of issues, inspire others, raise consciousness, provide mutual support, and use cooperation to achieve macro change.

I. Raise critical thinking questions concerning task groups.

Critical thinking questions concerned involvement in a team or task group, evaluation of an agency policy covering exclusion of clients from treatment conferences, and issues faced by a social action group working to improve state laws regarding how sexual assault perpetrators and survivors are treated.

Looking Ahead

This chapter discussed the various types of groups existing in the macro social environment. The next chapter will introduce knowledge and theories about organizations in the macro social environment.

For Further Exploration on the Internet

See this text's website at **www.cengage.com/social_work/kirst-ashman** for learning tools such as tutorial quizzing, Web links, glossary, flashcards, and PowerPoint® slides.

5 CHAPTER | Knowledge and Theories about Organizations

Organizations and people's status within them may be viewed in many ways.

CHAPTER CONTENTS

Beverly Hill received her social work degree last month and was ecstatic. She just got the job of her dreams as a counselor at Gridlock Meadows (GM), a residential treatment center for adolescent males with serious behavioral and emotional problems. She would be doing individual and group counseling with residents, providing consultation for behavioral planning on two residential units, and running some parent groups. Beverly loved working with young people and their families. She couldn't wait to start. It was too good to be true.

Three weeks after her first day on the job, Beverly knew the job was too good to be true. She was seriously wondering whether accepting the position was such a good idea. Her experiences at GM were unlike any she had before in work, educational, or volunteer positions. Every morning when she arrived at GM, she felt like she was in jail. GM required all employees to sign in and out. One minute late meant being docked a half hour's pay.

But that was only a minuscule part of the problem. Beverly felt she couldn't breathe without her supervisor Bambi's approval. Bambi insisted on attending all Beverly's adolescent and parent group sessions and proceeded to take over running them. Beverly had little chance to get a word in edgewise.

Every progress note, letter, and report Beverly wrote, Bambi insisted on seeing, approving, and initialing. Beverly felt like Bambi thought her an incompetent idiot. Beverly had little chance to get a cup of coffee without Bambi's explicit approval.

When Beverly gently approached Bambi about these and several other similar issues, Bambi blew up. "How dare you contradict me after being here a measly couple of weeks," she exclaimed. "You're under a strict three-month probationary period. I can fire you anytime. You'd better start paying attention to company policy and watch your Ps and Qs."

Beverly never thought an organization could be run like that. She felt thwarted and trapped. She didn't know if she could work under such circumstances even for a short time. Maybe she should quit and start her job search over again. Now, she felt she knew much more when considering a job about what to look for in an agency and how it was run. She would give the possibility of quitting very serious thought.

Organizations—including social service agencies—vary dramatically in structure and managerial style. Perhaps Beverly would not have been so shocked had she better understood organizational dynamics and the potential problems she might encounter. No organization is perfect. Some organizations are more productive and better places to work than others.

Human behavior in organizations involves people using their skills and working together to meet goals and provide services. Communication channels and a hierarchy of authority coordinate this process. Understanding how organizations function requires a focus on "the behavior, attitudes, and performance" of the people who work in them (Champoux, 2006, p. 7).

Social service organizations, as macro systems in the social environment, have major impacts on clients and other community residents. They establish services and develop means to deliver them. Because the organizational environment provides the context and structure for social workers to provide services, it is critical for workers to understand organizations' internal functioning.

Despite the difficulties, people within organizations can work to improve organizational effectiveness and efficiency. Social workers have the serious ethical responsibility to enhance agency functioning. The National Association of Social Workers (NASW) *Code of Ethics* states that "social workers should work to improve employing agencies' policies and procedures and the efficiency and effectiveness of their services" (NASW, 2008, 3.09b)

We have established that this book does not try to teach *how* to do social work practice and implement changes in communities, organizations, or groups. However, it does intend to provide a *foundation* upon which to build such system-changing skills. Before you can plan and implement changes in organizations on clients' and communities' behalf, you must understand how these macro systems work. This and the next three chapters will address a range of problems and issues relevant to how organizations function in the macro social environment.

This chapter focuses primarily on organizations related to social services. However, much of the content also is relevant to understanding any type of organization as a macro system.

Learning Objectives

A. Define *organization*
B. Describe organizations providing social services.
C. Discuss several organizational theories, including classical organizational theories (scientific management, the administrative theory of management, and bureaucracy), neoclassical organizational theories, human relations theories, Theory X and Theory Y, feminist theories and organizations, the cultural perspective, political-economy theory, contingency theory, culture-quality theories, Theory Z, and ecosystems theories.
D. Propose the dynamics of gender-based power in organizations.
E. Demonstrate the application of ecosystems concepts to organizations and social agencies.
F. Introduce various critical thinking questions.
G. Focus on ethical issues.

Defining Organizations

Organizations are "(1) social entities that (2) are goal directed, (3) are designed as deliberately structured and coordinated activity systems, and (4) are linked to the external environment" (Daft, 2007, p. 10). Four elements stand out in this definition.

First, organizations are *social entities*. That is, organizations are made up of people, with all their strengths and failings. Organizations dictate how people should behave and what responsibilities employees must assume as they do their jobs. Individuals bring to their jobs their own values and personalities. Thus, patterns of behavior develop in organizational environments, which Chapters 7 and 8 discuss further.

Second, organizations are *goal-directed*. They exist for some specified purpose. An organization specializing in stock brokering exists to help clients develop financial packages that make money. Social service organizations exist to provide services and resources to help people with designated needs. An organization must clearly define its goals so that workers can evaluate the extent to which it achieves these goals.

The third key concept in the definition is that organizations are *deliberately structured and coordinated activity systems*. Activity systems are clusters of work activities performed by designated units or departments within an organization. Such systems are guided by a technology, the practical application of knowledge to achieve desired ends. Organizations coordinate the functioning of various activity systems to enhance efficiency in attaining desired goals. Organizations have structures that include policies for how the organization should be run, hierarchies of how personnel are supervised and by whom, and different units working in various ways to help the organization function.

An intake unit for a large county Department of Social Services is an example of an activity system. Workers under supervision process new cases by following established procedures, obtaining required information, and making referrals to the appropriate service providers.

Another example is a family services organization that has a number of activity systems, including one staff unit providing marriage and family counseling, another providing family life education,[1] and still another focusing on community activities aimed at family advocacy, recreation, and support (Barker, 2003). Each unit pursues different functions in order to achieve the agency's general goal of providing family services.

Of course, organizations other than those providing social services also have activity systems. For example, consider a factory, also an organization, that specializes in producing customized wash baskets. One activity unit is responsible for designing baskets, one for manufacturing them, and another for marketing them.

The fourth concept inherent in the definition of organizations is *linkage to the external environment*. Thus, an organization is in constant inter-action with other systems in the social environment, including individuals, groups, other organizations, and communities. Agencies providing social services interact dynamically with clients, funding sources, legislative and regulatory agencies, politicians, community leaders, and other social service agencies.

Organizations Providing Social Services

This and the next three chapters focus on organizations that provide social services to clients. *Social services* include the tasks that social work practitioners and other helping professionals perform with the goal of improving people's health,

---

[1] *Family life education* is a group learning program that focuses on addressing a wide range of life issues and crises (Barker, 2003; Harris, 2008). It is typically led by a social worker or other helping professional in any of a variety of settings, including health care centers, schools, churches, and community centers. Virtually any important life issue can be addressed, ranging from newborn care to child management to preparation for retirement.

enhancing their quality of life, increasing autonomy and independence, supporting families, and helping people and larger systems improve their functioning in the social environment (Barker, 2003; Popple, 2008). That is quite a mouthful. In essence, social services include the wide range of activities that social workers perform in their goal of helping people solve problems and improve their personal well-being.

Social services may be *institutional*, that is, those provided by major public service systems that administer such benefits as financial assistance, housing programs, health care, or education (Barker, 2003). They might also include *personal social services* that address more individualized needs involving interpersonal relationships and people's ability to function within their immediate environments. Such services usually target specific groups (such as children or older adults) or particular problems (such as family planning or counseling) (Barker, 2003).

Social Agencies

A *social agency*, or *social services agency*, is an organization providing social services that typically employs a range of helping professionals, including social workers in addition to office staff, paraprofessionals (persons trained to assist professionals), and sometimes volunteers (Barker, 2003). Social agencies generally serve some designated client population who experience some defined need. Services are provided according to a prescribed set of policies regarding how the agency staff should accomplish their service provision goals. Highlight 5.1 discusses some related terms.

A number of different concepts can characterize social agencies. For example, social agencies can be either public, private, or proprietary. *Public* social agencies are run by some designated unit of government and are usually regulated by laws impacting policy. For example, a county board committee oversees a public welfare department and is responsible for establishing its major policies. (Of course, such a

---

| Highlight 5.1 | **Common Terms** |

Note that the terms *social services, human services*, and sometimes *social welfare* are often used interchangeably when referring to organizations, agencies, and agency personnel. Human services are "programs and activities designed to enhance people's development and well-being," including the provision of financial help and social support when they're needed (Barker, 2003, p. 204). Since the terms *social services agency*, *social services organization*, and *social agency* mean essentially the same thing, these three terms will be used interchangeably.

Social welfare is the "nation's system of programs, benefits, and services that help people meet those social, economic, educational, and health needs that are fundamental to the maintenance of society" (Barker, 2003, p. 6). Social welfare, then, is a broad concept related to the general well-being of all people in a society. Inherent in the definition are two basic dimensions: (1) what people get from society (in terms of programs, benefits, and services) and (2) how well their needs (including social, economic, educational, and health) are being met.

committee must function in accordance with state or federal governments, which often provide at least some of the money for the agency's programs.)

Private social agencies, on the other hand, are privately owned and run by people not employed by government. They are *nonprofit social agencies*. That is, they are run to accomplish some service provision goal, not to make financial profit for private owners. They usually provide some type of personal social services. Funding for services can include tax moneys, private donations, grants, and service fees. A board of directors presides over a private agency, formulating policy and making certain that agency staff run the agency appropriately.

Proprietary, or *for-profit*, social agencies provide some designated social services, often quite similar to those provided by private social agencies. However, a major purpose for the existence of a proprietary social agency is to make a profit for its owners.

Organizational Theories and Conceptual Frameworks

Organizational theories are ways to conceptualize and understand how organizations function by stressing specific concepts and explaining how these concepts relate to each other. They provide a lens through which to view the organizational environment and direct you as to which aspects of that environment should be your focus of attention. The remainder of this chapter explores a range of ways in which organizations can be viewed and examined.

Organizational behavior "is the study of human behavior in the workplace, the interaction between people and the organization, and the organization itself. . . . The major goals of organizational behavior are to explain, predict, and control behavior" (Dubrin, 2007, p. 2). What components in the organizational environment are significant to those who work there? What issues do they face and how do they tend to react? *Management* "is the attainment of organizational goals in an effective and efficient manner through planning, organizing, leading, and controlling organizational resources" (Daft, 2010, p. 5). Here attention is focused on the interaction between managers, those in power, and workers, those who directly accomplish the organization's goals through doing various tasks. Later chapters will further explore organizational behavior, dimensions and structure of the organizational environment, and management.

In order to work within organizations, evaluate them, and sometimes work to change them, it is helpful to understand the major theories regarding how organizations operate. Such a perspective is also useful to determine what kinds of organizational structures are most effective for specific client situations.

Many organizational theories have been borrowed from the business and management literature. Businesses and social service organizations have much in common. Both need resources, namely money, to function. Likewise, both produce results or products via some kind of process. For example, a business might manufacture the product of burglar alarms. A social services organization might furnish the product of improved family functioning.

There is a wide range of theories concerning how organizations work. Some of them directly contradict others, probably because there is such a vast array of organizational structures, functions, and goals. There are tremendous differences among social service organizations in terms of structure and function, and more so among all types of businesses and organizations. The important thing for you is to think about how organizations work, because you will be working in one.

Some theories emphasize similar dimensions such as expectations for staff treatment, the importance placed on profits, or the degree to which new ideas are encouraged. However, each theory stresses various concepts somewhat differently.

One means of considering the wide variety of organizational theories is to place them on one of two continuums (Burrell & Morgan, 1979; Netting & O'Connor, 2003). One is adherence to traditional rigid structure, on the one hand, versus seeking fundamental change for the better on the other. The second continuum involves a focus on human individuality and well-being on one side, and a focus on objective, efficient completion of tasks on the other.

The following theories are reviewed here. Classical organizational theories developed early in the last century include scientific management, the administrative theory of management, and bureaucracy. They reflect rigid structure in addition to emphasis on productivity and task completion. Neoclassical organizational theory portrays a later shift in perspective to theory that's more oriented toward human relationships and motivation. Human relations theories and feminist theories stress the importance of the human component in organizational functioning. Feminist theories, of course, focus on the empowerment of women. The cultural perspective emphasizes the importance of expectations in the organizational environment and culture to maintain the organization's the status quo. Political-economy theory emphasizes how organizations must adapt to their external environments, stressing the effects of resources and power. The institutional perspective also focuses on external pressures—not resources and power, but social institutions and their demands. Contingency theory stresses careful analysis of all variables to determine those that relate directly to an issue or problem (which could involve either "personal" or "situational factors") (Vecchio, 2006, p. 11). Culture-quality theories, characterizing the end of the last century, emphasize the importance of establishing a positive organizational culture that promotes worker motivation and improves the quality of their work. Finally, ecosystems theory provides a perspective for understanding organizational functioning that fits well with social work. It provides a structured way of viewing organizations, yet focuses on how change might occur. It also can involve both the importance of human well-being and the accomplishment of organizational tasks and goals.

Classical Organizational Theories

Classical management theories emphasize that specifically designed, formal structure and a consistent, rigid organizational network of employees are most important in having an organization run well and achieve its goals (Griffin & Moorhead, 2010; Hodge, Anthony, & Gakes, 2003). In general, these early theories saw each employee as holding a clearly defined job and straightforwardly being told exactly how that job should be accomplished. These schools of thought call for minimal independent functioning on the part of employees. Supervisors closely scrutinize the latter's work. Efficiency is of utmost importance. Performance is quantified (that is, made very explicit regarding what is expected), regulated, and measured. How people feel about their jobs is insignificant. Administration should avoid allowing employees to have any input regarding how organizational goals can best be reached. Rather, employees should do their jobs as instructed and as quietly and efficiently as possible. Early proponents of these theories included Frederick W. Taylor, Henri Fayol, and Max Weber (Champoux, 2006; Netting & O'Connor, 2003).

Scientific Management   Frederick W. Taylor introduced the concept of *scientific management* (Champoux, 2006, p. 11). Developed in the early twentieth century, it reflected a time when there was often great hostility between management and employees. Management pushed employees to work as hard as possible to maximize company profits. In response, employees, to protect themselves, worked as slowly and did as little as possible. They figured that working faster and becoming more productive would endanger their own and other workers' jobs if management could get more work out of fewer people. Management sought high profits and workers wanted high wages. Both were working against each other.

Four principles characterize Taylor's scientific management style (Champoux, 2006):

1. Jobs and tasks should be studied scientifically to "develop" and "standardize" work procedures and expectations.
2. Workers should be chosen on a scientific basis to maximize their potential for being trained and turned into productive employees.
3. Management and employees should cooperate with each other and work together following standardized procedures.
4. Management should make "plans" and "task assignments," which workers should then "carry out" as instructed. (p. 12)

The Administrative Theory of Management   Also in the early twentieth century, Henri Fayol proposed an *administrative theory of management* (Champoux, 2006). His ideas focused on the administrative side of management rather than the workers' performance. He proposed five basic functions that management should fulfill, including "planning, organizing, command, coordination, and control" (Champoux, 2006, p. 12). He concluded that all managers should abide by the following six basic principles, although he did indicate that they should use discretion (the opportunity to make independent judgments and decisions) concerning the intensity of their actions (Champoux, 2006):

1. *Division of labor.* Workers should be divided up into units so that they might perform specialized instead of more general tasks. He posed that specialization would lead to greater productivity.
2. *Authority and responsibility.* Management should have the authority to give orders to workers, oversee their activity, and make them comply with these orders. In response, workers would assume responsibility for completing their assigned work.
3. *Centralization.* Depending on what would maximize productivity, management should centralize authority (that is, place decision-making power and

responsibility at the top of the organization's power hierarchy) or decentralize such authority (give power and responsibility to lower-level managers and workers in the organization's power hierarchy).

4. *Delegation of authority*. Upper-level management should have the responsibility of delegating responsibility and work assignments to managers and workers lower in the power hierarchy. Management should carefully analyze organizational processes and delegate authority as it saw fit.

5. *Unity of command*. Each worker should have one designated supervisor to whom he or she should report. This should avoid confusion and give consistent messages and orders to workers.

6. *Unity of direction*. Each unit in the organization (which is specialized under the division of labor) should have a single designated goal. This also should avoid confusion and inconsistency.

In essence, these principles should work together. High-level management should give authority to lower-level management (authority and responsibility) as it saw fit (centralization or decentralization; delegation of authority). Workers should be specialized (division of labor) and work in designated units. There should be a clear hierarchy of authority regarding who is responsible for each worker (unity of command) and each unit (unity of direction) to avoid confusion, enhance consistency, and maximize productivity.

Bureaucracy   Initiated by Max Weber in the early twentieth century, "*bureaucracy is an administrative structure with well-defined offices or functions and hierarchical relationships among the functions. The offices or functions have clearly defined duties, rights, and responsibilities. Each office or function is designed without regard for who will hold the office. Relationships within a bureaucracy are impersonal. Decisions are made according to existing rules, procedures, and policies. Bureaucracies attain goals with precision, reliability, and efficiency*" (Emphasis added) (Champoux, 2006, p. 14).

In summary, traditional bureaucracies emphasize the following (Griffin & Moorhead, 2010):

- Highly specialized units performing clearly specified job tasks
- Minimal discretion on the part of employees
- Numerous specific rules to maintain control

The Social Security Administration, the Detroit Department of Social Services, and the Federal Bureau of Investigation are examples of large bureaucracies. Chapter 8 will address what it's like to work in an organization with a bureaucratic style of management.

Neoclassical Organizational Theories

Originating during the mid-twentieth century, neoclassical theories were reactions to classical management thought and represented "a transition in the theoretical movement from the overly simplistic, mechanistic perspectives of the classical theorists to more contemporary thinking about complex organizations" (Netting & O'Connor, 2003, p. 106). They addressed problems and omissions in classical theories. Criticisms of classical theories involved lack of attention to human needs and individuality, coordination of work and goals among various bureaucratic units, the importance of relationships among organizations in the larger macro environment, and the need to comprehend the decision-making processes in organizations (Netting & O'Connor, 2003, pp. 105–106).

Champoux (2006) describes the ideas expressed by one of the leaders of this movement, Chester I. Barnard. Barnard defined an organization as a deliberately structured system of tasks and activities undertaken by two or more people. The implication is "that any system of two or more people with consciously coordinated activities is an organization. Organizations are based on cooperation and have a conscious, deliberate purpose" (p. 16). In order to achieve coordination and cooperation, organizations "offer inducements in exchange for contributions. *Inducements* include salary and fringe benefits. *Contributions* are things such as the work to be done. Barnard felt a person joined an organization when the inducements exceeded the contributions" (p. 16). Management's goal should be maintenance of this balance.

Barnard proposed that organizations functioned on the basis of two types of motivation—motivation to participate and motivation to perform (Champoux, 2006). "*Motivation to participate* is the motivation of an individual to join and stay with the organization and perform at a minimally acceptable level" (p. 16). Various organizations maintain different expectations regarding what is minimally acceptable performance. It is the responsibility of managers to balance inducements and contributions to retain staff and motivate them to complete their work. After management attends to workers' motivation to participate, they then should direct their attention to workers' motivation to perform; *motivation to perform* involves inducements to produce contributions that are greater than minimal performance expectations (p. 16).

Barnard's contributions changed how organizations were viewed from the classical organizational perspectives in various ways (Champoux, 2006). First, he emphasized deliberately coordinated tasks that required cooperation between two or more people. Thus, the theoretical focus was changing from production results to how people work together in an organizational environment. Second, he stressed the need to induce people by providing incentives (salary and benefits) to reinforce their contributions (work performance). This began to change the focus from controlling worker behavior and performance to motivating workers to perform. An emphasis on motivation reflected the beginning of a shift toward considering workers as individuals with emotions, needs, and desires instead of as mindless entities requiring control and direction.

Human Relations Theories

Human relations theories reflect the result of this shift to focus on "human relations" within the organizational environment. As Netting and O'Connor (2003) reflect:

> It was at this stage that classical organizational theory was actually displaced, making room for the more creative approaches to understanding organizations. At this juncture,

theorists realized that organizations were much more than variables to manipulate in order to change behavior of organizational members. Instead, organizations were understood as contexts within which behavior occurs. The people and the organization represent mutual, interactive influences through which people are shaped by the organization and the organization is shaped by the people within its boundaries. (p. 107)

Griffin and Moorhead (2010) explain that human relations theories assume

that employees want to feel useful and important, that employees have strong social needs, and that these needs are more important than money in motivating employees. Advocates of the human relationship approach advised managers to make workers feel important and allow them a modicum of self-direction and self-control in carrying out routine activities. The illusion of involvement and importance were expected to satisfy workers' basic social needs and result in higher motivation to perform. For example, a manager might allow a work group to participate in making a decision, even though he or she had already determined what the decision would be. The symbolic gesture of seeming to allow participation was expected to enhance motivation, even though no real participation took place. (p. 85)

Likewise, the immediate work group, a mezzo system, is critical in human relations theories. If workers were satisfied with their interpersonal relationships with their supervisors and in their work groups, they would become more productive; in this context, virtually all workers theoretically could become productive employees (Dubrin, 2007).

Theory X and Theory Y   The management styles of administrators and supervisors in organizations have considerable impact on the productivity and job satisfaction of employees. Douglas McGregor (1960) developed two theories of management style. He hypothesized that management thinking and behavior are based on two different sets of assumptions, which he labeled Theory X and Theory Y. Theory X reflects aspects of classical scientific management in its focus on hierarchical structure, providing a contrasting approach to Theory Y, which focuses on human relations. These theories are addressed here because they emphasize the treatment of employees.

Theory X managers view employees as being incapable of much growth. Employees are perceived as having an inherent dislike for work, and it is presumed that they will attempt to evade work whenever possible. Therefore, X-type managers believe that they must control, direct, force, or threaten employees to make them work. Employees are also viewed as having relatively little ambition, wishing to avoid responsibilities, and preferring to be directed. X-type managers therefore spell out job responsibilities carefully, set work goals without employee input, use external rewards (such as money) to induce employees to work, and punish employees who deviate from established rules. Because Theory X managers reduce responsibilities to a level where few mistakes can be made, work can become so structured that it is monotonous and distasteful. The assumptions of Theory X, of course, are inconsistent with what behavioral scientists assert are effective principles for directing, influencing, and motivating people.

In contrast, Theory Y managers view employees as wanting to grow and develop by exerting physical and mental effort to accomplish work objectives to

> **Critical Thinking Questions 5.1**
>
> Compare and contrast classical organizational theories and human relations theories. What are the strengths and weaknesses of each?

which they are committed. Y-type managers believe that the promise of internal rewards, such as self-respect and personal improvement, are stronger motivators than external rewards (such as money) and punishment. A Y-type manager also believes that under proper conditions, employees will not only accept responsibility but seek it. Most employees are assumed to have considerable ingenuity, creativity, and imagination for solving the organization's problems. Therefore, employees are given considerable responsibility in order to test the limits of their capabilities. Mistakes and errors are viewed as necessary phases of the learning process, and work is structured so that employees can have a sense of accomplishment and growth.

Feminist Theories and Organizations   Chapter 3 discussed feminist theory with respect to groups and established that there are a range of feminist theories that emphasize various concepts (for example, women's individual rights, economic status, or cultural contexts). Feminist theories emphasize interpersonal relationships and respect for each other's right to be heard and contribute. Highlight 5.2 discusses the dynamics of gender-based power in organizations.

The Application of Feminist Principles to Organizations

In order to counteract the types of gender-related power dynamics discussed in Highlight 5.2, a number of feminist principles can be applied to organizations.

At least five basic feminist concepts and related recommendations for organizational improvements are relevant:

- *Using a gender filter* (Hyde, 2008). Feminist theories focus on the rampant sexism existing in the macro social environment and the need to stress women's conditions, needs, and opportunities. Therefore, within organizational contexts, management and workers must be vigilant regarding the treatment of women in a fair, nondiscriminatory manner.

   Powell and Graves (2003) recommend that organizational leaders:

   promote nondiscrimination in treatment of people and decisions about people. This means promoting compliance by all employees with federal, state, and local equal employment opportunity (EEO) laws. Such laws ban discrimination on the basis of sex, race, ethnicity, national origin, age, religion, and other personal characteristics that are not relevant to the job at hand. It also means refraining from discrimination on the basis of job-irrelevant personal characteristics even if it is not illegal. For example, there is no U.S. federal law banning discrimination on the

| Highlight 5.2 | The Dynamics of Gender-Based Power in Organizations |

Burk (2009) proposes and discusses some of the dynamics involved in organizations that sustain men in positions of power. To begin with, "males, much more so than females, are conditioned almost from birth to view the world in terms of hierarchies, power relationships, and being winners" (p. 483). Consider the following five dynamics:

1. *"Power re-creates itself in its own image"* (p. 483). Burk (2009) states that, psychologically, people tend to be drawn to other people who resemble themselves. Therefore, in organizations where men already assume most of the powerful positions, there is a tendency to promote other men to maintain that status quo. Often, diversity in terms of gender and race characterize the lower echelons of organizational power structures. The higher up in management you go, the less diversity there is. Consider how there are only nine women chief executive officers (CEOs) in all of the Fortune 500 companies (p. 483).

2. *"Power elites enforce norms and systems that guarantee continued power"* (p. 483). Boards of directors (as discussed in Chapter 4) often govern organizations, select top administrators, and recruit for their own replacements. Therefore, a board of white males (who make up the majority of most boards) will tend to seek other white males to "fit in" with the board culture. Even when diverse people in terms of gender or race are brought into a board, they are 'trained' through mentoring and role modeling" regarding how to act (p. 484). Thus, they will be taught board expectations and be encouraged to conform. This would likely serve to discourage people characterized by some aspect of diversity from bringing in other people like themselves. They would not want to be seen as someone who will cause trouble and "rock the boat."

3. *"Power creates a sense of entitlement"* (p. 484). People who are in powerful positions become accustomed to having that power. They begin to assume they are naturally entitled to maintain that power over others. Consider how the average pay of a CEO in 2003 is "300 times that of the average worker," up from 42 times more in 1982 (p. 484). Such huge salaries become a general expectation.

4. *"Power creates invulnerability, leading to a flaunting of society's standards"* (p. 484). People with great power have the authority to exercise their own will. They are able to surround themselves with people who flatter and reinforce them because of their power. Powerful leaders may have the ability to isolate themselves from authorities that could affect or sanction them. They may feel invulnerable and capable of doing whatever they choose, regardless of the rules. A former Illinois governor comes to mind who allegedly participated in a wide range of illegal activities. One of these alleged activities involved trying to sell President Barack Obama's prior Senate seat to the highest bidder. Or consider the mortgage companies' CEOs who received huge bonuses upon their already huge salaries after allowing their companies to verge on or fall into bankruptcy. I never cease to be amazed at what some people (who already have so much) think they can get away with (and often do).

5. *"Loyalty to power overshadows other loyalties, including gender"* (p. 484). Women who attain higher levels of authority and power tend to lose their interest in helping other women advance (Burk, 2009). Perhaps, the dynamics involve how more powerful women begin to identify with others in the power structure, primarily white men. Such women may seek validation from their powerful peers and assume attitudes more like these peers in order to increase their own personal power.

Critical Thinking Questions 5.2

What do you think of these five proposed dynamics of gender-based power in organizations? Do they make sense to you, or are they too extreme? Explain why. What are the reasons women make up such a relatively small percentage of people with the greatest political and corporate power, despite making up more than half the population?

basis of sexual orientation,[2] but such discrimination is just as unacceptable as sex or race discrimination. (p. 218)

- *Empowerment.* Power should be distributed and equalized to whatever extent possible within an organization. This would support a decentralized organizational structure that provides great discretion on the part of workers throughout the organization. Organizations should also empower women to be promoted and assume leadership positions (Netting & O'Connor, 2003).

  Gutierrez and Lewis (1999) suggest that "attention should be paid to staff development," including "access to conferences, training workshops, and other educational opportunities . . . Staff can also be supported through flex time and other policies that encourage flexibility and self-care. Similarly, providing opportunities for staff to develop programs and professional skills that match their own personal interests is an important part of the empowerment of staff within an agency" (pp. 83–84).

- *The personal as political* (Bricker-Jenkins & Netting, 2009, p. 279; Fisher & Burghardt, 2008). Feminist theories emphasize that women become aware of their own opinions, feelings, and situations (consciousness raising). They stress that the condition of women goes beyond one's personal situation and that women should strive to improve conditions for all women. The implication is that workers should try to combat sexism wherever it occurs in an organization, not just on their own personal behalf.

- *The importance of process.* Feminist theories emphasize that the process of *how* things get done is just as important as *what* gets done (Hyde, 2008). The implication in an organizational context is that management should involve workers in decision making and planning to the greatest extent possible. Workers should feel like important participants in the organizational environment.

  Organizational administrations should "*promote inclusion* of employees from all groups in the organizational culture. The focus of promoting inclusion is on the nature or *quality* of work relationships between employees who belong to different groups" (Powell & Graves, 2003, p. 219). Teamwork should be emphasized (Gutierrez & Lewis, 1999).

---

[2] "As of April 2008, twenty states and the District of Columbia have outlawed employment discrimination based on sexual orientation, and twelve states and the District of Columbia ban it based on gender identity" (Human Rights Campaign, 2009).

- *"Diversity is strength"* (Bricker-Jenkins & Netting, 2009; Hyde, 2008). Feminist theories stress unity and harmony, on the one hand, and appreciation of diverse characteristics on the other. Women should appreciate each other's differences and work together for the benefit of all. In organizational contexts, diversity (for example, gender, race, ethnicity, age, and sexual orientation) should not only be appreciated but actively sought out and encouraged.

    Administrations should "*promote diversity* among employees in all jobs and at all levels. The focus of promoting diversity is on the number or *quantity* of employees from various groups in different jobs and at different organizational levels" (Powell & Graves, 2003, p. 218).

In summary, Powell and Graves (2003) recommend that "*all* organizations—large or small, public or private, profit or nonprofit—set the goals of being nondiscriminatory, diverse, and inclusive in their employment practices. . . . [Organizational] communications should convey the message that promoting non-discrimination, diversity, and inclusion are important organizational goals. These communications may include speeches by top executives, with transcripts or videos available to internal and external groups, newsletters, status reports, recognition events, special awards, and publicity for employees who have done good work toward these goals. The *mission statement* [a declaration of an organization's purpose and goals] of the organization should state that the organization regards achievement of these goals as critical to its success" (Emphasis added) (pp. 231–232).

The Cultural Perspective

Organizational culture is the constellation of "values, beliefs, and assumptions about appropriate behavior that members of an organization share" (Lussier, 2009, p. 46). The cultural perspective on organizations assumes that each organization develops a unique mixture of values, standards, presumptions, and practices about how things should be done that eventually becomes habit.

Management and other personnel may not be consciously aware that such patterns and expectations have developed. They become ingrained in established means of accomplishing tasks and goals. If it worked before, it'll work again. "If it ain't broke, don't fix it." The result is the establishment of an ideological structure that frames how organizational members think about the organization and how it should work. This perspective not only guides people's view of current practices but also shapes how they think about new issues. Employees tend to view new ideas by shaping them to conform to old, tried-and-true practices.

An advantage of the cultural perspective may be that performance becomes predictable, thus requiring less effort to develop new approaches. However, a

 Critical Thinking Questions 5.3

How do men fit into the application of feminist theories to organizations?

disadvantage is that such an established view may squelch innovative ideas. There's pressure to retain the old way of thought. For example, an energized worker in a social services organization might come to a staff meeting with a brilliant new treatment approach (in his opinion). The cultural perspective suggests that staff will tend not to evaluate the new approach fairly and impartially. Rather, they might nod pleasantly in feigned mild agreement and proceed to recycle the new approach into the same old routine.

It should be noted that the organization's culture might support "innovation" and "risk-taking" instead of the status quo (Johns, 1996, p. 289). If this were the case with the group just discussed, staff would enthusiastically welcome the new treatment idea the worker presented. Personnel would shy away from old techniques and search for new ones. In this case, the advantages and disadvantages would be reversed. An advantage, then, would be development of fresh, more effective intervention modalities. A disadvantage would be lack of stability and predictability.

Political-Economy Theory

Political-economy theory emphasizes how organizations must adapt to their external environments, stressing the effects of resources and power. Schmid (2009) explains political-economy theory as it applies to social services organizations:

> Political-economy theory (Wamseley & Zald, 1976; Zald, 1970) recognizes that in order to survive and produce services, the organization must garner two fundamental types of resources: legitimacy [having appropriate legal status and justification for existence] and power (i.e., political) and production resources (i.e., economic). The underlying premise of this approach is the organization's dependence on resources controlled by agents and interest groups in the external environment. The greater the organization's dependence on these resources, the stronger the influence of external interest groups on processes within the organization. (p. 418)

Political-economy theory stresses how an organization is dependent on external resources for survival. Therefore, it is subject to pressure from resource providers in terms of how it functions. "The greater the resource dependency of the organization on an element in the environment (e.g., governmental funding agency, regulatory organization, professional association, providers of clients), the greater the ability of the element to influence organizational policies and procedures" (Hasenfeld, 2009, p. 62).

Therefore, an organization is in a constant struggle to negotiate with resource providers and other controlling systems to gain as much control over its functioning as possible (Hasenfeld, 2009; Patti, 2008). An organization can do this in various ways (Patti, 2008). To gain power, an organization will strive to compete effectively with other agencies providing similar services. Or an organization might form *coalitions,* alliances of individuals, groups, and organizations with similar goals that become more influential and powerful when united. Organizational leaders might bargain with external controlling elements to negotiate for more power and control in exchanges of services for resources.

Political-economy theory also characterizes the internal agency environment. Hasenfeld (2009) explains:

> The internal dynamics of the organization will also reflect the power relations of different interest groups and individuals within the organization. Some of these groups (e.g., profession staff, executive[s] . . .) derive their power from relations with important external organizations, others because they possess personal attributes, control internal resources (e.g., information and expertise), or carry out important functions (e.g., manage the budget). (p. 62)

Focus on Ethics 5.1 raises some ethical questions concerning political-economy theory.

The Institutional Perspective

Like political-economy theory, the institutional perspective emphasizes the importance of external pressures on an organization. However, instead of focusing on power and resources, this perspective accentuates the pressures imposed by social institutions (Patti, 2008). *Social institutions* are established constellations of roles, expectations, values, groups, and organizations that are instituted to meet basic societal needs. Examples include "religion, the family, military structures, government, and the social welfare system" (Barker, 2003, p. 404). Social institutions are reinforced by various "social rules"; social rules govern society's expectations for behavior through laws, regulations, values, and assigned statuses (Hasenfeld, 2009, p. 65).

The institutional perspective assumes that "the more organizations adhere to the rules of these institutions—by embedding the rules in their structures—the greater will be their legitimacy and chances of survival" (Hasenfeld, 2009, p. 65). Schmid (2009) explains the application of an institutional perspective to social services agencies:

> For example, to ensure a steady flow of resources, human services organizations often adopt the espoused ideologies and goals of the government, which are not always attainable. These ideologies and goals can be expressed as 'closing social gaps and

---

Focus on Ethics 5.1 | **Power versus Service Provision**

Political-economy theory has been criticized for the emphasis placed on power and access to resources instead of effective service provision to clients (Patti, 2008). This theory obviously poses difficulties for social workers who maintain professional values and ethics. How does the use of power and its relationship to resources relate to saving a three-year-old from neglect and abuse? Or how do you determine the significance and cost of helping an adult with bulimia nervosa control the disorder? (*Bulimia nervosa* is a condition occurring primarily in females that is characterized by uncontrolled overeating followed by purging activities such as self-initiated vomiting and the use of diuretics, as well as excessive guilt and shame over the compulsive behavior.)

reducing inequality between haves and have nots,' 'the need to redistribute power and transfer it to peripheral units,' 'integration of populations,' and 'changing attitudes toward minorities.' Organizations that succeed in achieving those goals increase their legitimacy and, consequently, their prospects for survival, irrespective of the immediate efficacy of the required practices and procedures. (p. 421)

In other words, these ideals and social rules may sound good. However, for an organization actually to comply with them and achieve actual results through service provision is often a difficult, and perhaps impossible, task (Hasenfeld, 2009; Patti, 2008; Schmid, 2009). Thus, what often really happens is that organizations establish goals in concordance with social rules and receive the resulting legitimacy and support. However, such stated goals may have little to do with actual results achieved.

Contingency Theory

Contingency theory maintains that each element involved in an organization depends on other elements; therefore, there is no one perfect way to accomplish tasks or goals (Daft, 2007; Hasenfeld, 2009; Schmid, 2009). Each organization with its units or subsystems is unique. Thus, the best way to accomplish goals is to make individual determinations in view of the goal's context. The behavior of personnel is too varied and "complex to be explained by only a few simple and straightforward principles" (Vecchio, 2006, p. 11). Daft (2007) clarifies:

> *Contingency* means that one thing depends on other things, and for organizations to be effective, there must be a "goodness of fit" between their structure and the conditions in their external environment. What works in one setting may not work in another setting. There is not one best way. Contingency theory means "it depends." (p. 27)

Therefore, different means are required to solve various problems depending on all of the variables involved. Daft (2007) continues:

> For example, some organizations experience a certain environment, use a routine technology, and desire efficiency. In this situation, a management approach that uses bureaucratic control procedures, a hierarchical structure, and formal communication would be appropriate. Likewise, free-flowing management processes [with few standardized routines and much worker discretion] work best in an uncertain environment with a nonroutine technology. The correct management approach is contingent on the organization's situation. (p. 27)

A strength of this theory is its flexibility. It can be applied to any situation in any organization. However, a potential weakness is its lack of direction. The core idea suggests that all variables should be evaluated and any may be significant. Where does one start when evaluating a problem or planning a procedure? Staff? Input? Output? Process? It's difficult to determine.

Focus on Ethics 5.2 addresses evaluating a number of the theories we've discussed concerning the application of social work values and ethics.

| Focus on Ethics 5.2 | **Organizational Theories and the NASW *Code of Ethics*** |

Chapter 2 introduced the following six core values emphasized in the NASW *Code of Ethic* (NASW, 2008):

1. *Service*: Providing help, resources, and benefits so that people may achieve their maximum potential.
2. *Social justice*: Upholding the condition that in a perfect world, all citizens would have identical "rights, protection, opportunities, obligations, and social benefits" regardless of their backgrounds and membership in diverse groups (Barker, 2003, pp. 404–405).
3. *Dignity and worth of the person*: Holding in high esteem and appreciating individual value.
4. *Importance of human relationships*: Valuing the dynamic reciprocal interactions between social

workers and clients, including how they communicate, think and feel about each other, and behave toward each other.

5. *Integrity*: Maintaining trustworthiness and sound adherence to moral ideals.
6. *Competence*: Having the necessary skills and abilities to perform work with clients effectively.

To what extent do the following theories comply with these professional values? Explain.

- Classical organizational theories
- Human relations theories
- Feminist theories
- The cultural perspective
- The institutional perspective
- Contingency theory

Culture-Quality Theories

Theories stressing organizational culture and quality improvement characterized the final two decades of the twentieth century and paved the way for future approaches (Vecchio, 2006). These views

> focused on how to build a strong set of shared positive values and norms within a corporation (that is, a strong corporate culture) while emphasizing quality, service, high performance, and flexibility. Simultaneously, Western industry developed an interest in designing an effective response to growing global competition. High quality was seen to be related to high employee commitment and loyalty, which were believed to result, partially, from greater employee involvement in decision making. In order to establish new mechanisms for employee involvement, changes were seen as being necessary in existing corporate cultures, and the establishment and maintenance of new cultures became the goal. Some organizations now seek to have employees openly discuss aspects of corporate culture and suggest techniques for achieving a culture that emphasizes greater teamwork and cooperation. (Vecchio, 2006, p. 12)

One application of culture-quality theories is total quality management, described in Chapter 8. Theory Z, described in Highlight 5.3, provides an example of a theory emphasizing culture and quality (Vecchio, 2006).

Ecosystems Theories

Chapter 1 established that ecosystems theory serves as an umbrella approach for defining and understanding the functioning of macro systems, including organizations. We have established that ecosystems theory assumes a systems theory

Highlight 5.3 | Theory Z

Theory Z proposes a theoretical perspective relating to organizational culture and quality based on several assumptions initiated in Japanese industry. Developed by Ouchi (1981), these assumptions about human behavior within organizations clash poignantly in several ways with many traditional assumptions about organizational behavior espoused by U.S. and Canadian organizations (Griffin & Moorhead, 2010; Lewis et al; 2007; Ouchi, 1981). Note that we are emphasizing differences between Theory Z and traditional organizational perspectives here. The organizational management scene constantly changes. Any particular agency can adopt a hybrid combination of theoretical assumptions and management styles.

First, Theory Z views workers as long-term employees instead of people having a series of short-term jobs in different organizations over a career's time. It emphasizes job security as a major component of employee satisfaction and, hence, motivation for productivity.

A second presumption in Theory Z is that employees undergo long periods of evaluation and are not promoted quickly. This is in contrast to U.S. organizations, which tend to evaluate regularly and after relatively brief periods of time. For example, it is not uncommon for workers in social service agencies to undergo a six-month probationary period during which management can discharge them with relative ease. Also in contrast to Theory Z, U.S. workers hope for promotions more quickly in order to progress along salary and career paths.

Collective decision making is a third tenet of Theory Z. Instead of higher levels of management imposing decisions on employees, groups of workers collectively address issues and arrive at some consensus regarding how to proceed.

In contrast, U.S. organizations historically have emphasized decision making on the individual level. Each employee has discretion for performing his job as he sees fit as long as he remains within the boundaries of his job description. Job descriptions usually describe the general goals and tasks inherent in a particular job. Similarly, individuals in higher levels of U.S. management are generally given greater individual power to affect the work of employees below them in the organizational power structure. The chief executive officer of a U.S. organization might decide that Fridays are casual days where employees should not wear high heels, ties, or three-piece suits. She could make such a decision independently and would expect employees to follow her directive automatically.

A fourth assumption in Theory Z (one related to collective decision making) is collective responsibility. Theory Z emphasizes the importance of all workers being responsible for the successful functioning of the organization. High-level management does not drop arbitrary decisions and policies upon workers without extensive worker input. Since employees expect to have a long-term job, consensus is important because workers will have to live with decisions for a long time. In contrast, U.S. organizations have traditionally emphasized individual responsibility. Each employee is responsible for making his or her own decisions within the parameters of his or her job expectations.

Lewis, Packard, and Lewis (2007) summarize the significance of Theory Z for today's organizations and their management:

> While the term *Theory Z* is rarely used today, its most valuable principles have been incorporated in other ways in many American organizations. Principles of Japanese management have been summarized for use in the human services by Keys (1995), who studied their use in Japanese social welfare agencies. These include flexible job descriptions; informal decision-making processes to build consensus before formal decisions are made; training and team building to foster shared values, consensus, and high morale; . . . and total quality management. (p. 82)

perspective but integrates a number of relevant ecological concepts. Other theories can be explained using concepts and terms inherent in ecosystems theory.

Ecosystems theories focus on how organizations take resources (input) and process them into some kind of product or service (output) (Daft, 2010). They emphasize how all parts of the organization (subsystems) are interrelated and function together to produce output (Daft, 2010; Patti, 2008).

Ecosystems theories stress the interactions of the various subsystems involved. Additionally, the importance of the environment and the impacts of other systems upon the organization are also stressed. In some ways, ecosystems theories are more flexible than many other theories. Irrational, spontaneous interactions are expected rather than ignored. Ecosystems theories emphasize constant assessment and adjustment.

Undertaking Organizational Change from an Ecosystems Perspective Social workers want to provide clients the best services they can. Because practitioners generally work under the auspices of organizations, they want those organizations to be as effective as they can be. Other organizations with which clients have transactions should also be as effective as possible. The underlying theme is to provide the best resources and services possible to help clients.

For whatever reasons, organizations may not provide the best service possible. An agency director may make decisions in the best interest of a grant funding source instead of clients. Procedures may be out of date and bogged down. Resources might shrink so critical decisions must be made about which programs to support and which to cut. The NASW *Code of Ethics* states that social work practitioners should advocate for "open and fair" resource allocation procedures; "when clients' needs can be met, an allocation procedure should be developed that is non-discriminatory and based on appropriate and consistently applied principles" (NASW, 2008, 3.07b). Thus, practitioners have an ethical responsibility to advocate on the behalf of clients when those clients are not being served adequately. Social workers are expected to work with larger systems to improve service provision. If the agency isn't doing its job well enough, then it's the worker's responsibility to initiate and undertake positive changes. In order to undertake such change, you must understand how organizations function as systems. Highlight 5.4 applies ecosystems concepts both to organizations and social service agencies.

Which Organizational Theory Is Best?

No one really knows which organizational theory is best. As time passes, theoretical perspectives rise and fall in terms of their popularity. Daft (2007) reflects: "Today, almost all organizations operate in highly uncertain environments. Thus, we are involved in a significant period of transition, in which concepts of organization theory and design are changing as dramatically as they did with the dawning of the Industrial Revolution" (p. 27).

Most organizations probably reflect a mixture of concepts derived from various theories. It is outside the scope of this text to explore organizational theory

| Highlight 5.4 | Applying Ecosystems Concepts to Organizations and Social Service Agencies |

Ecosystems concepts can be applied to social service and other organizations such as businesses and industry. We've established that they help structure ways to think about how any organization works. Organizations in general take *input*, process it, and produce some *output*. Input is the energy, information, or communication flow received from other systems. Output is what happens to input after it has gone through and been processed by some system.

Consider an industrial organization that manufactures earplugs called Plugitup. Plugitup is a *system*, a set of elements that are orderly and interrelated and a functional whole. The system's purpose is for its elements, including employees, management, and machinery, to work together to manufacture earplugs. The system is delineated by its *boundaries*, the repeatedly occurring patterns that characterize the relationships within a system and give that system a particular identity. People working for Plugitup are within the system's boundaries. People not working there are outside those boundaries. Boundaries determine who is and is not part of the system. Within these boundaries are various *subsystems*, secondary or subordinate systems. These include employees working on the plant floor, engineers, and management.

Plugitup's *input* is raw materials necessary for producing earplugs. Processing involves converting raw materials into a liquid formula, pouring it into molds, and refining the final product in preparation for sale. Plugitup's *output* is the final earplug products ready for sale.

As does any company, Plugitup has a *relationship* with its consumers. A relationship is the dynamic interpersonal connection between two or more persons or systems that involves how they think about, feel about, and behave toward each other. To establish *homeostasis*—the tendency for a system to maintain a relatively stable, constant state of balance—the company must preserve lines of communication with its public and respond to the public's wants.

A *role* is an expected behavior pattern based on individuals' positions or status within the group. Part of Plugitup's management's role is to monitor public demand. Management finds that the public desires more variety in earplugs than it did two decades ago. It sponsors market surveys to get *feedback* from consumers. Feedback is a special form of input by which a system receives information about that system's own performance. Sometimes consumers give *positive feedback*, the informational input a system receives about what it is doing correctly in order to maintain itself and thrive. For example, consumers say they particularly love fluorescent orange earplugs. This tells Plugitup what it is doing well and encourages the company to continue producing orange ones. *Negative feedback*, on the other hand, is informational input received by a system that criticizes some aspect of its functioning. For instance, consumers might indicate that the earplugs are too small for people with exceptionally large ear canals. Plugitup would then have to address the issue of earplug size. It might start offering earplugs that are more flexible in terms of size or provide a range of earplug sizes.

That there are many ways of producing and marketing earplugs reflects *equifinality,* the fact that there are many different means to the same end. Earplugs can be made in various colors and shapes, and with varying pliability. Various production procedures can be employed. In Plugitup's case, the end or goal is to produce marketable earplugs regardless of the final product's specifications and how that product is made. Therefore, instead of manufacturing only one type of earplug as it originally did decades ago, the company sustains six different lines of earplugs using somewhat different production procedures. This reflects *differentiation*, a system's tendency to move from a more simplified to a more complex existence.

The *interface* between the company and earplug consumers is the stores selling earplugs to the public. An interface is the point where two systems (including individuals, families, groups, organizations, or communities) come into contact with each other, interact, or communicate.

If Plugitup's management does not effectively respond to public demand, the company may experience *entropy,* the natural tendency of a system to progress toward disorganization, depletion, and death. Rather, management strives to achieve *negative entropy*, the process of a system toward growth and development. Company management wants to continue growing and increasing earplug profits.

Now compare Plugitup with a counseling center called Happyhelp. Happyhelp is a *system* whose purpose is to help clients solve problems. People working for Happyhelp are within the system's *boundaries*. People not working for Happyhelp are not part of the system. Various *subsystems* including social workers, accounting staff, support staff, and management work within Happyhelp's boundaries to provide service.

Happyhelp's *input* into the helping process includes its staff and all their skills. Plugitup's process is the conversion of raw materials into earplug products. Happyhelp's process is the application of intervention skills to help clients with many different problems, including depression, mental illness, eating disorders, and substance abuse. Happyhelp's *output* is the extent to which clients' goals are achieved and problems alleviated.

Relationships are formed between Happyhelp's social workers and its clients. Relationships are also formed among staff and between practitioners and management. Practitioners' *roles* include helping clients work on and solve problems. Role expectations include having effective skills in addition to conducting oneself professionally and ethically. Goals include helping clients regain their *homeostasis* so that they might maintain stable and productive lives. Happyhelp also strives to maintain its own homeostasis so that it can continue to function as a helping agency. Happyhelp seeks to avoid *entropy* because it wants to continue functioning as a productive system. Thus, it strives for *negative entropy* by adding new staff and innovative programs. Such development reflects *differentiation* as service provision becomes more complex.

The *interface* is the contact between client and social worker, the agency's representative. Workers provide clients with *feedback* about their thoughts and behavior. Workers endeavor to give *positive feedback* to clients whenever possible to reinforce clients' strengths and positive efforts.

Various Happyhelp social workers use different treatment approaches and techniques to help people solve problems. This reflects *equifinality*, as there are many different ways to conceptualize issues and pursue goals.

beyond providing a foundation to help you understand human behavior within the context of organizational macro systems.

Because of its flexibility and the complexities of working with real clients, this book will primarily view organizations from an ecosystems perspective. As we have discussed, various organizational theories emphasize different aspects of organizations in terms of how you should view their functioning and what you should consider most significant. Regardless of the theory chosen, you can use an ecosystems approach to readily describe the processes involved in organizational life. The *Encyclopedia of Social Work* stresses the significance of systems theories and the ecological perspective in framing social work practice, including social services management (Gitterman & Germain, 2008a; Patti, 2008). Each management theory can be examined using concepts inherent in ecosystems theories. Additionally, accreditation standards for social work programs emphasize the importance for social workers to understand "the range of social systems in which people live" and "the ways social systems promote or deter people in maintaining or achieving health and well-being" (CSWE, 2008, p. 6).

Concept Summary 5.1	Organizational Theories

Theories	Major Concepts
Classical Organizational	Specifically designed formal structure Consistent, rigid organizational network of employees Clearly defined job descriptions with little discretion Efficiency; close supervision
Neoclassical Organizational	Inducements and contributions Emphasis on coordination and cooperation Motivation to participate and motivation to perform
Human Relations	Focus on human relations Strong emotional needs of employees Symbolic participation by employees in decision making
Feminist	Dynamics of gender-based power Using a gender filter Empowerment The personal as political The importance of process Diversity is strength Promotion of nondiscrimination, inclusion, and diversity
Cultural Perspective	Organizational development of a unique mixture of values, standards, presumptions, and practices about how things should be done Predictable performance
Political-Economy	Organizational adaptation to the external environment Emphasis on resources and power Constant struggle to gain power
Institutional Perspective	Organizational adaptation to the external environment Responses to social rules imposed by social institutions Search for external legitimacy and support
Contingency	All organizational elements dependent on all other elements Complexity of employee behavior No one best approach
Culture-Quality	Emphasis on organizational culture and quality improvement
Ecosystems	System Boundaries Input and output Interrelated subsystems Relationships Homeostasis Roles Positive and negative feedback Equifinality Differentiation Interface Entropy and Negative entropy

Critical Thinking Questions 5.4

Which organizational theory or theories do you think are most effective and practical? What are your reasons for thinking so? What concepts do you think are most important? What type of organizational environment would you prefer to work in? What experiences in working for businesses or organizations have you had that influence your opinions?

Chapter Summary

The following summarizes this chapter's content as it relates to the learning objectives presented at the beginning of the chapter. Objectives include the following:

A. Define *organizations*.

Organizations are "(1) social entities that (2) are goal directed, (3) are designed as deliberately structured and coordinated activity systems, and (4) are linked to the external environment" (Daft, 2007, p. 10).

B. Describe organizations providing social services.

Social services include the tasks that social work practitioners and other helping professionals perform with the goal of improving people's health, enhancing their quality of life, increasing autonomy and independence, supporting families, and helping people and larger systems improve their functioning in the social environment.

C. Discuss several organizational theories, including classical organizational theories (scientific management, the administrative theory of management, and bureaucracy), neoclassical organizational theories, human relations theories, Theory X and Theory Y, feminist theories and organizations, the cultural perspective, political-economy theory, contingency theory, culture-quality theories, Theory Z, and ecosystems theories.

Organizational theories include classical organizational theories that reflect rigid structure in addition to emphasis on productivity and task completion. Examples are scientific management, the administrative theory of management, and bureaucracy. In contrast, neoclassical organizational theory represents a later shift in perspective to theory that's more oriented toward human relationships and motivation. Human relations theories and feminist theories stress the importance of the human component in organizational functioning. Feminist theories, of course, focus on the empowerment of women. The cultural perspective emphasizes the importance of expectations in the organizational environment and culture in order to maintain the organization's status quo. Political-economy theory focuses on how organizations adapt to external systems in the macro environment that have resources and power. The institutional perspective also focuses on organizations' adaptation to the external environment, but in response to social rules imposed by social institutions. Contingency theory stresses careful analysis of all variables to determine those that relate directly to an issue or problem involving either personal or other organizational factors. Culture-quality theories, characterizing the end of the last century, emphasize the importance of establishing a positive organizational culture that promotes worker motivation and improves the quality of their work. Theory Z, developed by Ouchi (1981) and focusing on organizations in Japan, emphasizes long-term employment, long periods of employee evaluation, collective decision making, and collective responsibility. Finally, ecosystems theory provides a perspective for understanding organizational functioning that fits well with social work. It provides a structured way of viewing organizations, yet focuses on how change might occur.

D. Propose the dynamics of gender-based power in organizations.

Dynamics include: (1) "Power re-creates itself in its own image"; (2) "power elites enforce norms and systems that guarantee continuous power"; (3) "power creates a sense of entitlement" (4) "power creates invulnerability, leading to a flaunting of society's standards"; and (5) "loyalty to power overshadows other loyalties, including gender" (Burk, 2009, pp. 483–484).

E. Demonstrate the application of ecosystems concepts to organizations and social agencies.

The ecosystems concepts—including system, boundaries, input, output, subsystem, relation-ship, homeostasis, role, positive and negative feedback, and equifinality—were applied to an industrial organization and to a social service agency.

F. Introduce various critical thinking questions.

Critical thinking questions addressed comparing and contrasting theories, evaluation of the proposed dynamics of gender-based power in organizations, the application of feminist theories to men, and the usefulness of organizational theories.

G. Focus on ethical issues.

Ethical issues addressed included power versus service provision in political-economy theory, and the relationship between organizational theories and the NASW *Code of Ethics*.

Looking Ahead

This chapter discussed the various theories concerning how organizations function. The next chapter will address social service organizational settings, goals, and contexts in the macro social environment.

For Further Exploration on the Internet

See this text's website at **www.cengage.com/ social_work/kirst-ashman** for learning tools such as tutorial quizzing, Web links, glossary, flashcards, and PowerPoint® slides.

Social Service Organizational Settings, Goals, and Environmental Contexts

Organizations respond to human needs. Here people demonstrate on the behalf of Social Security to emphasize the importance of saving it.

CHAPTER CONTENTS

A pink slip. Perry could not believe it. He went to his mailbox today at work just like he did every weekday, and there it was. The pink slip said he was being laid off in two weeks.

Perry had been a social worker for a Protective Services unit at Rutabaga County Department of Social Services for four years. Although very demanding, he loved his job. He worked in a special program stressing family preservation that emphasized keeping families together if at all possible. It involved intensive work with families over limited time periods. Perry's goal was to help families get back on their emotional feet and function permanently without social service assistance.

With a relatively small caseload of families, he could provide the intensive services families at risk of child abuse or neglect desperately needed. Sometimes, he served as an educator, providing help with child management, anger control, or budgeting. He usually served as counselor and support system, focusing on family strengths and assisting with members' problem solving. Other times, he was a broker, linking families with needed resources like health care or grants for paint and home repairs to comply with building codes. He even helped families paint rooms and fix windows to avoid having children removed for neglect because of inadequate housing conditions. The intent was to help families in crisis and under extreme economic and emotional pressure become stronger, healthier, and independent. As a result, the risk for child abuse or neglect was significantly decreased and the need for placement of children in foster care at the county's great expense eliminated. Perry felt he had provided enormous help to many families over the years.

In the past, getting people off expensive assistance and service-provision roles had delighted county administrators gravely focused on budget crises. The external environmental climate, however, had abruptly changed. Severe budget cuts forced agency administrators to make tough decisions. They decided Perry's family preservation program was much too expensive to continue. He served too few clients to warrant his salary. Perry no longer had a job. His clients would no longer receive the services they needed.

It was not Perry's fault that he lost his job. Nor was it his fault that he could no longer help his clients as he had in the past. His agency's external environment had shifted and resources had been reduced. The result was a change in the agency's goals that no longer made his program a priority. Forces in the external environment had direct impacts on his agency's ability to provide services.

Chapter 5 discussed organizational theories and some basic knowledge about organizations. This chapter will continue examining organizations within the social environment, both internally and externally. Two important concepts concerning the internal environment are agency setting and organizational goals. A range of variables in the external environment directly affects structure and human behavior in the internal environment.

Learning Objectives

A. Examine primary and secondary agency settings.
B. Define and discuss organizational mission statements, goals, and objectives for achieving goals.
C. Describe faith-based services.
D. Discuss goal displacement.
E. Explore the external macro environment of social service organizations, including resources, legitimation, client sources, and relationships with other organizations.
F. Examine the impact of social and economic forces on social service organizations.
G. Provide case examples concerning working in a secondary setting, goal displacement, personnel resources, and competitive relationships among organizations.
H. Examine how federal social legislation, Temporary Assistance to Needy Families (TANF), and managed care impact agency service provision.
I. Focus on ethical issues in managed care and national health care coverage.
J. Raise various critical thinking questions.

The Importance of Organizations for Social Workers

Organizations are particularly important to practitioners for three basic reasons. First, they employ workers. An organization's policies, goals, and restrictions will directly affect what work practitioners can and cannot do with clients. The second reason for an organization's significance is that frequently the organization and not the client will be the source of problems. Workers therefore need to evaluate how well their organizations are functioning in order to do their own work effectively. Third, it's necessary to analyze and understand an agency's functioning prior to undertaking any macro-level changes. We have established that the NASW *Code of Ethics* obligates social workers to advocate and work for improvements in their agency settings when necessary.

Social workers may need to participate in organizational change in order to enhance agency functioning and effectiveness (Packard, 2008). This section's purpose is not to provide a detailed explanation of organizational behavior. Rather, it is to alert new social workers to internal organizational factors that can affect their ability to do their jobs. Two primary concepts important in understanding the internal environment of organizations are agency settings and organizational goals.

It is necessary to briefly comment about the terms used in this book. Organizational theories are taken primarily from the business and management literature. However, they may apply to all organizations, including social services agencies. For our purposes, we will use the terms *organization, social services agency, social service agency, social agency*, and *agency* interchangeably. The chapters on organizations in this book focus on the social services agencies in which social workers practice and clients receive services.

Agency Settings

Social workers usually work within one of two types of organizational settings, primary or secondary. Each type of setting has implications for effective practice and for how workers experience their work environment.

Primary Settings

Primary settings are those agencies where social work is the main or primary profession employed. Most public social service agencies are primary settings. It is common for the administrators, supervisors, and most of the workers to be social workers with social work degrees and titles. While there may be other occupations or professions present (for example, homemaker service providers[1] or psychologists), they represent a minority of the staff.

Because most of the staff and administrators are social workers, they tend to share similar professional values and perspectives. Their education and training are typically similar. One benefit of these settings is that workers never have to explain what social workers do. Everyone knows and understands the social work role. This cannot be said for secondary settings.

Secondary Settings

Secondary settings are characterized by the presence of a variety of professional staff. The main service provided by the agency is not social services. Typical examples are hospitals and schools. In a hospital, medical care of patients is the primary service. Medically trained personnel (for example, nurses and physicians) comprise the largest segment of the professional staff. Most of the administrative staff and supervisors will have a medical background. Social work is just one of several ancillary professions contributing to the overall goal of medical care provision. Other professions include dietitians, pharmacists, and chaplains, to name a few.

The wealth of disciplines and professional perspectives can produce a challenging environment for social work. Typically, social workers must learn the language (for instance, medical terminology or relevant abbreviations) used by the other professions. Unlike primary settings, a secondary setting such as a hospital is usually operated within a definite pecking order controlled by other professions. Physicians are at the top of that hierarchy. Social workers are not. This sometimes means that social work values and perspectives will clash with those of the physicians and other medical personnel. Highlight 6.1 provides an example illustrating how this can work.

---

[1] *Homemaker services* help clients reside in their own homes by providing necessary assistance such as meal preparation, laundry, shopping, cleaning, or transportation (Barker, 2003).

Highlight 6.1 | Case Example—Working in a Secondary Setting

Cristina, a hospital social worker, was working with Tyrone, a sixty-one-year-old patient with Parkinson's disease, along with his family. *Parkinson's disease* is "a progressive disease of the nervous system marked by tremor[s], muscular rigidity, and slow, imprecise movement, chiefly affecting middle-aged" and older people (Lindberg, 2007, p. 998). Tyrone had been hospitalized for a malfunctioning of his kidneys that had nothing to do with his Parkinson's disease. However, nurses referred Tyrone to Cristina when they observed him falling several times while walking from his bed to the bathroom. These nurses felt that Tyrone would have difficulty returning home without special equipment such as a walker or a wheelchair. They indicated he might even require some special placement instead of returning to his home.

Cristina met with Tyrone. She found it very difficult to understand him, as the Parkinson's disease was seriously affecting his ability to formulate words. However, with some difficulty she was able to discuss his situation with him. He stated vehemently that he wanted to return home. He emphasized how the disease "wasn't that bad." He stressed that he would be all right now that the kidney problem had subsided, if he could just get home!

Cristina also spoke alone with Tyrone's wife, Ursula, age fifty-nine. Ursula felt that Tyrone was denying the seriousness of his condition. She said that his muscular control and balance had deteriorated significantly in the past four months. Ursula told Cristina that Tyrone had been a university professor in engineering at a prestigious private college. She explained that it was very difficult for him to admit to his increasingly serious weakness. Ursula also expressed concern about her ability to care for him adequately at home. Tyrone was a large hulk of a man. Ursula indicated that it was impossible for her to lift him if he should fall. She felt that someone needed to be with him at all

times. Yet, she hesitated to take him out of the home and place him in a health care facility. She felt it might break his spirit and his heart.

Cristina met with Tyrone and Ursula individually one more time and, finally, together for their last encounter. She discussed with them a variety of possibilities. These included obtaining supportive equipment, widening the doorways in their home, installing ramps for wheelchair accessibility, and referring them to various other supportive service providers. The latter included a beeper Tyrone could use to call for help in the event he fell. Additionally, Cristina began arranging for a visiting nurse to assist Ursula with Tyrone's care and to provide respite care one afternoon each week to give Ursula a break.

Cristina felt good about her work with Tyrone and Ursula. She felt she had helped them establish a viable plan for the present. It could maintain Tyrone in his own home until his increasing disability required more extensive treatment and, possibly, placement in some special facility. Cristina had already contacted the recommended services to establish their availability and viability in Tyrone's case. The next step was to finalize the plans and put them into place before Tyrone's upcoming discharge.

Cristina came to work the next morning and went around as usual checking her patients' charts to see what was happening and monitor progress. When she got to Tyrone's room, it was empty. Initially, Cristina assumed that a nurse or volunteer had taken him for a walk in order to get some daily exercise.

However, Cristina was shocked as she found and read his chart. It stated he was being transported this very day to a health care facility. What about the plans she had made with Tyrone and Ursula? What about Tyrone's adamant feelings about remaining in his own home? In disbelief she stared at the signature of Tyrone's attending physician, Dr. Strangelove. Dr. Strangelove had totally ignored all that she had written in the chart about Tyrone's discharge planning. A deepening fury began to paint her emotions. How dare Dr. Strangelove do this! How dare he act as if she did not even exist.

Luckily, Cristina became so busy that day that she had little more time to think about Tyrone, Ursula, or Dr. Strangelove. By the next morning she had simmered down quite a bit. After all, Tyrone and Ursula had the right to choose their own destinies. She was just there to help them if she could.

When she later talked to the head nurse about the matter, Cristina was enlightened about what it meant to work in a secondary setting. She abruptly found out that the physician's word ruled in a medical facility. Apparently, Dr. Strangelove was personal friends with Ursula's son Devin, who was also a physician. Dr. Strangelove and Devin sat down first with Ursula and later with Tyrone to discuss their feelings about Tyrone's condition and his and Ursula's future. Both physicians felt strongly that it was ridiculous for Tyrone to return home. Both felt it was far beyond Ursula's marital responsibility to "sacrifice" herself for Tyrone. They apparently had urged and eventually persuaded Ursula to pursue placing Tyrone in a residential facility. It was the head nurse's opinion that Tyrone felt too weak to fight all three of these people and voice his own desires. So, defeated, he complied with their recommendations.

Cristina was not convinced that the decision was the correct one for either Tyrone or Ursula. However, she understood that they had every right to make their own decisions, regardless of the dynamics involved in the decision-making process. Cristina also learned that she had significantly less status than physicians did in this secondary setting.

Mission Statements, Goals, and Objectives

Every social services agency should develop a *mission statement*, a declaration of the organization's purpose that "establishes broad and relatively permanent parameters within which goals are developed and specific programs designed" (Kettner, Moroney, & Martin, 2008, p. 121). It also includes what client populations are to be served and provides general guidance for what needs should be met.

For example, Lad Lake, Inc., a private nonprofit social services agency, has a mission statement saying it "provides living and learning environments for at-risk youth and families in preparation for responsible living in our communities" (Lad Lake, Inc., undated). This is a broad statement that encompasses a range of programs, including the following:

- A residential treatment center for adolescents with severe behavioral and emotional problems
- Special education programs and an alternative school in the community
- Independent living services to support children transitioning out of the foster care system as they approach age eighteen
- Outreach services offering "guidance, therapy, and even friendship" to young people and families (p. 19)
- An in-home therapy program
- A mentoring program serving youth ages seven to twenty-one "with a history of substance abuse, truancy, disorderly conduct, or an unstable family life" (p. 23)

- A "Brighter Future Initiative" program offering "intervention services" to youth "who have committed their first minor delinquent offense" and to their families (p. 23)
- Parent training classes
- A number of other creative initiatives (Lad Lake, 2005)

Kettner and his colleagues (2008) provide two other examples of mission statements. One concerns a family service agency whose mission is "to promote family strength and stability in a manner that allows each individual to achieve his or her potential while, at the same time, supporting strong and productive interrelationships among family members" (p. 122). Still another mission statement involves an agency offering services to alcohol and drug addicts. Its mission is "to promote and support the achievement of a positive and productive lifestyle, including steady employment and stable relationships, for those formerly addicted to chemical substances" (p. 122). The "key" to a mission statement is that it "should focus on what lies ahead for its clients or consumers if the agency is successful in addressing their problems and meeting their needs" (Kettner et al., 2008, p. 122).

Organizational Goals

Mission statements identify the organization's basic goals. Kettner et al. offer this definition of *organizational goals*: "Goals are statements of expected outcomes dealing with the problem that the program is attempting to prevent, eradicate, or ameliorate. They are responsive to problems and needs, and represent an ideal or hoped-for outcome (Coley & Scheinberg, 2000). Goals need not be measurable or achievable. They tend to be more general and provide a sense of programmatic direction" (Kettner et al., 2008, p. 123).

Organizational goals serve at least three major purposes (Etzioni, 1964). First, they provide guidelines for the kinds of functions and activities organizational workers are supposed to pursue. Second, organizational goals "constitute a source of legitimacy which justifies the activities of an organization and, indeed, its very existence" (p. 5). Third, goals can "serve as standards by which members of an organization and outsiders can assess the success of the organization—i.e., its effectiveness and efficiency" (p. 5).

How does an organization establish its mission statement and goals? As services must be in line with current social welfare policy and legislation, so must the mission statement and official goals. Mission and goals will also reflect the organization's stance in terms of treatment modality and values.

Social service organizations and agencies, then, formulate goals in order to address any of a wide range of needs and problems concerning human well-being. Social service organizations are supposed to use their resources to address these needs and remedy problems. The establishment of goals directs this process.

In order to understand an organization's functioning, it is helpful to think in terms of "official" goals and "operative" goals (Perrow, 1961, p. 856). *Official* goals "are the general purposes of the organization as put forth in the charter [or *mission statement*], annual reports, public statements by key officials and other authoritative pronouncements; *operative* goals, on the other hand, "designate the ends sought through the actual operating policies of the organization" that entail what the organization does in its everyday practice (p. 856).

Why must we make the distinction between official and operative goals? The problem is that "official goals may predict little about organizational behavior" (Hasenfeld, 1983, p. 87). In other words, official goals may have very little to do with an agency's actual operative goals. Reasons for this will be discussed more thoroughly later when we address the concept of goal displacement.

Goals provide social services agencies with general direction concerning *what* should happen, but not with specific guidance regarding *how* it should be done. Highlight 6.2 discusses how agencies structure the process of carrying out goals by identifying objectives.

One aspect of many private organizations that involves organizational goals concerns a spiritual dimension. Some social service organizations are faith-based— that is, sponsored by or affiliated with a religious or spiritual organization. Such organizations "may contain elements that are guided by the faith assumptions of the group or some form of spirituality," which are reflected in the organization's goals (Barker, 2003, p. 154). The following section discusses faith-based social service organizations.

Mission and Goals Involving Spirituality: Faith-Based Social Services   A common context in which social workers face up to issues in spirituality and religion involves faith-based organizations. *Spirituality* concerns people's "values, beliefs, mission, awareness, subjectivity, experience, sense of purpose and direction, and a kind of striving toward something greater than oneself"; *religion* is "a set of beliefs and practices of an organized religious institution . . . It is important to note that *religion* is one form of spirituality. The two concepts are not mutually exclusive" (Frame, 2003, pp. 3–4).

To varying degrees, faith-based social services often incorporate aspects of spirituality and religion into their mission statement and goals. For example, a mission statement might include "spiritual nurture" as one of the agency's goals or describe a "program as 'Christ-centered'" (Hartford Institute, 2006).

Faith-based social services have gained much attention, support, and flexibility in recent years (Lupu & Tuttle, 2008). Because it is possible that you will either work in faith-based agencies or be working with them in some capacity, we will spend some time describing them here. Cnaan and Boddie (2002) explain the policy scene. The Personal Responsibility and Work Opportunity Reconciliation Act (PRWORA) of 1996 that structures the social welfare public assistance system in the United States includes a section known as "Charitable Choice." Before PRWORA was implemented, "a faith-based organization contracting with the government had to remove all religious symbols from the room where service was provided; forego any religious ceremonies (such as prayers at meals); accept all clients— even those opposed to the beliefs of the providers; hire staff that reflected society at large and not the organization's spirit and belief system; adhere to government contract regulations; and incorporate separately as . . . [a] nonprofit organization" (p. 225). The idea was clearly to maintain the separation between church and state. Charitable Choice, however, permits "faith-based service providers [to] retain their religious autonomy. . . . In addition, the government cannot curtail the religious

| Highlight 6.2 | Objectives Indicate How to Achieve Goals |

Goals are general statements about what an organization wants to accomplish. They usually don't specify exactly how to achieve them. *Objectives* are smaller, behaviorally specific subgoals that serve as stepping stones on the way to accomplishing the main goal. Brody (2005) explains:

> Typically, goals represent long-term endeavors, sometimes as long as three to five years, and may even be timeless. Examples of these goals statements would be "improving access to health care services for low-income persons" or "reducing racism in our community." . . . Objectives represent relevant, attainable, measurable, and time-limited ends to be achieved. They are relevant because they fit within the general mission and goals of the organization and because they relate to problems identified by the organization. They are attainable because they can be realized. They are measurable because achievement is based upon tangible, concrete, and usually quantifiable results. They are time limited (usually a year); this time frame helps the organization demonstrate concrete results within a specified period. (pp. 58–59)

Kettner and his colleagues (2008) recommend that the following questions be asked in order to establish "clear, specific measurable, time-limited, and realistic" objectives that the agency is committed to achieve:

- "Is the objective clear? Does it mean the same thing to anyone who reads the statement?"
- "Does the objective specify results to be achieved, including numbers and changes in conditions?"
- "Is the objective written in such a way that it can be measured? Are measurement criteria incorporated into the objective?"
- "Does the statement indicate a time limit within which or a target date by which the objective will be achieved?"

- "Is the objective realistic given our technology and knowledge as well as available resources?" (p. 125)

Brody (2005) identifies four basic types of objectives used in social service agencies—*impact, service, operational*, and *product*:

Impact objectives specify outcomes to be achieved as a result of program activities. They detail the return expected on the organization's investment of time, personnel, and resources.

The following are examples:

- To place 20 children in adoptive homes in one year
- To secure jobs for 35 juvenile delinquents in 5 months
- To increase the number of foster children reunited with their natural parents from 40 to 50 by June 30

Service objectives are the organization's tally of activities provided or services rendered. Sometimes these are referred to as *activity* or *process* objectives. Examples include the following:

- To serve 300 clients in the program year
- To conduct 680 interviews
- To provide 17 neighborhood assemblies
- To interview 20 children needing foster homes . . .

Operational objectives convey the intent to improve the general operation of the organization. Examples include the following:

- To sponsor 4 in-service training workshops for 40 staff
- To obtain a pilot project grant of $10,000 within 6 months
- To increase the number of volunteers by 150
- To reduce staff turnover from 20% to 10% annually

Operational objectives are essential to enhance the way an organization functions. They are a means to the end for which the organization was established. By providing in-service training, for example, an organization improves the way it serves its target populations.

Product objectives are designed to provide a tangible outcome to benefit a target population or a community. . . . The following are examples of product objectives:

- To obtain passage of House Bill 41
- To develop a neighborhood family support system
- To review and critique a specific piece of legislation
- To open four schools in the evening for recreation
- To provide a media effort on teen pregnancy prevention . . .
- To sponsor a communitywide campaign on mental health (pp. 59–60).

expression or practice of faith-based services providers by requiring them to change their internal governance or remove from their property any 'religious art, icons, scripture, or other symbols.' (S104 (a)(2)) . . . [The legislation also] allows faith-based organizations to have discretion in hiring only those people who share their religious beliefs or traditions and to terminate employees who do not exhibit behavior consistent with the religious practices of the organization" (p. 226).

Faith-based organizations may offer a broad assortment of services. These include "job-search, job-readiness, job-skills training programs; Literacy, General Education Development (GED) and English as a Second Language (ESL) programs; food, shelter, and clothing; social services and referral; child care and transportation: and counseling services among others" (Texas Workforce Commission, 2004).

Tangenberg (2005) provides some examples of how diverse faith-based programs can be in terms of service programming, conceptualization of faith, and expression of spirituality:

> The Daylight Shelter organization provides overnight shelter and meals to homeless individuals and families. Prayer occurs before meals, and evening worship services open to the public are offered five times each week. Engagement in religious activities is optional. Men and women also may choose to participate in 12-step recovery programs that are separated by gender and have a strong religious focus. Religious activities in the recovery programs are required and are discussed before participation so referrals to secular programs can be made if necessary. . . . Describing the program's spiritual base, the Director said:
>
> "Our program is Christ-centered. . . . [Program participants] have to go to church—they pick their own churches—we do devotions every morning, we have Bible studies threes times a week, we have Bible classes." . . .
>
> [In contrast,] [t]he Jackson Community Center is an organization with no religious references in its name or program activities, although it is closely affiliated with a large Protestant denomination. Primary services include adult basic education and employment preparation. . . .
>
> Some board members must be members of the founding Christian denomination, and ties to the denomination are strong, although there are no expectations regarding the faith commitments of staff members. Values of dignity, care, and compassion are

emphasized rather than a specific religious ideology, and financial and volunteer support is frequently sought from the religious community. . . .

[Yet, another example involves] Peace House [which] is a drop-in center that provides meals and emergency services for homeless men and women and outreach to former center guests who are in jail or prison. . . .

Although it originated under Catholic auspices, Peace House includes staff from various faith traditions sharing spiritual values of compassion and service. No organized religious programs are available for guests, and no religious symbols are displayed, although staff meet daily for meditation and prayer and have a small weekly liturgy. (pp. 203–204)

Many issues can surface when social workers enter the realm of spirituality in a faith-based setting. Questions can arise regarding how the worker's own sense of spirituality coincides or contrasts with the host agency's perspective. There are no easy answers to such questions. A worker may struggle with personal views that are at odds with the agency's. A practitioner must always address such issues in an ethical and professional manner. If views between the agency and the worker are too incongruent, leaving the agency may be an appropriate solution.

Derezotes (2006) reflects upon spiritually oriented social workers:

From a spiritual perspective, the common denominator of all religions should be kindness. The spiritually oriented social worker respects the diversity of doctrines, rituals, and beliefs found in the religions of the world and she or he realizes that all religions can either foster and/or hinder spiritual development. The social worker never tries to change the religion of an individual or community, but may work to help make that religion more of a [supportive] Community of Spiritual and Universal Diversity. The social worker refuses to practice "religionism"; she or he does not evaluate a person or group based upon religion, but does evaluate the individual or group's unique expression of that religion. . . . [The] worker also respects the client's spiritual faith system, and will ask the client . . . if he wants to work toward his own spiritual growth and transformation. (pp. 260–261)

Multiple Goals

Social service organizations usually are complex entities. Therefore, they frequently aim to accomplish multiple goals (Austin, 2002; Ginsberg, 1995). There are a number of reasons for this. First, agencies must hold themselves accountable to legislative requirements and constraints. For instance, an organization providing group homes for children with cognitive disabilities must conform to a range of state licensing rules that mandate the minimum standards for service provision. These include the maximum number of clients in any particular residence, the amount of space required per child, the staff-to-client ratio, how the kitchen and dining areas should be equipped, and even the requirement that toilet seats be open or split in the front instead of closed.

Multiple goals also occur because many social service agencies may serve a range of client groups. For example, one organization may provide day care services, vocational training, adoption services, and foster care all at the same time. Lad Lake, Inc., described earlier, provides another example of an organization sponsoring a wide range of programs pursuing many goals. Each segment of the agency pursues its own goals within the context of the larger organizational environment that has more encompassing organizational goals.

Additionally, organizations may be held accountable to different segments of the public, each making its own demands upon an agency's performance and subsequently its goals. Such publics can include "other human service organizations, interest groups, legislative bodies, and professional associations" in addition to clients being served (Ginsberg, 1995; Hasenfeld, 1983, pp. 90–91). For example, a child advocacy group may pressure a social services agency specializing in helping survivors of domestic violence to increase its standards for temporary shelter of mothers and their children. Likewise, professional organizations may require the same agency to provide minimum in-service training sessions for staff in various job positions. We have established that in-service training is instructional programming provided by an employer that brings in experts to help employees develop skills and understanding intended to help them improve their work performance. Hence, the agency must pursue both of these goals in addition to many other goals established for numerous other reasons.

Goal Displacement

A major problem encountered by workers in organizations involves *goal displacement*. Goal displacement was originally defined as "substitution of a legitimate goal with another goal which the organization was not developed to address, for which resources were not allocated and which it is not known to serve" (Etzioni, 1964, p. 10). Goal displacement "occurs when an organization moves in different directions from its original purpose. For example, the leaders of an alternative agency could become so concerned over being able to survive financially that they might apply for any available funds [in the form of grants], even if receiving the grant will mean taking the agency in a different direction from its original cause or purpose" in order to comply with the grant's requirements (Netting & O'Connor, 2003, p. 51). Another example is an organization that begins pursuing its leaders' personal interests rather than achieving its official goals (Netting, Kettner, & McMurty, 2008).

In other words, goal displacement occurs when an organization continues to function but no longer achieves the goals it's supposed to. Sometimes, it happens when the *process* of achieving goals takes precedence over the actual goal *attainment*. A typical scenario in social service organizations is when the rules and following those rules become more important than providing services to clients.

It should be noted that goal displacement can also involve positive changes in goals. A classic example is the March of Dimes, which began as an organization dedicated to raising money to eradicate polio, historically a major childhood disease. With the discovery of a polio vaccine, the disease ceased to be a major health problem in the United States and Canada. Instead of going out of business, however, the organization shifted its goal to raising money to combat birth defects. The new goal had one advantage over the polio-related goal. Instead of focusing on a single disease, the organization now directed its attention to a large category of problems. With such a broad scope, the organization would probably never run out of new childhood health problems to combat. Therefore, it would be unlikely that it would ever again face a similar dilemma of goal displacement.

This commentary is not intended to be critical of the March of Dimes, or any other organization. It is a fact of organizational life that agencies seldom go out of existence. Once a goal is achieved, most organizations do not disappear. Instead, they shift their attention to new goals. This process only becomes a problem when the means to the goals assume a life of their own. When this happens, agencies may place greater emphasis on getting the files up-to-date than on providing effective service to clients.

People's access to resources has major impacts on the options available to them and, in effect, how they behave. Poverty and lack of resources will be at the root of many of your clients' problems. Therefore, it is crucial to understand how organizations affect resource provision and clients. Such a background can enable you to identify ways to make changes in systems so that your clients are better served.

For instance, consider the example concerning the county social services department in Highlight 6.3. As a worker in that agency, there are several things you might target for change. These include working with other workers and administration to shorten significantly the tedious forms. You might also explore ways to get information out to community residents regarding the documentation and needed information they must bring when applying for services. Simple things like putting up clearly visible signs instructing people where to go when they first enter the building might be helpful. Even advocating for waiting room chairs made to make people comfortable might be useful.

Ecosystems Theory, Organizations, and Goal Displacement

We have established that it is helpful to view social service organizations in terms of ecosystems theories' concepts. Many of the notions involved are similar to those used in reference to business and industry. For example, in industry, resources or *input* are *processed* by the organizational system, which turns out some product or *output*. Figure 6.1 illustrates this sequence as "ecosystems concepts." Essentially, the same thing happens in social service organizations. They take resources (*input*) and, in response to social forces and institutionalized values, apply some *process* (procedures for providing services) to produce *output* (actual service provision or some other benefits for clients).

Often when goal displacement occurs, however, the emphasis is placed on the process rather than the product. The organizational system begins to consider the rigid process of providing services as its major function. The *process*, rather than effective provision of services, then becomes the organization's *product*.

Goal attainment comprises what is supposed to happen through the intervention process. Illustrated in Figure 6.1, the input (in the form of resources) is supposed to be used on behalf of clients in the intervention process. Hence, "$" refers to resources with an arrow pointing to "clients" in the top box in the goal attainment process. The result is supposed to be positive benefits for clients. Thus, an arrow points from the "$ to clients" box to the middle box that refers to

| **Highlight 6.3** | **An Example of Goal Displacement— Process Supersedes Progress** |

A large county Department of Social Services (previously referred to as "the public welfare department") comes to mind. It is located in the shell of an old department store with high ceilings and a myriad of small worker cubicles somewhat resembling a mammoth beehive. All outside windows have been sealed with bricks because of "the heating and ventilation problems." No one really knows what that means. However, everyone inside the building knows that the building's interior is isolated from the outside world.

When entering the main door of the building, it is extremely difficult to figure out where to go for what kind of services. This is true even if you're a professional social worker, let alone if you're a client entering the building for the first time. Consider what it would be like if you were a client applying for services from this agency. You probably have to stand in line for fifteen or twenty minutes simply to get the information you need to find out where to go.

When you finally wander into a waiting area for the services you need, you have to stand in line again for another twenty minutes or so to get the forms you must fill out for the services you need. You then take the twenty pages of complicated forms, which you must fill out meticulously, and take a seat. The chairs are made of hard plastic. There are large "dust bunnies" (sometimes referred to as "dinosaur dust bunnies") rolling around your feet. It then takes

approximately an hour to fill out the forms. This is assuming you can read well in English. You probably do not understand some of the questions, so you leave the spaces blank. You then take the forms up to the desk, where they are placed in a pile. You must wait your turn in order to see an intake worker (that is, someone who begins the process to provide services). You wait two to three hours.

Finally, your name is called and you are instructed to go to Cubicle 57 to see Ms. Hardmoney. You enter Cubicle 57 and see Ms. Hardmoney sitting at her desk and reading your forms. You then begin a discussion with her concerning the additional information she needs in order to process your application for services. It seems, she indicates, that a number of critical elements of information are missing. Look at those blanks. She then says you must get the critical information before you can continue the application process. The critical information is somewhere at home. Well, that's all right. Just go home, get it, and start this whole process over again tomorrow. At least you know where the waiting room is now.

In this example, the organization was supposed to be providing services to people in need. However, the complicated process, commonly called "red tape," became much more important to the organization's staff than whether clients received needed services or not.

the "intervention process." The intervention process involves whatever treatment process or technology the organization uses to help its clients. Finally, an arrow points from the "intervention" box down to the "benefits for clients" box, illustrating what is supposed to happen in an agency's goal attainment process.

Figure 6.1 also illustrates *goal displacement* on the far right. Here, input (in the form of resources) is used to maintain the *process* of what is done with those resources. In essence, the process becomes the *product*. The positive impacts upon clients are somehow lost and forgotten as agency personnel strive to maintain and complete the process. Figure 6.1 depicts this with arrows leading down from the "$ to clients" box to the "process becomes product" box. The arrow leading from the

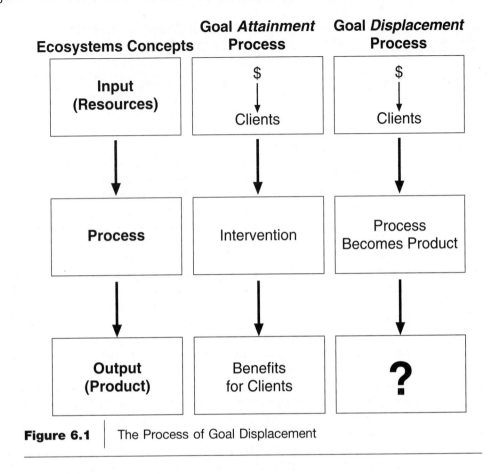

Figure 6.1 | The Process of Goal Displacement

latter box down to the "?" box reflects how the actual results for clients become relatively unimportant and possibly unknown.

Goal Displacement and Generalist Practice

This discussion's intent is to enhance your awareness of problems often encountered in organizational service provision. Understanding the dynamics of organizational behavior is a prerequisite to changing an organization's behavior for the clients' benefit. When a social service agency ceases to serve clients as effectively as possible, it is your job as a generalist practitioner to try to improve service provision. This may involve advocating with administrators for a new program, suggesting and promoting agency policy changes, or initiating a fundraising project to provide Christmas toys for needy families.

The Environmental Context of Social Service Organizations

The environmental context in which a social services organization functions is critically important to the organization's ability to pursue and attain its goals. It is essential for you to understand at least four environmental dimensions impacting organizations: available resources, (Alter, 2009; Holland & Petchers, 1987; Schmid, 2009), legitimation (Holland & Petchers, 1987; Schmid, 2009), client sources (Holland & Petchers, 1987; Schmid, 2009), and relationships with other organizations (Alter, 2009; Holland & Petchers, 1987; Schmid, 2009).

Resources

Resource inputs are "those external units" that supply an agency with (1) financial support and (2) personnel (Hasenfeld, 1984, p. 24). First, a social services agency must have money to function. It needs to pay staff salaries, rent and/or for building maintenance, for supplies, telephone, and a myriad of other expenses.

The second type of resource critical for a social services agency involves personnel. What kind of staffing does the agency have? What are their professional credentials? Are staff qualified and plentiful enough to carry out their duties effectively? Highlight 6.4 provides a case example involving personnel resources.

Legitimation

A second environmental dimension impacting social service agencies is *legitimation* (Schmid, 2009, p. 412). We have already briefly mentioned the importance of legislative requirements and constraints with respect to an agency's organizational goals. Legitimation is the condition where the external environment provides an agency with the appropriate status or authorization to perform agency functions and pursue agency goals. An agency must be legally viable. Once established, the agency must continue to abide by the rules upon which its existence is based.

Consider, however, if an agency does not follow the appropriate rules and regulations. For example, a health care center for older adults failed to follow the rules concerning maintenance of its bedridden patients, especially those with Alzheimer's disease. Clients' relatives visiting the center reported to the state's licensing agency that they had observed a number of seriously disturbing incidents during their visits. These observations included clients having wallowed in their own feces for over a day, staff slapping clients in the face when these clients refused to cooperate, and employees depriving clients of food to punish them for poor behavior. Needless to say, once the health care center's practices became known and were investigated by state authorities, the agency was closed. It no longer possessed the legitimation and accountability needed to support its existence.

Client Sources

The third environmental dimension affecting agencies involves the availability of clients. A range of client resources is necessary to provide enough clients to keep the agency financially afloat. Client resources include other public and private agencies that make referrals. They also include individual potential clients who seek services for themselves. In other words, an agency cannot last very long without enough clients to sustain it.

Highlight 6.4 | Case Example—Personnel Resources

A debate raged in one state between professional social workers, on the one hand, and certain county social services agency administrators on the other. (It might be noted that many of the latter administrators were not social workers by profession.) The battle ensued when professional certification for social workers was first initiated in the state. Most professional social workers adamantly maintained that it was critically important for workers calling themselves "social workers" to have graduated from accredited social work programs and have the requisite experience.

Some rural county social service agency administrators, on the other hand, staunchly maintained that there were not enough graduates from professional social work programs to fill all of the positions available in their rural agencies. They declared that the only workers they could attract to fill their agencies' job positions were graduates having other degrees, such as those in sociology and psychology. These administrators emphasized that most social work graduates were attracted to the state's larger, more exciting urban areas.

Much to the dismay of professional social work educators, a faction of sociologists teaching in local universities supported the county administrators' view and politically lobbied on the former's behalf. In reality, these sociologists were concerned that graduates with sociology degrees would be able to find employment as easily as graduates with social work degrees. To a great extent, this approach coincided with the sociologists' own interests, namely, to maintain a higher number of sociology majors.

Most professional social workers and social work educators were appalled. None of the sociology programs were accredited. Therefore, these programs were held accountable to no standards such as those mandating the teaching of practice skills, the infusion of professional values and ethics throughout the curriculum, a substantial field internship, and a focus on human diversity. All social work programs, on the other hand, were required to adhere faithfully to such standards.

Upon further investigation, the state association of social workers established that the major reason the complaining rural county administrators were unable to recruit social work graduates was that these administrators paid near-to-minimum-wage salaries. Additionally, the state Social Work Education Association determined that virtually hundreds of graduates were being turned out from several state universities within one hundred miles of these counties. In reality, there were plenty of graduates available to fill positions—that is, if the counties would pay salaries appropriate for professional social workers.

This environmental dimension substantially affected the ability of county social service agencies to provide professional services. If agencies were not required to hire professional social workers, but could employ sociology or psychology graduates, regardless of their training in skills and values, quality of service would be seriously curtailed. The agencies' personnel resources would directly affect the agencies' ability to provide service to clients.

One agency, for example, provided special therapy services (including social work, occupational, speech, and physical) to school children in a variety of rural counties. The counties initially did not each have enough clients to hire their own full-time therapists. Therefore, each county respectively purchased from the agency whatever therapists' time was needed.

For instance, a social worker or occupational therapist might serve clients in a particular county only one or two days each week. Because of a limited number of clients, this might be all the service that the county needed. Together, the counties provided enough work for the agency to maintain several full-time therapists in each discipline. However, new state requirements to provide adequate service to children were put into place. More children became eligible for service. The counties also began to develop enhanced assessment techniques and procedures. As a result, a number of counties subsequently identified enough of their own clients to hire their own full-time therapists. Hence, the agency providing special services no longer had access to enough clients in enough counties. It simply had to shut down.

Relationships with Other Organizations

The fourth environmental dimension affecting organizations involves relationships with other agencies in the macro environment. Analysis of this organizational environment is essential to understand any particular organization's functioning. How does the social service agency interact with other organizations within its macro environment? Such relationships may fall under the category of *uninvolved, complementary*, or *competitive* (Holland & Petchers, 1987, pp. 208–209).

Uninvolved Relationships among Organizations   Organizational involvement can be placed on a continuum (Emery & Trist, 1961). At one end of this continuum are agencies that are integrally involved with each other and, in essence, can't function without each other. Such complementary relationships are discussed next. On the other end of this continuum lie agencies that have virtually nothing to do with each other except for brief, haphazard encounters. Therefore, there is little need to focus much attention on such *uninvolved* relationships. Finally, in the middle of this continuum lie those organizations that are competitive with each other. This latter type will also be discussed next.

Complementary Relationships among Organizations   Complementary organizations are different agencies that work together in some way. "Organizations must build collaborations and networks with other organizations to manage the external task environment [for example, lobby for legislation that is supportive of social services, or work together to serve the same clients with multiple needs], adapt to fast-changing conditions, and acquire resources essential for the organization's survival" (Alter, 2009, p. 435). Agencies are not islands. Often, they cannot function in isolation. They need referral sources for clients. Alternately, they need appropriate resources to which they can refer clients whose needs they cannot meet.

Consider a sheltered employment facility where adults with cognitive disabilities are trained in basic work skills and function under comprehensive supervision. Such an agency needs other agencies that run group homes and institutional facilities where clients can reside when not at work. If clients have nowhere to live, then they can't take advantage of the sheltered employment facility activities.

Another example is an organization providing in-service treatment for alcoholic clients. This organization receives virtually all of its referrals from local family services agencies providing family counseling and local hospitals. Without the cooperation of these referral agencies, the inpatient program would cease to exist.

Likewise, the local family services agencies and hospitals would be unable to serve alcoholic clients adequately if the in-service alcohol treatment program did not exist.

Competitive Relationships among Organizations   Social service agencies may compete with each other for clients (Alter, 2009). If the number of clients is relatively limited, the competition may be quite fierce. We have established that agencies need clients to survive and thrive. Highlight 6.5 provides a case example of competitive relationships among organizations.

The Impact of Social and Economic Forces on Social Service Organizations: The Shifting Macro Environment

Social service organizations function within the larger macro environment and must respond to shifting social and economic forces. Social forces include societal expectations regarding who is eligible to receive benefits and what types of benefits are appropriate. People vote for politicians who support their ideas and, it is

---

| Highlight 6.5 | Case Example—Competitive Relationships among Organizations |

One state supported a number of privately run residential treatment centers for boys, ages twelve to seventeen, who had serious behavioral and emotional problems. The state purchased services from these agencies because the state did not provide these services itself. *Purchase-of-service* involves a financial agreement or contract where one agency, often a public agency, agrees to purchase services from another agency. It may be cost effective for the public agency to purchase the services from the other agency rather than to develop and provide those services itself. The agency from which services are purchased then assumes responsibility for developing and overseeing service provision.

For many years the state and counties provided enough clients to maintain all of the centers. No new centers opened because the number of agencies approximately matched the number of clients. No new agencies were needed. The status quo, or homeostasis, was maintained.

However, when the state decided to build and open its own extremely large treatment complex, the number of clients available to privately run treatment centers was significantly decreased. Thus,

approximately half of the residential centers were forced to close. They could not solicit enough clients to sustain themselves. The other half of the centers that continued to exist did so because they quickly decided to specialize their services. For instance, one center specialized in serving clients who had dual diagnoses of both behavioral disorder and cognitive disability. Another center specialized in boys needing treatment because they had been sexually abused.

The new state treatment complex was not large enough to accommodate all of the state's clients who needed treatment. These clients had to go somewhere. The state determined that it was in the state's best fiscal interest to continue purchasing services for some clients who fell in certain categories. The fact that various centers decided to specialize in treating certain problems facilitated the state's decision-making process concerning which clients to treat in its own facility and which to refer elsewhere. Children with special needs and problems were referred to those centers that specialized in the treatment of those respective needs and problems.

hoped, will implement social policies agreeing with these conceptions. Economic forces involve how many resources are allocated to agencies for service provision. Social service agencies can only provide resources that are available and administer services in legally prescribed ways.

Social and economic forces may affect social service provision in at least three major ways. First, resources and funding may be limited. For example, a funding cut may result in the elimination of one of several programs in a domestic abuse shelter. Second, policies, regulations, and the wishes of political leaders determine what agencies can and cannot do. For instance, a child protection agency may be required by law to address a child maltreatment complaint within twenty-four hours. Third, social service agencies may be pressured to conform to public expectations. For example, the encompassing community might expect a large private mental hospital to sponsor an annual triathlon for fundraising.

As the population continues to expand worldwide, resources continue to shrink. Decreasing resources means that funding and financial support become more and more difficult to get. It also means that competition becomes more and more intense. It then makes sense that organizations producing higher-quality products (more effectively) at lower costs requiring lesser input (more efficiently) will be more likely to survive than those that are less effective and efficient. Likewise, social service organizations providing more effective and efficient services will probably outlive less effective and less efficient counterparts.

Understanding social and economic forces affecting social service organizations provides insights into organizational behavior and individual behavior within organizations. Whenever possible, social workers have a professional obligation to improve organizational systems' performance and enhance service provision to clients. This is difficult to do within the macro context because social service organizations' external environment is constantly in flux. Social forces impact other macro organizations and influence political policies which, in turn, modify the availability of funding. Social service organizations must continue seeking out and nurturing funding resources, while at the same time responding to changes in legislation and regulation.

Funding mechanisms vary widely. Social and economic forces jar social service organizations with unpredictability, suddenness, and severity. Thus, to survive and effectively meet their goals of helping clients, these organizations must maintain keen awareness of external influences and their effects. Organizations must also readily react to changing requirements and demands, as people's needs, values, and conditions change over time. Two major social and economic thrusts seriously impacting and, in many ways, restricting service provision today are federal social legislation and managed care.

Federal Social Legislation: Temporary Assistance to Needy Families (TANF)

Federal social legislation has major effects on what programs social service agencies can provide. Therefore, when legislation changes, agency services are identified and limited by that legislation. The underlying theme is that social legislation may significantly enhance or severely cut benefits to people in need. Agencies and their workers must comply with regulations whether they like them or not and whether they think such regulations are fair or not.

The current major public assistance program for children and families living in poverty is Temporary Assistance to Needy Families (TANF), which replaced the former program Aid to Families with Dependent Children (AFDC) in 1996. TANF was created by the Personal Responsibility and Work Opportunity Reconciliation Act of 1996 (also known as PRWORA). In February 2006, President George W. Bush signed into law the Deficit Reduction Act (DRA) of 2005 that reauthorized the TANF program (Administration for Children and Families [ACF], 2009). The result was a $39 billion cut in federal spending over the subsequent five years (Keene, 2006).

It's important to review the history of public assistance to understand the issues involved. Americans have a long-established record of ambivalence about providing poor people with financial assistance. Karger and Stoesz (2010) explain:

> On the hostility side, the argument goes like this: If privilege is earned by hard work, then people are poor because they are lazy and lack ambition. Those driven by the powerful American spirit of competitiveness see the inability of the poor to compete as a serious character flaw. On the other hand, only a few paychecks separate the welfare recipient from the average citizen—thus the compassion. Although democratic capitalism is rooted in the belief that hard work guarantees success, real life often tells a different story. (p. 277)

AFDC, originally established as Aid to Dependent Children (ADC) by the Social Security Act of 1935, was a program providing payments funded by federal and state governments to children deprived of parental support because a parent was absent from the home, had died, or was incapable of managing the household for physical or mental reasons. Most families receiving benefits were single mothers whose partners were not in the home.

AFDC established eligibility standards based on income level, family configuration, number and age of children, motivation to participate in work programs, and willingness to comply with paternity determination and solicitation of child support (Abramovitz, 1995). Eligible families passed an income test, that is, an eligibility guideline that establishes the maximum amount of income a family may earn without losing benefits. Those who made too much money were ineligible for benefits.

Eligible families could potentially receive financial assistance for many years in addition to Medicaid,[2] food stamps,[3] and partial financial support for housing, (with the exception of a few states that subtracted the amount received in food stamps and housing assistance from the AFDC grant) (Abramovitz, 1995). Note that how long families can continue receiving public assistance is a matter of strong debate. Facts indicate that before TANF, half of all AFDC recipients left welfare

---

[2] *Medicaid* is a program funded by federal and state governments that pays for medical and hospital services for eligible people who are unable to pay for these services themselves and are determined to be in need.

[3] *Food stamps* are coupons distributed through a federal program to people in need who use them like cash to purchase primarily food, plants, and seeds (Barker, 2003).

rolls within one year, the number rising to 70 percent after two years; however, 75 percent of welfare recipients did eventually return to AFDC rolls (Karger & Stoesz, 2010).

A number of issues characterize the public assistance debate concerning the effectiveness, fairness, and humaneness of TANF and its effects on children and families in need. They include adequacy of funding, time limits, work requirements, child care, education and training for better jobs, job quality and availability, health insurance after TANF, encouraging healthy marriages, and equitable treatment by states.

Adequacy of Funding   DiNitto (2007) describes some aspects of TANF spending. Note that the 2006 Deficit Reduction Act (DRA) allows for no increase in TANF funding for five subsequent years (CWLA, 2006). First, TANF requires states to spend at least 75 percent of what they spent on AFDC in 1994. States can then choose to contribute more if they wish. However, most states have continued to fund TANF at the 1994 level; although some have increased benefits, five states and the District of Columbia essentially decreased benefit levels. When adjusting for inflation, the real dollars allocated to recipients has significantly decreased over time. After adjustments, the actual monthly benefits per family in 2002 ($355) were 121 percent lower than those in 1969 ($803 in 2002 dollars) (Karger & Stoesz, 2006, p. 273). "TANF benefits are exceedingly small; the maximum monthly benefit for a family of three with no income in most states in 2006 was between $300 and $500 a month" (Karger & Stoesz, 2010, p. 279).

With state budgets continuing to shrink, it's highly unlikely that states will divert proportionately more funding than they have in the past to address additional public assistance needs. Instead, they are likely to supply only the minimal funding required, which means fewer resources for potential recipients. TANF also permits states to impose tighter restrictions regarding who is eligible for benefits. Many social service agencies providing benefits have serious concerns about these restrictions and the negative effects on clients. Will TANF benefits be adequate during tough economic times? Less than one-fourth of all families living below the poverty line receive TANF benefits (The *poverty line* is the minimal annual cash income level established by the federal government and based on family size that determines whether or not people are living in poverty) (Karger & Stoesz, 2010). Additionally, as of 2006, twenty-one states had established family caps that banned families from receiving additional benefits for any children born after the family's initial involvement in the program (Karger & Stoesz, 2010).

   Critical Thinking Questions 6.1

Do you feel that children and families living in poverty should be supported by the government? If so, to what extent and under what circumstances? If not, why not?

Critical Thinking Questions 6.2

Should time limits be imposed upon how long a recipient can receive assistance? If so, what should they be?

Time Limits   TANF also establishes time limits for receipt of benefits (ACF, 2008b). Clients must find work within two years of beginning the program (or less if the state so chooses) and can receive no more than five years of benefits in their lifetime. Beyond five years, states may opt to extend assistance to no more than 20 percent of their caseload, or they may continue funding recipients through state funds alone. This is a huge change from AFDC, through which "people received assistance as long as they satisfied the program's eligibility rules, which were set by the individual states under federal guidelines" (Abramovitz, 1997, p. 312). "Seventeen states or jurisdictions have TANF time limits of less than five years," but nine other states have continued providing benefits funded solely by the state after the five years were up (DiNitto, 2007, p. 238). A concern is that agencies may have to turn away people in desperate need because these people have depleted their time allocation. What happens when time limits run out?

Work Requirements   According to the Center on Budget and Policy Priorities (CBPP) (2006):

> Under the DRA, states must have 50 percent of all adults receiving TANF assistance— and 90 percent of two parent households receiving assistance—in a set of work activities defined in the law. The work requirements are lower for states that reduce their TANF caseloads below 2005 levels, but few states are likely to accomplish this unless they choose to restrict poor families' access to assistance, given that caseloads already are at historic lows.

States face financial penalties if they don't comply. It is questionable regarding how many states will be able to meet the standard that requires work participation in 90 percent of two-parent households.

Child Care   TANF maintains strict work requirements to make people eligible for financial assistance compared to AFDC. "Single parents are required to work 20 to 30 hours per week, depending on the age of their child, and two-parent families must work 35–55 hours (combined) per week" (Berrick, 2009, p. 34; CBPP, 2007). Questions concern how parents will cope with child care needs, work stress, homemaking responsibilities, and parenting.

 Critical Thinking Questions 6.3

Should public assistance recipients be required to work? If so, what do you think this requirement should be?

Critical Thinking Questions 6.4

Who will provide all the additional child care services for newly working mothers?

Will funding be adequate in view of the huge potential influx of children requiring care?

What if no adequate day care is available?

Will centers accept infants or toddlers who are not yet toilet-trained, children many current child care facilities reject?

How will these services be monitored for adequacy, safety, and quality?

How will parents adjust to separation from their children?

How will children be affected by limited access to their single parent?

How does this policy affect children's welfare?

TANF will not allow mothers with children age six or older to cite lack of adequate child care as their rationale for not working outside the home (Karger & Stoesz, 2010; Marx, 2004). Although states are not required to provide child care for working parents as AFDC did, states are allowed to transfer up to 30 percent of TANF funds for its provision; $2.6 billion was spent on child care in 1999, but this decreased to only $1.9 billion in 2002 (DiNitto, 2007, p. 243). Slashing child care expenditures has been connected to economic declines and resulting state budget deficits (DiNitto, 2007). When states need money to provide cash assistance and health care to recipients, child care may get a much lower priority.

The DRA reauthorized the child care program with few changes and marginal funding increases; child care funding was increased less than 5 percent in 2006 and had no increases planned from 2007 to 2010 (CWLA, 2006).

Education and Training for Better Jobs States spend comparatively small amounts on providing education and training for participants. According to DiNitto (2007), less than 2 percent ($462 million) of the total TANF budget was used to enhance skills in 2002, and similar amounts ($584 million) were spent on transportation and supportive services (p. 243). How can former TANF recipients seek better jobs and experience upward mobility with little or no education and training? In contrast, pregnancy prevention programs received over a sevenfold increase from 1999 to 2002, resulting in 2.6 percent of total TANF funding (DiNitto, 2007, p. 243).

Critical Thinking Questions 6.5

To what extent should the public pay for education and training for public assistance recipients?

Job Quality and Availability   Hagen and Lawrence (2008) summarize the plight of people after TANF. Only one-third of people leaving TANF rolls work the entire subsequent year, although about 75 percent work at some time during that year. They tend to earn low incomes, live near the poverty line, and frequently suffer serious food and housing shortages. Often obstacles to employment include problems that are difficult to solve, such as low educational levels, little work experience and training, and serious health conditions.

Gilbert and Terrell (2010) suggest that:

> A portion of those transitioning from welfare to work . . . simply trade public assistance for low-wage, dead-end jobs. Many of the jobs secured by ex-welfare clients, roughly a third are part time. And many of the available full-time jobs—clerks, cooks, fast-food, telephone sales reps, and the like—pay the minimum wage, or just above, and provide few benefits. . . . New workers, in addition, are often burdened by significant job-related expenses for transportation, daycare, clothing, and meals. . . . [M]any remain close to destitution, churning through an uncertain job market, struggling with the routine hardships of utility and car insurance bills, rent, daycare, and the cost of family meals. (pp. 260–261)

Realistically, how good is the potential for upward mobility offered by most low-paying jobs? Also, as the economy slows as it has in recent years, how much more difficult is it to find jobs while competing with qualified workers who have been laid off? Research shows that the sluggish economy between 1999 and 2002 resulted in former TANF recipients finding it increasingly difficult to find employment; many were likely to return to TANF—that is, if they hadn't already exceeded TANF's time limits (Loprest, 2003).

Health Insurance after TANF   Only a third of employed former TANF recipients work in jobs providing health insurance benefits (Hagen & Lawrence, 2008). We've established that this is due to getting low-paying or minimum-wage jobs that have poor or no benefits. After leaving TANF, families can continue receiving Medicaid for twelve months if their income does not surpass 185 percent of the poverty line (DiNitto, 2007, p. 235). For many families, what happens after that? To what extent does TANF force single mothers to deprive themselves of future health care by accepting low-paying jobs without benefits—the only jobs they can get?

Note that at the time of this writing, the provision of national health care for all is under heated debate. It is unclear what access to health care might be available for former TANF recipients in the future.

 Critical Thinking Questions 6.6

What could be done to improve the quality of jobs for public assistance recipients?

Critical Thinking Questions 6.7

Should health insurance be made available to all citizens like it is in many other industrialized countries? If so, how should it be paid for?

Encouraging "Healthy Marriages"   TANF's stated goals are as follows:

1. Assisting needy families so that children can be cared for in their own homes
2. Reducing the dependency of needy parents on government benefits by promoting job preparation, work, and marriage
3. Preventing incidence of out-of-wedlock pregnancies
4. Encouraging the formation and maintenance of two-parent families (ACF, 2008a).

Three of these goals relate directly to the support of "healthy marriages" (ACF, 2006). The initiative designed by President George W. Bush and administered by the Administration for Children and Families provides funding for "marriage education services" to married couples and initiatives to promote "responsible fatherhood" (ACF, 2006).

Equitability among States   TANF "eliminated the federal income test that previously determined eligibility for AFDC" (Abramovitz, 1997, p. 312). Instead, TANF permits states to establish their own eligibility rules. However, with budget pressures, states could establish eligibility levels so low that only the very poorest of the poor would receive benefits. Additionally, benefit levels vary appreciably from state to state, which raises questions regarding the program's fairness (DiNitto, 2007; Karger & Stoesz, 2010). "For example, the maximum monthly benefit may be $691 in New York, $625 in New Hampshire, and $640 in Vermont, but it is just $215 in Alabama, $204 in Arizona, and $170 in Mississippi" (Karger & Stoesz, 2010, p. 279).

In contrast to AFDC, TANF limited the amount of federal funding given to states and allowed states greater discretion in benefit distribution. Gilbert and Terrell (2010) explain:

> Under AFDC, welfare, by and large, *was* the monthly cash benefit. But under TANF, states employ their spending for a multitude of antipoverty purposes—many not targeted specifically on welfare recipients at all. Some states, for example, have invested in wage supplements through a state version of the Earned Income Tax Credit,[4] in order

---

[4] *The Earned Income Tax Credit (EITC)* provides "a refundable tax credit to 'families whose incomes fall below the federal poverty line even though they are supported by full-time workers' (Jouzaitis, 1993, p. 17). Although this tax credit is modest and did not significantly reduce poverty, it established the principle of using the tax system, administered through the Internal Revenue Service, to provide resources to low-income citizens. This approach, similar to . . . other welfare programs for wealthy and middle-class families, reduces the stigma of assistance and helps people realize that the tax system is a method for providing welfare and that most people are likely welfare recipients themselves" (Chapin, 2007, pp. 66–67). Essentially, for families with incomes under about $43,000, "when the value of the credit exceeds the amount of income taxes owed, the worker receives a cash rebate" (Gilbert & Terrell, 2010, p. 95).

Critical Thinking Questions 6.8

To what extent does the government have the right to try to coerce people into marriage? Explain your answer.

Critical Thinking Questions 6.9

To what extent should benefits provided to public assistance recipients be equal in all the states?

to increase salaries for low-wage earners. Others, such as New York, have created public jobs. Still others have expanded day care, transportation, counseling, and job training. (p. 252)

What Is the Answer?   We have touched upon only a few of the many issues involved in TANF. Legislation governs programs and service provision in the macro social environment. The following are suggestions to consider when making future legislative decisions:

1. Provide adequate funding and build in adjustments for inflation in future years.
2. Reduce current weekly work requirements.
3. "Require states to emphasize education and job training" that can lead to career advancement and better occupational opportunities.
4. Increase the opportunities that can be involved in "work" to include "participation in an education program" leading to a degree or involvement in vocational or technical training so that recipients have access to a better, more productive future.
5. Eliminate time limits or make them more flexible so that recipients can actually have enough time to become educated and develop career skills.
6. Abolish "marriage promotion" pressures that have "not been proven to be an effective measure in reducing poverty and enabling welfare recipients to become economically self-sufficient."
7. "Increase child care funding" to support working parents and their children. (Women Work!, 2006)

Critical Thinking Questions 6.10

How would you restructure the public assistance system if you had the power? What are your values concerning what's important?

Managed Care Reflects Social and Economic Forces

Another major social and economic force that affects many agencies' service provision is managed care. The concept serves as an umbrella for many different types of health agencies and health care services. *Managed care* is "any medical insurance plan that controls costs through monitoring and controlling the decision of health care providers" (Mooney, Knox, & Schacht 2009, p. 55). These include decisions "about medical procedures, diagnostic tests, and other services that should be provided to patients" (Kendall, 2007, p. 233). Kornblum and Julian (2007) explain that managed care involves

> a wide range of health plans and practices that depart from the traditional model of private health insurance provided by one's employer. In the traditional model, insured patients chose their physician; physicians treated patients with absolute clinical autonomy; insurers generally paid physicians whatever they billed on a fee-for-service basis; and employers paid premiums for their workers to private insurers, regardless of the cost. Managed care has altered all these arrangements by setting limits on individual medical visits or treatments—that is, by managing care. (p. 60)

Managed care has become an integral part of social work practice in numerous fields, including health care, mental health, work with older adults, public assistance, and child welfare (Corcoran, 1997). All people, including all clients, need health care to one extent or another. Gilbert and Terrell (2010) explain the significance of managed care:

> Managed care is basically a form of human services organization . . . that has become institutionalized in the health care economy, where about two thirds of Americans are now enrolled in networks of health care providers that contract with managed care organizations and abide by managed care rules. These rules have created an apparatus of incentives, procedures, and structures that revolutionized the nature of American health care, fundamentally altering relationships among doctors, hospitals, drug and insurance companies, and employers, and putting cost considerations front and center in the decision-making process. (pp. 184–185)

Managed care involves health insurance companies, hospitals, networks of physicians and other treatment providers, and *health maintenance organizations (HMOs)*. HMOs (one type of managed care that is quite common) "are prepaid group plans in which a person pays a monthly premium for comprehensive health care services. HMOs attempt to minimize hospitalization costs by emphasizing preventive health care. *Preferred provider organizations (PPOs)* are health care organizations in which employers who purchase group health insurance agree to send their employees to certain health care providers or hospitals in return for cost discounts. In this arrangement health care providers obtain more patients but charge lower fees to buyers of group insurance" (Mooney et al., 2009, p. 55).

Managed care fundamentally altered traditional relationships between clients and social work practitioners. Historically, social workers in agency settings established treatment plans (that could address health and mental health concerns) in conjunction with clients, in addition to stressing informed consent and confidentiality to comply with ethical standards. Managed care takes these decisions out of workers' and clients' hands and puts them into the hands of removed third-party decision makers. A managed care representative, often a utilization reviewer or case manager, then reviews documentation and regulates "the services that clients receive, especially what specific services will be provided and at what cost" (Corcoran, 1997, p. 194). To some, managed care "represents the complete (and seemingly sudden) triumph of financial management concerns over virtually all other professional considerations" (Lohmann, 1997, p. 202).

Two primary principles promoted by managed care are *retention of quality and access* while *controlling cost*. That is, health and mental health services should be of high quality and readily accessible to clients, on the one hand. Yet, they should be very cost effective, on the other.

Managed Care's Means of Controlling Costs   Managed care employs several approaches to control costs. One method is the practice of *capitation*, "the provision of fixed payments made on a per-member per-month basis regardless of the use of services. In other words, the physician receives a fixed amount of money each month for every member of the [managed care plan]. . . . Whether the member seeks care every day or never seeks care at all, the amount of money that the physician receives does not vary" (Kongstvedt, 2009, p. 69).

A second approach to controlling costs involves *gatekeeping*, the required authorization by a designated primary care physician to make all decisions about "prescriptions, referrals to specialists, or hospital care" (Gilbert & Terrell, 2010, p. 185). This prevents patients from seeking out alternative care and care providers on their own.

A third cost-preventive mechanism is *utilization management*, where a health provider "often must apply to a utilization manager for approval to initiate a particular treatment regimen. This oversight by external cost-oriented monitors diminishes the degree of autonomy exercised by professionals and may also erode the professional's ability to maintain client confidentiality"; the managed care staff often have access to all of a patient's health information (even that not clearly related to the treatment request) in order to make a determination about treatment provision (Gilbert & Terrell, 2010, p. 185).

The Pros and Cons of Managed Care   Those supporting managed care state that it has decreased the cost of health care and emphasizes the importance of prevention (DiNitto, 2007; Karger & Stoesz, 2010). However, the research has been mixed regarding whether it really is less expensive and more efficient than traditional fee-for-service health insurance (Kornblum & Julian, 2007; Vandiver, 2008).

Physicians indicate that the quality of health care has decreased since the advent of managed care due to "limitations on diagnostic tests, length of hospital stay, and choice of specialists" (DiNitto, 2007; Karger & Stoesz, 2010; Mooney et al., 2007, p. 57). Karger and Stoesz (2010) explain further:

> Managed care plans generally gate-keep the access to specialists for consumers. These plans do this by pressuring primary physicians not to refer or by limiting specialist care to one or two visits. Some managed care plans are reluctant to cover costly procedures or experimental treatments, especially those relating to cancer. Still other plans refuse to pay for medical care clients receive while out of state, even if it was required in an

Focus on Ethics 6.1 | ## Ethical Issues in Managed Care

Generalist practitioners must work within social service agencies that employ them. They are supposed to follow agency and other regulatory policy. However, they are also responsible for maintaining ethical practices and making certain clients' needs are met. Several ethical issues may be raised concerning managed care and how it affects agency service provision.

The first involves the potential conflict between "the gatekeeping role of some managed care organizations and client self-determination" (Corcoran, 1997, p. 196). When subject to managed care, clients no longer have the right to choose their service provider. Rather, the managed-care utilization reviewer makes this determination. Redmond (2002) reflects how "hospital social workers face serious ethical dilemmas when patients are forced out of the hospital before they or their families are ready or when resources have not been put into the home" (p. 23).

Similarly, managed care may conflict with the ethical principle of informed consent. Corcoran (1997) remarks:

Informed consent requires that the client know in advance the clinical procedures, the risk of those procedures, and the available alternative procedures. Managed care may destroy informed consent by restricting the available procedures to a limited number. For example, a managed care company may determine the preferred practice and the preferred providers, with little consideration or disclosure of alternative procedures. (p. 196)

Managed care also has the potential to violate client confidentiality (Corcoran, 1997). Social workers are bound by the code of ethics, which emphasizes how "social workers should respect clients' right to privacy" and "should not solicit private information from clients unless it is essential to providing services" (NASW, 2008, 1.07a). If a managed care organization demands information before providing services, what should the worker do? What if the worker does not agree with the organization's demand for information and feels the regulations violate clients' rights to privacy? Workers may be required to report confidential information, whether they feel it's ethical or not.

emergency. Other enrollees complain that managed care forces them to use only primary care physicians, hospitals, and specialists that are on an approved list, which restricts their freedom of choice. . . . Critics also note that the size of managed care operations has led to greater bureaucratization and impersonality. (p. 320)

Focus on Ethics 6.1 discusses some ethical issues in managed care.

The Future of Managed Care: Advocacy for Patients' Rights No one knows what the future of managed care will be (Vandiver, 2008). However, "both physicians and patients have come to believe that managed care is leading to a reduction in the quality of health care" (Kornblum & Julian, 2007, p. 61).

Consumer groups are pursuing legislation to address such issues as lack of provider choice and managed care organizations' denial of treatment options (Vandiver, 2008). Social workers can actively advocate for improvements (Galambros, 2008). They can help clients understand health care provision processes. They can help clients fight to get the treatment they need. They can join health organization advisory boards to provide input into organizational policy (Vandiver, 2008). They can pressure legislators for positive change.

At least five specific provisions could improve legislation to protect clients and their rights ("Managed Care," 1998):

- Guarantee patients the right to choose a doctor outside their health plans' networks if they agree to share the cost of services.
- Ensure patients access to detailed information about coverage, treatment options [Vandiver, 2008].
- Require companies to cover emergency care without prior authorization.
- Make health plans comply with state and federal laws that protect the confidentiality of . . . health information.
- Require companies to set up procedures under which providers could appeal denials of coverage [Chapin, 2007]. (p. 1)

Chapin (2007) adds that "statements of patient rights need to be developed and enforced. For example, some states have passed laws that prohibit gag clauses in [managed care] . . . contracts with health care providers. Gag clauses prohibit physicians from telling patients about expensive or alternative options not covered" by the managed care organization (p. 277).

Problems with Access to Adequate Health Care   Regardless of what happens in the managed care arena, health care generally in the United States remains a major concern (Karger & Stoesz, 2010; Mizrahi & Gorin, 2008; Mooney et al., 2009). Millions of people have no health insurance (Kendall, 2007). Additionally, many Americans are underinsured (Karger & Stoesz, 2010; Kendall, 2007). This includes having exceedingly high deductibles; paying high co-payments on drugs and treatments; having strict limits on hospital stays; being excluded from certain drugs, tests, and treatments; and having no benefits for vision or dental care (Karger & Stoesz, 2010).

Additionally, disparities exist among population subgroups. People with lower income levels and minorities, especially Hispanics, have less access to health care, and the services they receive are often of lower quality (Kendall, 2007; Galambros, 2008).

The United States spends a higher proportion of its gross national product (Galambros, 2008) and more than twice as much per person on health care than any other industrialized nation (Mooney et al., 2009). Yet, so many citizens live with no or inadequate health care.

Congress continues to debate potential solutions to this health care crisis (Galambros, 2008). Some type of national or universal health care coverage that would be available to all, or at least most, has been discussed for decades. Various

Critical Thinking Questions 6.11

How would you structure the managed care system if you had the power to do so?

Focus on Ethics 6.2	The Need for National Health Care Coverage

What is your opinion about the provision of national health care coverage? Is it the nation's ethical responsibility to provide adequate coverage for all its citizens? Why or why not? If it should be provided, who should pay for it?

specific proposals to provide better coverage have surfaced, but to date no political consensus has emerged (Mizrahi & Gorin, 2008). Focus on Ethics 6.2 addresses your opinion on the matter.

Chapter Summary

The following summarizes this chapter's content as it relates to the learning objectives presented at the beginning of the chapter. Objectives include the following:

A. Examine primary and secondary agency settings.

Primary settings are those agencies where social work is the main or primary profession. Secondary settings are characterized by the presence of a variety of professional staff.

B. Define and discuss organizational mission statements, goals, and objectives for achieving goals.

An organizational mission statement is a declaration of the organization's purpose that "establishes broad and relatively permanent parameters within which goals are developed and specific programs designed" (Kettner et al., 2008, p. 121). Organizational "goals are statements of expected outcomes dealing with the problem that the program is attempting to prevent, eradicate, or ameliorate" (Kettner et al., 2008, p. 123). Social service organizations are usually complex with multiple goals. Objectives are smaller, behaviorally specific subgoals that serve as stepping stones on the way to accomplishing the main goal.

C. Describe faith-based services.

Faith-based social service organizations are agencies sponsored by or affiliated with a religious or spiritual organization. To varying degrees, faith-based social services often incorporate aspects of spirituality or religion into their mission statement and goals.

D. Discuss goal displacement.

Goal displacement is the "substitution of a legitimate goal with another goal which the organization was not developed to address, for which resources were not allocated and which it is not known to serve" (Etzioni, 1964, p. 10). A typical scenario in social services is when the rules and following those rules become more important than providing services to clients. Ecosystems concepts can be applied both to social service and business organizations.

E. Explore the external macro environment of social service organizations, including resources, legitimation, client sources, and relationships with other organizations.

Social service organizations must have access to adequate resources in order to function. Legitimation is the condition where the external environment provides an agency with the appropriate status or authorization to perform agency functions and pursue agency goals. A range of client resources is necessary to provide enough clients to keep the agency financially afloat. Social service organizations experience uninvolved, complementary, or competitive relationships with other organizations in the macro social environment.

F. Examine the impact of social and economic forces on social service organizations.

Social service organizations function within the larger macro environment and must respond to shifting social and economic forces. Resources and funding may be limited. Policies and regulations determine what agencies can do. Social service organizations may be pressured to conform to public expectations.

G. Provide case examples concerning working in a secondary setting, goal displacement, personnel resources, and competitive relationships among organizations.

A case example of working in a secondary setting concerned a social work practitioner working in a hospital setting. An example of goal displacement involved the situation where the process of providing services had become more important than helping clients in the context of a large public welfare department. An example of conflict over personnel resources involved social work educators working to establish the credibility of formal education in social work. A competitive relationship example concerned public and private agencies competing to provide services to adolescents with behavioral and emotional problems.

H. Examine how federal social legislation, Temporary Assistance to Needy Families (TANF), and managed care impact agency service provision.

TANF replaced Aid to Families with Dependent Children (AFDC) as one primary means of reducing poverty. Major issues include adequacy of funding, time limits, provision of child care, education and training for better jobs, job quality and availability, health insurance after TANF, encouragement of marriage, and equitability of benefits among states.

Managed care is "any medical insurance plan that controls costs through monitoring and controlling the decision of health care providers" (Mooney et al., 2009, p. 55). Managed care has become an integral part of social work practice in many fields. Managed care organizations attempt to retain quality by controlling costs. Means of controlling costs include capitation, gatekeeping, and utilization management. Physicians and patients generally feel health care has declined since the advent of managed care. The future of managed care is uncertain. Social workers can actively advocate for improvements. The problem of access to adequate health care is a major problem in the United States, especially for people with low incomes and minorities. Congress continues to debate potential solutions, with no consensus as of yet.

I. Focus on ethical issues in managed care and national health care coverage.

Ethical issues in managed care include the potential clash between gatekeeping, on the one hand, and client self-determination, informed consent, and client confidentiality on the other. The question regarding the ethical responsibility of the federal government to provide universal health care was raised.

J. Raise various critical thinking questions.

Critical thinking questions focused on various aspects of TANF (including public support, time limits, work requirements, working mothers, education and training, job quality, encouraging marriage, equitability among states, and restructuring the public assistance system) and managed care.

Looking Ahead

This chapter addressed social service organizational settings, goals, and contexts in the macro social environment. The next chapter will explore organizational structure and dynamics.

For Further Exploration on the Internet

See this text's website at **www.cengage.com/ social_work/kirst-ashman** for learning tools such as tutorial quizzing, Web links, glossary, flashcards, and PowerPoint® slides.

7 CHAPTER | Organizational Structure and Dynamics

Interpersonal communication and dynamics characterize organizations.

CHAPTER CONTENTS

"I just can't tolerate Mr. Biff," Brunhilda proclaims to Stanwood, one of her social work colleagues in a large private social services organization providing numerous services, including counseling, substance abuse programs, vocational training, and community-based facilities, for people with developmental disabilities. Mr. Biff, whose real name is Bufford Bifford, is the manager of the agency's accounting department. Mr. Biff is very impressed with his own accomplishments, but unfortunately has extremely poor social interaction skills. With a superior demeanor, he typically commands Brunhilda and other social workers to scurry about and do his bidding when he determines that some billing matter needs immediate attention. He expects workers to drop everything else they're doing and obey his command on the double.

Stanwood tries to soothe Brunhilda's ruffled feathers. "After all," he stresses, "Mr. Biff is not our immediate supervisor." Social workers must maintain positive working relationships with other agency staff, including Mr. Biff, because financial accountability is so important. However, other staff like Mr. Biff have little direct power over what social workers in the agency can, cannot, will, or will not do. Social workers must work directly with their own supervisor to develop appropriate treatment and referral plans and respond to agency needs. Stanwood urges Brunhilda to "be cool." He adds, "Our own supervisor is a pretty good egg. The bottom line is you don't have to obey Mr. Biff. You could just choose to smile, nod, and ignore him. You know, there are no jerk-free work environments."

This vignette does not imply that all organizational environments have Mr. Biffs, although many probably do. However, it focuses on the importance of agency expectations, structure, and interpersonal dynamics when you're trying to get your job done. Depending upon your agency environment, you can feel supported and energized or angry and thwarted.

Chapter 5 defined *management* as "the attainment of organizational goals in an effective and efficient manner through planning, organizing, leading, and controlling organizational resources" (Daft, 2010, p. 5). Simply put, management is "the art of getting things accomplished in organizations through others" (Johns, 1996, p. 10). Managers in organizations accomplish this by setting goals for the entire organization or agency units, acquiring and allocating resources, coordinating employees' work, monitoring progress, and improving efficiency and effectiveness where possible (Daft, 2010; Daft & Marcic, 2009). This says *what* management does, but it doesn't say *how* managers do it. This is where management style comes in. Equifinality applies here in that there are many ways to manage an organization.

Ginsberg (1995) maintains "that strict adherence to a hierarchy often is dysfunctional, and the bureaucratic element of organizations can be harmful" (p. 15). However, he continues that "the principle of maintaining some unity of command is important, and failure to maintain a division of labor can lead to conflict and to some functions not being performed. The need for an organizational structure that separates tasks and maintains distinct responsibilities is probably as important as it always was" (p. 15).

Thus, elements of organizational structure are necessary to hold an agency together regardless of variations in management style, that is, how staff and clients

are viewed and services provided. This chapter investigates organizational culture, structure, and interpersonal dynamics. Chapter 8 will further explore management approaches and means of empowering staff.

Learning Objectives

A. Describe organizational culture and structure, and discuss how lines of authority and channels of communication are involved.
B. Discuss supervision and consultation in organizational settings.
C. Discuss centralized versus decentralized organizations.
D. Examine interpersonal communication within social service agencies.
E. Describe the perceptual process during communication.
F. Identify interpersonal barriers to communication.
G. Describe the importance of power in organizations and identify its various types.
H. Explain organizational politics and their dynamics.
I. Suggest tactics for using agency politics for positive change.
J. Focus on ethical issues concerning the use of distortion, enhancement of ethical communication, political behavior, and problematic unethical behavior.
K. Raise various critical thinking questions.

Organizational Culture

Organizational culture is "the set of key values, beliefs, understandings, and norms shared by members of an organization. . . . Culture is a pattern of shared values and assumptions about how things are done within the organization. Members learn this pattern as they cope with external and internal problems and teach it to new members as the correct way to perceive, think, and feel" (Daft & Marcic, 2009, p. 63). Many aspects of culture entail unwritten rules, traditions, and practices that hold the organization together (Hellriegel & Slocum, 2009). Organizational culture can include expectations for level of performance, interpersonal communication and interaction, management style, and appropriate dress.

Organizational culture, then, involves many facets. For example, what kind of attire is expected and considered appropriate within the organization's cultural environment—suits or jeans? A hospital social worker might choose to dress more formally because the environment is full of uniformed professionals. Contrasting informal dress might appear "unprofessional." A residential treatment center for males with behavioral disorders, on the other hand, might manifest a very informal organizational culture, at least concerning dress. The latter culture expects social workers and counselors to participate in a range of activities, including informal group sessions in the living units, recreational activities, and administration of consequences for poor behavior. It makes sense to dress comfortably and informally in such an environment.

Another facet of organizational culture is the agency's "personality." Each agency has its own personality. That is, it is more formal or informal, structured or unstructured, innovative or traditional than other agencies. From the first day of work within an agency, it is important to explore and begin understanding that agency's character. What tasks are considered the most important (for example, documentation of treatment effectiveness, other record keeping, administrative conferences, or number of hours spent with clients)? How much freedom do workers have in conducting daily professional activities? Daft and Marcic (2009) comment:

> In some organizations, a basic assumption might be that people are essentially lazy and will shirk their duties whenever possible; thus, employees are closely supervised and given little freedom, and colleagues frequently are suspicious of one another. More enlightened organizations operate on the basic assumption that people want to do a good job. In these organizations, employees are given more freedom and responsibility and colleagues trust one another and work cooperatively. (pp. 63–64)

Organizational culture is a common concept addressed in studying organizations, regardless of the theoretical perspective assumed. The cultural theoretical perspective on organizations discussed in Chapter 5, of course, emphasizes culture as the primary dimension for understanding organizational functioning. Other theories give the concept of culture less emphasis in relationship to the numerous other dimensions involved in organizations.

Organizational Structure

Organizational structure is "the system of task, reporting, and authority relationships within which the work of the organization is done" (Griffin & Moorhead, 2010, p. 407). All large agencies (and many smaller ones, as well) have a *formal* structure specifying how management thinks the organization should be run (Jaskyte, 2008). Most often formal structure is explicated in an organizational chart showing who reports to whom (Griffin & Moorhead, 2010; Hodge, Anthony, & Gates, 2003). Such charts depict designated lines of authority and communication within the agency. A later section of this chapter will discuss organizational charts more thoroughly. Frequently, the agency operates in accordance with this chart, at least with respect to some functions, such as how information is disseminated, either from the top down or bottom up. For example, a social work supervisor might be expected to give appropriate information directly to supervisees. Likewise, those supervisees might expect the supervisor to convey their concerns up the administrative ladder. Highlight 7.1 discusses an important dimension of agency structure—the degree to which the organization is centralized or decentralized.

Agencies also develop *informal* structures and lines of communication. For example, it is typical for an agency to structure its units so that all workers in the unit report to one supervisor. Consider the case of the Humdrum County Foster Care Unit. Five workers and a supervisor comprise this unit. When workers have questions or problems, they are supposed to bring these to Henry, the Foster Care Unit Supervisor. Often, however, Henry's supervisees discuss their cases with other workers in the unit or with Tiffany, the senior worker in the agency's Adoptions Unit. This means that the Foster Care Unit Supervisor is deprived of information that might be important to doing his job.

While superficially confiding in Tiffany may seem like a bad arrangement, it has some beneficial aspects. Workers who are sometimes uncomfortable talking

| **Highlight 7.1** | **Centralized versus Decentralized Organizations** |

One other aspect of agency structure merits brief commentary. A continuum can depict organizations and their degree of centralization. On one far side are extremely centralized organizations. These organizations resemble those run according to classical scientific management theories. Their lines of authority are clearly established. There is a strict hierarchy designating who has power over whom. The units in centralized organizations are clearly defined and cleanly separated. Workers have little discretion to make their own decisions. Responsibilities are defined and overseen from above.

A probation and parole department provides an example of centralization. Clients assigned to workers in a designated unit reflect very similar characteristics. Procedures and treatment plans are relatively uniform in approach. Clients and workers must abide by clearly defined rules and regulations. Little worker discretion is possible.

On the opposite side of the centralization continuum are extremely decentralized organizations, contrasting sharply with centralized organizations in flexibility. Decentralized organizations provide and encourage broad worker discretion. They likely serve a wide variety of clients with vastly different problems, issues, and backgrounds. Workers in such organizations need discretion to make plans for viable solutions. For example, extreme decentralization might characterize a community crisis-intervention organization. Clients coming in for help might have problems ranging from depression to illness to job loss to executive-level stress. Workers need a broad range of discretion to address a wide variety of problems.

with their supervisor can get help from other more experienced workers. Maybe Henry is not competent to provide answers or is too lazy or busy to take the time. Tiffany might be an extremely knowledgeable, pleasant person who likes to help her colleagues. Sharing ideas and problems helps to produce a camaraderie among the workers. This decreases their stress levels and often leads to better job performance. Human relations theories stress the importance of such interpersonal communication and support in organizations.

The point here is not to praise or criticize the existence of informal structures and communication channels. Instead, it is to acknowledge that they do exist and are a reality with which practitioners must deal within a social service agency's context. In practice, being aware of both formal and informal avenues within an agency strengthens social workers' ability to do their job. Once practitioners know the options and alternatives, they can make more informed choices. This is, after all, a major goal of the intervention process.

Three concepts are especially significant when appraising an agency's formal and informal structures. These are *lines of authority, channels of communication,* and *dimensions of power.*

Lines of Authority

All large agencies (and many smaller ones) have a formal structure. An agency's formal structure involves *lines of authority* (Daft, 2007; Griffins & Moorhead 2010). For our purposes, authority concerns the specific administrative and supervisory responsibilities of supervisors involving their supervisees. Authority entails who is designated to supervise whom. Agency policy usually specifies in writing these lines of authority.

We have established that often an agency's formal structure is explained in an organizational chart. Job positions held by individual staff members are portrayed by squares or circles that are labeled according to their respective job positions. A formal hierarchy of authority in an organizational chart is depicted by vertical lines leading from supervisors down to supervisees (Griffin & Moorhead, 2010; Jansson, 2008). Generally, job positions higher on the chart have greater authority than those placed lower on the chart. Lines drawn from higher figures to lower figures identify the supervisors of staff holding job positions located lower on the chart and having less responsibility and power. In essence, these lines represent "who oversees and assumes direct responsibility for the specified employees directly below them. The formal organizational structure as demonstrated by an organizational chart, then, dictates how control and supervision are supposed to flow.

Highlight 7.2 discusses the significance of supervision in social services agencies and how in many ways it is similar to supervision in any other organizational setting. It also defines *consultation*, describes how it differs from supervision, and explains its potential benefits.

Highlight 7.2 | **Supervision and Consultation in Organizational Settings**

This book stresses the importance of interpersonal dynamics and relationships in the macro social environment. In the organizational context, social workers practice under supervision. *Supervision* is the process by which a designated supervisor watches over and evaluates a worker's performance, directs and coordinates activities, and provides feedback. The ultimate goal of supervision is to maximize performance and make certain that activities are conducted and services are delivered effectively and efficiently. A good supervisor can be invaluable in helping practitioners get their work done successfully in agency settings.

You've most likely worked in some kind of job or, perhaps, many jobs, although such jobs were not necessarily in social services. Regardless of what type of job you held, you had a supervisor to oversee your work. The skills used and responsibilities assumed in different jobs obviously vary widely. However, many aspects of the interpersonal relationship between an employee and a supervisor are the same regardless of job setting. You may have had what you considered a good supervisor or a bad supervisor. Such experiences provide you with insight for understanding the importance of supervision in any work environment, including social services settings. Working under and with supervisors is an important facet of the organizational macro social environment.

Effective supervisors manifest a range of qualities (Kirst-Ashman & Hull, 2009a). First, they are competent in that they understand your job and generally know what they're doing. Second, they provide help and support when you need it. Third, they supply a communication link between you and higher levels of administration and management. This allows you to find out what's going on in the organization and, in turn, provides a means for administrators to learn about your concerns. Fourth, effective supervisors facilitate cooperation among you and other workers (e.g., addressing and resolving disputes and conflicts). Fifth, they evaluate your job performance fairly. Ideally, on the one hand, this should help improve your performance in areas where you are weak. On the other hand, it should provide a means for you to get credit when you've done a good job. Sixth, supervisors

should help you develop new skills and enhance your effectiveness. For example, an effective supervisor might teach you new skills directly or provide training opportunities for you.

There are also many reasons why supervisors are ineffective (Kirst-Ashman & Hull, 2009a). They may have gotten the job for whatever reason, despite the fact that they are not competent to do it. Thus, they're incapable of providing you with the help you need. Sometimes, supervisors take credit for their employees' work, which of course causes resentment on the employees' part. Some supervisors don't like to work very hard. You may feel that they're not doing their job the way they should. A supervisor may dislike conflict and shy away from it. Such a supervisor may provide no help in resolving interpersonal disputes among staff. Finally, supervisors may have difficulty delegating work to supervisees. They may not trust in your competence to do a good job. They may monitor your work too closely and "breathe down your neck" at every opportunity.

The supervisory relationship represents one significant aspect of generalist practice in organizational macro environments. Another important concept is consultation, described next.

Consultation in Organizational Settings

Consultation is the process of seeking out and receiving expert help from an individual, group, or organization in order to resolve an identified problem or address a designated issue. Supervision also should provide skilled assistance in order to improve job functioning. However, our definition of *consultation* differs from that of *supervision* in two ways (Barker, 2003). First, supervision is an ongoing process inherent in an organization's structure that addresses supervisees' overall work performance and many specific practice matters. Second, consultation is sought outside of ongoing administrative relationships to address a designated, explicit problem or issue. A consultant has no administrative power over the recipient of consultation. The recipient can choose to use the consultant's input and suggestions or not.

Consultation can be useful when an individual, group, organization, or even a community is

Critical Thinking Questions 7.1

Supervision is an important aspect of working in an organizational context, whether it is a social services agency, business, or any other organization. What types of jobs have you held? In what types of organizations (e.g., businesses) have you worked? What were your supervisors like? One by one, picture each supervisor in your mind. Evaluate each according to the following variables and explain your reasons; to what extent was this specific supervisor:

- Competent?
- Capable of providing you with help when you needed it?
- Supportive of your work?
- A good communication link between you and upper levels of management or administration?
- A good facilitator of cooperation among you and other staff?
- Effective at resolving intra-staff conflicts?
- A fair and reasonable evaluator of your job performance?
- Effective at providing you with positive feedback about good performance?
- Helpful in terms of facilitating the development of new skills?

addressing a problem that is beyond its ability to solve. Additional expertise and solutions are sought, often at some financial cost.

For example, social work programs seeking accreditation often hire an expert consultant from an outside source to help them through the complex accreditation process. (*Accreditation* is an official body's formal recognition that some organization has met all the standards required by the accrediting body.) Accredited social work programs must provide evidence that their students have mastered various competencies necessary for social work practice (e.g., application of critical thinking skills and ethical principles), and that the learning environment satisfies established standards (e.g., the program has appropriate admissions procedures for students, faculty assignments, and resources) (CSWE, 2008).

A Case Example: The Idle Ness Center

The chart in Figure 7.1 reflects the hierarchy of authority for the Idle Ness Center for Diagnosis and Treatment, an agency providing assessment and therapeutic treatment to children with multiple developmental and physical disabilities. Parents bring children with a wide range of physical and behavioral difficulties to the agency to assess the children's abilities in a variety of areas, plan treatment programs, and provide the appropriate therapies.

Rectangles in Figure 7.1 designate those job positions having some degree of administrative responsibility within the agency system. The bolder the rectangle, the more authority and responsibility the position entails.

The Executive Director has the most authority and is responsible for the overall performance of the Idle Ness Center. Below him are five agency directors, including the Medical Director (a physician), and those for accounting, maintenance engineering, food services for clients and staff, and transportation services for clients. Each director (except accounting) is, in turn, responsible for the supervision of other staff further down the hierarchy of authority. The Medical Director is responsible for overseeing the entire clinical program, including the work of the various departmental supervisors. Departments include occupational therapy, physical therapy, speech therapy, psychology, and social work. Circles at the very bottom of the chart represent line staff who are providing services directly to or concerning clients.

By examining this chart, it is painfully clear how this agency is run, correct? If you look at the Social Work Department, there are two direct service workers who report directly to their Social Work Supervisor. It is obvious how these social workers go about their business of providing services to clients, look to their own supervisor for direction, and live happily ever after, right? The chain of command is so blatant you may think this entire discussion borders on, if not engulfs itself in, monotony.

The "catch" is that formal organizational charts depict lines of *formal* authority within agencies. Such formal lines of authority dictate how communication and power are *supposed* to flow. Sometimes, an agency's actual chain of command follows the formal chart fairly closely. Equally often, however, agencies develop *informal* channels of communication and power that are very different from those stated on paper. As an example, we will explore the Idle Ness Center's informal channels of communication and dimensions of power.

Channels of Communication

All agencies have numerous, complex systems of communication whereby staff members convey and receive information. *Communication*, of course, is "a process by which information is exchanged between individuals through a common system of symbols, signs, or behavior" (Mish, 2008, p. 251). Communication, then, involves the many nuances regarding how information is conveyed verbally and nonverbally. It entails subtle inflections, comfort level between communicators, and multitudes of minute gestures. Communication will be explored further later in the chapter.

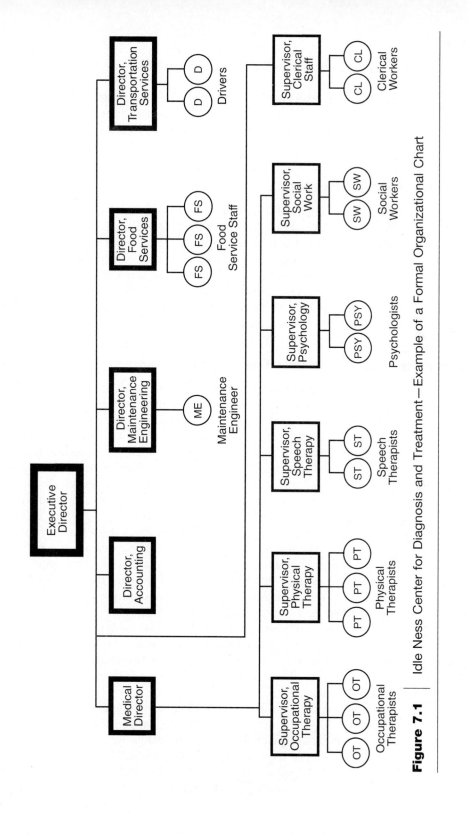

Figure 7.1 | Idle Ness Center for Diagnosis and Treatment—Example of a Formal Organizational Chart

Formal lines of authority might imply that such communication channels are supposed to flow harmoniously and synchronously along with these lines of authority. In other words, supervisees are *supposed* to communicate primarily with their identified supervisors for direction and feedback. Likewise, supervisors are *supposed* to communicate directly with their supervisees and the managers who supervise them. As we will see, this is not the case in the Idle Ness Center.

Power in the Formal Structure

Power is the potential ability to move people on a chosen course to produce an effect or achieve some goal (Griffin & Moorhead 2010; Homan, 2008). Like channels of communication, dimensions of power are supposed to follow the established lines of authority. In the organizational chart, those in supervisory positions above their employees are supposed to have actual power (that is, clear-cut influence and control) over those employees. In real-life agency environments, this may or may not be the case. Note that many other facets of power and organizational politics will be explored later in the chapter.

Example of Informal Structure: The Idle Ness Center

Direct your attention to the Social Work and Psychology Departments illustrated in Figure 7.2. We will concentrate on this smaller portion of the organizational chart concerning the informal structures of communication and power within the agency. Figure 7.2 contrasts the formal and informal structures for these two agency departments. The *real* channels of communication and dimensions of power among supervisors and direct service staff are very different than those illustrated in the formal organizational chart. The real relationships reflect the personalities and interactions among people who have unique perspectives and identities, strengths, weaknesses, problems, and needs of their own.

The formal structure pictures Ellen, the Psychology Department Supervisor, as being responsible for the administration and supervision of both LaVerne and Shirley's job performance. Both the latter have a master's degree in psychology. Likewise, the formal structure portrays Roseanne, the Social Work Department Supervisor, as having direct supervisory authority over both Karen and Susan, each of whom has a master's degree in social work.

The lower box portrays the real-life informal structure of these departments. Karen, one of the social workers, has become good friends with Ellen, the Psychology Department Supervisor. Both single, they frequently socialize together and even vacation together. Their positive relationship is reflected by the bold line connecting them in Figure 7.2.

Karen, on the other hand, gets along terribly with Roseanne, her own supervisor. It is difficult to define what "having a personality conflict" really means. However, this concept could be used to define Karen's and Roseanne's relationship. For whatever reason, they do not personally like each other. Additionally, Karen views Roseanne as basically being incompetent, lazy, and interested in doing as little work as possible. On the other hand, Roseanne perceives Karen as an overly energetic, impulsive "go-getter" who acts "just like a bull in a china closet."

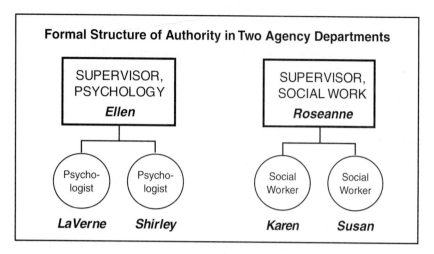

Formal Structure of Authority in Two Agency Departments

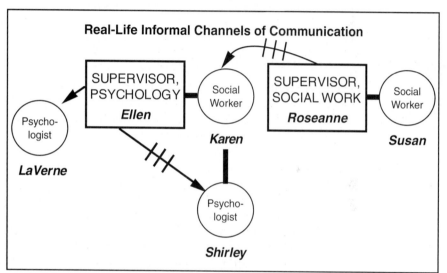

Real-Life Informal Channels of Communication

Figure 7.2 | Organizational Charts Contrasting Formal and Informal Structures in Agencies

Both interact as little as possible with each other. Most communication between them takes place in memo form, with Roseanne issuing Karen direct commands regarding what should and should not be done. Figure 7.2 illustrates Roseanne and Karen's relationship by the arrow that swoops up from Roseanne and down again to Karen. Communication and power consistently flow downward from Roseanne to Karen in a dictatorial, hierarchical fashion. Cross lines on the arrow indicate conflict.

Roseanne, on the other hand, has much in common with Susan, the other social worker. They frequently spend much time together and go out to lunch. Roseanne views Susan as a calmly competent worker who communicates well and provides enjoyable company. In effect, Roseanne treats Susan like a friend and equal. Figure 7.2 illustrates this relationship with the thick linear bond linking Roseanne and Susan horizontally.

Now, let's investigate the informal relationship within the Psychology Department. Supervisor Ellen sees LaVerne, one of her supervisees, as a competent professional colleague. Hence, Figure 7.2 portrays LaVerne slightly below Ellen. The connecting arrow flows from Ellen down to LaVerne because Ellen maintains her supervisory and administrative status with respect to LaVerne. They essentially like each other on a professional basis. However, neither considers herself a personal friend of the other.

Ellen, on the other hand, perceives Shirley, her other supervisee, in a much different light. Ellen regrets hiring Shirley and has begun to document Shirley's difficulties in performance in preparation for "letting her go" (dismissing her or firing her from the agency). Thus, Shirley is positioned significantly below Ellen, the arrow connecting them running from Ellen down to Shirley. The chain of communication and power clearly positions Ellen in the more powerful, communication-controlling position, and Shirley in an inferior, less powerful, communication-receiving status.

However, the plot is even more complicated. Karen, who is substantially younger than Ellen, is about the same age as Shirley, who is also single. Karen and Shirley have much in common and have established a firm friendship. They, too, occasionally spend time and socialize with each other. Thus, a bold vertical line connects them. This indicates that they consider each other equals, friends, and colleagues. This is despite the fact that Ellen and Shirley's relationship is poor and quickly deteriorating. Cross lines on the arrow again indicate conflict.

Karen is in an uncomfortable and tenuous position. On the one hand, she values her friendship with Ellen. She also sees Ellen as a professional ally within the agency who provides her with some leverage against Roseanne. On the other hand, Karen likes Shirley. Karen understands that Ellen is not perfect (nor is she). Thus, Karen can listen to Shirley's complaints against Ellen and provide some sympathy. Karen, however, must take extreme care not to speak against either Ellen or Shirley to the other. It is not easy to maintain such a balancing act.

The point here is neither to praise nor criticize the existence of informal structures of communication and authority. Instead, it is to acknowledge that they do exist and pose a reality to deal with in any agency, including yours. In practice, being aware of both formal and informal agency structures may strengthen your ability to do your job. Once you know the options and alternatives open to you, you can make better informed, more effective choices.

What eventually happened at the Idle Ness Center described here? Shirley quit and left for another position in a different state. Shirley and Karen soon lost contact. Six months later, Karen also left the agency for another social work position that more closely matched her more energetic, enthusiastic style. She became a counselor for teens with serious behavioral and family problems. Karen and Ellen continued to maintain their personal friendship for many years after Karen left the agency. No one knows what became of Roseanne, Susan, or LaVerne.

Informal assessment of your agency environment can help you determine how you can best do your job. It can help you to decide the extent to which you "fit in" or should look for another job somewhere else.

The next sections of the chapter will explore in greater depth the processes of interpersonal communications, power, and politics as they occur in social service agencies.

 Critical Thinking Questions 7.2

Have you ever worked in an environment where the actual channels of communication differed significantly from those proposed by the formal agency structure? If so, in what ways did they differ?

Interpersonal Communication in Social Service Organizations

We've established that communication involves "the process of transmitting information from one person or place to another" (Williams, 2009, p. 747). Such transfer occurs in the context of the perception of both the person sending information and those receiving it. The sender's *intent* is the information that the sender is trying to communicate. The receivers' *impact* is what the receivers actually comprehend.[1] The communication's effectiveness involves the extent to which the sender's intent matches the receiver's impact. The receiver may *perceive* what the sender is saying in a very different way than what the sender is trying to say.

Williams (2010a) clarifies:

> *Perception* is the process by which individuals attend to, organize, interpret, and retain information from their environments. And since communication is the process of transmitting information from one person or place to another, perception is obviously a key part of communication. However, perception can also be a key obstacle to communication. (p. 365)

People are exposed to multiple stimuli at the same time. They may be talking on the phone while reading their email while someone knocks at their door. They thus must filter all the input they're getting and focus on what they perceive as the most significant or attention-grabbing aspects of that communication. People participating in the same group or watching the same event may have totally different perceptions or be in total disagreement about what's occurring.

Williams (2010a) explains:

> For example, every major stadium in the *National Football League* has a huge TV monitor on which fans can watch replays. As the slow motion videotape is replayed on the monitor, you can often hear cheers *and* boos [at the same time], as fans of both teams perceive the same replay in completely different ways. This happens because the fans' perceptual filters predispose them to attend to stimuli that support their team and not their opponents. (p. 365)

---

[1] The concepts of *intent* and *impact* were taken from the film *Behavioral Interviewing with Couples*, available from Research Press, Dept. 98, P.O. Box 9177, Champaign, IL 61826.

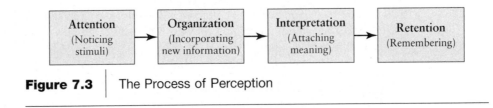

Figure 7.3 | The Process of Perception

The filtering process involves four phases (Williams, 2010a):

Attention is the process of noticing or becoming aware of particular stimuli. Because of perceptual filters, we attend to some stimuli and not others. *Organization* is the process of incorporating new information (from the stimuli that you notice) into your existing knowledge. Because of perceptual filters, we are more likely to incorporate new knowledge that is consistent with what we already know or believe. *Interpretation* is the process of attaching meaning to new knowledge. Because of perceptual filters, our preferences and beliefs strongly influence the meaning we attach to new information ([For example,] 'This must mean that top management supports our project.'). Finally, *retention* is the process of remembering interpreted information. In other words, retention is what we recall and commit to memory after we have perceived something. Of course, perceptual filters also affect retention, that is, what we're likely to remember in the end. [Figure 7.3 depicts the process of perception.]

In short, because of perception and perceptual filters, people are likely to pay attention to different things, organize and interpret what they pay attention to differently, and, finally, remember things differently. Consequently, even when people are exposed to the same communications (for example., organizational memos, discussions with [supervisors] . . . or [clients]) . . . , they can end up with very different perceptions and understandings. (pp. 365–366)

Just as families or couples have misunderstandings (potentially resulting in fights), so do people communicating in organizations have problems "hearing" the meaning of what others are saying. For example, a supervisor may say to her social work supervisees, "The agency director is coming to talk to us tomorrow." One of the workers may perceive that she said, "The director probably wants to break some bad news to us." A second worker might think, "The director's going to pat us on the back for the nice job we did on that fundraising dinner." Still another worker may interpret, "The director's coming and I never can understand a thing she says because she's such a jumbled speaker."

Interpersonal Barriers to Communication in Agencies

At least four barriers can inhibit effective communication in social service organizations. These include noise, personality factors, individual perceptual errors, and lying and distortion (Hellriegel & Slocum, 2009, pp. 230–231). Figure 7.4 illustrates how each of these barriers can negatively impact effective communication. They distort the congruence between the sender's *intent*, what the sender wants to communicate, and the receiver's *impact*, what the receiver actually interprets.

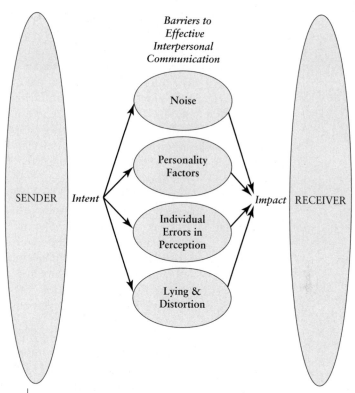

Figure 7.4 | Barriers to Effective Interpersonal Communication

Noise The first barrier to effective interpersonal communication in agencies is *noise*, "any interference with the intended message" while a sender is trying to get his or her message across (Hellriegel & Slocum, 2009, p. 231). We've already established that people in work settings must sift through multiple stimuli to focus on, organize, interpret, and retain what has been said. Distractions can involve any number of circumstances. Several people may be talking at once. Someone may drop a large metal box filled with office equipment. Outside an office window, a car may crash into a lamp post.

Personality Factors Personality factors are the second type of barrier to effective interpersonal communication (Dumler & Skinner, 2008). We all know people who are popular and other people whom everybody tries to avoid. Personality factors are a major dimension in any interpersonal relationship, including those developed in organizations. This is true both for social workers providing direct service and for people holding management positions. Five personality factors can either enhance or interfere with effective communication (Hellriegel & Slocum, 2009):

1. "*Emotional stability* is the degree to which a person is calm, secure, and free from persistent negative feelings" (p. 44). People with high levels of emotional stability can be described as calm, unexcitable, level-headed, and steady in

their interpersonal interactions. They are easier to work with than people who "fly off the handle" when the least bit flustered.

2. "*Agreeableness* is a person's ability to get along with others." Highly agreeable people are often described as "considerate, friendly, helpful, and willing to compromise their interests" (p. 45). On the other hand, people with low levels of agreeableness are frequently characterized "as short tempered, unco-operative, and irritable" (p. 45). People who are highly agreeable are better at forming relationships with others. Other people are more likely to feel comfortable with them instead of being defensive and are more likely to communicate openly their feelings and ideas.

3. "*Extraversion* is the degree to which a person seeks the company of others" (p. 45). Extraverts (people who are socially outgoing) eagerly seek out and socialize with others. They generally develop good interpersonal skills and nurture relationships. Introverts (people who are socially withdrawn), on the other hand, tend to isolate themselves and avoid interaction with others.

4. "*Conscientiousness* " involves "self-discipline, acting responsibly, and directing our behavior" (p. 46). A conscientious person places importance on achieving goals and getting things done. Conscientious people are often described as organized and thorough. They take their responsibilities seriously and can be depended upon to carry out their tasks. A person who lacks conscientiousness tends to assume a laid-back attitude in which promptness and attention to detail are not all that important. It's much more difficult to work with, communicate with, and trust unreliable people than conscientious people.

5. "*Openness* describes imagination and creativity" (p. 46). An open person actively seeks out others' ideas and is open-minded about trying to understand them. Openness implies having the potential to change in response to new concepts and information. An individual who lacks openness can be described as closed-minded and unreceptive to new ways of thinking and doing things.

 Critical Thinking Questions 7.3

How would you describe yourself in terms of emotional stability, agreeableness, extraversion, conscientiousness, and openness? How do these personality variables relate to how you see yourself interacting with others in a work setting?

Individual Errors in Perception   Individual errors make up the third category of perceptual mistakes involved in agency interpersonal communication. As people organize and interpret information, inaccuracies and errors in both perception and judgment may occur (Dumler & Skinner, 2008; Hellriegel & Slocum, 2009).

Accuracy of judgment is important because perceptions affect how people are treated in organizations. For example, a supervisor who attends to or emphasizes the wrong factors in a supervisee's performance could cause an inaccurate perception of how well that employee is functioning in the agency. This could result in a poor performance review of that employee instead of a good one. (Note that this book uses the terms *employee* or *worker* to refer to people who directly serve clients and other staff generally at the bottom of an organizational chart. The terms *manager* and *supervisor* refer to people higher in the organizational chart who have supervisory responsibility and authority over other employees. Specific agencies may choose one of the latter two terms over the other in their job titles and descriptions. The term *manager* can also refer to people in management higher in the organizational structure who have direct authority over supervisors or other managers.)

Another example of inaccurate judgment involves an employer interviewing a potential employee for a job. The interviewer may selectively focus on characteristics that are insignificant or simply miss out on the interviewee's best qualities because of perceptual errors and erroneous judgment. Several errors commonly occur in such job interview situations (Hellriegel & Slocum, 2009, p. 79). First, *similarity error* happens when interviewers place too much importance on the similarities and differences between themselves and the interviewees. People are naturally drawn to others whom they perceive as being similar to themselves. Once, a job candidate was interviewing for a social work position. The candidate had mentioned on his resume that one of his personal areas of interest was flying airplanes recreationally. It just so happened that the interviewer was also a recreational flier. They "hit it off" immediately while talking about flying and the candidate was hired. The candidate, who was qualified for the job along with many others, felt strongly that having flying in common with the interviewer gave him an edge over other candidates and got him the job.

Contrast error, a second type of error of judgment, involves placing too much emphasis on how a job candidate compares with other candidates in the pool of those who applied. Every job search has a pool of candidates who apply. (Sometimes, no one applies and the job search must be done over.) It's unpredictable who will be in the pool. Pools vary dramatically regarding the quality of applicants. An average candidate (in terms of qualifications such as education, experience, and interpersonal skills) may look terrible in a pool composed of applicants with stellar qualifications but look terrific compared to a group of very poorly qualified candidates.

Third, *first-impression error* happens when, for whatever reason, an interviewer formulates an initial impression based on the perceptions of some variables and then refuses to change that impression. For example, an interviewee might be wearing orange earrings, a color the interviewer despises. It's neither fair nor logical, but the interviewer forms a negative impression of the interviewee right from the beginning of the interview. This view may be highly resistant to change, regardless of the interviewee's relevant qualifications.

Hellriegel and Slocum (2009) suggest guidelines to help make more accurate judgments in job interviewing situations: "(1) Avoid generalizing from an observation of a single trait (e.g., tactful) to other traits (e.g., stable, confident, energetic, dependable); (2) avoid assuming that a behavior will be repeated in all situations; and (3) avoid placing too much reliance on physical appearance" (p. 79).

Highlight 7.3 reviews several other specific perceptual errors that can occur in interpersonal communication in an agency context.

Critical Thinking Questions 7.4

We probably all have been interviewed for a job at some time or another. Some of us have had many job interviews. If you've had such experience, picture a specific situation where you were interviewing for a job. To what extent do you think the interviewer's perceptions of you and your abilities were accurate? To what extent do you think that the interviewer made similarity, contrast, or first-impression error? Did you get the job? Why or why not?

Highlight 7.3 | # Specific Types of Individual Perceptual Errors in Agency Settings

Some other specific types of inaccurate judgments can occur in agency settings and interfere with effective interpersonal communication. These include stereotyping, the halo effect, projection, and assumptions about ethnicity and culture.

Stereotyping

We've established that a *stereotype* is "a fixed mental picture of a member of some specified group based on some attribute or attributes that reflect an overly simplified view of that group, without consideration or appreciation of individual differences" (Kirst-Ashman, 2010, p. 53). For example, if an agency worker maintains the stereotype that women make poor supervisors regardless of their practice and interpersonal skill levels, that worker will probably resent a woman being hired as his or her supervisor. Similarly, consider a young employee who automatically assumes that a person in his or her seventies is probably "getting senile." That young employee is unlikely to place any confidence in colleagues over seventy. Additionally, the employee will likely have perceptual distortions about the abilities and strengths of senior clients.

Halo Effect

"The *halo effect* refers to evaluating another person solely on the basis of one attribute, either favorable or unfavorable" (Hellriegel & Slocum, 2009, p. 80). For example, if Jadwiga, an agency worker, perceives her colleague Mohammad as having trouble being punctual in meeting deadlines, that impression may color her impression of other aspects of Mohammad's personality and behavior. Jadwiga may display impatience whenever Mohammad volunteers to get something done for their *social work department* (a group of social workers clustered together under one supervisor in the organizational power structure and organizational chart). She may not listen to Mohammad's contributions during staff meetings, because she automatically assumes he's a poor worker. She may perceive everything Mohammad does negatively even when his work is done well and punctually.

Projection

"Projection is the tendency for people to see their own traits in other people" (Hellriegel & Slocum, 2009, p. 82). This is especially true for negative traits including hostility, vengefulness, miserliness, disorganization, or the need to control others. In effect, projection reverses the truth. For example, consider a worker who savers manipulating colleagues to do work for him. He may also project this trait onto his colleagues and feel that they are trying to manipulate him into doing their work.

Assumptions about Ethnicity and Culture

Hellriegel and Slocum (2009) explain how perceptions are influenced by ethnicity and culture:

> Misinterpretation of the situation occurs when an individual gives certain meaning to observations and their relationships. Interpretation organizes our experience and guides our behavior. Read the following sentence and quickly count the number of Fs:
>
> FINISHED FILES ARE THE RESULT OF YEARS OF SCIENTIFIC STUDY COMBINED WITH THE EXPERIENCE OF YEARS.
>
> Most people who do not speak English see all six Fs. By contrast, many English speakers see only three Fs; they do not see the Fs in the word *of*. Why? Because English-speaking people do not think that the word *of* is important for them to understand the meaning of the sentence. We selectively see those words that are important according to our cultural upbringing. (pp. 77–78)

The role of culture is important in organizational settings concerning both staff and staff/client interactions. For example, differences in cultural perceptions exist regarding what is appropriate behavior for people in the United States compared to those in Saudi Arabia (Hellriegel & Slocum, 2009, p. 78). A common behavior in the United States is to shake hands upon meeting. In Saudi Arabia, a male should not shake hands with a female unless she extends her hand first. Verbal greetings are appropriate. Under no circumstances should a male being introduced to a female greet her by kissing her. In the United States, it is generally customary to open a gift in front of the gift giver when it is received. Arabian people do not do so in organizational settings, but open gifts later when the giver is no longer present. Gifts involving alcohol or pork should never be given to Arabian people.

    Critical Thinking Questions 7.5

Have you had interactions in work settings that involved inaccuracies of judgment such as stereotyping, the halo effect, projection, or ethnic and cultural assumptions? If so, what were they? Did they involve misperceptions on your part or on the part of other staff? If you could go back and improve the communication and interaction both on your part and on the part of the other people who were involved, what would you change?

Lying and Distortion   A fourth barrier to effective interpersonal communication in agencies, unfortunately, involves lying and distortion (Hellriegel & Slocum, 2009, p. 231). *Lying* is the use of communication to deceive information receivers into believing something that is not true. In contrast, honesty involves stating what one considers to be true in the most straightforward manner possible. *Distortion*, as defined by Hellriegel and Slocum, "represents a wide range of messages that a sender may use between the extremes of lying and complete honesty" (2009, p. 232). The intent is to slant information in a particular direction.

The NASW *Code of Ethics* instructs social workers to "act honestly and responsibly and promote ethical practices on the part of the organizations with which they are affiliated" (NASW, 2008). Furthermore, it directs social workers not to "participate in, condone, or be associated with dishonesty, fraud, or deception" (NASW, 2008, 4.04).

However, just as organizations are imperfect, so are the people who work in them. The *Code of Ethics* cannot guarantee that all professionals will always function in an ethical manner. We address the issues of lying and distortion because you may be confronted with these in the agency where you work.

Hellriegel and Slocum (2009), commenting from a business management perspective, note that "the use of vague, ambiguous, or indirect language doesn't necessarily indicate a sender's intent to mislead" (p. 232). In fact, they continue:

> This form of language may be viewed as acceptable political behavior. Silence may also be a form of distortion, if not dishonesty. Not wanting to look incompetent or take on a manager [or supervisor] in a departmental meeting, a subordinate may remain quiet instead of expressing an opinion or asking a question. (p. 232)

Sometimes, distortion provides a means of "*impression management*—the process whereby a sender purposefully tries to manipulate the perceptions of another person (that person's impression) about the sender (Hellriegel & Slocum, 2009, p. 82). The following are three tactics reflecting forms of impression management:

1. *Ingratiation* is the act of seeking acceptance and support through deliberate efforts such as "using flattery, supporting others' opinions, doing favors," or "laughing excessively at others' jokes" (Hellriegel & Slocum, 2007, p. 329).
2. *Self-promotion* is the act of describing oneself in an unwarranted and overly positive manner (Hellriegel & Slocum, 2009, p. 83). It might be considered a form of bragging.
3. *Face-saving* is behavior that attempts to avoid being accountable for the full consequences of one's negative behavior, decisions, and performance (Hellriegel & Slocum, 2009, p. 83). People using face-saving strategies will try to make their actions look better than they really are. This might involve making excuses for why things turned out badly, blaming others for negative results, minimizing negative consequences by disguising them as not really being that bad, or denying that the problem really exists at all.

Lying is clearly unethical. Levels of distortion are more complex. For example, you don't necessarily say to someone you really don't like, "I really can't stand you. Shut up." In this instance it's not that you're lying. Rather, it does not necessarily facilitate an agency's functioning to say every negative thing that comes to mind. However, on the continuum from mild distortion to lying, the more distortion strategies approach lying, the more unethical they are. The more that distortion and lying occurs in an agency environment, the worse the agency's potential for effective interpersonal communication. Focus on Ethics 7.1 addresses the ethics of using distortion. Focus on Ethics 7.2 suggests tactics for enhancing ethical communication in agency settings.

Focus on Ethics 7.1 | **Using Distortion to Manipulate Others**

To what extent do you feel distortion tactics are ethical or unethical? Are any such tactics ever useful or necessary? If so, which ones, and in what situations? Have you ever had experience using distortion tactics? If so, which ones and under what circumstances? Have distortion tactics ever been used on you? If so, what were your reactions?

Power and Politics in Social Service Organizations

We have established that *power* is the potential ability to move people on a chosen course to produce an effect or achieve some goal. Power is an important concept regarding social service organizations. Who has power and how it's used directly affects how workers can do their jobs. Management has power over workers (including you when you get a job). However, we determined earlier that there are various types of power that don't necessarily coincide with the formal organizational chart. Therefore, a discussion of power in organizations is relevant to you for at least two reasons. First, management has the potential to empower you to do your job well. Second, as a worker you can think in terms of your own power and how you can strive to improve agency functioning. You may also develop tactics to influence people in power when advocating for clients or improved service provision. For example, you might feel that agency hours should be extended to better accommodate clients' schedules. Or you might feel clients' needs are not being met adequately in some area (for example, counseling, transportation, financial support) and you decide to advocate on their behalf. Acquisition of a power base may also be useful when requesting benefits such as a raise or select vacation times.

Focus on Ethics 7.2	Enhancing Ethical Communication in Agencies: Means to Empowerment

There are a number of guidelines to improve ethical interpersonal communication in agencies. These are important both for management and other staff to implement.

1. "Be honest" (Vecchio, 2006, p. 308). Simply put, honesty enhances open communication and increases trust. Colleagues are more likely to work together when they trust and like each other.
2. Practice empathy in your interpersonal work relationships (Dumler & Skinner, 2008; Vecchio, 2006). *Empathy* is the interpersonal practice not only of *being in tune* with how another person feels, but also *conveying* to that person that you understand how he or she feels (Kirst-Ashman & Hull, 2009b). People are more likely to communicate with you and feel comfortable with you if they think you understand them.
3. Workers should work at listening carefully to each other and trying to understand what each other is really trying to say (Daft & Marcic, 2009; Dumler & Skinner, 2008; Vecchio, 2006). Daft and Marcic (2009) explain that an important aspect of communication is *active listening*, the process of "asking questions, showing

interest, and occasionally paraphrasing what the speaker has said to ensure acute interpretation" (p. 508). They continue:

> Senders and receivers should make a special effort to understand each other's perspective. Managers [and supervisors] can sensitize themselves to the information receiver so they will be able to target the message, detect bias, and clarify misinterpretations. When communicators understand others' perspectives, semantics can be clarified, perceptions understood, and objectivity maintained. (p. 509)

4. Management should work to establish an environment that encourages a *climate of trust and openness*: "Open communication and dialogue can encourage people to communicate honestly with one another. Subordinates will feel free to transmit negative as well as positive messages without fear of retribution. Efforts to develop interpersonal skills among employees can also foster openness, honesty, and trust" (Daft, 2010, p. 492; Vecchio, 2006). (Chapter 8 will discuss management approaches.)

Types of Power

Chapter 3 discussed the five types of power that group leaders may have. These types of power also apply to people working in organizations (Champoux, 2006; Daft, 2010; Dumler & Skinner, 2008; Lussier, 2009). Sources of power include the following:

- *Legitimate power* (that attained because of one's position and vested authority)
- *Reward power* (that which stems from the ability to provide positive reinforcement and rewards to others)
- *Coercive power* (the capability of dispensing punishments in order to influence others' behavior)
- *Referent power* (that held as a result of other group members' respect and high esteem)
- *Expert power* (that based on established authority or expertise in a particular domain)

Supervisors and managers usually are given legitimate power. They also often have reward and coercive power. Anyone, including direct service workers and supervisors or managers, can develop referent and expert power.

The concept of power is quite complex. Vecchio (2006) explains:

Power is an essential feature of a manager's [or supervisor's] role. Without some degree of power, a [supervisor] . . . would find it difficult to direct the efforts of subordinates. Thus, power underlies a [supervisor's] . . . effectiveness. Subordinates also possess forms and degrees of power. For example, subordinates can control the work flow or withhold support from their [supervisor]. . . . Therefore, to some extent, each member of an organization possesses power.

Because power is intangible, it is very difficult to define clearly and precisely. Also, our language has several similar terms that we tend to confuse with power, such as authority and influence. . . .

Power is not always legitimate. Therefore, we speak of *authority* as the right to try to change or direct others. Authority includes the notion of legitimacy. It is the right to influence others in the pursuit of common goals agreed upon by various parties. [For example, supervisors have authority by virtue of their job titles and descriptions.] Power, in contrast, does not always pursue common goals and may, at times, be clearly directed to pursuing only a single individual's goals.

Another term, *influence*, is also frequently used when discussing the notion of power. Influence tends to be subtler, broader, and more general than power. Although both influence and power can be defined as the ability to change the behavior of others, power embodies the ability to do so with regularity and ease. Influence is weaker and less reliable than power. . . . Influence relies on particular tactics and often employs face-to-face interactions. Thus, the exercise of influence tends to be more subtle than the exercise of power. (p. 124)

Determining who has power can be tricky. Sometimes, people with important titles or placement high in the organizational structure have little ability to influence and control subordinates' behavior in reality. Because people in power have the potential ability to influence your work behavior and how clients are served, it's important to know who has this power. Aldag and Kuzuhara (2005) explain:

How can you tell who has power in an organization? Job titles may help; so may status symbols. Still, we know these things can be deceptive and that some people with a lot of power don't have fancy titles or big offices. Some other signs of managers' power include the abilities to do the following:

- Intercede favorably on behalf of someone in trouble with the organization
- Get a good placement for a talented subordinate
- Gain approval for expenditures beyond the budget
- Obtain above-average salary increases for subordinates
- Place items on the agenda at policy meetings
- Get fast access to top decision makers
- Have regular, frequent access to top decision makers
- Obtain early information about decisions and policy shifts (pp. 370–371; Kanter, 1979; Rynecki, Smith, Shanley, & Wheat, 2003)

Critical Thinking Questions 7.6

Power relationships characterize all organizations, including social services and businesses. Most of us have had work experience. Think of a job you've had. What types of power did your direct supervisor have? Who else in the organization had influence or power, and how did they use it?

Politics in Social Service Organizations

Aldag and Kuzuhara (2005) describe *organizational politics*:

When we hear someone speak of organizational politics, we probably think of such things as "passing the buck," "apple polishing," "backstabbing," and other "dirty tricks" we use to further our selfish interests. We use the term organizational politics more broadly, to refer to activities that people perform to acquire, enhance, and use power and other resources to obtain their preferred outcomes in a situation where there is uncertainty or disagreement. Because the focus is on people's preferred outcomes, rather than organizational outcomes, this may or may not involve activities contrary to the best interests of the organization. (p. 378; Pfeffer, 1981)

Don't automatically think that organizational politics are always evil and self-serving (Aldag & Kuzuhara, 2005). Sometimes, agency problems or needs should be addressed. A policy might not be working or a supervisor might not be performing all her responsibilities. It's beyond the scope of this book to teach you *how* to advocate for positive changes, but you should be aware of organizational politics as an important aspect of human behavior in the macro social environment. For one thing, most people prefer to be somewhat "political" by avoiding "criticizing your boss in public, losing control of your emotions during meetings, or challenging sacred beliefs or values of the organization" (Aldag & Kuzuhara, 2005,

p. 379). Therefore, being aware of politics may be important, "if only to be alert for the political actions of others and to avoid personal embarrassment" (Aldag & Kuzuhara, 2005, p. 379).

Dynamics Contributing to Political Behavior in Agencies   DuBrin (2007) cites at least two reasons why politics occur in organizations:

1. Organizations are by nature political (Griffin & Moorhead, 2010). They are made up of a range of units or departments, each striving to achieve its own goals and competing for resources. Competition is a fact of life when resources are limited or scarce. Power enhances the ability to compete.
2. Some people are more power-oriented than others. When power is limited, power-oriented workers, supervisors, or managers will often try to expand their influence. "Power-oriented managers [or supervisors] sometimes cope with the limited amount of power available by expanding their sphere of influence sideways. For example, the director of the food stamp program in a government agency might attempt to gain control over the housing assistance program, which is at the same level" (Dubrin, 2007, p. 270). (*Food stamps* are credits distributed through a federal program to be used like cash to purchase primarily food, plants, and seeds [Barker, 2003]. *Housing assistance* often involves rental subsidies or vouchers by which government programs assist with rent, mortgage payments, and low-rent public housing, or block grants to state and local governments for developing affordable housing [Dolgoff & Feldstein, 2007; Kirst-Ashman, 2010].) Some people who are extremely concerned with gaining power are characterized by "Machiavellianism, a tendency to manipulate others for personal gain" (Dubrin, 2007, p. 270). Such people thrive on gaining power for power's sake.

Focus on Ethics 7.3 addresses the issue of political behavior in organizations.

Focus on Ethics 7.3 | **Political Behavior in Organizations**

Champoux (2006) reflects:

> Political behavior in organizations raises many questions about what is ethical and what is not. . . . Using power and political behavior in an organization to serve self-interest is unethical . . . Similarly, political behavior that uses excessive organizational resources to reach a personal goal is also unethical. These observations suggest that any political strategy and its associated tactics are unethical if they do not serve the organization's goals or at least the goals of a larger group [(clients or staff serving clients on the clients' behalf). (p. 372)

Champoux (2006) suggests considering the following characteristics to determine that political behavior in an organizational context is ethical:

*   The behavior should serve people outside the organization [(clients), not just the person using politics for personal gain] . . .
*   Individuals should clearly know the person's intent and give their consent . . . to be influenced. . . .
*   Administering the organization's resources, procedures, and policies should allow fair treatment of all affected people. (p. 372)

Using Agency Politics for Positive Change   We've indicated that as an agency worker, you may be in the position to advocate for positive change on the behalf or clients or agency personnel. The following are tactics to establish a power base within an agency setting so that you might have greater influence with decision makers.

First, conduct a *political diagnosis*, an assessment of "the location of power in an organization and the type of political behavior that is likely to happen" identifying "politically active individuals and coalitions in the organization, the amount of power they have, and the likely ways they will use their power" (Champoux, 2006, p. 367).

You can pursue several strategies to identify individuals who have power; start with the "organization chart and a description of titles and duties" (Champoux, 2006, p. 367). Then interview people in various organizational units to determine how decisions are made, who has decision making responsibility for distributing resources, how identified people generally use their power or are likely to, and what their goals are for their performance and status within the organization.

It is also important to identify any coalitions within the agency. "A *coalition* is an alliance of individuals who share a common goal. Coalitions are also interest groups that try to affect decisions in the organization. Coalitions can have members from widely scattered parts of the organization" (Champoux, 2006, p. 368). Assessing coalitions should involve the same strategies used in assessing the power of individuals within the organization. This should help establish the agency's "political network," the system of "affiliations and alliances of individuals and coalitions" within the social service organization's environment (Champoux, 2006, p. 368).

A second tactic for enhancing power and influence involves developing contacts and relationships with people in power (Dubrin, 2007). Such people can provide you with support and information to help achieve your goals.

Third, to increase your power base, form coalitions yourself (Lussier, 2009; Vecchio, 2006). This may be as simple a thing as forming a coalition to have enough votes to get a proposal passed in a committee. Or it may involve a coalition approaching an administrator with a new idea to persuade him or her to adopt it. Involving more people tends to enhance your credibility and validity.

Fourth, get information about what's going on (Aldag & Kuzuhara, 2005; Dubrin, 2007). Keeping current helps you develop believable arguments on your behalf. Being knowledgeable inspires people's confidence in you.

Fifth, provide positive feedback where warranted (Aldag & Kuzuhara, 2005). Positive feedback can be given concerning others' statements, support, and performance; it should be "a straightforward and specific declaration of what the person did right" (DuBrin, 2007, p. 273). Positive feedback helps to strengthen interpersonal relationships. Persistent complainers tend to turn other people off. People with positive proposals who are known to be supportive are more easily heard.

Sixth, use assertive communication (DuBrin, 2009; Vecchio, 2006). "*Assertiveness* involves being able to state your thoughts, wants, and feelings straightforwardly and effectively. It concerns the ability to establish an appropriate stance between being too aggressive and too timid. . . . The implication is that you take both your needs and the needs of others into account" (Kirst-Ashman & Hull,

2009b, pp. 164–165). Of course, being assertive does not mean that you should avoid tact. Always consider the communication receivers' feelings. Effective assertive communication means thinking about the best way to state your ideas at the most appropriate time.

Focus on Ethics 7.4 describes some tactics *not* to use when engaging in agency politics.

Focus on Ethics 7.4 | ## Tactics *Not* to Use in Agency Politics: Problematic Unethical Behavior

We've noted that behavior can occur in organizations that is inappropriate and unethical. Some political tactics are designed to hurt other people. Others are intended for selfish advancement. Some tactics can ruin your reputation or have very negative consequences in the future. The following six strategies should not be used when involved in agency politics.

1. *Don't engage in "backstabbing"* (Dubrin, 2007, p. 274). Backstabbing "requires that you pretend to be nice but all the while plan someone's demise. A frequent form of backstabbing is to inform your rival's superior that he or she is faltering under the pressure of job responsibilities" (p. 274). People backstab to make themselves look better or more important to get ahead in competitive situations. Backstabbing is devious, self-serving, and unprofessional. It usually results in deterioration of interpersonal relationships and the ability to function as a team. "The recommended approach to dealing with a backstabber is to confront the person directly, ask for an explanation of his or her behavior, and demand that he or she stop" (p. 274).

2. *Don't set up a person for failure* (Dubrin, 2002, p. 247). "The object of the setup is to place a person in a position where he or she will either fail outright or look ineffective. For example, a supervisor who the agency head dislikes might be given responsibility for a troubled department. The newly appointed supervisor cannot improve productivity, is then reprimanded for poor performance, and the negative evaluation becomes part of the person's permanent record" (p. 247).

    At one point I was a newly promoted supervisor of a social work unit in a day treatment center for youth having serious emotional and behavioral problems. The center provided therapy and special education for troubled youth residing in the community. The program's two primary components were social services and therapy under my direction, and the school under its principal's direction. I was young and didn't know much about supervision or agency politics. For whatever reason, the school principal was not supportive of my promotion. The director informed the principal and me (who were equals on the organizational chart) that new recording requirements of clients' progress would require twice as much time and work as before. None of the staff—teachers, teaching assistants, or social workers—would be at all happy about that news. The principal asked me to make the announcement at an all-staff meeting. I foolishly did what he told me to and made the announcement both to my social work supervisees and to his teaching staff. Everyone immediately viewed me as the bringer of bad tidings and "the bad guy," an image that persisted for months. The principal benefited in at least two ways by setting me up for failure. First, he avoided being "the bad guy" himself; second, he enhanced his power base by making me look worse than him.

3. *Don't "divide and conquer"* (Vecchio, 2006, p. 131). This strategy "usually involves creating a feud among two or more people so that they will be continually off balance and thus unable to mount an attack against you" (p. 131). They are essentially kept busy fighting with each other, allowing you to go about your business. Unfortunately, this tactic hurts interpersonal

relationships. It also takes time and energy away from doing a good job.

I once worked in a social work department supervised by Fred. Fred's approach to supervision was control by dividing and conquering. Two of the workers, Jethrow and Davida, had been good friends for a long time. Fred told Jethrow that Davida had been criticizing his work. Fred then told Davida that Jethrow had been critical of her work. None of this was true. By disrupting Jethrow's and Davida's friendship, Fred broke up the coalition of support that they formed. In this way, Fred felt he had greater control of what went on in the department. It eventually backfired for Fred, however. A third worker, Cathy, talked both to Jethrow and Davida, who told her what Fred had been saying. Cathy subsequently told Jethrow and Davida what each other had shared. The result was that they confronted each other and discovered that Fred had been lying. They then confronted Fred, who consistently denied that he had said anything like that. Eventually, the entire department formed a coalition and sought help from the administration concerning Fred for this and many other behavioral problems. Fred was fired.

4. *Don't "exclude the opposition"* (Vecchio, 2006, p. 131). Another underhanded technique is to exclude a rival or adversary from participation in meetings, agency functions, or social events. One approach is to schedule an important decision making meeting "when the opposition is out of town (on vacation . . .) or attending another meeting. With the opposition absent, it is possible to influence decision making or to take credit for a rival's efforts" (p. 131).

5. *Don't go over your supervisor's head without first exhausting all other options* (Vecchio, 2006). There are times when it might be necessary to go over your supervisor's head and complain to his or her supervisor. Some employees do this to complain about the supervisor's performance or how the supervisor is treating them. Consider the earlier example with Fred, Jethrow, and Davida when staff formed a coalition and sought help from administration. However, the staff first confronted Fred, who did not respond. The entire staff formed a coalition to address the issue the only way they knew how. Only then did they "air dirty laundry" about the department to higher levels of administration. Supervisors hate it when supervisees go over their heads and "narc" about their performance. It's much wiser to try to work out whatever the problem is internally before going outside of the department. Making an enemy of a supervisor by making him or her look bad can make your life miserable in the future. Additionally, often administration will side with the supervisor, as people in management tend to stick together. The result might be a decrease rather than an increase in your power and potential to influence.

6. *Don't throw "temper tantrums"* (Vecchio, 2006, p. 132). Emotional volatility may earn you the reputation of being overly emotional and overreactive. People tend to see the emotions and miss out on the content of what you're trying to communicate. You don't want to establish a reputation of being hard to work with. That will only encourage others to avoid you and not provide you with support when you need it.

Critical Thinking Questions 7.7

Most of us have likely had work experiences. Have you ever been in a position to observe the use of either the negative or positive tactics described here? If so, explain the circumstances. To what extent were the tactics effective? To what extent were they ethical?

Chapter Summary

The following summarizes this chapter's content as it relates to the learning objectives presented at the beginning of the chapter. Objectives include the following:

A. Describe organizational culture and structure, and discuss how lines of authority and channels of communication are involved.

Organizational culture is "the set of key values, beliefs, understandings, and norms shared by members of an organization" (Daft & Marcic, 2009, p. 63). Organizational structure is "the system of task, reporting, and authority relationships within which the work of the organization is done" (Griffin & Moorhead, 2010, p. 407). Lines of authority reflect the formal agency structure of administrative and supervisory responsibilities. Channels of communication involve numerous, complex systems of communication in an organization whereby staff members convey and receive information.

B. Discuss supervision and consultation in organizational settings.

Supervision is the process by which a designated supervisor watches over and evaluates a worker's performance, directs and coordinates activities, and provides feedback. Consultation is the process of seeking out and receiving expert help from an individual, group, or organization in order to resolve an identified problem or address a designated issue.

C. Discuss centralized versus decentralized organizations.

Centralized organizations are clearly defined with a strict hierarchy that allows little discretion. Decentralized organizations have flexibility and allow for great worker discretion.

D. Examine interpersonal communication within social service agencies.

The communication sender's intent is the information that the sender is trying to communicate. The receiver's impact is what the receiver actually comprehends. The sender's intent should closely match the receiver's impact in effective communication. A case example (the Idle Ness Center) provides an examination of formal and informal channels of communication among staff.

E. Describe the perceptual process during communication.

Perception is "the process by which individuals attend to, organize, interpret, and retain information from their environments" (Williams, 2010a, p. 365). The process of perception involves attention, organization, interpretation, and retention.

F. Identify interpersonal barriers to communication.

Barriers to communication in agencies include noise, personality factors, individual errors in perception, and lying and distortion.

G. Describe the importance of power in organizations and identify its various types.

Power is the potential ability to move people on a chosen course to produce an effect or achieve some goal. The concept of power, which can be used in many ways, is complex. Types of power include legitimate, reward, coercive, referent, and expert.

H. Explain organizational politics and their dynamics.

Organizational politics are "activities that people perform to acquire, enhance, and use power and other resources" to attain their goals (Aldag & Kuzuhara, 2005, p. 378). Organizations are by nature political. Some people are more power-oriented than others.

I. Suggest tactics for using agency politics for positive change.

Tactics include conducting a political diagnosis, developing contacts with those in power, forming coalitions, being informed, providing appropriate positive feedback, and using assertive communication.

J. Focus on ethical issues concerning the use of distortion, enhancement of ethical communication, political behavior, and problematic unethical behavior.

Questions were raised concerning the ethics of distorting communication with the intent of manipulating others. Means of enhancing ethical communication in agencies include being honest, using empathy, employing active listening, and establishing a "climate of trust and openness" (Daft, 2010, p. 492). Political behavior should not be used in organizations to pursue self-interests at the expense of others. Unethical political tactics include backstabbing, setting others up for failure, creating divisions between other staff, excluding the opposition from decision making, going over your supervisor's head, and throwing temper tantrums.

K. Raise various critical thinking questions.

Critical thinking questions focused on experiences with supervisors, organizational communication channels, one's own personality factors, job interview experience, experiences with inaccuracies of judgment, power relationships, and observations of positive and negative tactics used in an organizational context.

Looking Ahead

This chapter discussed social service organizational settings, goals, and contexts in the macro social environment. The next chapter will explore human behavior, management, and empowerment in organizations.

For Further Exploration on the Internet

See this text's website at **www.cengage.com/social_work/kirst-ashman** for learning tools such as tutorial quizzing, Web links, glossary, flashcards, and PowerPoint® slides.

8 | CHAPTER | Human Behavior, Management, and Empowerment in Organizations

© Jon Feingersh/PhotoLibrary

Organizations can empower their members. Awards for achievement can enhance internal environments in all types of organizations.

CHAPTER CONTENTS

Have you ever worked in an organization or business where you heard the following complaints, or perhaps made them yourself?

"My boss is so . . ."

- *Bossy*
- *Inconsiderate*
- *Disorganized*
- *Unfair*
- *Incompetent*
- *Pea-brained*
- *Unethical*
- *Screwed up*

Critical Thinking Questions 8.1

Have you ever worked in an organization or business where you or other employees had difficulties with a supervisor? If so, what did the problems involve? How might they have been solved and the situation improved?

All organizations, including social service organizations, are governed by the orientation or style of their management. Supervisors, as part of management, function within the organizational culture and expectations. For any variety of reasons, you yourself may have experienced having a poor supervisor. Management in social service settings can empower practitioners to work more effectively and efficiently, ultimately benefiting their clients. The internal functioning of organizational systems can promote or deter workers' ability to perform effective interventions and link clients with needed resources. Because management is so important for how workers function in organizations, it is critical to understand the dynamics of management and how they relate to worker behavior in the macro social environment.

Learning Objectives

A. Explain the significance of management in social service organizations.
B. Describe traditional bureaucracies, orientation discrepancies between social work and bureaucracies, and common behavior patterns found in bureaucracies.
C. Critique the U.S. health care system's clash with Asian and Pacific Islander (API) cultural values.
D. Discuss problems frequently encountered by and in social service organizations.
E. Describe newer concepts involved in management and employee empowerment.
F. Discuss the situation encountered by women in social services management.

G. Describe two examples of common management and leadership approaches—total quality management (TQM) and servant leadership.
H. Introduce various critical thinking questions.
I. Focus on an ethical issue.

The Importance of Management

Management is the "attainment of organizational goals in an efficient and effective manner through planning, organizing, leading, and controlling organizational resources" (Daft & Marcic, 2009, p. 8). Management involves how employees are thought of and treated. Management style provides important clues for understanding people's behavior in the organizational environment. Often, an organization's management approach reflects some combination of the organizational theories described in Chapter 5. Numerous bureaucracies continue to exist, with all their strengths and weaknesses, but alternative organizational perspectives and management styles are continuously being developed.

For example, management by objectives (MBO) was a popular approach used in the last quarter of the twentieth century (Albrecht, 1978). It focused on goals as the primary driving force of agency life, measuring organizational success in terms of how effectively the organization achieved these goals (Netting, Kettner, & McMurtry, 2008). MBO encouraged organizational employees to arrive at an agreement about what objectives or results they want to accomplish, specify what organizational resources each goal requires, and establish how long the goal-attainment process should take (Barker, 2003).

The following sections will address various aspects of management. First, traditional bureaucracy will be discussed. Subsequently, some problems organizations face in the macro social environment will be addressed. The remainder of the chapter will focus on new methods of management aimed at empowering workers to provide better services to clients.

Working in a Traditional Bureaucracy

The concept of bureaucracy was introduced in Chapter 5 under classical management organizational theories. It reflects a traditional approach to management. Because it is such a commonly used concept, we will spend some time here addressing practice within bureaucracies.

What words come to mind when you hear the term "bureaucracy"? Dullness? Tediousness? Boredom? Repetitiveness? Red tape? Sludge?

For whatever reason, most of us have a terrible opinion of bureaucracies. Even one dictionary definition labels bureaucracy "a system of administration marked by officialism (lack of flexibility and initiative combined with excessive adherence to regulations in the behavior of usually government officials), red tape (official routine or procedure marked by excessive complexity which results in delay or inaction), and proliferations ([growth] by rapid production of new parts, cells, buds, or offspring)" (Mish, 2008, pp. 165, 861, 993, 1044). Even reading this definition is rather dull.

As classical organizational theories propose, bureaucratic management style emphasizes the importance of a specifically designed, formal structure and a consistent, rigid organizational network of employees to make an organization run well and achieve its goals (Dubrin, 2007; Hellriegel & Slocum, 2009). Each employee has a clearly defined job and is told exactly how that job should be accomplished. This school of thought calls for minimal independent functioning on the part of employees. Supervisors closely scrutinize the latter's work. Efficiency is of utmost importance. How people feel about their jobs is insignificant. Administration avoids allowing employees to have any input regarding how organizational goals can best be reached. Rather, employees are expected to do their jobs as instructed as quietly and efficiently as possible.

Traditional bureaucracies are made up of numerous highly specialized units that are supposed to perform specific job tasks. In the formal structure, there is supposed to be little communication among horizontal units, that is, units of approximately equal status that perform different functions. Employees are supposed to "stick to their own business" and get their own specifically defined jobs done within their own units. That's it. Discussion is unnecessary.

Traditional bureaucracies allow very little discretion on the part of workers. Policies and procedures for how to accomplish tasks are clearly specified. In other words, what any particular worker is supposed to do in any particular situation is designated ahead of time. Employees are allowed little, if any, ability and opportunity to be able to think for themselves and make their own decisions concerning their work. They are simply supposed to follow instructions.

The policies and procedures are infinitely complex and detailed. Regardless of what new situation might come up, workers should be able to consult the "rule book" regarding how they should deal with it.

Value Orientation Discrepancies between Workers and "The System"

Helping professionals (including social workers) have a value orientation that can clash with the traditional bureaucracy's reality (Knopf, 1979; Lewis, Lewis, Packard, & Souflee, 2001). Expecting the values of a large bureaucracy to coincide with your own simply sets you up for disappointment.

Examples of discrepancies are many. For instance, helping professionals believe that the primary goal of bureaucracies should be to serve clients, while the actual goal of bureaucracies is to survive. Helping professionals believe bureaucracies should change to meet the emerging needs of clients, while bureaucracies resist change and are most efficient when no one is "rocking the boat." Helping professionals believe bureaucracies should personalize services to each client and convey that "you count as a person," while bureaucracies are in fact highly depersonalized systems in which clients (and employees) do not count as persons but are only tiny components of a mammoth system. Highlight 8.1 lists additional conflicting orientations between helping professionals and bureaucratic systems (Gibelman & Furman, 2008; Knopf, 1979).

Any of these differences in orientation can become an arena of conflict between helping professionals and the bureaucracies in which they work. A number of

| Highlight 8.1 | **Value Orientation Conflicts between Helping Professionals and Bureaucracies** |

Orientation of Helping Professionals	Orientation of Bureaucratic Systems
Desire a democratic system for decision making.	Most decisions are made autocratically.
Desire that power be distributed equally among employees (horizontal structure).	Power is distributed vertically.
Desire that clients have considerable power in the system.	Power is held primarily by top executives.
Desire a flexible, changing system.	System is rigid and stable.
Desire that creativity and growth be emphasized.	Emphasis is on structure and the status quo.
Desire that communication be on a personalized level from person to person.	Communication is from level to level.
Desire shared decision making and a shared responsibility structure.	A hierarchical decision making structure and a hierarchical responsibility structure are characteristic.
Desire that decisions be made by those having the most knowledge.	Decisions are made in terms of the decision making authority assigned to each position in the hierarchy.
Belief that clients' and employees' feelings should be highly valued by the system.	Procedures and processes are highly valued.

helping professionals respond to these orientation conflicts by erroneously projecting a "personality" onto the bureaucracy. The bureaucracy is viewed as being "mixed in officialism," "uncaring," "cruel," and "the enemy." A negative personality is sometimes also projected onto officials of a bureaucracy, who may be viewed as being "paper shufflers," "rigid," "deadwood," "inefficient," and "unproductive." Knopf (1979, p. 25) states:

> The HP (helping person) . . . may deal with the impersonal nature of the system by projecting values onto it and thereby give the BS (Bureaucratic System) a "personality" [It is interesting how Knopf refers to a bureaucracy as BS]. In this way, we fool ourselves into thinking that we can deal with it in a personal way. Unfortunately, projection is almost always negative and reflects the dark or negative aspects of ourselves. The BS then becomes a screen onto which we vent our anger, sadness, or fright, and while a lot of energy is generated, very little is accomplished. Since the BS is amoral [that is, the BS can be neither moral nor immoral so the concept of morality does not apply to it], it is unproductive to place a personality on it.

A bureaucratic system is neither good nor bad. It is simply a structure with certain expectations for how to carry out various tasks. However, practitioners may have strong emotional reactions to these orientation conflicts between the helping professions and bureaucracies. Common reactions are anger at the system, self-blame ("It's all my fault"), sadness and depression ("Poor me," "Nobody appreciates all I've done"), and fright and paranoia ("They're out to get me," "If I mess up, I'm gone").

Behavior Patterns in Bureaucratic Systems

Helping professionals often adopt one of several types of behavior patterns while coping with bureaucracies that don't enhance organizational effectiveness; they include "the warrior," "the gossip," "the complainer," "the dancer," "the machine," and "the executioner" (Knopf, 1979, pp. 33–36).

The Warrior   The *warrior* leads open campaigns to destroy and malign the system. A warrior discounts the value of the system and often enters into a win-lose conflict. Warriors loudly and outspokenly complain about almost everything. Because of their overt "bad attitude," warriors rarely, if ever, get promoted. In fact, the warrior generally loses and is dismissed.

The Gossip   The *gossip* is a covert warrior who complains to others both inside and outside of the agency (including clients, politicians, and the news media) about how terrible the system is. A gossip frequently singles out a few officials to focus criticism upon. Bureaucratic administrators generally hate gossips because gossips try to air internal "dirty laundry" outside of the agency. Therefore, supervisors and administrators in bureaucracies often make life very difficult for gossips by assigning them distasteful tasks, refusing to promote them, giving them very low salary increases, and perhaps even dismissing them.

The Complainer   The *complainer* resembles a gossip, but confines complaints internally to other helping persons, to in-house staff, and to family members. A complainer wants people to agree in order to find comfort in shared misery. Complainers want to stay with the system, and generally do. Since they primarily keep their complaining secretive and internal, they usually avoid antagonizing the administration, and therefore maintain their anonymity (and their jobs).

The Dancer   The *dancer* is skillful at ignoring rules and procedures. Dancers are frequently lonely, often reprimanded for incorrectly filling out forms, and have low investment in the system or in helping clients. However, once inside of a bureaucratic system, dancers often manage to "just get by." In essence, they are usually lazy. Dancers generally don't really cause any trouble. They just don't do their jobs very well. It generally goes against the bureaucratic principle of maintaining the status quo to exert the energy necessary to fire a dancer.

The Machine   The *machine* is a "typical bureaucrat" who takes on the orientation of the bureaucracy. A machine's intent is to abide by the official bureaucratic rules no matter what. Machines dislike conflict. To them, obeying the rules to the letter of the law is much safer. Often a machine has not been involved in providing direct services for years. Machines are frequently named to head study committees and policy groups, and to chair boards. Machines often rise in the organizational power structure to the level of their incompetence ("The Peter Principle"[1]), where they often remain until retirement.

The Executioner   The *executioner* is a tremendously enthusiastic and self-motivated individual who has managed to gain some power, status, and advancement within the bureaucratic organization. Executioners have no real commitment to the value orientations of the helping professionals or to the bureaucracy. However, they have learned how to "play the game." They have managed to hide their anger toward bureaucratic control and red tape. They have succeeded in disguising their manipulative ploys and have fooled many of those around them about their true self-centered, hostile motives. Especially when threatened, executioners attack other targeted persons within an organization with energized, impulsive vigor. An executioner abuses power by not only indiscriminately assailing and dismissing employees but also slashing services and programs.

A Final Commentary on Bureaucracies

The description of bureaucratic systems presented here stresses a number of the negatives about such systems, particularly their impersonalization. In fairness, Lewis and colleagues (2001) stress that there are some positive aspects of bureaucracy, particularly as it "provides a foundation for personnel practices that all workers appreciate" (p. 74). These include "clear job roles and performance expectations, fair treatment, and due process" (p. 74). They continue, however, that it surely doesn't focus enough on the importance of interpersonal processes and the "uniqueness" of each individual (p. 74). In a later section, this chapter will address newer, more relationship-focused management approaches.

Also note that another advantage of being part of a large bureaucracy is the existing potential for changing a powerful system to clients' advantage. In small or nonbureaucratic systems, a social worker may have lots of freedom but little opportunity or power to influence large macro systems or mobilize extensive resources on behalf of clients.

 Critical Thinking Questions 8.2

If you were to work in a traditional bureaucracy, what aspects of that bureaucracy would be most difficult for you and why? How might you cope with the problem?

Highlight 8.2 discusses problems inherent in the U.S. health care system with respect to Asian and Pacific Islander cultural values. In many ways the health care system functions as a large bureaucracy. It also proposes ways to improve its functioning to empower this macro client system.

---

[1] The Peter Principle was developed by Laurence J. Peter in 1968 (Mish, 2008, 1995, p. 865).

full
vel
ch
wit
ex
th
19

Pi
Al
ge
th
ce
tic
e:
c(
m
e
h
a
ir
()
h
l(
c
v
:
\
t
(

1
1

made uniform. Effectiveness can be evaluated in terms of the machine's accuracy and efficiency (that is, how fast and perfectly the machine can punch out slabs). In this context, unlike that of the social services, work routines are predictable, repetitive, and relatively easy to monitor and control.

Additionally, professional staff in social service organizations vary widely in terms of intervention approaches, techniques used, priorities, and personality styles. Clients probably vary even more widely in terms of characteristics and needs. Therefore, social service organizations bring multiple, immeasurable, human factors to the intervention process. Because people vary drastically more than inanimate materials like metal slabs, practitioners who work with people must have much more flexibility than metal slab punchers. That is, workers in organizations need to have some degree of discretion in working with their clients. This, in turn, makes the monitoring of the intervention process more difficult. Social service organizations must constantly strive to define the process by which they deliver services to enhance social workers' ability to function effectively.

Impersonal Behavior

The goals of accountability and efficiency can create difficulties for workers and clients. Sometimes agencies engage in behavior intended to be businesslike but perceived by the workers as impersonal. It's easy, for example, for administrators to make arbitrary decisions where the workers feel left out. One agency director wanted to reduce costs such as postage and cut the time workers spent performing clerical tasks. He decided to eliminate the appointment letters that workers would type on their computers and send to clients who lacked phones. The letters told the client when the worker was planning to visit and asked the client to notify the worker if this was not satisfactory.

No one quarreled with the wish to save money, but many workers were upset because the new mandate would force them to make home visits without giving clients prior notice. To many workers this seemed inappropriate and unprofessional behavior, even a violation of clients' rights. It could also be more time consuming. The director did not share these opinions, and he overruled the workers' objections. Finally, tired of arguing social work values against business values, one worker calculated the cost of driving across the county to see a client who wasn't home. The wasted mileage cost exceeded the cost of sending out the appointment letters. After some discussion and debate, the director canceled the policy and allowed workers to send out appointment cards once again.

Management can minimize impersonal behavior by enhancing workers' involvement in planning and decision making. It can also strive to address and improve internal channels of communication. Newer trends in management discussed later in the chapter address this issue.

Another example of impersonal behavior involves a foreign adoptions unit in a private child welfare agency. Unit staff felt like their supervisor, Keung, was disinterested in their work and their needs. Keung spent most of his time in meetings with administration. Other times, he seemed preoccupied, gave little eye contact to supervisees, and enclosed himself in his office whenever possible. By demonstrating such impersonal behavior, his staff felt he just didn't care. In reality, Keung was power structure to the level of their incompetence ("The Peter Principle"[1]), where they often remain until retirement.

The Executioner The *executioner* is a tremendously enthusiastic and self-motivated individual who has managed to gain some power, status, and advancement within the bureaucratic organization. Executioners have no real commitment to the value orientations of the helping professionals or to the bureaucracy. However, they have learned how to "play the game." They have managed to hide their anger toward bureaucratic control and red tape. They have succeeded in disguising their manipulative ploys and have fooled many of those around them about their true self-centered, hostile motives. Especially when threatened, executioners attack other targeted persons within an organization with energized, impulsive vigor. An executioner abuses power by not only indiscriminately assailing and dismissing employees but also slashing services and programs.

A Final Commentary on Bureaucracies

The description of bureaucratic systems presented here stresses a number of the negatives about such systems, particularly their impersonalization. In fairness, Lewis and colleagues (2001) stress that there are some positive aspects of bureaucracy, particularly as it "provides a foundation for personnel practices that all workers appreciate" (p. 74). These include "clear job roles and performance expectations, fair treatment, and due process" (p. 74). They continue, however, that it surely doesn't focus enough on the importance of interpersonal processes and the "uniqueness" of each individual (p. 74). In a later section, this chapter will address newer, more relationship-focused management approaches.

Also note that another advantage of being part of a large bureaucracy is the existing potential for changing a powerful system to clients' advantage. In small or nonbureaucratic systems, a social worker may have lots of freedom but little opportunity or power to influence large macro systems or mobilize extensive resources on behalf of clients.

 | **Critical Thinking Questions 8.2**

If you were to work in a traditional bureaucracy, what aspects of that bureaucracy would be most difficult for you and why? How might you cope with the problem?

Highlight 8.2 discusses problems inherent in the U.S. health care system with respect to Asian and Pacific Islander cultural values. In many ways the health care system functions as a large bureaucracy. It also proposes ways to improve its functioning to empower this macro client system.

---

[1] The Peter Principle was developed by Laurence J. Peter in 1968 (Mish, 2008, 1995, p. 865).

Highlight 8.2 | The U.S. Health Care System, and Asian and Pacific Islander Cultural Values

The U.S. health care system is a huge bureaucracy reflecting many of the characteristics of traditional bureaucracies. Although management approaches do vary within its many organizational structures, strict regulations and decision making hierarchies for health care provision tend to dominate. A problem commonly faced by such bureaucracies is the lack of cultural sensitivity. Rigid rules do not provide flexibility for adapting to culturally diverse values and needs. A major goal in social work is to enhance service provision for clients. Lack of responsiveness to clients' cultural values and belief systems can erect major barriers to receiving effective services.

McLaughlin and Braun (1999) critique the appropriateness of the U.S. health care system concerning its responsiveness to Americans of Asian and Pacific Islander (API) cultural heritage. More specifically, concerns focus on how "the system" emphasizes individual autonomy, which may conflict with "collectivist decision making norms" inherent in API cultures (p. 321). The concept *collectivist* refers to giving greater consideration to group goals, needs, and issues over those of the individual (Sue, 2006). The following discussion first describes five dimensions important in understanding API cultures with respect to involvement in the health care system. Second, three conflicts with U.S. health care policy are addressed—medical informed consent, advance directives, and decisions about nursing home placement. Third, implications for improved health care provision are proposed.

Value Dimensions in API Cultures Relating to Health Care Provision

At least five major concepts inherent in API cultures relate directly to U.S. health care provision: shared decision making in families, "filial piety," "silent communication," "preservation of harmony," and "delayed access but great respect" for health care (Brammer,

2004; McLaughlin & Braun, 1999, pp. 323–325; Mokuau, 2008; Paniagua, 2005; Weaver, 2005).

Shared Decision Making in Families

In contrast to the individualist perspective emphasized in U.S. health care, Asian Americans and Pacific Islanders rely on the family or larger group to make ultimate decisions about any individual member's care. In the U.S. health care system, individual patients are subject to *informed consent*. That is, physicians and health care staff must inform an individual patient about her "diagnosis, prognosis, and alternatives for treatment" (McLaughlin & Braun, 1999, p. 322). A patient then has the right to provide consent for continuation of the treatment process. In many API cultures, this assumption does not comply with values and norms. For instance, "unlike the custom among white people, for whom the individual patient is the decision maker, many Japanese and Chinese families assign decision making duties to the eldest son. In Pacific Islander families, it may be less obvious who the decision maker is" (McLaughlin & Braun, 1999, pp. 323–324). The entire family may share duties and assume designated responsibilities like getting food. Because of the collective nature of decision making, in API cultures it is customary for "all family members" to "receive the same level of detail about the patient's diagnosis, prognosis, and treatment options" (Braun, Mokuau, & Tsark, 1997; McLaughlin & Braun, 1999, p. 324).

A Cautionary Note

Note that when speaking about any racial, ethnic, or cultural group, it is important not to overly generalize. Here we talk about general value dimensions evident in API cultures. However, individuals or families from any ethnic or racial group may embrace traditional cultural norms to various degrees. They may also experience *acculturation*, "the loss of traditional cultural attitudes, values, beliefs, customs, behaviors, and the acceptance of new cultural traits" (Lum, 2005, p. 101). In other words, members of a diverse group may gradually blend into and adopt the values and customs of the larger society. When thinking about a racial, ethnic, or cultural group, it is therefore important not to assume that all members comply with all cultural values or conform to the same extent. Being of German ethnic heritage does not automatically mean a person loves sauerkraut, liver sausage, and raw ground beef with onions on rye bread just because these are traditional ethnic foods. The trick is to open-mindedly view each person as a unique personality, yet be sensitive to the possible cultural values and beliefs that person may hold.

The other word of caution concerns differences among the many cultures included under the API umbrella. For example, Balgopal (2008) cites several variations evident in specific groups. Japanese Americans are more likely than other Asian-American groups to marry outside of their ethnic group and are more likely to divorce at some point in their lives. Filipino-American couples maintain a more egalitarian relationship than most other Asian-American groups. Indian Americans are more likely to wear clothing based on cultural expectations in India, consume a vegetarian diet, and participate in arranged marriages.

Filial Piety

A second value dimension in API cultures is *filial piety*, "a devotion to and compliance with parental and familial authority, to the point of sacrificing individual desires and ambitions" (Kirst-Ashman & Hull, 2009b, p. 432; Wong, 2005). Paniagua (2005) explains:

> Traditional Asians believe that children's primary duty is to be good and to respect their parents. Parents are expected to determine the course of their children's lives, without consulting the children

about their own desires and ambitions, and any failure on a child's part to comply with parent's expectations is seen as a threat to the parents' authority. (p. 76)

Silent Communication

A third value inherent in API cultures is silent or nonverbal communication. Paniagua (2005) explains:

> Asians often respond to the verbal communications of others by being quiet and passive; they may go to a great deal of effort to avoid offending others, sometimes answering all questions affirmatively to be polite even when they do not understand the questions, and they tend to avoid eye contact. . . .
>
> Among Asians silence is a sign of respect and politeness; it also signals an individual's desire to continue speaking after making a point during a conversation (Sue & Sue, 2003). In Western cultures, eye contact during direct verbal communication is understood to imply attention and respect toward others. Among Asians, however, eye contact is considered a sign of lack of respect and attention, particularly to authority figures (e.g., parents) and older people. (p. 77)

Leong, Lee, and Chang (2008) elaborate:

> Asian Americans tend to communicate in a high-context style with context as the primary channel for communication. Direct and specific references to the meaning of the message are not given. Receivers are expected to rely on their knowledge and appreciation for nonverbal cues and other subtle affects for interpreting message meaning. [In contrast,] [t]he Euro-American culture tends to focus on communication through a low-context style, where words are the primary channel of communication. Direct, precise, and clear information is delivered verbally. Receivers can expect to simply take that which is said at face value. The high-context communication style can be seen as an elaborate, subtle, and complex form of interpersonal communication. (p. 117)

continued

Therefore, much can often be learned by carefully observing silent responses and subtle nonverbal gestures. For example, it is "improper" for children "to discuss issues of death and dying with parents, yet concern by either party may be expressed by nonverbal cues such as bowing of the head or eye contact" (McLaughlin & Braun, 1999, p. 324).

Preservation of Harmony

API cultures emphasize *harmony*, the importance of getting along peacefully and not causing trouble for the family (Brammer, 2004; Weaver, 2005). This concept characterizes collectivist societies. The implication, then, is "to endure hardship and pain," especially if addressing issues that might cause discomfort or disturbance for other family or group members (McLaughlin & Braun, 1999, p. 325). For example, in Vietnamese culture the "desire to achieve harmony between the self and the non-self remains an essential preoccupation of the Vietnamese in interpersonal relations outside the family group" (Vietnam-culture.com, 2009). Such interpersonal harmony involves being courteous, truthful, and diplomatic (DuongTran & Matsuoka, 1995). In Hawaiian culture, "contributions to unity and harmony are more valued . . . than are competitive success or self-satisfaction" (Ewalt & Mokuau, 1996, p. 260). Many values in Hawaiian culture reflect the importance of harmony and affiliation, including generosity, honesty, and helpfulness (Mokuau, 1995).

There also tends to be respect for clearly defined family structure and hierarchy of authority, arrangements that tend to clarify expectations and encourage predictability of behavior (Balgopal, 2008; Sue, 2006). For instance, Samoan culture stresses "hierarchical systems with clearly defined roles. The highly structured organization of the family defines an individual's roles and responsibilities and guides the individual in interactions with others" (Ewalt & Mokuau, 1996, p. 261).

Delayed Access to But Great Respect for Health Care

API values include emphasis on family, cooperation, harmony, and aversion to causing trouble. All these contribute to avoidance of the U.S. health care system if at all possible. Asian Americans and Pacific Islanders generally experience shame at the inability to handle their own problems and the need to seek help from formal outside sources (Balgopal, 2008; Fong, 2008; Paniagua, 2005). Thus, family and group members strongly prefer to deal with issues and illnesses internally within the family and avoid exposing problems to outsiders. For example, Chinese Americans suffer disgrace when forced to communicate personal information about family problems, including cognitive disability, mental illness, and school or work failures (Lum, 1995).

When it becomes obvious to family members that the family is incapable of resolving health problems, they hesitantly turn to health care providers. For example, Japanese Americans will only seek mental health help when the problem becomes extraordinarily unmanageable (Murase, 1995). Asian and Pacific Islanders who experience mental or emotional stress often transform this into physical symptoms (Fong, 2008).

For physical illness, API families pursue external health services "only if emergency care is needed"; once that step is taken, however, group members view the physician "as a wise and benevolent authority figure" (McLaughlin & Braun, 1999, p. 325). Health care professionals are expected to make collectivist decisions, that is, those "in the best interest of the greatest number of people involved with the patient" (McLaughlin & Braun, 1999, p. 325).

Conflicts between Cultural Values and the U.S. Health Care System

Conflicts between API cultures and U.S. health care system policy and practice focus on at least three areas—informed consent, advance directives, and decisions about nursing home placement (McLaughlin & Braun, 1999). The following discussion relates how the five value dimensions discussed earlier can clash with that system. The point is not to condemn the U.S. health care system, but rather to examine how it can either detract from the health and well-being of Asian Americans and Pacific Islanders or empower them. The subsequent section will suggest recommendations for improvement.

Informed Consent

Four problematic issues relate to informed consent (McLaughlin & Braun, 1999). First, consider Asian Americans' and Pacific Islanders' emphasis on harmony and conforming to group wishes. Patients may feel obligated to sign consent papers presented to them when they really don't want to. The API cultural orientation is to cooperate and not cause trouble. Second, cultural norms emphasizing silence and inconspicuousness may prevent patients from voicing contrary opinions, asking questions about illnesses, and refusing to sign papers. Third, health care personnel are often unaware of how API cultural values can affect the consent process and interfere with its integrity.

Fourth, although physicians generally tell family members about a terminal illness, informing the patient about ensuing death is taboo for many Asian Americans and Pacific Islanders. Reasons can be "that the family does not want the patient to become disheartened and give up on living, that the family feels it is disrespectful to speak of such things to an elder, or that talking about death is 'polluting' or will cause bad luck" (McLaughlin & Braun, 1999, p. 330). Health care personnel thus face an ethical dilemma. Policy and professional ethics may assert that a patient be informed of a terminal diagnosis in order to discuss and weigh treatment options. However, culturally, the patient may not want to know and may well choose ignorance if given that option.

Advance Directives

A second problematic issue concerning API cultures and the health care system involves advance directives. An *advance directive* is a person's formally recognized statement signed before witnesses that gives instructions for what medical alternatives should be pursued in the event that the person becomes incapable of making such choices. Two issues tend to surface here (McLaughlin & Braun, 1999). First, health care facilities are legally required to "to approach patients for copies of advance directives" (McLaughlin & Braun, 1999, p. 331). However, in Chinese, Japanese, and Hawaiian cultures, people seriously avoid discussing death for fear of inviting it or suffering negative consequences. A second issue is that it is pointless for Asian Americans and Pacific Islanders to discuss such issues because of their collectivist approach. They assume that family members will take care of those issues appropriately when the time comes.

Decisions about Nursing Home Placement

Many Asian Americans and Pacific Islanders embrace filial piety and firmly believe that children should care for aging parents (Balgopal, 2008; Brammer, 2004; Wong, 2005). To them, nursing home placements should be avoided at all costs. Thus, there is some tendency for API families to wait until situations reach crisis proportions before initiating possible nursing home placement (McLaughlin & Braun, 1999; Murase, 1995). Stress may escalate from economic pressure to work outside the home, caring for both children and aging parents, and increasing physical and cognitive health problems experienced during the aging process.

Interestingly, in contrast to Western culture, "many traditional API cultures expect death to occur at home and have mourning traditions that involve keeping the body at home for a number of days before burial" (McLaughlin & Braun, 1999, p. 331; Nichols & Braun, 1996). Thus, ensuing death may not spur API families to remove the dying member to a nursing or hospital facility.

Critical Thinking Questions 8.3:
Implications for an Improved Health Care System

Large service provision systems are never perfect. There are always quirks and problems because such diverse people are involved. Bureaucracies have established rules to assist in their ongoing functioning. A large health care system cannot adapt itself perfectly to all its beneficiaries' needs. However, a continuous concern for social workers is the need to assess large systems' functioning, recommend improvements, and work to achieve positive changes. This is especially true in view of the U.S. population's wide range of cultural diversity.

How can the U.S. health care system become more sensitive to API and other cultures? How would you address this issue? What recommendations would you make to improve service access and provision to people of API cultural heritage? Four recommendations are proposed here.

First, training should be provided for health care personnel that sensitizes them to API cultural values and issues (Fong, 2008; McLaughlin & Braun, 1999; Patti, 2008; Yamashiro & Matsuoka, 1997). Staff should be taught to carefully observe periods of silence, nonverbal behavior, and family or group interaction for clues to understand such behavior.

Second, the health care system should encourage personnel to "begin addressing end-of-life planning issues with whole families (not just individual patients) earlier in the life course (rather than waiting until the end) and in nonhospital venues" (McLaughlin & Braun, 1999, p. 333). Agency policy should encourage staff to tune in to cultural values regarding collectivist versus individual perspectives on decision making, and work with families accordingly.

Third, the health care system should begin investigating the adoption of family-centered rather than individual-centered decision making models for virtually any health-related decisions (Fong, 2008; McLaughlin & Braun, 1999; Mokuau, 1995). Health care personnel should seek to understand individual's and family values, and work within that value system to the greatest extent possible. The health care system should respect both the individual's and the family's right to self-determination (Ewalt & Mokuau, 1996).

Fourth, social workers should pursue ongoing advocacy for positive policy and practice changes in the health care system. Health care should respect and appreciate cultural diversity and self-determination, not pretend they don't exist.

Problems Frequently Encountered by and in Social Service Organizations

Regardless of an agency's structural type and managerial approach, a number of obstacles can hinder social workers' ability to do their best possible job. As social service agencies struggle to provide efficient and effective services within the larger macro environment, they are often plagued by internal problems and issues. These include vagueness of goals, vagueness of process, impersonal behavior, lack of rewards and recognition, agency policy and worker discretion, and traditions and unwritten rules.

Vagueness of Goals

From a social work perspective, *accountability* is an individual worker's and the profession's responsibility to clients and the community to work effectively and achieve the goals that have been established. Individual practitioners and whole agencies are called upon to prove that their performance is productive and valuable. A major way of doing this is to define specific, measurable goals and monitor the extent to which these goals are achieved. Chapter 1 introduced the concept of *research-informed practice*. This means social workers should use the approaches and interventions in their practice that research has determined are effective. Social workers should employ "research findings to improve practice, policy, and social service delivery" (CSWE, 2008, p. 5).

Superficially, this sounds good. However, think about it. How can a practitioner prove that a client has been helped? One way is to define specific behavioral goals. This takes substantial time, effort, and expertise.

For instance, if you're teaching physically abusive parents child management techniques, how do you know when you've been successful? When they can pass a written test quizzing them on specific techniques? When the parents strike their children only on the hands and rump instead of on the head? When they only strike their children once each day instead of at least a dozen times, as they did in the past? Human behavior simply is difficult to define and measure.

Evaluating the outcomes of an entire organization (or even a single program), including goals, effectiveness, and efficiency, is infinitely more difficult than evaluating the outcomes of micro or mezzo interventions. This is because of the strikingly increased number of variables involved. In order to evaluate program outcomes, first, the program's goals must be clearly specified and understood. Brueggeman (2006) reflects:

> Often, however, the program goals are vague and nonspecific. For example, an organization may state that its goals are to reduce crime, assist the homeless, or support victims of domestic violence. These are worthy endeavors, but they are not goals that you can easily assess. . . . [T]he first task, therefore, is to assist the organization's key *stakeholders* [those who have something to gain from the program's effectiveness], including clients and the community in general, social workers, and other staff, and the board and administration, in stating their goals in clear, specific, and measurable terms, and help them decide which are the most practical and important. Other stakeholders are funding agencies and other social organizations and governmental agencies that partner with the social organization. (p. 332, emphasis added)

Specifying measurable goals is not an easy task, although social service agencies continue to make progress in the area despite all the difficulties involved. Effective definition, measurement, and attainment of goals enhance workers' ability to do their jobs.

Vagueness of Process

Interventions performed by a variety of individual practitioners and other staff are very difficult to measure and monitor. They are not like manufacturing machinery that punches out slabs of metal. Such slabs can be measured. Raw materials can be made uniform. Effectiveness can be evaluated in terms of the machine's accuracy and efficiency (that is, how fast and perfectly the machine can punch out slabs). In this context, unlike that of the social services, work routines are predictable, repetitive, and relatively easy to monitor and control.

Additionally, professional staff in social service organizations vary widely in terms of intervention approaches, techniques used, priorities, and personality styles. Clients probably vary even more widely in terms of characteristics and needs. Therefore, social service organizations bring multiple, immeasurable, human factors to the intervention process. Because people vary drastically more than inanimate materials like metal slabs, practitioners who work with people must have much more flexibility than metal slab punchers. That is, workers in organizations need to have some degree of discretion in working with their clients. This, in turn, makes the monitoring of the intervention process more difficult. Social service organizations must constantly strive to define the process by which they deliver services to enhance social workers' ability to function effectively.

Impersonal Behavior

The goals of accountability and efficiency can create difficulties for workers and clients. Sometimes agencies engage in behavior intended to be businesslike but perceived by the workers as impersonal. It's easy, for example, for administrators to make arbitrary decisions where the workers feel left out. One agency director wanted to reduce costs such as postage and cut the time workers spent performing clerical tasks. He decided to eliminate the appointment letters that workers would type on their computers and send to clients who lacked phones. The letters told the client when the worker was planning to visit and asked the client to notify the worker if this was not satisfactory.

No one quarreled with the wish to save money, but many workers were upset because the new mandate would force them to make home visits without giving clients prior notice. To many workers this seemed inappropriate and unprofessional behavior, even a violation of clients' rights. It could also be more time consuming. The director did not share these opinions, and he overruled the workers' objections. Finally, tired of arguing social work values against business values, one worker calculated the cost of driving across the county to see a client who wasn't home. The wasted mileage cost exceeded the cost of sending out the appointment letters. After some discussion and debate, the director canceled the policy and allowed workers to send out appointment cards once again.

Management can minimize impersonal behavior by enhancing workers' involvement in planning and decision making. It can also strive to address and improve internal channels of communication. Newer trends in management discussed later in the chapter address this issue.

Another example of impersonal behavior involves a foreign adoptions unit in a private child welfare agency. Unit staff felt like their supervisor, Keung, was disinterested in their work and their needs. Keung spent most of his time in meetings with administration. Other times, he seemed preoccupied, gave little eye contact to supervisees, and enclosed himself in his office whenever possible. By demonstrating such impersonal behavior, his staff felt he just didn't care. In reality, Keung was faced with some major issues in terms of keeping his unit intact and healthy. International political problems were causing difficulties in foreign adoptions, making many fewer children available for U.S. adoption. Keung was struggling with administration, trying not to lay off workers and instead providing transfer alternatives for them to other agency units. Keung appeared impersonal, but he was really very concerned. He was preoccupied with helping his workers keep their jobs.

Thus, workers should be sensitive to the position and needs of supervisors and administrators. The latter may indeed appear preoccupied or aloof. However, they must attune themselves to external social and economic forces that affect the entire agency and its operation. If they don't keep the agency running, no one has a job.

Lack of Rewards and Recognition

Another impediment in many organizational environments is management's failure to distribute rewards and recognition as frequently and consistently as most workers would like. In school, it is common for you to get periodic feedback on your performance. Papers are returned with comments and a grade. Exams are returned soon after they are given with the grade very evidently displayed. After each grading period, instructors give grades in each course. Many people prefer this regular system of positive reinforcement and expect something like it to exist in the agencies where they work.

Unfortunately, much of the good work that social workers do will never be recognized. It is simply not acknowledged in the busy life of the agency. Other good work will be noticed, but for many reasons no one will comment on it. Supervisors may come to take the good work for granted, not believing it needs regular reinforcement. Clients may appreciate our efforts but are too involved in their own situations to show their gratitude. Sometimes, supervisors like practitioners' performance but clients do not. For example, probation and parole workers taking clients back to court because of clients' violations are unlikely to have such clients praise their efforts. Consequently, a good guiding principle is to learn to reinforce yourself. This means you must take pride in work you do well, accepting that your work will not always be acknowledged to the extent you would like.

A guiding principle is for supervisors, managers, and even colleagues to emphasize strengths whenever possible, just as workers should do with clients. In a busy, demanding work environment, they are easily overlooked. However, the extent to which management can emphasize strengths generally enhances workers' morale and ability to function well.

Agency Policy and Worker Discretion

Agency policies and worker discretion can pose another obstruction to effective work. Practitioners may either feel squelched by policy restrictions about what they can and can't do, or be floundering because policies don't provide enough guidance.

Agencies establish and operate within a system of policies that guide workers' behavior and provide direction in situations commonly encountered. For example, an agency may have a policy that requires workers to sign out when they leave the building. This policy makes it easier for supervisors, administrators, and clients needing help to know a worker's location at any given moment. In effect, it is a form of accountability and makes sense to most workers.

Many new workers feel overwhelmed with all the policies, rules, regulations, and procedures they must learn and abide by. They may think that policies control or constrain their every action. In reality, workers have enormous discretion about how they do their jobs, because policies, by their very nature, must be general enough to apply in many different situations. This means that no policy can foresee all the possible events, nuances, and complexities that arise in any given case. Policies establish general guidelines, but workers are responsible for using their discretion or judgment with specific cases. Thus, these policies do not present a real barrier to effective social work. Workers must be prepared to apply their professional knowledge and skills and cannot rely on agency policy to dictate each decision in the field.

For example, consider being a practitioner working for a family services agency that specializes in helping parents learn how to control their children's behavior. Agency policy might prescribe eight weeks to work with parents and demonstrate improvements in their children's behavior. However, you and the parents have relatively wide discretion in determining what specific behaviors to work on. Should you focus on the children's tantrums, their refusal to eat anything but pizza and Krispy Kreme double-chocolate cream-filled donuts for supper, or their almost constant nagging for attention? The decision is a matter of discretion.

It is important for management to monitor the effectiveness of policy on all aspects of agency functioning. Outdated policies should be identified and changed. Cumbersome policies should be simplified if possible. Vague policies should be clarified to provide workers with adequate direction, even in view of their need to use discretion.

Traditions and Unwritten Rules

Unobtrusive, hidden traditions and unwritten rules are other potential problems in agency environments. The written rules frequently appear in some sort of regulation manual or personnel handbook. The unwritten rules are related to the organization's informal structure reflecting who has power and who communicates with whom. As in families, the traditions and unwritten rules are often learned only through verbal exchanges with more experienced group members. Sometimes they are learned only when the novice worker inadvertently violates the rule or tradition.

A case in point was a situation that arose when a new MSW graduate, Butch Cassidy, took his first job at a huge state mental hospital. Each Wednesday afternoon at 2:00 p.m., all the social workers at the hospital gathered around a large conference table. The meeting's purpose was to improve communication among the social work staff. The hospital's social services director, Frank Enstein, and formal policy encouraged social workers to feel free at these meetings to raise issues that were causing them problems or making their jobs more difficult. Butch was confused. Frank, the supervisor of four social work units, had offered Butch a job right out of graduate school. Butch had done his first field placement at the hospital and Frank had liked the quality of his work.

Butch's direct social work supervisor, Danielle Pricklesteel, seemed distant and acted as though she resented Butch's presence. Although she was always polite and professional, Butch felt Danielle did not really want him around. Finally, Butch decided to use the next Wednesday afternoon meeting to discuss his feelings. All social work staff, supervisors, and Frank attended these meetings.

At the meeting, Butch shared his feelings with the assembled group. Danielle tactfully acknowledged she felt as though Frank had "dumped" Butch in her unit without talking to her about Butch's status beforehand. Danielle apologized for taking out her anger at Frank on Butch. Frank apologized to Danielle for not consulting her before assigning Butch to her unit. The air appeared to clear, and Butch felt much better.

After the meeting, Danielle took Butch aside and told him that she was very upset because he had brought the topic up at the meeting. She stressed, "We never discuss anything important at these meetings. We just meet because Frank likes us to get together. If you have a concern, please talk it over with me first and we'll work it out." Later, Butch learned from talking to other workers that Danielle was right. The group had an informal rule that they never discussed anything important at these meetings. To do so was to violate the workers' informal policy and expectations.

The point of this example is that informal rules and traditions can affect social workers' ability to function effectively. We learn best by observing others and asking privately about things that appear to be rules. Learning about informal rules by breaking them can be painful. The extent to which management can identify expectations and clearly communicate them to new staff enhances workers' ability to function effectively.

Critical Thinking Questions 8.4

Have you ever worked in an organization or business where you experienced any of these problems—vagueness of goals, vagueness of process, impersonal behavior, lack of rewards and recognition, vague or restrictive work policies, or hidden traditions and unwritten rules? If so, what were the circumstances? How did you deal with the problem?

Newer Approaches to Management and Worker Empowerment

We've discussed bureaucracy and some of the problems inherent in bureaucracies and any organization providing social services, regardless of its management approach. We'll now turn to addressing some of the new management trends in social service and other organizations. In contrast to bureaucracy, a number of new approaches have been developing that serve to empower workers. Here we will explain five of them: constructing a culture of caring, the learning organization, teamwork and team empowerment, managing diversity, and client system empowerment within the organizational context. There are also dozens of specific methods of management. Two will subsequently be explained here—total quality management and servant leadership. Note that because all of these management trends and specific approaches focus on worker motivation, needs, and interpersonal dynamics, there's overlap in some of the concepts involved.

Constructing a Culture of Caring

Chapter 7 defined *organizational culture* as "the set of key values, beliefs, understandings, and norms shared by members of an organization" (Daft & Marcic, 2009, p. 63). Organizational culture provides guidelines and establishes expectations for how people should behave while at work (Brueggemann, 2006). Brody (2005) recommends developing a "culture of caring" in the social service agency setting. When staff feel connected with and supportive of each other, they can become a strong, cohesive force in achieving agency goals together.

Five core values characterize a caring organization (Brody, 2005). First, *job ownership* is the situation where workers feel that their job and their work performance is an important part of their identity (p. 152). They will strive hard to achieve goals and excellence in their work.

Organizations can promote job ownership by encouraging a second key value, *seeking a higher purpose* (p. 153). A caring culture encourages employees genuinely to feel that they're making a difference through their participation. It makes them feel like an integral, important part of a larger system. This can motivate them to work hard and learn new skills, not because management orders them to, but because they have a genuine desire to do so.

A third core value promoting a caring organizational culture is *emotional bonding* (p. 153). This means the organizational culture supports an environment in which people truly care about and experience a vital feeling of connection with each other. This can be especially helpful in agencies where workers experience exceptional pressures to work with demanding clients.

The fourth core value is *trust*, the condition where people feel they can depend on each other to follow through on tasks and be supportive of one another (p. 153). They then don't have to waste energy on negative interpersonal interactions, conflicts, complaints, and criticisms.

Pride in one's work, the fifth core value, is the condition where workers feel high self-esteem regarding and have great respect for their accomplishments at work (p. 153). Feeling good about yourself and being proud of the job you're doing motivates you to continue doing a good job.

The Learning Organization

A second management trend related to empowering workers is the concept of the learning organization. The *learning organization* is one "in which everyone is engaged in identifying and solving problems, enabling the organization to continuously experiment, change, and improve, thus increasing its capacity to grow, learn, and achieve its purpose" (Aldag & Kuzuhara, 2005; Daft, 2010, p. 50).

Daft (2010) further explains:

> The essential idea is problem solving, in contrast to the traditional organization designed for efficiency. In the learning organization all employees look for problems, such as understanding special [client] . . . needs. Employees also solve problems, which means putting things together in unique ways to meet a [client's] . . . needs. (p. 50)

At least five primary concepts characterize the learning organization. First, power is redistributed from higher levels to lower levels in the organizational structure through increased worker participation (Daft, 2010; Daft & Marcic, 2009; Jaskyte, 2008). Workers providing services directly to clients are given greater discretion to make their own decisions and plans. Power to provide input into and pursue organizational goals is distributed among all staff instead of being concentrated in management (Daft, 2010).

> *Empowerment* means unleashing the power and creativity of employees by giving them the freedom, resources, information, and skills to make decisions and perform effectively. Traditional management tries to limit employees while empowerment expands their behavior. Empowerment may be reflected in self-directed work teams, . . . job enrichment, and employee participation groups as well as through decision making authority, training, and information so that people can perform jobs without close supervision. In learning organizations, people are a manager's primary source of strength, not a cost to be minimized. (Daft & Marcic, 2009, p. 27)

A second concept involves how learning organizations nurture the development of new ideas. Employees are encouraged to be creative and share their ideas with others (Daft & Marcic, 2009; Jaskyte, 2008). Risk taking on the behalf of improvement is encouraged (Hellriegel & Slocum, 2009; Lussier, 2009). Learning organizations "encourage employees to be creative without fear of punishment if they fail. Mistakes and failure are viewed as learning experiences" (Lussier, 2009, p. 208).

Third, learning organizations emphasize the *effectiveness* of service provision to clients instead of the *process* of service provision (Jaskyte, 2008). Clients' perceptions about services are sought out so that improvements in quality and effectiveness can be made.

Fourth, the use of teams is encouraged (Daft & Marcic, 2009; Yaskyte, 2008). Teams are encouraged to make recommendations and decisions that management takes seriously and implements. Teams are charged with regularly assessing processes and procedures in order to make improvements. In social service organizations *multidisciplinary teams* (those including representatives from a variety of fields and with a range of backgrounds) can help improve insight into service provision. Thus, change occurs continuously. This contrasts strongly with traditional bureaucracies, which usually work to maintain the status quo.

Fifth, "open information" is promoted (Daft & Marcic, 2009, p. 27). "A learning organization is flooded with information. To identify needs and solve problems, people have to be aware of what's going on. They must understand the whole organization as well as their part in it" (Daft & Marcic, 2009, p. 27).

Sixth, as in a caring organizational culture, a learning organization encourages individuals to "lead because they want to serve one another as well as a higher purpose" (Aldag & Kuzuhara, 2005, p. 588). Their motivation focuses on the organization's greater good rather than on their own personal power and gain. Servant leadership, discussed later in the chapter, reflects this type of approach. (Highlight 8.3 explains four major types of leadership often identified in the context of organizational management.)

"Learning Disabilities" Working against Learning Organizations   Senge (1990) identifies at least six "learning disabilities" that may occur in organizations and work against learning organization culture (pp. 18–25):

- *I am my position.* This means that each worker has tunnel vision, focusing only on the tasks required in his or her position. Workers neither feel part of the greater whole nor feel that have input into the organization's vision for the future.
- *The enemy is out there.* It's not my fault. It's his. Or it's hers. Blaming others for the consequences of your own behavior works against the learning organization. People don't learn from their mistakes and improve their behavior. Blaming others only weakens interpersonal relationships.
- *The illusion of taking charge.* Sometimes it appears that organizational leaders are taking charge of situations when they lash out at others while trying to solve problems. Superficially, they look like they're in control because they're calling attention to themselves. However, people who are really in charge don't react with emotional outbursts. Rather, they carefully think issues through, assess their own conduct, and make rational decisions.
- *The parable of the boiled frog.* As unappealing as this analogy is, it paints a poignant picture. If you throw a frog into a pot of boiling water, it immediately reacts by jumping out. However, if you put a frog in cold water and gradually heat it to boiling, the frog will just stay put and come to an unfortunate end. That's because frogs have adapted to react to abrupt changes in temperature, not gradual ones. The analogy between this parable and organizational behavior is that management often reacts to a crisis or some other situation and shifts its focus on events as they occur. For example, an important, highly skilled employee quits. New legislation requires recording procedures radically different from the old ones. Huge funding cuts loom on the horizon. Senge (1990) would say that the major issues affecting organizations are ongoing, gradual developments. Of course, management must react to events, but managers should never lose sight of the long haul, ongoing processes, and longer-term, distant goals.
- *The delusion of learning from experience.* Hopefully, each of us learns from our experiences so that we make better, wiser choices in the future. However, after a change (such as making a policy decision or implementing a new program) is made in an organization, it often takes years to determine whether that change was effective or not. Thus, organizations don't necessarily learn from experience very quickly.

| Highlight 8.3 | **Leadership Styles** |

Leadership is "a process whereby an individual influences a group of individuals to achieve a common goal" (Northouse, 2007, p. 3). Four leadership styles will be described here—directive, supportive, participative, and achievement-oriented (House & Mitchell, 1974; Lussier, 2009; Northouse, 2007; Williams, 2009, 2010a). They are based on a theoretical approach to leadership called *path-goal theory*. Williams (2010b) explains:

> Just as its name suggests, *path-goal theory* states that leaders can increase subordinate satisfaction and performance by clarifying and clearing the paths to goals and by increasing the number and kinds of rewards available for goal attainment. Said another way, leaders need to clarify how followers can achieve organizational goals, take care of problems that prevent followers from achieving goals, and then find more and varied rewards to motivate followers who achieve those goals. (p. 261)

As Northouse (2007) explains, the path-goal theory of leadership "is about how leaders motivate subordinates to accomplish designated goals."; he continues:

> Path-goal theory emphasizes the relationship between the leader's style and the characteristics of the subordinates and the work setting. The underlying assumption of path-goal theory . . . suggests that subordinates will be motivated if they think they are capable of performing their work, if they believe their efforts will result in a certain outcome, and if they believe that the payoffs for doing their work are worthwhile. (p. 127)

The following four leadership styles are based on path-goal theory:

1. *Directive leadership* "involves letting employees know precisely what is expected of them, giving them specific guidelines for performing tasks, scheduling work, setting standards of performance, and making sure that people follow standard rules and regulations" (Williams, 2009, p. 528).

2. *Supportive leadership* "involves being friendly to and approachable by employees, showing concern for them and their welfare, treating them as equals, and creating a friendly climate" (Williams, 2009, p. 528). "Leaders using supportive behaviors go out of their way to make work pleasant for subordinates" (Northouse, 2007, p. 130). "Supportive leadership often results in employee satisfaction with the job and with leaders. This leadership style may also result in improved performance when it increases employee confidence, lowers employee job stress, or improves relations and trust between employees and leaders" (Williams, 2009, p. 528).

3. *Participative leadership* "involves consulting employees for their suggestions and input before making decisions. Participation in decision making should help followers understand which goals are most important and clarify the paths to accomplishing them. Furthermore, when people participate in decisions, they become more committed to making them work" (Williams, 2009, p. 529).

4. *Achievement-oriented leadership* "means setting challenging goals, having high expectations of employees, and displaying confidence that employees will assume responsibility and put forth extraordinary effort" (Williams, 2009, p. 529).

Note that these categories are not mutually exclusive. People's personalities, values, and behaviors vary dramatically. Each person is unique. It is certainly possible, indeed probable, that a particular leader may reflect aspects of more than one leadership style.

Critical Thinking Questions 8.5

What type or types of leadership do you think characterizes leaders in a learning organization? Explain.

- *The myth of the management team.* Some teams (defined in Chapter 4 and discussed further in the next section) are made up of members with hidden agendas who engage in power struggles and attempted manipulation. Management should look beyond the external appearance of a team's functioning and carefully evaluate its accomplishments.

Teamwork and Team Empowerment

Chapter 4 established that a *team* is a group of two or more people gathered together to work collaboratively and interdependently with each other to pursue a designated purpose. Teams can provide a useful means of empowerment in organizations by giving the responsibility for service provision to designated groups that work together (Daft, 2010; Daft & Marcic, 2009; Lussier, 2009; Williams, 2009). In effect, it means giving power to teams of agency workers rather than individual managers or workers. Teams can identify problems and issues, discuss potential alternatives, make decisions about how to proceed, set goals, and evaluate progress.

Specific teams might consist of groups of staff members who either provide similar services or serve the same category of clients. Teams generally meet regularly and are expected to work cooperatively together on the clients' behalf. Ongoing resolution of any conflicts occurring among team members is emphasized. Negative internal staff conflict does not benefit clients. Therefore, it is not tolerated.

Teams are most effective and empowered when used under four circumstances (Williams, 2009). First, a "clear, engaging reason or purpose [should exist] for using them. . . . Teams are much more likely to succeed if they know why they exist and what they are supposed to accomplish, and more likely to fail if they don't" (p. 354).

"Second, teams should be used when the job can't be done unless people work together. This typically means that teams are required when tasks are complex, require multiple perspectives, or require repeated interaction with others to complete" (p. 354). Tasks requiring specific skills that can be undertaken by a single worker don't necessarily require the multiple sources of energy and ideas generated by a team.

"Third, teams should be used when rewards can be provided for teamwork and team performance. Team rewards that depend on team performance, rather than individual performance, are the key to rewarding team behaviors and efforts" (p. 355). An agency might reward teamwork by giving the team's efforts and accomplishments public recognition in the form of praise, progress reports in an agency newsletter, or plaques that can be displayed in an office. Bonuses and raises also provide means of rewarding effective teamwork.

The fourth circumstance under which teams can function well is when they have clear authority to make recommendations or implement their decisions as a result of their efforts. Teams function most effectively when left to their own devices to determine their own processes and procedures (Williams, 2009).

Working as a team has several advantages to working as separate individuals. First, a team allows for the presentation and sharing of many ideas, perspectives, and experiences. Second, team members have a wider repertoire of skills than any one individual. Third, the entire team should "own" its conclusions, recommendations, and results. Fourth, members can teach each other skills in addition to sharing knowledge and information.

The *team* concept should be distinguished from that of a *group*. A team is always a group, but a group might not be a team. Groups do not necessarily work cooperatively, individual roles may be unclear, participation of individual members may be hampered or discouraged, and frequently individual group members are seen as "stars" instead of cooperative co-participants. The team perspective, on the other hand, should encourage performance of the team allowing the entire team to gain recognition and respect within the agency environment.

Managing Diversity

"Diversity exists in an organization when there is a variety of demographic, cultural, and personal differences among the people who work there" and the clients who receive services there (Williams, 2010b, p. 215). Lussier (2009) reflects:

> When we talk about diversity, we are referring to characteristics of individuals that shape their identities and their experiences in the workplace. *Diversity* refers to the degree of differences among members of a group or an organization. People are diverse in many ways. Within the workforce, people differ in their race/ethnicity, religion, gender, age, and ability. They also differ in their military status, sexual [orientation] . . . , expectations and values, lifestyle, socioeconomic status, work style, and function and/or position within the organization. (p. 210)

In contrast to traditional approaches to management, which stressed conformity, current thought focuses on the appreciation of diversity. "*Valuing diversity* emphasizes training employees of different races and ethnicities, religions, genders, ages, and abilities to function together effectively. To be creative and innovative and to continuously improve [service delivery] . . . , employees must work together . . . in an atmosphere of dignity and trust" (Lussier, 2009, p. 211).

Daft (2007) concludes: "Diversity is a fact of life for today's organizations, and many are implementing new recruiting, mentoring, and promotion methods, diversity training programs, tough policies regarding sexual harassment and racial discrimination, and new benefits programs that respond to a more diverse workforce" (p. 421).

Highlight 8.4 addresses the status of women in social services management.

Highlight 8.4 Women in Social Services Management

Gardella and Haynes (2004) explain the situation concerning women, social work, and social services management:

> Women represent nearly 70 percent of all paid employees in human services organizations, and more than 79 percent of social workers in the National Association of Social Workers (NASW) are women. Even so, men hold most of the managerial positions. In comparison to women in human services, men move into management earlier in their careers, are promoted faster, and earn significantly higher salaries at every occupational level. (p. 7)

Gardella and Haynes (2004) also note:

> Few books encourage women in human services to become leaders. . . . Management literature provides more information than inspiration for women with social work values and goals. Most research on women leaders has taken place in large corporations, where, in contrast to women in human services, nearly all the managers are affluent and [W]hite. . . .
>
> Although corporate managers and human services managers perform many similar tasks, books by and for women corporate leaders do not address the particular challenges of leading human services organizations. Many women who advance into leadership positions must resist prejudice and discrimination in their careers, but from a social work perspective, women leaders in human services have the greater responsibility 'to strive to end discrimination, oppression, poverty, and other forms of social injustice,' which is the professional mission of social work [NASW, 1999]. (pp. xiii–xiv)

Management Approaches Used by Women Who Are Leaders

To explore further the dynamics of women in social services management, Gardella and Haynes (2004) invited twenty-three women leaders in the human services to become members in one of three focus groups, two that met face-to-face and one online. *Focus groups* are those formed to discuss some topic in depth, clarify issues, and significantly enhance understanding of the topic (Toseland & Rivas, 2009). Group members in Gardella's and Haynes's groups came from racially diverse backgrounds, and all participants had substantial leadership experience in organizations. These groups were formed to discuss the career paths followed and the issues faced by these women as they progressed up the career ladder.

Findings revealed that group members' leadership experience reflected the theme of "inclusion," a pattern of behavior emphasizing "connection" and "collaboration" with others, "commitment" to professional values, and "optimism" (p. 102). "Inclusive leaders cultivate relationships with and among various communities and groups, using relationships to gather information, to enhance resources, and to form political alliances for their organizations" (p. 139). They took their "social responsibility" very seriously and strove to empower their clients, students, staff, organizations, and communities (p. 102). These leaders believed in "participatory decision making" and "an appreciation for diversity," which of course coincides with a culture of caring, employee empowerment, and advocating for diversity (p. 102). "Responding to obstacles with perseverance and hope, they were optimists who learned to fit into human services organizations while also trying to change them. . . . They advanced their causes along with their careers, pursuing changes 'to make the workplace more equitable and inclusive'" (p. 103; quote from Meyerson & Scully, 1999).

Austin (2002) comments on how these findings clash with perspectives adopted by many workers and managers in human service organizations:

> Executive positions in human service organizations, as well as in much of the rest of society, are still perceived as being embedded in a White, male, heterosexual culture . . . One of the factors in the resistance of many White heterosexual men, who are otherwise reasonable individuals, to the demographic

changes that are now taking place within many organizations is anxiety over the possibility of having to adapt to different expectations in organizational settings in which *it is not taken for granted* that the White, male, heterosexual culture is dominant at the executive level. Anxiety may be particularly acute in male-dominated organizations that have traditionally been organized as a hierarchical, command-and-control structure in which a gender change in leadership positions is accompanied by a change to a low-profile interactive management style. Such culture changes have already occurred in some human service organizations in which women predominate in executive and in policy-making roles as well as in direct service roles. (p. 349)

What Organizations Can Do to Empower Women as Leaders

What should be done to empower women as leaders in organizational settings? First, an organization's management should conduct an audit or analysis of the status of women within itself (Powell & Graves, 2003). This should go beyond counting the number of women in specific job categories:

> Organization analysis also includes a cultural audit, a snapshot of the current organizational culture. It assesses the nature of the organizational culture as experienced by employees, which is not necessarily what top management thinks the culture is or should be. It also assesses how the organizational culture influences the treatment of members of different groups. Surveys, interviews, focus groups, and meetings may be used to gather information for the audit. . . . A successful audit uncovers obstacles to the full attainment of diversity goals. Obstacles may include stereotypes and prejudices that affect employees' interactions with one another and managers' decisions regarding recruitment, performance appraisals, promotions, compensation, and other employment practices. (Powell & Graves, 2003, p. 233)

A second suggestion is for an organization to establish clear-cut objectives for each management unit (Powell & Graves, 2003). "Managers will put more effort into promoting nondiscrimination, diversity, and inclusion if they are expected to meet concrete objectives in pursuit of each of these goals" (Powell & Graves, 2003, p. 233).

A third suggestion involves encouraging employee involvement in the diversity-enhancement process by establishing "employee network groups" composed of women or people with the same cultural background (Powell & Graves, 2003, p. 235). These groups can provide "career development and networking opportunities" (Powell & Graves, 2003, p. 235). However, Gardella and Haynes (2004) warn that this process can isolate women or ethnic groups of color. They indicate that "ethnic niche experience is considered marginal experience with little relevance to the rest of the organization. Knowledge related to women or ethnic minority communities is seen as specialized knowledge, applicable only to those groups. Knowledge related to majority or mainstream groups is seen as general knowledge, applicable to all" (p. 111).

Encouraging Women in Social Work to Pursue Careers in Management

Gardella and Haynes (2004) make several suggestions for female social workers to consider in pursuing a career in organizational management or to support other women who want to do so:

- "Identify a woman leader who may be a role model for you in the future or, alternatively, who has been a role model for you in the past. Invite your role model to lunch. Ask about her career path, accomplishments, and future goals, and thank her for her example" (p. 13).
- Develop a list of your personal strengths. What qualities do you have that enhance your ability to set and achieve goals? Go over the list with a person you respect to assess its accuracy and expand it if possible.
- If you ever have the opportunity, "reach out" to another woman "as a mentor" (p. 53). Offer her support and the chance to solicit information and help from you. Help her integrate herself into a professional network where she can make additional contacts and establish her professional identity. "Mentoring relationships" are "essential" for "success" (Gibelman, 1998, p. 161).

continued

Highlight 8.4 | *continued*

- Think about and articulate what "personal and professional goals" you would like to achieve within "the next five years" (p. 76). Identify the "barriers and opportunities" that may confront you. Develop a strategy for how to deal with them (p. 76).
- Select a community club or professional organization and join it. This can expand both your personal and professional networks. Networking often opens up exciting opportunities.
- Meet with other women who are in professional circumstances similar to your own. You can talk about issues, provide support, and make suggestions for how to cope with problems and develop your personal and professional life.

Client System Empowerment by Management

We have defined *power* as the potential to move other people on a chosen course to produce an effect or achieve some goal, and *empowerment* as the "process of increasing personal, interpersonal, or political power so that individuals can take action to improve their life situations" (Gutierrez, 2001, p. 210). Chapter 1 established that a *client system* is any individual, family, group, organization, or community who will ultimately benefit from social work intervention. *Macro client systems* include communities, organizations, and larger groups of clientele with similar issues and problems. Despite typical organizational problems and wide variations in management style, social workers are responsible for client-system empowerment.

By orienting their management approaches, organizations can serve as empowerment mechanisms for large groups of clients. A major goal of social work is to enhance clients' right of choice, participation in decision making concerning their own well-being, and the availability of resources for them. A "goal of effective practice is not coping or adaptation but an increase in the actual power of the client or community so that action can be taken to change and prevent the problems clients are facing" (Gutierrez, GlenMaye, & DeLois, 1995, p. 250). How then can organizational management as a mightier force than individual practitioners encourage the empowerment of large groups of clients and citizens?

Gutierrez and her colleagues (1995) identify a range of elements working for and against an agency's ability to empower large groups of clients. They selected six private social service organizations that oriented themselves to serving client "populations that have been associated with empowerment-based services" (p. 251). Empowerment-oriented intervention involves educating clients so that they understand their social environment, helping them acquire "concrete skills for surviving and developing social power," emphasizing strengths upon which to build skills, and using democratic processes to involve clients in decision making (p. 250).

Selected agencies included two focusing on women's services, two on people of color, one on young people, and one on older adults. The researchers interviewed both direct-service staff and administrators, using taped interviews with an established format to identify environmental variables working for and against client empowerment. They identified four obstacles to empowerment—expectations of funding sources, the macro social environment, intrapersonal issues, and interpersonal issues. Three positive supports for client empowerment included staff development, an enhanced collaborative approach, and appropriate administrative leadership and support.

Factors Working against Client Empowerment   The first barrier to empowerment is *expectations of funding sources* (p. 252). Funding agencies do not necessarily give precedence to encouraging client participation. Involving clients in the decision making and service provision process on a large scale takes more time and energy. More people are involved. More communication is necessary. Therefore, the empowerment process is time-consuming. Funding sources must be sensitive to the significance of empowerment. They must consider it valuable enough to pursue despite increased costs in time and money.

The second impediment to empowerment is the *social environment*, the macro context in which organizations function (p. 252). Other agencies not supportive of the empowerment concept may not encourage referrals to or from empowerment-based agencies. Likewise, competition among agencies works against client empowerment in that empowerment is best established when people and agencies work together.

Rivalry for people's time and participation in the community social environment also obstructs the client-empowerment process. Community residents and practitioners have just so much time and energy. It becomes more difficult to involve people in the empowerment process who are also integrally involved in other organizations and processes. These might include neighborhood centers, advocacy groups, professional organizations (such as the National Association of Social Workers), or parent/teacher organizations.

Intrapersonal issues make up the third barrier to an organization's ability to seek client empowerment (p. 253). Sometimes, the basic attributes of clients or workers interfere with the empowerment process. For example, to what extent can people with serious mental or physical disabilities participate in the empowerment process? Some practitioners express frustration at the time and energy involved in pursuing empowerment, especially when they only find limited success.

The fourth obstacle to organizational empowerment consists of *interpersonal issues* (p. 253). These involve the interactions and relationships between clients and practitioners. Some workers express serious concerns about how difficult it is to let go of their own control and direction in the intervention process. This is especially so when empowered clients choose alternatives placing their own well-being at risk. For example, a client who is a survivor of domestic violence might *choose* to return to a destructive, abusive situation. It is difficult for some workers to accept their clients' right to choice when the workers feel the choice is inherently bad.

Organizational Conditions Enhancing Client Empowerment   In contrast to the obstacles, three supports are identified for client empowerment in organizations.

The first key to client empowerment is *administrative leadership and support* (p. 255). When administrators encourage the nurturance of client empowerment and practitioners feel this, "an atmosphere of empowerment" is established (p. 255).

A second support for client empowerment is *staff development* (p. 254). This includes the in-service training and other educational activities the agency provides both to empower the staff themselves and to teach staff how to incorporate approaches for empowering clients. Management should develop means of soliciting and improving client input into service provision, and teach these methods to staff.

A third support for client empowerment is an *enhanced collaborative approach* (p. 254). This involves the importance of a teamwork perspective infiltrating the agency environment. Staff understand the concepts of input and shared decision making because they're living it. They, in turn, can use these concepts to involve and empower clients. Gutierrez and her colleagues (1995) conclude that "those organizations that empower workers by creating an employment setting that provides participatory management, the ability to make independent decisions about their work, communication and support from administrators, and opportunities for skill development will be more capable of empowering clients and communities" (p. 256).

These suggestions sound positive and logical. However, despite good ideas, ethical and other problematic issues may surface in the course of service provision. Focus on Ethics 8.1 considers a scenario where a client is dissatisfied with a social services agency and its worker's approach in dealing with her.

Focus on Ethics 8.1 | **Client Dissatisfaction**

Consider the following scenario.

Yoko is furious. She is the single mother of three young children and a client at Penniless County Department of Social Services. She is currently receiving public assistance and is enrolled in a work preparation program teaching her skills in food preparation.

She has tried to see her assigned social worker Gunter eight times without success. The man is simply never there. Twice she's tried to complain to a supervisor but was cut off at the pass by secretarial sentries who adamantly declared that all supervisors were busy at the moment. They added she could make an appointment in three weeks or so.

Yoko's problem is that she discovered she hates food preparation and the training program in which she was arbitrarily placed. She wants to work and needs training, but couldn't it involve office work or

sales or anything but food preparation? She has little time to make a change. She will only qualify for a few more months of assistance before she is required to work and her assistance is terminated.

Yoko doesn't know whom she can turn to. The agency has no client advisory group or formal appeal process for clients to use. Clients must work through their designated worker. Yoko feels frustrated, angry, and powerless.

What is the ethical thing for the Department of Social Services and the social worker to do? How might management improve "the system" to include procedures and opportunities for Yoko's empowerment? How might she be allowed better opportunities to voice her opinions, make her own decisions, and have direct access to people in power making decisions about her?

Specific Management Approaches

We've discussed some major themes in current management thought. Now we'll turn to two of the dozens of specific management approaches being used today that apply some of these themes—total quality management and servant leadership. Note that these two theoretical approaches simply provide examples of how management can be used to empower staff in organizations.

Total Quality Management[2]

The first of two specific approaches to management and leadership discussed here is *total quality management (TQM)*. Developed by W. Edward Deming (1982, 1986) and others (Crosby, 1980; Feigenbaum, 1983; Juran, 1989), "TQM is a philosophy or overall approach to management that is characterized by . . . customer focus and satisfaction, continuous improvement, and teamwork" that entails employee involvement and empowerment (Daft, 2009; Williams, 2010b, p. 673). It "focuses on managing the total organization to deliver quality to customers" (in the social services context—clients) (Daft, 2009, p. 49). TQM involves both the application of systematic research and statistical analysis to determine what quality service involves, reflecting a scientific management approach, and an emphasis on human relations (Austin, 2002; Kronenberg & Loeffler, 1991; Martin, 1993). We have also established that many of the principles proposed by Theory Z (discussed in Chapter 5) apply as well.

"TQM means that the organization's culture is defined by and supports the constant attainment of customer satisfaction through an integrated system of tools, techniques, and training. This involves the continuous improvement of organization processes, resulting in high quality products and services" (Sashkin & Kiser, 1993, p. 39). Bedwell (1993) provides an even more straightforward description of TQM by stating, "The essence of total quality is simple: Ask your customers what they want; then give it to them!" (p. 29).

TQM is a management approach especially significant in social service agencies, because many of their administrators view TQM "as a preferred leadership model" (Bailey & Uhly, 2008, p. 67). TQM is also often used as a means of organizational development in social services as a long-term approach to improve service delivery (Packard, 2008). Another application of TQM and its principles involves the organizational assessment approach of quality assurance, frequently employed in social services agencies (Poertner, 2008). *Quality assurance* is a technique used to assess "organizational processes and systems" (as opposed to organizational outcomes or goals) to make certain these processes and systems meet expected standards; problems are identified, changes in organizational practices are made, and subsequently reassessment of those practices is done to determine whether effective improvements have been made (Lewis, Packard, & Lewis, 2007, p. 233).

It is beyond the scope of this book to describe in detail the implementation process of a TQM philosophy and program. However, to begin understanding

---
[2] The author wishes to thank the administrators for Lutheran Social Services of Wisconsin and Upper Michigan, 3200 W. Highland Blvd., P.O. Box 08520, Milwaukee, WI 53208, and Family Counseling Service, 148 Prospect St., Ridgewood, NJ 07450, who readily shared their ideas and materials.

how TQM is implemented and how it affects human behavior in a real agency, we will discuss a number of concepts. These include a focus on clients as customers, quality as the primary goal, employee empowerment and teamwork, TQM leadership, and continuous improvement.

A Focus on Clients as Customers   The central theme of TQM is the importance of the customer or client (Austin, 2002; Daft & Marcic, 2009). The quest for quality should be focused on what clients need and how effective and efficient they perceive service provision to be. Since staff who provide service directly to clients are central to client satisfaction, such staff are considered critical TQM stresses that they should have high status and receive good, supportive treatment.

TQM maintains that *customer satisfaction*, the condition where an organization's "services meet or exceed customer expectations," is paramount (Williams, 2009, p. 673). Therefore, agencies must solicit information from customers in order to strive for greater effectiveness (Austin, 2002; Sluyter, 1998). This can be done in a variety of ways (Albrecht, 1988; Martin, 1993). For one thing, the agency can administer customer satisfaction surveys or community surveys that solicit information from customers or residents about agency services. Staff can also conduct extensive interviews with individual customers to identify and examine their feelings. Likewise, the agency can focus on customer complaints and undertake extensive investigations. Suggestion boxes for anonymous feedback can be placed in accessible places. Finally, the agency can assemble groups of customers (focus groups) to discuss services and to make suggestions for quality improvement.

It should be emphasized that not only is customer feedback regularly solicited, but that the agency *uses* this feedback to improve its service provision. There are many ways an agency might incorporate feedback: by prioritizing client and agency needs, planning new goals, and undertaking new projects and procedures. Since this book's purpose is not to teach you how to be a manager but rather how to understand and work within an organizational environment, we will not discuss these processes here.

Highlight 8.5 identifies seven interactions between workers and customers that should never occur in an organization espousing total quality management.

Quality as the Primary Goal   In TQM, quality is the primary goal (Daft, 2010; Williams, 2009). However, quality is a difficult term to define. There is "no universally accepted definition" (Martin, 1993, p. 27). Each organization must determine for itself what quality means in terms of its own service provision.

For example, the Lutheran Social Services of Wisconsin and Upper Michigan define six components of quality: "accuracy," "consistency," "responsiveness," "availability," "perceived value," and "service experience" (LSS, 1993, p. 8).

- *Accuracy* measures the extent to which actual service provision matches customers' expectations. To what extent do customers feel they are getting the services they sought and hoped to receive?
- *Consistency* is "service accuracy over time" (LSS, 1993, p. 8). Are customers consistently getting the appropriate services, or is service provision inconsistent?

Highlight 8.5 | "The Seven Sins of Service"

Albrecht (1988) maintains the need to focus consistently on the quality of service provided to customers (or clients). He identifies "seven sins of service" that organizations commonly commit that work against maintenance and enhancement of service quality: "apathy," "brush-off," "coldness," "condescension," "robotism," "rule book," and "runaround" (pp. 14–16).

Of course, according to professional social work ethics, our clients or customers should always be our top priority. In an ideal world this would be so. In the real world, however, staff members are individuals with individual weaknesses and failings. These seven sins of service can and do occur. From an organizational perspective, of course, "staff" includes everyone from the agency director to various levels of administrative staff to professional social workers and other helping professionals to clerical staff to maintenance staff. Regardless of job title and responsibilities, each is, in essence, a representative of the agency. Albrecht maintains that it is absolutely essential for all staff to avoid committing any of the seven sins described here.

Of course, as professional social workers, we are supposed to be warm, empathic, and genuine. We are to always treat the customer with respect. However, these values are more difficult to maintain when we have twenty-three customers waiting in line impatiently for service, or if we absolutely have to finish by 4:30 p.m. today an eight-page report that we haven't started yet, or if we have an excruciatingly painful migraine headache. During these times, Albrecht would say that it's especially important to be vigilant about not committing any of the seven sins. Each of the seven organizational sins is explained here.

1. *Apathy.* Albrecht describes this as the "DIL-LIGAD" syndrome, or "Do I Look Like I Give Damn?"–à la comic George Carlin (p. 15). In other words, it's easy for staff to focus on getting their jobs over with so that they can go home and live their own lives. Apathy involves boredom with customer interactions and almost total lack of concern regarding the *quality*, usefulness, or effectiveness of the service provided.

2. *Brush-off.* This consists of getting rid of the customer by passing the buck and doing the smallest amount of work feasible. For example, a staff member might tell a customer that he can't answer her questions accurately and send her off to another department, probably on a wild goose chase.

3. *Coldness.* This "kind of chilly hostility, curtness, unfriendliness, inconsiderateness, or impatience" is intended to convey to the customer, "You're a nuisance; please go away" (p. 15). It is difficult to maintain a warm, interested interpersonal stance every minute of the day. Some customers may be hostile, feisty, or demanding, on the one hand. On the other, you as a worker may be tired, fed up, or disgusted.

4. *Condescension.* Treating customers with a disdainful, patronizing attitude implies you as the worker are more knowledgeable and, essentially, better than the customers are. When you condescend, you treat people as if they're not very bright. It might be characterized by the phrase, "Now don't you worry your stupid little head about it. I know best and I'll take care of everything. Trust me."

5. *Robotism.* When you treat each customer identically, without changes in facial or verbal expression, or ask the same questions over and over to different customers, you are not responding to individual differences. Such differences don't concern you. Your main intent is to get the job done as fast and efficiently as possible while using as little brain power as possible.

6. *Rule Book.* If you want to think as little as possible, use the rule book to give the

continued

Highlight 8.5 | *continued*

organization's rules and regulations absolute precedence. "Go by the book" totally and completely without any hint of compromise. I once called a weight control clinic for information on exercising and maintaining my weight. A young woman answered the phone, obviously reading a boilerplate blurb about losing weight at the clinic. I asked her if the clinic also helped people *maintain* their current weight, not lose anymore. She answered by rereading the identical blurb she just had read to me. I asked her the same question two more times, after which she repeated the same blurb. Finally, exasperated, I said, "Can't you think for yourself or what?" and abruptly hung up.

Although this situation does not reflect a social work context, it does exemplify the sin of rule book. The young woman answering the phone apparently was instructed to read her blurb and not say anything else. As a result, trying to get any help from her (in this case, information) was totally useless and frustrating.

7. *Runaround.* Stalling customers is a common sin. Workers tell a customer to call someone else for the information first, or to go to Window 217 and fill out the appropriate twenty-seven page form. Runaround entails using as little of your own time as possible, on the one hand, and wasting the customer's time, on the other.

- *Responsiveness* refers to timeliness of service provision. How long do customers have to wait before they get the attention and services they need?
- *Availability* is the ease with which customers can obtain services. To what extent are the services actually delivered to customers who request and need them?
- *Perceived value* is the extent to which customers feel the service is worth it. To what extent are the services they received worth the expense, time, and energy, and possible annoyance or frustration they experienced? To what extent is the service's value worth its total cost?
- The *service experience* sums up the total treatment experience with all of its nuances and subtleties. What is the customer's sum total evaluation of each word spoken with staff? How do customers perceive the agency, taking into account all their experiences with it? This covers each moment of interaction with the agency and each tiny aspect of their experience. For example, what was the time like that they spent sitting in a waiting room chair? How clean were those chairs, anyhow? Where they comfortable? How long were they forced to wait? How were the clients greeted when they finally met with their workers? What is their summary impression of their total treatment experience?

Employee Empowerment and Teamwork   We stress repeatedly that empowerment involves providing people with authority or power so that they might have greater control over what they do. A TQM approach means that workers must be "empowered" to make decisions about how to do their jobs; they "need to be encouraged constantly to develop pride in their work and their organization" (Dumler & Skinner, 2008, p. 359; LSS, 1993; Sluyter, 1998). Management places the major responsibility for effective service provision on direct-service workers. TQM not only emphasizes the importance of customers, but also employees in the agency units providing services directly to these customers. Likewise, other agency units providing input to direct-service units are considered important because of their support to the service providers. For example, supervisory input is considered important primarily because it should aid in the service-provision process.

In some ways, you might envision TQM as an upside-down pyramid. In a typical bureaucratic organization, the power structure as reflected in a formal organizational chart is in the form of a triangle or pyramid. The agency director sits at the pinnacle. Below her might be assistant directors, beneath them managers, below them supervisors, and, finally, at the very bottom, the many workers. The pyramid's shape, of course, reflects the relative number of persons involved at each level. There is only one agency director. There are fewer supervisors than direct-service workers. Finally, there are fewer direct-service workers than there are clients. In TQM, because the client customers or consumers are given precedence, those providing service directly to them are considered, in a way, the most important. The agency's clients as customers thus form the top level of the inverted pyramid because they are considered the most significant. Right below them would be the direct-service workers, beneath them the supervisors, and so on in the reverse order of the bureaucratic pyramid. The agency director and, perhaps, the board of directors would be placed at the very bottom of the inverted pyramid.

TQM emphasizes each employee's importance. Matza (1990) describes empowerment as "getting employees—especially front line employees—to take care of the customer" (p. 21).

TQM espouses not only empowerment of individual employees, but also "team empowerment" (Daft, 2010; Ginsberg, 1995; LSS, 1993, pp. 20–27; Williams, 2009). As already discussed, this involves giving the responsibility for service provision to designated groups that work together. TQM emphasizes cooperation instead of competition (Martin, 1993; Muckian, 1994). Such teamwork also means that all organizational employees from top management to direct-service workers are "given the incentive to work together and the responsibility and authority to make improvements and solve problems" (Williams, 2009, p. 674).

A Total Quality Approach to Leadership   Strong support and leadership from top management is critical in implementing TQM (Dumler & Skinner, 2008; Martin, 1993; Sluyter, 1998). Dumler and Skinner (2008) explain:

> Supervision has been widely practiced as a traditional method of keeping an eye on workers—that is, looking for mistakes [a method often practiced in traditional bureaucracies]. Some managers have even resorted to using information technologies to eavesdrop on employees. This type of practice has debilitating effects on performance and is ethically questionable. . . .
>
> The responsibility for quality control ultimately rests with management; however, managers must also promote worker self-management. To further employee self-management, managers must develop worker participation programs and policies. With knowledge of the [organization's] . . . costs and goals, workers can practice control with minimal supervision. Management's job is to ensure that workers have the knowledge, the tools, and the power to prevent problems from arising. Managers must also

encourage employee's suggestions . . . by recognizing and implementing worker quality improvement decisions. And, if there are problems, management should give workers the first opportunity to solve them. (p. 358)

One task leaders must accomplish is the establishment of a "culture of quality" (Martin, 1993, p. 80). We've established that *organizational culture* is "the set of key values, beliefs, understandings, and norms shared by members of an organization" (Daft & Marcic, 2009, p. 63). A culture reflecting a total quality perspective is one "characterized by teamwork, cooperation, open communication, flexibility, autonomy and empowerment" (LSS, 1993, p. 74). "As all employees must be involved in the total quality approach, agency leaders must visibly demonstrate their commitment to TQM" (Brown, Hitchcock, & Willard, 1994, p. 3). Leaders are responsible for "changing the organizational culture from one that dwells on *status quo* to one that gets excited about change" (Bedwell, 1993, p. 30).

For example, one agency director whose private, nonprofit family services organization had adopted a TQM perspective illustrated her commitment in a very concrete way. Historically, staff would park in the best spots in the parking lot each workday morning because they always got there first. Clients (or customers in TQM terminology), who regularly got there later, would get the parking spots furthest from the building—if there were any spots left at all. Traditionally, the agency director assumed "ownership" of the best parking spot right by the agency's main door. The assistant director (no. 2 in the agency's hierarchy) then took the second-best spot, and so it went on down the line. The daytime janitor was assigned the very worst spot.

Reflecting the TQM philosophy, the director decided to demonstrate the importance of serving customers and giving them priority by ordering that customers should be left the very best parking spots. Staff were relegated to the worst. The director herself chose the spot in the farthest corner of the lot, next to an appallingly foul-smelling dumpster. She also rallied some of the agency's precious funds to purchase extra parking spaces for customers in a lot adjacent to the agency. She felt that clients should no longer suffer from parking scarcity problems.

Another example of how agency leaders can demonstrate their commitment to TQM principles involves a family services agency that had held its board of directors meetings at noon each Friday since 1946. The boardroom where their meetings were held was the only large meeting facility in the agency. Therefore, it was used for a variety of agency activities and business, including staff meetings, treatment conferences concerning individual cases, and educational activities for clients. When the agency adopted the TQM management philosophy, the board solicited and received feedback from clients. One recommendation was a stress management class that, ideally, would be held at (yes, you guessed it) noon on Fridays. Because TQM emphasizes clients' importance, the board changed its meeting time to another day and another time. This was done despite some inconveniences for board members.

Note that the board of directors in a traditionally bureaucratic agency would likely assume the topmost status in an agency. In effect, the board functions as the agency director's boss. In traditional bureaucracies, top leaders usually receive top priority for access to agency resources such as prime meeting space.

Continuous Improvement   "*Continuous improvement* is an ongoing commitment to increase product and service quality by constantly assessing and improving the processes and procedures used to create those products and services" (Williams, 2010b, p. 333). TQM is not a "quick fix" (Daft, 2010, p. 49). Rather, it involves an ongoing commitment to the principles involved.

In the context of social services agencies, one indication that improvement is needed involves "variation" in service provision (Williams, 2010b, p. 333). If service provision is uneven and unpredictable, then attention should be focused on improving the processes concerned to make them more consistently effective. Quality of effective service provision is the ongoing goal.

 Critical Thinking Questions 8.6

What are the pros and cons of total quality management? To what extent would you feel comfortable either being an employee or a manager in an organization employing total quality management principles?

Servant Leadership

Another approach to the leadership aspect of management "that has gained increased popularity in recent years" (Northouse, 2007, p. 348) is *servant leadership*, developed by Robert Greenleaf (1970, 1977). Northouse (2007) explains:

> Servant leadership emphasizes that leaders should be attentive to the concerns of their followers and empathize with them; they should take care of them and nurture them.
>
> Greenleaf (1970, 1977) argued that leadership was bestowed on a person who was by nature a servant. In fact, the way an individual emerges as a leader is by first becoming a servant. A servant leader focuses on the needs of followers and helps them to become more knowledgeable, more free, more autonomous, and more like servants themselves. They enrich others by their presence.
>
> In the novel *The Journey to the East*, by Herman Hesse (1956), there is an example of leadership that was the inspiration behind Greenleaf's formulation of servant leadership. The story is about a group of travelers on a mythical journey who are accompanied by a servant who does menial chores for the travelers but also sustains them with his spirits and song. The servant's presence has an extraordinary impact on the group, but when the servant becomes lost and disappears, the group of travelers falls into disarray and abandons their journey. Without the servant, they are unable to carry on. It was the servant who was leading the group. He emerged as a leader by caring for the travelers. (pp. 348–349)

In addition to serving, the servant leader has a social responsibility to be concerned with the have-nots and to recognize them as equal stakeholders in the life of the organization. Where inequalities and social injustices exist, a servant leader tries to remove them (Graham, 1991). In becoming a servant leader, a leader uses less institutional power and less control, while shifting authority to those who are being led. Servant leadership values everyone's involvement in community life because it is within a community that one fully experiences respect, trust, and individual strength. Greenleaf places a great deal of emphasis on listening, empathy, and unconditional acceptance of others.

Qualities of a Servant Leader Barbuto and Wheeler (2005, A-15) cite eleven characteristics that make one a good servant leader. Some are inherent qualities that really can't be taught. Others are behaviors that can be learned and enhanced.

1. *Calling.* Becoming a servant leader is more than just choosing that course. You must have an innate desire to forgo your own needs. Instead, you must put the well-being of others in the organization and the organization itself before yourself. You must have a genuine desire to improve the lives and functioning of workers. Therefore, it's like a calling instead of a choice.

2. *Listening.* We've established that listening is a vital communication skill. Servant leaders are exceptional listeners (Dubrin, 2009). They seek out information from others in the organization and strive to understand what others are trying to say.

3. *Empathy.* Empathy involves not only *being in tune* with how others feel, but also *conveying to them* that you understand how they feel (Kirst-Ashman & Hull, 2009b).

4. *Healing.* Servant leaders encourage emotional healing. They are supportive people who are easy to talk to and trust. People are naturally drawn to them.

5. *Awareness.* Servant leaders have a keen awareness of what's going on around them. They look beyond superficial appearances and explore issues and situations in depth.

6. *Persuasion.* Servant leaders are experts at using persuasion. They avoid making commands, but rather explain their views carefully and help others see their point of view.

7. *Conceptualization.* Servant leaders look at the organization's total picture and have vision about what the organization might become (Daft & Marcic, 2009). They encourage others to be creative and dream of how things could or should be. Their conceptualization of the organization's operation and environment is clearly articulated to others.

8. *Foresight.* Servant leaders look ahead and prepare for what might happen in the future. Others look to them for guidance and depend on them to anticipate upcoming issues.

9. *Stewardship.* Stewardship is the condition and act of caring for the basic daily needs of others. It involves planning activities, managing processes, and helping to make other people's lives run smoothly (Daft & Marcic, 2009). Stewardship involves a strong desire to serve and assist.

10. *Growth.* Servant leaders view others as being capable of growth and improvement. They maintain a positive perspective and encourage skill development and confidence building in others.

11. *Building Community.* A "*community* consists of a number of people with something in common that connects them in some way and that distinguishes

them from others" (Homan, 2008, p. 8). Servant leaders encourage a sense of community among all the people who work in an organization. They urge others to work together as a part of something bigger and more important than any single individual could be.

 Critical Thinking Questions 8.7

What are the pros and cons of servant leadership? To what extent would you feel comfortable either being an employee or a manager in an organization employing servant leadership principles?

Chapter Summary

The following summarizes this chapter's content as it relates to the learning objectives presented at the beginning of the chapter. Objectives include the following:

A. **Explain the significance of management in social service organizations.**

Management is the "attainment of organizational goals in an efficient and effective manner through planning, organizing, leading, and controlling organizational resources" (Daft & Marcic, 2009, p. 8). Management style provides important clues for understanding people's behavior in the organizational environment, including social services agencies.

B. **Describe traditional bureaucracies, orientation discrepancies between social work and bureaucracies, and common behavior patterns found in bureaucracies.**

Bureaucratic management style emphasizes the importance of a specifically designed, formal structure and a consistent, rigid organizational network of employees to make an organization run well and achieve its goals. This allows for very little discretion on the part of workers. Value orientation discrepancies between social work and bureaucracies focus on decision making, distribution of power, flexibility, communication, and consideration of people's opinions and feelings. Common behavior patterns manifested by bureaucrats include the "warrior," the "gossip," the "complainer," the "dancer," the "machine," and the "executioner" (Knopf, 1979, pp. 33–36).

C. **Critique the U.S. health care system's clash with Asian and Pacific Islander (API) cultural values.**

Important values in API culture include shared decision making in families, filial piety, silent communication, preservation of harmony, and delayed access to but great respect for health care. Conflicts between API cultural values and the U.S. health care system include those focusing on informed consent, advanced directives, and decisions about nursing home placement. Suggestions for improvement include providing training for health care personnel, addressing end-of-life issues with whole families, adopting family-centered versus individual-centered decision making models, and pursuing ongoing advocacy for positive changes.

D. **Discuss problems frequently encountered by and in social service organizations.**

Problems frequently encountered by social service organizations include vagueness of goals, vagueness of process, impersonal behavior, lack of rewards and recognition, agency policy and worker discretion, and traditions and unwritten rules.

E. Describe newer concepts involved in management and employee empowerment.

Newer management concepts include constructing a culture of caring, the learning organization, teamwork and team empowerment, managing diversity, and client system empowerment by management. According to path-goal theory, leadership styles include "directive," "supportive," "participative," and "achievement-oriented leadership" (Northouse, 2007, p. 127).

F. Discuss the situation encountered by women in social services management.

Women managers tend to assume management styles that focus on "inclusion," "connection," "collaboration," and "commitment" to professional values (Gardella & Haynes, 2004, p. 102). Organizations can empower women by analyzing women's status within the organization, establishing clear objectives for improvement, and encouraging employee participation in the diversity-enhancement process.

G. Describe two examples of common management and leadership approaches—total quality management (TQM) and servant leadership.

"TQM is a philosophy or overall approach to management that is characterized by . . . customer focus and satisfaction, continuous improvement, and teamwork" that entails employee involvement and empowerment (Williams, 2010b, p. 673). Important principles inherent in TQM include a focus on clients as customers, quality as the primary goal, employee empowerment and teamwork, a total quality approach to leadership, and continuous improvement.

"Servant leadership emphasizes that leaders should be attentive to the concerns of their followers and empathize with them: they should take care of them and nurture them" (Northouse, 2007, p. 348). Important concepts include calling, listening, empathy, healing, awareness, persuasion, conceptualization, foresight, stewardship, growth, and building community (Barbuto & Wheeler, 2005, A-15).

H. Introduce various critical thinking questions.

Critical thinking questions in this chapter include having difficulties working in an organization, working in a traditional bureaucracy, working in organizations experiencing problems, leadership in a learning organization, and the pros and cons of TQM and servant leadership.

I. Focus on an ethical issue.

An ethical issue involved a scenario where a client is dissatisfied with the social services agency and its worker's approach in dealing with her.

Looking Ahead

This chapter discussed human behavior, management, and empowerment in organizations. The next chapter shifts the focus from organizations to communities. It examines theoretical perspectives on communities, and explores variations in geographic, rural, urban, and nongeographic communities.

For Further Exploration on the Internet

See this text's website at **www.cengage.com/social_work/kirst-ashman** for learning tools such as tutorial quizzing, Web links, glossary, flashcards, and PowerPoint® slides.

Communities
in the Macro Social
Environment:
Theories and Concepts

Student members of a Hispanic community demonstrate at a rally on the behalf of immigrants.

CHAPTER CONTENTS

Samura had an idea. For years she had worked for an alternative school in a large city. Her clients were teenagers coming from poor socioeconomic backgrounds and, frequently, troubled families. They had experienced little scholastic success and had usually begun participating in a range of illegal activities. Samura felt these young people needed direction, support, a sense of competence, and paid work.

At the same time, Samura was concerned about the urban community, which she felt was deteriorating. She spent substantial time thinking about what could be done to help both her clients and the community in which they lived.

Finally, she came up with the idea for a community project. She met with a group of social workers from the local National Association of Social Workers chapter. Responding to her initiative, these workers formed a coalition, that is, a union of various individuals or groups who come together in order to accomplish some designated goal. Coalition members identified people with power in fifty-five local organizations and businesses. They contacted these people, solicited supportive funding, and discussed potential ideas for community improvement. Thirty-five contacts become active members in the coalition. Together coalition members raised enough money to pay four hundred community young people to participate in community-enhancing projects within a designated geographical area. Projects included "building a cement basketball court for a church, rehabilitating housing, painting murals, designing puppets for a parade, developing a 'toxic tour' of the city's hazardous neighborhood, and educating residents about health issues" (Kretzmann & McKnight, 1993, p. 35).

Samura was thrilled that so many good works were performed as a result of her initiation. She also felt the young people involved learned much about what it was like to be an active, concerned, and committed community citizen.

Communities are primary settings for human behavior in the macro social environment. Understanding communities is essential for understanding why people behave as they do. This book does not try to teach *how* to do social work practice and implement changes in communities, organizations, or groups. However, it does intend to provide a *foundation* upon which to build such system-changing skills. Generalist practitioners are then better prepared to plan for and implement changes in communities to enhance people's well-being and improve their quality of life.

Learning Objectives

A. Explain the concept of community.
B. Explore several conceptual frameworks of communities, including social systems, human ecology, social-psychological, structural, functionalist, conflict, symbolic interaction, and empowerment theories.
C. Describe geographical and nongeographical contexts for communities.
D. Discuss nongeographical communities, including professional, spiritual, ethnic and racial, and those based on sexual orientation.
E. Describe rural communities, including population trends, employment issues, some inherent problems, and generalist social work practice within them.

F. Describe urban communities, including some inherent problems and social work practice within them.
G. Explain people's membership in multiple communities.
H. Raise critical thinking questions.
I. Focus on ethical issues.

Defining Communities

We have established that a *community* is "a number of people who have something in common with one another that connects them in some way and that distinguishes them from others" (Homan, 2008, p. 8). A key feature of a community is the fact that participants share some mutual characteristic. Common features might include "location, interest, identification, culture, and/or common activities" (Fellin, 2001a, 2001b, p. 118).

Thus, communities can be of two primary types—those based on geographic vicinity and those on common ideas, interests, loyalty, and a feeling that one belongs (Streeter, 2008). Locality-based communities include smaller towns such as Crouch, Idaho, Eggemoggin, Maine, and Necessity, Louisiana. Larger communities include mammoth cities such as the greater Los Angeles Metropolitan Area or New York City. Still other locality-based communities include smaller portions of larger cities, such as a struggling inner-city ghetto or a posh suburban neighborhood.

Nongeographical communities are based on some commonality other than location. For example, African Americans might form a community based on racial identification, mutual history, and culture. Similarly, a community of professional social workers shares common values, beliefs, and generalist practice skills. Additionally, there are gay communities and military communities where members share many common goals, values, and functions (Harrison, 1995). Even scuba divers make up a community based on common interests, activities, and experiences.

A major social work perspective views communities as entities where citizens can organize or be organized in order to address mutual concerns and improve their overall quality of life. You, as a social worker, have the responsibility to examine the community macro environment in which your clients reside. Certainly, you are concerned about how specific clients will function as individuals. However, the effects of the environment in which they live, such as access to resources, cannot be ignored. Assessment of human behavior within the community context is necessary to propose solutions in your practice that address larger issues affecting a broad range of clients. Social workers can use generalist practice skills to mobilize citizens within communities in order to accomplish the goals these citizens define for themselves.

Conceptual Frameworks of Communities

Conceptual frameworks provide means to view, analyze, and understand communities. You might think of them as theories offering a wide range of lenses, each focusing on alternate aspects or characteristics, and thus affording different outlooks. Viewing the same picture through a red wide-angle lens poses a distinctly different picture than looking at the same scene through a dark blue telephoto lens. Because theories may be applied either to geographical or nongeographical communities, the term *member* rather than *resident* will be used regarding people involved. The eight conceptual frameworks introduced here are social systems, human ecology, social-psychological, structural, functionalist, conflict, symbolic interactionist, and empowerment.

Social Systems Theories

The first conceptual framework identified here concerning communities involves thinking of them as social systems (Streeter, 2008). This view is based on systems theory, the major concepts of which were introduced in Chapter 1 and applied to organizations in Chapter 5. We defined a *system* as a set of elements that are orderly, interrelated, and a functional whole. Each community has *boundaries*, borders or margins that separate one entity from another, that define it. For example, a specific location lies within city limits or a specific county. Or you are either a member of the National Association of Bungee Jumpers or you are not. Anderson, Carter, and Lowe (1999) comment on the internal boundaries of geographical communities:

> Boundaries within the community include those between [social] institutions that differentiate tasks. [Remember from Chapter 1 that a *social institution* is an established and valued practice or means of operation in a society resulting in the development of a formalized system to carry out its purpose.] These horizontal boundaries include, for example, the uniform worn and the choice of specific colors and tasks. Firefighters' gear is adapted to their task, but it also distinguishes them from police. Their distinctive gear says, "We fight fires. We don't baptize children with our hoses, pick up garbage with our trucks, or fight off mobs with our axes and poles!"
>
> Sometimes boundaries between differentiated institutions are not so clear: . . . Should police conduct drug education programs? Should health clinics do AIDS testing and should they be required to report the results to federal agencies? These continue to be controversial questions in many communities. (p. 84)

The social systems perspective emphasizes analyzing how the various social *subsystems* within the community interact with each other. A subsystem is a secondary or subordinate system within a larger system. Fellin (2001a) explains the importance of examining a community's functioning from a social systems perspective:

> We are interested in examining the activities of the various social units which make up the subsystems in order to determine how well these subsystems are carrying out their community functions. The major social units within each of these subsystems are formal organizations, such as businesses, governmental units, churches, schools, health care organizations, and social welfare agencies. A significant aspect of a community social system also involves the functioning of informal groups, including families and other social groups. . . . [T]hese groups contribute to the functioning of community subsystems, e.g., parents' activity in relations to schools, and residents' contributions to the community as a whole through civic involvement and voluntary associations. (pp. 82–83)

Viewing communities from a social systems perspective can aid you in assessing your clients' community and their involvement in that community. A social systems perspective can help you formulate a range of questions to help you assess your clients' situations and figure out what you can do to assist them among your various options (*equifinality*). You might ask yourself what *inputs* the community has in terms of resources available to clients and other citizens. How effectively does the community process these *inputs* into *outputs* to meet its citizens' needs? Are enough resources entering the community to keep it healthy and thriving (thereby experiencing *negative entropy* and growth)? Is the community or possibly some of its *subsystems* progressing toward disorganization and *entropy*? For instance, are farmers moving out of a rural community because they can no longer make ends meet on family farms owned for generations? Are high crime rates driving residents out of a large segment of an urban community, leaving behind deserted, dilapidated shells of buildings? How do the answers to these questions affect your clients' *homeostasis*? What clues do they provide concerning what you can do on your clients' behalf? What actions might you consider taking (a form of *output* on your behalf that results in *input* into the community) to improve the community and how it affects your clients' quality of life?

Human Ecology Theories

Recall the ecological concepts reviewed in Chapter 1. A human ecology perspective of community "focuses on the relationship of populations to their environment, especially in regard to . . . how people and services are distributed" (Fellin, 2001b, p. 119). This view emphasizes how communities are complex organisms. Their members are integrally involved in transactions with each other in the surrounding social environment. How clusters of people and organizations are arranged in the community's space becomes important.

Demographics, facts about population characteristics and distribution, are very important from the human ecology perspective (Streeter, 2008). Environmental issues such as pollution, depletion of scarce resources, and overpopulation are especially relevant.

For example, a human ecology approach might focus attention on the exodus of community residents from inner-city neighborhoods to outlying suburbs. Emphasis is placed on the relationship between people and their environment, including the resources available in that environment. Inner-city buildings might be deteriorating rapidly. Businesses and industries might be moving to new, more spacious facilities allowing for more parking, greater growth potential, better consolidation of shopping areas, and improved access for workers and consumers. Often when jobs—and hence, resources—leave an area, so do residents. People move where they can find work. The human ecology perspective might help frame subsequent questions. For example, how can the inner-city environmental deterioration be reversed to provide necessary resources and allow people to thrive there once again?

Competition, Segregation, and Integration   In addition to some basic ecological concepts identified in Chapter 1, three more terms based in human ecology that apply to community macro systems include *competition, segregation*, and *integration* (Fellin, 2001b, p. 119). *Competition* concerns the condition where community members must vie for control over land use and seek the most advantageous locations "for commercial, industrial, institutional, and residential purposes" (Fellin, 2001b, p. 119). Space and resources within communities are inevitably limited. Therefore, individuals and groups within a community must typically vie for them. Community members with greater resources and power can gain greater space and larger resources. It follows, then, that poorer residents have access only to less desirable space and significantly poorer resources. For example, richer community members can afford to acquire grander houses in the suburbs while poorer residents might be clustered in crowded urban ghettos.

Competition is often related to *social class*, the ranking of people in society based on their wealth, power, and family background. Indicators of social class usually include job type, educational level, amount of income, and typical lifestyle. People of higher social class generally have a higher standard of living than those of lower social class.

Segregation is the detachment or isolation of some group having certain common characteristics such as race, ethnicity, or religion through social pressure, restrictive laws, or personal choice. *Integration*, on the other hand, refers to the process of bringing together and blending a range of groups (including people of different races and ethnic backgrounds) into a unified, functional whole.

Such ecological concepts as competition, segregation, and integration can help you as a social worker analyze a community in terms of its fairness and support to all of its members. Fellin (2001b) explains:

> Membership in these groups affects the quality of life of people in positive and negative ways. People benefit or suffer as a result of their social positions within communities, through differential life chances, employment opportunities, access to social and material resources, and social relationships. (p. 121)

Viewing communities from a human ecology perspective helps you to focus in on the inequities and problems faced by people who have fewer resources (in effect, less energy) than others in the community. It provides a useful assessment mechanism for understanding why people act as they do within the context of the larger community macro system.

Concept Summary 9.1 | # New Human Ecology Concepts

Demographics: Facts about population characteristics and distribution.

Competition: The condition where community members must vie for control over land use and seek the most advantageous locations "for commercial, industrial, institutional, and residential purposes" (Fellin, 2001b, p. 119).

Segregation: The detachment or isolation of some group having certain common characteristics such as race, ethnicity, or religion through social pressure, restrictive laws, or personal choice.

Integration: The process of bringing together and blending a range of groups into a unified, functional whole.

Social-Psychological Theories

A social-psychological perspective emphasizes how each community member feels about him- or herself and how they interact with others. Beyond mere structural, territorial, or functional concerns, this perspective views community members as bound together for psychological and social reasons (Longres, 2008; Martinez-Brawley, 1995). People feel they are part of a community to experience a sense of belonging, importance, and being part of "we."

One aspect, then, of a social-psychological approach involves the extent to which community members feel they have similar concerns. Do people perceive that the community has a sense of identity? Do individuals feel that they are truly a part of the community along with the other members? To what extent do community members agree about how well the community is running or how it should be run?

Another aspect of the social-psychological perspective involves individuals' sense of well-being within the community. Do people feel protected and secure? Or, do they feel they imperil themselves by just walking the streets? Are fellow community members perceived as "friends" or as "foes"?

Still another social-psychological approach to communities involves the standards, expectations, routines, and practices community members expect of each other (DeFilippis & Saegert, 2008; Rothman, 1987). How do community members expect each other to behave? Which behaviors and attitudes are considered appropriate and which are not? To what extent do community members feel that they fit into the community social environment?

Martinez-Brawley (2000) notes:

> Traditional communities play an important part in defining identity . . . and stressing normative [expected] behavior. They bond the members through a strong sense of what came before or through a strong personal commitment to maintaining the culture— rituals, lore, and folklore. Ethnic group practices that emphasize a sense of who the individual is, given a role in group rituals, also function as an antidote for the sense of normlessness and confusion that often plagues modern societies. The more traditional Indian tribes in Arizona, for example, offer their members a continued sense of belonging by adherence to the rituals that have been, through the ages, a mark of tribal continuity. Among the Hopi in Arizona, even among tribe members who would be considered "modern" because they dwell and earn a living outside the reservation, the maintenance of ritual has great significance. (p. 114)

Structural Theories

Generally, the term *structure* refers to how the parts of any community are organized to become one whole. Additionally, structure involves how the components of the whole relate to each other. Although a bit vague, the point is that there are many ways of viewing a community's structure, three of which we identify here.

The first structural approach is the *political perspective* that focuses on various units defined by law, such as village, town, municipality, and county (Rothman, 1987). Each legal entity has its own governing political structure that oversees

Highlight 9.1	Structural Theories and Social Action

Healy (2005) maintains that social workers adopting a structural perspective "are primarily concerned with analyzing and confronting structural injustices, particularly 'how the rich and powerful within society constrain and define the less powerful' (p. 178; Martin, 2003, p. 24). She continues that "structural social workers draw on the insights of a range of critical social work theories including . . . antiracist and feminist social work, noting that structural social workers 'promote consciousness' because the social structure may hide inequities from people" (p. 178). Social workers serve as catalysts to mobilize people to change the power structure to make it more equitable.

individuals and links them with state and national government. Communities, then, are smaller political subsystems within larger systems, namely, state and national governments. When thinking about such entities, concepts such as the public, taxes, and voting come to mind.

A second means of viewing communities from a structural perspective focuses on *geographical organization*. How are properties and tracts of land arranged within the community's geographical area? How are roads arranged? Is the community geographically organized like Tokyo, which developed over centuries and is composed of an endless maze of winding, confusing streets and alleys? Or, is the community structured in terms of equally square blocks of land where an address such as "South 2230 East 14791" pinpoints an exact location?

A third way of viewing the community from a structural perspective stresses *power structure*. A community can be assessed according to which of its units have the most power and influence over what happens within it. For instance, wealthier residents typically have greater power. It's likely, then, that they will exert greater influence over decisions made in the community than will the community's poorer citizens. "Power groups" within a community involve members "who, because of their social status and positions, influence the decisions made on behalf of the community and who have greatest access to resources"; power group members include elected officials, influential businesspeople and professionals, religious leaders, and other locals who have developed influence (Barker, 2003, p. 334). Highlight 9.1 addresses the relationship between structural theories and social action.

   Critical Thinking Questions 9.1

In what ways are social systems, human ecology, social-psychological, and structural theories similar? In what ways do they differ?

Functionalist Theories

Functionalist theories emphasize a community's purpose or *function* and how that community can continue working to attain that purpose. A community must operate well enough to maintain its population, such as having enough food and other resources available (Harrison, 1995). The functionalist perspective views society as "a stable, orderly system composed of a number of interrelated parts, each of which performs a function that contributes to the overall stability of society" (Kendall, 2007, p. 11; Parsons, 1951).

A functional community is one that "includes groups of people who share some common interest or function, such as welfare, agriculture, education, [or] religion" (Ross, 1967, p. 42). The primary functions of the community over time directly impact the actions a community chooses to take. For instance, historically, farming community members would assist a new neighbor in building a barn. The community's *function* focused on farming. Community *actions* were used to support that function.

Another example concerns looking at various dimensions of an individual's life in a geographical community, including family, schools, the economy, the political system, and religion. It involves "how the family is a system to ensure the care and raising of children, how schools provide young people with the skills they need for adult life, how the economy produces and distributes material goods, how the political system sets national goals and priorities, and how religion gives our lives purpose and meaning" (Macionis, 2008, p. 11). Each dimension of life serves some function to sustain an individual as a member of a community.

A functionalist approach also focuses on how the community has grown, acted, and matured over time. Because decisions and maneuvers change as time passes, taken collectively the actions become a process. These processes are intimately linked to a wide range of the community's structures, all serving to carry out designated functions. For example, churches of various denominations in a community may informally work together to raise funds and provide food, shelter, and clothing to the community's homeless population. More formal community structures include school boards to supervise the provision of education and social service agencies to provide services and resources (Harrison, 1995).

Manifest and Latent Functions   Not all social functions work out as they're planned. Kendall (2007) explains:

> *Manifest functions* are intended and recognized consequences of an activity or social process. A manifest function of education, for example, is to provide students with knowledge, skills, and cultural values. In contrast, *latent functions* are the unintended consequences of an activity or social process that are hidden and remain unacknowledged by participants (Merton, 1968). The latent functions of education include the babysitter function of keeping young people off the street and out of the full-time job market and the matchmaking function whereby schools provide opportunities for students to meet and socialize with potential marriage partners. These functions are latent because schools were not created for babysitting or matchmaking, and most organizational participants do not acknowledge that these activities take place. (p. 11)

Positive and Negative Social Functions   A society's functions can be either positive or negative. Positive functions are purposeful dynamics that serve to sustain people in the community context (Macionis, 2008). Negative functions, or *dysfunctions*, according to Kendall (2007): "are the undesirable consequences of an activity or social process that inhibit a society's ability to adapt or adjust (Merton, 1968). For example, a [positive] function of education is to prepare students for jobs, but if schools fail to do so, then students have problems finding jobs, employers have to spend millions of dollars on employee training programs, and consumers have to pay higher prices for goods and services to offset worker training costs. In other words, dysfunctions in education threaten other social institutions, especially families and the economy" (p. 11).

Sometimes, trying to address and fix a social dysfunction results in unpredictable other problems. As Coleman and Kerbo note (2002):

> Things get out of whack. Even when things are going well, changes introduced to correct one imbalance may produce other problems. . . . [Education for all citizens is a valued social function. The educational system develops programs to train people for jobs. However,] educators may train too many people for certain jobs. Those who cannot find positions in their area of expertise may become resentful, rebelling against the system that they feel has treated them unfairly. Thus, "over-education" may be said to be a dysfunction of our educational institutions. Functionalists also realize there are sometimes unintended consequences from our efforts to change society. For example, the effort to reduce the amount of drugs available on the street may work to push up the crime rate. As the supply of illegal drugs is reduced, the street price of drugs goes up, and addicts may have to commit more crimes to pay for their drug habit. (p. 12)

The functionalist perspective stresses that before making major changes in society, it is vital to analyze carefully the potential repercussions. Bad consequences or dysfunctions may result from well-intended attempts at making positive changes. Highlight 9.2 discusses the relationships among social dysfunctions, social problems, and social disorganization.

Focus on Ethics 9.1 addresses the ethics of assuming a functionalist perspective about homelessness.

Conflict Theories

Conflict theories pose direct opposition to functionalist theories. Kendall (2007) explains:

> The conflict perspective is based on the assumption that groups in society are engaged in a continuous power struggle for control of scarce resources. Unlike functionalist theorists, who emphasize the degree to which society is held together by a consensus on values, conflict theorists emphasize the degree to which society is characterized by conflict and discrimination. According to some conflict theorists, certain groups of people are privileged while others are disadvantaged through the unjust use of political, economic, or social power. (p. 13)

| Highlight 9.2 | **Social Dysfunctions, Social Problems, and Social Disorganization** |

Coleman and Kerbo (2002) describe the relationship between social dysfunctions, social problems, and social disorganization from a functionalist perspective:

> Functionalists see a common set of norms and values as the glue that holds groups, [social] institutions, and whole societies together. Small tribal societies in which everyone is in constant close contact usually have little difficulty in maintaining these common ideals, but as the great French sociologist Emile Durkheim pointed out, as societies have become ever larger and more complex, it has become increasingly difficult to maintain a social consensus [agreement by all of society's members about what's valued and what's not] about basic norms and values [Durkheim, 1947]. Thus, one of the major sources of contemporary social problems is the weakening of the social consensus. [A *social problem* is "a social condition that a segment of society views as harmful to members of society and in need of remedy" (Mooney, Knox, & Schacht, 2009, p. 3).] Functionalists can cite considerable evidence to show that when the social rules lose their power to control our behavior, people become lost and confused and are more susceptible to suicide, mental disorders, and drug problems.
>
> Functionalists also feel that social problems arise when society, or some part of it, becomes disorganized. This *social disorganization* involves a breakdown of social structure, so that its various parts no longer work together as smoothly as they should. Functionalists see many causes of social disorganization: Young people may be inadequately socialized because of problems in the institution of the family, or society may fail to provide enough social and economic opportunities to some of its members, thus encouraging them to become involved in crime or other antisocial activities. Sometimes a society's relationship to its environment may be disrupted so that it no longer has sufficient food, energy, building materials, or other resources. However, in modern industrial societies, one cause of social disorganization—rapid social change—promotes all [the other social problems]. (pp. 12–13)

Leon-Guerrero (2009) adds:

> The functionalist perspective, as its name suggests, examines the functions or consequences of the structure of society. Functionalists use a macro perspective, focusing on how society creates and maintains social order. Social problems are not analyzed in terms of how "bad" it is for parts of society. Rather, a functionalist asks, How does the social problem emerge from the society? Does the social problem have a function?
>
> . . . [For example,] [a] social problem such as homelessness has a clear set of dysfunctions but can also have positive consequences or functions. One could argue that homelessness is clearly dysfunctional and unpleasant for the women, men and children who experience it, and for a city or community, homelessness can serve as a public embarrassment. Yet, a functionalist would say that homelessness is beneficial for at least one part of society, or else it would cease to exist. The population of the homeless supports an industry of social service agencies, religious organizations, and community groups and service workers. In addition, the homeless also highlight problems in other parts of our social structure, namely the problems of the lack of a livable wage or affordable housing. (pp. 13–14)

| Focus on Ethics 9.1 | **A Functionalist Perspective on Homelessness** |

To what extent do you think it is ethical to view the social problem of homelessness from a functionalist perspective that focuses on its positives? Explain. To what extent are "social service agencies, religious organizations, and community groups and service workers" dependent on the homeless for their existence (Leon-Guerrero, 2009, p. 14)?

Concept Summary 9.2	Functionalist Theory Concepts

Manifest functions: "Intended and recognized consequences of an activity or social process" (Kendall, 2007, p. 11).

Latent functions: "Unintended consequences of an activity or social process that are hidden and remain unacknowledged by participants" (Kendall, 2007, p. 11).

Positive functions: Purposeful dynamics that serve to sustain people in the community context.

Dysfunctions (negative functions): "The undesirable consequences of an activity or social process that

inhibit a society's ability to adapt or adjust" (Kendall, 2007, p. 11).

Social problem: "A social condition that a segment of society views as harmful to members of society and in need or remedy" (Mooney et al., 2009, p. 3).

Social disorganization: "A breakdown of social structure, so that its various parts no longer work together as smoothly as they should" (Mooney et al., 2009, p. 3).

Functionalists assume that society maintains itself on the basis of a configuration of stable rules and consensus. In contrast, Robbins, Chatterjee, and Canda (2006) reflect:

> Conflict theorists see stability as a temporary and unusual state. . . . [C]onflict rather than consensus is assumed to be the norm, and coercion rather than cooperation is considered the primary force in social life. Conflict theorists are primarily interested in two phenomena—power and change. More specifically, they are interested in the ways that people use power to resist or create change. (p. 63)

An example of how functionalism and conflict theories starkly contrast involves how people view the law (Coleman & Kerbo, 2002). Functionalists maintain that people obey laws because they value them and know they're supposed to do the right thing. There is a social consensus that law is important to maintain the social structure. Conflict theorists, on the other hand, affirm that people avoid committing crimes because they're afraid of the negative consequences such as jail. It's not so much that they want to be "good," but rather that they want to avoid potential conflict.

Four concepts are vital dimensions of all conflict theories—conflict, power, minority, and change; Robbins and her colleagues (2006) define them from the conflict perspective:

> *Conflict* is a clash or struggle between opposing forces or interests. *Power* is the ability to control and influence collective decisions and actions. *Minority* refers to groups that have limited access to power even when they represent a numerical majority. *Change* is a transition or transformation from one condition or state to another. Change can be either rapid or slow, radical or conservative, evolutionary or revolutionary. Some conflict theories perceive change as rapid and radical while others see slow, incremental change as the norm. Change, however, is seen as normative and healthy and the central propositions listed above are at the core of most conflict [theories]. (p. 66)

Society is viewed as being composed of various competing groups. These groups are in constant conflict, grappling with each other for power and resources. Some groups such as minority groups have less access to power, which means they must struggle to get it. Such struggling results in ongoing conflict. Ongoing conflict, in turn, means constant pressures for change in the distribution of power and resources.

Class Conflict   Conflict theories can be divided into two broad categories—those focusing on "class conflict and the other on interest group conflict" (Robbins et al., 2006, p. 66). Karl Marx (1818–1883), a German philosopher, economist, and activist, began to conceptualize conflict theory based on class differences and conflict. Marx identified basic differences in *social class*, which we have established as the ranking of people in society based on their wealth, power, and family background. He proposed that society was basically divided into the "haves," those with access to wealth and power, and the "have-nots," those with little or no access to such resources. Marx theorized that the wealthy, whom he called the capitalist *bourgeoisie*, owned the factories and businesses, and ran the government. (*Capitalism* is "an economic system in which businesses are privately owned by people called *capitalists* who operate them for profit" [Macionis, 2008, p. 12]). The bourgeoisie then wielded power over the workers, whom he called the *proletariat*, and exploited them at low wages for profit. Marx maintained that the capitalist system only resulted in the exploitation and poverty experienced by the proletariat.

Robbins and her colleagues (2006) explain the resulting conflict:

> Because a small privileged group owns the means of production and exploits others for their profit, a class struggle becomes inevitable as people struggle against exploitation. During this struggle the owners and the laborers become increasingly polarized and antagonistic toward each other. A class consciousness—an awareness of class position—develops among the bourgeoisie, who consolidate their common interests based on their need to exploit others for profit. Their economic monopoly, however, manifests itself not only in the work arena but also in the political arena. Through their consolidation of interests they transform their economic power into political power and dominate the political institutions that then become subservient to them. (p. 67)

The result is ongoing conflict between various groups in society based on their social class and the resulting access to power. Marx proposed that the only solution would be revolution and the demise of capitalism so that resources and power could be more equally distributed (Robbins et al., 2006). This, of course, has not happened.

Out of the perspective of conflict theory comes the troubling idea that capitalism encourages "corporate violence" (Mooney et al., 2009, p. 12). Mooney and her colleagues (2009) reflect:

> Corporate violence can be defined as actual harm and/or risk of harm inflicted on consumers, workers, and the general public as a result of decisions by corporate executives or managers. Corporate violence can also result from corporate negligence; the quest for profits at any cost; and willful violations of health, safety, and environmental laws (Reiman, 2007). Our profit-motivated economy encourages individuals who are otherwise good, kind, and law-abiding to knowingly participate in the manufacturing and marketing of defective brakes on American jets, fuel tanks on automobiles, and contraceptive devices (e.g., intrauterine devices [IUDs]). The profit motive has also caused

| Focus on Ethics 9.2 | **Corporate Accountability for Production** |

To what extent should corporations be held account-able for the production and distribution of harmful goods nationally and internationally? If they should be held accountable, in what ways? Who should hold them accountable?

individuals to sell defective medical devices, toxic pesticides, and contaminated food to developing countries. (p. 12)

Focus on Ethics 9.2 addresses the ethical responsibilities of corporations concerning production of goods.

Interest Group Conflict   The second broad category of conflict theories involve those focused on conflict resulting from *contradictory values and interests among social groups* rather than among *social classes*. Such groups and coalitions may be based on race, ethnicity, gender, sexual orientation, religion, politics, or values (for example, the National Rifle Association or the National Abortion and Reproductive Rights Action League).

For example, consider the abortion controversy. People who maintain an anti-abortion stance feel strongly that a fetus is a human being from the moment of conception when sperm meets egg. Pro-choice proponents, on the other hand, emphasize that a woman has the basic right to choose what she wants done with her own body.

Another example involves *affirmative action*, the "broad range of policies and practices in the workplace and educational institutions to promote equal opportunity as well as diversity" (Mooney et al., 2009, p. 373). People who support affirmative action often feel that it's a necessary approach to fight discrimination against people of color, promote equality, and help level the playing field for oppressed populations. People against affirmative action often maintain that it's unfair to provide privileges unavailable to white people because that in itself is a form of discrimination.

Still another conflict-laden issue concerns same-gender marriage. People supporting it feel that marriage is a basic right regardless of sexual orientation and that it is discriminatory to deny that right to people of the same gender. On the other hand, people against gay marriage may claim that marriage, often portrayed in a biblical context, can only occur between a man and a woman.

 Critical Thinking Questions 9.2

What are the similarities and differences between functionalist and conflict theories with respect to communities?

| Concept Summary 9.3 | Conflict Theory |

Conflict: "A clash or struggle between opposing forces of interest" (Robbins et al., 2006, p. 66).

Power: "The ability to control and influence collective decisions and actions" (Robbins et al., 2006, p. 66).

Minority: "Groups that have limited access to power even when they represent a numerical majority" (Robbins et al., 2006, p. 66).

Change: "A transition or transformation from one condition or state to another" (Robbins et al., 2006, p. 66).

Social class: The ranking of people in society based on their wealth, power, and family background.

Corporate violence: The "actual harm and/or risk of harm inflicted on consumers, workers, and the general public as a result of decisions by corporate executives or managers" (Mooney et al., 2009, p. 12).

Bourgeoisie: Wealthy, powerful people who own factories and businesses, and run the government.

Capitalism: "An economic system in which businesses are privately owned by people called *capitalists* who operate them for profit" (Macionis, 2008, p. 12).

Proletariat: Workers who live in poverty and earn low wages, and whom the bourgeoisie exploit for profit.

Interest groups: Groups and coalitions based on race, ethnicity, gender, sexual orientation, religion, politics, or values.

Affirmative action: The "broad range of policies and practices in the workplace and educational institutions to promote equal opportunity as well as diversity" (Mooney et al., 2009, p. 373).

Symbolic Interactionist Theories

Both functionalists and conflict theorists maintain a macro focus on communities and the total society. In contrast, symbolic interactionist theories emphasize using "a microlevel analysis of how people act toward one another and how they make sense of their lives. The symbolic interactionist perspective views society as the sum of the interactions of individuals and groups" (Kendall, 2007, p. 16).

Leon-Guerrero (2009) explains:

> An interactionist focuses on how we use language, words, and symbols to create and maintain our social reality. This perspective highlights what we take for granted: the expectations, rules, and norms that we learn and practice without even noticing. In our interaction with others, we become the products and creators of our social reality. (pp. 15–16)

Our communities and our society, therefore, are based on how we construct and perceive what exists, what is important, and what is expected behavior. "The concept of role is central to symbolic interactionism"; "a *role* is a social category or position with a set of expected behavior patterns. Roles, however, do not exist in isolation and are, to a great extent, defined by their relationship to one another" (Robbins et al., 2006, p. 310). Therefore, according the symbolic interactionist theories, "our identity or sense of self is shaped by social interaction. We develop our self-concept by observing how others interact with us and label us. By observing how others view us, we see a reflection of ourselves" that determines who we are (Mooney et al., 2009, p. 13). It's almost like we are actors playing a part, trying to "present a self that will be accepted by others" (Robbins et al., 2006, p. 305).

Leon-Guerrero (2009) continues:

> How does the self emerge from interaction? Consider the roles that you and I play. As a university professor, I am aware of what is expected of me; as university students, you are aware of what it means to be a student. There are no posted guides in the classroom that instruct us where to stand, how to dress, or what to bring into class. Even before we enter the classroom, we know how we are supposed to behave and even our places in the classroom. We act based on our past experiences and based on what we have come to accept as definitions of each role. But we need each other to create this reality; our interaction in the classroom reaffirms each of our roles and the larger educational institution. Imagine what it takes to maintain this reality: consensus not just between a single professor and her students but between every professor and every student on campus, on every university campus, ultimately reaffirming the structure of a university classroom and higher education. (p. 16)

Deviant Behavior   Appropriate behavior can be interpreted and learned, but so can deviant behavior. Consider drug addiction or delinquency (Leon-Guerrero, 2009). Symbolic interaction theory maintains that no one begins life as a drug addict or a delinquent. Rather, such behavior is perceived and learned. Drug addicts and delinquents learn and establish their destructive behaviors through interaction with others. They construct and view their realities to support their patterns of behavior.

Labeling Theory   *Labeling theory*, which has developed from symbolic interactionism, indicates that no behavior is inherently bad (Leon-Guerrera, 2009; Robbins et al., 2006). Rather, society determines which behaviors it considers deviant and labels them as such. Thus, when an individual is labeled as "being mentally ill" or a "criminal," these labels reposition that person from being thought of as normal to being considered deviant. Robbins and her colleagues (2006) note:

> A deviant role then carries with it a special status and role expectations that the deviant person is expected to fulfill. Often, these role expectations become a self-fulfilling prophecy for both the individual and the social audience. Further, labeling theorists point out that these roles are stigmatized and are usually not reversible. Thus, once labeled, the stigmatized person is rarely, if ever, allowed to resume a normal role or position in society. (p. 309)

 Critical Thinking Questions 9.3

To what extent do you agree with the comment, "Once a person is labeled as having a deviant role, that label is impossible or nearly impossible to escape"? Explain.

Empowerment Theories

Chapter 2 introduced the concepts of empowerment, strengths, and resiliency, the latter two being important aspects of empowerment theories. Chapters 3 and 5 related empowerment theory to groups and organizations, respectively. The concept of empowerment was integrated throughout Chapter 8, focusing on its importance for both workers and clients in the organizational context. Empowerment is just as important in the context and understanding of communities.

We have established that empowerment involves supporting the development of self-confidence, establishing control over one's life, working together to improve the quality of life, and gaining political power to enhance input and equality. Empowerment theories support the attainment of these goals in communities. Chapter 10 explores community empowerment in greater depth.

The Strengths Perspective and Communities   The strengths perspective, which provides a basis for empowerment, focuses on a community's assets rather than its problems. Here, six principles championed by the strengths perspective are applied to communities (Saleebey, 2009, pp. 15–18):

1. Each community has assets and strengths. The important thing is to identify them, then use them.
2. Community problems (for example, crime, delinquency, drug addiction, unemployment, poverty, lack of resources and services in a geographical community, and conflict among factions in a nongeographical community) may be detrimental to the community's well-being, but they can also be viewed as jumping-off points for improvement and growth. For example, if crime and delinquency are problems in a geographical community, then citizens can band together to form neighborhood watch organizations to look out for each other. (*Neighborhood watch organizations* are voluntary groups of neighborhood residents who help each other by keeping a careful eye on each other's property for potential damaging criminal activity, and report any suspicious incidents to each other and police.) Residents can work together to advocate for youths' recreational opportunities and job training to provide positive alternatives to delinquency and employment potential. Citizens can work with school personnel to educate children about drugs, abuse, and prevention. Residents can work together with various facets of the community for improved services and resources.

   Similarly, the strengths perspective views conflict in a nongeographical community such as a professional or special interest organization as providing the opportunity to address differences, make compromises, and collaborate to improve the community's functioning. For example, two factions in a professional organization that differ regarding preferred meeting times—mornings or evenings—may need to meet and discuss a potential compromise. This provides the opportunity for both factions to explain their needs, get information on the other's perspective, review the purpose for meetings, and make compromises that both factions can live with.
3. You never can fully realize how far a community can grow and improve itself. Instead of focusing on limitations and what a community cannot

| **Highlight 9.3** | **Using Resiliency to Enhance Communities: Kwanzaa as an Example** |

Chapter 2 defined *resiliency* as the ability of any size system, including a community, to recover from adversity and resume functioning even when suffering serious trouble, confusion, or hardship. Greene (2007) discusses how one means of strengthening and developing a community is to combine the seven resiliencies of Kwanzaa. Kwanzaa, meaning "first fruits of the harvest" in Swahili, is a week-long celebration of life, culture, and history for many African Americans (Woodword & Johnson, 1995, p. 88). Greene (2007) indicates that geographical communities and their members can become more resilient when they abide by the tenets inherent in Kwanzaa (quoted from Karenga, 1997):

1. *Umoja* (unity): believing that the community, family, nation, and ethnic group of which a person is a part may become whole

2. *Kujichagulia* (self-determination): accomplishing goals that are self-selected

3. *Ujima* (collective work and responsibility): working together to solve problems and make the community a safe and productive place

4. *Ujamma* (collective economics): building and maintaining community-based businesses and profiting from them together

5. *Nia* (purpose): planning for the future and being willing to help others to succeed

6. *Kuumba* (creativity): doing as much as they can to leave the community a better, more beautiful place

7. *Imani* (faith): believing with all their heart in their people and in the righteousness of their struggle (p. 35)

do, the strengths perspective seeks out and enhances ideas about what it can do.

4. Social workers are most effective when working together collaboratively with clients. Social workers can work with community members to identify issues, develop plans, and achieve results.
5. Each community has multiple resources. The trick is to identify them and establish ways to use them.
6. It's critical to care about the community's overall well-being and provide community members with support and help.

Resiliency, a concept introduced earlier in the book, is related to the strengths perspective. Highlight 9.3 discusses how community resiliency can be enhanced through the celebration of Kwanzaa.

Which Conceptual Framework Is Best?

There is no answer to this question. Conceptual frameworks simply give you ways of examining things. They give you ideas about how to think and what to look for. Thinking about communities or assessing them in different ways can give social work practitioners ideas about what could be done to improve life for large groups of people in communities. Highlight 9.4 provides a summary of the theories identified here, their foundation principles, and some of their major concepts.

Critical Thinking Questions 9.4

Of the theories portrayed in Highlight 9.4, which theories and concepts do you think have the most relevance to social work practice in communities? Explain your reasons. Which theories and concepts do you think have the least relevance? Explain.

Community Context: Nongeographical Communities

We have established that in addition to geographical communities such as a small town or large city, a community may also be based on some commonality other than location, such as a belief system, cultural background, area of interest, or common experience. These are also referred to as "communities of interest" (Streeter, 2008, p. 348). Examples include professional communities, racial-ethnic communities, religious groups, friendship networks, groups of patients experiencing common problems, and groups of workplace colleagues (Longres, 2008).

Nongeographical communities can serve a number of purposes to enhance members' sense of well-being, all relating to each other. First, they provide an arena for forming relationships where a person can receive support, encouragement, praise, and information. Relationships can provide feelings of belonging and connectedness that most people seek in one way or another. Second, nongeographical communities can also offer a sense of identity, of who members are. People can view themselves as Roman Catholics, gay men, lesbians, Chicanos/Chicanas, massage therapists, or rocket scientists, depending on the communities to which they belong. Third, nongeographical communities make people feel that they belong and are an integral part of the community even when apart from other members. You don't have to be standing next to another member to experience being part of the community. Regardless of where nongeographical community members are, their community membership and its contribution to their identity as community members remains intact.

Four examples of nongeographical communities will be presented here. These include professional communities (specifically, the National Association of Social Workers), spiritual communities, ethnic communities and communities of people of color, and communities based on sexual orientation.

Professional Communities:
The National Association of Social Workers

One type of nongeographical community is a professional or special interest organization. The National Association of Social Workers (NASW) has already been mentioned several times, especially with respect to its *Code of Ethics*. Established in 1955, NASW is the major social work organization with the largest and broadest membership in the profession. Persons holding bachelor's or master's degrees in

Highlight 9.4	**Comparison of Community Theories**

Community Theories	Foundation Principle	Some Major Concepts
Social Systems	A system as a set of elements that are orderly, interrelated, and a functional whole.	Boundaries Subsystems Inputs/outputs Entropy Negative entropy Homeostasis Equifinality
Human Ecology	Emphasis on the relationship between populations and their environment, especially regarding how resources are distributed.	Competition Segregation Integration
Social-Psychological	Emphasis on how community members feel about themselves and on their interactions with others.	Sense of "we" Having similar concerns Sense of well-being
Structural	Emphasis on the structure of the community and how various parts are organized to make a unified whole.	Political structure Geographical structure Power structure
Functionalist	Emphasis on a community's purpose or function and how the community works to continue functioning.	Functions • Manifest and latent • Positive and negative (dysfunctions) Social problems Social disorganization
Conflict	Emphasis on how groups in communities and society are in constant conflict and in a power struggle for scarce resources.	Conflict Power Minority Change Class conflict Interest group conflict
Symbolic Interaction	Emphasis on interpersonal interaction and how communities and society in general are based on people's interpretations of these interactions.	Roles Defining deviant behavior Labeling theory
Empowerment	Emphasis on supporting the development of self-confidence, increased control over personal destiny, working together, and increased political power.	Strengths Resiliency

social work and students in accredited social work programs can join. It is called an "organization" and does have an internal management structure. However, like many other professional and special interest organizations, it also provides a community for members to share information concerning common issues and to provide each other with support.

Like other professional organizations, NASW fulfills at least five purposes in establishing a professional community. First, membership in such a professional organization lends credibility as a social work professional. Most, if not all, established professions have an organization to which members can belong. Such membership bolsters members' professional identity, helps them identify with other members, and enhances the visibility of a profession.

NASW's second purpose is to provide opportunities for networking. State, regional, and national conferences and meetings enable members to talk with each other and share news and ideas. Such meetings also provide a means for finding out about new career and job opportunities.

NASW's third purpose is to provide membership services. These include *Social Work*, a quarterly journal that addresses various aspects of practice; the *NASW News*, a national newspaper published almost monthly that focuses on relevant research, social welfare policy and service issues, and social workers' accomplishments around the country and the world; and newsletters published by some state chapters.

NASW's fourth purpose is to sponsor organized efforts for lobbying on behalf of socially responsible social welfare policies and services. NASW exerts influence in support of causes and political agendas concurrent with professional social work values. It has also helped states establish licensing or certification regulations for social workers.

NASW's fifth purpose is to publish policy statements on various issues (e.g., youth suicide, health care, people with disabilities, affirmative action, and environmental policy) to help guide members in their practice (NASW, 2009) and a professional *Code of Ethics* (NASW, 2008).

A number of other organizations reflect more specific facets or subsets of social work. Examples include the Association of Community Organization and Social Administration (ACOSA) and the National Association of Black Social Workers (NABSW).

Spiritual Communities

Religion and spirituality reflect yet another aspect of human diversity. *Religion* involves people's spiritual beliefs concerning the origin of, character of, and reason for being, usually based on the existence of some higher power or powers, that often involves designated rituals and provides direction for what is considered moral or right. *Spirituality*, a related concept, is "one's values, beliefs, mission, awareness, subjectivity, experience, sense of purpose and direction, and a kind of striving toward something greater than oneself. It may or may not include a deity" (Frame, 2003, p. 3). Religion implies membership in a spiritual organization with customs, traditions, and structure. Spirituality may involve religion, or it may reflect a personal, internalized view of existence.

Gotterer (2001) explains: "For some people, religion fosters a spirituality that serves as a bastion of strength. It can provide emotional consolation, inspiration, guidance, structure and security. It can foster personal responsibility, identity, respect for ethical codes, meaningful ritual, and community building" (p. 188).

People involved in formally organized religious denominations or sects become part of that religious community. Hugen (2001, p. 11) cites five ways religion can maintain a sense of community:

- Religion serves an integrative function by establishing norms and values, making for moral character and for ethical relations with others.
- Religion serves a social control function by fostering order, discipline, and authority.
- Religion provides the individual believer with emotional support when needed.
- Religion confers on believers a sense of identity.
- Religion can serve as a source of positive physical and mental health. It can contribute to happier, more stable families, marriages, and communities.

Religion may also provide an important source of community for ethnic and racial groups. Solomon (2002) describes the church's importance for many African Americans:

No African religious cults were established in the United States during slavery. However, with the coming of Baptist and Methodist missionaries, the slaves found an avenue for the expression of emotion as well as bonds of kinship with their fellow slaves. After emancipation, the enlarged church organizations played an even more important role in the organization of the African American communities. They promoted economic cooperation for the purpose of erecting and buying churches, establishing mutual assistance and insurance companies, and building educational institutions (Leigh & Green, 1982). As the main form or focus of organized social life, the church has been both a secular and a religious institution, a fact that may well account for its playing a broader role in African American communities than in white communities. . . .

The spiritual side of the African American church is far more personal than that of the traditional white church: God is never an abstraction apart from the here and now. He is personalized and included in daily life situations. . . . Prayer is a frequent response to everyday crisis, even by those who do not profess to any deep religious convictions. Comments like "I prayed that my husband would find a job," or "I prayed that my child would get well," may be heard. The church provides significant services in African American communities that can be utilized by creative social work practitioners seeking to enhance social functioning in those communities. For example, Leigh and Green [1982] point out that churches have served to develop leadership skills and mutual aid activities, as well as emotional catharsis for those in need of some release of emotional tensions. If social workers routinely assess the significance of the church in the lives of African American clients, they may find avenues for enhancing their service effectiveness through collaborative activity. (pp. 302–303)

As indicated, spirituality can also be expressed in ways other than those determined by formal religions. Another example is Kwanzaa, described earlier in its role of providing a source of strength and resilience. We described how Kwanzaa "emphasizes spiritual grounding" for many African Americans in their communities (Karenga, 2000, p. 62). Karenga (2000) explains its conceptualization and how it is key to a sense of community:

> Kwanzaa [first celebrated in 1966] was created first as a fundamental way to rescue and reconstruct African culture in the midst of a movement for re-Africanization. It was to recover a valuable and ancient way of building family and community, shaped so it spoke to current needs and aspirations as a paradigm of possibility. Second, I created it to introduce the Nguzo Saba (The Seven Principles [noted earlier]) and to reaffirm the centrality of communitarian values in building and reaffirming family, community and culture. Kwanzaa was also created to serve as a regular communal celebration which reaffirmed and reinforced the bonds between us as African people both nationally and internationally. And finally, Kwanzaa was created as an act of self-determination as a distinct way of being African in the world. It was conceived as a cultural project, as a way to speak a special African truth to the world by recovering lost models and memory, reviving suppressed principles and practices of African culture, and putting them in the service of the struggle for liberation and ever higher levels of human life. (p. 57)

Sometimes, people's spiritual community involves a combination of religion and spirituality. Consider the First Nations people, the Lakota (Teton Sioux). (Other terms that refer to the indigenous people of North America include American Indians and Native Americans.) Brave Heart (2001) describes the spiritual orientation of the Lakota people:

> For the Lakota and many other Native peoples, spirituality is an integral part of culture and of one's sense of self and worldview. Lakota spirituality is based upon the Seven Sacred Rites brought by the White Buffalo Calf Woman. . . . Inherent in this spiritual tradition are the sacredness of women, the sacred relationship with the Buffalo Nation, the values manifested in the ceremonies of self-sacrifice for the good of others, and the importance and sacredness of relationship with all of creation. The Seven Laws (*Woope Sakowin*) of the Lakota include generosity; compassion; humility; respect for all of creation; the development of a great mind through observance, silence, and patience; bravery in the face of adversity in order to protect the nation; and wisdom. The Lakota embrace principles of *non-interference* [the concept that people should be able to make their own decisions without meddling from others (emphasis added)] and tolerance. . . . Traditionally, all decisions are made with the next seven generations in mind. (p. 19)

Ethnic Communities and Communities of People of Color

People may also be part of nongeographical communities based on ethnicity or race. For example, many large cities sponsor a range of ethnic festivals such as Italian Fest, Polish Fest, or African-American Fest. People who identify with their ethnic heritage may belong to an organized community group that celebrates its heritage and provides opportunities for socializing.

People may also feel part of that community based on their race. However, it may depend on the degree that an individual continues to identify with that racial group's traditional heritage and customs. *Acculturation*, as defined by Lum (2004) is

> an ethnic person's adoption of the dominant culture in which he or she is immersed. There are several degrees of acculturation; a person can maintain his or her own traditional cultural beliefs, values, and customs from the country of origin to a greater or a lesser extent. (p. 202)

For example, people initially immigrating to the United States from Mexico might maintain a strong identity with their Mexican heritage and culture when they first arrive. However, the subsequent generations may lose some of their adherence to traditional culture as they become acculturated.

Weaver (2005) describes how First Nations people often strive to maintain their sense of traditional community:

> Native communities continue to exist as distinct cultural entities with many strengths. Even when federal policies interrupted values transmission, wisdom, beliefs, and practices are strengths that have survived (Long & Curry, 1998). Communities are striving to revitalize traditions through programs that teach language and culture. Many youth now participate in kindergarten or grade school immersion programs that teach language. The importance of the group reinforces socially acceptable behaviors and emphasizes the value of learning traditions (Swinomish Tribal Mental Health Project, 1991).
>
> First Nations people of all ages are seeking and reclaiming cultural knowledge and traditions. A study of Native women (predominantly Oneida) revealed they handle multiple roles through integration and balance of traditional and contemporary feminine strengths in a positive, culturally consistent manner. Healing the spirit is done through returning to traditions to reclaim the self (Napholz, 2000). (p. 94)

Communities Based on Sexual Orientation

Communities based on sexual orientation reflect another type of nongeographical community (Longres, 2008). Chapter 2 introduced terminology used in referring to gay, lesbian, bisexual, and transgender (GLBT) people and explained the concept of homophobia. Because GLBT people live in a world that's primarily heterosexual, they frequently seek out others of the same sexual orientation. They then often can feel more comfortable, feel free to be themselves, and avoid the scrutiny of critical heterosexuals.

Hunter and Hickerson (2003) discuss the significance of community for many GLBT people:

> The lesbian and gay community is essentially based on a shared sense of identity instead of on residential areas or territories (Bernard, 1973). The solidarity of an identificational community flourishes in large part through its culture or the values, common experiences, and sentiments that it produces (Gruskin, 1999). This includes art, music, literature, and jewelry; groups and organizations, including political associations, baseball teams, and choruses; and special events including music festivals and marches. The lesbian and gay community is also a subculture of the larger American culture and thus shares many broader social values (Murray, 1992).
>
> Just as no unified American culture or community exists, no monolithic gay and lesbian culture or community exists. "Community" can mean different things to

different persons, for example, being a member of the worldwide population of lesbian and gay persons versus the population of lesbian and gay persons in the San Francisco Bay area. It can mean participation in a social network, the social "scene," or the lesbian and gay institutions operating in a certain area (Saulnier, 1997). Cultural norms and behaviors also vary because of factors including social class, ethnicity, and residential area (Appleby & Anastas, 1998). Diversity is evident in large events such as Lesbian and Gay Pride Day that is celebrated every year across the United States with parades. Although "solidarity" is present in rhetoric, considerable diversity and pluralism are evident among the parade participants (Herrell, 1992). (p. 22)

Hunter and Hickerson (2003) note that GLBT people can reach out in a number of ways to become part of a community:

> In this time of expanding technology and media, LGBT persons have been able to interact with others in their groups via print publications, e-mail, and the Web. Yet, the most enduring connection of these groups remains proximity as they gather in urban areas and neighborhoods to build an infrastructure that offers not only individual support, but also public identity and a sense of pride. Intersex persons also experience these kinds of connections. (p. 29)

Community Context: Geographical Communities

Geographical communities, the second major type of community, are based on location. "Population size, density, and heterogeneity" are the most frequent demographic variables used to characterize geographical communities (Fellin, 2001a, p. 89). Such communities are also referred to as "place communities" (Anderson et al., 1999, p. 73). *Population size*, of course, is the total number of persons living in a designated community. The communities may be large, widely spread out farming areas or counties within an urban area.

Density is the ratio of people living within a particular space. The density of a heavily populated inner-city area is much higher than a suburb where all residences contain single families and are built on two-acre lots. Population size and density are often closely related. Extremely dense areas usually have high populations.

Heterogeneity refers to the extent to which community members have diverse characteristics. A community may vary in its level of heterogeneity depending on its residents' socioeconomic status, racial and ethnic background, or age range.

The largest communities are *metropolitan*, traditionally those with at least 50,000 people (Davenport & Davenport, 2008; Ginsberg, 2005). The U.S. Census Bureau now uses a more complex definition that divides urban areas into metropolitan and micropolitan areas (U.S. Census Bureau, 2008). *Metropolitan* statistical areas are locales that "have at least one urbanized area of 50,000 or more inhabitants" (p. 877). *Micropolitan* statistical areas, on the other hand, are locales that "have at least one urban cluster of at least 10,000 but less than 50,000 population. . . . As of November 2004, there are 363 metropolitan statistical areas and 577 micropolitan statistical areas in the United States. In addition, there are eight metropolitan statistical areas and five micropolitan statistical areas in Puerto Rico" (p. 877).

This book will consider both metropolitan and micropolitan areas as *urban* communities. Rural communities, discussed later, are generally considered as having 2,500 residents or less (Ginsberg, 2005; Johnson & Yanca, 2004). Because communities differ so widely, Highlight 9.5 identifies a number of terms that reflect some of the differences in communities that don't necessarily fit clearly the categories we've identified thus far.

Urban communities then are usually composed of many smaller neighborhoods, communities, and even smaller cities enveloping a central nucleus of social, business, and political activity. Cities making up a large metropolis may include suburban and satellite communities. Suburban communities directly adjoin large urban centers, while satellite communities are located near but not directly next to the metropolitan area.

For example, Metropolis, a large metropolitan city of two million people, comprises numerous smaller communities, including downtown Metropolis, Wauwatosa, Cudahy, and Wayside. Directly adjacent to the central Metropolis area are less densely populated suburbs with generally higher socio economic levels, including Mequon, Pinegrove, and Menomonee Falls. Satellite communities located thirty to forty miles from central Metropolis are Sheboygan, Oconomowoc, and Ixonia. Many people working in central Metropolis actually live in these

| Highlight 9.5 | **Variations in Communities** |

Communities vary widely. The following are terms used to identify some of these distinctions (Johnson & Yanca, 2004, p. 142):

1. *Small cities* are units of 15,000 to 20,000 people. They generally have internal operations, with their own police department, post office, and other systems (Kirst-Ashman & Hull, 2006a). They may be satellite communities to metropolitan areas.

2. *Small towns* have between 8,000 and 20,000 people. Unlike small cities, they do not operate independently. Services are few, with residents depending on the encompassing county or larger cities close by.

3. *Bedroom (or satellite) communities* usually grow up near larger urban areas. They are what the name implies, primarily residential communities where people reside, sleep, and enjoy recreational activities. Residents work in nearby urban centers that harbor businesses and industry.

4. *Institutional communities* contain "a large institution such as a state mental hospital, an educational institution, or a government site (state capital), which is the major employer in

that community" (Johnson & Yanca, 2004, p. 142). Smaller communities with large universities or prisons are other examples. Residents in such communities are dependent on the institution for their economic well-being. Most often, these are located in rural environments.

5. *Reservation communities* are areas that are recognized by the federal government where First Nations people reside. The largest concentrations of their population are in California, Arizona, and Oklahoma, respectively (U.S. Census Bureau, 2008). Note the significance of the concept of *sovereignty* with respect to First Nations peoples (Weaver, 2008). Sovereignty means that they are considered part of separate nations, and so maintain a distinctly different legal standing from other ethnic groups. Thus, tribal governments control some aspects of tribal life such as law enforcement. The federal government has a role in assisting their communities "by providing financial and medical services" (Kirst-Ashman & Hull, 2009a, p. 277).

outlying communities and commute. Suburbs and satellite communities often offer less population density, more services, and a generally higher quality of life. They also usually cost much more to live in.

Heterogeneity or the opposite, *homogeneity* (having like or similar characteristics), also comes into play. Returning to the Metropolis example, South Metropolis, the southern portion of the central city, comprises mostly Hispanic residents; Babblebrook, a northern suburb, people of Jewish descent; Pinegrove, a western suburb, White Anglo-Saxon Protestants (WASPS); and the old fifth ward in the central city, people of Italian descent. Wayside on the east side of central Metropolis is the home of a large university and, hence, is a congregating place for intellectuals, artists, and more trendy people. It is known for great diversity in its racial, ethnic, and vocational composition.

Rural Communities

We've established that rural communities have traditionally been characterized as having 2,500 residents or less. They usually include a small town, which might consist of a grocery store, gas station, and tavern. However, such communities often do not offer a wide variety of specialized services. Residents depend on the county and neighboring towns for resources.

People in a rural social environment live under very different circumstances than those in urban areas. These conditions directly affect resource availability, and hence the way social workers practice. Three variables tend to characterize communities in rural areas (Davenport & Davenport, 2008). First, population density is low as people either live relatively far apart or relatively few people populate the entire community area. Second, rural communities tend to be geographically distant from larger urban areas. Third, rural communities tend to be more specialized in function than urban centers, which have both population and room to achieve diversity. For example, a farming community's resources would focus on those supporting farming needs, such as feed, seed, and farm implements like tractors and harvesting equipment. Such a community would probably not be able to support a gourmet jelly bean and cappuccino shop. There would be too few people to support such a specialized interest. A generic Super Duper Value grocery store offering a wide range of basic daily foods would probably achieve greater success.

Population Trends in Rural Areas   Lohmann and Lohmann (2005) report the following population trends in rural areas:

1. "The actual number of rural residents has grown slowly but steadily since the first census in 1790 right to the present" (p. xv). So, although people have steadily migrated to urban areas over the past two centuries, the total number of people living in rural areas has actually grown. The rural environment is not a desolate wilderness void of people.
2. "At the same time, the proportion of rural population has declined steadily for more than a century, and at least four states (California, New York, Florida, and Massachusetts) are now over 90 percent urban" (p. xv). So, it is

indeed true that the *proportion* of urban residents has grown in comparison to that of rural residents. Also note that the proportion of people who work as full-time farmers is less than 1 percent, the lowest proportion ever (p. xxi).

3. "Each of those 90 percent-plus urban states (like most other large urban states) also has a rural population that, in actual numbers, exceeds the total population of the smallest state(s)" (p. xv). Therefore, even in states where the number of urban residents vastly exceeds the number of rural residents, a significant number of people still reside in rural areas.

4. "For the country as a whole, and for most states, the proportion of the rural population living outside any 'organized' place (small town or village) is almost four times the number of rural people living in towns and villages of 2,500 or less" (p. xv). Therefore, many people live in places with very low population density.

So, when we talk about the rural social environment, we're referring to a significant number of people. We've defined the rural community in terms of numbers, but looking at the microcosm of life there is much more complex. The next sections will discuss employment issues, problems faced, and generalist social work practice in rural communities

Employment Issues in Rural Communities Lohmann and Lohmann (2005) report on the labor force participation in rural areas:

> In earlier, simpler times, labor force participation in rural areas was concentrated heavily in the so-called primary industries: fishing, mining, and most especially farming. However, we easily underestimate how long ago declines in employment in these industries began occurring and the continuing impact this has had on rural life for many decades. Historians now generally agree that the market revolution in American society that transformed farming and fishing from subsistence activity to employment probably began around 1800. Prior to that time, rural living truly may have been the fully self-sufficient way of life of a cashless existence where things were grown, made at home, or done without. But at least, since that time, rural life for most has included a strong, if sometimes minor dimension of 'store-bought goods,' and most rural communities moved from simple villages to towns where organized buying and selling occurred regularly. Only in a relative few backwoods areas was this not the case even by 1920.
>
> There is almost nowhere in the United States where urban markets and consumer goods (and accompanying jobs in sales and service occupations) do not reach today. While certainly not an unmixed blessing, as illustrated by concerns with Walmarts and MacDonalds, access to national markets is a reality of rural life. It is certainly also the case that mechanization, increased productivity and relocation of industries [many to foreign countries], particularly over the past half-century, have taken a ferocious toll on the number of traditional rural jobs. . . .
>
> And yet, through such wrenching declines in traditional rural employment, the total numbers of people living in rural areas have increased. How do rural people survive? In the case of many Native American reservations (almost all of which are located in rural areas) and other distressed communities, the answer is that many rural people barely survive and do so only on the basis of public aid and their own grit despite staggering barriers and challenges. (pp. xxiii–xxv)

The result is that many people are forced to live on "Social Security, pensions, Temporary Assistance to Needy Families (TANF), food stamps," and other cash benefits (Lohmann & Lohmann, 2005, p. xxv). Ginsberg discusses the impact of social welfare:

> In rural areas, social welfare programs are often the most important economic factor in the community. . . . [Cash benefits], along with the in-kind economic impact of the Food Stamp Program, may drive the retail industry in the community, provide much of the tax revenue, and serve as factors in real estate and other aspects of the community's economy. (pp. 7–8)

Some people in rural environments may work for businesses where they may earn near minimum wages and receive no health care benefits. Ginsberg (2005) reflects on the rural employment scene:

> Many small communities are one- or two-industry towns ("company towns"). . . . However, there are many other kinds of rural community industries, such as tourism, services to retirees, and, to some extent, warehousing and manufacturing. Many smaller communities do not provide a diversity of employment, though, and young people often find that they must either find a job within the limited number of local industries or move elsewhere for work. Rural employment for well educated people is often available only in public schools, churches, colleges and universities, or social service agencies. Much employment in rural areas may also require extensive commuting. Trains and buses are not generally available in smaller towns, particularly in the South and West. Therefore, commuting is often by private automobile, which is expensive and often unreliable. Therefore, transportation resources are often considered a major deficiency in rural areas. (p. 8)

The United States Department of Agriculture (USDA) has established an identification system for work in rural areas that can give us clues about where people find employment (Olaveson, Conway, & Shaver, 2004). They classify rural counties by "economic activity and policy traits . . . Economic types are farming-dependent, mining-dependent, manufacturing-dependent, government-dependent, services-dependent, and non-specialized. The policy types are retirement-destination, federal lands, commuting, persistent poverty, and transfer-dependent (more than 25 of the population receives public funds)" (p. 12).

Other Problems and Issues Faced by Rural Communities   People have similar problems whether they live in rural or urban environments. However, there are generally fewer services available in rural areas, and those that do exist are often not readily accessible. Therefore, it's often more difficult for rural residents to get what they need. Carlton-LaNey, Edwards, and Reid (1999) explain:

> The list of problems with which rural and small town residents must cope includes poverty, lack of transportation, inadequate childcare, unemployment, substandard housing, and insufficient health care. Problems of access and adequacy, for example, remain critical issues that need to be addressed in rural social work practice. Krout (1994) noted that access problems add time and expense to service delivery efforts, ultimately discouraging both the development of new services and the expansion of existing services into rural areas. For example, rural homebound individuals who could benefit from home-delivered meals and thereby maintain independence are denied this

service because it is too expensive. The cost of delivering meals to remote areas can significantly limit the amount of money available for the service itself.

Health care is another significant problem. Rural areas, particularly low-income areas, are underserved because of a lack of physicians and other healthcare providers. (p. 7)

It is also important to note that access to medical specialists is limited in rural areas, often posing additional difficulties for rural residents.

Generalist Social Work Practice in Rural Communities   Social workers practicing in rural communities must address at least four special issues. First, they must be true generalists who are prepared to work with individuals, families, groups, local organizations, and the community, using a wide range of skills to meet clients' diverse needs (Daley & Avant, 2004; Davenport & Davenport, 1995, 2008; Carlton-LaNay et al., 1999). We've established that because of lower population densities, rural environments usually have fewer resources.

A large metropolitan area with dense population generates lots of tax moneys and resources. Such a county can afford to support a large urban Department of Social Services that may have a huge number of workers. Large numbers enable such a department to diversify. For example, public and private social service agencies might provide specific, separate services such as substance abuse counseling, protective services for older adults, services for people with cognitive disabilities, foster care, crisis counseling for victims of sexual assault, shelter for victims of domestic violence, and so on. Urban workers may become more specialized in the problems they address depending on their assigned unit.

In contrast, rural environments usually can't sustain large social services departments with numerous workers. Rather, practitioners must use a wide range of skills to help clients address a broad arena of issues. In a single day, a rural worker may deal with child maltreatment, elder abuse, substance abuse, and foster care issues.

A second special issue for social workers in rural communities involves *interagency cooperation* (Carlton-LaNay et al., 1999, p. 10). Because fewer, more general services are usually provided by public agencies, it's critical for agencies and their staffs to work more closely together than in many urban communities. It's common for practitioners and agency administrations "to know each other and to reach out to each other regularly" to meet clients' diverse needs (Carlton-LaNay et al., 1999, p. 10). In urban areas with hundreds of available services, this may not be the case.

A third issue involving social work in rural communities is the importance placed on understanding the community, knowing its values, and developing relationships with rural residents (Daley & Avant, 2004). People living in rural communities have different life experiences than those living in bustling cities. Because there are fewer people, social interaction and relationships tend to be much more informal. Rural social workers and their family members might attend the same church or school, participate in the same civic clubs and organizations, and shop at the same grocery store as clients. Therefore, a rural practitioner must be careful to portray an image that reflects positively on his or her agency (Daley & Avant, 2004).

| **Focus on Ethics 9.3** | **Ethical Issues Involved in Dual Relationships in Rural Communities** |

Because of the close interpersonal nature of rural communities, there is a strong likelihood that dual relationships exist (Davenport & Davenport, 2008). *Dual* or *multiple relationships* occur when "a practitioner is in a professional role with a person in addition to another role with that same individual, or with another person who is close to that individual" (e.g., both social worker and neighbor, or member of the same church, temple, mosque, or synagogue) (Corey, Corey, & Callanan, 2007, p. 262). Especially in rural communities, dual and multiple relationships may be unavoidable. Watkins (2004) suggests that social workers in such situations "above all, do no harm; practice only with competence; do not exploit;

treat people with respect for their dignity as human beings; protect confidentiality; act, except in the more extreme instances, only after obtaining informal consent; [and] practice, insofar as possible, within the framework of social equity and justice" (p. 70).

It's very important for workers to separate their personal relationships from their professional to the greatest extent possible. For example, consider a worker and a client who attend the same church and serve on the same committee there. This does not mean that the worker should become "friends" with the client. That would bias the worker's objectivity and threaten the effectiveness and fairness of the worker–client relationship.

Private lives might be more public—some say as if "living in a fishbowl" (Davenport & Davenport, 2008). For example, it would not be impressive for a social worker counseling a client with an alcohol problem to be cited in the local newspaper for driving under the influence (DUI). Focus on Ethics 9.3 addresses the ethical issue of dual relationships in rural communities.

The fourth issue important for social work in rural communities involves emphasizing the strengths inherent in rural communities. Because of the informal nature of relationships, rural clients are often integrally involved with informal support systems or social networks of other people willing to help them out—sometimes referred to as *natural helping networks* (Tracy, 2002; Watkins, 2004). Such networks can include family members, neighbors, coworkers, fellow church members, community benefactors, and others not providing formal agency services who are willing to volunteer assistance.

Highlight 9.6 discusses potential advantages for social workers in rural environments.

Urban Communities[1]

Urban communities provide very different settings for generalist social work practice than rural communities. *Urban social work* is practice within the context of heavily populated communities, with their vast array of social problems, exceptional diversity, and potential range of resources. Phillips and Straussner (2002) stress how urban social workers "need to be sensitive to the situations commonly

---

[1] Note that many of the ideas in this section are taken from *Urban Social Work: An Introduction to Policy and Practice in the Cities,* by N. K. Phillips and S. L. A. Straussner (Boston: Allyn & Bacon, 2002), unless otherwise indicated.

Highlight 9.6	Advantages for Social Workers in Rural Environments

Despite the challenges inherent in working in rural environments, there are often several positive aspects as well (Ginsberg, 2005). First, workers usually have greater independence because of broader job descriptions and less complex bureaucratic structures in social service organizations. This may be a great advantage for people who appreciate having discretion over what they do and how they accomplish goals. A second advantage is that it may be easier to advance in the social services organizational power structure and get a management position. Competition may not be nearly as strong or plentiful. Third, social workers may be more likely to see the fruits of their efforts with clients more quickly and clearly. "The dearth of services and the smaller scale, which often permits rapid implementation of plans, can allow social workers to see what they have done early in their assignments" (p. 10).

found in the cities and to be knowledgeable about the nature of urban life and the range of impact that the urban environment can have on people" (p. 20). Work in urban communities is important in view of how both the national and global population has been shifting from rural to urban settings. People often flock to cities in search of new opportunities, higher-paying jobs, and greater access to activities and services. Many times, although hopes are high, actual opportunities are scarce or nonexistent, which results in a "disproportionate number of the poor" in the "country's largest cities" (p. 107).

Urban communities are characterized by a number of conditions (Marsella, 1998). First, population is denser and often contains diverse population subgroups (for example, ethnic, racial, cultural, age, sexual orientation). Second, urban economic conditions involve a range of industries, businesses, rent levels, and transportation availability and costs. Third, urban communities often involve a bustling tangle of concrete, traffic, noise, and questions about air quality—in sharp contrast to the more natural rural environment. Fourth, an urban lifestyle entails more condensed interaction and contact with many people. Fifth, the political situation may be intense, with many layers of bureaucracy and numerous people in "the system" who have various amounts of power. Sometimes crime, corruption, and social injustice are evident.

Watkins (2004) explains:

Urbanization brought dramatic changes in the way people interacted with each other. Individuals moved away from extended family and other primary relationships to cities where primary relationships were replaced by more role-based interactions [for example, employee, renter, customer, student]. Population density and crowding were accompanied by emotional distancing to preserve a sense of privacy and individuality. In low-income neighborhoods, needs overwhelmed the resources of neighbors. Many persons in need were new to the cities and had no support networks. Formalized or institutionalized social services were a rational response to the peculiar social patterns and needs of these urban residents. . . . However, when federal, state, and local governments increased their role in providing services, the programs were no longer tailored to a specific community. In efforts to increase efficiency and fairness, services became more bureaucratic and standardized. The new model of service delivery that developed preferred secondary, "professional" relationships and interactions that were rule- and role-based rather than more personal [and individualized]. Needy individuals were depersonalized into "clients." (p. 67)

Problems Inherent in Urban Communities   At least five problems tend to characterize urban areas more than rural areas (Phillips & Straussner, 2002). Even though "problems such as poverty, discrimination, overcrowded housing, crime and violence, homelessness, high rates of school dropouts, substance abuse, and HIV/AIDS exist in communities of all sizes," it is important to note that "they occur with greater frequency and therefore are more visible in the cities" (Delgado, 2008; Phillips & Straussner, 2002, p. 25).

A second problem is the widespread occurrence of discriminatory behavior because of the wide variety of ethnic, racial, religious, and cultural groups living in cities (Delgado, 2008). Groups may be in conflict and fighting for power and resources. Often public schools are disadvantaged because of inadequate funding, resulting in poorer buildings, libraries, laboratory equipment, and technology, as well as underpaid staff.

"Migration of people unprepared" for the pressures and demands of urban living is a third problem characterizing cities; Phillips and Straussner (2002) explain:

With their promise of freedom and opportunity, the cities have always been magnets for both the adventurous and the desperate. Most people move to urban areas in search of better opportunities for work or for education, either for themselves or their families, and for many, the cities have served and continue to serve as gateways to success.

However, some who migrate to urban areas, whether from other parts of the United States or from other countries, are faced with unemployment, underemployment, discrimination, poor housing, and language barriers. Those without families or social supports to help them make the transition to the new culture and to city life are at greater risk for poverty, social isolation, and personal and family problems. (p. 27)

As Phillips and Straussner (2002) point out, financial shortfalls or unavailability of resources make up a fourth problem characterizing urban areas:

Some cities do not have the financial resources to provide services that would assist people in maximizing their potential, while other cities may have the resources, but do not choose to provide services, particularly for the poor. Consequently, there may be a lack of affordable, good-quality housing, or a lack of adequate police protection, schools, or recreational facilities. For example, preschool children and their parents are underserved in many urban communities. (p. 28)

Because of cities' dense population, service gaps can affect huge numbers of people.

The fifth problem characterizing cities involves greater amounts of psychological stress. Stressors including noise, dirty streets, abandoned buildings, overcrowded housing, lack of geographic mobility, and substance abuse can impose psychological pressure and increase general anxieties (Phillips & Straussner, 2002, p. 29).

Highlight 9.7 describes some of the skills involved in urban social work practice.

| Highlight 9.7 | **Generalist Social Work Practice in Urban Communities** |

As in other types of social work, urban social workers use micro practice skills in their work with clients in the community, including establishing and working toward goals, using effective communication and interviewing techniques, respecting client values and perspectives, emphasizing strengths, expressing empathy, and "developing self-awareness" to combat biases and effectively understand clients' perspectives (Phillips & Straussner, 2002, p. 201). Thus, "social workers need to constantly reflect on their work, talk with supervisors or consultants, discuss their concerns with colleagues, and, as students, engage in classroom discussion and exercises that promote the development of self-awareness" (Phillips & Straussner, 2002, p. 201).

Additionally, urban social workers must focus on using skills in at least four major arenas (Phillips & Straussner, 2002):

1. *Paying close attention to human diversity.* Because urban environments more likely have a wider variety of ethnic, racial, and religious backgrounds, urban social workers must be sensitive to the wide range of cultural differences, become knowledgeable about their various clients' cultures, and focus on the identification and use of clients' respective cultural and personal strengths. Urban practitioners must also be attuned to the potential discrimination experienced by people "based on race, ethnicity, culture, age, gender, religion, sexual orientation, disability, poverty, or language spoken. While historically various immigrant groups such as the Irish, the Jews, the Italians, the Chinese, and the Japanese have experienced discrimination in the United States, the most persistent discrimination today is experienced by Native Americans; blacks, including African Americans, people from the Caribbean, and people from Africa;

Latinos; Asians; and people of Middle Eastern backgrounds" (p. 26).

2. *Understanding their agency environment.* Urban agencies may be large and complex, or may serve large client populations. Urban workers must understand the intricacy of their agency's power structure, who has decision making power about what they can and can't do, and where resources are located. Large bureaucracies are often highly impersonal. They tend to emphasize following rules and regulations to coordinate their complex maze of service provision. Often workers are called on to work with other personnel they don't know. Workers must then be sensitive to other staff's roles and use good communication skills to work effectively in collaboration with other service providers. Even smaller agencies in urban settings must work within a complex interplay of numerous organizations also addressing client needs. Urban social workers must understand the functioning of other agencies serving the same clients and work carefully with other staff to coordinate service provision.

3. *Seeking resources in the external urban environment.* Urban social workers often function in a complex labyrinth of many public and private agencies, each providing specialized services in one of a broad range of areas (for example, mental health counseling, administration of public assistance, domestic violence shelter, sexual assault hotline, or adolescent pregnancy prevention). This differs from rural agencies, which frequently provide a broader range of services to a smaller population; in other words, they are less likely to specialize to the degree that urban agencies can. In their broker role, urban social workers must often seek resources in a confusing tangle of red tape and available services.

continued

Highlight 9.7 | *continued*

4. *Using advocacy.* Note that just because urban areas tend to have larger and more numerous services, this does not mean that there are no significant gaps in service due to limited or lacking resources. Such gaps may involve massive numbers of people. At the agency level, an urban practitioner may need to develop a coalition with colleagues and approach decision making administrators with suggestions for positive changes. On another level, public policy may not serve clients' best interests. Therefore, strategies to change legislation may include the use of letter-writing or email campaigns to lawmakers, *lobbying* (seeking direct contact with legislators to influence their opinions), or using the mass media to publicize clients' needs and issues to gain public support for positive change.

Membership in Multiple Communities

Remember that each individual is probably a member of multiple communities. You are probably a member of the university or college community, your residential community, the social work professional community, possibly a work group community, and any number of others. Involvement in multiple communities reinforces an individual's sense of belonging and expands potential access to resources and support provided by various communities. For example, the college community provides you with access to library resources and knowledge about values and skills. The residential community gives you neighborly support and potential friendship. The professional community furnishes you with information about jobs, ethical decision making, relevant legal issues, and new work skills.

 Critical Thinking Questions 9.5

To which geographical and nongeographical communities do you belong? Describe each.

Chapter Summary

The following summarizes this chapter's content as it relates to the learning objectives presented at the beginning of the chapter. Objectives include the following:

A. Explain the concept of community.

A community is "a number of people who have something in common with one another that connects them in some way and that distinguishes them from others" (Homan, 2008, p. 8).

Communities include those that are geographic and nongeographic.

B. Explore several conceptual frameworks of communities, including social systems, human ecology, social-psychological, structural, functionalist, conflict, symbolic interaction, and empowerment theories.

Conceptual frameworks offer theoretical ways to view, analyze, and understand communities.

Social systems theories emphasize the concepts of system, boundaries, subsystem, input and output, entropy, negative entropy, homeostasis, and equifinality. Human ecology focuses on the relationship between populations and the environment. Major concepts include competition, segregation, and integration. Social-psychological theories stress how community members feel about their interactions with others in the community and their overall sense of well-being. Structural theories underscore various structural aspects of communities, including political, geographical, and power structures. Functionalist theories focus on the community's purpose and dynamics. Major concepts involve manifest and latent functions, positive functions, dysfunctions, social problems, and social disorganization. Conflict theories emphasize how various community groups are in constant conflict in a power struggle over scarce resources. Primary notions include conflict, power, minority, change, class conflict, and interest group conflict. Symbolic interaction theories stress interpersonal interaction and the interpretation of this interaction for defining roles and deviant behavior, and the labeling of behavior. Empowerment theories emphasize strengths, resiliency, and the development of self-confidence, increased control over personal destiny, working together, and increased political power.

C. Describe geographical and nongeographical contexts for communities.

Geographical communities are based on location and focus on demographic variables such as "population size, density, and heterogeneity" (Fellin, 2001a, p. 89). Nongeographical communities are based on some commonality other than location, such as a belief system, cultural background, area of interest, or common experience.

D. Discuss nongeographical communities, including professional, spiritual, ethnic and racial, and those based on sexual orientation.

Professional communities such as the National Association of Social Workers are based on membership and professional status. Spiritual communities are based on having common "values, beliefs, mission, awareness, subjectivity, experience, sense of purpose and direction, and

a kind of striving toward something greater than oneself" (Frame, 2003, p. 3). For example, Kwanzaa "emphasizes spiritual grounding" for many African Americans in their communities (Karenga, 2000, p. 62). People involved in formally organized religious denominations or sects become part of that religious community.

Nongeographical communities may also be based on common racial identity or ethnicity. Communities based on sexual orientation include people with common orientations, values, and a sense of identity.

E. Describe rural communities, including population trends, employment issues, some inherent problems, and generalist social work practice within them.

Rural communities have traditionally been characterized as having 2,500 residents or less. Although the actual number of rural residents has increased, the proportion of people living in rural areas has decreased. Rural areas often suffer unemployment problems and decreased access to resources. Generalist social workers in rural communities should be prepared to work with a wide range of clients and issues, readily work together with other social service organizations, understand the community and its values, and emphasize the strengths inherent in rural communities.

F. Describe urban communities, including some inherent problems and social work practice within them.

Urban locales include metropolitan and micropolitan communities (U.S. Census Bureau, 2008). Metropolitan communities are those with at least 50,000 residents. Micropolitan communities "have at least one urban cluster of at least 10,000 but less than 50,000 population" (U.S. Census Bureau, 2008, p. 877). Multiple problems often characterize densely populated urban communities. Urban social workers should closely attend to aspects of human diversity, understand their agency environment, actively seek out resources available from other agencies, and advocate for improved policy, services and resources.

Other types of community variations include "small cities," "small towns," "bedroom communities," "institutional communities," and "reservation communities" (Johnson & Yanca, 2004, p. 142).

G. Explain people's membership in multiple communities.

Any individual is likely to be a member of many kinds of communities at once, including geographical and nongeographical communities.

H. Raise critical thinking questions.

Critical thinking questions addressed comparing and contrasting various theories, the labeling of an individual as "deviant," and the relevance of various theories to social work.

I. Focus on ethical issues.

Ethical issues involved a functional perspective on homelessness, corporate accountability for the safe production of goods, and dual relationships in rural communities.

Looking Ahead

This chapter shifted the focus from organizations to communities. It examined theoretical perspectives on communities, and explored variations in geographic, rural, urban, and nongeographic communities. The next chapter discusses power and empowerment in communities; including mapping community assets.

For Further Exploration on the Internet

See this text's website at **www.cengage.com/ social_work/kirst-ashman** for learning tools such as tutorial quizzing, Web links, glossary, flashcards, and PowerPoint® slides.

Assessment of Geographic Communities and Empowerment

Communities can help and empower their residents. Here volunteers work for Habitat for Humanity to build homes for Hurricane Katrina victims.

CHAPTER CONTENTS

Brutus, age seventy-seven, lives in a rundown two-story home in an ancient residential section of Bumrap, a large metropolitan city. Chenequa, his neighbor, is very concerned about Brutus and his situation. Twice she found Brutus had fallen helplessly on the ground while walking out to get his mail. She practically had to drag Brutus into the house. Brutus has rheumatoid arthritis, which makes it very difficult to walk even with his two canes. Additionally, his eyesight is poor. Chenequa has questions about Brutus's ability to shop and cook for himself.

Brutus's wife, Olive, died two years ago after a long bout with intestinal cancer. Since her death, Brutus has remained isolated and alone. His two children live in other states and are busy with their own families and careers.

Brutus considers himself an intelligent, independent man who worked hard most of his life as a house painter. However, since his arthritis took a turn for the worse ten years ago, he has had to stop actively working. He is now facing financial difficulties. He's experienced many years of little income and high health costs for both him and his wife. He is becoming increasingly depressed at his failing health. However, he clings doggedly to the notion he must remain in his home. To do otherwise, he thinks to himself, would mean giving up and accepting certain death. Brutus is aware of the Heavenly Happy Haven Health Care Center, the only nursing home in the area. He has sadly watched some of his friends enter it and dreads the thought of having to go himself. He misses the old days when he was an active breadwinner who loved to play stud poker and drink Miller GD.

Luckily for Brutus, Chenequa is a natural helper[1] who is concerned about her neighbors' well-being and is well acquainted with a series of neighborhood services available for older adults. Chenequa made a "neighborly visit" and forced Brutus to address his needs and situation. Although reticent at first, Brutus succumbed to her persuasive encouragement that his life could be better than it is. She emphasized he would not have to enter a nursing home if he didn't want to.

Chenequa made a number of suggestions regarding how Brutus might tap community resources. First, a local neighborhood center sponsored hot meals each weekday noon for senior residents at nominal cost. Volunteers were available to transport people like Brutus who had difficulty walking even a couple blocks. Brutus had to admit he was tiring of his repetitive diet of baked beans and sauerkraut. Hot cooked meals with some kind of meat sounded pretty good to him. Some company with others his age didn't sound that bad either. The center also sponsored a cooking group that taught citizens basic cooking techniques and provided some free canned goods and other staples.

Chenequa was also aware of a special outreach program sponsored by a local hospital that provided affordable basic medical care for seniors. Seeing a physician there might help Brutus deal more effectively with his arthritis, or, at least, get him some pain medication for those days when it was really bad. The local library

---

[1] *Natural helpers* are "'ordinary' individuals identified by others in the community as being good listeners and helpers"; natural helpers typically "provide social support consisting of alleviation of social isolation, emotional support (encouragement, reassurance), communication activities (confidante, listening), and problem-centered services (light housekeeping, errands, transportation, cooking)" (Biegel, Shore, & Gordon, 1984, p. 97).

sponsored a day periodically when practitioners from a local eyecare center volunteered their time to "screen seniors for cataracts" and provide updated eyeglass prescriptions (Kretzmann & McKnight, 1993, p. 58). The center subsequently discounted seniors' fees for new glasses.

Chenequa indicated that a local church sponsored biweekly lectures and discussion groups on wellness for senior citizens. Brutus expressed some interest in this but indicated he would rather play poker and drink beer. Chenequa noted that another church sponsored bingo parties for seniors, which held more appeal for Brutus.

Chenequa kept popping in on Brutus to see how he was doing. As a result of her efforts and his involvement with a range of neighborhood services and activities, he attained a consequentially better quality of life for a number of years. He significantly benefited from community empowerment.

Chapter 9 provided descriptive and theoretical information about communities and how they function. This chapter focuses on community empowerment. It emphasizes the importance of assessing a geographic community, not only in terms of its problems and needs, but also concerning its strengths and assets.

Learning Objectives

A. Examine the significance of power in communities, who has it, and why.
B. Discuss the importance of citizen participation and social networks.
C. Explain natural helping networks.
D. Describe personal empowerment, social empowerment, and the relationship between the two.
E. Provide a format for assessing communities and describe data-gathering procedures.
F. Explain community building and highlight the primary principles involved.
G. Relate President Barack Obama's experience in community organizing and community building.
H. Provide examples of community building in rural communities.
I. Explain mapping community assets and suggest methods for collecting information.
J. Provide examples of how individuals, groups, associations, organizations, and social institutions can work together for community empowerment.
K. Raise critical thinking questions.
L. Focus on ethical issues.

People and Power in Communities

As a generalist practitioner, you must understand how communities work. Accurate assessment of community functioning can provide you with a foundation to initiate community change. One aspect of communities that you must understand is power. *Power* is the potential ability to move people on a chosen course to produce an effect or achieve some goal (Homan, 2008; Martinez-Brawley, 1995). Three concepts are important in this definition. First, power involves *potential ability* or other people's perception that power exists. Even if power is not used, the potential for use is there.

For example, a major religious leader may have the power to influence heavily a decision regarding whether to allow women in the clergy. He might have the power to make this decision independently or to exert pressure upon others to comply with his wishes. However, that same leader may choose to remain neutral on the issue and, hence, not use his potential power. Potential ability means the opportunity to use power is there, but there is no guarantee regarding whether this power will be used or to what extent it will work.

The second concept involved in the definition of power is that of *moving people on a chosen course*. People having power can influence, that is, direct or sway, people's actions, thoughts, or decisions in some desired direction. Consider a practitioner working for a public social service agency who wants that agency to earmark more resources for poor people in the community. She must somehow engender some power to obtain that end. She must write a grant for funding, persuade the agency's board of directors[2] and administrative leaders of the idea's value, or lobby with local politicians to divert funding for her proposal.

The third important concept in the definition of power involves the idea that power is used to *produce an effect or achieve some end*. The worker just described above might have specific programmatic ideas about helping poor people in her community. For example, she might think a community food pantry or a homeless shelter is the best way to spend funds after they're attained.

A community's power structure involves who makes decisions about what can and can't be done in a community. It is eminently important for social workers to understand the power structure—including who may potentially be helpful and valuable allies, and who may be potential causes of vicious conflict (Streeter, 2008). Such information is vital for establishing effective strategies for positive change.

Who Has Power in Communities and Why?

At least seven rationales explain why some people in communities have greater power than others. Remember these reasons only reflect potential power. Even a person who has power may or may not get what he or she wants in the end. The rationales are information, wealth, reputation, high status, decision-making positions, laws and policies, and interpersonal connections.

1. *Information* (Homan, 2008, p. 136). You might think of the old cliché "knowledge is power." Information provides insight into an issue. It might provide greater access to ideas or help one choose allies to enhance power. For example, perhaps you happen to be a great grant writer and can expertly use the Internet to locate information such as grant sources. This gives you an advantage over someone without this knowledge. It gives you greater power to achieve your goals for acquiring funds. Other examples of people whose access

---

[2] Chapter 4 established that a *board of directors* is a group of people authorized to formulate an organization's mission, objectives, and policies, and to oversee the organization's ongoing activities.

to information gives them power includes "newspaper editors, talk show hosts, educators, gossips, gatekeepers (those who control the flow of information to decision makers), preachers, computer wizards, and political confidants" (Homan, 2008, p. 137).

2. *Wealth* (Homan, 2008; Martinez-Brawley, 1995). Think of another old cliché, "money is power." People with lots of money have many more choices regarding how they will live their lives than poor people. Rich people can choose to live in Boca Raton, Florida, Beverly Hills, California, or Aspen, Colorado, if they want. Money provides them with that power.

    Likewise, having money affects interaction with those who don't have it. People without enough money must go to other people who have money to get what they need to achieve goals. For example, people who can't afford to pay cash for a home must go to a bank or mortgage broker and apply for a loan. The lending institution has power over those requesting money. It can determine whether a potential borrower is a good credit risk or not. The lender also has the power to determine conditions for the loan, namely, how much interest the borrower must pay in order to use the borrowed money for some designated time period.

3. *Reputation* (Hardcastle & Powers, 2004; Martinez-Brawley, 1990, 1995). People who are highly thought of have greater power to influence others than people with shoddy reputations. Consider the milk advertisements in national news magazines where famous athletes, celebrities, and even politicians pose smiling ear to ear with blatant milk mustaches. The advertisers obviously are trying to communicate nonverbally that milk is good for you. You're supposed to believe this based on the celebrities' great reputations.

    Liking and respecting a person probably makes you more likely to go along with that person's ideas. This reflects one type of interpersonal power. On the other hand, a politician who you feel has lied to you or participated in some sleazy, unethical behavior probably would not command much of your attention.

4. *High Status* (Hardcastle & Powers, 2004; Homan, 2008; Martinez-Brawley, 1990, 1995). People who have high social status can command power over those with less social status. Sometimes, such people are in professional or work positions commanding respect because of their high earnings, their degrees, the difficulty it takes to get these degrees, or their sterling accomplishments. They might be CEOs of huge corporations, Supreme Court justices, physicians specializing in breakthrough health care arenas, nuclear physicists, astronauts, or university presidents. Other times, people have high status because of popular political support and acclaim. At varying levels, presidents of nations, state governors, and town board chairpersons have positions assuming status because of the popular support necessary to achieve such positions.

    Sometimes, conditions for enhancing power overlap. For example, an extremely wealthy automobile manufacturer with a high public profile might command power based on wealth, reputation, and resulting high status. Similarly, the director of the CIA might command power based on ready access to lots of information, popular reputation, and high status related to that position.

5. *Decision-Making Positions* (Hardcastle & Powers, 2004; Homan, 2008; Martinez-Brawley, 1990, 1995). People holding important positions in organizational hierarchies have automatic decision-making power as part of their job descriptions. By definition, agency executive directors, company or professional organization presidents, elected politicians, and labor leaders have power and decision-making authority over those below them in their respective hierarchies. People in lower positions are dependent upon those above to make effective decisions regarding how organizations and communities are run.

6. *Laws and Policies* (Hardcastle & Powers, 2004; Homan, 2008). Public laws and organizational policies dictate how such macro systems are organized and run. "The ability to make, interpret, and enforce the policies governing a community confers a great measure of authority" (Homan, 2008, p. 137). A law or policy can swiftly determine whether you win or lose a child custody suit or an agency grievance concerning sexual harassment. Being associated with formal legal processes gives politicians power. Greater knowledge about legal issues gives lawyers power. Ability to enforce laws gives police officers power. If the blue and red flashing lights have ever overtaken you as you were passing on a curvy rural road on the yellow line, you would be well aware of how it feels to be at the mercy of legal power. It is even worse when the middle-aged officer says, "You're getting a ticket, young lady" when the "young lady" is forty-seven.

7. *Connections* (Hardcastle & Powers, 2004; Homan, 2008). Interpersonal connections and affiliations with others in the community can enhance your power base. This is true concerning both large numbers of contacts and supporters, on the one hand, and fewer but more powerful contacts, on the other. "Good ol' boy" networks are alive and well, while good ol' girl connections are developing (Homan, 2008). When trying to change a community policy or develop a community service, soliciting others' collaboration and support can significantly strengthen a macro change effort. Other people can provide support, money, votes, information, and extended networking contacts (that is, people they know but you don't).

 Critical Thinking Questions 10.1

Think of a person in your own geographical or university community who has power. What are the sources of that power in terms of the seven sources just described?

Citizen Participation

Individuals and people banding together in community groups can develop and wield significant power. *Citizen participation* is the dynamic, voluntary involvement of community members to address issues and concerns affecting their community and improve social policies, laws, and programs. Several aspects of this definition are significant. First, participants are voluntary, that is, they are committed to expend their efforts. Second, the focus is on the community members

---

Focus on Ethics 10.1 | # Informed Consent and Community Action

Citizen participation is an essential aspect of community improvement. Yet, what does this really mean? Does it mean community members with the most *power*, the *majority* of community members, or *all* community members? What about community members who simply don't care about the issue one way or another? Dolgoff, Loewenberg, and Harrington (2009) address the ethical issue of informed consent when pursuing community action:

> The ethical dimensions of obtaining informed consent are especially problematic when the client is a community or a neighborhood, as may be the case for social workers engaged in community organizing. A social worker involved in a neighborhood renewal program must consider whether the elected representatives really represent all residents. Does their informed consent suffice or must every resident consent? What is the situation when the initiative for intervention comes from the outside? What does it mean "to obtain informed consent" when the social worker's initial objective is to raise the residents' consciousness to the fact that there is a problem in their community and that they can do something about it? Requiring every person's consent in this latter situation may be

tantamount to ruling out any intervention activity, yet intervening without informed consent is a violation of professional ethics. What should a social worker do in these circumstances? Hardina (2004) suggests that the best method for ensuring that most participants agree with an approach is to hold a "meeting in which all members debate risks and benefits of the proposed action and attempt to reach a consensus" (p. 599). This approach can be time consuming, and there is no guarantee that consensus can be reached, however "constituents should be fully informed about the consequences of their actions, especially when personal sacrifices (such as job loss, arrest, or social stigma) are great" (Hardina, 2004, p. 599). (p. 93)

It's no newsflash that people in general are complex. Social workers' charge is to work with the client system (be it a community, organization, group, family, or individual) to determine the most effective course of action that will protect people's lives, equality, autonomy, and rights; improve their quality of life; yet cause the least harm (Dolgoff et al., 2009). Consider when legislation is passed at the state and national levels. To what extent is there ever 100 percent consensus on any issue?

---

themselves, not on outside help. Community members work to make their own changes and improvements. Third, members are aware of issues and problems confronting the community. Often, this requires the education of community members by providing factual information and discussing specific change tactics. Fourth, citizen participation targets laws, rules, and regulations affecting the community in order to make them serve the community and its members better.

Social workers who strive to improve community macro systems often employ the concept of citizen participation. Social workers can encourage and enable community members to improve community conditions for themselves. Highlight 10.1 provides examples of how young people can contribute to their communities. Focus on Ethics 10.1 explores the issue of informed consent when pursuing community action.

Social Networks

We have established that interpersonal connections provide people with one source of power. The extent of support, both formal and informal, evident in any community usually contributes strength to community citizens. When residents work together, it's usually easier to get more accomplished than when isolated individuals work alone.

A term related to interpersonal connections is that of a social network. For any individual, a *social network* is a "formal or informal linkage of people or

Highlight 10.1	**The Power of Youth**

Community involvement is not limited to adult residents. Creative, energetic, concerned young people can also provide great citizen participation and service. Young people can potentially undertake a number of projects (Agrest, 1997).

Janet, age eight, noticed some of her classmates were going without the clothes, toys, and attention she so much enjoyed. The inequities continued to bother her until age fifteen, when she took the initiative to visit a shelter for homeless people. There she met many children and gave them gifts of colorful crayons, markers, and paper with which they could draw. Some of the drawings, reflecting their life experiences, were intense, moving, and distressing. For the next half of a year, she continued to visit the shelter on a weekly basis, playing with and reading to the children. Then she got an idea. She organized a group at school to help her carry it out. First, she took the pictures the children had drawn and used them as illustrations on calendars. Her start-up money was about $300, most of which she had earned working part-time. She then organized her schoolmates to sell them. The two purposes were to raise money for the shelter and to educate the public about homelessness. When Janet left for college, she made certain that the club would continue. She trained officers, transferred records, and recruited a faculty advisor.

Jacques, age fifteen, knew that the Special Olympics existed for people with cognitive disabilities, but he never really attended functions or helped out. Jacques was very active in high school basketball, football, and tennis. Accidentally, he found out about Unified Sports, a Special Olympics program that paired people who had a disability with those who performed actively in competitive sports. The intent was to provide opportunities for sports participation and simply to have fun. As Jacques's mother was a special education teacher, he put up a sign-up sheet in her classroom. Seven students with various learning and cognitive disabilities were interested. Jacques then recruited two friends and established the community's first Unified Sports team. Now two hundred community citizens are actively involved in Unified Sports basketball, track, soccer, bowling, baseball, and tennis. Jacques still allocates thirty hours each week in a variety of sporting activities.

Yael, age seventeen, attended a multiracial high school in which the student population was 45 percent Hispanic, 24 percent Asian, 25 percent African American, and 6 percent White. She became increasingly distressed by the serious racial tensions engulfing all aspects of school life. Racial groups put pressure on individuals, including Yael, not to associate across racial lines. More and more fights were breaking out. Finally, Yael had enough. She started with six interested people, a number that grew to over forty. Every day they have lunch together, discussing issues and ideas. She also started publishing a newsletter where students could share their ideas and suggest improvements.

Abdu, age sixteen, was saddened at the condition of a triangular plot of city land compressed where two city streets came together. It was scattered with junk—old refrigerators, tires, twisted pieces of metal that came from who knows what, and basic garbage. One day while reading the paper, Abdu ran across an article describing a national organization aimed at helping poor neighborhoods improve their conditions. It sparked an idea. Why couldn't he get some volunteers and money together to help fix up that miserable piece of property? Abdu worked with school officials, city administrators, other students, teachers, and community residents to completely refurbish the lot into an attractive, well-kept little park. He managed to solicit over $10,500 in donations, grants, and material contributions and helped organize volunteers to develop and use skills. Together, they seeded grass, planted shrubs, erected basketball hoops, and installed playground equipment. Thanks to Abdu's efforts, the community could be proud of its new park.

Other social networks are informal or more casual associations. Most social networks, for example, are "individuals or groups linked by some common bond, shared social status, similar

continued

Highlight 10.1 | *continued*

or shared functions, or geographic or cultural con- nection" (Barker, 2003, p. 405). Such networks are based on either interest or need and can include family, friends, neighbors, volunteers, or work groups (Barker, 2003; Fellin, 2001a). Usually, there is no formal membership list or hierarchy of author- ity. An example is an Internet talk group or "chat room" addressing some common interest such as Christmas ornament collecting or the hottest Hawaiian fishing spots.

organizations that may share resources, skills, contacts, and knowledge with one another" (Barker, 2003, p. 405). A core concept is the establishment of communi- cation channels with others based on common characteristics, interests, or needs.

Social networks vary according to the number of people involved, the frequency of their contact or communication with each other, how strongly members feel about being part of the network, strength of common bonds or characteristics (such as reli- gious commitment, age, or cultural heritage), and geographic distance among mem- bers (Fellin, 2001a). An example of a formal social network is a professional association such as the American Public Human Services Organization. Formal social networks may have established membership dues, prerequisites for membership, or lists of members' names. Note that professional organizations also serve as profes- sional communities. Social networks, however, imply more intercommunication and interaction than the concept of community. One can be a member of a professional community, for example, and have very little involvement with other members.

     Critical Thinking Questions 10.2

With what social networks are you involved? In what ways do they serve to support you?

The Relationships among Power, Citizen Participation, and Social Networks

The concepts of power, citizen participation, and social networks often relate to each other. Community members come together in citizen participation. They form a social network of support for each other and establish their power base. They then can confront a formal power structure (for example, the mayor's office) and pressure this structure to make policies fairer and to distribute community re- sources more equitably.

Natural Helping Networks

One form of informal social network is the *natural helping network,* a group of nonprofessional people volunteering their time and resources to help either an individual or group of people in need; this might involve "small loans, baby sitting, help in combating alcoholism, [or] a place to stay when funds are short" (Rubin & Rubin, 2008). The emphasis here is on a network *helping* designated individuals who require resources or support instead of a group networking on the basis of some other common interest. The help usually focuses on at least two functions (Lewis & Suarez, 1995). First, the network can provide support, either emotional or in the form of resources. For example, Zebb, a young man leaving prison on parole, has a natural helping network back in his home community consisting of concerned family members and clergy. Zebb depends on his family to provide a place to live, food, clothing, and emotional support to help him get back on his feet and live independently. A second function of natural helping networks is to provide information and help connect people with other needed resources. Zebb can rely on his rabbi to help link him with potential jobs made available by other members of the synagogue.

One example of establishing a natural helping network in a community neighborhood involves a protective services worker, Olga, who "was aware that a particular neighborhood needed more day care services and had a high incidence of child abuse" (Halley, Kopp, & Austin, 1998, pp. 407–408).[3] Olga received a number of referrals to investigate alleged child maltreatment. She made numerous visits to the neighborhood and talked to many residents. Olga found out that many residents had an excellent grasp of what was happening there, including incidents of family violence and neglect. Olga thought that if she could find out about potentially explosive situations before they "blew," she could help prevent placement of many neighborhood children in foster care.

A number of residents often referred to two strong, independent community women, Lolita and Pat, as "people in the know." They were *natural helpers*, that is, " 'ordinary' individuals identified by others in the community as being good listeners and helpers"; natural helpers typically "provide social support consisting of alleviation of social isolation, emotional support (encouragement, reassurance), communication activities (confidante, listening), and problem-centered services (light housekeeping, errands, transportation, cooking)" (Biegel, Shore, & Gordon, 1984, p. 97).

Lolita and Pat, who were good friends, each managed an eight-family rental property located near a large public housing project. Apparently, community residents, including those in the project, knew that they could turn to Lolita and Pat for help and support when they were down and out. For example, one resident, Jewel, mentioned to Olga that when her thirteen-year-old daughter became pregnant last year, Lolita lent Jewel money for an abortion. Another neighborhood resident, Lakeesha, told Olga how Pat helped her out last year. When Lakeesha couldn't make the rent one month and was evicted from her tiny apartment, Pat let Lakeesha stay with her for a couple weeks until Lakeesha found another place to live.

Olga contacted Lolita and Pat, set up informal meetings, and talked to them about neighborhood issues. Olga slowly approached them about the possibility of

---

[3] This vignette is loosely adapted from one described in *Delivering Human Services: A Learning Approach to Practice* (4th ed.), by A. A. Halley, J. Kopp, and M. J. Austin (New York: Longman, 1998).

becoming identified neighborhood helpers. She explained that residents would informally come to know such helpers as people to whom they could turn for help, advice, information, and support. Lolita and Pat could act as brokers to link community residents with needed daycare services and other resources aimed at combating child maltreatment. Olga emphasized that she would continue to be available to Lolita and Pat to provide information about resources or intervene in crisis situations they felt were too difficult to handle.

Both Lolita and Pat were wary at first. However, upon understanding Olga's idea more fully, Lolita was flattered. It surprised her that a person representing "the system" would recognize her in this manner. Pat was more hesitant. She didn't feel she was qualified to pull off such a role. After all, Pat told Olga that she only had a high school education.

Olga, Pat, and Lolita continued to talk. They discussed how Pat and Lolita were essentially neighborhood helpers already. The new ideas Olga was suggesting were to reinforce this fact, help spread the word farther, and have Olga provide them with help from a formal institution when they needed it. Pat's and Lolita's relationship with Olga evolved and was strengthened. They effectively put the plan into action for the general betterment of community residents' health and well-being.

The extent of support, both formal and informal, evident in any community usually contributes strength to that community. When residents work together, it's easier to get more accomplished than when isolated individuals work alone.

Critical Thinking Questions 10.3

Are you aware of any natural helping network in your community? If so, describe it and how it works.

Empowerment and Communities

We have established that *power* is the potential ability to move people on a chosen course to produce an effect or achieve some goal (Homan, 2008; Martinez-Brawley, 1995). We have also defined *empowerment* as the "process of increasing personal, interpersonal, or political power so that individuals can take action to improve their life situations" (Gutierrez, 2001, p. 210). It involves "an intentional, ongoing process centered in the local community, involving mutual respect, critical reflection, caring, and group participation, through which people lacking an equal share of valued resources gain greater access to and control over those resources" (Cornell University Empowerment Group, 1989, p. 2). Social workers seek to empower client systems, including individuals, families, groups, organizations, and communities, depending on who benefits from the change effort.

Social workers do not hand power over to people. Rather, they help people identify potential courses of action and make decisions about which options result in greater benefits, giving them more power over their own lives and futures. In community settings, social workers can help people become empowered in two basic ways, by achieving personal empowerment and social empowerment (Cowger & Snively, 2002, p. 108).

Personal Empowerment

People have *personal empowerment* when they can directly control what's happening in their own lives. For example, on a simple level, a person can choose whether to order a cherry-chocolate double-nut ice cream cone topped with butterscotch-flavored jimmies or a peanut butter and pumpkin cone covered in chopped walnuts. Likewise, people are empowered when they can choose in which neighborhood they want to live or which job offer to accept.

Social Empowerment

Social empowerment is the condition in the social environment where people have access to opportunities and resources in order to make personal choices and maintain some control over their environment. Personal empowerment is limited if people don't first possess social empowerment. Laws and policies often regulate people's ability to make choices. For example, people under age eighteen do not have the right to vote. Thus, they do not have the social empowerment necessary to provide input for selecting government officials.

Similarly, several decades ago many southern states restricted the use of water fountains either to people of color or White people. People were not empowered in the social environment to make their own decision regarding which water fountain to use. People choosing to use the one not designated for persons with their skin color potentially subjected themselves to severe criticism, ridicule, and even physical endangerment.

Still another example involves professional women working in an agency setting. Agency decision makers follow an unspoken rule that women make ineffective supervisors and administrators because of stereotyped gender-related characteristics. For example, administrators think women get crabby when they have their periods or they aren't strong enough to back up their decisions. Thus, women in that agency are not empowered to move up the career ladder. They do not have social empowerment.

The prior examples of social empowerment or the lack thereof primarily involve opportunities. People can also gain social empowerment by having adequate access to resources. Resources and opportunity are often integrally entwined. For example, people who earn minimum wages do not have the option of buying Rolex watches and Porsches or of living across from Central Park in Manhattan (unless they're servants or enjoy rent freezes established many years ago). Likewise, consider people who live in poverty-stricken areas that provide relatively poor educational backgrounds. School systems might have extremely large class sizes, giving teachers little chance of providing students with individual attention. Scarce resources result in fewer educational supplies and limited access to current technology. Because of poorer educational preparation, students attending such schools are less likely to do as well on college entrance examinations, and therefore are less likely to be accepted into college. Additionally, the poorer people are, the more difficulty they have paying for higher education and vocational training. Statistics clearly establish that the more education you have, the higher your income is likely to be. Lack of current resources subsequently blocks the acquisition of future resources.

The Interrelationship of Personal and Social Empowerment

Individual and social empowerment are interrelated. It is often hard to determine where one leaves off and the other begins. When a person has social empowerment, it is much more possible to enjoy personal empowerment by exercising personal choice. More personal choices are available.

Community empowerment is a primary social work task. We have established that people are not isolated individuals doing whatever they want like mosquitoes buzzing around potential targets. Rather, each aspect of life depends on people's involvement in the communities, organizations, and groups encompassing them. The macro social environment sets the stage for what resources and opportunities are available. A focus on community empowerment enhances professional social workers' ability to help people gain better access to resources, opportunities, and, subsequently, choices.

Assessment of Communities

Essentially, there are two ways of looking at a community in order to understand it (Kretzmann & McKnight, 1993: Naparstek & Dooley, 1997; Rapp, 1998; Saleebey, 2009). First, there is the traditional focus on *community problems and needs*. This problem- or deficit-based perspective directs social workers' focus to stressing what's wrong or missing in a situation. "*Need identification* describes health and social service requirements in a geographic or social area, whereas *need* [or *needs*] *assessment* is aimed at estimating the relative importance of these needs" (Siegel, Attkisson, & Carson, 2001, p. 105).

Consider the terms "South Bronx," "South Central L.A.," or "public housing," which, for many, prompt immediate thoughts of a host of problems—gangs, poverty, substance abuse, crime, unemployment, welfare, homelessness, truancy, slums, child maltreatment, broken families, and poor health care (Kretzmann & McKnight, 1993, p. 2). An analogy is looking at a glass as being half empty instead of half full (Kretzmann & McKnight, 1993). Not only is this problem-focused perspective overwhelming, but it encourages a spectrum of segmented services each aimed at addressing some designated, isolated problem or need. Service is provided to eligible individuals who may see themselves as service consumers or victims with little or no power to control their own destiny.

For example, a Protective Services agency may see Nicole, age twenty, as a client who appears to be using illegal drugs and is neglecting her two small daughters. The agency's primary goal is to stop the neglect. Its purpose is to ensure survival rather than to improve Nicole's overall quality of life. Agency workers may refer Nicole to counseling, a parent effectiveness training group, or a substance abuse program, and help her receive a public assistance grant. They might threaten to place her children in foster care. However, with large caseloads, there may be little they can do to help Nicole get her GED (general education diploma or high school equivalency), seek employment with good health care benefits, find adequate daycare, locate better housing, improve her cooking and child care skills, or provide her with an improved social support system. With Nicole, service provision to meet specific individual needs or address designated problems is the focus.

An alternative to viewing a community and its clients from a problem-focused perspective is appraisal of and emphasis on *assets and strengths*. *Mapping assets* is an assessment of a community that emphasizes that community's "capacities, skills, and assets" instead of the community's problems and weaknesses (Kretzmann & McKnight, 1993, p. 5). This approach stresses the importance of looking at the strengths of individuals, community organizations, and social institutions[4] when analyzing any community. It helps practitioners focus on what's going right for people in a community, what resources exist, and what opportunities might be developed. Capacity building then can result. *Capacity building* "is the ability to increase the leadership and organizational skills of local people for the purpose of strengthening their own organizations and networking capacities" (Gamble & Hoff, 2005, p. 178). By identifying and focusing on a community's and its residents' assets, you can build people's capacity to empower themselves and improve their lives and living conditions.

Nicole, introduced earlier, for example, has strengths including love for her children, a foundation of parenting and homemaking skills upon which to build, friends and two sisters in the community who might help and support her, completion of her sophomore year in high school, and a strong desire to keep her two little girls. Potential community organizations to which she might turn for support include an outpatient substance abuse clinic, a vocational education and job placement program, daycare centers, support groups for single mothers held at the local YWCA,[5] and a church to which she belongs. Local institutions potentially available for her and her children's use include public social services, the school system (including an adult education program), hospitals, libraries, and parks.

The following sections will discuss community assessment. First, the many dimensions of a community will be identified to help you understand its essence and how it functions. This kind of information forms the basis for a needs assessment. The final two sections will focus on approaches concerned with community empowerment, community building, and mapping assets.

---

[4] We've established that a *social institution* is an established and valued practice or means of operation in a society resulting in the development of a formalized system to carry out its purpose. Examples include "religion, the family, military structures, government, and the social welfare system" (Barker, 2003, p. 404).

[5] *YWCA* (Young Women's Christian Association), established more than 150 years ago, refers to organizations around the world that serve to "eliminate racism and empower women" by providing education, social activities, recreation, and other types of support (YWCA, 2006) in the pursuit of "justice, peace, health, human dignity, freedom, and care for the environment" (World YWCA, 2006).

Understanding the Dimensions of a Community

There are many dimensions of a community to explore that are important to fully understand that community. Questions posed here should provide a foundation for how to identify and subsequently assess community needs. Sheafor and Horejsi (2009, pp. 236–238) propose twelve dimensions to consider.

1. *Demographics.* What are the community's boundaries and basic demographic characteristics (Netting, Kettner, & McMurtry, 2008; Rubin & Rubin, 2008; Sheafor & Horejsi, 2009)? Think about the type of community it is. This includes determining the community's *population size* (the total number of persons living in a designated community), *density* (the ratio of people living within a particular space), and *heterogeneity* (the extent to which community members have diverse characteristics). What ethnic groups live in the community? Do they speak languages other than English?

   Identify the names given to various parts of the community. Are different areas known for having their own characteristics? For example, if it's a larger community, is there an industrial area with several factories? Are there some neighborhoods characterized by blue-collar families and others by wealthy professionals and businesspeople? Does one section have a university with its accompanying academic and student populations and activities? Where is the community located with respect to other communities, towns, and cities? Is it relatively isolated or close to other communities that could provide resources and services?

   What is the area's history? How old is the community? How has it developed over time? What changes have occurred regarding who has populated the area? Have certain groups moved away and others moved in? If so, why?

2. *Geography and environmental influences on community.* What kind of environment encompasses the community (Rubin & Rubin, 2008)? Is it in the middle of the central prairies, connected by interstate highways with other communities at great distances? Is it located on an ocean, major river, or one of the Great Lakes, where shipping and boating are primary economic and recreational activities, respectfully? Is it located in the mountains where winter might cause transportation difficulties? Are there recreational areas such as parks available? To what extent is the community experiencing environmental hazards such as pollution, smog, or tainted water, or deprivations such as power shortages?

3. *Beliefs and attitudes.* What are the "cultural values, traditions, and beliefs" that matter to various segments of the population (Netting et al., 2008, p. 206)? What are the spiritual and political values of the various factions of community residents? What social service agencies are available in the community and how do residents receive and value them? To what extent do residents feel an integral and supported part of the community? Or do they feel isolated and alone?

4. *Local politics.* How is the government structured? For example, cities, towns, and counties can be structured quite differently in terms of who has decision-making power and control. Are there any major issues currently under debate? For example, residents might have conflicting views regarding paying for a new middle school or rezoning a residential area to a business one.

5. *Local economy and businesses.* What businesses, factories, and other sources of employment characterize the community? Is the local economy thriving or in a major slump? Are businesses owned by local residents or huge conglomerates based in other states? What kinds of jobs exist in the community? Do people work inside the community or simply live here and work somewhere else? Is there adequate public transportation for people to get to and from work? What is the unemployment rate?

6. *Income distribution.* To what extent do community residents receive cash and in-kind (goods and services) public assistance benefits? What are the median income levels for men, women, and various ethnic groups? What percentage of people live in poverty?

7. *Housing.* What are housing conditions like in the community? Is it a relatively new community with low population density? Or it is an aging, economically deprived community with a high population density and deteriorating, dilapidated housing? What are the "types of housing" characterizing the area ("for example, single-family dwellings, apartments, public housing") (Sheafor & Horejsi, 2009, p. 237)? What are average rents and costs for real estate? Is there a shortage of low-income housing?

8. *Educational facilities and programs.* An educational system can be assessed in at least four ways. The first involves its context. What is the educational system like? Are schools well supported by the community, or are they experiencing funding cut after funding cut? Where and in what types of neighborhoods are schools located? Are they public, private, or charter schools? A *charter school* is a public school supported by tax dollars but allowed to be managed (chartered) outside of the jurisdiction of the local school board but in accordance with state regulations; its curriculum, targeted population, or educational philosophy usually diverges from other schools in the system (Massat, Constable, McDonald, & Flynn, 2009).

   The second way an educational system can be assessed involves its treatment of special populations of children (Naparstek & Dooley, 1997) and its attention to cultural differences. How are children with special needs treated? To what extent are programs available for preschool children to prepare them for school entry? For instance, are Headstart programs available? Are there diagnostic and treatment services available for children who have developmental disabilities? Are schools perceptive regarding the ethnic and cultural makeup of their students? Do they celebrate or discourage diversity? If needed, are bilingual programs available?

   A third way to assess the functioning of a community's educational system is the extent to which the school system enables students to do well (Naparstek & Dooley, 1997). How do children typically score on standardized achievement tests compared to other communities in the United States and Canada? How well do community students compete with students from other communities in events such as science fairs, spelling competitions, and other contests? How well prepared for high school and college are students? How many students graduate and go on to college? Does elementary school provide them with a solid foundation for future levels of higher education, vocational education, and job training? What is the drop-out rate?

A fourth assessment aspect concerns a community educational system's attention to its adult residents (Naparstek & Dooley, 1997). On the one hand, to what extent do parents understand their children's development? On the other, how well do community educational programs adequately prepare adults to enter the labor force?

9. *Health and welfare systems.* A community's strengths concerning residents' health primarily involve access to and quality of care. Are there adequate numbers of health professionals and specialists? Are hospitals and clinics readily accessible to area residents? Are residents adequately covered by private insurance or public programs? Especially important is "the prevention and treatment of those conditions that afflict inner-city and poor people of color at disproportionate rates" (Naparstek & Dooley, 1997, p. 84).

   What social service programs are available and where are they located? What specific types of services exist (for example, crisis intervention, substance abuse treatment, and public assistance)? How accessible and well publicized are these programs? To what extent are they adequate, or are there substantial gaps in service? To what extent are "service providers sensitive to special needs or concerns of minority and ethnic groups" (Sheafor & Horejsi, 2009, p. 237)? If the community has non-English-speaking residents, are translators available? Are "self-help groups and informal helping networks" available in the community (Sheafor & Horejsi, 2009, p. 237)?

10. *Social control and safety.* To what extent are fire and police protection adequate? To what extent is the environment safe? Are housing standards and codes being followed? How do community residents view the justice system and feel they are treated by it and by police officers? Are the public safety and justice systems sensitive to the needs and issues faced by minorities in the community?

11. *Sources of information and public opinion.* Are there "influential TV and radio stations and newspapers to which the people look for information and perspectives on current events" (Sheafor & Horejsi, 2009, p. 237)? We have established that knowledge is power. It is therefore important to ask how members of the community learn what is going on in the community as well as in the world at large (Rubin & Rubin, 2008). Are there neighborhood organizations or other active community groups whose purposes are to keep on top of what's going on within the community? For example, are residents aware that commercial developers are planning to build a toxic waste plant in the near vicinity? Do residents know that school classroom populations have climbed to a ratio of one teacher for every forty-five students? Do community members know about a job training program subsidized by the county and targeting people in need?

   To what extent does the community have human resources? *Human resources* are the knowledge and abilities characterizing some people that can be used to enhance other people's quality of life (Barker, 2003). Human resources are people who can act as advocates, initiators, planners, educators, leaders, and workers for positive social changes. Are there significant community political, religious, or other informal community leaders who speak for various subgroups and minorities in the population and to whom people look to for help and support?

12. *Summary assessment of community issues.* What is your overall assessment of the community's functioning? To what extent is it good or inadequate? What serious social problems (for example, "inadequate housing, inadequate public

transportation, lack of jobs, youth gangs, poverty, teen pregnancy, domestic abuse, etc.") do community residents face (Sheafor & Horejsi, 2009, p. 238)? What primary "gaps" are evident in "social, health care, and educational services" (Sheafor & Horejsi, 2009, p. 238)?

 Critical Thinking Questions 10.4

How would you analyze your own community in terms of these twelve criteria? How would you summarize the information? What are your community's primary problems, needs, and strengths?

Highlight 10.2 discusses ways to gather data about a community.

Highlight 10.2 | **How to Gather Data about a Community**

There are many ways of collecting data to assess a community. Three will be introduced here that are often used in conducting a needs assessment.

First, you can hold a *community forum*, which is "an open meeting of all members of a community" (Siegel et al., 2001, p. 120). Any community member may be a valuable source of information. "The perspectives of residents concerning the accessibility, availability, acceptability, and organization of services comprise indispensable clues about the human service needs of the community as a whole" (p. 119). Although probably no individual can give you the "total picture" of what a community needs, he or she might provide some valuable insights. Getting information from a variety of residents can result in a general picture of community needs.

A second needs assessment approach is the *nominal group technique* (Siegel et al., 2001; Zastrow, 2009). Here group members are gathered and asked to silently "list their needs on paper without group discussion" so that "each member's personal views can be ascertained" without influence from the others (Zastrow, 2009, p. 98). Members are asked to write down what they feel are the community's major needs. After members have completed their list, the group leader asks them to go around one at a time and share one of their ideas with the

rest of the group. Ideas are then recorded on a blackboard, on large sheets of paper, or electronically so that they are visible to the group. After all ideas have been recorded, group members participate in a discussion regarding their feelings about the needs that have been shared. After the leader determines that discussion has been adequate, he or she asks group members to prioritize and write down what they feel are the community's most pressing needs. The leader then collects the lists and can combine them to determine the group's overall impression of community needs.

A third needs assessment approach is the *key informant technique* (Kirst-Ashman & Hull, 2009a; Siegel et al., 2001). Here ten to fifteen individuals are identified "who have extensive first-hand knowledge of the community and who either live or work in the community" (Siegel et al., 2001, p. 126). Participants might include service providers such as police officers or teachers, residents who have resided in the community a long time and have been active in community activities, and workers in community service agencies. Participants who serve as key informants are then interviewed in depth concerning their perceptions of community needs. A summary regarding their impression of community needs can subsequently be established.

Community Building

Community building, a vital concept in an empowerment approach, is the process of enhancing a community's strengths by linking community residents, organizations in the community, and external resources to tackle community problems and working together toward positive change (Briggs, 2008; Milligan, 2008; Rubin & Rubin, 2008). All communities obviously have problems and needs. The trick is to scrutinize potential strengths, often easily overlooked, and to get relevant entities to work together on behalf of community growth and improvement. Saleebey (2006) explains:

> Community building refers to the reality and possibility of restoring or refurbishing the sense and reality of community in neighborhoods. It involves among other things helping neighbors—individuals, families, and associations—in a community to strengthen relationships with one another usually around mutually crafted projects. The idea is to replace the notion that they must be completely dependent on outside or professional organizations and institutions for help with the assumptions that they have internal assets and capacities that can be developed and used in increasing the human and social capital of the community. The upshot of this is an increase in the sense of self-efficacy and power in the individuals, families, and associations of the community—they believe that they can make things happen! (p. 255)

Chapter 1 introduced the concept of community organization. Essentially, community building is a dimension of community organizing and macro practice. Highlight 10.3 discusses President Barack Obama's experience in community building in his role as a community organizer.

Naparstek and Dooley (1997) emphasize four major principles in establishing a healthy, productive, integrated community: working together, developing new alliances that work in cooperation, targeting neighborhoods, and building on neighborhood strengths.

Working Together

First, community building involves many components of a community and other systems with which it's involved working synchronously together. If community resource systems don't work together, nothing much gets done. For example, a community high school may have a strong vocational component aimed at training for and placing students in jobs upon graduation. Related components are adequate employment opportunities, affordable housing, and availability of health care. The high school's efforts are virtually useless if no adequately paying jobs for high school graduates exist in the area and no public transportation is available for workers to get to jobs located elsewhere. What good is a job if no affordable housing is available? Where would workers live? Or, how useful is it to get a young single parent of a chronically ill child a job paying minimum wages and offering no health care benefits? She wouldn't make nearly enough to cover even minimal health expenses and keep her family afloat financially.

| Highlight 10.3 | **President Barack Obama's Experience in Community Organization and Community Building** |

Some might say that an effective community organizer is "a combination of educator, confessor-priest, social activist, motivational expert, mediator, and campaign leader"; thus one of his colleagues described President Barack Obama during Obama's experience in community organizing and community building (Walsh, 2007).

Walsh (2007) depicts Obama's history. Obama graduated from Columbia University in 1983, having majored in political science. Initially, he worked in New York City as a financial consultant, a job of which he soon tired. He then moved to Chicago in 1985 to work for the newly established Developing Communities Project (DCP) as a community organizer. DCP was "a community group based in the churches of the region, an expanse of White, Black and Latino blue-collar neighborhoods that were reeling from the steel-mill closings" (Moberg, 2007). His salary was $10,000 a year with an additional $2,000 thrown in to purchase "a beat-up blue Honda Civic" (Moberg, 2007) so he could get around and do his job. There Obama worked among the "seemingly endless clumps of drab brick apartment buildings and patchy lawns on Chicago's South Side" (Walsh, 2007). He served among the 5,300 African Americans who lived "amid shuttered steel mills, a nearby landfill, a putrid sewage treatment plant, and a pervasive feeling that the white establishment of Chicago would never give them a fair shake" (Walsh, 2007).

Obama (1990) comments on the meaning of community organizing:

> In theory, community organizing provides a way to merge various strategies for neighborhood empowerment. . . . This means bringing together churches, block clubs, parent groups and any other institutions in a given community to pay dues, hire organizers, conduct research, develop leadership, hold rallies and education campaigns, and begin drawing up plans on a whole range of issues—jobs, education,

crime, etc. Once such a vehicle is formed, it holds the power to make politicians, agencies and corporations more responsive to community needs. Equally important, it enables people to break their crippling isolation from each other, to reshape their mutual values and expectations and rediscover the possibilities of acting collaboratively—the prerequisites of any successful self-help drive.

Obama (1990) speaks of DCP's accomplishments that include establishing job training programs in schools, repairing and restoring housing, improving city services, developing parks, and curbing crime and drug trafficking. He worked on such issues as getting potholes filled, developing summer jobs for youth, and urging housing managers "to repair toilets, pipes, and ceilings" (Walsh, 2007). Possibly, Obama's most contentious experience involved organizing residents to confront public housing administrators about removing dangerous asbestos from area housing (Walsh, 2007). He led residents—although "far fewer than Obama had anticipated—to challenge authorities downtown. Ultimately, the city was forced to test all the apartments and eventually begin cleaning them up" (Moberg, 2007).

Ultimately, Obama left DCP for other pursuits (Walsh, 2007). In 1988 he began law school at Harvard, in 1990 he "became the first African-American president of Harvard Law Review," and in 1991 he graduated with his law degree (Walsh, 2007). He then became a civil rights lawyer in Chicago and taught law at the University of Chicago. In due course, he became an Illinois state senator and eventually a U.S. senator in 2004.

Some claim Obama's community organizing work taught him how to listen well, minimize conflict, and involve a wide range of people in establishing a consensus (Lawrence, 2008; Moberg, 2007). This experience may be what made him decide to devote his life to public service (Moberg, 2007).

New Alliances and Cooperation

A second principle basic to community building is that it requires new alliances and cooperation. These relationships involve both those among agencies within the community and those between community agencies and external, larger systems.

The first dimension of this principle, *internal cooperation* among community organizations and groups, might involve new creative ways in which they can work together to serve residents. For example, a church, YMCA,[6] and outpatient substance abuse counseling center might combine their efforts in outreach for youth. They might work together contributing staff time, resources, and space to establish a program offering a series of services. These may include drug education provided by counseling center staff at the church and the YMCA, supervised social activities cosponsored by all three agencies, space provided by the YMCA for recreational activities for youth involved in both church groups and abuse counseling, and publicity developed and distributed by the church and the YMCA. These three agencies have no formal connections with each other. Yet, they could potentially work together to establish a unified program available to a wide spectrum of community youth.

Another dimension of establishing new alliances in community building is *external cooperation*. This concerns how organizations and groups in the community must work well together with external macro systems in order to meet community needs. Community residents know what they need and are experts on how public resource systems work or do not work on their behalf. A high-level White male policy maker in Washington, D.C., likely has little insight into the life of a single African-American mother of three who has an eleventh-grade education and lives in a tiny two-room apartment in a huge urban hub. How could that administrator know the myriad of details and problems she must address every day to stay alive? There's a crack house next door. She's afraid of what would happen to her kids if they wander too near the dealers and the addicts. Prostitutes walk the streets every night. She's not certain how well her baby-sitter attends to her kids while she's at work. She can just barely make the rent and the grocery bill each week. She's afraid to tell the landlord someone broke her back window because she fears he might evict her. Sometimes, she's late with the rent and doesn't want to make any waves.

The point is that community residents usually have the best understanding about what affects their lives. They really need to provide input into decisions made far above in the bureaucratic structure that have major and sometimes ominous effects on their lives. Hence, we heavily emphasize community resident involvement and leadership.

However, major resources flow into communities from larger city, state, and national macro systems. Communities depend on these resources. Bureaucratic structures are complicated, and regulations for funding distribution complex.

---

[6] *YMCA* (Young Men's Christian Association), initiated over 150 years ago, refers to organizations in over 120 countries that provide a wide range of educational, recreational, social, and supportive services to community residents including "all people of all faiths, races, ages, abilities and incomes" (YMCA, 2006).

Communities don't have the power and influence to formulate policies and make decisions about how public funds at national and state levels are spent. Community residents and leaders generally have a more limited perspective on what's going on outside of their community and "are less likely to produce the comprehensive policy changes that are needed to address more complex realities" (Naparstek & Dooley, 1997, p. 80). Therefore, community residents and leaders must work together with decision makers in external systems to understand processes and obtain resources the community deserves.

The Importance of Targeting Neighborhoods

The third principle involved in community building is the importance of targeting neighborhoods to undertake positive change on behalf of the community. Successful macro changes "must focus on a distinct geographic area whose residents are linked by, and who identify with, a cluster of local institutions such as schools, churches, or community centers" (Naparstek & Dooley, 1997, p. 81). Chapter 11 examines more thoroughly how neighborhoods function and can empower residents.

Building on Neighborhood Strengths

Neighborhoods are central to the fourth salient principle in community building. The foundation for positive macro change rests on neighborhood strengths and assets. Neighborhood residents know the most about their needs. They have much in common in that they experience similar living conditions. The basic social work values of self-determination and empowerment dictate that neighborhood residents should have maximum choices about what happens in their own lives.

Mapping assets is a tool to prepare for community building. The subsequent section elaborates upon this approach.

Focus on Ethics 10.2 helps explore the extent to which community building in all its facets complies with professional ethics.

Community Building in Rural Communities

Much of the literature on community building is oriented toward urban development (Merritt & Collins, 2008; Messinger, 2004). Therefore, we will spend some time here elaborating on the potential for community building in rural communities. First, we will review briefly the context of the rural community. Then we will provide some examples of community building approaches that have been used effectively in rural communities.

Chapter 9 examined rural communities and identified some of the differences between them and urban environments (Davenport & Davenport, 2008). Population density is low in rural communities compared with urban. They tend to be located far from urban centers and lack much diversity in functioning. For example, a farming community and any services it has would be oriented toward the support of farming. Similarly, a mining community would focus on sustaining mining.

| **Community Building and Professional Ethics**

We have established that the six core values in the NASW *Code of Ethics* include (NASW, 2008):

1. *Service:* Providing help, resources, and benefits so that people may achieve their maximum potential.
2. *Social justice:* Upholding the condition that in a perfect world, all citizens would have identical "rights, protection, opportunities, obligations, and social benefits" regardless of their backgrounds and membership in diverse groups (Barker, 2003, pp. 404–405).
3. *Dignity and worth of the person:* Holding in high esteem and appreciating individual value.

4. *Importance of human relationships:* Valuing the dynamic reciprocal interactions between social workers and clients, including how they communicate, think and feel about each other, and behave toward each other.
5. *Integrity:* Maintaining trustworthiness and sound adherence to moral ideals.
6. *Competence:* Having the necessary skills and abilities to perform work with clients effectively.

To what extent does the concept of community building comply with these principles? Explain.

Additionally, lack of employment and poverty often characterize rural areas (Merritt & Collins, 2008). Resources are scarcer than in urban hubs, and therefore services are fewer and less specialized.

Rural residents often have a different perspective on life and the environment than their urban counterparts. Merritt and Collins (2008) remark that it is:

possible that rural residents define their relationship with the natural environment differently than urban residents. For a trivial, but maybe meaningful example, consider the nicknames of rural high school sports teams such as the Farmington Farmers and the Hoopeston Cornjerkers in Illinois, the Hematites [a type of local mineral often used in making jewelry] of Ishpeming, Michigan and the Biglerville Canners in the apple orchards of Pennsylvania. These nicknames denote rural communities closely connected to their surrounding natural environment and economic base. (p. 151)

Subsequent sections provide case examples of and suggestions for rural community building.

Case Example: The Warren Family Institute

Messinger (2004) describes a grant-funded demonstration project that established the Warren Family Institute (WFI) in Warren County, a rural county in eastern North Carolina. As a *comprehensive community initiative (CCI)*, WFI "strategy uses coalitions of public and private agencies, religious organizations, neighborhood groups, community leaders, and individuals in the community to work together on neighborhood councils, task forces, planning committees, and advisory boards to identify needs in the community and to develop and implement a comprehensive plan for multisystem change. . . . Rather than using a single strategy targeting one 'cause' of a social problem, CCIs offer a comprehensive systems approach that attacks complex problems on a variety of fronts" (p. 535).

Messinger (2004) describes the context of Warren County:

Like many rural areas in the southern United States, Warren County suffers from the replacement of small family farms by corporate agribusiness, sparse economic development, and substandard and inadequate housing. The county's poverty is evidenced by the dubious honor of having the highest percentage of privies [outdoor toilets or, in more colloquial language, outhouses] in the state. (p. 537)

Many of the impoverished residents were isolated and located far apart. Whereas much "community building" is oriented toward empowering urban neighborhoods (as Chapter 11 will explain), the neighborhood concept doesn't readily apply to many rural communities because of the demographics. Rural residents generally don't live that close together.

Social services agencies serving Warren County also often were responsible for several other counties on a regional basis. This resulted in sparse service provision in Warren County. There were only a few small manufacturers in the county that served as employers and provided some tax revenues, although there was a prison, some nursing homes, and some small businesses.

Community strengths included "the presence of good neighbors," the quiet rural setting, and, for some, the support of an extended family network (Messinger, 2004, p. 540).

The WFI planning group initially included representatives from nonprofit social services agencies, "churches, and service organizations, along with county officials" (Messinger, 2004, p. 538). Low-income county residents at first participated by conducting a door-to-door needs assessment. Because citizen participation is so essential, eventually residents became involved at all levels of the organization. Some became members of the board of directors. Others served as representatives at public meetings. Still others became employed as WFI staff.

> The institute attacked the roots of the social and economic problems of low-income families through a three-pronged approach. They partnered low-income families with the institute's family services coordinators, caseworkers who provided support to family members, advocated on the families' behalf with local agencies' staffs, and mentored family leaders to help them be more self-sufficient. The institute also facilitated interorganizational collaboration and coordinated joint projects among local agencies to make better use of their combined resources. Finally, the institute worked to change policies at local and regional agencies that were damaging to low-income families, collaborative planning efforts, and overall development of the county. (Messinger, 2004, p. 538)

Issues that WFI addressed included "unemployment and underemployment, lack of education, poor health care, lack of community involvement, disorganized service provision, and inadequate and substandard housing, with the ultimate purpose of helping low-income families become self-sufficient" (Messinger, 2004, p. 536).

WFI was able to implement a range of programs and projects, including:

- housing repair days
- a first-time homebuyer education and counseling program
- a locally administered, tenant-based rental assistance program
- tenant–landlord mediation services
- transitional housing services
- re-establishment of a county housing authority
- creation of evening family health assessment
- information and referral services
- leadership development training with low-income residents

- the establishment of a summer program for youths
- the creation and coordination of VISTA[7] . . . volunteer opportunities
- the creation of instructional programs and community-building events
- the purchase of a van to transport low-income residents to and from job training and community college classes (Messinger, 2004, p. 541)

Enhancing Rural Youths' Interest in Higher Education

Poole and More (2004) address the problem of encouraging rural youths' interest in higher education. "Rural youth are half as likely to obtain a college degree as their peers in urban and suburban communities. The situation is worse for rural African Americans and Hispanics, only 4% of whom graduate from college" (p. 147).

Reasons Why Rural Youth May Not Seek Higher Education   A number of factors operate against rural young people aspiring for college degrees. These involve a wide range of factors (Poole & More, 2004). *Institutional factors* include:

- "As a group, rural youth tend to be less academically prepared for college than their peers in urban school systems. Rural students generally have lower achievement scores on standardized tests and less access to advanced preparatory courses, which deter them from attending college" (p. 148).
- Rural students may experience less encouragement from teachers to attend college and may not receive adequate information about college and potential careers initiated in college.
- College costs may be prohibitive to rural youth, who are more likely than many urban and suburban youth to come from families with lower incomes.

Community factors working against college enrollment include:

- Since many jobs in rural areas do not require a college education, rural youth may not have adequate exposure to role models—people with a college education. Youth may not clearly see the benefits of attaining a college degree.
- "Community members without a college degree sometimes do not recognize the benefits of higher education" (p. 149). Therefore, they would be less likely to encourage college attendance. Community residents may also be hesitant to encourage youth to leave the rural community because it further depletes the population and potential community resources.
- Often rural communities are located far from colleges and universities, posing geographical obstacles to college attendance.

Family factors against higher education include:

- If parents don't have college degrees, they may be less likely to encourage their children to pursue them.

---

[7] *VISTA* is a national service program to fight poverty in the United States, established in 1965, in which volunteers "commit to serve full-time for a year at a nonprofit organization or local government agency, working to fight illiteracy, improve health services, create businesses, strengthen community groups, and much more" (Corporation for National & Community Service, 2009b).

- "Rural parents often lack information about available resources for college" (p. 150).
- Rural families may have less access to financial resources.

Individual factors inhibiting college enrollment include:

- "Many rural youth are not confident that they can compete successfully in a college environment" (p. 150).
- "Rural students often have low educational and occupational aspirations" due partially "to socioeconomic status" (p. 150).
- "Educational achievement levels are low among rural females," many of whom decide to marry early (p. 151).
- We've already established that rural African-American and Hispanic youth are even less likely to get college degrees than their White counterparts.
- It is often very difficult for rural youth to leave their home communities for a radically different college environment, often in an urban setting. They just don't feel they can handle the "culture shock" of it all (p. 151).

So What Is the Answer?   Poole and More (2004) propose a number of community-building suggestions to encourage college attendance by rural youth. Educational institutions and the community can address the issue in a number of ways. Schools can raise expectations for academic performance. They can offer college preparatory courses to begin socializing students for college involvement. One means of doing this is to provide Web-based courses. Schools can also accelerate efforts to provide information about colleges and careers to students early on. Rural students may then be more likely to see college as a viable option. Schools can also provide workshops for school staff, providing them with current information about college and teaching them ways they can portray college attendance in a positive light. Scholarships can be established to assist rural students in financial need. Additionally, schools can identify and link rural students with college-educated mentors where available.

Family strategies include providing workshops for and meetings with rural parents. These can be used to educate parents about opportunities available with a college education, the college application process, and financial planning for college. Individual strategies to encourage rural youths' college potential include inviting college faculty to meet with students and talk to them about the college experience. Students require self-confidence that they can indeed be successful in college. "Tutoring, academic advising, SAT preparation, and [teaching] problem-solving" skills may also enhance motivation to attend college (p. 154). Campus visits also can acquaint students and their families with the college environment and college life. The unknown is often scary. The more familiar students are with the idea of college attendance and what it might be like, the more comfortable they will likely feel.

The idea here is that generalist social workers can help rural communities to develop innovative strategies for addressing problems. This example, of course, focuses on the educational dimensions of a rural community. Highlight 10.4 provides one school social worker's perspective on working in a rural community.

| Highlight 10.4 | Working as a Rural School Social Worker |

Line (2005) talks about her experience as a school social worker in the rural Upper Peninsula of Michigan.[8] She describes the area as "about as rural an area as one can get. Some would even call it a wilderness area"; she was one of three school social workers in a three-county school district covering 4,000 square miles that "had more deer than people" (p. 105).

Line (2005) describes the community's residents:

> People who lived in this area were very independent and proud. They had been used to working their land, bartering for their needs with their neighbors, and surviving as a result of their own efforts. They all lived like one big, extended family and helped each other without being asked. (p. 106)

It was very difficult for residents to ask for help from "outsiders" whom they neither knew nor trusted; this included school staff although "the school was the focal point for community life" (Line, 2005, p. 106). Having moved from the urban bustle of Detroit, a rural community was quite a change for Line. Because of the huge area and low population density, the job required a lot driving, both traveling between schools and doing home visits. She remarks:

> Some of the home visits were memorable, to say the least. Directions to homes were given by landmarks, not by miles or road names. One went to a home based on: "It is the first white house on the right, after the dairy farm. If you go up the hill, you have gone too far. There is a blue pickup in the driveway. (p. 106)

Line describes some of her various home visit experiences of being welcomed by a flock of lookout geese in addition to "a variety of dogs, goats, and sheep" (2005, p. 107). She indicates that these creatures weren't posted to "get the social worker,"

but rather they just meandered about the yard at will as a normal part of the scheme of things. She indicated she learned to wear only washable clothing and to not take along anything she "could not do without, in the event it was eaten" (p. 107).

Line stressed that doing her job necessitated true generalist skills in working with various size systems; she was frequently required "to work with individuals, groups of parents, staff or administrators, agencies, and communities" (2005, pp. 107–108). She emphasized how fast information traveled by word of mouth. If something happened one night, the whole community seemed to know about it by the next morning. Because of this communication system, it was very important to establish a good reputation. Only then would community members begin to trust and work with you. Reputation was also important in work with other agencies because networking and working together in rural communities are critical.

Line also underscored the importance of confidentiality. Everyone seemed to know everyone else. So, if one person asked how another was doing, it was important not to violate anyone's privacy. She prepared herself with pat responses like, "I am sorry but I cannot talk about my clients" or "Isn't the weather awful today?" (the latter is actually answering one question with another question, which is quite a tricky maneuver) (2005, p. 107).

Line indicates that one dynamic in her rural community experience is that "EVERYONE KNOWS your personal beliefs" (2005, p. 109). Therefore, it is important distinguish personal from professional values, and remain nonjudgmental in interventions with clients. She concludes that she is quite satisfied with her practice in a rural community. To her "people everywhere are just people and need to be respected for the individuals that they are" (p. 109).

---

[8] The contents of this highlight are taken from the book *Days in the Lives of Social Workers* (3rd ed.), written by Linda May Grobman (ed.) and published by White Hat Communications in Harrisburg, PA. It provides an excellent source of a wide range of interesting "real-life" stories about social work practice.

Additional Development Strategies for Rural Communities

Industrialization and capitalist competition have not been very helpful to rural communities. Such "progress" made it difficult for small family farmers to compete with "corporate agribusiness" (Messinger, 2004, p. 537). Merritt and Collins (2008) propose at least three potential ways that rural communities can develop their resources. Generalist social work practitioners can help community members organize themselves and pursue these ideas.

First, "community-supported agriculture" involves:

> a consumer cooperative where a farmer sells subscriptions or shares to several dozen households. The farmer takes this money and buys seeds and other inputs to start the growing season. As crops ripen, subscribers can expect a weekly basket of vegetables, fruits, herbs, cut flowers and other items. The farm and subscribers both share the agricultural bounty and the risks. (p. 153)

A second development strategy concerns "agritourism," where:

> farmers can offer educational experiences to urban tourists who are willing to pay to learn about agriculture and country life. Activities include barn tours, hayrides, u-pick gardens, orchards, hiking, horseback riding, and mountain biking. To teach student where their meals come from, some farmers have planted 'pizza farms,' a circular plot divided into wedges. Each wedge is planted with an ingredient used to make pizza. One wedge might have herbs; another might have wheat. Yet others might have tomatoes or a grazing dairy cow as the source of cheese. Each wedge is divided by a pathway so tourists can get close to each ingredient. In Massachusetts, the Hyland Orchard and Brewery combines a brewpub with a petting zoo so parents and children can have fun. (153–154)

A third approach to rural development concerns "producer cooperatives"; Merritt and Collins (2008) explain:

> Instead of shipping raw commodities such as soybeans elsewhere for processing, farmers are forming so-called new generation cooperatives (NGCs) to process locally-grown commodities in the community. This increases on-farm profits, generates local jobs, and increases the local tax base, while taking advantage of the rural competitive advantages in crop production. NGCs also lessen the risk of capital flight [where rural residents migrate to cities in search of better jobs and financial prospects] because farmers and other community investors own the processing facilities. (p. 154)

Mapping Community Assets and Empowerment

Earlier we indicated that Kretzmann and McKnight (1993) have established a capacity-building approach to community assessment called *mapping assets*. It emphasizes the community's "capacities, skills, and assets" instead of the community's problems and weaknesses (p. 5). *Assets* are potential persons, groups, and resources in a community that can help a community function and grow. It contrasts with the community-assessment approach we reviewed earlier that focused primarily on figuring out a community's problems and gaps in services. Saleebey (2002a) explains mapping assets:

> Three principles define this approach. First, it is *assets and strengths based*. Community workers start with what resources are present in the community and not with what is

missing, what is wrong, or what the community needs. Second, this approach to community development is *internally focused*. That is, it is very important to know what is going on within the community, what assets are available, and what individual and group capacities exist. The role of external factors and institutions is, for the time being, ignored. Rather the focus on the inner life of the community demonstrates the centrality of local control, local capital, local vision, and local ownership. Finally, if the first two elements of the assets-based scheme are to hold, then the process must clearly be *relationship driven*. If people are to be pulled into the life of the community and share their capacities, it will be done through the medium of relationship. A gift is given from hand to hand. (p. 236)

Mapping assets concerns at least two domains—"releasing individual capacities" and empowering local associations, organizations, and institutions (Kretzmann & McKnight, 1993, p. 13; Saleebey, 2009).

Releasing Individual Capacities

Each community resident has positive qualities and capacities that can contribute to the community's well-being. If those capacities are identified and appreciated by fellow citizens, the individual will feel like an important community member who feels a sense of connection with other citizens. Kretzmann and McKnight (1993) provide a detailed framework for assessing individual capacities that can be administered to a community resident. These capacities reflect many dimensions of abilities and skills.[9]

Health   Individuals, family members, neighbors, or volunteers can provide help to those who need it in a community. This may take the form of assisting people who are seniors, have mental disorders, have physical or cognitive disabilities, or have other health problems.

Administrative and Interpersonal Work Skills   Individuals may also have organization and office skills that could help in developing a neighborhood organization or supporting a social service or health care agency through volunteering. Such skills might include computer proficiency, budgeting, planning, telephone communication, marketing and sales, writing reports, and organizing data and records.

Construction and Repair   Being handy at building and fixing things can be helpful. Repairing buildings, improving homes, and fixing electrical and plumbing fixtures are skills that can contribute to community well-being. Consider Habitat for Humanity, an international organization whose overarching goal is "to eliminate poverty housing and homelessness from the face of the earth by building adequate and basic housing" (Habitat for Humanity, 2005). To do this, the organization solicits donations from sponsors and help from volunteers. People skilled in construction and repair have valuable assets to contribute.

---

[9] Note that the headings of *health, construction and repair, maintenance,* and *food* were taken directly from Kretzmann and McKnight (1993, pp. 19–21). Ideas presented under *administrative and interpersonal work skills,* and *assistance in daily activities* were also based on those presented in this source.

Kretzmann and McKnight (1993) provide another example involving how a "group of residents in a public housing project organized and became powerful enough to gain control of their buildings." They describe how "their association took over the management and finances of the project" and how subsequently "they were able to employ residents to carry out the maintenance functions such as painting rooms, fixing broken windows, running a laundromat, etc." (p. 26). The group used information from a questionnaire addressing individuals' assets to identify who had which strengths, skills, and assets (p. 19).

Even without working within a formal structure, community residents can help their neighbors by using specific skills. Staff in one community social services organization wrote and received a grant for starting a tool library. Community residents could "take out" tools and use them for household construction and repair. They later would return them to the tool library, as they would books from a traditional library.

Maintenance   Community residents may contribute time and effort to help maintain and clean up buildings, parks, and public facilities. For example, various groups, businesses, or families volunteer to clean up garbage along highways in Adopt-a-Highway programs. Or a group of community residents could volunteer to renovate a park area.

Food   Some people are skilled at food preparation. People can volunteer to set up, cook, barbeque, and clean up for a neighborhood picnic or other community event.

Recreation and Entertainment   Community volunteers could organize sports teams and events for youth or adults. One neighborhood organization in an impoverished community of a large city established sports teams for high-school-age youth. This provided an excellent alternative to participating in illegal and idle activities. All participants were required to maintain at least a B average in school. Volunteer coaches were supportive and worked hard at reinforcing positive behavior, not only on the court, but also in terms of conflict resolution and interpersonal skills. The tallest team member was only 6'2", which, as we know, is not very tall in the basketball world. However, the team managed to make it to and compete in the national championship against players who loomed above them. Although they didn't quite win, they became the much-applauded and well-respected underdogs. They beamed with self-confidence and pride at their accomplishments.

Some community residents may be musically talented. They can organize into an orchestra or a band and give concerts or play during parades. One neighborhood resident was highly skilled at playing the piano. She gave monthly concerts to all neighbors who were interested in attending.

Assistance in Daily Activities   There are many other arenas of life where community residents can help each other. Working parents might provide child care for each other. Or senior residents might volunteer to provide daycare for children. A resident with a car could volunteer to take another resident who doesn't have one to a doctor's appointment. One neighbor could mow another neighbor's lawn or help change the oil in his car. One community member might help another with sewing or mending clothing.

Anything Else   Potential sources of individual assets and contributions are infinite. Asking individuals what they feel their strengths are and how they could help might result in answers that never would've occurred to you.

 Critical Thinking Questions 10.5

How would you assess your own individual capacities with respect to the just dimensions cited? What do you consider as your most important three assets?

Highlight 10.5 suggests ways to undertake mapping assets in a community.

Highlight 10.5 | Mapping Assets of Local Associations, Organizations, and Institutions: Gathering Information

In addition to assessing individual capacities, it is important to find out what associations, organizations, and institutions exist in the community and how they function; there are at least four ways to do this. First, look to media such as newspapers and newsletters for printed information (Kretzmann & McKnight, 1993). Service directories might be available. The internet also is an excellent source of information. Most agencies have Web pages.

A second way to find out about community services is to use the library. "Your public library has a treasure trove of information about your community, and so does your college or university library"; Homan (2008) reflects:

> Prepare some questions in advance. This will give the librarian a better idea of how to help you. It will also help you focus your inquiry. Most librarians are very helpful. Not only do they know books and where to find them, but they enjoy helping people uncover information and discover the other wonders of their library, such as audiovisual resources, computer data banks, and much more. (p. 119)

A third way to gather information about services and organizations is to talk "to people at local institutions" such as parks and churches (Kretzmann & McKnight, 1993, p. 113). To what groups do people belong in the community? These may be political, recreational, volunteer, or social. You can also contact individual leaders of various organizations for their insights. Finally, you can simply start conversations with people you run into as you go about your daily business (Homan, 2008). You might be sitting at the bus stop or standing in line at Wal-Mart. Informal conversation can provide you with valuable insights and ideas.

A fourth means of gathering information about services is to conduct a telephone survey (Homan, 2008; Kretzmann & McKnight, 1993). A "scientific sampling procedure" should be used so that "answers from a modest number of people can be generalized to a larger number with a specified degree of accuracy" (Rubin & Rubin, 2008, p. 161). There are several other suggestions for enhancing the effectiveness of surveys (Rubin & Rubin, 2008). Make certain that the questions are clear and that respondents can clearly understand their meaning. Only collect the information that you really need. Don't waste respondents' and your time. Make sure that the categories of answers are simple and distinct. For example, "strongly agree," "mildly agree," "mildly disagree," and "strongly disagree." Use open-ended questions carefully because you might get much too much information or information that's irrelevant.

Mapping Assets of Associations, Organizations, and Institutions: Forming Community Linkages

After it's determined what associations, organizations, and institutions exist in the community by using processes such as those suggested in Highlight 10.4, a list of strengths can be established for each organization. Creative ideas about how to get these systems to work together to provide services and meet needs are endless. For example, each organization may have assets including "personnel," "space and facilities," "materials and equipment," "expertise," and "economic power" (Kretzmann & McKnight, 1993, pp. 144–145). Personnel, of course, are people who are members of an organization or who work for an organization. They reflect a potential for volunteer service. Space and facilities refer to rooms that are not being used all the time. An organization may give other organizations and groups access to space at unused times. An organization may also have a special space such as a gym that it could share when not in use. Materials and equipment include copying machines, writing utensils, computers, kitchens, tables, chairs, DVD equipment, and sports equipment (Kretzmann & McKnight, 1993). Any of these could be shared with other groups. Expertise means specialized knowledge or skills that also can be shared with other groups and organizations. Finally, economic power means access to resources. Organizations may have membership dues or contributions, grant money, or the ability to conduct fundraising activities.

Community associations, organizations, and institutions can use these assets to work together with other groups and organizations to benefit community residents, both as groups and as individuals. For instance, a religious organization can provide space for Alcoholics Anonymous support group meetings or recreational activities for community youth. (*Alcoholics Anonymous* is a nationwide self-help organization, also sponsoring chapters in many other countries, that provides support, information, and guidance necessary for many recovering alcoholics to maintain their recovery process.) Similarly, a church can sponsor a fundraising drive for a homeless shelter.

Public parks can be used in conjunction with other community groups and organizations to sponsor activities and provide space. For example, a park offered its meeting room facility to a group of seniors for their weekly support meeting; another worked with a local museum to sponsor displays and offer crafts classes (Kretzmann & McKnight, 1993).

Schools provide communities with another source of strengths and assets; consider the following examples (Kretzmann & McKnight, 1993). A school can work with a local hospital to provide an opportunity for health professionals to offer pregnancy prevention information. A retired business executive offers to provide tutoring to students at a school. A school's chorus gives concerts to nursing home residents.

Police departments provide yet another source of community assets, as illustrated by the following examples (Kretzmann & McKnight, 1993). Police officers distribute Thanksgiving turkeys provided by a local grocery among senior and "blind neighborhood residents" (p. 249). Police provide training in tactics to reduce substance abuse at a local high school. A police department works together with local neighborhood associations to motivate "at-risk" children by rewarding them with bicycles for improved school performance (p. 247). In reaction to a crime wave in an urban community, police work with neighborhood residents to establish an information network. Residents telephone others they've been assigned to announce when safety meetings are being held in local churches.

Hospitals also provide a source of community assets (Kretzmann & McKnight, 1993). For example, a hospital works with local churches to sponsor and publicize blood pressure screenings at the religious facilities or supports a Hispanic culture festival with Hispanic neighborhood associations at a local park. Another hospital hires a person with mild cognitive disabilities to do filing in one of its administrative offices.

Community colleges and universities are yet another source of community assets (Kretzmann & McKnight, 1993). For example, faculty can provide educational

---

Highlight 10.6 | **A Case Example: Macro Systems Working Together**

Improving communities often requires creative thinking about how to use existing political and other public structures, residents' energy, and other resources. One example is the unlikely association between a Housing Authority in a large, well-established, southern city and a major university in that city—"a highly selective, overwhelmingly white, old-line Southern school situation in a picturesque neighborhood" (Gwynne, 1998, p. 74). The city's "government-subsidized apartments were consistently rated among the country's worst" (Gwynne, 1998, p. 74). One of the largest projects having 1,800 apartment units, ironically named Desire, was infamous as one of the worst in the country.

Gwynne (1998) explains the scenario. The Housing Authority, a fifty-eight-year-old agency, was "a political hornet's nest of patronage and chronic mismanagement" that "was so inept at making repairs that tenants routinely waited years for simple services. Hundreds of tenements were literally falling down" (Gwynne, 1998, p. 74). At its wits' end, the Housing Authority had two choices. It could either put the projects under the authority of a federal judge or find some outside agent to take control. A major university in the city turned out to be that outside agent. Many might ask, "What does a university know about running public housing projects?" Apparently, a lot.

University representatives approached the U.S. Bureau of Housing and Urban Development (HUD)

with a proposal to assist with one project. HUD and the mayor of the city took it much further and gave the university authority over ten projects and 55,000 residents. The new association allowed for the newly appointed Housing Authority vice-president to reorganize the agency's total structure and approach.

First tasks included expelling drug dealers and criminals, drastically reducing the backlog of residents' requests for service, and dramatically improving how long it took to get repairs such as plumbing leaks and broken windows accomplished. Instead of months and years, such repairs now might take days or even hours. Future plans included building new, better single-family apartment units after tearing down old, dilapidated ones.

Importantly, the university and the Housing Authority worked closely with the projects' resident association. Community residents became actively involved in running the projects where they lived. Additionally, they helped with maintenance, security, and finding residents employment.

Hundreds of university faculty and students volunteered to provide residents with tutoring and information on "health, parenting, job training, teen pregnancy and high school equivalency" (Gwynne, 1998, p. 74). The volunteers have helped hundreds of adult residents find jobs and placed hundreds of young people in basketball and other sports programs.

presentations on any number of topics to community groups. One college established a lecture series presented each fall at a nearby nursing home. One instructor who was certified in sex education volunteered to help a residential treatment center for male adolescents with severe behavioral and emotional problems develop a sex education program. Highlight 10.6 provides a more detailed example of macro systems—including a university—working together.

  Critical Thinking Questions 10.6

In what ways does your college or university work with individuals, groups, and organizations in the community to empower the community?

Chapter Summary

The following summarizes this chapter's content as it relates to the learning objectives presented at the beginning of the chapter. Objectives include the following:

A. Examine the significance of power in communities, who has it, and why.

Concepts important in the determination of power include potential ability, the movement of people on a chosen course, and the result of producing an effect or achieving some end. Sources of power include information, wealth, reputation, high status, decision-making positions, laws and policies, and connections. These reflect only potential power, not absolute determination of power.

B. Discuss the importance of citizen participation and social networks.

Citizen participation is the dynamic, voluntary involvement of community members to address issues and concerns affecting their community and improve social policies, laws, and programs. A social network is a "formal or informal linkage of people or organizations that may share resources, skills, contacts, and knowledge with one another" (Barker, 2003, p. 405). The concepts of power, citizen, participation, and social networks often relate to each other.

C. Explain natural helping networks.

A natural helping network is a group of nonprofessional people volunteering their time and resources to help either an individual or group of people in need.

D. Describe personal empowerment, social empowerment, and the relationship between the two.

Personal empowerment occurs when a people can directly control what's happening in their own lives. Social empowerment is the condition in the social environment where people have access to opportunities and resources in order to make personal choices and maintain some control over their environment. Personal and social empowerment are integrally related and often difficult to distinguish from each other.

E. Provide a format for assessing communities and describe data-gathering procedures.

Mapping assets is an assessment of a community that emphasizes that community's "capacities, skills, and assets" instead of the community's problems and weaknesses (Kretzmann & McKnight, 1993, p. 5). Capacity building "is the ability to increase the leadership and organizational skills of local people for the purpose of strengthening their own organizations and networking capacities" (Gamble & Hoff, 2005, p. 178).

Communities can be assessed in terms of demographics, geography and environmental influences on community, beliefs and attitudes, local politics, local economy and businesses, income distribution, housing, educational facilities and programs, health and welfare systems, sources of information, elements of safety, and a summary evaluation (Sheafor & Horejsi, 2009, pp. 336–338). Data-gathering techniques include holding a community forum, using the nominal group technique, and employing the key informant technique.

F. Explain community building and highlight the primary principles involved.

Community building is the process of enhancing a community's strengths by linking community residents, organizations in the community, and external resources to tackle community problems and work together toward positive change. Primary principles include working together, the formation of new alliances, the use of cooperation, the importance of targeting neighborhoods, and building on neighborhood strengths.

G. Relate President Barack Obama's experience in community organizing and community building.

President Obama served as a community organizer on Chicago's South Side in the mid-1980s. It provided a means for him to learn how to use good listening skills, minimize conflict, and establish a consensus among many dissenting elements.

H. Provide examples of community building in rural communities.

Examples of community building in rural communities include a grant-funded comprehensive community initiative, approaches to enhance rural youths' interest in higher education, "community-supported agriculture," "agritourism," and "producer cooperatives" (Messinger, 2004, pp. 153–154).

I. Explain mapping community assets and suggest methods for collecting information.

Mapping community assets is a technique that emphasizes the community's "capacities, skills, and assets" instead of the community's problems and weaknesses (Kretzmann & McKnight, 1993, p. 5). Mapping assets involve both "releasing individual capacities" and empowering local associations, organizations, and institutions (Kretzmann & McKnight, 1993, p. 13). Releasing individual capacities can include the areas of health, administrative and interpersonal work skills, construction and repair, maintenance, food, recreation and entertainment, and assistance in daily activities, among others. Information for mapping aspects of local associations, organizations, and institutions can be obtained from the media or the local library, by simply talking with people, and by conducting a telephone survey.

J. Provide examples of how individuals, groups, associations, organizations, and social institutions can work together for community empowerment.

Examples of how youth can empower the community include raising money for the homeless, providing opportunities for participation in Special Olympics, addressing racial issues in schools, and transforming abandoned community property into a park. An example of a natural helping network involved two natural indigenous leaders in a community neighborhood. Organizations can share assets involving "personnel," "space and facilities," "materials and equipment," "expertise," and "economic power" (Kretzmann & McKnight, 1993, pp. 144–145). One case example reflected how a university worked together with a housing authority to improve living conditions.

K. Raise critical thinking questions.

Critical thinking questions addressed community power, social networks, natural helping networks, community analysis, releasing one's own individual capacities, and ways your college can work to empower the community.

L. Focus on ethical issues.

Ethical issues addressed informed consent and citizen participation, and the extent to which the concept of community building complies with professional ethics.

Looking Ahead

This chapter discussed power and empowerment in communities, including mapping community assets and community building. The next chapter will explore various facets of neighborhood empowerment within communities.

For Further Exploration on the Internet

See this text's website at **www.cengage.com/ social_work/kirst-ashman** for learning tools such tutorial quizzing, Web links, glossary, flashcards, and PowerPoint® slides.

11 CHAPTER | Neighborhood Empowerment

Neighborhoods and neighborhood centers can improve the quality of life in communities. Here neighborhood residents work together to paint a mural on a community center wall.

CHAPTER CONTENTS

Neighborhood residents can:

- *Start up a new radio station that plays ethnic music and discusses topics of interest to residents.*
- *Initiate a campaign to clean up and preserve the downtown riverfront area.*
- *Help entrepreneurs start up new businesses.*
- *Organize community celebrations and events.*
- *Conduct fundraisers to support community goals and projects.*
- *Identify employers and link them with community citizens needing jobs.*
- *Develop a network of community experts that residents can contact for help in their areas of expertise (for example, electrical repair, writing, wellness, or investment).*
- *And do much more.*[1]

Because of a neighborhood's critical significance in community building and empowerment, we will discuss neighborhoods in some detail here. The subsequent section emphasizes the importance of neighborhood centers as facilitators of empowerment.

Learning Objectives

A. Define *neighborhoods* and examine how they provide a vital context for human behavior.
B. Review the functions of neighborhoods and how they can enhance residents' quality of life.
C. Identify the qualities of strong neighborhoods.
D. Describe two conceptual frameworks for examining neighborhood structure.
E. Discuss neighborhoods, ethnicity, and social class, including the strengths of ethnic and cultural solidarity, and segregation.
F. Describe projects that can enhance neighborhood strengths.
G. Examine processes of change in neighborhoods, including those based on the invasion-succession, life cycle, and political capacity models.
H. Describe neighborhood centers and examine their origin in the settlement house movement.
I. Examine the assumptions upon which neighborhood centers are based today.
J. Specify the types of activities neighborhood centers can sponsor to improve living conditions for neighborhood residents.
K. Provide specific examples of neighborhood and community projects reflecting empowerment.
L. Raise critical thinking questions.
M. Focus on an ethical issue.

---

[1] These ideas are based on those described by J. P. Kretzmann and J. L. McKnight in *Building Communities from the Inside Out* (Chicago: ACTA Publications, 1993).

Defining Neighborhoods

A *neighborhood* is a "community of place within a larger community" (Fellin, 2001a, p. 128) where residents "share certain characteristics, values, mutual interests, or styles of living" (Barker, 2003, p. 292). There are three important points to this definition. First, a neighborhood is based on a physical area. Second, neighborhoods provide places for people to reside and go about their daily living tasks. Third, neighborhood residents share something in common, such as religious affiliation, racial identity, socioeconomic status, or concerns about encroaching crime. Neighborhood is an especially important concept when talking about geographical communities because of its immediate significance to clients' lives. It is the immediate social environment in which they live, eat, sleep, and interact on a daily basis.

A geographical community may consist of a number of neighborhoods. There are several types of neighborhoods based on size (Fellin, 2001b, p. 127). An *immediate neighborhood* is one consisting of a limited number of family units and lodgings located in a relatively small area. A three-block-long city street might exemplify an immediate neighborhood. An *extended neighborhood* is larger than an immediate neighborhood and might include several square blocks. Finally, a *community neighborhood* includes thirty square blocks or even more.

Neighborhood boundaries are determined in various ways (Fellin, 2001a; Homan, 2008). Neighborhoods are based upon residents' common characteristics, values, interests, or lifestyles. Therefore, the concept of neighborhood is more complex than *x* number of square feet, homes, or blocks. For example, Hmong immigrants from Southeast Asia might relocate in the same neighborhood based on common heritage, culture, and language. The immediate neighborhood might end abruptly in the middle of an urban block where people who are not Hmong reside in the event there is little interaction or common interest between the two groups.

Likewise, consider a single-home neighborhood populated primarily by older adults. A government housing project for families with young children is built on the next block. The immediate neighborhood for the older residents might end where the housing project begins if the divergent groups have little in common and virtually nothing to do with each other. You might view a neighborhood and its boundaries as how residents define it (Homan, 2008). How would you define the boundaries of your own neighborhood?

Functions of Neighborhoods: Promoting Optimal Health and Well-Being

Neighborhoods can perform a variety of functions (Fellin, 2001a; Homan, 2008; Rubin & Rubin, 2008; Warren, 1977; Warren & Warren, 1977). First, a neighborhood can be an arena for social interaction. It can be a place where people feel comfortable and that they belong. Residents might use each other as their primary context for socializing. A neighborhood block party in Madison, Wisconsin, comes to mind. Each year residents on three blocks of Mifflin Street banded together, obtained permission from the city, and hosted a block party where residents contribute resources and "party hearty" to celebrate the coming of spring.

A second neighborhood function is the provision of mutual aid. Residents can help each other in any number of ways. Homan (2008) reflects:

> Neighbors can provide one another with a range of practical and emotional support. Borrowing a cup of sugar, helping out in times of emergency, establishing social contact over a cup of coffee, or helping to fix a leaky toilet are some of the common forms of assistance neighbors provide to each other. The benefits of these commonplace activities, of course, extend beyond eggs and coffee and functional flushing. These connections provide psychological benefits by strengthening our attachments to a wider human community and by helping us recognize the reality and importance of our interdependence. More effectively functioning neighborhoods are more likely to offer their members the benefits of "neighboring." (p. 373)

The following are other examples of mutual aid. A neighborhood in a metropolitan suburb filled with young families who have small children can provide each other child care when they need it. An urban neighborhood can form a "Neighborhood Watch" organization where residents keep a careful eye out on each others' homes to report suspicious strangers and prevent crime. In a northern suburban neighborhood, one neighbor snowplows another's driveway when the latter takes a winter vacation. This helps conceal the fact that residents aren't home and decreases their vulnerability to thieves and vandals.

A third function of neighborhoods is provision of an arena for people to communicate and share information. We have noted that information can provide power. Therefore, neighborhood residents with access to information can share that information and thereby increase their neighbors' and ultimately the neighborhood's power. For example, Harry, a neighborhood resident in a small town, has a good friend, Ernest, a town board member (the decision-making body responsible for planning town projects). Harry finds out from Ernest that the Town Board is planning to rezone a lot in the neighborhood from residential to commercial, requiring that a business and not a personal residence be built on the lot. The implication for the neighborhood is that property values may plummet. The neighborhood's property is valuable because it boasts a pleasant, laid-back residential area for families. A business in its midst implies more traffic, more congestion, and less daily living appeal. Thus, with this information Harry and his neighbors can band together, confront the Town Board, and initiate whatever action is necessary to halt the rezoning plan.

A fourth function of neighborhoods is to allow people to congregate with other people having similar status, cultural backgrounds, or interests as themselves (Rubin & Rubin, 2008). For better or for worse, a neighborhood can establish certain standards and strive to admit residents who comply with the prerequisites. A common example is a suburban neighborhood that promotes residents who are White and who have achieved a prescribed level of socioeconomic status. Current residents can work to keep out potential residents who don't comply. High property prices and taxes can exclude people from lower socioeconomic levels. Derogatory comments and even threats can act to deter people of color from moving into such neighborhoods. Obviously, this function does little to comply with the social work values of self-determination and the right to equal opportunity. Preserving social status can be an oppressive function that can counteract optimal health and well-being for people who are excluded from neighborhoods.

Consider one such suburban neighborhood. Neighborhood residents all have one-acre lots on a lake and huge, expensive homes with intricately manicured landscaping. All the neighborhood residents are White. Typically, residents make racial slurs and steadfastly discourage people of color from becoming interested in purchasing homes or empty lots. When one resident family moved because of a job relocation, a rich single White female owner of a large trucking firm, Lullabelle, purchased the family's home. The neighbors had seen Lullabelle, who was obviously White, and thus had few, if any, negative comments to make about her. They were, however, interested in determining what Lullabelle was like and how she would "fit into" the neighborhood. Unfortunately for them, they discovered that Lullabelle was a one-sided, perpetual talker who limited herself to various complaints and excessive detail about how much money she made. Lullabelle also had numerous men friends ranging in age from about seventeen to seventy-one frequently stay with her and roam about the property. Neighbors were mortified as these men regularly spewed forth vulgarities and felt perfectly comfortable urinating on the garage or on the faultlessly trimmed bushes. Lullabelle could afford to hire a professional landscaper to maintain her yard. Lullabelle built a small, ugly warehouse-like structure in the front yard to house her old junker cars and used appliances. She kept the remaining three "junkers" out in the driveway. Then she placed several dozen plaster of paris and wooden lawn ornaments about the property. These included the ones where the backsides of "Ma" and "Pa" bending over are viewed so that you can see their polka-dotted underwear. No, the neighborhood residents didn't want any persons of color living in their neighborhood.

A fifth function of neighborhoods is provision of an organizational and political base. Neighborhood residents may choose to join a neighborhood organization or center. Such organizations are groups formed to address common needs of or establish goals for the neighborhood. Examples of goals are cleaning up rubbish, improving the conditions of older buildings, enhancing voter registration and voting, or targeting and abolishing crack houses. This chapter later discusses neighborhood centers much more thoroughly as a means of neighborhood empowerment.

As a group, neighborhood residents may also push politicians and community decision makers to make changes on their behalf. They may advocate for heavier police protection through increased patrolling of the area, or enforcement of property requirements such as maintaining buildings' compliance with minimal codes (for example, all windows must have screens, lead paint must be removed, or outside doors must be operational).

Qualities of Strong Neighborhoods

Strong, healthy neighborhoods that support residents and enhance their quality of life have the following eight basic characteristics (Homan, 2008; Wireman, 1984):

1. A good school system with high standards, good resources, and well-trained teachers who respond to the neighborhood's cultural composition and needs.

2. Good, safe areas for children to participate in play, sports, and other positive recreational and cultural activities.
3. Effective management of children's behavior by presiding adults.
4. Ready availability of and access to good health care facilities and services, especially in times of emergency.
5. Easily accessible public or other community transportation so residents can go to work or school, access health care, and undertake other necessary activities for daily life.
6. Good availability and facilities to meet daycare and other child care needs.
7. Strong support network of families and adults to watch over children, provide support, and serve as positive role models.
8. A reasonably safe environment with low or nonexistent levels of criminal activity, hazardous environmental dangers (such as potholes in streets or bridges lacking railings), and racial conflict.

 Critical Thinking Questions 11.1

To what extent does the neighborhood you live in reflect the eight strengths mentioned here?

Describing Neighborhood Structure

Several conceptual frameworks have been developed to describe neighborhoods' structure and composition (Fellin, 2001a, pp. 137–140; 2001b, pp. 123–125). Such approaches focus our attention on various dimensions of neighborhoods so we can evaluate how well they provide for residents' health and well-being. Two will be described here. The first emphasizes interpersonal interaction, identification, and connections. The second approach focuses on neighborhood groups and value implementation.

Conceptual Framework One:
Interpersonal Interaction, Identification, and Connections

One approach to assessing neighborhoods focuses on three conditions (Fellin, 2001a, 2001b; Warren & Warren, 1977). The first is the degree of interpersonal interaction among residents. To what extent do they socialize with each other and provide each other with support? The second condition is the residents' identification with the neighborhood and each other. To what extent do they identify with and feel a part of their neighborhood? The third condition involves the neighborhood's connections with the larger encompassing community. This last variable involving *social connectedness* concerns how neighborhoods have varying degrees of access to politicians who wield power, resources, needed services, and other systems in the larger community. Each of these variables can be appraised along a continuum from low to "neutral" to high (Fellin, 2001a, p. 138).

Critical Thinking Questions 11.2

To what extent do you socialize with and get support from your neighbors? To what extent do you identify with and feel an integral part of the neighborhood where you live? To what extent is your neighborhood connected with other systems in the larger community environment? Explain your answers.

Neighborhoods can then be categorized into six basic types—integral, parochial, diffuse, stepping-stone, transitory, and anomic—based on residents' social interaction, sense of belonging, and connections with others (Fellin, 2001a, pp. 138–139). Highlight 11.1 summarizes how each type of neighborhood reflects the degree of interpersonal interaction, residents' identification with the neighborhood, and social connectedness with other systems outside of the neighborhood.

Integral Neighborhoods *Integral* neighborhoods are those manifesting high levels of all three conditions. Neighborhood residents are highly involved with each other. They readily identify themselves as part of the neighborhood. Espousing "positive values toward education, participation in community life, community improvement, and maintenance of law and order" can add to a neighborhood's cohesion (Fellin & Litwak, 1968, p. 79). Additionally, an integral neighborhood is clearly linked with the encompassing larger community. For example, neighborhood residents may sit on governing groups or agency boards in their town, city, or state. Or, residents may regularly write letters or editorials for the media.

Parochial Neighborhoods A *parochial* neighborhood is one high on interaction and identification but low on community connections. In such a neighborhood, residents may interact frequently, identify with each other, and advocate for positive neighborhood goals and changes. Yet, they may neither have any involvement with the larger community nor have access to many resources. For instance, residents in

Highlight 11.1 | Communities Based on Interpersonal Interaction, Identification, and Social Connections

	Interpersonal Interaction	Identification with Neighborhood	Social Connectedness
Integral	High	High	High
Parochial	High	High	Low
Diffuse	Low	High	Low
Stepping-Stone	Low	High	High
Transitory	Low	Low	High
Anomic	Low	Low	Low

an urban Hispanic neighborhood where most residents speak only Spanish may have little opportunity or ability to communicate with English-speaking decision makers in the larger community. Yet, these residents may feel very bonded with each other and be extremely supportive among themselves.

Diffuse Neighborhoods   A *diffuse* neighborhood offers residents a strong sense of neighborhood identification. However, residents experience little social interaction. They feel they do not need the neighborhood for support or help, and require low levels of connections to resources and services outside of the community. These are usually exclusive suburban neighborhoods or opulent luxury apartment buildings in urban settings. Residents may have money, power, and perceived identification with the neighborhood yet not feel interaction is essential. They already have what they need and more; therefore, they find it unnecessary to expend energy for advocacy or change.

Stepping-Stone Neighborhoods   A *stepping-stone* neighborhood is characterized by the temporary nature of residents. They may positively identify themselves with the neighborhood but have low levels of commitment to interact with other residents or to work on the neighborhood's behalf because they simply won't be there that long. Residents of stepping-stone neighborhoods often are moving up in their careers and possibly starting and raising families. Because they're "on the way up," they usually have high levels of connection with other resources and systems in the larger community environment. Their efforts are directed elsewhere than neighborhood involvement and improvement. These are poor social environments for people seeking permanent residence or social belonging.

Transitory Neighborhoods   A *transitory* neighborhood resembles a stepping-stone in terms of the transitory nature of residents. However, residents in such neighborhoods have much less access to resources and are probably not moving up in the world. They're just moving. In such a neighborhood, residents have low levels of social interaction and identification with the neighborhood. However, because of their serious needs, they frequently have high linkages with the wider community with its resources and services.

Anomic Neighborhoods   Finally, an *anomic* neighborhood is dysfunctional and provides little social support. *Anomie* is a sociological term that means "social instability resulting from a breakdown of standards and values" often involving "personal unrest, alienation, and uncertainty that comes from a lack of purpose or ideals" (Mish, 2008, p. 51). Despite residents' geographical proximity, the feeling of being in a neighborhood does not exist. It differs from a transitory neighborhood in that people may live here for long periods of time. An example of such a neighborhood is a huge urban public housing project for people with very low incomes. Gangs, guns, and drugs may infest its corridors. Many residents may feel little identification with other residents yet have nowhere else to go. They may live in constant fear, often for good reason. The larger community may provide little support.

Highlight 11.2 | **Brief Commentary on the Nature of Neighborhoods**

It should be noted that these neighborhood types are not necessarily distinct from each other. The degree to which a neighborhood has social interaction, resident identity, and community linkages varies from one to another. Thus, neighborhood types may overlap or change over time (Fellin, 2001a, 2001b).

Understanding a neighborhood can help social workers determine an intervention strategy to improve the neighborhood's functioning and enhance residents' quality of life. For example, in an anomic neighborhood, a generalist practitioner might seek to improve residents' involvement and identification with the neighborhood. One way is to identify potential community leaders who are interested and have a stake in community improvement. The worker could then help to organize residents, "provide expertise in developing leadership within the neighborhood, and promote participation by residents" (Fellin & Litwak, 1968, p. 79).

 Critical Thinking Questions 11.3

Of these six neighborhood categories—integral, parochial, diffuse, stepping-stone, transitory, diffuse, and anomic—how would you describe your neighborhood and why?

Highlight 11.2 addresses the issue of how neighborhoods don't always fall clearly into one category or another.

Conceptual Framework Two: Neighborhood Groups and Value Implementation

The second approach to describing and understanding neighborhoods focuses on two dimensions—the structure and connections of formal and informal groups in neighborhoods, and how these groups implement the neighborhood's primary values. The basic idea is that formal and informal groups in neighborhoods can "play a significant role in the attainment of individual and social goals in American society" (Fellin & Litwak, 1968, p. 73). Such goals may concern "education, participation in community life, community improvement, and maintenance of social order" (Fellin, 2001a, p. 141). Fellin (2001b) explains:

The organizational base of neighborhoods involves informal contacts and local formal organizations, such as voluntary associations. Neighborhoods can be classified in terms of both their level of organization and their capacity to implement their values, such as orientations toward education, good citizenship, and crime and violence. Recognition of the values of residents in a neighborhood is helpful for both interpersonal and community practice. For example, in areas with high rates of crime and delinquency, the social worker can assess the values of residents toward law and order and toward the tolerance of deviant behavior, and their willingness to organize to implement values to combat violence and crime. (p. 128)

Examples of informal neighborhood groups include groups based on friendship or shared caregiving for children or ailing older adults. Other organized groups might involve support groups, Neighborhood Watch organizations, or social groups such as the Red Hat Society (a nationally based organization with local groups of women who are middle-aged and older that congregate for social activities whose hallmark is the wearing of red and purple clothing—hence the name "Red Hat").

Fellin and Litwak (1968) stress the significance of neighborhood groups:

> In the use of expertise, formal organizations provide for problem-solving most efficiently in dealing with uniform tasks, while the neighborhood group is likely to be equal to or better than the formal organization when there is no real knowledge available, when problems are simple, and when they are idiosyncratic in nature. The neighborhood can handle problems of a diffuse nature and, owing to small size and common values, can gain quick consensus for action. Thus, a variety of crisis situations can be handled by the neighborhood group, such as emergency first aid, baby-sitting, and immediate advice. (pp. 76–77)

Problems often facing neighborhoods, especially urban ones, include mobility and impersonality (Fellin & Litwak, 1968, p. 74). Mobility involves a continuous flux in a neighborhood's population. Fellin and Litwak (1968) explain: "Since it generally has been assumed that relatively permanent membership is a condition of group cohesion, the question becomes one of how well the neighborhood primary group can function when members move in and out of the group" (p. 74). A second problem, impersonality, involves lack of connection and caring among neighborhood residents. It implies deficient social interaction and even isolation from each other. Without cohesion, it's difficult for neighborhood residents to bond together and provide each other with help and support.

By strengthening neighborhood groups and their links with formal organizations, neighborhoods can address and help resolve these problems to empower residents. Social workers can enhance this process. Residents can address the problem of mobility by discussing issues openly, developing welcoming attitudes and behaviors, and using informal groups and local voluntary organizations to reach out to new residents. Neighborhoods can address the issue of impersonality by strengthening their informal group structures, associating and bonding with each other, and offering support.

 Critical Thinking Questions 11.4

What are the strengths and weaknesses of the two conceptual frameworks describing neighborhood structure—the first emphasizing interpersonal interaction, identification, and connections, and the second focusing on neighborhood groups and value implementation?

Neighborhoods, Ethnicity, and Social Class

Neighborhoods are often characterized by ethnicity and social class. (Fellin, 2001a, 2001b; Rubin & Rubin, 2001). Fellin (2001a) explains:

> The most common criteria used for classifying neighborhoods are social class, ethnicity, and culture. Neighborhoods may be distinguished by social class through the use of census data regarding occupational status, household income, education, and lifestyle. Residents usually refer to one or more of these factors in assigning social class names to their neighborhoods. Class names include terms such as wealthy, middle-class, working class, poor, underclass, and skid row neighborhoods. Names for ethnic neighborhoods include those of White ethnic groups, religious ethnic groups, and ethnic minority groups. Use of ethnic/cultural labels for neighborhoods usually indicates that members of a specific group are over-represented in relation to the general population, such as an African American neighborhood or a Hispanic/ Latino neighborhood. Religious or white ethnic labels are usually used when a substantial portion of the population, even if not a majority, are members of a specified group, such as Jewish, Catholic, Italian, Polish, or Irish neighborhoods. (p. 149)

Strengths of Ethnic and Cultural Solidarity

Rubin and Rubin (2008) elaborate on the strengths of community neighborhoods characterized by ethnicity, culture, and religion:

> *Solidarity communities* are constructed as people see themselves, or are labeled by others, as being part of the same racial or ethnic group, or who accept that they share a similar history, cultural traditions, language, or religion [emphasis added] . . .
>
> Solidarity ties are usually based on birth, and for some are seen as given . . . You are born from Irish, or Ethiopian, or Thai ancestry, or your religion of birth is Hindu, Catholic, Dutch Reform, or whatever. . . .
>
> With solidarity communities, cultural pride and ethnic identity provide the social glue that enables people to come together. People are likely to give to charities sponsored by their solidarity group, even if the contributors don't foresee that they themselves are likely to need support. Or people of a given ethnic neighborhood may rally when a hurricane devastates their ancestral homeland, collecting food and clothes in local churches.
>
> Members of solidarity communities reinforce their connectedness through shared rituals, holidays, festivals, and evocations of a common history. To build a sense of community within a solidarity group, organizers encourage social events during which members relate shared historic sufferings to one another. Such narratives replace past traumas and humiliations: forced migrations for Native Americans, incarceration in concentration camps for Japanese Americans during World War II, slavery for African Americans. . . . These historic, mutual experiences can be simultaneously a cause for pride—we went through this and survived—as well as a cause for rebellion. Native American organizers build solidarity within the group by narrating how the mainstream society stole Native American lands and deceived members of the group. Then by orchestrating actions on these same lands, demand that government must now restore traditional hunting, fishing, and land rights that it had taken away.
>
> By reframing how the past is understood, solidarity groups turn prior humiliation into a source of pride. (pp. 82–83)

Understanding the history and interconnections within a solidarity community is vital for social workers. Community organizers such as social workers can identify, convene, and mobilize neighborhood residents and resources both to help celebrate their origins and make them responsive to unmet community neighborhood needs.

Highlight 11.3 describes three types of projects neighborhoods can undertake to build assets, the first of which emphasizes embracing one's cultural heritage and pride.

Social Class

"Attention to the social class level of neighborhoods is important for social workers, since neighborhood location and social class have a powerful effect on the resources and liabilities that affect the quality of life of neighborhood residents" (Fellin, 2001b, p. 129). The proportion of homes owned and the quality of those homes usually reflect the social class level of a neighborhood. Both social class and home ownership are related "to some combination of occupational status, household income, and educational level of members of a household" (Fellin, 2001a, p. 150). Houses and social class reflect social status. Higher social status implies greater access to resources.

Social workers are especially concerned with building assets in poorer community neighborhoods because these generally have the greatest needs. Fellin (2001a) reflects:

> Studies of inner-city poverty areas show a decline in status in these neighborhoods, due to the decline in employment and increase in welfare dependency among residents, as well as the departure of upwardly mobile individuals and families (Wilson, 1996). At the same time, many working- and middle-class ethnic minority neighborhoods have been able to maintain their status because of residential stability and strong institutional supports from schools, churches, medical and social service institutions, and neighborhood voluntary organizations. Many urban neighborhoods that have become more integrated racially have managed to maintain their class status through institutional and voluntary group efforts that support integration. [*Integration* is the process of assembling diverse groups of people including different races into a cohesive whole.] (pp. 153–154)

Segregation

Segregation, the opposite of integration, is "the detachment of isolation of some group having certain common characteristics (such as race, ethnicity, or religion) through social pressure, restrictive laws, or personal choice" (Zastrow & Kirst-Ashman, 2010, p. 36). Segregation, therefore, may be imposed upon a group or it may be voluntary. Segregation continues to be a major problem in terms of housing and geographical community location (Kornblum & Julian, 2007; Mooney, Knox, & Schacht, 2009). Fellin (2001b) explains:

> The concepts of segregation and integration serve to describe these neighborhood communities, with segregated neighborhoods having a high proportion of ethnic minority and/or cultural group membership (Rusk, 1993). Empirical studies of housing patterns in North American communities continue to leave no doubt that housing segregation is due in large part to discrimination and prejudice based on race and/or ethnicity. (p. 129)

| **Highlight 11.3** | **Projects to Enhance Neighborhood Strengths** |

Delgado (2000) suggests at least three types of projects that community neighborhoods can undertake to enhance their strengths and assets. These include murals, gardens, and playgrounds. The idea behind such projects is for neighborhood residents to express themselves and their culture, thereby enhancing their sense of presence, cultural pride, and self-esteem.

The concept of *community built* means that a project is undertaken with the support and under the direction of a community neighborhood (Delgado, 2000, p. 75). This can mean that the entire project is completed by neighborhood residents or that the residents choose to bring in experts to complete a project. To be labeled community built, the project must meet the following eleven criteria (Arie-Donch, 1991; Delgado, 2000, p. 76): "(1) A concrete product is the end result, (2) the project is built primarily by volunteers, (3) successful completion is dependent on the participation of a wide sector of the community (the wider the better), (4) the project's scale corresponds to the size of the community to increase accessibility, (5) the project has distinct phases (a beginning, middle, and end), (6) the project develops in the community a sense of ownership, (7) the project is spatially defined, (8) the project has significance (social, political, and psychological) for the community, (9) the final form of the project reflects the needs of the community, (10) the final project can last long enough to be enjoyed by future generations, and (11) the project is permanent and creates a sense of permanence and long-term community commitment."

Murals

Large pictures painted or drawn on walls or ceilings, known as murals, can provide an important means of self-expression and cultural pride. Delgado (2000) explains:

> A mural is an art form that is expressed on a building's walls as opposed to a canvass" (Barnett, 1984). Murals represent a [neighborhood] community effort to utilize cultural symbols as a way of creating

an impact internally and externally. Murals should not be confused with graffiti. A mural represents an artistic impression that is not only sanctioned by a [neighborhood] community, but often commissioned by it ("California Town Hopse," 1996; Madden, 1996) and invariably involve a team of artists. Graffiti, on the other hand, represent an artistic impression (sometimes referred to as "tagging") that is individual centered and manifested on subway trains, doors, mailboxes, buses, public settings, and other less significant locations. Their content generally focuses on the trials and tribulations associated with urban living, issues of oppression, or simply a "signature" of the artist. (p. 78)

Delgado and Barton (1998) describe six basic types of mural content. First, murals can illustrate "symbols of ethnic and racial pride" (p. 348). For example, concerning Chicanos and their pride in their history, Treguer (1992, cited in Delgado & Barton, 1998, p. 348) notes that pre-Columbian themes are common, with frequent ancient Aztec motifs (taken from or inspired by Aztec manuscripts and temples) and references to the Spanish conquest and images of the Virgin of Guadelupe, which he describes as "a cherished Mexican icon" (p. 23).

A second theme often evident in murals involves religious symbols. Delgado and Barton (1998) remark in the context of Latino culture:

> Spirituality, in the form of religion and folk beliefs, plays an important role in the lives of Latinos (Coleman, 1994; Cooper & Sciorra, 1994; Treguer, 1992). Religious and spiritual symbols often represent a community's hopes for the future, its history, and, depending on the symbols, the value it places on the metaphysical. (p. 349)

The third type of content often portrayed in murals involves "issues related to social justice" (Delgado & Barton, 1998, p. 349). This may include "scenes of police brutality, arson, alcohol and other drug abuse, prison, U.S. imperialism" and "infant

continued

Highlight 11.3 | *continued*

mortality," scenes that Delgado and Barton characterize as "based on historical events" and "a daily reminder of the trials and tribulations" experienced by people of color in "the search for social justice" (p. 349).

A fourth theme displayed in murals involves beautification and decoration for its own sake. Murals don't have to be a statement of great social, political, or religious impact. Rather, they can serve to make a neighborhood a more pleasing and nice looking place to live.

The fifth type of content displayed in murals concerns "homages to national and local heroes" (p. 350). Delgado and Barton (1998) explain:

> Communities of color rarely have the opportunity to honor their own. With the exception of national heroes like Rev. Martin Luther King, Jr., Malcolm X, Cesar Chavez, and so forth, many local heroes never make it into history books. Consequently, murals provide local residents the opportunities to validate their experiences through their heroes. (p. 350)

The sixth theme for a neighborhood mural involves "memorials commissioned by local residents," which may honor "a dead relative, close friend, or gang member" (p. 350). "The number and extent of murals dedicated to community residents who have died," note Delgado and Barton, "can be an excellent indicator of key issues within the community," an assessment of which "can provide important data on gender, age, cause of death, as well as other information" (p. 350).

Delgado and Barton (1998) also note that mural production can provide the opportunity for neighborhood youths to develop a number of skills in the process. These include:

- "research skills" to define content
- "negotiation skills" to help neighborhood residents come to a consensus regarding what the mural should entail
- "safety consciousness and following rules"
- "teamwork"
- "starting and completing a project"

- "development of proper work habits"
- improvement of "communication skills"
- "knowledge of math and chemistry" when designing content and preparing paints
- "budgeting and scheduling abilities" when finding resources to finance the project and scheduling a plan for completion
- becoming effective contributors to the neighborhood and community by assuming responsibility as active participants in the project's completion

Gardens

Gardens in urban areas are very important (Delgado, 2000; Hynes, 1995). "Urban gardens are an essential part of an ecological system that fosters the development of community, relationships, and capacity enhancement" (Delgado, 2000, p. 88). Gardens are grown for three basic purposes (Delgado, 2000). First, they can be visually appealing. Second, people can grow gardens as a type of recreation. Third, gardens can be grown for food. Sometimes, gardens serve two or all of these purposes.

Neighborhood residents usually get together to develop a garden under four different circumstances (Delgado, 2000). A local empty or cleared plot of land might become available for their use. An institution such as a hospital, church, or school might seek a beautification project. Neighborhood residents might decide to grow a garden for residents in need. Or funding becomes available from grants or other public or private sources to support a neighborhood gardening project.

There are many benefits from community gardens. Gardens can provide opportunities for residents to work together toward a common goal. We've already noted that gardens can both provide food and improve a neighborhood's appearance. They can improve residents' sense of self-worth and self-esteem. Gardens can help people living in urban settings experience and appreciate nature.

Neighborhood House of Milwaukee, Inc., a neighborhood center located in an impoverished inner-city community, provides a good example of encouraging urban gardening and the appreciation of nature.[2] (Neighborhood centers established in the settlement house tradition are described later in the chapter.) Neighborhood House's mission is to provide "social, educational and recreational activities to improve the quality of life in the community" (Neighborhood House, 2006b).

One of its programs involves Outdoor/Environmental Education (Neighborhood House, 2006a). The agency's property includes a "32,000 square foot outdoor habitat, including butterfly gardens, art sculptures, and pizza gardens" (where pizza ingredients such as tomatoes and herbs are grown) (Neighborhood House, 2006a). A primary purpose is to encourage young people's appreciation and enjoyment of nature. Children ages six weeks to six years are introduced to this habitat and encouraged to explore. The Gardening Programs offer opportunities for children and teens up to age eighteen to participate in all aspects of gardening, including "choosing the plants, sprouting seeds, planting seedlings, growing plants, harvesting the vegetables, weeding the beds, adding compost to the soil [which they observe being processed right there in the garden], and . . . eating the products from the garden" (Neighborhood House, 2006b). The program also sponsors School-Age and Teen Programs that include camping and other outdoor experiences at a rural site owned by the agency.

Community Playgrounds

Developing and improving "community playgrounds" can provide excellent opportunities for enhancing a neighborhood's assets. Delgado (2000) explains:

> Although community playgrounds primarily target the recreational needs of children, they also fulfill other functions that rarely get noticed in the everyday life of a community. The structures can play a central role in connecting residents with each other and provide an outlet for families to do some activity together that does not require the expenditure of funds. (pp. 95–96)

It is vital that neighborhood residents make their own decisions regarding what the playground should be like—what types of equipment should be included and how it should be arranged. It's crucial that the area meet the individual neighborhood's and its residents' needs. Delgado (2000) likens a neighborhood's development of a playground to an old-fashioned barn raising. He continues:

> Simply described, a barn raising brings all members of a rural community, regardless of age, gender, and skills, together for a concentrated period (usually one or two days) to help a fellow neighbor who has suffered some tragedy, like a fire, to build a barn. It serves to help a neighbor in need, reaffirms a community's definition of itself, and ensures the members that they do, in fact, belong to a community that cares. (p. 97)

He concludes, "Community-built playgrounds . . . reflect a community's desire to claim their own space and control the activities within this area. Thus, the presence of such playgrounds can serve as excellent indicators of a community's capacity to rally for a common good" (Delgado, 2000, p. 102).

 Critical Thinking Questions 11.5

Have you noticed any murals, neighborhood gardens, or playground development in your community neighborhood? If so, what were your thoughts about it?

---

[2] Many thanks to Bradley Blaeser, Program Director of the Outdoor and Environmental Education Department and School-Age Program, Neighborhood House of Milwaukee, Inc. (2819 W. Richardson Place, Milwaukee, WI 53208-3546) for his excellent explanation of this program. Further information about Neighborhood House can be retrieved from http://www.nh-milw.org.

Focus on Ethics 11.1 | **Is Segregation Ethical?**

What do you think are the dynamics involved in seg-regation? To what extent is it ethical for communities to allow segregation to continue in neighborhoods?

Explain. What, if anything, should be done about segregation?

There are other rationales for the existence of neighborhoods where residents have the same racial heritage. Fellin (2001a) explains:

> Some members of ethnic minority groups prefer to reside in neighborhoods populated mainly by members of their own group. These individuals . . . reside in and are posi-tively identified with the minority community. These neighborhoods also receive people who are unable to move into other neighborhoods due to economic factors and/or dis-crimination in housing. There is strong evidence that societal and community barriers to residential mobility prohibit some persons from 'leaving the "hood" ' and [entering more mainstream society]. These barriers include not only financial constraints and housing discrimination. (p. 158)

  | **Critical Thinking Questions 11.6**

Think of a large city with which you're familiar. To what extent do neighborhoods reflect ethnic, cultural, and class distinctions? To what extent is segregation apparent?

Processes of Change in Neighborhoods

By nature, systems are subject to change. Levels of input and output change. Exter-nal factors affecting the system are altered. So it is with neighborhoods. Neighbor-hoods' social, economic, and political environments are in constant flux. People move in and out. Jobs are developed or businesses leave the area. Buildings get older and require repair. Sometimes, old buildings are torn down and new ones built. Other times, old buildings are refurbished. Still other times, old buildings rot and stagnate in deteriorating states.

Homan (2008) cites three theories that explain neighborhood change: the "invasion-succession," "life cycle," and "political capacity" models (p. 375).

The Invasion-Succession Model

The invasion-succession model is based on the idea that conflict occurs when new groups of people reflecting certain racial, cultural, or religious characteristics move into areas already inhabited by people with different characteristics. A new group will invade and the other will withdraw. *Invasion is* "the tendency of each new group" of people coming into an area "to force existing groups out" (Kirst-Ashman & Hull, 2009a, p. 284). *Succession,* then, is "the replacement of the original occupants of a community or neighborhood by new groups" (Kirst-Ashman & Hull, 2009a, p. 284). For example, a neighborhood might first be populated by people of German descent, followed by African Americans, and later by Eastern Europeans. A concern is that "if the withdrawing group takes valuable resources from the community (for example, family income, shop ownership, political clout) before these can be effectively replaced, the neighborhood is likely to decline" (Homan, 2008, p. 375).

The Life Cycle Model

The life cycle model views neighborhood change as a decline, with a neighborhood undergoing predictable phases from birth until death. These phases include the following five (Downs, 1981; Homan, 2008).

1. A stable and viable neighborhood
2. A minor decline
3. A clear decline
4. A heavily deteriorated neighborhood
5. An unhealthy and nonviable neighborhood (Homan, 2008, p. 375)

Homan (2008) explains:

A stable and viable neighborhood exists when no symptoms of decline have appeared and property values are rising. A period of minor decline may follow in which some minor deficiencies in housing units are visible and density is higher than when the neighborhood was first developed, but property values are stable or increasing slightly. A neighborhood in clear decline is marked by populations from lower socioeconomic groups. Renters are dominant in the housing market, and landlord-tenant relations are poor because of high absentee ownership. Other factors, such as higher density, low confidence in the area's future, and abandoned buildings, are also associated with this stage. In heavily deteriorated neighborhoods, housing is very run down and even dilapidated. Most structures require major repair. Subsistence level households are numerous, and profitability of rental units is poor. Pessimism about the area's future is widespread. An unhealthy and nonviable neighborhood is at the final stage of change. Massive abandonment occurs, and those residents who remain are at the lowest social status and incomes in the region. Expectations about the area's future are nil. (p. 375)

The Political Capacity Model

The political capacity model perceives a neighborhood as having the ability to pass through various stages as it develops its political viability and power (Homan, 2008; Taylor, 1979). Unlike the life cycle model, the focus is on growth rather than deterioration.

Initially, the neighborhood may be disorganized and lacking in leadership. At this stage, someone must function as a community organizer to encourage development of leadership potential in residents. The next stage involves the organizer identifying and working with a number of social institutions such as schools, churches, and clubs to develop social networking, cooperative interaction, and emerging leadership. The following phase concerns identifying and targeting some neighborhood issues for change. The organizer eventually develops a strong network of neighborhood groups and individuals who begin working together seriously in addressing neighborhood concerns and needs. The final stage involves a neighborhood with a strong leadership and a widespread, inclusive social network that can independently identify neighborhood goals and work cohesively to achieve them.

 Critical Thinking Questions 11.7

What are the strengths and weaknesses of each of the three models explaining neighborhood change—invasion-succession, life cycle, and political capacity?

Neighborhood Centers, Empowerment, and the Promotion of Health and Well-Being

A *neighborhood center* is a community-based agency that advocates for community residents and works with them to provide a wide array of services meeting their needs; it is funded primarily through government agencies, but also through some grants and the United Way[3] (Fabricant & Fisher, 2008; Smith 1995). Unfortunately, they are suffering from the effects of today's conservative climate and shrinking funding (Fabricant & Fisher, 2008). Services provided by neighborhood centers can potentially address numerous issues, needs, and developmental tasks from pre-birth to post-death. For example, a neighborhood center might offer family planning information to one family, while helping another plan a funeral (Smith, 1995). To understand the potential significance of neighborhood centers in the macro social environment, we will discuss three dimensions. These include a brief history of their development originating with settlement houses, a description of current services and structures and types of activities they sponsor, and a range of case examples.

---

[3] The *United Way* is a nationally based alliance of local agencies founded to organize and coordinate voluntary fundraising for many social agencies, including those providing health, educational, or recreational services (Barker, 2003).

Settlement Houses: A Response to Changing Social and Economic Forces

Settlement houses of the last century provided the ideological foundation for today's neighborhood centers (Fabricant & Fisher, 2008). They developed in response to three changing social and economic forces (Garvin & Cox, 1995). The first was industrialization. Mammoth growth in manufacturing and technology brought with it numerous social problems, including unemployment (as the production of goods moved from personal homes to manufacturing plants), and problems with working environments involving poor conditions, long hours, safety issues, and child labor (Day, 2006; Garvin & Cox, 1995).

The second primary change was urbanization. Concurrent with the centralization of industry within urban settings was tremendous growth of urban populations. Masses of people moved from rural to urban areas on quests for work and prosperity. Unfortunately, most were forced to move into the oldest, most crowded, and least sanitary portions of cities.

The third major change during this period was explosive immigration, primarily from northwestern Europe. Immigrants brought with them their own problems. Many came from poor rural environments and had little with which to start their lives in this country. Many became ill during the immigration process. When they arrived, poverty forced many immigrants to live under poor conditions and accept whatever work they could find.

Day (2006) explains that *settlement houses:*

> were run in part by client groups, and they emphasized social reform rather than relief or assistance. Three-fourths of settlement workers were women, and most were well-educated and dedicated to working on problems of urban poverty. Early sources of funding were wealthy individuals or clubs such as the Junior League, and at first their founders tried to provide "culture" to members, such as art, music, and lectures. When they found a need, they added new features such as playgrounds, day care, kindergartens, baths, and classes in English literacy. Other services included art exhibits, lectures, and classes in homemaking, cooking, [and] sewing . . . Settlement workers tried to improve housing conditions, organized protests, offered job training and labor searches, supported organized labor, worked against child labor, and fought against corrupt politicians. Over time settlement houses became centers of social reform, and clubs, societies, and political groups . . . used them as bases of operation. (pp. 229–230)

Settlement Houses and Generalist Social Work Practice

Settlement houses formed a strong partial foundation for generalist social work practice within communities in at least three ways (Fabricant & Fisher, 2008; Smith, 1995). First, the settlement house approach addressed the problems of people in an environmental context instead of focusing on individual pathology. Problems existed in the environment that created difficulties for individuals. Individuals were not viewed as the targets of blame, punishment, and change.

Settlements focused on social issues and improving living conditions, especially for those who were poor or less fortunate than most.

Second, an environmental focus led naturally to an emphasis on advocacy and social reform. The macro social environment required change in order to meet people's needs.

Third, settlement houses emphasized the empowerment of people. At its most basic level, empowerment involves providing people with authority or power. The settlement house perspective viewed people as having strengths and capabilities to effect their own change. Families and neighborhoods were seen as potential vehicles for positive change. The concepts of community organization and group work developed within the settlement house context. Jane Addams and Ellen Gates Starr began, perhaps, the most famous settlement house, Hull House, in Chicago in 1889.

Yan (2004) maintains that settlement houses can provide an important source of strength to neighborhoods and communities today. He explains:

> The settlement house can provide a physical platform for dialogue. The "neutral turf" of a settlement house allows it to function as a "living room" of the neighborhood, in which all members of the community, of different generations, racial, cultural, gender and political orientation, are welcome (Hiroto, Brown, & Martin, 1997). The settlement house's physical presence in the community also represents a symbolic figure of the community. The architectural image of many settlement houses and their history of working with members of the community have been inter-woven into the memories of several generations of members of the community.
> To newcomers in the community, the physical presence of, and the services provided by, a settlement house also provide a physical entry point for integration into the new environment. (p. 62)

Neighborhood Centers Today

Many of the social ills that settlement houses originally addressed no longer exist today. For example, child labor is illegal, and minimum requirements for work-place safety are in place. However, successful neighborhood centers, sometimes called community centers, organize community residents to meet new needs and demands. These include provision of daycare for working parents, preschool pro-grams, home support for older adults, family counseling, substance abuse education and counseling, health services, recreational activities for children and teens, food pantries, temporary shelter, vocational assessment and employment counseling, and meeting locations for various local organizations from the Boy Scouts to Alcoholics Anonymous (Smith, 1995).

Whereas the initial settlement houses were run by concerned volunteers and community residents, today's neighborhood center is typically run by professionals, although volunteers are often used. The executive director or chief executive officer is usually a social worker with a master's degree (Smith, 1995).

Community Neighborhood Residents Are Key Factors   Neighborhood centers are built on four assumptions (Smith, 1995). First, the core of a neighborhood cen-ter's existence and success rests on community people. It exists only to furnish service to community residents and to provide a mechanism for residents to organize themselves to get things done.

Emphasis on Community Neighborhood Assets   The second assumption upon which neighborhood centers are built is a focus on community assets. These include strengths and values that contribute to a community's progress, improvement, and development. The focus is on providing residents with what they need to survive and thrive.

For example, working single parents may require daycare and after-school care for their children in order to keep their jobs. Providing such services supports parents' strength in their capacity to work.

Older adults may be able to remain in their own homes if they receive minimal daily support, such as a daily hot meal delivered or someone to transport them to get groceries. A neighborhood center can build on strengths and help maximize people's potential to live independently.

Finally, a neighborhood center may sponsor a gang prevention and youth recreation program. Such a program could focus on the strengths of the community's young people. Services might include counseling children and teens concerning the legal repercussions of gang involvement and redirecting their energies to other, more productive social and recreational activities.

Neighborhood Centers Can Help Neighborhoods Work Together   A third assumption regarding neighborhood centers is that they are a means of unifying a neighborhood so it may work together with other neighborhood centers for the betterment of the entire community. The center can serve as the congregating place for residents to organize and hold meetings to address social, economic, and political issues. For example, several neighborhood centers could collaborate to develop "an inventory to initiate self-help, mutual support and exchange networks" for all the neighborhoods involved (Kretzmann & McKnight, 1993, p. 133). With consolidated resources, the neighborhoods could provide a wider range of services to address more specific identified needs.

One such neighborhood collective in an urban neighborhood initiated several self-help groups. These included Parents Anonymous to deal with parental stress and a Young at Heart group for victims of arthritis to discuss means of adjusting lifestyles to minimize discomfort and participate in strengthening exercises that maximize agility (Powell, 1995).

The collective also established a landlord assistance project where residents volunteered time and effort to help local landlords. Volunteers identified and made minor repairs on and in neighborhood homes to keep neighborhood residences operational and in compliance with local building codes. Landlords were responsible only for providing required materials at minimal costs. Prior to the landlord assistance project, landlords frequently avoided or "forgot" to make repairs and improvements, saying that it was too costly to repair old properties in low-rent neighborhoods. They threatened to allow foreclosure for unpaid taxes if upkeep became too expensive. Neighbors volunteering time significantly cut upkeep costs as landlords paid only for supplies, not for the expensive reimbursement required by skilled tradespeople.

Linkage among Neighborhood Units   A fourth foundation principle for neighborhood centers is linkage among various facets of the neighborhood. This includes individual families, local businesses, social service departments, schools, medical centers, religious organizations, and other public resources. For example, one neighborhood center established a neighborhood-based mental health referral group (Kretzmann & McKnight, 1993). The group identified businesses supportive of providing jobs to people with mental health problems; county social workers to assess, counsel, and refer; school social workers to identify clients and provide group counseling; psychiatrists and other physicians to assess, provide, and monitor appropriate psychotherapeutic drugs; and church groups providing facilities for support group meetings and recreational space and activities. After establishing relationships with relevant service and resource providers, the referral group publicized its existence with fliers to residents and ads in local papers. Neighborhood families with members suffering from mental health problems could then contact the referral group, which, in turn, would link people with necessary resources.

Highlight 11.4 identifies a number of goals that an effective community center can accomplish.

Critical Thinking Questions 11.8

Are you aware of or familiar with a neighborhood center in your neighborhood or campus community? If so, what types of programs does it provide? If you don't know of one, you might investigate where one exists in a town or city close to you.

Examples of Neighborhood and Community-Building Projects: Resident Empowerment

The following are some examples of projects pursued by neighborhood centers or other local organizations (Kretzmann & McKnight, 1993):

* Residents in a public housing project identified unemployment as a major problem. They banded together and formulated job training sessions that addressed issues such as developing resumes, preparing and dressing for interviews, answering questions asked during job interviews, emphasizing personal strengths, and establishing good work habits. Additionally, they developed a system for identifying job openings and referring residents to them for full- and part-time employment.

* Local chapter members of the National Association of Black Accountants volunteered time to help community residents and local businesses. They assisted with business start-ups, budget development, and other accounting tasks.

* A group of neighborhood residents living in a small town determined that they needed a place to hold community events. Thus, they established a reception center in a local church basement. They used the space for a wide range of

| Highlight 11.4 | What Effective Neighborhood Centers Can Do |

Neighborhood centers can provide support to residents and improve living conditions in a number of ways (Homan, 2008):

- *Establish a positive and effective sense of self as a neighborhood and as a resident of that neighborhood.* This can be done through publicity in local papers and newsletters, announcements posted in businesses, and decals and emblems placed throughout the neighborhood.

- *Social activities and celebrations.* Neighborhood centers can sponsor picnics, cultural events, dinners, recreational activities, and entertainment to provide opportunities for positive social interaction, networking, and bonding as a community neighborhood.

- *Maintenance and clean-up.* Neighborhood centers can form groups to pick up garbage, repair housing, plant trees and gardens, and rejuvenate parks, playgrounds, and other public spaces.

- *Opportunities for interpersonal interaction.* Neighborhood centers can sponsor and promote any number of chances for social interaction. These include establishing a program where older adults become foster grandparents to lonely children, sponsoring dances, providing information via newsletters about community events, and offering opportunities for residents to participate in the organization's decision making processes.

- *Sharing resources and organizing volunteer help.* Neighborhood centers can sponsor book, toy, or tool libraries. They can identify residents' skills and link these residents with others who need help.

- *Training and education.* Neighborhood centers can provide educational and training opportunities on any number of topics ranging from how to change the oil in your car to a discussion about a work of classic literature.

- *Support for various organized groups.* Neighborhood centers can provide facilities and promote publicity for neighborhood groups, including Boy Scouts, Gamblers Anonymous, or the local theater guild.

- *Evaluating services provided by the local government.* The quality of police and fire protection can be monitored, as can the neighborhood's general maintenance.

- *Protection and safety.* Neighborhood centers can initiate resident participation in crime prevention and monitoring. They can serve as advocates for environmental improvements where dangerous physical conditions exist.

- *Provision of various services.* Neighborhood centers can provide a range of services, including counseling, daycare, transportation, and emergency help.

- *Collaboration with managers of public programs.* Neighborhood centers can work with local government and service providers to develop needed programs and make certain laws and local codes are enforced.

- *Housing improvement and business development.* Neighborhood centers can advocate for upholding building codes, write grants to develop small businesses to help stimulate the local economy, and encourage resident involvement in public programs providing loans and other assistance.

- *Enhancement of political clout.* Neighborhood centers can encourage residents to participate in the political process through voting and forming coalitions to advocate for positive change.

- *School improvement.* Neighborhood centers can provide feedback to local schools and work with school personnel to develop programs and improve educational processes.

local festivities, including organizational banquets, fundraising festivities, neighborhood meetings, church events, and family reunions.

- A neighborhood center's members became concerned about teens having little to do when school was out. The neighborhood had virtually no places for young people to congregate other than in alleys or on storefront sidewalks. The center's members rented a deserted warehouse and volunteered time to fix it up and make it into a recreational center. They also volunteered time to coach youth and supervise activities. In addition, they organized interested young people into a work club that emphasized identifying skills and finding part-time employment.

- One neighborhood center identified homebound older adult residents' need for help plowing snow in winter and spading gardens in preparation for spring planting. Center members identified volunteers willing to participate in a mutual help program. Volunteers who did the physical labor for the older adults were called "The Earthmovers"; in return, older adults receiving help prayed for volunteers' well-being and were called "The Prayer Warriors" (p. 135). Each group's intent was to help the other.

- Residents of a suburban neighborhood concluded that they needed greater communication among themselves about community events and each other's activities. There was no local paper except one in the nearby big city, so they got little detail about issues, activities, concerns, and accomplishments in their smaller community. Few residents had ready access to computers. Starting a newsletter, *The Community Chitchatter*, a group of volunteer residents visited door-to-door soliciting subscriptions and approaching local businesses for financial backing to help with initial start-up costs. A local school allowed the group to use space for evening meetings. Volunteers formed an editorial staff that solicited news items and articles. Once the newsletter became known, neighborhood residents sent in dozens of news items. The volunteer staff was able to publish and distribute the newsletter for minimal cost.

- Community residents in St. Louis addressed the problems of teen pregnancy and school dropout by establishing the Teen Outreach Program (TOP) in 1978 (McDonald, 1998; NCSET, 2005). During one recent school year TOP served over 13,000 young people in sixteen states throughout the country (NCSET, 2005). Weekly classes are offered either as part of the school curriculum or after school, where participants "discuss topics such as communication skills, dealing with family stress, parenting, and understanding self and values"; volunteer experience such as "working as aides in hospitals and nursing homes, peer tutoring, and volunteer work in schools" is also required (NCSET, 2005). The program's strategy is that "the best way to help teenage girls avoid becoming pregnant is to involve them in voluntary activity, whether or not it is explicitly designed to point out the pitfalls of early parenthood" (McDonald, 1998, p. 48). TOP aims to reinforce members' self-esteem and change the way they view the world. It emphasizes participants' role in the community and the importance of caring for both others and themselves. One study found that TOP members were 40 percent less likely to become pregnant compared with a control group; other studies found decreased school dropout and suspension rates (NCSET, 2005). (Note that this does not mean that sex education is unimportant. TOP concepts mentioned here involving values, decision-making, and communication are important dimensions of effective sex education programs.)

Chapter Summary

The following summarizes this chapter's content as it relates to the learning objectives presented at the beginning of the chapter. Objectives include the following:

A. Define *neighborhoods* and examine how they provide a vital context for human behavior.

A neighborhood is a "community of place within a larger community" (Fellin, 2001a, p. 128). It is the significant immediate social environment in which people live, eat, sleep, and interact on a daily basis. Neighborhoods include "immediate," "extended," and "community neighborhoods" (Fellin, 2001b, p. 127).

B. Review the functions of neighborhoods and how they can enhance residents' quality of life.

Neighborhood functions include provision of: a place for interaction, mutual aid, an arena for people to communicate and share information, an opportunity for people to "assert their social status" (Rubin & Rubin, 1992, p. 89), and an organizational and political base.

C. Identify the qualities of strong neighborhoods.

Strong neighborhoods support residents through provision of good resources, strong support networks, and a safe environment.

D. Describe two conceptual frameworks for examining neighborhood structure.

One approach to examining neighborhood structure focuses on interpersonal interaction, identification, and connections. Integral neighborhoods are those manifesting high levels of all three conditions. A parochial neighborhood is one high on interaction and identification but low on community connections. A diffuse neighborhood offers residents a strong sense of neighborhood identification, but allows for little social interaction and few connections. A stepping-stone neighborhood is characterized by the temporary nature of residents. A transitory neighborhood is also transitory, but residents have much less access to resources and upward mobility. Anomic neighborhoods are dysfunctional and provide little support.

A second approach to examining neighborhood structure emphasizes the structure and connections of formal and informal neighborhood groups, and how these groups implement the neighborhood's primary values. Values may focus on goals involving "education, participation in community life, community improvement, and maintenance of social order" (Fellin, 2001a).

E. Discuss neighborhoods, ethnicity, and social class, including the strengths of ethnic and cultural solidarity, and segregation.

Neighborhoods are often characterized by ethnicity, culture, and religion. "Solidarity communities are constructed as people see themselves, or are labeled by others, as being part of the same racial or ethnic group, or who accept that they share a similar history, cultural traditions, language, or religion" (Rubin & Rubin, 2008, p. 82). A focus on social class is important for social workers in order to understand residents' access to resources and experience with liabilities. It's not news that poor neighborhoods generally have the greatest needs. Segregation is "the detachment of isolation of some group having certain common characteristics (such as race, ethnicity, or religion) through social pressure, restrictive laws, or personal choice" (Zastrow & Kirst-Ashman, 2010, p. 36).

F. Describe projects that can enhance neighborhood strengths.

Projects to enhance neighborhood strengths include the use of murals, and development of community gardens and playgrounds.

G. **Examine processes of change in neighborhoods, including those based on the invasion-succession, life cycle, and political capacity models.**

The invasion-succession model is based on the idea that conflict occurs when new groups of people reflecting certain racial, cultural, or religious characteristics move into areas already inhabited by people with different characteristics. The life cycle model views neighborhood change as a decline, with a neighborhood undergoing predictable phases from birth until death. The political capacity model perceives a neighborhood as having the ability to pass through various stages as it develops its political viability and power.

H. **Describe neighborhood centers and examine their origin in the settlement house movement.**

A neighborhood center is a community-based agency that advocates for community residents and works with them to provide a wide array of services meeting their needs. Settlement houses were developed in response to industrialization, urbanization, and explosive immigration. Although they provided a range of services, they "emphasized social reform rather than relief or assistance" (Day, 2006, p. 229). They formed a strong partial foundation for generalist social work practice within communities today and provided the underpinning for today's neighborhood centers.

I. **Examine the assumptions upon which neighborhood centers are based today.**

Neighborhood centers are based on four assumptions. First, the core of a neighborhood center's existence and success rests on community people. Second, neighborhood centers focus on community assets. Third, they provide a means for unifying a neighborhood so it may work together with other neighborhood centers for the betterment of the entire community. Fourth, neighborhood centers provide linkage among various facets of the neighborhood.

J. **Specify the types of activities neighborhood centers can sponsor to improve living conditions for neighborhood residents.**

Neighborhood centers can establish a positive sense of neighborhood identity, provide social activities and opportunities for social interaction, assist in neighborhood clean-up, share resources and volunteers, provide training and education, support various established groups, evaluate the local government's services, encourage neighborhood safety, provide various services including counseling, collaborate with managers of public programs, address housing improvement issues, enhance political clout, and work toward school improvement.

K. **Provide specific examples of neighborhood and community projects reflecting empowerment.**

Examples of empowerment include help with job searches, use of formal professional groups to assist local businesses, identification and provision of space for community events, the offering of opportunities for youth involvement, assistance to homebound older adults, development of neighborhood newsletters and communication channels, and launching of programs to address teen pregnancy and school dropout.

L. **Raise critical thinking questions.**

Critical thinking questions addressed: neighborhood strengths and neighborhood support systems; description of your neighborhood; comparison of theories describing neighborhood structure; neighborhood projects; ethnic, cultural, and class distinctions with respect to segregation; strengths and weaknesses of models of neighborhood change; and awareness of the existence of neighborhood centers.

M. **Focus on an ethical issue.**

Ethical questions concerned the extent to which it is ethical for communities to allow or maintain segregation in neighborhoods.

CHAPTER CONTENTS

Rivera and Erlich (1995, p. 204) cite the following empowerment approaches undertaken by various racial and ethnic groups:

- *An urban African-American community actively countered drug lords by undertaking an aggressive anti-drug campaign spearheaded by major community leaders.*
- *An African-American teacher promised her first-grade class that she would pay for their college education if they maintained "C" averages and made it to college. She saves $10,000 each year from her modest salary to fortify the fund.*
- *"Southeast Asian communities in Boston, New York, Houston, and San Francisco have organized legal immigration and refugee task forces to help fight the arbitrary deportation of undocumented workers."*
- *Isolated, poor urban neighborhoods in major cities throughout the United States have "revitalized themselves through cooperatives and community development activities."*
- *"Native-American tribes are attacking problems of alcoholism through indigenous healing rituals which utilize the sweat lodge ceremony as its core. Success rates are often dramatic."*
- *Boston's Latino community has initiated an effective health care program entitled "Mujeres Latina en Action." It emphasizes the importance of extended family in health care provision and uses "a culturally and gender-sensitive model of community organization . . . to reach women in the barrios."*

Each example above reflects a creative example of empowerment for various diverse populations within the macro social environment. The responses of macro systems to people in need often cannot be categorized neatly as a community, organizational, or group effort. Rather, responses and resulting activities reflect a combination of all three types of systems. Okazawa-Rey (1998) maintains that problems ranging "from addiction and mental illness to homelessness and poverty" all involve micro, mezzo, and macro variables. A need might be identified within a community context. Organizations and their staff may participate with citizens to develop programs in response to community needs. Task groups are formed to initiate, develop, and implement ideas. Sometimes groups focusing on treatment, support, education, personal growth, or socialization are formed to meet identified needs.

This chapter provides a range of examples regarding how communities and organizations can respond to the needs of citizens who are members of diverse groups.

Learning Objectives

A. Describe how groups, including African-Americans, Hispanics, GLBT people, women, and older adults, are populations-at-risk, discuss how empowerment can occur in the macro environment for each group, and provide some case examples demonstrating empowerment.

B. Provide examples of how spiritual communities can empower their members.

C. Define *developmental disabilities* and identify a range of disabilities clustered under this umbrella.

D. Examine the past history of how people with developmental disabilities have been treated by the macro social environment, and discuss current trends.

E. Describe generalist social work practice with people who have developmental disabilities.

F. Discuss avenues of legislative, community, and worker empowerment.

G. Examine the macro environment's potential for empowering people with visual impairment and intellectual disabilities.

H. Raise critical thinking questions.

I. Focus on ethical issues.

Empowerment in the Macro Environment for African-Americans

Consider the status of African-American citizens in the United States. Mooney, Knox, and Schacht (2009) remark:

> Despite significant improvements over the last two centuries, race and ethnic group relations continue to be problematic. The racial divide in the United States sharpened in 2005 in the wake of Hurricane Katrina, which left victims—who were predominantly black and poor—waiting for days to be rescued from their flooded attics or rooftops or to be evacuated from overcrowded "shelters" where there was no food, water, medical supplies, or working toilets. (p. 343)

A national survey administered after the disaster indicated that 71 percent of African-Americans felt that the Katrina experience demonstrated that racial inequality is still a major problem in the United States; in contrast, 56 percent of Whites indicated that the Katrina disaster provided no real evidence of racism (Mooney et al., 2009). Interestingly, the same survey found that 77 percent of African-Americans felt that the hurricane victims would've received better treatment had they been White; this stood in start contrast with the meager 17 percent of Whites who felt the same way (Mooney et al., 2009).

Despite major triumphs concerning legal and social racial equality, African-Americans still fall markedly behind their White counterparts in most measures of social and economic well-being; such indicators include health, educational attainment, employment, and income (Davis, Wallace, & Shanks, 2008).

African-American people (making up over 12.8 percent of the U.S. population) continue to suffer a range of injustices (U.S. Census Bureau, 2008). Over one quarter of African-Americans live below the poverty level, compared to 10.5 percent of Whites. Over one-third of African-American children live below the poverty level compared to 14.1 percent of White children. The median[1] family income for African-Americans is slightly more than 61 percent of that of their White counterparts.

---

[1] A *median* is the middle number in any ordered list of numbers, with one half of the other numbers below it and one half above it.

African-Americans are much more likely than their White peers to be incarcerated or on death row.

We have established that macro systems can develop policies and programs to enhance the well-being of various groups and populations-at-risk. Groups can be formed and services offered to address larger social issues facing African-Americans that benefit individual group participants. An example presented here concerns a program assisting African-American grandparents who are primary caregivers for grandchildren due to their own children's crack-cocaine abuse.

Empowerment of Grandparents Who Become Primary Caregivers of Grandchildren

There is a long and strong history of extended family members in African-American families supporting each other and helping care for children (Diller, 2007; Moore, 2008). Gibson (2004) explains the current scenario:

> According to the U.S. Census Bureau, there are 4.5 million children under the age of 18 living in grandparent-headed households; one-third of these children have no parents present in the home. . . . African-American grandmothers are coming to their grandchildren's aid in unprecedented numbers. . . . , and grandparent-maintained households with neither parent present are the most economically disadvantaged. (p. 21)

Okazawa-Rey (1998) provides an example of a community response to the needs of African-American grandparents who have become primary caregivers of their grandchildren. The initiating problem is one well established in the community and national scenes. Many people have become addicted to crack cocaine and are relinquishing their responsibilities as parents and productive citizens to pursue drug use. An example of a program responding to this problem is the Grandparents Who Care Support Network of San Francisco. Most members are "poor and working class, middle-aged and [older adult] . . . African-American women" (Cox, 2002; Okazawa-Rey, 1998, p. 54). They have gained custody of their grandchildren because of their own children's neglect. This is due to drug abuse, incarceration because of drug convictions, and the unwillingness to submit their grandchildren to strangers in the public foster care system.

These grandparents have found themselves in the strange and unusual circumstance of having sudden responsibility for small children at a stage in life when they feel they were done with all that. This situation can pose serious challenges, as Okazawa-Rey (1998) explains:

> Research on the issues confronting grandparents raising grandchildren reveals that these caregivers are prone to an increased incidence or exacerbation of depression and insomnia, hypertension, back and stomach problems [Miller, 1991] as well as increased use of alcohol and cigarettes [Burton, 1992]. In addition, grandparents tend to ignore their problems and the associated stresses to meet the needs of their grandchildren [Minkler & Roe, 1993]. (p. 46)

Problems are compounded with the health problems many children suffer due to poor prenatal care, drug use during pregnancy, and child neglect. These grandparents "desperately need day care, special education services, transportation, respite care, and money" (Okazawa-Rey, 1998, p. 54). To get services, they find themselves trying to negotiate the confusing maze of bureaucracies governing service provision.

Two health care workers, Doriane Miller and Sue Trupin, identified the problems and needs, and established Grandparents Who Care (Okazawa-Rey, 1998). The program is based on four philosophical principles. First, individual health problems transcend the fault of the individual. They are related to mezzo and macro conditions. Second, cultural, legal, and organizational barriers often hinder access to needed services. Third, even if people can get needed services, they may be inadequate and unable to meet needs. Fourth, empowerment at the micro, mezzo, and macro levels is necessary for maintaining optimal health and well-being (Breidenstein, 2003).

The project reflects an empowerment approach as described by Cox (2002):

> The immediate goals of empowerment practice are to help clients achieve a sense of personal power, become more aware of connections between individual and community problems, develop helping skills, and work collaboratively towards social change (Gutierrez, GlenMay, & DeLois, 1995). But, the gains of empowerment do not rest only with the individual (Lee, 1994). As empowered people work together on common issues and problems, the communities in which they live become empowered, further empowering those who reside there. (p. 46)

Grandparents Who Care established a series of support groups to provide information, emotional support, and practical advice. Groups consist of two to twenty-five grandparents, are co-led by professional health care personnel (including nurses or social workers), and meet weekly for ninety minutes. Grandparents Who Care has a board of directors made up of grandparents, citizens, and concerned health care professionals who advise the organization.

Group members provide each other with support and help addressing a range of issues. For example, "when one woman faces a particular problem with her grandchild in the school system, another one will describe her dealings with this system and offer suggestions concerning the most effective ways to intercede" (Okazawa-Rey, 1998, p. 58). Members can thus share their experiences with each other and help work through issues. The professional co-leaders can assist the group by providing technical information about service availability, eligibility, and accessibility.

Areas of relevant interest to participants include "(1) introduction to empowerment; (2) importance of self-esteem; (3) communicating with grandchildren; (4) dealing with loss and grief; (5) helping grandchildren deal with loss; (6) dealing with behavior problems; (7) talking to grandchildren about sex, HIV/AIDS, and drugs; (8) legal and entitlement issues; (9) developing advocacy skills; [and] (10) negotiating systems" (Cox, 2002, p. 47).

Grandparents Who Care expanded its work in several macro dimensions to further empower its members. First, grandparents were trained as group leaders who go out and form new groups. In this way, the program's supportive help spread to help grandparents elsewhere in the community.

Second, Grandparents Who Care undertook political advocacy and lobbying on its members' behalf. One problem advocates addressed involved the legal difficulties grandparents experienced in receiving foster care payments. As relatives, they did not technically qualify as foster parents. Other financial support available to them was not nearly as good as that provided to unrelated foster parents. Grandparents Who Care advocates lobbied with a state legislator to pass a bill allowing grandparents to receive greater benefits.

Empowerment in the Macro Environment for Hispanics

Over 45.5 million Hispanic people live in the United States (U.S. Census Bureau, 2008). The population varies immensely in terms of culture, race, and ethnic origin. Also, note that Hispanic people may also be of more than one race.

Highlight 12.1 addresses identifying terms used to describe Hispanics, and a subsequent section examines the oppression of Hispanic people in the macro environment. A discussion of empowering practices employed by Hispanic women and two case examples of how communities can empower Hispanic people follow.

Oppression in the Macro Environment

The economic and educational picture for the Hispanic population is much poorer than for Whites (U.S. Census Bureau, 2008):

- There's a significantly higher percentage of families earning lower incomes and a significantly lower percentage earning high incomes as compared to Whites: 35.7 percent of Hispanic families have annual incomes of less than $30,000 compared to 20.1 percent of Whites, while 30 percent of Hispanic families have annual incomes of $60,000 or more compared to 51.1 percent of Whites. Greatest disparities between Hispanics and Whites exist at the highest income levels.
- Of Hispanic families, 21.5 percent have incomes below the poverty level, compared to 9.3 percent of Whites. Of Hispanic groups, Puerto Rican families (21.8 percent) are most likely to be below the poverty level, followed by Mexican families (20.1 percent) and Cuban families (10.2 percent), respectively.
- The median income for Hispanic families is $40,000 compared to $62,280 for Whites.
- In terms of educational attainment, 58.2 percent and 62.5 percent of Hispanic men and women, respectively, graduated from high school or attained more education, compared to 85.3 and 87.1 percent for White men and women, respectively. Only 11.8 percent of Hispanic men and 13.7 percent of Hispanic women graduated from college or attained higher levels of education, compared to 29.9 and 28.3 percent for White men and women, respectively.

Although there is tremendous variation among Hispanics (Delgado, 2007; Longres & Aisenberg, 2008), several factors may operate to block socioeconomic success. First, lower educational rates fail to prepare Hispanics for higher-paying jobs (Leon-Guerrero, 2009). Second, poverty is related to the undocumented status of many Hispanic immigrants (Delgado, 2007). Without proper documentation, access to higher levels of employment is dubious. Third, some problems may be associated with acculturation issues (Furman et al., 2009; Longres & Aisenberg, 2008).

Highlight 12.1 | Identifying Terms

The U.S. government's Office of Management and Budget originally coined the term *Hispanic* in 1978 for use in the census (Green, 1999). The original definition defined Hispanic as "a person of Mexican, Puerto Rican, Cuban, Central or South American or other Spanish culture or origin, regardless of race" (Green, 1999, p. 256). However, the concept is much more complex than this. For example, does this umbrella term include Brazilian people who speak Portuguese, South American Indians whose original language is not Spanish, people from the Philippines who speak Spanish, or immigrants from Spain (Green, 1999)?

An alternate term is *Latino*, which makes reference both to the Latin languages including Spanish and to Latin America. (Note that the term *Latina* is the feminine form of *Latino*.) However, this term omits South Americans who speak English, such as those from Belize or the Guyanas, and "people whose family roots extend to Italy, Germany, and some areas of the Mediterranean" (Green, 1999, p. 256).

Still another term often used is *Chicano*, which refers to U.S. citizens whose heritage is based in Mexico. The obvious disadvantage of this is that it focuses only on Mexico and excludes people with origins in other countries, including those that are primarily Spanish speaking.

Essentially, no one term is acceptable to all groups of people. The three primary Hispanic groups in the United States in terms of size are Mexican Americans (almost 65 percent of all Hispanics), Puerto Ricans (8.6 percent), and Cuban Americans (3.7 percent) (U.S. Census Bureau, 2008). Other groups include those from the Dominican Republic and from other countries in Central and South America (Santiago-Rivera, Arredondo, & Gallardo-Cooper, 2002). However, for any particular family, Goldenberg and Goldenberg (2002) caution, "Socioeconomic, regional, and demographic characteristics vary among Hispanic American groups,

making cultural generalizations risky" (p. 326). Santiago-Rivera and her colleagues (2002) reflect:

> Perhaps no other ethnic group in the United States is as heterogeneous in its ethnicity, physical appearance, cultural practices and traditions, and Spanish language dialects as the Latino population. Latinos in the United States are a diverse group of multigenerational. . . . [people] from different Spanish-speaking countries as well as long-term residents in the southwest United States. All have unique social, economic, and political histories. Latino groups vary in their ancestry, blending indigenous [people originating in an area] (e.g., Aztec and Mayan) and Spanish cultural traditions and, for some Latino groups, African traditions. (p. 56)

It's important not to make stereotyped assumptions about such a diverse group. Santiago-Rivera and her colleagues (2002) continue:

> Although it is not often reported, Latinos may also be of Asian heritage. The Philippine islands, conquered by Spain, were populated by people of Asian heritage. Whereas the native language of the island is Tagalog, Spanish surnames are commonplace, and in the United States, Filipinos may claim either Asian or Latino heritage. In South America and Mexico, there are settlements of Chinese families as well. Peru is one such example. (p. 23)

It's probably best for social workers to listen to their clients concerning language and use the terms those clients prefer when referring to their ethnic heritage (Longres & Aisenberg, 2008). Despite the complexity and the need to appreciate differences within this population, the terms *Hispanic* and *Latino/a* have generally been used to refer to people originating in countries in which Spanish is spoken. Here the terms *Hispanic* and *Latino* will be used interchangeably unless a specific group (e.g., Puerto Rican Americans) is discussed.

We have noted that acculturation is the degree to which people take on the values and customs of the dominant culture. Recent immigrants or those who have not been acculturated may experience difficulties in feeling as though they fit in; they may receive inadequate support and may isolate themselves from integration into the economic and social structure (Diller, 2007).

Values Often Characterizing Hispanic Families

Keeping in mind that more specific variations exist within the many subgroups, we will discuss some cultural themes important to Hispanic families in general. Hispanic heritage is rich and diverse, but the groups tend to share similarities in terms of values, beliefs, attitudes, culture, and self-perception. These include the significance of a common language, the importance of family relationships including extended family and other support systems, spirituality, and the traditional strictness of gender roles.

Significance of a Common Language   The first theme important in understanding the environment for children growing up in Hispanic families is the significance of a common language (Delgado, 2007; Longres & Aisenberg, 2008). Almost 80 percent of Hispanics indicate they are proficient in Spanish (Longres & Aisenberg, 2008). English language use varies depending on whether people are native or foreign born (Pew Hispanic Center, 2006). Almost 36 percent of Hispanic native-born adults indicate that they speak *English only,* whereas only 4 percent of foreign-born adults do. Almost half of native-born adults feel they speak English *very well,* compared to 23 percent of those who are foreign born. Over half of children under age eighteen who are foreign born indicate they speak English *very well.* Thus, as less than a quarter of foreign-born adults in contrast to over half of foreign-born children feel they speak English very well, it appears that children pick up English faster. This may be due to school attendance and more exposure to the language that occurs earlier in life.

Social workers should "know that there is a growing population of bilingual Latinos who have varying degrees of language proficiencies in English and Spanish" (Santiago-Rivera et al., 2002, p. 121). For instance, recent immigrants may use little if any English, whereas people whose families have been here for centuries may be bilingual or lack any knowledge of Spanish. One strong implication of such diversity is the need for social workers to assess Latino clients' language history and use on an individual basis.

Arredondo and Perez (2003) point out that "language has always been made a political issue in the United States" so that many Latinos may "prefer to speak English versus Spanish" (pp. 120–121). They suggest that practitioners consider the following issues when working with Hispanic clients and communities:

1. Language use can be associated with generation in the United States. Recent immigrants may be monolingual Spanish speakers or speak English as a second language with a wide range of ability.

2. Many Latinos, particularly Mexican Americans, do not speak Spanish at all. These individuals were taught by their parents that in order to fit in and not be punished in school, as they had been, they could not learn to speak Spanish.

3. Being bilingual or speaking Spanish whenever possible can be viewed as an indication of comfort. However, speaking Spanish in the workplace has often been discouraged so as not to make "others" feel uncomfortable.

4. *Code-switching* refers to the use of Spanish and English in the same sentence [emphasis added]. Individuals engage in code-switching to emphasize a point with a particular English or Spanish word.

5. Bilingualism is an academic, psychological, social and economic asset, not a deficit. The need for Spanish-speaking professionals and workers continues to increase in all work environments in both urban and rural settings. (p. 121)

An important note is the fact that so many cultural activities and aspects of cultural pride are associated with Spanish. Consider the events and holidays (e.g., Cinco de Mayo for Mexican Americans, which refers to the celebrated day a small Mexican army defeated a French army battalion), common history, customs, beliefs, and cooking traditions related to Spanish-speaking origins that are so meaningful in daily cultural life (Longres, 1995).

The Importance of Family   A second theme reflecting a major strength in many Hispanic families is the significance placed on relationships within the nuclear and extended family, including "aunts, uncles, cousins, and grandparents, as well as close friends," referred to as *familismo* (Delgado, 2007; Santiago-Rivera et al., 2002, pp. 42–43; Weaver, 2005):

> Latino families are typically large, intergenerational, and interdependent, and offer an important source of support to their members. . . . Extended family ties are highly valued and serve as a source of pride and security. . . . This emphasis on respect and responsibility to family members often leads to . . . [older] adults both being cared for and taking on caregiving responsibilities within the family. . . . [Older adults] are often cared for within the family rather than through formal social services. When nursing homes are used, family members often continue to fulfill supportive caregiving responsibilities. (Kolb, 1999; Weaver, 2005, p. 148)

Another important related concept reflecting a cultural strength is *compadrazco* (godparentage). *Compadres* (godparents) often serve as substitute parents. According to Santiago-Rivera et al. (2002), godparents "may be prominent leaders or older people who hold some position of authority and respect within the Latino community" and "play an important role in the Latino family's life and are included in all traditional celebrations. The practice of godparentage formalizes relationships between the child's parents and the *compadres* and promotes a sense of community" (p. 44).

Other vital sources of strength involve the community support systems often available to Hispanic families. These include the following:

- *Botanicas:* "Shops that sell herbs as well as records and novels in Spanish."
- *Bodegas:* "Grocery stores" that "also serve as information centers for the Hispanic community, providing such information as where folk healers can be

found." (Mexican, Puerto Rican, and Cuban Hispanic cultures espouse folk healers who help people deal with physical, emotional, and spiritual difficulties).

- *Club sociales:* Settings that "provide recreation as well as links to community resources, including employment and housing" (Chilman, 1993, p. 160)

Personalismo *Personalismo* is "a preference by Latinos for forming personal relationships with others based on a strong sense of trust, cooperation, mutual help-giving, and inclusion rather than exclusion" (Delgado, 2007; Morales, 1996, p. 275). Ho, Rasheed, and Rasheed (2004) explain:

> Along with the concept of *familismo*, Latinos define their self-worth in terms of those inner qualities that give them self-respect and earn them the respect of others [emphasis added]. They feel an inner dignity (*dignidad*) and expect others to show respect (*respeto*) for that dignidad. Personalismo is also a cultural trait that reflects a collectivisitic worldview (Levine & Padilla, 1980) in which there is a great deal of emotional investment in the family. Positive interpersonal interaction will help to maintain mutual dependency and closeness for a lifetime. Hence, great importance is given to those positive interpersonal and social skills to facilitate warm, close relationships. (p. 152)

This value can provide a natural predisposition for practice in neighborhoods and communities where people work together and are concerned about each other.

Machismo and Marianismo Morales (1996) describes the concepts of *machismo* and *marianismo:*

> *Machismo* refers to a man's responsibility to provide for, protect, and defend his family. His loyalty and sense of responsibility to family, friends, and community make him a good man. The Anglo-American definition of *macho* that describes sexist, male-chauvinist behavior is radically different from the original Latino meaning of *machismo*, which convened the notion of "an honorable and responsible man."
>
> *Marianismo* refers to the responsibility of a woman to provide for, protect, and nurture her family and to value motherhood strongly. Her self-sacrificing dedication to the family and motherhood is viewed with great esteem and is expected of Latinas. The term comes from the biblical Virgin Mary (Maria) and refers to her purity and sanctity in relation to the family and her influence in maintaining high moral and ethical standards. (p. 274)

Santiago-Rivera and her colleagues (2002) reflect: "There is considerable debate over the extent to which Latinos adhere to traditional gender roles in contemporary U.S. society. Although evidence suggests that gender roles are undergoing transformation, the complexities surrounding this phenomenon are far from clear-cut" (p. 51).

Weaver (2005) indicates that "although distinct gender roles exist, it is important to recognize that not all Latinas fit these roles to the same extent," and gives the following example:

> Latinas are often stereotyped as passive and submissive, but many changes have taken place in marriages and families in the last decade. Many Latinas now work outside the home and may wield decision-making power about family finances. It is important to understand evolving gender roles within Latino families. (p. 146)

Today over 56.5 percent of Latinas are in the workforce compared to 61.1 percent of African-American women and 59 percent of White women, respectively (U.S. Census Bureau, 2008). From a strengths perspective, Latinas function as socializers, educators, and promoters of values and beliefs within family systems. Hispanic couples vary widely in terms of who assumes decision-making power and responsibility for family support, as do couples in any other ethnic or racial group. Other factors to consider that influence gender roles include educational level, income, location, history in this country, verbal communication, and family structure (Santiago-Rivera et al., 2002).

Spirituality   A third theme characterizing many Hispanic families is the importance of spirituality and religion (Delgado, 2007; Longres & Aisenberg, 2008). Weaver (2005) explains:

> Spirituality has a fundamental shaping influence on the lives of many Latinos. Catholicism is a defining force of family and gender roles for Latino people. . . . Latino Catholicism revolves around the concepts of life and death. This fatalistic belief system emphasizes that God will provide. There is a pervading sense that much of what happens is beyond an individual's personal control. Most Latinos are Roman Catholic, but many espouse beliefs and practices influenced by indigenous and African belief systems. (p. 147; Santiago-Rivera et al., 2002)

Negroni-Rodriguez and Morales (2001) give the following examples of such folk beliefs:

> *Espiritismo* (among Puerto Ricans): "The belief in spirits. Everyone is believed to have spirits of protection, and these can be increased by performing good deeds and decreasing evil. Latinos who ascribe to *espiritismo* believe that loved ones can be around in spirit after death and can lead one's life in times of difficulties. *Espiritistas* (spiritist healers) communicate with spirits and can be incarnated by them. Healing can take place with prescribed folk healing treatment" (p. 135).

> *Curanderismo* (among Mexican Americans and other Central and South Americans): The practice of curing "physical, emotional, and folk illnesses. *Curanderos/as* are healers who use a range of treatments, such as herbal remedies, inhalation, sweating, massage, incantations, and *limpieza* (a ritual cleansing)" (p. 135).

> *Santeria* (among Cuban Americans): Practices that combine "African deities with Catholic saints. The *santeros/as* are priests who function as healers, diviners, and directors of rituals" (p. 135).

Critical Thinking Questions 12.1

People of color have a long history of discrimination in the United States (Miller & Garran, 2008). How has discrimination and lack of appreciation for diversity negatively affected Hispanic people? How might obstacles to progress be demolished and improvements be made?

Case Examples Involving Empowerment for Latinos and Latinas

There are many ways communities can empower Latinos and Latinas. The next section reviews some research regarding Latinas' perceptions of their means of successfully helping to empower their communities. The subsequent two sections provide case examples of empowerment—one involving Latina-owned beauty parlors and the other community assets assessment conducted by Latino youths.

Latinas Empower Communities Lazzari, Ford, and Haughey (1996) studied twenty-one Latinas who were active in social-service-related employment and volunteer activities in a variety of Colorado communities. An old stereotype portrays "Hispanic men as macho and Hispanic women as passive and subservient" (Lazzari et al., 1996, p. 198; Melville, 1980). This research paints quite a different picture. The women interviewed were involved in activities that included "performing tasks for others (for example, teaching translating, connecting with resources), performing tasks for oneself to service others (for example, becoming certified in domestic violence counseling, developing leadership skills, learning Spanish), and performing tasks in groups to help others (for example, networking grassroots organizing, participating in decision making)" (Lazzari et al., 1996, p. 200).

These women indicated that factors supporting and sustaining them "in their extensive amount of community involvement included seeing the need, feeling personal satisfaction, receiving support from others, and having personal beliefs and obligations" (such as a sense of responsibility or spiritual beliefs) (Lazzari et al., 1996, p. 201). It is the social worker's task to identify such strong potential actors in community development, help them, and work with them on the behalf of communities.

Critical Thinking Questions 12.2

In what ways do these Latinas' perceptions concerning empowering communities differ from traditional male approaches?

Case Example: Latina-Owned Beauty Parlors and Empowerment We have established that there are many ways to empower people in communities. Some might not be that obvious. For example, one study of Puerto Rican–owned grocery stores and restaurants found that such small businesses can serve their communities in ways far beyond selling food. They can:

- Furnish credit and cash checks when necessary.
- Provide information about community issues and events.
- Supply information about what's going on in their homeland.
- Provide informal counseling to people in crisis.
- Furnish information about relevant, available social services.
- Help community residents interpret and fill out government forms.

- Provide "cultural connectedness to the homeland through the selling of video-tapes, publications," and so on. (Delgado, 1997, p. 447)

Targeting beauty parlors might not be the first approach that comes to mind when trying to empower a community. However, Delgado (1997) pursued this idea by identifying Latina-owned beauty parlors in Lawrence, Massachusetts, and interviewing their owners. Some findings were similar to those cited earlier concerning the expanded community roles of small businesses. Although no social service agency had approached any of the owners to solicit their involvement in formal community service roles such as task force or advisory board member, most owners expressed interest in assuming such leadership roles. Owners understood the impacts of the community's problems ("most notably alcoholism and family violence") on their customers and their families, and recognized the need to address these issues (Delgado, 1997, p. 449).

This research emphasizes the significant roles that small businesses such as beauty parlors can play in communities. Social workers who intend to strengthen communities can use innovative strategies to do so. Delgado (1997) suggests that social workers and social service organizations can pursue "sponsoring workshops for small business development, contracting with small businesses for goods and services whenever possible, and facilitating the provision of consultation for owners" (p. 450). Delgado notes that such efforts benefit both the businesses and the larger community:

> Latino [and Latina] small businesses can be organized into coalitions to increase their visibility, advocacy, purchase of supplies, and so forth. In turn, owners are an excellent community resource to be tapped for agency boards, advisory committees, task forces, and commissions. (p. 450)

Case Example: Latino and Latina Youth Conduct a Community Assets Assessment We have emphasized the importance of using community strengths to empower communities. Delgado (1998a) describes a project conducted by New Bridges (Nuevo Puente), an agency established by a Center on Substance Abuse Prevention grant. The grant targeted at-risk youth who are "vulnerable" to harm due to a variety of "medical, social, political, or environmental" conditions such as substance use, truancy, delinquency, depression, or suicide (Barker, 2003, p. 32). New Bridges' purpose is to identify and recruit natural helping resources to participate in substance abuse prevention activities. Other facets of New Bridges include provision of "cultural and educational activities"; opportunities to learn about "the effect of substance abuse on individuals, families, and communities; and training "to carry out school and community education on alcohol, tobacco, and other drugs" (Delgado, 1998a, pp. 204–205).

New Bridges hired six girls and four boys to conduct a community assets assessment of a forty-block urban community. Interviewers asked representatives of business establishments questions about type of business, when it initially opened, availability of contact people, social services provided (if a social services agency), and "willingness to collaborate with schools and agencies on community projects" (Delgado, 1998a, p. 205). Goals were to "provide youths with an appreciation of community strengths, raise school and human services agency awareness of community assets, and develop an assets directory" (Delgado, 1998a, p. 205).

Results indicated that "the use of Latino adolescents in community asset assessments offers much promise" for social work (Delgado, 1998a, p. 210). Although this assessment was conducted via a grant-created community agency, Delgado (1998a) presents a number of suggestions for implementation of community asset assessments. He suggests doing so through community schools because there is natural access to youth, including those at-risk.

First, school social workers can recruit youths to identify "potential student leaders, candidates for peer education programs, and possible projects involving natural support systems" (Delgado, 1998a, p. 209). For example, the young people involved in the New Bridges project decided they wanted to go on a trip and finance it by sponsoring a car wash. They asked identified Latino businesses to contribute a small amount of money (such as a nickel or a quarter) for each car washed. In return, the youth listed sponsors' names on a billboard to provide publicity for them. This is a good example of how a community can work together to enhance relationships among various facets (that is, this group of young people and local businesses) to reach mutually positive goals (that is, financial backing for the trip and positive publicity for the businesses).

A second idea for using assets assessment is for schools to invite interested business owners from the community in to talk about how they started their businesses. In this way owners could provide positive role models for young people and sow some seeds about career possibilities and goals.

A third idea for using the community assets assessment is to use information gathered to sponsor special school projects. Extra credit might be assigned to investigate community strengths in a social studies course. Students might videotape interviews with interested community residents or community service representatives. They might then share these tapes with other students or even social service agencies to provide education about social issues or cultural strengths.

 Critical Thinking Questions 12.3

In what ways might a project such as New Bridges serve to enhance young people's self-esteem?

Empowerment for Gay, Lesbian, Bisexual, and Transgender People Through Political Action Organizations

Earlier chapters introduced the concepts of sexual orientation, the expression of gender, and a number of related terms. We have defined *sexual orientation* as sexual and romantic attraction to persons of one or both genders.

Elze (2006) explains the historical context facing gay, lesbian, bisexual, and transgender (GLBT) people:

The history of gay, lesbian, bisexual, and transgender people in America is a history of oppression and resistance. Since colonial times, gender-variant people, and people who love and sexually desire those of the same sex, have been imprisoned, executed, witch-hunted, pilloried [placed in a frame with hands and head locked in as a means of public embarrassment], confined in asylums, fired, excommunicated, disinherited, evicted, extorted, entrapped, censored, declared mentally ill, drugged, and subjected to castration, hormone injections, clitoridectomy [surgical removal of the clitoris], hysterectomy [surgical removal of the uterus], ovariectomy [surgical removal of the ovaries], lobotomy [surgical cutting of the nerves connecting the brain's two frontal lobes], psychoanalysis, and aversive therapies such as electro-shock and pharmacologic shock. (p. 43)

A *political action organization* is based on the concept of a social action group. It is an organization that conducts "coordinated efforts to influence legislation, election of candidates, and social causes" (Barker, 2003, p. 330). Changing legislation and social policy on the behalf of GLBT people can involve the provision of due and equal rights, the purging of discrimination, and the enhancement of overall well-being.

The National Association of Social Workers *Code of Ethics* states that "Social workers should not practice, condone, facilitate, or collaborate with any form of discrimination on the basis of . . . sexual orientation" (NASW, 2008, 4.02). It continues that "social workers should act to prevent and eliminate domination of, exploitation of, and discrimination against any person, group, or class on the basis of . . . sexual orientation" (NASW, 2008, 6.04d). It is the ethical obligation of social workers to advocate on the behalf of GLBT people so that they have the right to self-determination and equal treatment under the law.

Important Issues for GLBT People

Many issues concerning GLBT people require attention, six of which are mentioned here (Barusch, 2009; Messinger, 2006). They include the need for nondiscrimination laws, the recognition of same-sex relationships, family policies for GLBT parents, harassment and violence against GLBT people, housing, and employment.

Need for Nondiscrimination Laws   First, there is a need for nondiscrimination laws. Although debates are currently taking place at the state level, there is no federal legislation prohibiting discrimination against GLBT people in employment (Messinger & Brooks, 2008). Barusch (2009) continues:

A review of legislation affecting GLBT Americans reveals the oppressive role of some state and federal government authorities. In sharp contrast to its policies concerning people of color and even women, the government seems to have adopted a much more hostile posture toward homosexuals. This hostility is manifested in [issues that] . . . include sodomy laws;[2] state initiatives to limit rights of people who identify as gay or lesbian; the Defense of Marriage Act [to be discussed]; legal issues in family formation, including child custody and adoption; discrimination in employment and volunteer work; treatment of gays in the military; hate crime legislation; and policies related to HIV/AIDS. (p. 327)

---

[2] *Sodomy laws* make it illegal to practice certain sexual behaviors, such as oral or anal intercourse, even in the privacy of one's own home.

Note that some state and local governments have taken various steps forward to secure some of these rights, such as legal employment protections (Messinger & Brooks, 2008). In lieu of a federal law, political action organizations can work to establish laws enhancing rights at the state and local levels.

Recognition of Same-Sex Relationships A second issue involves the recognition of same-sex relationships, particularly the legalization of gay marriage. The possibility is being hotly debated at local, state, and national levels. In terms of all federal legislation, the federal Defense of Marriage Act (DOMA) identifies marriage as an officially authorized union between a man and a woman; additionally, it allows states to reject marriages performed in other states that allow same-sex marriages (DOMAwatch, 2008). DOMAwatch (2008) reveals the following facts:

- To date, thirty states have constitutional amendments that define marriage as being between a man and a woman only;
- Thirty-seven states have state DOMA legislation;
- A mere five states—Massachusetts, New Jersey, New Mexico, New York, and Rhode Island—have neither legislation nor constitutional amendments that, in effect, prohibit gay marriage;
- Only two states legally allow gay marriage—Massachusetts and Connecticut.

Recent Gallup Polls revealed a somewhat negative picture of same-sex marriage (PollingReport.com, 2009). Fifty-four percent of people polled feel that persons of the same gender do not have the constitutional right to marry, whereas 45 percent think they do, and 1 percent are uncertain. Only 38 percent of people surveyed said they would support a state law that allowed same-sex marriages, 55 percent opposed such a law, and 7 percent were uncertain. Inability to marry denies GLBT couples, among many other things, potential income tax, health insurance, and Social Security (upon death of a spouse) benefits in addition to decision-making rights when partners are seriously ill and are unable to make decisions for themselves.

Family Policies for GLBT Parents A third issue involves family policies for GLBT parents. Thirty percent of same-sex couples have children under the age of eighteen living in their households; of those who have children, over half (56 percent) have two or more living with them (Gay Demographics, 2006). Some research proposes that about "30 percent of all lesbian and bisexual female parents have been threatened with loss of custody. Fathers, known sperm donors, female co-parents, grandparents and other relatives all have the potential of bringing custody challenges against lesbian mothers" (Cahill, Ellen, & Tobias, 2002, p. 74, cited in Messinger, 2006, p. 441).

Harassment and Violence against GLBT People A fourth area threatening the rights of GLBT people involves harassment and violence (Martin, 2008). Messinger (2006) explains:

Hate crimes legislation at the state and federal levels is designed to impose additional penalties for certain crimes that are based on . . . [spiteful ill will] toward some element of a person's identity, specifically an identity of a population that is oppressed. While all but five states have some sort of hate crimes legislation, only seven states have statutes against hate crimes that are based on prejudice toward gender expression, and twenty-nine states have statutes against hate crimes that are based on prejudice toward sexual orientation . . . The federal statute used to prosecute hate crimes does not include sexual orientation or gender expression as protected categories. . . . GLBT activists have been working with friendly politicians to pass federal hate crimes legislation that would include sexual orientation and gender expression. (pp. 444–445)

Housing A fifth area of concern involves housing, as Messinger (2006) explains:

Most GLBT families have no legal remedy if they encounter discrimination in purchasing or renting a dwelling. There is no federal law banning discrimination in housing that is based upon sexual orientation or gender expression, though ten states and the District of Columbia ban discrimination on the basis of sexual orientation (Cahill et al., 2002). (Messinger, 2006, p. 448)

Employment A sixth issue relevant to GLBT people involves employment. Barusch (2009) explains:

With the exception of those states that include sexual orientation in their human rights statutes, employment discrimination against homosexuals is perfectly legal. A man or woman can be denied a job or a promotion, or be fired, for being homosexual. It is difficult to document the extent of employment discrimination against homosexuals; nonetheless, survey results suggest that between 16 and 44 percent of gay and lesbian workers have experienced some form of employment discrimination . . . Gays and lesbians who work with children as teachers, counselors, and coaches are especially vulnerable. Job discrimination against homosexuals also takes the form of verbal harassment. . . .

Laws governing employment discrimination on the basis of sexual orientation vary across the nation. Some openly homosexual teachers enjoy the protection of non-discrimination cases that include sexual orientation, and others are subject to dismissal . . .

In addition to employment discrimination, homosexuals are subjected to discrimination in volunteer activities, most notably those sponsored by the Boy Scouts of America. (pp. 335–336)

 Critical Thinking Questions 12.4

What are your personal views concerning each of the six issues mentioned concerning GLBT people? Explain.

Political Action Organizations

Political action organizations working on the behalf of GLBT people to address these and other issues can function in at least three ways. These include providing direct support to political candidates, educating the public to gain support, and conducting legislative advocacy (Barker, 2003; Messinger, 2006).

Providing Support to Political Candidates   Political action organizations can identify and support the campaigns of political candidates advocating for GLBT rights. Haynes and Mickelson (2003) describe candidate selection:

> Because it is not unusual for a political candidate to slant a position on a particular issue in order to gain the support of specific groups, often it becomes necessary to determine how a politician really stands on issues that may not be of major campaign interest. In the case of incumbents, the best measurement is action already taken. Consequently, to give a clearer picture of the candidate's position on certain issues, PACs often prepare and publicize a record of the candidate's votes on relevant pieces of legislation—sometimes referred to as the "report card." (p. 155)

Questions can be posed. To what extent did the candidate support GLBT rights in the past? What is the candidate's verbal stance and/or voting record on such issues as anti-hate legislation and gay marriage?

Because political campaigns cost money, a primary means of supporting political candidates is through financial support. This is often done by forming and working through a *political action committee* (PAC), a group whose purpose is to raise money and provide support for designated political candidates (Barker, 2003; Haynes & Mickelson, 2003). PACs may be formed within a political action organization or in other organizations pursuing a broader range of goals than exclusively political action. A PAC can participate in any number of fundraising activities, from bake sales to walk-a-thons to direct solicitation for financial support.

Political action organizations can also provide candidates support by endorsing them. The "PAC can endorse the candidate by stating that the membership organization (for example, NASW [National Association of Social Workers]) recommends that social workers vote for that candidate" (Haynes & Mickelson, 2003, p. 159). Haynes and Mickelson (2003) elaborate:

> Services and support can be offered [by a PAC], including mailing and telephone lists. Candidates are aware that the endorsement alone will not guarantee membership votes, but mailing lists and telephone numbers facilitate the candidate's ability to reach PAC members and to gain their support and labor. . . .
>
> A PAC can recruit and assign volunteers from its membership to assist candidates, thereby increasing the effect of the endorsement. PACE [Political Action for Candidate Endorsement, NASW's political action component] has found this to be most effective because candidates have discovered that social workers have excellent campaign skills. Social workers listen well, are organized, are trained to take a broad perspective, and can work well with a variety of individuals (Wolk, 1981). Some candidates enlist social workers as campaign managers. Also after an election, social workers often are hired as aides to work out constituent problems. (pp. 159–160)

Educating the Public to Gain Support   A political action organization can work to influence public opinion to enlighten citizens about GLBT issues and mobilize citizens to vote on GLBT people's behalf. Citizens support politicians who, in turn, formulate laws that govern our macro social environment. Social workers can urge voters to critically think about issues of self-determination and expand their perceptions about human rights with respect to GLBT people.

In order to educate effectively, it's first important to define the issues and know the relevant facts. Myths and stereotypes that support prejudice against gay and lesbian people must be identified and disputed. The following facts should be emphasized (Morrow, 2006):

- Sexual orientation is "an innate orientation," not "a lifestyle choice" (p. 4). Significant research supports a strong biological component in the development of sexual orientation. "The term *sexual orientation* is more appropriate than the term *sexual preference*," explains Morrow:

  Preference implies ease and simplicity of choice or selection, while *orientation* more accurately connotes the innate essence of a person's intimate and affectional nature. Perhaps the best way to understand the role of choice in relation to sexual orientation is that people must choose whether to embrace or reject whatever is their essential orientation. (p. 4)

- Sexual orientation is a normal facet of human diversity. Chapter 2 established that the expression of gender is a complex concept. Van Wormer, Wells, and Boes (2000) explain that in a homophobic society that has much anxiety about sexuality, "sexual expression is often perceived as dirty, disgusting, and lustful, particularly same-sex sexuality (p. 89). They continue:

  Although sexual behaviors are similar across sexual orientations, the assumptions are that gay males and lesbians engage in homosexual behaviors that differ vastly from heterosexual behaviors when, in fact, sexual behaviors that people engage in are more appropriately deemed as human sexual behaviors. Gay men and lesbians do differ sexually from their heterosexual counterparts in that they are less goal oriented, communicate more, use more erotic words, [and] do not let interruptions ruin the mood . . . Gays and lesbians more often include pleasure, intimacy, and emotions into their definitions of sexuality than do heterosexuals. (p. 89)

- GLBT people are just as likely to be good parents as heterosexual people (Mallon, 2008; Morrow, 2008). Good parenting skills have no relationship to sexual orientation. GLBT parents are not more likely to molest children. In reality, the majority of child sexual abuse is committed by heterosexual men who usually are people trusted and close to the child (for example, a family friend, a father, stepfather, or brother) (Carroll, 2010; McCammon & Knox, 2007). There is no evidence to support a number of false homophobic stereotypes about gay parents (Mallon, 2008; Morrow, 2008). Children are no more likely than those raised in heterosexual families to become gay or lesbian. Children who have gay parents are just as psychologically healthy as those with heterosexual parents. They are just as socially well adjusted and experience no greater frequency in behavioral problems than children with heterosexual parents.

- Same-sex couples "develop long-term, committed relationships" just like heterosexual couples do (Morrow, 2006, p. 6). Relationships are complex. Just as heterosexuals, GLBT people may enter permanent relationships or may have a series of shorter-term relationships. However, GLBT people lack the social and legal supports provided to married heterosexuals.

Legislative Advocacy *Advocacy* is the practice of actively intervening on the behalf of clients so that they get what they need (Kirst-Ashman & Hull, 2009b). *Legislative advocacy* is the process of influencing legislators to support legislation promoting specific goals. *Lobbying* is the practice of seeking "direct access to lawmakers to influence legislation and public policy"; the expression originated when people seeking to influence lawmakers met with them in the lobbies of legislative houses (Barker, 2003, p. 253). Political organizational members can lobby legislators or testify before legislative committees to educate decision makers about issues and encourage them to vote in GLBT people's best interest. The same principles involved in the earlier discussion concerning educating the general public also apply here.

An example of a political action organization activity is to establish a statewide telephone network where members contact designated other members who in turn would initiate their own designated telephone contacts and so on. Before legislative decisions are made, members can alert each other to the issues via the network.

Highlight 12.2 | **Empowerment of GLBT People through Special Social Services**

There are many ways social services can respond to the needs of GLBT people. Special social services can be developed to lessen oppression and educate the general public about the need for gay rights. Mann (1997) identifies projects including a national organization and two community initiatives pursuing these ends on their behalf.

The Bridges Project sponsored by the American Friends Service Committee (AFSC), a Quaker organization, serves as a "national clearinghouse" to provide "information, resources, referrals and assistance to LGBT and their allies nationwide" (Mann, 1997, p. 96). The project serves to "support the formation of new youth-led organizations; enable mainstream organizations to effectively accept their LGBT youth; work with adult LGBT groups to include LGBT youth as leaders within their organizations; refer individuals and groups to sources that can help answer questions; and link groups working on similar issues" (pp. 96–97).

A second example of how special services can be developed to address issues is the Rural Transportation Program "sponsored by the State of Nevada's Bureau of Disease Control and Intervention Services" (Mann, 1997, p. 98). The program's purpose is to assist HIV-positive people who live in

rural areas in transporting themselves to medical or social services appointments in urban areas. The program provides a credit card to eligible service recipients that can be used to pay "for transportation related purchases by the consumer and/or a family member, a friend, or volunteer assisting the consumer"; purchases can include "gas, oil, windshield wiper fluid, anti-freeze, food, water, sodas and juices" (Mann, 1997, p. 99).

A final example of how a community has developed special services to meet lesbian and gay persons' needs is Beyond the Closet, a rural central Oregon organization. Its goals are to educate citizens, advocate for lesbian and gay rights, and provide support where needed (Mann, 1997). The organization has achieved the following accomplishments:

> the organizing of the premiere gay and lesbian lecture series in rural Oregon; the facilitation of a meeting between area clergy and Beyond the Closet spokespersons; . . . and the organization of several events such as a "queer" book sale and film series, concerts by out lesbian performers, and the distribution of radio, television and printed interviews and opinions regarding issues relevant to the LGBT community. (Mann, 1997, pp. 99–100)

Members can then exert immediate pressure upon legislative decision makers by writing letters, emailing, or phoning in their pleas advocating for whatever GLBT rights issue has current legislative attention.

We've established that empowerment can be pursued in many ways. Highlight 12.2 provides examples of programs empowering GLBT people through special social services.

Empowerment for Women in the Macro Environment

Lorber (2005) comments on the status of women:

> As a *social institution* [an established and valued practice or means of operation in a society resulting in the development of a formalized system to carry out its purpose], gender determines the distribution of power, privileges, and economic resources [emphasis added]. Other major social statuses combine with gender to produce an overall stratification system, but gender privileges men over women in most social groups.
>
> Through parenting, the schools, and the mass media, gendered norms and expectations get built into boys' and girls' sense of self as a certain kind of human being. Other social statuses, such as racial ethnic identification and religion, are similarly socially constructed and reproduced, but gender is so deeply embedded that it is rarely examined or rebelled against. By the time people get to be adults, alternative ways of acting as women and men and arranging work and family life are literally unthinkable. (p. 242)

Many facts support the existence of oppression for women:

- The median income of women who work full-time is 77 percent of what men earn (Brandwein, 2008).
- Women of color are significantly more disadvantaged than White women. Hispanic women earn less than African-American women, and both groups earn less than White women (U.S. Census Bureau, 2008).
- For all races, women earn significantly less than men do at every educational level. The average annual earnings for women with a high school degree or a bachelor's degree are about 62 percent of what men earn at that same educational level (U.S. Census Bureau, 2008).
- Women are clustered in low-paying supportive occupations such as clerical workers, teachers, and service workers while men tend to assume higher-paying occupations such as managers, professionals, and construction workers (U.S. Census Bureau, 2008).
- Women earn significantly less than men in the same job category (U.S. Census Bureau, 2008).
- Women are significantly more likely to be poor than men (U.S. Census Bureau, 2008).
- Women of color are significantly more likely to be poor than White women (U.S. Census Bureau, 2008).
- Similar disparities prevail in the household:

> Women perform more household work than men do, with the figure averaging out at around two-thirds. The other third tends to be shared by men and children,

with female children performing a greater amount of housework than male children. In addition, men tend to overestimate the work they do in the home and women underestimate it . . . [Additionally, women and men tend to do different kinds of tasks where women] "do the repetitive, ongoing, daily kinds of tasks, and men are more likely to perform the less repetitive or seasonal tasks. . . . Women are much more likely to 'multitask' or perform a series of tasks simultaneously. This means, for example, that they might be folding laundry at the same time that they are feeding the baby, or are cooking dinner at the same time that they are vacuuming. (Shaw & Lee, 2004, pp. 324–325)

 Critical Thinking Questions 12.5

What are the reasons for these differences in income, employment, poverty, and contribution to household work? To what extent do you feel women are oppressed and why?

Because women are an oppressed population-at-risk, it is social workers' responsibility to work in the macro environment for positive change. Earlier chapters introduced a number of feminist principles that can be applied to the treatment of women by macro systems. These include using a gender lens, the end of patriarchy, empowerment, consciousness raising, the personal is political, the importance of process, unity in diversity, and validation. The following section presents a case example for empowering at-risk pregnant women.

Empowering At-Risk Pregnant Women

Prenatal care is critically important for mothers and infants. The Centers for Disease Control (CDC) divides the states into two groups concerning the provision of prenatal care: pregnant women receive less care in eighteen states and slightly better care in the remaining thirty-two states. In eighteen states, 31 percent of pregnant women receive no prenatal care during the first trimester; in the remaining states, 17 percent receive no prenatal care during that period (CDC, 2009b). In eighteen states, 7.9 percent of pregnant women receive either late or no care; in the remaining thirty-two states, 3.6 percent receive either late or no care (CDC, 2009b). Good prenatal care "can help prevent maternal, prenatal, and infant death and other complications of birth. . . . Poor women who get prenatal care benefit by being put in touch with other needed services, and they are more likely to get medical care for their infants after birth" (Papalia, Olds, & Feldman, 2007, pp. 100–101). "Teenage and unmarried women, those with little education, and some minority women" are "least likely to receive" prenatal care (Papalia et al., 2007, p. 102).

Shared Beginnings, a Denver program, provides a good example of how various facets of a community have come together to address this issue (Balsanek, 1998). Initial consciousness raising occurred through extensive media coverage of the problem, alerting the public to the fact that increasing numbers of poor, single, and young mothers failed to seek or receive prenatal care. The project was spearheaded by a concerned volunteer philanthropist who brought citizens, social services representatives, health care personnel, and potential financial backers together to initiate the project. Fundraising projects included a luncheon program supported by influential community members and solicitation of financial donations.

Participants involved in the project established five basic program goals. The first was to educate the community concerning the importance of prenatal health care and to alter attitudes on health care's behalf. A second goal was the initiation of a "Sharing Partners" program where volunteer paraprofessionals would go out into the community to educate residents about prenatal care and encourage them to use services (p. 414). The third goal was to establish an ongoing agency complete with director, administrative assistant, and volunteer coordinator to oversee progress. The fourth was the creation of a "Baby Store" located in a local hospital where "coupons could be redeemed for new baby care items to reinforce health care appointment attendance before the baby is born and immunizations after the baby is born" (p. 414). The final goal was to integrate a research component to evaluate the program's effectiveness and provide suggestions for improvement. In summary, "Shared Beginnings represents a grassroots approach to providing the community support that poor and at-risk families need to raise healthy children" (p. 418).

Empowerment of Older Adults

At each age, people have different needs and experience different conditions. McInnis-Dittrich (2009) explains the significance of generalist practice with older adults:

> One of the greatest challenges of the twenty-first century will be the tremendous increase in the number of persons over the age of 65. Due to both the graying of the baby boomer generation (those persons born between 1946 and 1964) and improvements in health and medical care, the sheer numbers of persons entering "the third age" [often referred to as "old age" in an unflattering manner] will be staggering. Social institutions, including the health care system, education, income maintenance and social insurance programs, the workplace, and particularly social services, are bound to be radically transformed. Current and future generations of older adults will undoubtedly forge new approaches to the aging process itself and demand services that reflect positive and productive approaches to this time in their lives. As major providers of service to older adults and their families, social workers need a wide variety of skills and resources to meet these demands. (p. 1)

Generalist practitioners must advocate for the rights of older adults and help to address the negative attitudes they often face. McInnis-Dittrich (2009) continues:

> The term *ageism* refers to the prejudices and stereotypes attributed to older persons based solely on their age (Butler, 1989). These stereotypes are usually negative and convey an attitude that older adults are less valuable as human beings, thus justifying inferior or unequal treatment. These attitudes develop early in life as children observe parental, medical, and social attitudes toward older adults. Parents may unintentionally send the message that aging parents and grandparents are a nuisance to care for, demanding, needy, or unpleasant. Even simple comments such as "I hope I never get like

Grandma" or "Put me to sleep if I ever get senile," may be interpreted literally by children. Every time parents refer to aches and pains as "I must be getting old," the subtle message becomes clear that aging is destined to be painful and debilitating. (p. 20)

Aging is part of life, with its pros and cons. Each stage of life tends to be characterized by positive and negative experiences. It is the generalist practitioner's job to emphasize "the dignity and worth of the person" of any age; "each person regardless of position in society, has basic human rights, such as freedom, safety, privacy, an adequate standard of living, health care, and education" (CSWE, 2008, pp. 2, 5).

Needs of Older Adults

The traditional approach to "caring for" older adults provides a wide continuum of care to meet their needs as these needs change over time (Greene, Cohen, Galambos, & Kropf, 2007; Morrow-Howell & Hasche, 2008). As people get older, they tend to experience increasing health issues and therefore require more services. Most older adults requiring care receive it from family members (Morrow-Howell & Hasche, 2008). However, when this is not available or caregivers are no longer able to provide care, older adults may enter the formal service system that provides the following services, among others (Morrow-Howell & Hasche, 2008, pp. 112–114):

- *Homecare services*—"Home health care agencies [for example, the Visiting Nurses Association] often work with interdisciplinary teams that include nurses, social workers, and physicians. In addition, home health care agencies also employ trained nonprofessional workers, such as home health aides and homemakers. Home health aides . . . assist clients with the performance of activities of daily living, for example, bathing, toileting, and dressing them (Martin, 2000). Homemakers and chore workers assist their clients with light housekeeping tasks such as preparing meals, going shopping, and doing the laundry. However, homemakers are usually not qualified to perform any personal care activities" (Naleppa & Reid, 2003, p. 29).
- *Senior centers*—Senior centers are facilities that "offer older adults an opportunity to come together and fulfill many of their social physical, and intellectual needs . . . They offer a wide range of services and activities for older adults . . . that include social and recreational activities, educational programs, health and nutritional programs, and information and referral" to help people find and use relevant services (Naleppa & Reid, 2003, p. 20).
- *Congregate and home-delivered meal services*—"Congregate meals are often offered in senior centers as well as in some alternative living arrangement, such as retirement communities . . . In most communities home-delivered meals (meals-on-wheels) are provided by private nonprofit agencies funded through the OAA" (Older Americans Act) (Naleppa & Reid, 2003, p. 21).
- *Adult day services*—As "a setting for older adult care that falls between independent living and skilled nursing care," "adult day health care can provide individually designed programs of medical and social services for frail older adults who need structured care for some portion of the day. . . . These older

adults do not need full-time nursing care or even full-time supervision but do require assistance with some of the activities of daily living" (McInnis-Dittrich, 2009, p. 12).

- *Respite services*—Older adults "may have a number of conditions that prevent them from staying at home alone when their caregivers are at work. Other caregivers may simply need a respite [or break] from the highly demanding tasks of caring for" an older adult in poor health (Naleppa & Reid, 2003, p. 23). Most respite care is provided in the home by "companions, home-makers, home-health aides, or nurses for several hours at a time" (Morrow-Howell & Hasche, 2008, p. 112).

- *Hospice*—Hospice programs provide end-of-life care to terminally ill people. The intent is to make people as comfortable as possible during their final days. Services may be provided either in a comfortable setting outside the home or in the home.

- *Supportive housing*—"A living arrangement favored by more and more older adults who are able to live independently is the planned retirement community. These retirement communities usually have a minimum age requirement . . . Planned retirement communities often have extensive social and recreational offerings" (Naleppa & Reid, 2003, p. 23).

   One older widow comes to mind. When it became too difficult for her to take care of her single-family home by herself, she moved into an apartment in a retirement community. She was delighted to find out that not only were numerous social activities (for example, card-playing groups, bingo, and lectures on a wide range of topics by professors from a local university) and opportunities for social interaction (for example, afternoon "teas," holiday parties, and receptions) available, but the facility also offered weekly church services. As she was no longer driving, for a number of years she had been forced to depend on friends or relatives to drive her to church when they were available. Now that problem was solved. All she had to do each Sunday was walk down the hall.

   "*Continuing retirement communities* offer a continuous range of living alternatives, from independent living to residence in a nursing home [emphasis added]. Older adults can move from one level of supported living to the next according to their individual needs" (Naleppa & Reid, 2003, p. 23).

- *Nursing homes*—"The nursing home or long-term care facility offers the most comprehensive level of care. In a skilled nursing home, all aspects of life and care are fulfilled by the facility. The target groups of the nursing home are frail elderly persons who need around-the-clock nursing care and extensive assistance in daily living" (Naleppa & Reid, 2003, p. 24).

New Strengths-Based Perspectives on Aging: Means to Empowerment

The traditional approach to working with "the elderly" focuses on identifying weaknesses and on finding substitutions to make up for what older adults *cannot* do. Even the term *the elderly* conjures up visions of limitations, helplessness, and inability. Following this view, older adults are assessed in terms of their deficits and subsequent needs. Kaye (2005) proposes a very different "strengths-based perspective" to viewing and celebrating older adulthood (p. 8). This new outlook emphasizes hope, development, autonomy, activity, and empowerment (Kaye, 2008). He explains:

> This perspective embraces growth and capacity, potential yet to be realized, and the continuing aspirations and enhancements of people over time, regardless of their relative age and health. It dwells less on consolidating and coming to terms with past accomplishments or failures, but rather it integrates present-day and future-oriented perspectives. . . .
>
> Social workers . . . have a more explicit role to play in a variety of nontraditional settings, including retirement planning, travel and recreational programming, employment training and counseling, volunteer services, self-help programming, exercise programs, and continuing and lifelong learning programs. Such programs emphasize active engagement in community life and societal interaction. Increased social work involvement in these fields of practice will translate into more direct contact with and, ultimately longer-term engagement of active elders in the very programs that reinforce and reward productive older adult behavior. . . .
>
> A productive aging perspective may also be viewed as having greater relevance to financially secure and physically robust adults. To the contrary, it is believed that a productive aging perspective has universal relevance. All older persons will benefit enormously from a philosophy that promotes choice, opportunity, creativity, and personal development regardless of financial well-being or health status. Regardless of the degree of physical, functional, and emotional health, all persons as they age, are challenged to sustain a high quality of life, set genuine goals for themselves, structure their daily lives meaningfully, and remain engaged in community and family life. It is crucial that we remember that the manner in which active engagement is framed can vary dramatically from one person to the next. Furthermore, the ability to remain productive and vital will be determined by a host of personal factors, including but not limited to attitude, physical and emotional well-being, motivation, education and experience, and changing societal attitudes and expectations. For this reason, work with productive elders can and must take place in traditional settings in which a large proportion of geriatric social workers are already employed (for example, long-term care facilities, adult day care, senior citizen centers, hospices, chronic and acute care hospitals, and in-home programs). In these settings, the capacity of social workers to identify, to reinforce, and to help preserve those dimensions of older adult capacity that reflect a productive aging philosophy is particularly crucial. (pp. 8–10)

Spiritual Communities and Empowerment

We've established that *spirituality* "includes one's values, beliefs, mission, awareness, subjectivity, experience, sense of purpose and direction, and a kind of striving toward something greater than oneself" (Frame, 2003, p. 3). Chapter 9 addressed the importance of spiritual values and religion for many African-Americans and First Nations Peoples. The following two case examples reflect how spiritual communities can empower their members. First, an African-American spiritual community serves as a safe haven for its youth. Second, a Navajo spiritual and cultural community empowers its senior citizens through the provision of spiritually and culturally sensitive care to nursing home residents.

A Spiritual Community as a Haven for African-American Youth

A common theme in the lives of many African-Americans involves strong religious beliefs and a close relationship with the church, especially an African-American church (Davis et al., 2008; Dhooper & Moore, 2001; Diller, 2007). Many African-American families consider the church to be a part of the extended family, providing similar nurturance and support (Paniagua, 1998). Dhooper and Moore (2001) explain:

> The African-American church continues to address not only the religious and spiritual needs of the individual, family, and community, but also their social needs. It serves as a coping and survival mechanism against the effects of racial discrimination and oppression and as a place where African-Americans are able to experience unconditional positive regard. (p. 101)

The following is an example of how social workers can help enhance a community's functioning, in this case, an African-American spiritual community in Utah. Social workers can serve as human resources in a wide range of capacities. First, a study is discussed that explores the values and opinions of the spiritual community's members. Subsequently, a project is described that demonstrates how social workers can creatively work with a spiritual community to help meet its needs.

Haight (1999) conducted an ethnographic study targeting African-American youth belonging to the First Baptist Church in Salt Lake City, Utah. The church was established over 100 years ago by "'a Baptist Prayer Band,' a group of African-Americans who, excluded from worshipping in the white churches, met in one another's homes" (p. 247). Haight (1999) notes that "African-American Utahns, like African-Americans in other parts of the country, experience racial discrimination in employment, housing, education, and everyday social interactions" (p. 248). African-Americans are a tiny minority in Utah. Additionally, most of the Utah population belongs to the Church of Jesus Christ of Latter-Day Saints, a tightly knit spiritual community that sponsors a wide realm of social and cultural activities for its members.

Extensive interviews with First Baptist Church members revealed a local environmental context for children that was "negligent at best and virulently racist at worst" (p. 249). Of special concern was the perceived "negative expectations" of White educators in the public school system (p. 249). In response, First Baptist Church members felt the church's spiritual community provided a safe haven where children could learn about their cultural heritage in a safe, supportive environment. Emphasis was placed on "helping children understand the relevance of, and then apply, biblical concepts to their own lives" (p. 252). Additionally, children were strongly encouraged to participate in ongoing learning activities. One illustration is that children were expected to respond to a series of "call-and-response sequences." Haight gives an example: "When the teacher said that they would no longer be fishermen, but that they would be fishers of ———?, the class responded that they would be fishers of men" (p. 253). In this way, each individual was expected to actively participate. The nurturing spiritual community provided children with an environment where they could develop resilience to cope with any rejection, isolation, or discrimination they experienced in the external environment.

Church members also placed great importance on positive, supportive relationships between adults and children.

Along with First Baptist Church leaders, social workers initiated and developed "an intervention, informed by knowledge generated through the ethnographic study, to support the development of children's resilience" (p. 253). This intervention strategy was the establishment of a "Computer Club" (p. 254). First Baptist Church members "both prioritized educational achievement and identified school as problematic for African-American children" (p. 254). Furthermore, children's computer literacy was perceived as "a specific area of need, and learning more about computers as an opportunity that children and families would embrace" (p. 254). Thus, members felt that enhancing children's competence in using computers was a valuable goal. Although the Computer Club's primary focus was educational computer games, student volunteers from a local university also participated with children in a range of activities, including field trips, parties, picnics, computer-generated art shows, African dance groups, and a gospel choir (p. 254). The activities provided a healthy atmosphere for students and children to enjoy mutual experiences, share ideas, and develop positive relationships.

The workers portrayed in this example first explored the values and strengths of the community and then worked together with community members toward a mutually desirable goal. The process was based on mutual respect and cooperation. Haight (1999) concludes that

> the ability of social workers to develop knowledge of cultural beliefs and practices relevant both to African-American communities in general and to the unique African-American communities in which they are practicing is critical to the development of ethnic-sensitive social work interventions such as the Computer Club. (p. 255)

The Navajo Community, Spirituality, and Respect for Older Adult Members

Sue and Sue (2008) reflect on Native Americans' (First Nations Peoples) view of spirituality and life:

> The sacred Native American beliefs concerning spirituality are a truly alien concept to modern Euro-American thinking. The United States has had a long tradition in believing that one's religious beliefs should not enter into scientific or rational decisions (Duran, 2006). Incorporating religion in the rational decision-making process or in the conduct of therapy has generally been seen as unscientific and unprofessional. The schism between religion and science occurred centuries ago and has resulted in a split between science/psychology and religion (Fukuyama & Sevig, 1999). This is reflected in the oft-quoted phrase "separation of Church and State." The separation has become a serious barrier to mainstream psychology's [and medicine's] incorporation of indigenous forms of healing into mental health [and other health] practice, especially when religion is confused with spirituality. While people may not have a formal religion, indigenous helpers believe that spirituality is an intimate aspect of the cognitive, and affective realms, it only makes passing reference to the spiritual realm of existence. Yet indigenous helpers believe that spirituality transcends time and space, mind and body, and our behaviors, thoughts, and feelings (Lee & Armstrong, 1995; D. Smith, 2005). (pp. 225–226)

The Navajo community traditionally has maintained a rich fabric of spiritual beliefs intertwined with its cultural traditions and values. It is a community because of its intricate interpersonal relationships, sense of identity, and recognition of members' belonging regardless of where they reside. Many Navajos live on the Navajo reservation, a large geographical community located in the south central Colorado Plateau including parts of Arizona, New Mexico, and Utah.

An ongoing theme in social work practice is the importance of responding to diverse ethnic, cultural, and spiritual values and needs. This example portrays how the Navajo community has responded to meet the needs of aging members in ways differing from commonly held European Caucasian traditions. First, values focusing on spiritual beliefs and family centrality are discussed. Subsequently, a Navajo community's nursing home's responsiveness to meeting Navajo residents' needs is explored.

Traditional Navajo elders, referred to here as "Grandparents," adhere to cultural values that differ from European Caucasian traditions. For one thing, Mercer (1996) explains that

> traditional Navajo religion deals with controlling the many supernatural powers in the Navajo world. Earth Surface People (living and dead humans) and Holy People (supernatural beings) interact. . . . Navajos abide by prescriptions and proscriptions (taboos) given by the Holy People to maintain harmony with others, nature, and supernatural forces. . . . The goal of traditional Navajo life is to live in harmony and die of old age. If one indulges in excesses, has improper contacts with dangerous powers, or deliberately or accidentally breaks other rules, then disharmony, conflict, evil, sickness of body and mind, misfortune, and disaster result. (pp. 182–183)

Thus, when an imbalance occurs, a person may become sick, which can be attributed to "infection by animals, natural phenomena, or evil spirits such as ghosts (*chindi*) and witches" (p. 183). Preventive ceremonies can address the root of the illness, involve the appropriate Holy People, seek to restore harmony, and avoid ill fortune. "As major social and religious events involving entire communities, ceremonies are a major investment of time and resources for the afflicted person, extended family, and clan" (p. 183).

Another primary traditional value in Navajo life is the importance placed on the extended family. Referred to as a clan, such families include a much more extensive membership than that of grandparents, parents, and children. The Navajo community has "over 60 clan-based kinship groups." A related concept is the importance of the *hogan*, or home, as the center of Navajo family life.

Mercer (1996) explored the treatment of senior Navajo people, the Grandparents, who reside in the Chinle Nursing Home, a nonprofit agency whose Board of Directors is composed solely of Navajos. She investigated how treatment for Grandparents in the Chinle home differed from typical treatment provided outside of the reservation. She found that, essentially, the Chinle home emphasized the importance of spiritual values and *cultural care*, "the learned and transmitted values and beliefs that enable people to maintain their well-being and health and to deal with illness, disability and death" (Leininger, 1990, 1992; Mercer, 1996, p. 186).

Mercer (1996) found that culturally and spiritually sensitive care is applied in at least six major areas: "communication; clan associations and social structure;

personal space, modesty, privacy, and cleanliness; traditional food; dying and death; and cultural rituals" (pp. 186–188).

1. *Communication.* Few Navajo Grandparents are fluent in English, so translators are used. Such translation is done with great sensitivity, as often the Navajo language has no word that means exactly what an English word does. Additionally, sensitivity is important while listening, as interrupting a speaker is considered extremely rude.

2. *Clan associations and social structure.* Clan associations are very important to Navajo people. Upon introduction, Navajos traditionally announce their clan membership. Nursing home staff are sensitive to the fact that Grandparents would often have many visitors from their clan who traveled great distances at significant cost.

3. *Personal space, modesty, privacy, and cleanliness.* The Grandparents value personal space. They often find it difficult and uncomfortable to sleep in the high nursing home beds, having been accustomed to mattresses or sheep skins on the floor. Staff comply with Grandparents' wishes to sleep where they want and usually find that Grandparents eventually adjust to sleeping in beds.

   Grandparents value modesty and privacy. Therefore, communal showering is a problem. Rather, Grandparents often prefer sweat baths, which they feel cleanse them both physically and spiritually. The nursing home provides saunas to simulate these sweat baths and offers showers to residents twice each week.

   Finally, Grandparents often prefer sleeping in their daytime clothes rather than changing into nightgowns or pajamas. Staff allow Grandparents to sleep in whatever they want. In due time, most come to choose night clothes.

4. *Traditional food.* Grandparents prefer "grilled mutton [meat of a mature sheep], mutton stew, fry bread, corn, fried potatoes, and coffee" (p. 187). In response, nursing home staff serve lamb three times a month and usually bake fresh bread. Staff also encourage family members to bring foods the Grandparents prefer (that is, those that comply with health-related dietary constraints).

5. *Dying and death.* "Traditional Navajo people have many restrictions regarding contact with the dead. They do not talk about death, believing that discussing death may 'bring it to you'" (p. 187). Navajo families will usually move a dying person to a nearby brush shelter to avoid having death occur in the *hogan.* In the event of a home death, that *hogan* is usually deserted and even demolished.

   Traditionally, people touching a dead body followed specific rituals to avoid taboos. Similarly, most Grandparents and staff want to avoid touching a dead person or a dead person's clothing. Usually, a dying Grandparent is transferred to a hospital so that death will not occur in the nursing home. If a death does occur there, cleansing rituals are performed before other residents inhabit the room.

   Because of their aversion to talking about death, no Grandparents will discuss such issues as living wills or power of attorney. Staff respect this value and do not pressure residents to do so.

6. *Cultural rituals.* In order to hold cultural rituals, a *hogan* was constructed near the Chinle home and is made available for ceremonies and prayers that remain important aspects of Grandparents' lives.

The point here for social workers is the importance of understanding, appreciating, and respecting the values inherent in any spiritual community. Practice should then focus on emphasizing clients' strengths and meeting clients' needs within their own value system.

Empowerment of People with Developmental Disabilities

Bill, age thirty-five, has always lived with his parents. He has an energetic, upbeat personality and a moderate intellectual disability (traditionally referred to as mental retardation). His favorite activity is delivering mail as a volunteer to staff and patients at a local hospital. This is a bit tricky as he can't read. However, hospital staff, who appreciate his efforts and enthusiasm, have established a special color coding system to help him through the delivery process. Hospital staff all know him, watch for him, and assist him in carrying out his task.

Bill loves wearing the special red vest declaring him an official deliverer of the mail. He enjoys talking to patients and staff, and considers himself an integral part of the hospital environment.[3]

The hospital environment identified in this vignette provides an empowering organizational environment for Bill, an adult with an intellectual disability. People enjoy Bill's presence, support him, and include him in daily hospital life. Bill feels like he belongs.

A primary goal of social work education is "to promote human and community well-being . . . Each person regardless of position in society, has basic human rights, such as freedom, safety, privacy, an adequate standard of living, health care, and education" (CSWE, 2008, pp. 1, 5). Thus, social workers should "advocate for human rights," "engage in practices that advance social and economic justice," and work "to improve practice, policy, and social service delivery" (CSWE, 2008, p. 5).

People with developmental disabilities are a population-at-risk, as they likely experience more difficulties in daily living, discrimination, and lack of adequate services to address their disabilities. Therefore, social workers must maintain sharp awareness of how the macro social environment affects people with developmental disabilities, their choices, and their behavior (Rothman, 2003). Communities and organizations in the macro social environment can serve to promote or deter their optimal well-being. Bill's example shows how an organization in a community has adapted itself to empower Bill. Means of empowerment in organizational and community environments for people with developmental disabilities is the primary theme of the remainder of this chapter. This topic is given significant attention here because of its importance to practitioners and because it often receives minimal coverage in other social work textbooks.

---

[3] This vignette is loosely adapted from one described by J. P. Kretzmann and J. L. McKnight in *Building Communities from the Inside Out* (Chicago: ACTA Publications, 1993).

Defining Developmental Disabilities

Five attributes characterize people with developmental disabilities (CDC, 2009a; Maryland Developmental Disabilities Council, 2006; P.L. 101–496, 104 Stat. 1191, 1990). First, the disability is both severe and chronic, resulting from some mental or physical impairment. Second, the disability occurs before age twenty-two. Third, the conditions are likely to be permanent. Fourth, the disability "results in substantial functional limitations in three or more of the following areas of major life activity: (i) self-care, (ii) receptive and expressive language, (iii) learning, (iv) mobility, (v) self-direction, (vi) capacity for independent living, and (vii) economic self-sufficiency" (P.L. 101–496, 104 Stat. 1191, 1990). Fifth, a developmental disability demonstrates the need for lifelong supplementary help and services.

Examples of developmental disabilities are intellectual disabilities (sometimes referred to as cognitive disabilities), cerebral palsy, epilepsy, hearing impairment or deafness, visual impairment or blindness, and autism spectrum disorders (CDC, 2009a). Each results in serious implications for living in the macro social environment that will be discussed in the following sections.

Intellectual Disabilities *Intellectual disabilities* involve a condition defined by three criteria. First, there is "significantly subaverage general intellectual functioning (Criterion A) that is accompanied by significant limitations in adaptive functioning in at least two of the following skill areas: communication, self-care, home living, social/interpersonal skills, use of community resources, self-direction, functional academic skills, work leisure, health, and safety (Criterion B). The onset must occur before age 18 years (Criterion C)" (American Psychiatric Association [APA], 2000, p. 41). Highlight 12.3 discusses the use of terms to refer to this population-at-risk.

The first criterion for intellectual disabilities concerns scoring significantly below average on standard intelligence tests. The second criterion involves adaptive functioning, which the APA defines as

Highlight 12.3	Terms for People with Intellectual Disabilities

Note that the technical medical diagnosis for intellectual disabilities is still *mental retardation*. As legislation also uses that term, it will not go away. Because of the term's negative connotations, a preferred term is *intellectual disabilities* (Friend, 2008; Noble, 2008). You may also "hear the term *cognitive impairment* or *cognitive disability* or *mental impairment* or *mental disability*" (Friend, 2008, p. 240). We need to choose some specific term so we know what type of developmental disability we're talking about. The term *developmental disability* is much too broad, as it comprises various disabilities.

An empowerment perspective focuses on abilities, not on retardation. It is also important to refer to *people* with intellectual disabilities as people before referring to any disability they might have. For example, referring to them as *mentally* or *cognitively challenged* people tends to emphasize the disability because the disability is stated first. Our intent is simply to respect their right to equality and dignity. As there is no easy answer, we will continue using the term *intellectual disabilities* here.

how effectively individuals cope with common life demands and how well they meet the standards of personal independence expected of someone in their particular age group, sociocultural background, and community setting. Adaptive functioning may be influenced by various factors, including education, motivation, personality characteristics, social and vocational opportunities, and the mental disorders and general medical conditions that may coexist with Mental Retardation. Problems in adaptation are more likely to improve with remedial efforts than is the cognitive IQ, which tends to remain a more stable attribute. (APA, 2000, p. 42)

Individuals with intellectual disabilities, to some degree, are unable intellectually to grasp concepts and function as well and as quickly as their peers. It is estimated that between 1 and 3 percent of the population has intellectual disabilities (Goldenring, 2004).

Cerebral Palsy   *Cerebral palsy* is a disability involving problems in muscular control and coordination resulting from damage to the brain before it has matured, that is, before or during birth. Problems include lack of balance, problems walking, paralysis, weakness, uncontrolled or restricted movements, and psychological impairment, depending on where the brain damage occurred (DeWeaver, 1995; Hallahan & Kauffman, 2006). It should be emphasized that people with cerebral palsy may experience only motor impairment, with cognitive ability being unaffected.

Seizure Disorder   *Seizure disorder* (often referred to as *epilepsy*) is an abrupt change in one's conscious state that may involve unconsciousness, convulsive and/or jerky motor activity, or sensory distortions (Friend, 2008; Hallahan & Kauffman, 2006). Seizures are caused by sudden bursts of electrical activity in some brain cells causing reaction in other brain cells. Epilepsy can result from virtually any type of injury inflicted on the brain, including insufficient oxygen, chemical imbalances, infections, or physical damage (Hallahan & Kauffman, 2006).

Hearing Impairment   *Hearing impairment* is a general concept indicating a hearing loss that can range from mild to extremely severe (Friend, 2008; Hallahan & Kauffman, 2006). Friend (2008) explains:

> People may describe themselves as being deaf, Deaf, hard of hearing, hearing impaired, or having a hearing disorder. Initially, you might think that deafness would be a simple concept describing a condition that could be diagnosed through administration of a hearing test. However, the psychological, cultural, and educational issues that are unique to individuals who have a hearing loss make it more difficult to define; it is not a simple matter of saying that an individual has a particular percentage of a hearing loss. Examples of considerations include the age of onset of the hearing loss, the cause of the hearing loss, the age at which intervention began, the family response, the hearing status of the family, the presence of additional disabilities, and the type of education program attended. (p. 310)

Highlight 12.4 addresses the significance of the Deaf community and Deaf culture.

Visual Impairment   *Visual impairment* is difficulty in perception compared to the norm that is experienced through sight. Many people have a mild visual

Highlight 12.4	The Significance of the Deaf Community and Deaf Culture

Friend (2008) describes the importance of the Deaf community:

> It is . . . important to recognize use of the term *Deaf* with a capitalized *D.* This term is used to refer to members of the **Deaf community** who embrace **Deaf culture,** a unique subset of American society (Padden & Humphries, 1988). Membership in the Deaf community varies from place to place. Factors often mentioned as important for Deaf culture identity include (1) being deaf; (2) using **American Sign Language (ASL)** as a primary means of communicating, which is a visual-gesturing language that has its own rules of grammar distinct from English; and (3) attending a residential school for the deaf (Lane, Hoffmeister, & Bahan, 1996).
>
> However, the fundamental value of Deaf culture is that deafness is not a disability—that it is not a condition that needs to be "fixed." Instead, deafness is viewed as an identity with its own rich history, traditions, and language. The Deaf community often organizes local, regional, state, national, and international events such as conferences, athletic competitions, art shows, plays, and pageants. (p. 311)

impairment correctable by glasses or contact lenses. People of special concern here are those whose vision cannot be corrected and therefore experience significant functional limitations. *Legal blindness* is the condition where a person

> has visual acuity [sharpness of perception] of 20/200 or less in the better eye even with correction (e.g., eyeglasses [or contact lenses]) or has a field of vision so narrow that its widest diameter [extends] . . . a distance no greater than 20 degrees. The fraction 20/200 means that the person sees at 20 feet what a person with normal vision sees at 200 feet. (Normal visual acuity is thus 20/20.) The inclusion of a narrowed field of vision in the legal definition means that a person may have 20/20 vision in the central field but severely restricted peripheral vision. Legal blindness qualifies a person for certain legal benefits, such as tax advantages and money for special materials. (Hallahan & Kauffman, 2006, p. 361)

Autism and Autism Spectrum Disorders   *Autism* is characterized by at least three conditions (NICHHD, 2008; Sigelman & Rider, 2009). The first is the inability to participate in normal social interaction. Austistic children have trouble "responding appropriately to social cues" and "sharing social experiences with other people" (Sigelman & Rider, 2009, p. 473). It's difficult for them to share their emotions with others, and to comprehend other people's thoughts and feelings (NICHHD, 2008). The second characteristic of autism is the inability to communicate with others. This involves the interpretation of and ability to use both verbal and nonverbal communication. The third condition characterizing autism is the demonstration of repetitive movements and rigid routines. For example, people who are autistic might "engage in stereotyped behaviors such as rocking, flapping their hands in front of their faces, or spinning toys; if they are more intellectually able, they may carry out elaborate rituals such as a particular sequence of getting-dressed activities. They also become obsessed with particular objects and interests and can become highly distressed when their physical environment is altered (as when a chair in the living room is moved a few feet)" (Sigelman & Rider, 2009, p. 474).

Autism is one of a range of conditions on what has more recently been referred to as *autism spectrum disorders*. This is a group of disorders having characteristics similar to those of autism that range from very mild to very severe (Friend, 2008; NICHHD, 2008). Note that each person with any of these disabilities "may have a unique combination of strengths and needs" (Friend, 2008, p. 383). In addition to autism (or autistic disorder), autism spectrum disorders include:

- *Asperger syndrome* (AS), or Asperger's disorder—much like mild autism, but usually without significant delays in cognition and language [For example, a person with AS might do reasonably well in school and be fairly adept at communication. However, that person might also find it difficult establishing "normal" interpersonal relationships in addition to feeling the compulsive need to control his or her environment.] [Note that autism and AS are the most prevalent disorders in the autism spectrum.]
- *Rett Syndrome*—normal development for five months to four years, followed by regression and mental retardation; much more prevalent in females
- *Childhood disintegrative disorder*—normal development for a least 2 and up to 10 years, followed by significant loss of skills; much more prevalent in males
- *Pervasive developmental disorder not otherwise specified* (PDD-NOS)—persons who display behaviors typical of autism but to a lesser degree and/or with an onset later than three years of age. (Hallahan & Kauffman, 2006, p. 399; Smith, 2007)

Concept Summary 12.1 | **Developmental Disabilities**

Developmental disability: A condition that is severe and chronic, occurs before age twenty-two, is likely permanent, results in functional limitations in at least three areas, and demonstrates the need for lifelong supplementary help and services.

Intellectual disabilities: A condition where there is "significantly subaverage general intellectual functioning . . . accompanied by significant limitations in adaptive functioning" in at least two areas, and that has an onset occurring before age eighteen (APA, 2000, p. 41).

Cerebral palsy: A disability involving problems in muscular control and coordination resulting from damage to the brain before it has matured, that is, before or during birth.

Seizure disorder (epilepsy): An abrupt change in one's conscious state that may involve unconsciousness, convulsive and/or jerky motor activity, or sensory distortions.

Hearing impairment: A general concept indicating a hearing loss that can range from mild to extremely severe.

Visual impairment: Difficulty in perception compared to the norm that is experienced through sight.

Autism: A condition characterized by the inability to participate in normal social interaction, the inability to communicate with others, and the demonstration of repetitive movements and rigid routines.

Autism spectrum disorders: A group of disorders having characteristics similar to those of autism that range from very mild to very severe. (These include *Asperger syndrome*, a condition "much like autism, but usually without significant delays in cognition and language" [Hallahan & Kauffman, 2006, p. 399]).

Critical Thinking Questions 12.6

Do you know of anyone who has one of these developmental disabilities? If so, which one? Describe the person's characteristics. What kinds of support does the person need and get? What difficulties, if any, does the person experience? What are the person's strengths, and how can they be used to empower the person?

Treatment of People with Developmental Disabilities Yesterday and Today: Quests for Social and Economic Justice

Because of the difficulties experienced by people with developmental disabilities, community support systems and available agency resources are extremely important. How community residents and macro-level decision makers view people with developmental disabilities has tremendous implications concerning the latter's quality of life. To more fully understand the macro social environment's impacts, Mary (1998) describes in the following sections how community attitudes and resulting social policies have changed over recent decades.

Prior to the Late 1960s

Until the late 1960s, community treatment and public policy emphasized individual pathology. The medical model formed the basis for conceptualizing developmental disabilities. People were considered "patients," with caregivers focusing on individual diagnoses and the resulting problems (Mary, 1998, p. 249). Many people with developmental disabilities were placed in large state or regional institutions where they received custodial care and were kept clean and safe. These times obviously did not foster the current strong professional values of client self-determination and empowerment.

The 1970s and 1980s

The 1970s to early 1980s saw significant changes in how people with developmental disabilities were viewed. Principles becoming important, especially for people with intellectual disabilities, were "normalization," deinstitutionalization, "individual program planning," and "the developmental model" (Mary, 1998, p. 249).

Normalization *Normalization* is the belief "that every individual, even [those with the most severe disabilities] . . . should have an educational and living environment as close to normal as possible" (Hallahan & Kauffman, 2006, p. 537). Prior to the late 1960s, people with developmental disabilities were placed out of sight and mind in obscurely located institutions. During the 1970s and 1980s, however, communities and organizations started viewing such people as clients who had a right to live as normally as possible. Clients now had rights. This approach "shifted much of the problem from the individual to the environment" (Mary, 1998, p. 250). Instead of focusing on people's negative diagnoses, emphasis was placed on the importance of the social environment for an individual's quality of life.

Deinstitutionalization   A parallel concept to normalization is *deinstitutionalization*, the process of providing services and care for people within their own communities rather than in institutional settings. Their residences included "both large and small intermediate care facilities and group and family care homes" (Mary, 1998, p. 250). Sometimes, these facilities are referred to as community-based residential facilities (CBRFs). As explained earlier, this concept assumes that the more people with developmental disabilities can be assimilated into the community and live "normal" lives, the better their quality of life will be.

Although the thought to deinstitutionalize services was good and there were many successes, there were also significant problems. For one thing, clients simply being placed in the community did not necessarily mean integration or acceptance in that community (Mary, 1998). It did not mean automatic attitude readjustments on the part of community residents to alter their old stereotypes and unfounded fears about people with developmental disabilities.

Another problem with deinstitutionalization concerned inadequate community resources and services. Institutions were expensive, but so were community-based services. People could get lost and be severed from service provision altogether. Frequently, community-based services were furnished "by a complex and often fragmented set of local and state agencies" providing an unevenly distributed conglomeration of public and private services (Freedman, 1995, p. 722). Service provision could be confusing to clients and their families, as some services were available to the general public and others only to those with specific disabilities (DeWeaver, 1995). (Sometime, try calling the Social Security Office to get some specific information about a case. See how well you understand what's going on—and you're a current or future social worker at that.) Other criticisms of deinstitutionalization included people being discharged too quickly and sometimes inappropriately (for example, without adequate planning or resources for continued community service provision) (DeWeaver, 1995).

Individual Program Planning   Social workers, often functioning as case managers, developed *individual programs*, a second principle espoused in the 1970s and 1980s. (A *case manager* is a designated person who seeks out services, plans how they might be delivered, coordinates service provision, and monitors progress on the behalf of a client, usually one having ongoing multiple needs [Kirst-Ashman & Hull, 2009b].) Such individual programs emphasized people's environments and intervention results that would enhance people's functioning within those environments. Intervention stressed helping people with disabilities "achieve their maximum potential in the least restrictive setting possible" (Mary, 1998, p. 150). The concept of *least restrictive environment* concerns the encouragement of clients to enjoy as much freedom and make as many decisions for themselves as they can. This concept is related to normalization and deinstitutionalization. People living in the community should be more likely to live "normal" lives and make their own decisions than those living in institutional care. Program evaluation for organizational effectiveness was also stressed.

The Developmental Model   The fourth important concept during the 1970s and 1980s was that treatment should be based on a *developmental model* that espoused a continuum of service. People received services depending on the intensity and type of their needs. People with developmental disabilities were *clients* whom professionals assessed in terms of their needs. These professionals then determined necessary services depending on where the clients fell on the developmental continuum of service. You might picture a ruler. If a client was assessed as functioning at the 6.25-inch point, then that client would receive the services appropriate for that exact point. Likewise, a client at the 10-inch point would receive services designated for that level of assessment. Emphasis was not placed on the individual as a unique personality, but rather on the assessed level of need and the designated services available to address that need.

Often, clients' needs change over time. One assumption was that many clients made progress toward greater independence in a step-by-step process. A client had to master one skill first before attempting a more difficult one. For example, a young woman with mild intellectual disabilities might start out living in a group home where she could learn basic housekeeping, cooking, and self-care skills, including shopping and paying bills. She might then move to an apartment complex or boarding house for people with intellectual disabilities. Houseparents or residential caregivers would not be living with her, but they would be available in another apartment to help her with problems or questions. Eventually, the woman might achieve enough self-care mastery to live on her own or with a roommate.

Other clients' needs change over time but require increasing levels of help and assistance. A person with a deteriorating orthopedic problem involving his knees might require increasingly more intensive help as he loses mobility. Depending on his assessed state of need at any point in time, in the 1970s and 1980s he would receive a designated level of service.

The 1990s and Beyond: Consumer Empowerment

The 1990s brought with them a significantly greater emphasis on individual choice and personalized planning for people with developmental disabilities than there was in earlier decades (Freedman, 1995; Mary, 1998; Raske, 2005; Rothman, 2003). Essentially, such an emphasis laid the foundation for an empowerment approach. Before, people with developmental disabilities were *clients* whom professionals assessed and provided services prescribed for their level of functioning. There was relatively little variation of service provision at the assessed level. Today's perspective reflects three new important concepts—consumers, choice, and innovation.

Clients as Consumers   Today, practitioners should stress a much more individualized approach, characterized by two major principles (Mary, 1998; Mackelprang & Salsgiver, 2009). First, "services are driven by client needs, and clients are viewed as *consumers* with choices" (p. 253). The term *consumer* implies greater power and choice than does the term *client*. Consumers choose their purchases or resource providers within a competitive market rather than having someone else make these choices for them. Second, "service delivery mechanisms allow for innovative provision of supports to help children stay with families, and adults live as independently as possible" (p. 253). Innovation is stressed to develop unique avenues of service provision in response to individual needs.

Emphasis on Choice   One key word here is *choice*. Here the ruler concept explained earlier no longer applies. Rather, clients are encouraged to assess the choices available and decide what supports they want and what goals they wish to pursue.

Mackelprang and Salsgiver (2009) promote the "independent living model"; they reflect:

> Traditional models view people with disabilities as patients and clients. The independent living model views persons with disabilities as individuals, citizens, consumers, and/or participants in service. The roles of professionals . . . are also different. They may be considered experts in their field; however, that expertise does not translate into control over people's lives (White, Gutierrez, & Seekins, 1996). Instead, they act as consultants and assistants. Their roles are akin to those of financial investment consultants, who educate and sell investment packages to consumers. However, decisions rest with consumers, who decide whether they act on the advice of their consultants. (p. 429)

Consider Bertram, age forty-four, a quadriplegic whose condition is the result of a congenital spinal cord malformation. Instead of professionals assessing his capabilities and designating where it is best for him to live, he can make that decision himself. With practitioners and other caregiving professionals' input regarding what resources and services are available, Bertram can determine the environment providing him with what he perceives as the highest quality of life. Of course, his choices are influenced by his own capabilities and the resources available. It is impossible for Bertram to live in an apartment alone with no supportive help. His viable choices might include living in a nursing home or a group home for people with severe physical disabilities, staying in an apartment with the necessary supportive attendants, or living with his family whose members would serve as primary caregivers (assuming, of course, that they were willing to do so).

   Critical Thinking Questions 12.7

If you were Bertram, what alternative would you prefer? What do you think your major concerns would be?

Another example is Heriberto, who has cerebral palsy resulting in major difficulty controlling his arm movements. With professional help and practice, he has learned to dress himself if his clothes have zippers and no buttons. However, it takes him over an hour each time and leaves him physically exhausted. A personal care attendant can do the job in about four minutes. Heriberto might choose to have the attendant help him dress even though this option reflects less independence. His choice might be in his best interest to save him substantial time and energy (Renz-Beaulaurier, 1998).

Critical Thinking Questions 12.8

If you were Heriberto, what choice do you think you would make for yourself and why?

Innovation A vital word in today's approach toward working with people with developmental disabilities is *innovation,* the initiation, development, and application of new ideas. Innovative service provision may involve a totally unique combination of services depending on what an individual wishes to accomplish. In other words, "consumers define their own vision of the future—where they want to live, learn, work, and recreate—in a community that they define" (Mary, 1998, p. 253).

For example, Emmaline, age seven, has spina bifida, "a condition in which the spinal column fails to close properly" (Hallahan & Kauffman, 2003, p. 118). The split may occur at any point along the bones supporting the spinal column; the unprotected spinal nerves may be exposed and damaged, resulting in paralysis below that point (Hallahan & Kauffman, 2003). Emmaline has an individualized service plan designed to meet her unique needs. She can live at home with an innovative combination of supports. A motorized wheelchair maximizes her mobility. Family counseling provides her parents with information and help in responding to Emmaline's special needs. A wheelchair-accessible van provides her with transportation to and from school. A teacher's aid assists her with any help she needs in completing school assignments. Designated medical staff help Emmaline and her family meet her special health and surgical needs.

Current Emphasis on the Empowerment Approach

The empowerment approach continues to reflect our most current perspective on service provision for people with disabilities (Mackelprang & Salsgiver, 2009; Rothman, 2003). It focuses on what people can do, not what they cannot. Pfeiffer (2005) discusses the misconceptions about disability:

(1) Disability is not a tragedy; (2) disability does not mean dependency; (3) disability does not mean a loss of potential, productivity, social contribution, value, capability, ability, and the like; (4) disability is a natural part of life, everyone's life; and (5) there is as much variation between people with disabilities as between people in general.

In other words, disability does not mean grief, guilt, and bitterness. People with disabilities are not courageous, noble, and brave any more than any one else. People with disabilities can be very sexual and sensual. People with disabilities can be very good parents. People with disabilities are not poor unless they are unemployed. People with disabilities are not ignorant unless they were segregated from mainstream education and even then many are quite brilliant in spite of so-called special education. People with disabilities do not have to be with "their own kind," whatever that means. (p. 38)

Critical Thinking Questions 12.9

What are your reactions to these statements about the misconceptions of disability? To what extent do you automatically respond positively or negatively to them? Explain why.

Rothman (2003) addresses the empowerment of individuals with disabilities:

The empowerment model assists clients to achieve their potential and to promote changes in their environment and in social policy that will promote social justice. (Lee, 1996, p. 230)

Society has described the person with disabilities as a "victim" or a "tragedy" with which one must cope. Critiques of this assumption present the concept that (1) disability is not always as disastrous a condition for the individual as . . . people [without disabilities] think and that (2) it is not the disabling condition itself, but societal reactions to it that create difficulties and victimize the . . . person [with a disability] (Black, 1994, pp. 409–410).

Redefining disability to focus not on what is "wrong" with the individual but rather on what limits his or her ability to function in society moves us away from the medical model and toward a more social work-appropriate model that involves the full range of both individual and environmental assessment that is an essential part of the social work processes (Black, 1994, pp. 396–397).

The strengths assessment is an especially useful tool in working with the empowerment model of practice. By focusing on the client's strengths, the worker can help the client to motivate and to see himself or herself as actor, rather than acted upon. Empowerment practice involves the worker in helping the client to act, rather than in acting on his or her behalf. (pp. 210–211)

Rothman (2003) continues by discussing an empowerment approach with respect to people with disabilities as a community:

The empowerment model for communities is an extension of the empowerment model for individuals and is built upon the same foundations: that human dignity and respect are an essential part of optimal functioning, and that oppression, exclusion, and discrimination undermine self-esteem. On this broader level, empowerment focuses on supporting a feeling of group competence, connectedness, and the group's ability to effect change for the good of all of the members of the group. The skills, abilities, and personal characteristics of each member of the group are used together to promote and achieve the mutually determined goals. (p. 226)

People with developmental disabilities continue to suffer widespread discrimination (Karger & Stoesz, 2010). Focus on Ethics 12.1 describes a case example of discrimination against a person with disabilities and raises questions about the ethics involved in decisions made about her.

Focus on Ethics 12.1	**Case Example: Discrimination against a Person with a Disability**

Sandra, a thirty-five-year-old woman with Down syndrome, was denied a heart-lung transplant even though insurance covered the $250,000 necessary for the operation (Shapiro, 1995). Down syndrome is a congenital type of mental retardation "characterized by moderate to severe mental retardation, slanting eyes, a broad short skull, [and] broad hands with short fingers" (Mish, 2008, p. 377). The two hospitals approved for conducting this type of surgery "made issue of her intelligence and rejected her" (Shapiro, 1995, p. 59). One hospital administrator allegedly said, "We do not feel that patients with Down syndrome are appropriate candidates for heart-lung transplantation" (Shapiro, 1995, p. 59). Others at the hospitals indicated that they doubted she could maintain the rigorous medical requirements involved in taking medication and monitoring her health after the operations.

Sandra and her doctor strongly disagree with these allegations. Sandra has bussed tables in a public cafeteria, lives in her own apartment, and has "testified eloquently before committees" on the behalf of people with developmental disabilities (Shapiro, 1995, p. 59). Sandra already had assumed responsibility for taking various medications and monitoring her blood pressure every day. Publicity compelled the hospitals to reconsider her plea. Without the surgery Sandra only had a few years to live.

To what extent do you feel that the hospitals' decisions and their rationales were reasonable? To what extent were these decisions fair and ethical? What do you think should or should not have been done? Explain your reasons.

Generalist Social Work Practice with People Who Have Developmental Disabilities

May (2005) comments on how people with disabilities are treated differently than other populations-at-risk:

> Great effort is expended to ensure that everyone understands the value of diversity (read "deviation") in contemporary U.S. Culture. Not so when disability is the issue. Here, the focus is on "restoring" the person who is labeled "disabled" so he or she no longer deviates from normative expectations. There is no systematic effort to identify sources of pride or to instill positive connotations on being "disabled."
>
> The implications for social workers and other intentional helpers are profound and require a "working with" orientation with the . . . client [who has a disability] versus a "working on" orientation. From this "working with" perspective, the client system is not merely the collection of difficulties or clinical symptomatology, but is one component of an interactive system that may produce impairment. Solutions, then, are not to be found solely in the person with the disability, but in the larger social environment. (p. 84)

Social workers often must use brokering, case management, and advocacy skills to provide effective services. *Brokering* is the linkage of clients (consumers) to needed resources. *Case management* is the process of organizing, coordinating, and maintaining "a network of formal and informal supports and activities designed to optimize the functioning and well-being of people with multiple needs" (Moxley, 1989, p. 21). Obviously, many people with developmental disabilities require an innovative range of services to maximize self-determination and pursue an optimal quality of life. The key here is coordinating and monitoring services so that clients with ongoing or changing needs get these needs met.

Advocacy is "a process of affecting or initiating change either with or on behalf of client groups to:

- *obtain services or resources that would not otherwise be provided*
- *modify or influence policies or practices that adversely affect groups or communities*
- *promote legislation or policies that will result in the provision of requisite resources or service*" (Hepworth, Rooney, Rooney, Strom-Gottfried, & Larson, 2010, p. 430)

There is usually no problem when adequate resources and services are available. However, in reality, this is usually not the case. When clients are not getting their needs met, it is the practitioner's responsibility to advocate on their behalf. Resources may require redistribution. Policies may require change and improvement. New services may need development.

One facet of advocacy is helping clients advocate for themselves when they are capable instead of doing everything for them (Mackelsprang & Salsgiver, 2009). This is another form of client empowerment. For example, it might be easy for Kofi, a social worker, to advocate for his client Thanasi, age thirty-eight, who has *muscular dystrophy*. This condition is "any of a group of hereditary diseases characterized by a progressive wasting of the muscles" (Mish, 2008, p. 818). Thanasi was diagnosed with the disease at age twelve. Although Thanasi can take a few steps by herself, it is very difficult for her and she usually uses a motorized wheelchair. Balance is difficult, as she has lost eight of her toes from the disease. She has little strength in her arms and hands and so accomplishes tasks such as writing and eating very slowly. As muscles deteriorate, her voice is weakening, so she tries to do most of her necessary talking earlier in the day when she is stronger. Thanasi is a strong, independent person who prides herself in accomplishing her goals. For example, she has earned a bachelor's degree in accounting and is able to work part-time at her own pace.

Thanasi lives in a group home where Kofi is the social worker with other people who have physical disabilities. Thanasi has several issues to address, including some funding glitches and the need for a new wheelchair and other medical equipment. Kofi talks to Thanasi about these needs and eagerly volunteers to make the calls, write the letters, and advocate on her behalf. He is taken aback when Thanasi responds with a dour look on her face and then avoids eye contact with him. He asks her what's wrong. She hesitantly responds that she would much rather do it herself, although she admits she probably needs help negotiating the complicated maze of services. Kofi suddenly grasps the issue like being hit by a two-by-four. He backs off and volunteers to help find out whom she needs to contact and what information she needs to present. Although it will be much slower for her to advocate for herself than for him to do it, the process will empower her. Kofi decides it's best for him to support her in her advocacy efforts instead of performing the primary advocacy role himself.

An Example of Positive Legislation:
Empowerment through Social and Economic Justice

A positive piece of legislation passed in 1990 is of special significance in terms of improving access to resources in the macro social environment (Barusch, 2009;

Karger & Stoesz, 2010). The Americans with Disabilities Act of 1990 (ADA) intends to provide people with physical or mental disabilities "access to public areas and workplaces" and to blast away barriers keeping these people isolated from "the mainstream of public life" (Smolowe, 1995, p. 54). The ADA defines people with disabilities as those who have substantial physical or mental difficulties that significantly hinder at least one primary life activity, have an established record of such hindrances, or are regarded by other people as demonstrating such difficulties (Asch & Mudrick, 1995; Kopels, 1995). Impairments include those that

> substantially limit major life activities such as seeing, hearing, speaking, walking, breathing, performing manual tasks, learning, caring for oneself, and working. An individual with epilepsy, paralysis, HIV infection, AIDS, a substantial hearing or visual impairment, mental retardation, or a specific learning disability is covered, but an individual with a minor, nonchronic condition of short duration, such as a sprain, broken limb, or the flu, generally would not be covered. (U.S. Department of Justice, 2002)

The act also forbids discrimination against people "with a record of a disability" such as "cancer or mental illness," and against people perceived of as having a disability such as those "with a severe facial disfigurement" (U.S. Department of Justice, 2002). "About twenty percent of the U.S. population have disabilities that limit their ability to work" (Karger & Stoecz, 2010, p. 94).

ADA Requirements   ADA provisions help people with disabilities in at least two major ways. First, the ADA "prohibits discrimination in all employment practices, including job application procedures, hiring, firing, advancement, compensation, training, and other terms, conditions, and privileges of employment" and "applies to recruitment, advertising, tenure, layoff, leave, fringe benefits, and all other employment-related activities" (U.S. Department of Justice, 2002).

The ADA's second major thrust requires that "workplaces and public facilities provide 'reasonable accommodation' and accessibility for people with disabilities" (Segal, 2007, p. 110; U.S. Department of Justice, 2002). This means that "discriminatory practices, such as environmental and telecommunication barriers, need to be replaced with accessible structures in instances where cost would not be prohibitive" (DePoy & Gilson, 2004, p. 100).

The ADA "has legitimized the idea that the fundamental problems facing people are less medical than social and structural" (Renz-Beaulaurier, 1998, p. 81). It redefines problems as belonging to the *community*, not people with disabilities living in the community. For example, "the problem of how to get up the steps (problem within the individual) changes to how to get a ramp installed (problem outside the individual)" (Renz-Beaulaurier, 1998, p. 80).

Jansson (2005) reports on some of the ADA's "remarkable improvements" for people with disabilities:

> Elevators and ramps were added to most public buildings. Work accommodations were provided by public and private employers, including use of computer-assisted technologies, flexible work assignments, and special training programs. Lifts were placed in buses, as were reserved seats. Kitchens and bathrooms were redesigned in housing units. (p. 335)

Countering this view, Karger and Stoesz (2010) indicate:

> Despite the ADA and other federal laws, discrimination is still widespread against people with disabilities. For instance, most buildings still do not meet the needs of [people with physical disabilities] . . . in terms of access, exits, restrooms, parking lots, warning systems, and so forth. Many apartment complexes and stores continue to be built without allowing for the needs of people with disabilities. The struggle for full social, political, and economic integration remains an ongoing battle. (p. 97)

 Critical Thinking Questions 12.10

To what extent do you think the ADA has been successful in fighting discrimination and increasing access to people with disabilities? Do you know anyone with a disability? If so, what is that person's opinion?

Supreme Court Decisions and the ADA   As you know, Supreme Court decisions can shape the application of policy and refine how it's interpreted. "The ADA has generated a large body of case law, of which only a few cases are discussed here. Most of these cases focus on defining terms in the act" (Barusch, 2009, p. 275). DiNitto (2005) summarizes some court activity:

> With a more conservative Supreme Court, White House, and Congress, recent decisions have diluted the ADA. Between 1999 and 2003 rulings have favored business defendants rather than plaintiffs. In a number of cases, the court has concluded that individuals whose impairment can be corrected with medication or eyeglasses are not "truly disabled" and therefore are not entitled to protection against employment discrimination under the ADA. The "catch-22" is that some people are not "disabled enough" to receive protection under the ADA, but they are disabled enough to be refused a job or fired from a job because their physical or mental limitations, in the employer's opinion, keep them from safely and/or effectively fulfilling job requirements. (p. 183)

Focus on Ethics 12.2 addresses a specific court decision concerning what constitutes a disability and what does not.

Focus on Ethics 12.2   **What Is a "Disability"?**

Barusch (2009) identifies a court case where the court declared that two sisters were not considered "disabled"; yet, they still were not "able" enough to get the job:

> Two 1999 cases, [including] *Sutton v. United Airlines* . . . introduced the notion of "corrective" or "mitigating" measures to narrow the definition of disability. In the *Sutton* case, two sisters who had applied for jobs as airline pilots were turned down because they did not meet the airline's uncorrected vision requirement. The court rejected their complaint, holding that with assistive devices (glasses) they could perform other jobs and so did not meet the ADA definition of disability. [Yet they still couldn't be hired as pilots because they had to wear glasses.] (p. 275)

To what extent do you think the court's finding in the Sutton v. United Airlines *case was fair and ethical? Explain your reasons.*

DiNitto (2005) continues:

> To date courts have ruled against individuals with visual impairments, high blood pressure, carpal tunnel syndrome, and liver disease, and a stroke victim. In a Tennessee case, a judge ruled that a 9-year-old with spina bifida . . . did not have a disability as defined by the ADA and therefore was not permitted to keep her service animal. The U.S. Supreme Court has supported a strict definition of disability, indicating that it must interfere with essential tasks such as brushing one's teeth or washing one's face.

Barusch (2009) cites a specific case:

> In 2002 the Supreme Court ruled on the case of *Toyota Motor Mfg., Ky. v. Williams*. Williams was employed at a Toyota plant and requested accommodation for carpal tunnel syndrome. She later sued, claiming that she had been denied ADA accommodation. The Supreme Court found that, although her disability did limit her ability to perform some manual tasks, it did not limit her ability to perform major life activities such as household chores, bathing, and brushing her teeth, so she was not eligible for ADA protections. (p. 274)

One positive note involves the *L. C. & E. W. v. Olmstead* case decision by the Supreme Court in 1999. Hayashi (2005) explains:

> L. C. and E. W. were patients in a state psychiatric hospital in Georgia. They challenged their placement in an institutional setting rather than in a community-based program. The Supreme Court decided that unnecessary institutionalization of individuals with disabilities is discrimination under the ADA, and that the state must provide services in the most integrated setting appropriate to individual clients. (p. 49)

Community Support and Empowerment

Communities and organizations in the macro environment can offer resources and support to people with developmental disabilities in at least two major ways. First, mandated federal and state legislation can provide for programs available to community residents with developmental disabilities. The last sections reviewed two major pieces of federal legislation passed on the behalf of this population. Second, community residents can work together to establish their own innovative resources within the community.

Some examples of how to make progress through legislation, direct community support, and social work advocacy are presented next. The populations-at-risk addressed include people with visual impairment and those with intellectual disabilities.

Legislative Empowerment for People with Visual Impairments

The Rehabilitation Act of 1973 and its 1992 amendments approve reimbursement for some services provided by agencies for people with visual impairment specifically designated to help this population (Asch, 1995). Section 508 of the act "requires that all federal government Web sites and related materials be accessible to persons with visual impairment" (Asch & Mudrick, 2008, p. 208).

Other examples of supportive legislation are two 1930s laws that provide special employment opportunities for people who have visual impairment; the Wagner-O'Day Act (P.L. 75–739) "established a system of sheltered workshops," and the Randolph-Sheppard Act (P.L. 74–734) "gives blind people preference in obtaining employment as operators of vending facilities on federal properties" (Asch & Mudrick, 2008, p. 209). *Sheltered workshops* or *sheltered employment* provide programs "involving work in a safe, closely supervised environment for people who have trouble functioning more independently" (Kirst-Ashman, 2010, p. 39).

Additionally, people who are legally blind, unemployed, and have assets falling below prescribed levels may receive Supplemental Security Income (SSI). SSI is "a federal public assistance program that provides a minimum income to poor people who are older adults, have a disability, or are blind" (Kirst-Ashman, 2010, p. 227). Benefits are provided on the basis of need instead of one's work history.

The 1931 Pratt-Smoot Act (P.L. 71–787) provides an example of legislation making reading material more accessible for people with visual impairment; it established a Library of Congress program that later formed the foundation for regional centers providing Braille and recorded materials to people with visual impairment (Asch, 1995).

Community Empowerment for People with Visual Impairment

Laws and mandated programs may make some resources available. However, communities themselves can also enhance and make easier the lives of people with visual impairment. Community groups and government units can disseminate information concerning the issues addressed and the strengths inherent in people with visual impairment. These people and their families require relevant knowledge about legislation, available resources, and alternative approaches to completing necessary tasks of daily living (for example, doing housework, getting places, or accessing information) (Asch, 1995). Communities can sponsor self-help groups where people with visual impairment can come together, discuss issues, provide each other with ideas, and find support. Schools who have students with visual impairment can make it a point to educate parents about services, resources, and aids. Schools can encourage students with visual impairment to participate in sports, recreation, and other extracurricular and educational activities just as children with perfect vision do.

Even such a basic thing as ensuring that public buildings use Braille next to the floor indicator buttons on elevators is very helpful. Esther, a student with a visual impairment, comes to mind. She attended a state university renowned for its support of and services for students with disabilities. Esther felt that the campus focused its attention on serving people with physical disabilities involving mobility and viewed people with visual impairment as less significant. All buildings and classrooms had been readily accessible for as long as anyone could remember. She advocated for years to have Braille information installed in elevators throughout the campus with little response by university administration. After persistent pressure, she finally was able to make her point and all elevators were furnished with Braille directions.

Empowerment for People with Visual Impairment and Social Work Practice

Social workers can serve as important advocates in their communities and agencies to provide needed services for people with visual impairment. People initially dealing with visual impairment in themselves or another family member will need time to adjust to the situation and cope with its ramifications. Social workers can help people realize that the long cane ("a mobility aid used by individuals with visual impairment who sweep it in a wide arc in front of them"), a guide dog, human guides, recorded information, adapted computers, and other technological devices (such as reading machines that convert print into spoken words) can help people organize home, work, and social lives in an effective, efficient, although different, manner (Asch, 1995; Hallahan & Kauffman, 2006, p. 378).

Community Empowerment for People with Intellectual Disabilities

Because people with intellectual disabilities constitute a large proportion of people with developmental disabilities, and because they are likely to use services provided by state agencies, we will spend considerable time discussing them (Freedman, 1995). As with people who have visual impairment, legislation provides some support and programs for people with intellectual disabilities who qualify for such services. Funding for people with intellectual disabilities comes from a range of sources depending on whether individuals fulfill eligibility criteria often related to their income level. For example, Supplemental Security Income (SSI) may be available to people with intellectual disabilities whose income and assets are low enough to meet established criteria (Meyer, 1995).

Communities can creatively develop resources and programs to integrate people with intellectual disabilities and enhance their quality of life. For instance, one state has a Community Options Program (COP) funded at the state level that "provides assessments, case plans, and community services as an alternative to nursing home placements" (ARC Milwaukee, undated, b, p. 2).

ARCs and Related Resources Can Empower People and Enhance Quality of Life

One excellent example of how a community can use a support system for people with intellectual disabilities is an organization called ARC. Historically known as the Association for Retarded Citizens, ARCs now are established in communities throughout the United States. The following discussion focuses specifically on ARCs. However, the types of services ARCs provide can certainly be sponsored by other organizations and community groups.

Typically funded through a variety of sources, including donations by private citizens, corporations, local service clubs, foundations, and by government service contracts, ARCs provide a wide range of services. They reflect a creative alliance of public services, private contributions, and community groups to provide services for this population-at-risk. Potential services include information and referral service, help lines, noninstitutional residential opportunities, vocational and employment programs, support services, intervention advocacy, volunteer programs, and recreational activities.

Information and Referral Services and Help Lines

An *information and referral service* "provides information about what services and resources are available in a community and assists people in accessing them" (Kirst-Ashman, 2010, p. 315). A *help line* is an information and referral system based on telephone contact. Persons requiring information about services, laws, or issues related to a specific problem or population, in this case, intellectual disabilities, call a trained professional who connects them with the appropriate resource or provides them with necessary information. Many ARCs develop an extensive computerized system that can quickly identify relevant linkages between questions, needs, information, and resources.

Provision of Noninstitutional Living Opportunities

One type of resource that can help people with a disability maintain maximum independence and self-determination is linkage with noninstitutional living opportunities. As we discussed earlier in the context of deinstitutionalization, the intent is to place people in the least restrictive setting possible. These placements include adult family care homes where clients reside in the home of caregivers who supervise and care for them. Another setting is a group home or community-based residential care facility (CBRF). Residents often are selected on the basis of having similar needs, such as required levels of supervision and support. For example, one CBRF might have residents capable of taking care of personal needs and working at a sheltered workshop. Another CBRF might have clients who require a higher level of supervision, where staff must provide more direct input concerning how they dress, eat, and interact.

Other even more independent, supported living options include living with a roommate or by oneself in an apartment. Some limited supervision and assistance such as help with paying bills or arranging transportation to work is usually needed in these cases.

Vocational and Employment Opportunities

ARCs are also quite creative regarding provision of vocational and employment opportunities. They can assist people in gaining community employment by preparing clients for the expectations of employment, assisting in placement, helping employers restructure jobs to maximize clients' abilities to complete job tasks, and providing job coaching concerning basic work skills (such as getting to work on time and following supervisory instructions).

Individuals may also gain employment in more structured settings such as sheltered workshops. One ARC agency developed an employment program where clients made and finished ceramic gifts for special occasions such as weddings and graduations. Another ARC organization developed a work setting where clients manufactured pillows for a major national airline.

People who are unable to function in more demanding settings may receive "day services"; these aim to "maximize an individual's independent functional level in self-care, physical and emotional growth, mobility and community transportation, socialization, recreation, leisure time, and education and pre-vocational skills" (ARC Milwaukee, undated, a, p. 2).

Other Support Services

Support services can have many facets. Organizations can provide outreach support services to clients in their own homes that involve instruction in daily living skills, budgeting and financial management, transportation, parenting skills, and personal issues including interpersonal interaction, leisure activities, self-esteem, and assertiveness. Respite care programs provide care-giving services to parents or other caregivers of persons with intellectual disabilities. Caregivers can take some time off from responsibilities to give them a break and refresh their efforts. Family services geared to senior caregivers can provide support to aging caregivers who find it increasingly difficult to provide the same level of care they could in the past. For example, because of increasing strength limitations, an aging caregiver might find it much more difficult to assist a person with a severe disability in dressing himself. Family services for older adult caregivers can also provide support during crises, such as a caregiver experiencing her own acute health problems. They can also be used to assist caregivers in long-term planning for and with the person who has the disability. A common concern of aging caregivers is what will happen to the individual with a disability when the caregiver can no longer assume that function.

Support groups are another support mechanism, and they can focus on many different issues. Parent support groups "provide parents with an opportunity to get together and share stories, concerns and achievements with other parents who are experiencing similar circumstances" (ARC, undated, a, p. 2). Support groups for seniors with disabilities can give them opportunities to share concerns, discuss suggestions, and talk about how to maximize their quality of life.

Advocacy

Intervention advocacy "is designed to respond to the needs of persons with disabilities and their families when serious problems arise affecting legal rights, safety and health, financial security, or access to community resources" (ARC, undated, c, p. 2). The service system is complicated, and clients along with their families may find it very difficult to negotiate. Advocacy is often necessary to link clients with services they need and deserve. Advocacy is also essential when needed services don't exist.

Using Community Volunteers

There are numerous ways in which volunteers can help ARC programming. These include performing clerical duties and answering the phone, caring for small children while parents attend support groups, serving as a matched "friend" with a person who has a disability to provide support and encouragement, giving support via telephone to persons needing intermittent help, participating in fundraising activities, assisting at supervision of events such as group outings, and helping with household upkeep and maintenance (ARC, undated, c).

Providing Recreational Activities

Recreational activities and functions provide still another means of enhancing the quality of life for people with disabilities. Examples include ongoing athletic programs, support for Special Olympics, and operation of a summer camp where groups of clients of any age group can interact socially, work on crafts, participate in games and plays, learn appreciation for nature, increase leisure skills, and gain confidence in expressing themselves (ARC, undated, c).

 Critical Thinking Questions 12.11

Do you know a person with an intellectual disability? If so, to what resources does that person have access? What resources does that person need, but doesn't get? What are the reasons for any unavailability of resources?

Highlight 12.5 provides a case example of how a community supports and fails to support a person with an intellectual disability in some of the areas just discussed.

More Examples of Community Integration for People with Intellectual Disabilities

Kretzmann and McKnight (1993) cite a number of situations regarding how adults with intellectual disabilities can be mainstreamed[4] and integrated as part of a large urban community. The following four are adapted from their ideas:

1. Perry, age twenty-eight, thrives at playing games. Perry's neighbor acquainted him with the local Boys Club. He now volunteers there regularly, teaching children games and supervising their activities.
2. Felicita, age twenty-two, spends most weekdays at a day program with other people who have intellectual disabilities. She passes much of her time coloring and watching other residents. She is an exceptionally warm person who will light up with a dazzling smile when spoken to or given any attention. One of the day program staff introduced her to a local daycare center to see if she could help out there.

---

[4] *Mainstreaming* is "bringing people who have some exceptional characteristics into the living, working, or educational environments to which all others have access" (Barker, 2003, p. 258). Examples of such special groups include people with intellectual and other developmental disabilities.

Highlight 12.5	A Case Example: A Community Helps and Hinders Hiroshi, a Person with Intellectual Disabilities

Consider Hiroshi and how the environment both succeeds and fails to support him. Hiroshi, age fifty-eight, lives in a midwestern town of about 8,000 people in a rural farming community. Hiroshi has mild intellectual disabilities. He graduated from high school but only because in those days students like him were passed on whether they could perform the work or not. He is very proud of the high school ring he purchased at graduation. The macro environment, especially the school system, did not serve him well. Instead of receiving special services and training that might now be available, the system basically ignored him and passed him on through.

A major problem for Hiroshi is his speech. He has difficulty forming words, and he takes considerable time to structure his sentences. His comprehension of verbal communication is good, however, and he has an excellent sense of humor. His difficult speech often fools people who don't know him well into thinking he is much less competent than he really is. Speech therapy may have helped if it had been available when he was young.

Hiroshi works at a sheltered workshop in addition to working six hours per week as a janitor at Bertha's Butter Burgers. Hiroshi has a strong work history. For almost twenty years, he worked at a local tanning factory hauling deer hides from one area to another as they proceeded through the leather-making process. It was gruesome, back-breaking work. The place was doused with various chemicals. When Hiroshi got home, he was exhausted. At the time, he was living with his father, who cooked for him, did his laundry, and helped him with other daily living tasks.

Work at the tanning factory had not been without its problems. Once Hiroshi confessed to his relatives a story about another "guy at work" who liked to pick on him. Hiroshi had lots of experience being picked on. The guy liked to draw a knife and tease

Hiroshi, pretending to cut him. Once, he made quite a slit in Hiroshi's right hand. Hiroshi's confession involved payback time. One night after work, he slit all "the guy's" tires. The guy, who was fired shortly thereafter, never did find out who did it.

Hiroshi was a saver. He would wear the same pair of polyester pants for years, until the threads in the hem seams gave way. Although Hiroshi made little more than minimum wage, he put almost all of it in savings. When the plant closed and he was laid off, he had accumulated over $40,000. Investing with the help of his brother Egbert and a slick certified financial planner brought his assets to almost $200,000 by the time he turned fifty-eight. Unfortunately, this prevented him from receiving public assistance and resources because he did not meet various programs' means tests. *Means tests* involve using established criteria to evaluate clients' financial resources and to decide whether they're eligible for service.

When his father died, with Egbert's help Hiroshi was able to live in and pay rent for his own apartment. He told Egbert he preferred living alone to living with a roommate. One of Hiroshi's strengths was his strong relationship with Egbert and his family, although they lived inconveniently about 185 miles away. Hiroshi didn't see his family as often as he liked since buses were deregulated and federal regulations no longer required companies to sponsor less popular runs. Egbert and his wife were periodically forced to endure a gravely dull three-hour trip through flat farmland to pick Hiroshi up and another three hours to drive him home.

A major strength in Hiroshi's life was his involvement with the local Center for People with Developmental Disabilities, an agency that did not have a means test. In its sheltered workshop, Hiroshi felt productive and established many social contacts. As one of the highest-functioning clients, he achieved significant social status. At the center's periodic social dances, he was quite accomplished

continued

Highlight 12.5 | *continued*

and admired. Hiroshi also had a knack for taking pictures and videos, which he did regularly at the center's events. The center sponsored or cosponsored numerous events, including Special Olympics, bowling tournaments, picnics, and outings to movies in nearby towns. Hiroshi was extremely proud of a Volunteer's Award Plaque he received from the center for all of the conscientious time he spent photographing and videorecording events.

At the center he was assigned a case manager, Cornelia, who evaluated his daily living skills. She linked him with a trainer who tried to teach him how to cook. However, Hiroshi didn't like to cook and so ended up subsisting mostly on TV dinners. It might be noted that Egbert, who had superior intelligence, did not "know how" to boil water. He didn't like to cook either. Cornelia also helped coordinate any other supportive services Hiroshi might need with Egbert and his family.

Although Cornelia and Egbert tried to encourage Hiroshi to manage his own finances and checkbook, this was too difficult for him. Hiroshi didn't like making computations or sending checks, and he typically made significant mistakes. When mail-ordering gifts for family members, he would always send cash despite the risk of losing it. Egbert finally gave up and determined that it was easier just to keep track of Hiroshi's finances himself than to keep after Hiroshi on a regular basis.

Another major community strength was the support Hiroshi received from his church. He attended services regularly and was involved in a group called The Sunday Evening Club, consisting of adult church members who met every other Sunday for a pot-luck dinner and a chance to socialize or hear speakers.

Hiroshi's work at Bertha's was helpful in terms of making him feel useful and conserving his savings. However, the six-hour weekly work allocation was minimal. The management could have given him many more hours if they had not viewed him as an inadequate, "retarded" person. The town provided no public transportation, so Hiroshi had to walk to get anywhere, including two miles to work.

In summary, community strengths for Hiroshi include the Center for People with Developmental Disabilities; its sheltered workshop; his case manager, Cornelia, responsible for Hiroshi's care; public recognition by receiving a Volunteer's Award; his spiritual involvement at church; his job at Bertha's; and strong connections with his family despite the fact that they lived so far away. For Hiroshi, weaknesses in the community include the history of inattention to his needs through decades of absent service, the community residents who demeaningly made fun of him whenever they had the chance, inadequate involvement in his paid work environment, and lack of public transportation. In some ways, Hiroshi's community environment supported and integrated him, thereby enhancing his quality of life. In other ways, lack of community support served to hinder his ability to live the most useful, productive, and happy life possible.

At first, the day program staff always accompanied her and provided some supervision. Now she goes to the daycare center by herself several times a week. The children love her and her attention. She always has time to listen to what they have to say and give them a hug when needed. They realize she's different than her other teachers because sometimes they have to help her out in completing activities. They don't care. They love her anyway.

3. Joe, age sixty-eight, lives in a group home. He loves to bowl. Julietta, a member of the area's neighborhood association, stopped by one day to see if there

was anything the association could do for Joe and the other residents. She found out about Joe's desire to bowl and remembered that a local church had a Thursday night bowling league. She talked to the team members and asked them if they would consider including Joe on their team. They were a bit hesitant, as they took bowling very seriously and played desperately to win. They were even more hesitant when they discovered Joe was not a very good bowler. However, Joe was obviously ecstatic about being on the team. Team members worked out a rotation system where Joe could periodically bowl but his score was omitted from the final total. Joe continued to beam as he proudly wore his Beaver's Bowling Buddies T-shirt.

4. Norma, age thirty-five, is a pleasant, soft-spoken, shy woman who had lived with her senior parents. She and her parents would often shop at a small local drug store and gift shop across the street from their modest home. Myrtle, who owned the store, got to know and like Norma and her family. Myrtle was concerned that Norma rarely got out of the house except for shopping and other errands with her parents. She started taking Norma out for lunch or a movie every other week or so. Although a busy businesswoman, Myrtle enjoys her time with Norma and feels Norma really appreciates it. She harbors some growing fears about what will happen to Norma when her parents die. Myrtle has become part of Norma's natural helping network.

   ## Critical Thinking Questions 12.12

Of these examples of how to integrate people with intellectual disabilities into the community, which do you feel are most creative and why? Can you think of any other creative ways to integrate people with intellectual disabilities? If so, describe them.

There are many ways community residents can discover and invent to help people with intellectual disabilities. Help can be given by formal groups such as ARCs or Social Service Departments, or by concerned individuals such as neighbors and fellow church members. The key is concern for the well-being of other community members, sensitivity to their needs, and the willingness to contribute precious energy on the behalf of others in need.

Chapter Summary

The following summarizes this chapter's content as it relates to the learning objectives presented at the beginning of the chapter. Objectives include the following:

A. **Describe how groups, including African-Americans, Hispanics, GLBT people, women,** and older adults, are populations-at-risk, discuss how empowerment can occur in the macro environment for each group, and provide some case examples demonstrating empowerment.

Despite major triumphs concerning legal and social racial equality, African-Americans still fall markedly behind their White counterparts in most measures of social and economic well-being. Means used to empower African-American grandparents who are primary caregivers for their grand children include establishing support groups, training grandparents as group leaders, and undertaking political advocacy.

The economic and educational picture for the Hispanic (or Latino/Latina) population is much poorer than for Whites. Values often characterizing Hispanic families include the significance of a common language, the importance of family, *personalismo, machismo* and *marianismo*, and spirituality. Latinas can empower people in their macro environment through community involvement. Latina-owned beauty parlors can provide a wide range of empowering services to their communities. Latino and Latina youth can empower their communities by conducting a community assets assessment and putting identified strengths to use in community projects.

Important issues for GLBT people include the need for nondiscrimination laws, the recognition of same-sex relationships, family policies for GLBT parents, harassment and violence against GLBT people, and housing and employment discrimination. Political action organizations can empower GLBT people by providing support to political candidates who advocate for GLBT rights, educating the public about GLBT issues, and providing legislative advocacy through lobbying. GLBT people can also be empowered through special social services.

Many social and economic indicators, including income, occupation, and household responsibilities, reflect women's oppression. At-risk pregnant women can be empowered through a community program that educates the public regarding issues and provides needed resources.

A continuum of services is available to meet the needs of older adults. A new strengths-based empowerment approach toward aging emphasizes hope, development, autonomy, and activity, regardless of personal situation. This is in contrast to the traditional perspective that focused on deficits.

B. Provide examples of how spiritual communities can empower their members.

An African-American Baptist church in Utah empowered its youth by assisting them in educational pursuits and providing a range of social activities aimed at improving self-confidence and competence. A Navajo community empowered its older adults in the Chinle Nursing Home by providing culturally and spiritually sensitive care in a range of areas.

C. Define *developmental disabilities* and identify a range of disabilities clustered under this umbrella.

Developmental disabilities are severe and chronic, occur before age twenty-two, are likely permanent, result in significant functional difficulties, and create the need for lifelong supplementary services and help. They include intellectual disabilities, cerebral palsy, seizure disorder, hearing impairment, visual impairment, and autism spectrum disorders. It's important to understand the significance of the Deaf community and Deaf culture.

D. Examine the past history of how people with developmental disabilities have been treated by the macro social environment, and discuss current trends.

Prior to the late 1960s, community treatment and public policy emphasized individual pathology. Trends during the 1970s and 1980s included normalization, deinstitutionalization, individual program planning, and the developmental model. Since the 1990s, approaches have emphasized clients as consumers, emphasis on choice, innovation, and empowerment.

E. Describe generalist social work practice with people who have developmental disabilities.

Generalist practitioners employ brokering, case management, and advocacy, among other skills, when working with people who have developmental disabilities.

F. Discuss avenues of legislative, community, and worker empowerment.

The Americans with Disabilities Act (ADA) provides an example of empowering legislation. Supreme Court debates and decisions have centered on the definition of *disability*.

G. Examine the macro environment's potential for empowering people with visual impairment and intellectual disabilities.

A number of laws have been passed that emphasize the rights and needs of people with visual impairments. It is social workers' responsibility to advocate in their communities and agencies to provide needed services.

ARCs, information and referral services, noninstitutional living opportunities, vocational and employment opportunities, other support services (such as outreach services and support groups), advocacy, the use of community volunteers, and the provision of recreational activities can empower people with intellectual disabilities in communities.

H. Raise critical thinking questions.

Critical thinking questions were raised concerning the effects of discrimination on Hispanic people, Latina community empowerment, a community project's enhancement of Latino and Latina youths' self-esteem, your personal views about GLBT issues, gender differences concerning economics and household work, what people with developmental disabilities are like, alternative choices for people with physical disabilities, misconceptions about disability, success of the ADA, resources available for a person with intellectual disabilities, and integration of a person with intellectual disabilities into the community.

I. Focus on ethical issues.

Ethical issues addressed discrimination against a person with disabilities and the meaning of "disability."

Looking Ahead

This chapter investigated human diversity, populations-at-risk, and empowerment for these populations in the macro social environment.

The next chapter will explore the macro environment and social justice on a global scale.

For Further Exploration on the Internet

See this text's website at **www.cengage.com/ social_work/kirst-ashman** for learning tools such as tutorial quizzing, Web links, glossary, flashcards, and PowerPoint® slides.

13 CHAPTER | Social Justice and the Global Community

Social injustice and poverty characterize much of the world. Pictured here are young beggar children in Karachi, Pakistan.

© Ilyas Dean/The Image Works

CHAPTER CONTENTS

"Obama hopeful on diplomatic message to Iran"
"UN to bridge funding gap on health"
"Global crisis leaves export economy badly exposed"
"Australians join global race to build biggest solar power plane"
"US should turn to Europe for help in caging serial jobs killer"
"Brazil and China challenge dollar"
"Europe needs to stop its pandering to China"
"Dollar and yen fail to gain from boost"
"China gets tough on climate talks"
"European capital markets: 'We're getting national banks—it's ridiculous in a time of globalisation'"[1]

Each of the above is a headline found in a major national newspaper, *The Financial Times*, over the course of four days. What do you think they all have in common? Each, in its own way, refers to the integral way our world is interconnected. Neither we nor citizens in any other country are isolated entities able to do whatever we please. The point is that we live in a global environment that is interconnected in a complex web of social, economic, and political policies.

Brueggemann (2006) paints a disturbing picture of this world:

If we could shrink the earth's population to a village of precisely 200 people, with all the existing human ratios remaining the same:

57 Asians

21 Europeans

14 from the Western Hemisphere, both north and south

8 Africans

52 would be female

48 would be male

70 would be non-White

30 would be White

70 would be non-Christian

30 would be Christian

89 would be heterosexual

11 would . . . [have a same-gender sexual orientation]

6 (all from the United States) would possess 59% of the world's wealth

80 would live in substandard housing

50 would suffer from malnutrition

1 would have a college education

1 would own a computer

70 would be unable to read or write

---

[1] Each of these quotations is a headline in the *Financial Times* on the following respective dates and pages, beginning with the first: May 19, p. 7, p. 7, p. 20, p. 2, p. 2, p. 6, p. 11; May 20, p. 20; and May 22, p. 2, p. 7.

If you have food in the refrigerator, clothes on your back, a roof overhead, and a place to sleep, you are richer than 75% of the world's people. If you have money in the bank, in your wallet, and spare change in a dish someplace, you are among the top 8% of the world's wealthy. If you woke up this morning with more health than illness, you are more blessed than the million who will not survive this week. If your parents are still alive and still married, you are very rare, even in the United States and Canada. If you have never experienced the danger of battle, the loneliness of imprisonment, the agony of torture, or the pangs of starvation, you are more fortunate than 500 million people in our global society. (pp. 457–458)

This chapter intends to expand your perspective from a local, state, and national one to a global one. The international macro environment affects every citizen on earth. We will address some of the global issues we all face, explore the concept of social justice, and discuss international social work.

Learning Objectives

    A. Describe globalization.
    B. Review social justice, define *human rights*, and stress these concepts' significance for international social work practice.
    C. Discuss the social issues of poverty and economic justice, global conflict, immigration status, and the forced migration of people in need.
    D. Define *community development* and *social development*, discuss their theoretical foundations and provide case examples.
    E. Examine a feminist perspective on global development.
    F. Define and explain international social work.
    G. Identify and describe international social work and social welfare organizations.
    H. Define *international nongovernmental organizations* and provide examples.
    I. Discuss social work values and cross-cultural values in global perspective.
    J. Identify some of the cultural differences existing in organizational contexts.
    K. Raise critical thinking questions.
    L. Focus on ethical issues.

We Live in a Global Macro Environment

We have emphasized the importance of social workers understanding their macro environment in order to practice effectively. We've discussed how social workers practice within organizational environments. Organizations exist in the context of neighborhoods and communities. Communities subsist in a state government environment, subject to state rules, regulations, and laws. Individual states, the District of Columbia, and Puerto Rico, in turn, exist within the national environment of the United States and must function under federal directives. The macro environment doesn't stop there, which is no news flash. The United States is part of a complex global network that is intricately involved with other countries economically, politically, and socially (Finn & Jacobson, 2003). *Globalization* is the "process of global integration in which diverse peoples, economies, cultures, and political processes are increasingly subjected to international influences"

(Midgley, 1997a, p. xi). In other words, it means that what happens in one part of the world directly influences what happens in other parts (Brueggemann, 2006, p. 458).

A friend of mine investing for retirement recently mentioned that in the past he had been very hesitant to invest in international stocks because he felt safer sticking to investments at the national level. He said a stockbroker friend of his told him, "Good luck. Almost everything's involved internationally now. Finding good investments at the national level is almost impossible." Although that might be a bit of an exaggeration, the point is that we live in a global environment with a global economy. We face soaring gasoline prices, the threat of terrorism, and global warming (which most claim is due to human activity and carbon dioxide emissions) on a daily basis. Isolation is no longer a viable option for your country or for you.

In a global economy, what social and economic forces impact one nation may well result in repercussions in many other nations. Hokenstad and Midgley (1997) explain:

> Social work is one of many players in the response to these realities of global interdependence. The scope of global poverty and the intensity of ethnic conflict require first political and economic responses by nations and international organizations. Global challenges require action on many levels by many actors. Nevertheless, these are problems that are directly related to social work commitment and expertise. Social workers at the local level are directly involved with the implications of international realities by working with refugees or helping displaced workers. At the national level in many countries, the profession is active in promoting economic and social justice policy. Internationally, social work organizations are increasingly active in combating human rights violations. Thus, it is essential for social workers to have an international perspective and understanding to be effective practitioners in today's world. (pp. 3–4)

Link, Ramanathan, and Asamoah (1999) assert that "through building a global perspective, [social work] students can add insights about the human condition and more adequately understand, analyze, and predict human behavior" (p. 31). They provide an example of the 18th Street Gang members in Los Angeles, whose families originated in El Salvador and who maintain an ongoing cultural connection with that country. Link and his colleagues (1999) stress how a global perspective helps social workers:

> recognize how artificial it is to see national borders as separations between micro or macro systems. . . . These disenfranchised young people are frequently rounded up and deported to El Salvador, where they pick up with another branch of their gang so that their interactions are seamless despite the structural efforts of immigration and law enforcement to disband or break them (DeCesare, 1993). (p. 31)

We have established that social work's mission "is to enhance human well-being and help meet the basic human needs of all people, with particular attention to the needs and empowerment of people who are vulnerable, oppressed, and living in poverty" (NASW, 2008). We have also ascertained that the National Association of Social Workers (NASW) *Code of Ethics* states that "social workers should advocate for resource allocation procedures that are open and fair. When clients' needs can be met, an allocation procedure should be developed that is non-discriminatory and based on appropriate and consistently applied principles" (NASW, 2008, 3.07b). We have indicated that the Code instructs:

> Social workers should promote the general welfare of society, from local to global levels, and the development of people, their communities, and their environments. Social workers should advocate for living conditions conducive to the fulfillment of basic human needs and should promote social, economic, political, and cultural values and institutions that are compatible with the realization of social justice. (NASW, 2008, 6.01)

Three key concepts inherent in these quotes are the terms *global*, *advocate*, and *social justice*. A *global* focus concerns looking beyond your immediate local, state, and even national environment. A basic social work value is the importance of focusing on human rights issues around the world, not just those affecting you in your own backyard. We have defined *advocacy* as the act of speaking up, pushing for change, or pleading the causes of clients and those in need (Hoefer, 2006). Finally, *social justice* involves upholding the condition that in a perfect world all citizens would have identical "rights, protection, opportunities, obligations, and social benefits" regardless of their backgrounds and membership in diverse groups (Barker, 2003, pp. 404–405). Thus, it is social workers' responsibility to attend to and advocate for social justice on a global basis.

Social justice is one of the six core values identified in the NASW *Code of Ethics* (NASW, 2008). The *Code* explains:

> Social workers pursue social change, particularly with and on behalf of vulnerable and oppressed individuals and groups of people. Social workers' social change efforts are focused primarily on issues of poverty, unemployment, discrimination, and other forms of social injustice. These activities seek to promote sensitivity to and knowledge about oppression and cultural and ethnic diversity. Social workers strive to ensure access to needed information, services, and resources; equality of opportunity; and meaningful participation in decision making for all people. (NASW, 2008, Ethical Principles)

Highlight 13.1 explores another concept critical whenever addressing social justice—global human rights. Subsequent sections will discuss issues concerning global human rights and organizations that strive to attain them.

Global Issues Affect Us All

Developing a global focus means becoming aware of the issues facing the human population in the twenty-first century. From a social work perspective, global problems are everyone's problems. We have established that it is the ethical obligation of social workers to do what they can to help solve them. Out of the multitude of social problems that should be addressed, we will arbitrarily choose three to identify here. These are poverty and economic inequality, global conflict, and forced migration of people in need.

Poverty and Economic Inequality

Poverty is the condition where people maintain "a standard of living below the minimum needed for the maintenance of adequate diet, health, and shelter"

Highlight 13.1	Global Human Rights

In response to the atrocities of World War II, the General Assembly of the United Nations adopted a Universal Declaration of Human Rights (UNDR) in December, 1948 (United Nations [UN], 1948). *Human rights* involve the premise that all people—regardless of race, culture, or national origin—are entitled to basic rights and treatment. Mapp (2008) elaborates:

> Within the UNDR, there are three areas of rights: [1] political and civil rights, [2] social, economic, and cultural rights, and [3] collective rights. Political and civil rights are often referred to as "negative

freedoms" as they require a government to refrain from an overuse of its power against individuals. Included in this are rights such as freedom of speech and the right to a fair trial. The second group of rights—social, economic, and cultural rights—are referred to as "positive freedoms" as they require a government to take action for them to be realized for individuals. They include such rights as medical care, the right to an education, and the right to a fair wage. The last group, collective rights, are rights for groups of people and include the rights to religion, peace, and development. (pp. 17–18)

(Eitzen & Zinn, 2006, p. 182). Poverty concerns lack of access to adequate resources. There are a number of terms related to poverty. "*Income* refers to the amount of money a person makes in a given year. *Wealth* is the total value of that person's assets: real estate and personal property, stocks, bonds, cash, and so forth" (Coleman & Kerbo, 2002, p. 222).

The Complexity of Defining Poverty   Poverty is not a perfectly clear-cut concept. Leon-Guerrero (2009) remarks:

> *Absolute poverty* refers to a lack of basic necessities, such as food, shelter, and income. *Relative poverty* refers to a situation in which some people fail to achieve the average income or lifestyle enjoyed by the rest of society. Our mainstream standard of living defines the 'average' American lifestyle. Individuals in this category may be able to afford basic necessities, but they cannot maintain a standard of living comparable to other members of society. (p. 38)

In the United States, the Social Security Administration (SSA) establishes an "*official poverty line*, or *poverty threshold*, [that] is based on the minimal amount of money required for a subsistence level of life" (Eitzen & Zinn, 2006, p. 182).

However, this has been criticized as underestimating the extent of poverty in the United States. The formula was initiated in 1955, at which time people spent about one-third of their income on food (Mooney, Knox, & Schacht, 2009). Although the index is adjusted each year, the amount of money necessary for adequate food is still multiplied by three based on the 1955 formula. Costs of food, however, have not risen nearly as fast as the costs of other necessary costs of living such as housing, fuel, transportation, child care, and health care. It is estimated that families now spend much less than one-third of what they need to live on food while other costs have risen dramatically (Mooney et al., 2009; Segal, 2010). Establishing the poverty line at three times what a family needs to spend on food simply won't cut it. The implication is that the poverty line should be adjusted to reflect the much higher costs of living. This would result in a significantly higher official poverty line and significantly more people officially living "in poverty." Using the current method, the U.S. Census Bureau indicates that 12.3 percent of the U.S. population lives below the poverty level (U.S. Census Bureau, 2008).

The Widening Gap in the United States   Another facet of economic inequality in the United States involves the widening gap between the very rich and very poor (Macionis, 2008; Mooney et al., 2009). Macionis (2008) explains:

> The highest-earning 20 percent of U.S. families (with income of at least $103,000 a year and with a mean or average of $176,000) received 48.1 percent of all income. At the other end of the hierarchy, the lowest-paid 20 percent (with income below $26,000 a year and averaging $15,000) received just 4.0 percent of all income. Comparing these categories, we see that the high-income families earn twelve times as much as the low-income families. From another angle, the highest-earning 20 percent of families earn almost as much as the remaining 80 percent of families combined. (p. 30)

Critical Thinking Questions 13.1

Where do you stand personally in terms of your overall wealth? What factors in your own background contributed to your current financial status and your potential future financial status?

A vast discrepancy in income is mirrored by compensation received by CEOs and ordinary workers (Mooney et al., 2009). In 2005, CEOs of the 350 biggest corporations in the United States received an average compensation of $11.6 million each; this amounts to 411 times the average compensation for other workers. The discrepancy is ten times larger than that existing in 1980. From 1990 to 2005 (after adjustments for inflation), the average CEO pay increased by almost 300 percent, whereas average workers' compensation increased by less than 5 percent. Minimum-wage earners' income *decreased* by more than 9 percent.

Other demographic variables affect a U.S. citizen's potential to be in poverty. Females and people of color are significantly more likely to be poor (Lean-Guerrero, 2009; Mooney et al., 2009). For example, African–American households have one-tenth the total net worth of White households (Texeira, 2005).

Poverty levels also vary by state. For example, 4.9 percent of the population fall below the poverty line in New Hampshire, whereas over 17 percent does so in Arkansas, Kentucky, New Mexico, and West Virginia; 19 percent fell below the poverty level in Louisiana and over 21 percent in Mississippi (U.S. Census Bureau, 2008).

Focus on Ethics 13.1 raises questions regarding how ethical it is for a government to allow such enormous discrepancies in resources.

Focus on Ethics 13.1	**Should the Government Allow Such Vast Discrepancies in Wealth?**

What do you think are the reasons for the widening gap in wealth in the United States? Is it fair and ethical for the government to allow these discrepancies? Can or should something be done about them (for example, via taxes, regulation, or increased service provision)? Explain.

Global Poverty   Poverty is defined differently depending on where in the world you are. Mooney and her colleagues (2009) describe the situation:

> The World Bank sets a "poverty threshold" of $1 per day to compare poverty in most of the developing world [in the past, referred to as "third world"], $2 per day in Latin America, $4 per day in Eastern Europe . . . , and $14.40 per day in industrial countries (which corresponds to the income poverty line in the United States). [The *World Bank's* formal name is the International Bank for Reconstruction and Development. Headquartered in Washington, DC. It has branches around the world that make loans and provide economic consultation to countries that have low per capita incomes and lack resources.] Another poverty measure is based on whether individuals are experiencing hunger, which is defined as consuming less than 1,960 calories a day. (p. 210–211)

"In South Asia 1 in 4 goes hungry, and in sub-Saharan Africa as many as 1 in 3 goes hungry" (Mooney et al., 2009, p. 212). Cox and Pawar (2006) summarize:

> Poverty, with its associated problems such as infant mortality, malnutrition, and vulnerability, is commonly regarded as the world's most serious problem. Depending on how poverty is defined and measured, no one would dispute the claim that, at the very least, approximately one in every three of the world's people lives in poverty. This is partly because many people around the globe exist so close to the poverty line that any one of a number of common occurrences, even at a minor level, will push them into poverty. Such occurrences include economic changes, such as increases in *inflation* rates ["a continuing rise in the general price level usually attributed to an increase in the volume of money and credit relative to available goods and services" (Mish, 2008, p. 641)], deteriorating trade arrangements, or reductions in a government's subsidies of basic necessities; ecological changes, such as deterioration of the environment or depletion of essential food sources; social conflict within a nation or war between nations; demographic changes through migration or natural increase; and natural disasters that destroy people's homes and livelihoods. (emphasis added) (p. 51)

Problems Related to Poverty   Numerous other problems, of course, are related to poverty. If people don't have the resources, they may not be able to get many of the things they need to survive and thrive. These related problems include hunger, homelessness, unsafe water supplies, and lack of health care, among many others, all of which are beyond the scope of this text. They all are serious issues that social workers around the world must address. Focus on Ethics 13.2 speaks to this issue. Highlight 13.2 stresses the significance of global conflict.

Focus on Ethics 13.2 | The Crisis of Global Poverty

What are the reasons for such extreme global poverty? Is it ethical for richer, industrialized nations to allow such conditions to continue? To what extent is it these wealthier nations' ethical responsibility to address global poverty? What, if anything, can or should be done to help?

Highlight 13.2 | Global Conflict

Cox and Pawar (2006) summarize the state of conflict in this and the past century:

> A reading of any global history reveals the extremely common inability of social groupings, nations, and empires to live at peace with their neighbors. In pursuit of territory, booty of all kinds, slaves, power, and status, conflict at all levels has been a significant aspect of the human story. The last century witnessed two of the worst wars known to history, and since the end of the Cold War in 1989 the scourge of civil war has intensified alarmingly. In recent times, the world has been experiencing upwards of 30 civil wars at any one time, with very high casualty figures, especially among civilians.
>
> A major goal of the UN [United Nations] is world peace, yet its work and that of national governments and regional associations, along with that of many organizations of civil society, have together failed to do more than perhaps contain many situations. Only when we add together the widespread consequences of conflict on people's personal lives and social contexts, economic conditions, physical infrastructure, and the environment, do we begin to appreciate the enormity of this global problem. Yet because conflict once again has many causes, it seems difficult for the international community to significantly reduce the impact of conflict in the foreseeable future. Finally, it has become clear in recent times that rebuilding a society after conflict is a complex, hugely expensive, and extremely difficult undertaking. (p. 52)

 | **Critical Thinking Questions 13.2**

To what extent do you or did you support the U.S. presence in places like Afghanistan and Iraq? What are your reasons? How would you articulate the U.S. rationale for being there? What are the global consequences for and resulting perceptions about the United States? What are the consequences for the citizens of such occupied countries?

Immigration Status: Forced Migration of People in Need

It is estimated that about 50 million people worldwide are displaced from their community of origin, although they would prefer to have remained at home (Cox & Pawar, 2006). Cox and Pawar (2006) explain why:

> One inevitable consequence of extreme poverty, widespread social conflict, serious natural disasters, ecological degradation, and low levels of development is that many

people are forced to leave their usual place of abode and seek refuge, assistance, or a better future elsewhere. (p. 53)

Immigration involves the permanent movement from one country to another. *Immigration status* is a person's position in terms of legal rights and residency when entering and residing in a country that is not that person's legal country of origin. Social workers are often called upon to work with immigrants, so it's important to understand the terms and issues involved. Potocky-Tripodi (2002) defines many of the important concepts when discussing these populations:

The fundamental distinction between immigrants and refugees is that *immigrants* leave their countries voluntarily (usually in search of better economic opportunities) whereas *refugees* are forced out of their countries because of human rights violations against them. . . . Refugees are also sometimes referred to, or refer to themselves, as *exiles* or *émigrés*. . . .

Legally, anyone who is not a citizen of the United States is termed an *alien*. Aliens are further classified as immigrants and nonimmigrants, and as documented or undocumented (Loue, 1998). In this classification, an *immigrant* is a person who has been legally admitted into the United States and granted the privilege to be a permanent resident (a 'green card' holder). A *nonimmigrant* is a foreign-born person who is in the United States temporarily, such as a tourist, a student or a journalist. Nonimmigrants also include temporary, or seasonal, workers, who come to the United States to work during certain periods of the year and return to their countries during the rest of the year. This typically refers to agricultural laborers.

A *documented alien* is one who has been granted a legal right to be in the United States. This legal right is determined by admissions policy. The admissions policy details many categories of people who are eligible to be legally admitted. It also specifies how many people from each country may be legally admitted into the U.S. each year. . . .

An *undocumented alien* is one who does not have a legal right to be in the United States. These people are also sometimes referred to as *illegal immigrants*. They are also referred to as *deportable aliens*, because if discovered by immigration authorities, they are subject to deportation, or forcible return to their countries of origin. There are two ways in which people become undocumented aliens. One is by entering the U.S. illegally. This means that the person has not received authorization to enter the United States. For example, people who cross the border from Mexico without going through the immigration authorities are undocumented aliens. The second way that people become undocumented aliens is by entering the U.S. legally, but then violating the terms of the visa (the authorization to stay in the U.S.). For example, a tourist may be granted a visa to stay in the United States for a limited period of time. . . . [Anyone staying longer than the specified time period then] becomes an undocumented alien. (pp. 4–5)

Potocky-Tripodi (2002) continues:

A foreign-born person's legal status can, and usually does, change over time. This is referred to as *adjustment of status*. After one year of residence, a refugee is eligible to become a permanent resident. Permanent residents (including those who were formerly refugees and immigrants) may be eligible to become U. S. citizens after five years of residence. . . . [Upon attaining] citizenship, they are referred to as *naturalized citizens*. Undocumented aliens may sometimes become eligible to become legal permanent residents. For example, a law passed in 1986 allowed a large number of undocumented aliens to change to legal status. (pp. 8–9)

Many people from other countries may receive or need social services. Sue and Sue (2008) report:

> There are over 33 million [legal and illegal] immigrants living in the United States, which is about 12 percent of the population. About half have arrived since 1990. Of these immigrants, it is estimated that 36 percent are legally documented or legally admitted as permanent residents [non-citizens who hold a green card. Another]. . . . [t]hirty-two percent of immigrants are *naturalized citizens*. . . . Approximately 28 percent of immigrants are undocumented. . . . Over half of the immigrant population originates from Latin America, with Mexico being the largest contributor. Other countries providing the most recent legal immigrants include India, the Philippines, China, El Salvador, the Dominican Republic, Vietnam, Columbia, Guatemala, and Russia. Immigrants, particularly those from Latin America, tend to earn lower wages and have a higher incidence of poverty. About one-third have not completed high school as compared to 12.5 percent of the total adult population. However, the percentage of immigrants with a bachelor's degree or advanced degree is slightly higher compared to those born in the United States. (p. 242)

People with different national origins often find it difficult to integrate themselves into the mainstream culture. This is intensified when the use of different languages is a factor (Gushue & Sciarra, 1995). Finding employment, accessing adequate housing, and "fitting into" the social fabric of neighborhoods and communities can be difficult. Kamya (1999) cites "social isolation, cultural shock,

---

Concept Summary 13.1 | **Immigration Status and Related Terms**

Immigration: The permanent movement from one country to another (immigrants in the United States hold a "green card").

Immigration status: A person's position in terms of legal rights and residency when entering and residing in a country that is not that person's legal country of origin.

Nonimmigrant: "A foreign-born person who is in the United States temporarily, such as a tourist, a student or a journalist."

Alien: "Legally, anyone who is not a citizen of the United States."

Documented alien: "One who has been granted a legal right to be in the United States."

Illegal immigrant (undocumented alien):   "One who does not have a legal right to be in the United States."

Deportable alien: One who is not a U.S. citizen and who is subject to deportation upon discovery.

Refugees (exiles or émigrés):   People who have been "forced out of their countries because of human rights violations against them."

Adjustment of status: "A foreign-born person's legal status" that does "change over time."

Naturalized citizens: "Permanent residents (including those who were formerly refugees or immigrants)" who "become U.S. citizens after five years of residence" (upon attaining citizenship). (Potocky-Tripodi, 2002, pp. 4–5, 8–9)

cultural change, and goal-striving stress as four significant experiences" newcomers often face (p. 607). They may have difficulties understanding new behavioral expectations imposed on them, interacting effectively with others in the new culture, and achieving the goals they had hoped for.

Critical Thinking Questions 13.3

What do you think the U.S. policy should be toward people migrating illegally across the southern border?

Community Development

What should be done in response to the turbulence and many issues faced by the global community? How can resources be distributed more equitably and enhanced social justice attained? Community development provides one positive avenue to help communities and nations in need.

Rivera and Erlich (2001) state:

> *Community Development* refers to efforts to mobilize people who are directly affected by a community condition (that is, the "victims," the unaffiliated, the unorganized, and the nonparticipating) into groups and organizations to enable them to take action on the social problems and issues that concern them. A typical feature of these efforts is the concern with building new organizations among people who have not been previously organized to take social action on a problem (emphasis amended) (Erlich & Rivera, 1981; Fisher, 1984). (p. 256)

Community development involves helping a designated community of people who share cultural values and experience similar social and economic conditions; goals are to improve living conditions and enhance residents' quality of life in the social environment by using a planned change process (Harrison, 1995, Healy, 2008).[2] Development entails growth, progress, and empowerment of community members through their active involvement. We have defined a *community* as "a number of people who have something in common with one another that connects them in some way and that distinguishes them from others" (Homan, 2008, p. 8). A key feature of a community is the fact that participants share some mutual characteristic. Common features might include "location, interest, identification, culture, and/or common activities" (Fellin, 2001a, 2001b, p. 118). The following section describes the theoretical functions of community that provide a context for community development. Such theory "provides practitioners with a coherent way to organize the variables that have a bearing on their work" (Kramer & Specht, 1983, p. 19).

---

[2] Planned change as described in Chapter 1 involves engagement, assessment, planning, implementation, evaluation, termination, and follow-up.

Theoretical Functions of Communities

An important theoretical perspective on communities that serves as a foundation for community development involves the functionalist perspective introduced earlier in Chapter 9. Warren (1983), one of the leading early theorists on communities, cited five basic functions that communities should serve:

1. "*Production-distribution-consumption* relates to local participation in the process of producing, distributing, and consuming those goods and services that are a part of daily living and access to which is desirable in the immediate locality" (pp. 28–29). People need access to goods such as food, clothing, and housing, in addition to services like police and fire protection. In various communities around the world, this function is seriously obstructed.

2. "*Socialization* involves a process by which society or one of its constituent social units transmits prevailing knowledge, social values, and behavior patterns to its members" (p. 29). People in communities, which may be local or national, are socialized regarding expectations for behavior and "appropriate" values. One primary method of socialization is education, which is sorely lacking in many areas of the world.

3. "*Social control* involves the process through which a group influences the behavior of its members toward conformity with its norms" (p. 29). The first thing that comes to mind might be the government with its branches of police and courts. However, "many other social units, including the family, the school, the church, and the social agency, also play a part" (p. 29). As of this writing, a critical issue in Iraq concerns who maintains social control. Is it the occupying U.S. government, the various newly formed facets of Iraqi government, or the diverse terrorist ethnic and religious groups fighting those in power?

4. "*Social participation*" concerns the involvement of citizens in social, political, and economic processes. Various social entities provide avenues for social participation, including churches and religious organizations, "businesses, government offices, . . . voluntary and public health and welfare agencies, . . . family and kinship groups, friendship groups, and other less formal groupings" (p. 29). From a global perspective, various local and national communities limit social participation based on gender, or ethnic or religious status. Social participation is often a primary goal in achieving social justice.

5. *Mutual support* involves encouragement, assistance, caring, and cooperation among people in communities (p. 29). "Traditionally, such mutual support, whether in the form of care in time of sickness, exchange of labor, or helping a local family in economic distress, has been performed locally very largely under such primary-group auspices as family and relatives, neighborhood groups, friendship groups, and local religious groups" (p. 29). Today, many mutual support functions, at least in wealthier industrialized nations, have been assumed by public welfare departments, private health and welfare agencies, governmental and commercial insurance companies, and other formalized organizational structures (p. 29).

Critical Thinking Questions 13.4

How does the community in which you live fulfill the five functions mentioned here? If something is lacking, how might community functioning be improved?

Community Development Practice

At least five basic principles characterize practice when undertaking community development. First, community development calls for *community members' active participation* (Butterfield & Chisanga, 2008; Harrison, 1995; Healy, 2008; Homan, 2008; Mathie & Cunningham, 2008). Social workers can use their leadership, organizing, problem-solving, planning, and communication skills to encourage community members to work together and achieve community goals. Community members must be integrally involved in each phase of the planned change process from initial assessment through planning and implementation to final evaluation of results. The idea is to enhance community functioning through participation of as broad a range of community members as possible.

A second principle concerns *establishing common goals* (Harrison, 1995). Tropman (2008) explains:

> Emphasis is placed on goal selection, prioritization, and goal application. . . . In some instances goal selection will already have occurred. Frequently, the very process of discussion of goal alternatives results, in an almost automatic way, in the clear selection or desirability of one particular goal over others.
>
> On the other hand, there may well be competing interests and competing perspectives with regard to which goal should be selected. The worker needs to continue a process of interaction and encouragement with community members around the process of selecting a goal and prioritizing the efforts needed to get to that goal. (p. 130)

Help in determining goals often involves the worker attending community meetings, working closely with community leaders, raising questions to community groups, suggesting alternatives, providing ongoing encouragement for consensus, and assisting in initial implementation of goals (Tropman, 2008).

A third practice principle involved in community development entails *reaching out to various diverse groups, constituencies, and organizations* within the community (Butterfield & Chisanga, 2008; Harrison, 1995; Homan, 2008). It's important to mobilize as many community factions as possible to work together toward community goals. Numbers and solidarity can enhance the power necessary to get and use resources for the community's benefit.

A fourth dimension of community development concerns an emphasis on *using community assets* (Hardcastle & Powers, 2004; Homan, 2008; Mathie & Cunningham, 2008). Strengths provide the foundation for development. "People in communities can organize to drive the development process themselves by identifying and mobilizing existing (but often unrecognized) assets, thereby responding to and creating local economic opportunity" (Mathie & Cunningham, 2008, p. 283).

A fifth community development practice principle involves the *empowerment of community members to help themselves* and become self-reliant (Butterfield & Chisanga, 2008; Homan, 2008). The community development process should enhance the self-confidence and competence of community members so that they can maintain the progress they made. The intent is for them to continue to grow and develop, initiating and supporting their own goals without being dependent on external professional leadership. Emphasizing the integral involvement of oppressed and powerless groups in the community is also essential as part of the empowerment process to provide them with access to resources and services.

Note that community development must progress within the value structure of the community's people. Values and priorities vary dramatically from one culture or location to another. A subsequent section addresses the issue of cross-cultural value differences.

Examples of Community Development   Midgley and Livermore (2004) provide examples of community development in Africa:

> In many African countries, social workers have mobilized local people to engage in small-scale agricultural activities, construct rural bridges and feeder roads, establish cooperative enterprises [a program owned and run by people receiving its services], and accumulate community assets. These projects have a direct and positive impact on economic development. Community built and owned feeder roads provide easier access to the markets in larger towns and ensure that farmers get their produce to these markets in a timely way. Community development has also been used to assist women to engage more effectively in agricultural activities and microenterprises [such as small businesses] and to become economically independent.
>
> Community development has . . . been used to promote social welfare projects that . . . contribute to economic development. Throughout Africa, local people have collaborated with both governmental and nongovernmental agencies to build community centers, schools and clinics, sanitary and other public health facilities, and to provide safe drinking water. The use of community development to provide safe drinking water in many rural areas in Africa has been particularly impressive. Many communities that relied on rivers, streams, and marshes were exposed to the hazard of being infected with waterborne diseases. Community participation has been vital in providing access to clean drinking water. Village people have played an important role by providing labor for the construction of wells and channeling clean water to local communities from unpolluted mountain springs. (pp. 124–125)

Sowers and Rowe (2007) provide other examples of community development in Carmelita (Guatemala), Ghana, and Indonesia:

> In Carmelita, the Guatemalan government has established 13 locally managed forest concessions [governmental grants of land for specified use] in the jungle village. The cooperative that works the 130,000-acre concession in the rain forest consists of 56 impoverished families from the jungle village. The concessions are logged in accordance with rules laid down by the Forest Stewardship Council, a nonprofit organization based in Bonn, Germany. Environmental organizations credit the approach with reducing deforestation and protecting watersheds and wetland areas while providing a steady income for local residents (Replogle, n.d.). . . .
>
> The Ghana Community School Alliances Project, a community-mobilization initiative funded by USAID, fosters community participation in more than 300 primary

schools throughout Ghana to build an environment of mutual respect, responsibility, and action among community members, schools, and education administrators as they work to meet the learning needs of Ghanaian children. [USAID, the United States Agency for International Development, is "the principle U.S. agency to extend assistance to countries recovering from disaster, trying to escape poverty, and engaging in democratic reforms" (USAID, 2009).] In addition, the project trains district-level education managers to use data for decision making at the local level (Educational Development Center, n.d.). . . .

In the aftermath of the December 2004 Indian Ocean tsunami, Mercy Corps field managers quickly mobilized local workers to rebuild schools, clean up water systems, and repair commercial fishing boats. [Mercy Corps is a charitable organization founded in 1979 that focuses on relief assistance and "long-term solutions to hunger and poverty" (Mercy Corps, 2009).] Through innovative cash-for-work programs, tsunami survivors earned income to support their families and reclaim their lives (Mercy Corps. n.d.). (p. 220)

Critical Thinking Questions 13.5

What is your opinion regarding FEMA's (Federal Emergency Management Agency) handling of the Hurricane Katrina disaster in New Orleans? What could have been done to improve effectiveness and efficiency?

Social Development

A term related to community development is social development, initially coined when the British colonial administration began promoting economic development in West Africa in the 1940s (Miah, 2008). *Social development* is a planned change process on the behalf of an entire population that emphasizes economic development based on two principles: first, economic development integrates social and economic policy, and, second, it sponsors investment-oriented social programs "that contribute positively to economic development" (Midgley & Sherraden, 2009, p. 283). At least four concepts are important here.

First, social development is pursued *on the behalf of the entire community* and all its residents. It involves comprehensive change that encompasses multiple systems and dimensions within a community.

Second, the definition stresses the *importance of economic development* for communities. Rothman (2008) reflects:

Community economic development . . . believes that what distressed communities need most is an upgrade of economic conditions. According to Soifer (2002), this means concentrating on housing development, land development, job creation, and setting up more relevant financial institutions—primarily banks. This is consistent with a U.N. study of intervention results, where experts who were surveyed indicated that project outcomes are better when there is adequate prior planning, including the preparation of supportive organizational and resource [economic] elements. (p. 154)

The third significant concept regarding social development emphasizes the importance of *linkage between social and economic policy*. Midgley and Sherraden (2009) remark:

> Integrating economic and social policy is . . . key . . . This requires the creation of formal arrangements that effectively link economic and social policies and programs. In many countries, governmental organizations concerned with social welfare have few ties to agencies engaged in economic development. The social development perspective seeks . . . to ensure that social policy is not [of secondary importance] . . . to the economy. Instead, it advocates an integrative approach that regards economic and social policies as two essential elements of a sustainable . . . development process. (p. 283)

A fourth major principle characterizing social development is that economic development sponsors *investment-oriented social programs*.
Midgley and Sherraden (2009) explain:

> Social development proponents believe that economic participation is the primary means by which most people meet their social needs. Unlike the traditional income maintenance and social service approaches [that some view as a "drain on the economy" (Gamble & Hoff, 2005, p. 170)], the social development perspective seeks to shift the emphasis from consumption-based and maintenance-oriented services [for example, Food Stamps and public assistance] to social programs that contribute directly to economic development[,] . . . enhance economic participation[,] and contribute to growth . . .
>
> [S]ocial development advocates do not merely urge social welfare clients to become economically productive; they argue that adequate investments should be made to ensure that people have the skills, knowledge, resources, opportunities, incentives, and subsidies to participate effectively in the productive economy. Of course, this principle applies not only to the consumers of welfare services but also to the population as a whole. Social development advocates require that government regulations, subsidies, and supports be provided to all to ensure that economic participation results in adequate living wages, access to universal health care, full educational opportunities, affordable housing, and the other dimensions of a decent and satisfying living standard. (pp. 282–283)

Wetzel (2004) provides an example where economic development in the social development process had a successful impact on social conditions:

> Probably the world's most successful economic development program is the Grameen Bank of Dhaka, Bangladesh, founded in 1976 by Muhammad Yunus, an economist who was making loans for commercial banks. (Grameen means "rural" or "village" in English.) Yunus was appalled by the living conditions of people in rural Bangladesh, the second poorest nation in the world. He was struck especially by the severe situation of women who are in a particularly precarious position when they are abandoned or divorced. They have no means of livelihood, and their families will not allow them to return to their homes. Consequently, the self-esteem of these women is as impoverished as their economic. . . . [resources]. Banks would not grant them loans without collateral guarantees, so Yunus decided to become a personal benefactor to the region for micro-enterprises for low-income women. His credit union was opened to men as well, but 77 percent of the loans continue to be granted to women. Their payback rate has proven to be even better than their male counterparts. Because people

without . . . [economic resources] seldom have access to credit, the Grameen model requires the group members themselves to become the collateral, promising to pay any outstanding debt that is not paid by the grantee [any individual who does not repay the loan]. It has seldom been necessary to do so. (pp. 108–109)

Consequently, the Grameen model has been used successfully in developing and industrialized countries to help impoverished people (Rosenberg, 2000). Success has been attributed to three aspects—an emphasis on enhanced "self-esteem," "group support," and "collaboration in reaching . . . goals" (Wetzel, 2004, p. 109).

Highlight 13.3 describes a feminist perspective on global development that can be used both in community and social development.

Distorted Development

Midgley (1997b) explains how sometimes economic development does not significantly improve social conditions:

Distorted development occurs through a mismatch between economic and social development. The problem in many countries is not an absence of economic development but rather a failure to harmonize economic and social objectives and to ensure that the benefits of economic progress reach the population as a whole.

Conditions of distorted development are widespread in the Third World. Perhaps the most dramatic examples have occurred in Latin America, where rates of economic growth have been impressive but where poverty and deprivation are . . . [widespread]. Despite a significant degree of economic development, housing standards are inadequate, the distribution of income and wealth is highly skewed, investments in education and the social services are low, and rates of unemployment and underemployment are high. Similar examples are found in Africa and Asia, particularly in countries where economic prosperity has been achieved through exploiting natural resources. In these nations, mineral wealth has provided high standards of living for a small minority of the population but left the majority in conditions of poverty.

Distorted development also persists in industrial countries such as the United Kingdom and the United States despite their high level of economic development. In these countries significant sections of the population do not benefit from economic growth. Distorted development is manifested in high rates of poverty in decayed inner city areas and deprived rural communities. Inner cities are increasingly devastated in both physical and social terms. Here poverty, unemployment, crime, family disintegration, violence, drug use, and social deprivation are most marked. (pp. 13–14)

International Social Work

International social work is "international professional action and the capacity for international action by the social work profession and its members. International social work has four dimensions: internationally related domestic practice and advocacy, professional exchange, international practice, and international policy development and advocacy" (Healy, 2008, p. 10). International social work involves adopting a global focus, whether working in one's own country or in an international context. It also means establishing the global goal of firmly establishing

Highlight 13.3 | A Feminist Perspective on Global Development

Wetzel (1995) discusses the importance of women's mental health on a global level as a necessity to maintain their optimal well-being. She cites several standards based on feminist principles that should govern the development of programs for women around the world. For each she provides an international example. Although programs may vary, they should address the improvement of women's self-concepts, increasing their ability to act assertively on their own behalves, and enhance supportive relationships.

Standard 1. "Raising consciousness regarding gender roles and the importance and worth of every female" (p. 181). Work that is traditionally "women's work" should be respected and appreciated as work just as traditional "men's work" (work outside of the home) is respected. The rights and emotional wellbeing of women deserve respect.

Filomena Tomaira Pacsi, a women's social action group in Peru, provides an example. The issue addressed the plight of the wives of rural miners who were traditionally belittled and abused by their spouses. *Filomena* consisted of a group of urban women from Lima who worked with these rural women "to reduce their feeling of isolation (negative aloneness), enhance their solidarity (positive connectedness), encourage social action, and increase their self-perception and sense of worth by recognizing how important their roles are to their husbands, children, and communities" (p. 182). Wetzel (1995) elaborates:

> The urban women of *Filomena* joined with these rural women to raise their consciousness and change their lives. When the mines were being closed without notice, the rural women encouraged their husbands and families to make sacrifice marches hundreds of miles to the city. With the help of *Filomena*, the women of Lima began to realize how important they were to the mining struggle. The rural women took charge of the marches, feeding their families in community kitchens and providing education for their children along the way. The women also took

responsibility for health care, surveying the needs of children and arranging for mobile health units staffed by paramedics . . .

> The presence of the urban women of *Filomena*, in the words of the rural women of the mines, brought them "tremendous joy, sweeping them off their feet." The solidarity and spirit of the two groups of women spread to the rural women's husbands, who stopped being violent toward their wives and showed them newfound respect. Respect for the rural women's roles was enhanced by bonding among the women and the recognition of their organizational expertise. It was the women who taught their husbands to advocate for better working conditions rather than to settle for their poor circumstances. The women opened their husbands' eyes to the responsibilities of companies and the rights of human beings in their employ. (p. 182)

Standard 2. "Forming interdisciplinary professional partnerships with poor women and training indigenous [those originating in the community] *trainers to serve their own communities"* (p. 182). It's important for professionals from various backgrounds to work together with poor women to train them. These poor women then, in turn, can return to and help their own communities by providing training for the women there.

The Women in Development Consortium of Thailand was a program co-sponsored by three Thai universities in conjunction with York University in Canada. The project, called "Train the Trainers," was undertaken by "Friends of Women, an interdisciplinary group of professional women and a few men who [were] . . . kindred spirits. These women and men [were] . . . devoted to working in partnership with low-income female factory workers who [were] . . . exploited. Using a nonhierarchical participative group approach, the professional facilitators train[ed] selected leaders from the factory, who in turn train[ed] the other female factory workers, hence, the Train the Trainer program title."

continued

Highlight 13.3 | *continued*

The training included five parts. First, the participants' feelings of isolation were addressed and their connectedness as a potentially supportive group emphasized. Most participants originated in rural areas and traveled to work in the relatively better economic urban environment. The second part of training involved health concerns in an industrial setting including "chronic exhaustion from devastating working conditions" (p. 182). The third training segment addressed participants' individual economic issues such as "personal incomes and expenses, analyzing their situations in the context of their poor status" (p. 182). Feminist labor lawyers and educators led the fourth phase, where labor laws and rights were discussed. Collective bargaining and lobbying in the political arena were also explained. The fifth training unit concerned a "synthesis" of all that participants had learned. Connections between personal and social problems and economic and political concerns were clearly identified, and the necessity of working individually and collectively for social change was emphasized (p. 183). The process resulted in participants' enhanced self-esteem and vision concerning what they might be able to achieve. Participants could then return to their factory environments and share what they learned with other workers.

Standard 3. "Teaching women that both personal development and action, as well as collective social development and action, are essential if their lives are to change for the better" (p. 186). We have identified feminist principles that stress how consciousness raising, an enhanced perception of one's life circumstances, and an increased understanding of self are extremely important for women. We have also emphasized that, according to feminist theories, the personal is political. Personal development is fine, but it must coincide with political and social action. Only then can conditions be improved and social justice be attained for all women.

An example of a program adopting this standard is *Stree Mukti Sanghatana*, a group that uses street theater to raise consciousness and advocate for women's rights in Bombay, India. Dramatic performances, entertainment, and other visual media such as posters serve as conduits to convey information and identify issues. Examples of performances include *No Dowry, Please; We Will Smash the Prison;* and *A Girl Is Born*; all of these performances "address traumatic examples of female subordination" (p. 187).

Critical Thinking Questions 13.6

To what extent do you agree with these three feminist principles? How valuable did the principles seem in implementing the three programmatic examples?

social work as a respected profession around the world (Cox & Pawar, 2006). The following content elaborates on the four dimensions inherent in international social work.

1. *Internationally related domestic practice and advocacy.* The first dimension inherent in the definition of international social work concerns advocating for domestic policy that supports international social justice. It also means educating others about international issues to solicit their support on behalf of global

social justice. This is true for social workers practicing primarily in the United States, Canada, Puerto Rico, the Caribbean, and anywhere else in the world.

One way of practicing international social work in one's own country includes "international adoption" (Turner, 2001, p. 4). From our perspective, "*international adoptions* are those in which children are brought from other countries and placed with adoptive couples in the United States" (Crosson-Tower, 2007, p. 345). Another way of practicing international social work here is by "working with refugees or immigrants" (Turner, 2001, p. 4).

2. *Professional exchange.* The second dimension of international social work involves developing international arrangements and structures to encourage travel among countries and communication among professional colleagues. Various international social work and related organizations are discussed later in the chapter. These organizations sponsor conferences and serve as clearinghouses for information and ideas concerning global issues. Other positive avenues of professional exchange include international field internships sponsored by social work programs, volunteer activities in international helping organizations, and international social work faculty exchange programs.

    Turner (2001) provides an example of a professional exchange concerning Robert Wiles, who was a graduate student at the University of Calgary (Turner, 2001). He entered a three-month practicum where he was involved in "the development of the practicum component of the Associate Degree in Social Work at the University College of Belize" (p. 5). He emphasized:

    "My experience in Belize was outstanding," . . . .[stated] Robert. "Certainly, the opportunity to work within another country was an incredible privilege, but being and living there was an intense learning experience. Beyond the classroom and university setting, interacting and learning about another culture was the most beautiful part of the experience." (p. 5)

3. *International practice.* Practicing in other countries can involve a wide range of social work activities, including participating in community development activities, working directly with individuals, families, and groups, assuming management positions, and assisting in policy development. Ways of getting your foot in the door for international social work positions include volunteering for or getting a job in a global social welfare organization such as CARE (a humanitarian organization dedicated to combating global poverty) or Save the Children (a humanitarian organization committed to helping children in need around the world and improving their potential for a better quality of life) (Brueggemann, 2006). Examples of potential paid positions include child protection officer, program director, education specialist, regional HIV/AIDS director, training manager, global challenge coordinator, community campaigns and organization manager, advocacy and policy advisor, and campaigner (CARE, 2006; Oxfam, 2006).

    Note that it's important to be prepared to face and overcome possible hurdles when practicing in other countries. These include potential resistance on the part of indigenous citizens; funding shortages; lower salaries; different certification, licensing, and credentialing regulations; and language barriers (Turner, 2001).

    Highlight 13.4 illustrates a case example in international social work practice.

| Highlight 13.4 | International Social Work: A Case Example in Mauritius |

Healy (2008) presents an example of social work practice in Mauritius, an island country in the Indian Ocean. She notes that it is in the midst of staggering changes as it makes the transition from an agricultural to an industrial society; skilled jobs are replacing unskilled, and family structures are being transformed from extended to nuclear.

Most Mauritian social workers are employed by public agencies such as Social Security and probation departments. Note that "no single case is typical of social work in a country" (p. 213). However, the case of "Jean," a four-year-old boy with a serious intellectual disability, is depicted here "because it illustrates Mauritian social work in transition, recognizing child development needs, yet hampered by incomplete service development and lack of resources" (p. 213).

The Case

Healy (2008) describes the case:

> Jean is a 4-year-old boy who lives with his father, 7-year-old sister, and grandmother in a three-room corrugated iron-sheet house. The parents are separated, and mother lives elsewhere. The case was reported to the Child Development Unit of the Ministry of Women, Family Welfare and Child Development by a medical worker in the hospital. A caseworker (a social worker whose practice primarily focuses on work with individuals and families) visited and found that Jean, mentally retarded, was being "grossly neglected." The house was filthy; according to the grandmother, the father is an alcoholic, and she said she is too old to care for such a child who needs constant care. The caseworker discovered that Jean could not speak. He made noises and followed the caseworker everywhere, touching him frequently. The child seemed to the worker to be deprived of affection. Making a second visit, the caseworker interviewed the father. The father said he had no objection to the child being placed in a home. Mother was summoned to the office, but she refused to take Jean.

> The caseworker tried to admit Jean to an institution but could not find a vacancy in a place equipped to care for handicapped children.

> Soon thereafter, Jean was left tied to a bed, unfed and unattended. He became ill and was admitted to a hospital. During his 2-month stay, no relative visited him. Discharge planning was challenging, as no placement could be found. The caseworker attempted to admit Jean to the Shelter for Women and Children in distress, a temporary shelter. However, the agency refused him admission, as they claimed they were not equipped to cope with Jean's multiple needs. The caseworker took the case to the Ministry's Permanent Secretary and to the magistrate [a judicial administrative official] to get an order to admit Jean to the shelter. Now, he is waiting while SOS Children's Village determines whether it will admit him for longer term care (Boodajee, 1997). (p. 214)

Commentary

Healy (2008) reflects:

> The case such as Jean's could occur in many societies. It illustrates the functions of the social worker in investigation, efforts at family intervention, referral, and finally case advocacy to secure needed services for the client. It points out the need for further advocacy for service development to ensure that the needs of children with disabilities can be addressed. The case also illustrates the transition being experienced in Mauritian social work. Rather than focusing on child survival, the caseworker is focusing on child protection. As more appropriate services can be developed, child development will increase in importance. (pp. 213–214)

4. *International policy development and advocacy.* International social work involves supporting positive policy development and advocacy in the pursuit of social justice at the global level. An aspect of international social work includes joining and actively working for global organizations just as one would a national organization. These organizations often encompass "coalitions of people who are concerned about peace, environment, labor, housing, hunger, and social justice" (Verschelden, 1993, p. 768). Supporting global organizations seeking positive humanitarian policy changes such as the United Nations is another facet of this dimension.

The National Association of Social Workers (NASW) has also become "a member of InterAction, a large alliance of U.S.-based international development and humanitarian nongovernmental organizations" (NASW, 2005, p. 1). Being a member of NASW indirectly supports InterAction's humanitarian efforts.

International Social Work Organizations

We've discussed organizations and communities in various contexts. When addressing the global community, it's important to understand how international organizations function within it. International social work organizations that actively engage social workers around the globe include the International Federation of Social Workers (IFSW) and the International Association of Schools of Social Work (IASSW). Two other international organizations that have values closely related to social work are the International Council on Social Welfare (ICSW) and the International Consortium for Social Development (ICSD) (Brueggeman, 2006).

International Federation of Social Workers (IFSW)

Established in 1956, the IFSW "is a global organisation striving for social justice, human rights and social development" through the support of effective social work practice and "international cooperation between social workers and their professional organisations" (International Federation of Social Workers [IFSW], 2009c). It focuses on improving "the quality of life," "achievement of social justice," and the development "of human potential" for people around the globe (IFSW, 2009b). It is especially involved in "protesting human rights violations" (Hokenstad & Midgley, 1997, pp. 4–5).

The IFSW consists of five regions—Africa, Asia and the Pacific, Europe, Latin America and the Caribbean, and North America. It publishes a monthly newsletter for members. The IFSW also sponsors regional and global conferences to teach skills, train educators to teach in various areas related to social justice, and provide a forum for the discussion and development of ideas for addressing critical global issues. The IFSW also "promotes Human Rights by publishing statements on human rights issues and related matters and by raising awareness within the profession about the profession's commitment to its Human Rights heritage" (IFSW, 2009a). It has also developed an "International Policy on Human Rights" to provide guidance concerning human rights issues to social workers and organizations around the world. (The IFSW's home website is http://www.ifsw.org.)

International Association of Schools of Social Work (IASSW)

The IASSW is a "worldwide association of schools of social work," "related educational programmes, and social work educators"; it "promotes the development of social work education throughout the world, develops standards to enhance [the] quality of social work education, encourages international exchange, provides forums for sharing social work research and scholarship, and promotes human rights and social development through policy and advocacy activities" (International Association of Schools of Social Work [IASSW], 2009b). It also serves as a consultant to the United Nations.

The IASSW is based on humanitarian values and the quest for social justice on the behalf of oppressed populations. It holds a biennial conference for social work educators, publishes a member newsletter, provides representation at the United Nations, co-sponsors with the IFSW and the ICSW (discussed in the next section) the journal *International Social Work*, sponsors various committees and task forces, and funds "small cross-national projects in social work education" (IASSW, 2009a). (The IASSW's home website is http://www.iassw-aiets.org.)

Other Global Organizations Dedicated to Social Welfare and Social Justice

Established in 1928, the International Council on Social Welfare (ICSW) is an international nongovernmental organization whose membership includes local and national organizations in over 70 countries (International Council on Social Welfare [ICSW], 2009a). (Highlight 13.5 describes international nongovernment organizations.) The ICSW's membership consists of "tens of thousands of community organisations that work directly at the grass-roots with people in poverty, hardship or distress" (ICSW, 2009a). The ICSW collects relevant information and dispenses it to various community groups, governments, and other organizations; provides training and support for members and other organizations; assists in policy development; sponsors global and regional meetings; publishes papers and reports on issues; and advocates for oppressed populations (ICSW, 2009b). (The home website is http://www.icsw.org.)

The International Consortium for Social Development (ICSD) consists of "practitioners, scholars, and students in the human services" and "serves as a clearinghouse for information on international social development" (International Consortium for Social Development [ICSD], 2009). The ICSD seeks to improve economic and social conditions in various parts of the world by building on community strengths, improving distribution of economic resources, encouraging peace, and fighting discrimination (ICSD, 2009). It links skilled members with communities and governments in need, offers opportunities for training and

International Nongovernmental Organizations

An *international nongovernment organization* (INGO) is a nonprofit agency whose purpose is to address designated social problems and issues (Cox & Pawar, 2006, p. 61). It is usually funded privately through such sources as donations and grants. An INGO's activities at the international level include advocating for human rights, assisting in economic development, providing education to citizens, helping people address crises, monitoring governments' treatment of their citizens, and providing consultation to national governments (Barker, 2003). Examples of goals include helping refugees relocate and providing assistance in reconstruction after a crisis such as a hurricane, earthquake, or war (Cox & Pawar, 2006). One of the oldest, most famous INGOs is the *International Red Cross*, originating in 1863 (Cox & Pawar, 2006). It is "concerned with the alleviation of human suffering and the promotion of public health and civil rights" (Barker, 2003, p. 362). However, "many Christian humanitarian organizations, Jewish welfare agencies, and the American Medical Association were founded even earlier" (Beigbeder, 1991; Cox & Pawar, 2006, p. 61).

Amnesty International (AI) provides another example of an INGO (Brueggemann, 2006). It is a global movement that "operates around the world, mobilizing an international base of human rights advocates who question individual states about their human rights practices and provide material resources and legal services for victims of human rights abuse" (AI, 2009a; Brueggemann 2006, p. 478).

Examples of AI's campaigns involve taking action to:

- Stop violence against women
- Defend the rights and dignity of those trapped in poverty
- Abolish the death penalty
- Oppose torture and combat terror with justice
- Free prisoners of conscience
- Protect the rights of refugees and migrants
- Regulate the global arms race (AI, 2009a)

One issue being addressed at the time of this writing is the crisis in Sri Lanka, where 250,000 civilians, including 80,000 children, are being detained in internment camps (AI, 2009b). These people have endured weeks of heavy fighting between the Sri Lankan government and opposing forces; their conditions include being "badly injured, malnourished, exhausted and traumatized" (AI, 2009b). Human rights violations consist of executions without trial, torture, use as "human shields," and mandatory, involuntary conscription into fighting factions (AI, 2009b). AI is appealing to the United Nations' (UN) Human Rights Council for it to demand that the Sri Lankan government provide the UN, the International Committee of the Red Cross, and other international observers immediate ready access to all locations where displaced people are being held. The intent is for these groups to monitor conditions and prevent further human rights violations. AI emphasizes that the history of human rights violations in Sri Lanka is long-standing and well established; as such, AI is requesting that the Council on Human Rights establish "an international commission of inquiry into allegations of serious violations of international human rights" (AI, 2009b). Such a commission could investigate human rights infringements and make recommendations regarding increased accountability for violence and mistreatment. (Amnesty International's home website is http://web.amnesty.org.)

curriculum development, and provides a forum for the development and application of new ideas. (The ICSD's home website is http://www.iucisd.org.)

Focus on Ethics 13.3 discusses international codes of ethics.

Focus on Ethics 13.3 | International Social Work: Codes of Ethics

Although the NASW *Code of Ethics* is the primary code followed by social workers in the United States, note that other ethical codes also are available in other nations and on an international basis (CSWE, 2008). Consider, for example, the Association of Canadian Social Workers (CASW) Code of Ethics accessible at http://www.casw-acts.ca/canada/codepage_e.html.

The IFSW and IASSW have developed an *Ethics in Social Work, Statement of Principles* that may be applied when addressing *international* (involving two or more nations) or *global* (involving the entire world) ethical issues (CSWE, 2008). Often, these issues concern human rights. The document, concurrently supported by both organizations, consists of the following five parts:

1. *Preface*
2. *Definition of social work*
3. *International conventions* (that refer to various organizations' specific statements of human rights)

4. *Principles*
5. *Professional conduct* (IASSW, 2009; IFSW, 2004)

The "principles" in the *Ethics in Social Work, Statement of Principles* include "human rights and human dignity" and "social justice." The former indicates how "social work is based on respect for the inherent worth and dignity of all people, and the rights that follow from this. Social workers should uphold and defend each person's physical, psychological, emotional and spiritual integrity and well-being." It continues that "social workers have a responsibility to promote social justice, in relation to society generally, and in relation to the people with whom they work"; this involves "challenging negative discrimination," "recognizing diversity," "distributing resources equitably," "challenging unjust policies and practices," and "working in solidarity" (i.e., social workers as a group have the responsibility to confront social injustice).

Social Work and Cross-Cultural Values in Global Perspective

"Social work practice does not follow the same patterns in all parts of the world. The form of social work that develops in any society is shaped by the prevailing social, economic, and cultural forces" (Doel & Shardlow, 1996; Sowers & Rowe, 2007, pp. 29–30). Therefore, it's of critical importance to view and understand community development within the context of the society where it's happening.

Sowers and Rowe (2007) maintain that "social work has been profoundly influenced by Western thought, values, and views" (p. 30; Sacco, 1996). They continue:

> Arising from the dominant Western cultural point of view, human needs are based on the assumption that each individual needs a decent standard of living, education, housing, medical care, and social services, and that the provision of universal services would lead to the elimination of poverty, the advancement of underprivileged groups, and the narrowing of gaps in income, education, and employment (Barretta-Herman, 1994). (p. 30)

Verschelden (1993, pp. 766–767) proposes the following as fundamental global social work values that transcend cultural and national differences:

1. Primary importance of the individual
2. Respect and appreciation for differences

| Highlight 13.6 | Cultural Differences in an Organizational Context |

Dubrin (2007) cites four cultural differences in the context of working with and in large organizations (Hofstede, 1980, 1993; Kennedy & Everest, 1991). These also are significant when working effectively with organizations in the community environment and with community citizens. It's essential to establish goals with community residents that fit well with their own value systems. It's also crucial for people commencing community development to be aware of their own value orientations so as not to impose them on people in the community.

1. *Individualism versus collectivism. "Individualism"* is "a mental set in which people see themselves first as individuals and believe that their own interests take priority. At the other end of the continuum, *collectivism* is a feeling that the group and society receive top priority . . . . Highly individualistic cultures include the United States, Canada, Great Britain, Australia, and the Netherlands. Japan, Taiwan, Mexico, Greece, and Hong Kong are among the countries that strongly value collectivism" (Dubrin, p. 386).

Sowers and Rowe (2007) comment concerning differences in how individual importance is perceived:

> For instance, within the African context, traditional African thinking understands human nature and human flourishing as a network of life forces that emanate from God and end in God, who is the source of all life forces. For many Africans, personhood is attainable only in community and the single most important concept within African traditional life is the inclusion of all into the community, (Senghor, 1966; Setiloane, 1986)

Van Wormer (2006) reflects on the value of collectivism for First Nations Peoples:

> The sense of interconnectedness is a staple of traditional indigenous culture. The First Nations people in North American rely on the metaphor of the Medicine Wheel, which exemplifies the

wholeness of all life. The Medicine Wheel teaches about the cycle of life, a cycle that encompasses infancy through old age, the seasons, and four directions of human growth—the emotional, mental, physical, and spiritual. This is not a linear system; all the parts are interconnected. American Indian teachings are traditionally presented as narratives and shared within a talking circle. . . . [V]alues are: a strong emphasis on *being* not doing and cooperation over competition; a group emphasis; working only to meet one's needs; nonmaterialism; . . . and living in harmony with nature. The theme of these values is social interconnectedness. (p. 57)

Sowers and Rowe (2007) conclude that "working out an understanding of human beings and personal development that incorporates cultural conceptions and beliefs is critical to effective social work practice, particularly in a global context" (p. 30).

2. *Materialism versus concern for others* (Dubrin, p. 386). *"Materialism"* is the value that material things and money are extremely important, much more so than humanitarian or spiritual pursuits. There is also a tendency to emphasize, "Me, Me, Me" rather than focus on other people's needs and issues. In contrast, *concern for others* refers to genuine, active concern for other people's well-being and a focus on the importance of interpersonal relationships. As Dubrin notes, "Materialistic countries include Japan, Austria, and Italy. The United States is considered to be moderately materialistic . . . Scandinavian nations all emphasize caring as a national value" (p. 386).

3. *Formality versus informality.* According to Dubrin, "A country that values *formality* attaches considerable importance to tradition, ceremony, social rules, and rank. At the other extreme, *informality* refers to a casual attitude toward tradition, ceremony, social rules, and rank . . . [People] in Latin American countries highly value

continued

Highlight 13.6 | *continued*

formality, such as lavish public receptions and processions. Americans, Canadians, and Scandinavians are much more informal" (p. 386).

4. *Urgent time orientation versus casual time orientation*. Dubrin notes that "individuals and nations attach different importance to time. People with an *urgent time orientation* perceive time as a scarce resource and tend to be impatient. People with a *casual time orientation* view time as an unlimited and unending resource and tend to be patient. Americans are noted for their urgent time orientation. They frequently impose deadlines and are eager to get started doing business. Asians and Middle Easterners, in contrast, are [much more] patient." (p. 387).

3. Commitment to social justice and the well-being of all in society
4. Willingness to persist despite frustration

Some research indicates that the last three are generally held by social workers around the globe; however, the first is addressed quite differently depending on the culture (Rowe, Hanley, Moreno, & Mould, 2000; Sowers & Rowe, 2007). Social workers must respond to the diverse cultural values of the societies in which they work. The ways in which individuals expect to be treated and the ways they prioritize their values vary from one culture to another. Highlight 13.6 identifies some cultural differences that must be taken into account when undertaking community development.

Critical Thinking Questions 13.7

How would you describe yourself concerning these four global social work value dimensions and why?

What You Can Do on the Behalf of Global Social Justice

There are at least five things that you can do to address and enhance social justice on a global basis. First, vote for political candidates who appreciate the importance of global cooperation to address human rights issues and solve social ills (Verschelden, 1993). Second, you can continue to become more knowledgeable about global issues and educate others including legislators about the issues' significance (Verschelden, 1993). Third, you can become politically involved yourself by actively participating in political debate and working to support political candidates (Shaefor & Horejsi, 2009). You might even decide to run for office yourself. Fourth, you can join organizations, several of which were mentioned earlier, that seek to help needy and hurting people around the world. Fifth, you can volunteer your time to support the work of international helping organizations. Sixth, you can become a macro practice social worker participating in community development in the international context.

Chapter Summary

The following summarizes this chapter's content as it relates to the learning objectives presented at the beginning of the chapter. Objectives include the following:

A. Describe globalization.

We live in a global environment with multiple interconnections. Globalization is the "process of global integration in which diverse people, economies, cultures, and political processes are increasingly subjected to international influences" (Midgley, 1997a, p. xi). The concepts—global, advocate, and social justice—are critical aspects of social work's global perspective.

B. Review social justice, define *human rights*, and stress the significance of the concepts for international social work practice.

Social justice involves upholding the condition that in a perfect world all citizens would have identical "rights, protection, opportunities, obligations, and social benefits," regardless of their backgrounds and membership in diverse groups (Barker, 2003, pp. 404–405). Human rights involve the premise that all people—regardless of race, culture, or national origin—are entitled to basic rights and treatment. Developing a global focus means becoming aware of the issues facing the human population in the twenty-first century. From a social work perspective, global problems are everyone's problems.

C. Discuss the social issues of poverty and economic justice, global conflict, immigration status, and the forced migration of people in need.

Poverty is the condition where people maintain "a standard of living below the minimum needed for the maintenance of adequate diet, health, and shelter" (Eitzen & Zinn, 2006, p. 182). The gap between rich and poor is widening in the United States, which raises questions concerning economic justice. Global poverty is a major problem with numerous consequences related to it. Global conflict is rampant, with the goal of peace being very difficult to attain.

Immigration status is a person's position in term of legal rights and residency when entering and residing in a country that is not that person's legal country of origin. Millions of people worldwide are involuntarily displaced from their country of origin. Related terms include legal and illegal immigrants, nonimmigrants, refugees, documented and undocumented aliens, deportable aliens, adjustment of status, and naturalized citizens.

D. Define *community development and social development*, discuss their theoretical foundations, and provide case examples.

"Community development refers to efforts to mobilize people who are directly affected by a community condition into groups and organizations to enable them to take action on the social problems and issues that concern them" (Rivera & Erlich, 2001, p. 256). Important concepts in the conceptualization of community development are production-distribution-consumption, socialization, social control, social participation, and mutual support. Community development practice is based on five basic practice principles: community members' active participation; establishing common goals; reaching out to various diverse groups, constituencies, and organizations; using community assets, and empowerment of community members to help themselves. Examples of community development in Africa, Guatemala, and Indonesia are provided.

Social development, a concept related to community development, is a planned change process

on the behalf of an entire population that emphasizes economic development based on two principles; first, economic development integrates
social and economic policy, and, second, it sponsors investment-oriented social programs "that
contribute positively to economic development"
(Midgley & Sherraden, 2009, p. 283). A case
example is the Grameen Bank of Dahka,
Bangladesh. Distorted development can occur
where economic conditions improve, but social
conditions do not.

E. Examine a feminist perspective on global development.

A feminist perspective on global development
involves "raising consciousness regarding gender
roles and the importance and worth of every
female"; "forming interdisciplinary professional
partnerships with poor women and training
indigenous trainers to serve their own communities"; and "teaching women that both personal
development and action, as well as collective
social development and action, are essential if
their lives are to change for the better" (Wetzel,
1995, pp. 181–186).

F. Define and explain international social work.

International social work is "international
professional practice and the capacity for international action by the social work profession and
its members. International social work has four
dimensions: internationally related domestic
practice and advocacy, professional exchange,
international practice, and international policy
development and advocacy" (Healy, 2008,
p. 10). A case example of social work in Mauritius is provided.

G. Identify and describe international social work and social welfare organizations.

International social work and social welfare
organizations include the International Federation of Social Workers (IFSW), the International
Association of Schools of Social Work (IASSW),
the International Council on Social Welfare
(ICSW), and the International Consortium for
Social Development (ICSD). Although each

focuses on its own goals, these generally include
the pursuit of social justice and the international
exchange of ideas to improve the human
condition.

H. Define *international nongovernmental organizations* and provide examples.

International nongovernment organizations
are nonprofit agencies whose purpose is to address
designated social problems and issues. Examples
include the International Red Cross and Amnesty
International (AI). A current concern addressed by
AI is the war in Sri Lanka and the conditions experienced by its displaced persons.

I. Discuss social work values and cross-cultural values in global perspective.

Social workers must be sensitive to the major
differences in cultural values around the world.
The IFSW and IASSW have developed an *Ethics
in Social Work, Statement of Principles* that may
be applied when addressing international or
global ethical issues.

J. Identify some of the cultural differences existing in organizational contexts.

Cultural differences in an organizational context include "individualism versus collectivism,"
"materialism versus concern for others," "formality versus informality," and "urgent time orientation versus casual time orientation" (Dubrin,
2007, pp. 386–387).

K. Raise critical thinking questions.

Critical thinking questions addressed personal
views on financial status, support of the U.S. military presence in various other countries, illegal
immigration, community functioning, FEMA's
handling of Hurricane Katrina's victims, feminist
principles concerning global development, and
agreement with proposed global social work
values.

L. Focus on ethical issues.

Ethical issues focused on the gap between
rich and poor in the United States, reasons and
responsibility for global poverty, and international codes of ethics.

In summary, this chapter explored the macro environment and social justice on a global scale. The intent is help you develop a perspective that extends far beyond that of your immediate environment—school, work, neighborhood, city or town, and even state and country.

For Further Exploration on the Internet

See this text's website at **www.cengage.com/ social_work/kirst-ashman** for learning tools such as tutorial quizzing, Web links, glossary, flashcards, and PowerPoint® slides.

References

Abramovitz, M. (1995). Aid to families with dependent children. In *Encyclopedia of social work* (Vol. 1, pp. 183–194).Washington, DC: NASW Press.

Abramovitz, M. (1997). Temporary assistance to needy families. In *Encyclopedia of social work supplement*, (19th ed., pp. 311–330). Washington, DC: NASW Press.

Abramovitz, M. (2007). Ideological perspectives and conflicts. In J. Blau (Ed., with M. Abramovitz), *The dynamics of social welfare policy* (2nd ed., pp. 126–183). New York: Oxford.

Administration for Children & Families (ACF). (2006). Welfare reform reauthorized. Retrieved June 27, 2006, from http://www.acf.hhs.gov/opa/spotlight/welfarereauthorized.htm.

Administration for Children & Families (ACF). (2008a). About TANF. Retrieved April 19, 2009, from http://www.acf.hhs.gov/programs/ofa/tanf/about.html.

Administration for Children & Families. (2008b). Major provisions of the Personal Responsibility and Work Opportunity Reconciliation Act of 1996 (P.L. 104-193). Retrieved April 27, 2009, from http://www.acf.hhs.gov/programs/ofa/law-reg/finalrule/aspesum.htm.

Administration for Children & Families. (2009). Mission statement. Retrieved April 19, 2009, from http://www.acf.hhs.gov/programs/ofa/about.html.

Agrest, S. (1997, December 15). Kids who care. *Time*, Special Report, unnumbered inset.

Albrecht, K. (1978). *Successful management by objectives: An action manual*. Englewood Cliffs, NJ: Prentice Hall.

Albrecht, K. (1988). *At America's service*. New York: Warner Books.

Aldag, R. J., & Kuzuhara, L. W. (2005). *Mastering management skills*. Mason, OH: South-Western.

Alter, C. F. (2009). Building community partnerships and networks. In R. J. Patti (Ed.), *The handbook of human services management* (2nd ed., pp. 435–454). Thousand Oaks, CA: Sage.

American Psychiatric Association. (2000). *Diagnostic and statistical manual of mental disorders: Text revision. DSM-IV-TR* (4th ed.). Washington, DC: Author.

Amnesty International (AI). (2009a). About Amnesty International. Retrieved May 25, 2009, from http://www.amnesty.org/en/who-we-are/about-amnesty-international.

Amnesty International (AI). (2009b). UN Human Rights Council should tackle Sri Lanka crisis. Retrieved May 25, 2009, from http://www.amnesty.org/en/news-and-updates/news/un-human-rights-council-should-tackle-sri-lanka-crisis-20090522.

Anderson, J. (1997). *Social work with groups: A process model*. New York: Longman.

Anderson, R. E., & Carter, I., & Lowe, G.R. (1999). *Human behavior in the social environment: A social systems approach* (5th ed.). New York: Aldine De Gruyter.

Appleby, G. A., & Anastas, J. W. (1998). *Not just a passing phase: Social work with gay, lesbian, and bisexual people*. New York: Columbia University Press.

ARC Milwaukee. (undated, a). *Employment programs*. Milwaukee, WI: Author.

ARC Milwaukee. (undated, b). *Figuring out funding*. Milwaukee, WI: Author.

ARC Milwaukee. (undated, c). *Services profile*. Milwaukee, WI: Author.

Arredondo, P., & Perez, P. (2003). Counseling paradigms and Latina/o Americans: Contemporary considerations. In F. D. Harper, & J. McFadden (Eds.), *Culture and counseling: New Approaches* (pp. 115–132). Boston: Allyn & Bacon.

Asch, A. (1995). Visual impairment and blindness. In *Encyclopedia of social work* (Vol. 3, pp. 2461–2468). Washington, DC: NASW Press.

Asch, A. & Mudrick, N. R. (1995). Disability. In *Encyclopedia of social work* (Vol. 1, pp. 752–761). Washington, DC: NASW Press.

Asch, A., & Mudrick, N. R. (2008). Blindness and visual impairment. In T. Mizrahi & L. E. Davis (Editors-in-Chief), *Encyclopedia of Social Work* (Vol. 1, pp. 206–214). Washington, DC: NASW Press.

Axelrod, N. R. (2005). Board leadership and development. In R. D. Herman (Ed.), *The Jossey-Bass handbook of nonprofit leadership and management* (2nd ed., pp. 131–152).

Austin, D. M. (1995). Management overview. In *Encyclopedia of social work* (Vol. 2, pp. 1642–1658). Washington, DC: NASW Press.

Austin, D. M. (2002). *Human services management: Organizational leadership in social work practice.* New York: Columbia.

Bailey, D., & Uhly, K. M. (2008). Leadership. In T. Mizrahi & L. E. Davis (Editors-in-Chief), *Encyclopedia of Social Work* (Vol. 3, pp. 62–67). Washington, DC: NASW Press.

Bales, R. F. (1950). *Interaction process analysis: A method for the study of small groups.* Cambridge, MA: Addison-Wesley.

Balgopal, P. (2008). Asian Americans: Overview. In T. Mizrahi & L. E. Davis (Editors-in-Chief), *Encyclopedia of Social Work* (Vol. 1, pp. 153–160). Washington, DC: NASW Press.

Ball, S. & Lipton, B. (1997). Group work with gay men. In G. L. Greif & P. H. Ephross (Eds.), *Group work with populations at risk.* New York: Oxford University Press. (pp. 259–277).

Balsanek, J. (1998). Addressing at-risk pregnant women's issues through community, individual, and corporate grassroots efforts. In P. L. Ewalt, E. M. Freeman, & D. L. Poole (Eds.), *Community building: Renewal, well-being, and shared responsbility.* Washington, DC: NASW Press. (pp. 411–419).

Barbuto, Jr., J. E., & Wheeler, D. W. (2005). *Becoming a servant leader: Do you have what it takes?* Lincoln,

NE: University of Nebraska-Lincoln Extension, Institute of Agriculture and Natural Resources, A-15 General.

Barker, R. L. (2003). *The social work dictionary* (5th ed.). Washington, DC: National Association of Social workers.

Barnett, A. W. (1984). *Community murals: The people's art.* Philadelphia: Art Alliance Press.

Barretta-Herman, A. (1994). Revisioning the community as provider: Restructuring New Zealand's social services. *International Social work, 37*(1), 7–21.

Barusch, A. S. (2009). *Foundations of social policy: Social justice in human perspective* (3rd ed.). Belmont, CA: Brooks/Cole.

Beckett, J. O., & Johnson, H. C. (1995). Human development. In R. L. Edwards (Eds.), *Encyclopedia of social work* (19th ed., Vol. 2, pp. 1385–1405).Washington, DC: NASW Press.

Bedwell, R. T., Jr. (1993). Total quality management: Making the decision. *Nonprofit World, 2*(3), 29–31.

Beigbeder, Y. (1991). *The role and status of international humanitarian volunteers and organisations.* Dordrecht, The Netherlands: Martinus Nijhoff.

Berger, R. J., & Kelly, J. J. (1995). Gay Men Overview. In *Encyclopedia of social work* (Vol. 2, pp. 1064–1075). Washington, DC: NASW Press.

Bernard, J. (1973). *The sociology of community.* Glenview, IL: Scott, Foresman.

Berrick, J. D. (2009). Income maintenance and support: The changing face of welfare. In J. Midgley & M. Livermore (Eds.), *The handbook of social policy* (2nd ed., pp. 336–346). Thousand Oaks, CA: Sage.

Biegal, D. E., Shore, B. K., & Gordon, E. (1984). *Building support networks for the elderly.* Beverly Hills: Sage.

Black, R. B. (1994). Diversity and populations at risk: People with disabilities. In F. Reamer (Ed.), *The foundations of social work knowledge.* New York: Columbia University Press.

Blythe, B., & Reighoffer, A. (2000). Assessment and measurement issues in direct practice in social work.

In P. Allen-Meares & C. Garvin (Eds.), *The handbook of social work practice* (pp. 551–564). Thousand Oaks, CA: Sage.

Boodajee, K. Y. (1997). *A critical appraisal of the functioning of the Child Development Unit of the Ministry of Women, Family Welfare and Child Development with reference to case studies showing strengths and weaknesses of the unit.* Social Work Diploma Project, University of Mauritius, Reduit.

Brammer, R. (2004). *Diversity in counseling.* Belmont, CA: Brooks/Cole.

Brandwein R. A. (2008). Women: Overview. In T. Mizrahi & L. E. Davis (Editors-in-Chief), *Encyclopedia of Social Work* (Vol. 4, pp. 281–290). Washington, DC: NASW press.

Braun, K. L., Mokuau, N., & Tsark, J. (1997). Cultural themes in health, illness, and rehabilitation for Native Hawaiians: Observations of rehabilitation staff and physicians. *Topics in Geriatric Rehabilitation, 12,* 19–37.

Brave Heart, M. Y. H. (2001). Lakota— Native people's spirituality. In M. Van Hook, B. Hugen, & M. Aguilar (Eds.), (pp. 18–33), *Spirituality within religious traditions in social work practice.* Belmont, CA: Brooks-Cole.

Breidenstein, J. L. (2003, Spring). Grandparents raising grandchildren. *The New Social worker, 10*(2), 5–7.

Breton, M. (2004). An empowerment perspective. In C. D. Garvin, L.M. Gutierrez, & M. J. Galinsky (Eds.), *Handbook of social work with groups* (pp. 58–75). New York: Guilford.

Bricker-Jenkins, M., & Lockett, P. W. (1995). Women: Direct practice. In R. L. Edwards (Ed.), *Encyclopedia of social work* (19th ed., Vol. 3, pp. 2529–2539). Washington, DC: NASW Press.

Bricker-Jenkins, M., & Netting, F. E. (2009). Feminist issues and practices in social work. In A. R. Roberts (Editor-in-Chief), *Social workers' desk reference* (2nd ed., pp. 277–283). New York: Oxford.

Briggs, X. S. (2008). Community building. In J. DeFilippes & S. Saegert (Eds.), *The community development reader* (pp. 36–45). New York: Routledge.

Bridgewater, D. (1992). A gay male survivor of antigay violence. In S. H. Dworkin & F. J. Gutierrez (Eds.), *Counseling gay men and lesbians: Journey to the end of the rainbow* (pp. 219–230). Alexandria, VA: AACD Press.

Brody, R. (2005). *Effectively managing human service organizations* (3rd ed.). Thousand Oaks, CA: Sage.

Brown, M. G., Hitchcock, D. E., & Willard, M. L. (1994). Why TQM fails and what to do about it. *Soundview Executive Book Summaries, 16*(5), 1–8.

Brueggemann, W. G. (2006). *The practice of macro social work* (3rd ed.). Belmont, CA: Brooks/Cole.

Burk, M. (2009). Power plays: Six ways the male corporate elite keeps women out. In S. Shaw & J. Lee (Eds.), *Women's voices: Feminist visions* (4th ed., pp. 483–485). Boston: McGraw-Hill.

Burrell, G., & Morgan, G. (1979). *Sociological paradigms and organizational analysis*. London: Heinemann.

Burton, L. M. (1992). Black grandparents rearing children of drug-addicted parents: Stressors, outcomes, and social service needs. *Gerontologist, 32,* 744–751.

Butler, R. M. (1989). Dispelling ageism: The cross-cutting intervention. In M. W. Riley & J. W. Riley, Jr. (Eds.), *The quality of aging: Strategies for interventions. Annals of the American Academy of Political and Social Science, 503,* 163–175.

Butler, S., & Wintram, C. (1992). *Feminist groupwork*. Thousand Oaks, CA: Sage.

Butterfield, A. K. J., & Chisanga, B. (2008). Community development. In T. Mizrahi & L. E. Davis (Editors-in-Chief), *Encyclopedia of Social Work* (Vol. 1, pp. 375–381). Washington, DC: NASW Press.

Cahill, S., Ellen, M., & Tobias, S. (2002). *Family policy: Issues affecting gay, lesbian, bisexual, and transgendered families*. New York: National Gay and Lesbian Task Force Policy Institute.

California town hopes eye-catching murals will put it on map. (1996, November 10). *New York Times,* p. 24.

Capuzzi, D., & Gross, D. R. (2006). Group work: Elements of effective leadership. In D. Capuzzi, D. R. Gross, & M. D. Stauffer (Eds.), *Introduction to group work* (4th ed., pp. 515–547). Denver: Love.

CARE. (2006). CARE. Retrieved September 10, 2006, from http://www.care.org.

Carlton-LaNey, I. B., Edwards, R. L., & Reid, P. N. (1999). Small towns and rural communities: From romantic notions to harsh realities. In I. B. Carlton-LaNey, R. L. Edwards, & P. N. Reid (Eds.), *Preserving and strengthening small towns and rural communities* (pp. 5–12). Washington, DC: NASW Press.

Carr, E. S. (2004). Accessing resources, transforming systems: Group work with poor and homeless people. In C. D. Garvin, L. M. Gutierrez, & M. J. Galinsky (Eds.), *Handbook of social work with groups* (pp. 360–383). New York: Guilford.

Carroll, C., Bates, M., & Johnson, C. (2004). *Group leadership: Strategies or group counseling leaders* (4th ed.). Denver: Love.

Carroll, J. L. (2010). *Sexuality now: Embracing diversity* (3rd ed.). Belmont, CA: Wadsworth.

Center on Budget and Policy Priorities (CBPP). (2006, May 9). Implementing the TANF changes in the Deficit Reduction Act: "Win-win" solutions for families and states. Retrieved June 27, 2006, from http://www.cbpp.org/5-9-06tanf.htm.

Center on Budget and Policy Priorities (CBPP). (2007, February). *Implementing the TANF changes in the Deficit Reduction Act: "Win-win" solution for families and states*. Washington, DC: Author.

Centers for Disease Control (CDC). (2009a). Developmental disabilities: Topic home. Retrieved May 20, 2009, from http://www.cdc.gov/ncbddd/dd/default.htm.

Centers for Disease Control (CDC). (2009b). Prenatal care. Available online at http://www.cdc.gov/nchs/FASTATS/prenatal.htm.

Champoux, J. E. (2006). *Organizational behavior: Integrating individuals, groups and organizations* (3rd ed.). Manson, OH: South-Western.

Chapin, R. (2007). *Social policy for effective practice: A strengths approach*. Boston: McGraw-Hill.

Child Welfare League of America (CWLA). (2006, February 1). Analysis and summary of Deficit Reduction Act. Retrieved June 27, 2006, from http://www.cwla.org/printable/printpage.asp.

Chilman, C. S. (1993). Hispanic families in the United States: Research perspectives. In H. P. McAdoo (Ed.), *Family ethnicity: Strength in diversity*. Newbury Park, CA: Sage.

Cnaan, R. A., & Boddie, S. C. (2002). Charitable choice and faith-based welfare: A call for social work. *Social Work, 47*(3), 224–235.

Coleman, J. W., & Kerbo, H. R. (2002). *Social problems* (8th ed.). Upper Saddle River, NJ: Prentice-Hall.

Coleman, S. (1994, December 11). Mission's marvelous murals if you go . . . *The Boston Globe,* p. B1.

Coley, S., & Scheinberg, C. (2000). *Proposal writing* (2nd ed.). Thousand Oaks, CA: Sage.

Compton, B. R., Galaway, B., & Cournoyer, B. R. (2005). *Social work processes* (7th ed.). Belmont, CA: Brooks/Cole.

Cooper, M., & Sciorra, J. (1994). *R.I.P. memorial wall art*. New York: Henry Holt.

Corcoran, K. (1997). Managed care: Implications for social work practice. In *Encyclopedia of social work supplement* (19th ed., pp. 191–200). Washington, DC: NASW Press.

Corey, G. (2008). *Theory & practice of group counseling* (7th ed.). Belmont, CA: Brooks/Cole.

Corey, G., Corey, M. S., & Callanan, P. (2007). *Issues and ethics in the helping professions* (7th ed.). Belmont, CA: Brooks/Cole.

Corey, M. S., Corey, G., & Corey, C. (2010). *Groups: Process and practice* (8th ed.). Belmont, CA: Brooks/Cole.

Cormier, S., & Hackney. H. (2008). *Counseling strategies and interventions* (8th ed.). Boston: Allyn & Bacon.

Cornell University Empowerment Group. (1989). *Networking Bulletin, 1*(2).

Corporation for National & Community Service. (2009a). Retrieved May 13, 2009, from http://www.americorps.gov/about/programs/national.asp.

Corporation for National & Community Service. (2009b). Retrieved May 13, 2009, from http://www.americorps.gov/about/programs.vista.asp.

Cournoyer, B. R. (2005). *The social work skills workbook* (4th ed.). Belmont, CA: Brooks/Cole.

Council on Social Work Education (CSWE). (2008). *Educational policy and accreditation standards (EPAS)*. Alexandria, VA: Author.

Cowger, C. D., & Snively, C. A. (2002). Assessing client strengths: Individual, family, and community empowerment. In D. Saleebey (Ed.), *The strengths perspective in social work practice* (3rd ed., pp. 106–123). Boston: Allyn & Bacon.

Cox, C. B. (2002). Empowering African American custodial grandparents. *Social work, 47*(1), 45–54.

Cox, D., & Pawar, M. (2006). *International social work: Issues, strategies, and programs.* Thousand Oaks, CA: Sage.

Cox, E. O. (1991). The critical role of social action in empowerment oriented groups. In A. Vinik & M. Levin (Eds.), *Social action in group work* (pp. 77–90). New York: Haworth.

Crooks, R., & Baur, K. (2008). *Our sexuality* (10th ed.). Belmont, CA: Wadsworth.

Crosby, P. (1980). *Quality if free.* New York: Mentor.

Crosson-Tower, C. (2007). *Exploring child welfare: A practice perspective* (4th ed.). Boston: Allyn & Bacon.

Daley, M. R., & Avant, F. L. (2004). Rural social work. In T. L. Scales & C. L. Streeter (Eds.), *Rural social work: building and sustaining community assets* (pp. 34–42). Belmont, CA: Brooks/Cole.

Daft, R. L. (2003). *Management* (6th ed.). Cincinnati, OH: South-Western.

Daft, R. L. (2004). *Organization theory and design* (8th ed.). Cincinnati, OH: South-Western.

Daft, R. L. (2007). *Organization theory and design* (9th ed.). Cincinnati, OH: South-Western.

Daft, R. L. (2008). *Management* (8th ed.). Mason, OH: South-Western.

Daft, R. L. (2010). *Management* (9th ed.). Mason, OH: South-Western.

Daft, R. L., & Marcic, D. (2004). *Understanding management* (4th ed.). Cincinnati, OH: South-Western.

Daft, R. L., & Marcic, D. (2009). *Understanding management* (6th ed.). Mason, OH: South-Western.

Davenport, J. A., & Davenport, J., III. (1995). In R. L. Edwards (Editor-in-Chief), *Encyclopedia of Social Work* (Vol. 3, 19th ed., pp. 2076–2085). Washington, DC: NASW Press.

Davenport, J. A., & Davenport, J., III. (2008). Rural practice. In T. Mizrahi & L. E. Davis (Editors-in-Chief), *Encyclopedia of Social Work* (Vol. 3, pp. 536–541). Washington, DC: NASW Press.

Davis, L. E., Wallace, J. M., Jr., & Shanks, T. R. W. (2008). African Americans: Overview. In T. Mizrahi & L. E. Davis (Editors-in-Chief), *Encyclopedia of Social Work* (Vol. 1, pp. 65–75). Washington, DC: NASW Press.

Day, P. J. (2006). *A new history of social welfare* (5th ed.). Boston: Allyn & Bacon.

DeCesare, D. (1993, March). El Salvador: War, poverty and migration: A photo essay. *Fellowship, 59*(3).

DeFilippis, J., & Saegert, S. (2008). Communities develop: The question is how? In J. DeFilippes & S. Saegert (Eds.), *The community development reader* (pp. 1–6). New York: Routledge.

Delgado, M. (1997). Role of Latina-owned beauty parlors in a Latino community. *Social work, 42*(5), 445–453.

Delgado, M. (1998a). Community asset assessments by Latino youth. In P. L. Ewalt, E. M. Freeman, & D. L. Poole (Eds.), *Community building: Renewal, well-being, and shared responsibility* (pp. 202–212). Washington, DC: NASW Press.

Delgado, M. (2000). *Community social work practice in an urban context: The potential of a capacity-enhancement perspective.* New York: Oxford.

Delgado, M. (2007). *Social work with Latinos: A culture assets paradigm.* New York: Oxford.

Delgado, M. (2008). Urban practice. In T. Mizrahi & L. E. Davis (Editors-in-Chief), *Encyclopedia of Social Work* (Vol. 4, pp. 251–254). Washington, DC: NASW Press.

Delgado, M., & Barton, K. (1998, July). Murals in Latino communities: Social indicators of community strengths. *Social work, 43*(4), 346–356.

DeLois, K. A. (1998). Empowerment practice with lesbians and gays. In L. M. Gutierrez, R. J. Parsons, & E. O. Cox (Eds.), *Empowerment in social work practice: A sourcebook* (pp. 65–72).

Deming, W. E. (1982). *Quality, productivity, and competitive position.* Cambridge, MA: MIT Center for Advanced Engineering Study.

Deming, W. E. (1986). *Out of the crisis.* Cambridge, MA: MIT Center for Advanced Engineering Study.

Denhardt, R. B., Denhardt, J. V., & Aristigueta, M. P. (2002). *Managing human behavior in public and nonprofit organizations.* Thousand Oaks, CA: Sage.

DePoy, E., & Gilson, S. F. (2004). *Rethinking disability: Principles for professional and social change.* Belmont, CA: Brooks/Cole.

Derezotes, D. S. (2006). *Spiritually oriented social work practice.* Boston: Allyn & Bacon.

DeWeaver, K. L. (1995). Developmental disabilities: Definitions and policies. In *Encyclopedia of social work* (Vol. 1, pp. 712–720). Washington, DC: NASW Press.

Dhooper, S. S., & Moore, S. E. (2001). *Social work practice with culturally diverse people.* Thousand Oaks, CA: Sage.

Diller, J. V. (2007). *Cultural diversity: A primer for the human services* (3rd ed.). Belmont, CA: Brooks/Cole.

DiNitto, D. M. (2005). *Social welfare: Politics and public policy* (6th ed.). Boston: Allyn & Bacon.

DiNitto, D. M. (2007). *Social welfare: Politics and public policy* (6th ed.). Boston: Allyn & Bacon.

DiNitto, D., M., & Cummins, L. K. (2006). *Social welfare: Politics and public policy* (6th ed.). Boston: Allyn & Bacon.

Doel, M., & Shardlow, S. (1996). Introduction to the context of practice learning: An overview of key themes. In M. Doel & S. Shardlow (Eds.), *Social work in a changing world: An international perspective on practice learning.* Brookfield, VT: Arena Ashgate.

Dolgoff, R., & Feldstein, D. (2007). *Understanding social welfare: A search for social justice.* Boston: Allyn & Bacon.

Dolgoff, R., Loewenberg, F. M., & Harrington, D. (2009). *Ethical decisions in social work practice* (8th ed.). Belmont, CA: Brooks/Cole.

DOMAwatch. (2008). DOMA watch: Your legal source for Defense of Marriage Acts information. Retrieved May 19, 2009, from http://www.domawatch.org/index.php.

Downs, A. (1981). *Neighborhoods and urban development.* Washington, DC: The Brookings Institution.

Dubrin, A. J. (2002). *Fundamentals of organizational behavior* (2nd ed.). Mason, OH: South-Western.

Dubrin, A. (2007). *Fundamentals of organizational behavior* (4th ed.). Mason, OH: South-Western.

Dubrin, A. (2009). *Essentials of management* (8th ed.). Mason, OH: South-Western.

Dumler, M. P., & Skinner, S. J. (2005). *A primer for management.* Mason, OH: South-Western.

Dumler, M. P., & Skinner, S. J. (2008). *A primer for management* (2nd ed.). Mason, OH: South-Western.

DuongTran, Q., & Matsuoka, J. K. (1995). Asian Americans: Southeast Asians. In *Encyclopedia of social work* (Vol. 1, pp. 249–255). Washington, DC: NASW Press.

Duran, E. (2006). *Healing the soul wound.* New York: Teachers College Press.

Durkheim, E. (1947). *Division of labor in society.* Glencoe, IL: Free Press.

Dworkin, S. H. (2000). Individual therapy with lesbian, gay, and bisexual clients. In R. M. Perez, K. A. DeBord, & K. J. Bieschke (Eds.), *Handbook of counseling and psychotherapy with lesbian, gay, and bisexual clients* (pp. 157–181). Washington, DC: American Psychological Association.

Eitzen, D. S., & Zinn, M. B. (2003). *Social problems* (10th ed.). Boston: Allyn & Bacon.

Elze, D. E. (2006). Oppression, prejudice, and discrimination. In D. F. Morrow & L. Messinger (Eds.), *Sexual orientation & gender expression in social work practice:*

Working with gay, lesbian, bisexual, & transgender people (pp. 43–77). New York: Columbia University Press.

Engelhardt, B. J. (1997). Group work with lesbians. In G. L. Greif & P. H. Ephross (Eds.), *Group work with populations at risk* (pp. 278–291). New York: Oxford University Press.

Ephross, P. H., & Vassil, T. V. (2004). Group work with working groups. In C. D. Garvin, L. M. Gutierrez, & M. J. Galinsky (Eds.), *Handbook of social work with groups* (pp. 400–414). New York: Guilford.

Equal Employment Opportunity Commission, U.S. Department of Justice Civil Rights Division. (1997, May). *The Americans with Disabilities Act: Questions and answers.* Washington, DC: Author.

Erhlich, J. L., & Rivera, F. G. (1981). Community organization and community development. In N. Gilbert & H. Specht (Eds.), *Handbook of the social services* (pp. 472–489). Englewood Cliffs, NJ: Prentice Hall.

Etzioni, A. (1964). *Modern organizations.* Englewood Cliffs, NJ: Prentice-Hall.

Ewalt, P. L., & Mokuau, N. (1996). Self-determination from a Pacific perspective. In P. L. Ewalt, E. M. Freeman, A. E. Fortune, D. L. Poole, & S. L. Witkin (eds.). *Multicultural issues in social work: Practice and research* (pp. 255–268). Washington, DC: NASW Press.

Fabricant, M., & Fisher, R. (2008). Settlements and neighborhood centers. In T. Mizrahi & L. E. Davis (Editors-in-Chief). *Encyclopedia of Social Work* (Vol. 4, pp. 17–22). Washington, DC: NASW Press.

Fatout, M., & Rose, S. R. (1995). *Task groups in the social services.* Thousand Oaks, CA: Sage.

Feigenbaum, A. (1983). *Total quality control* (3rd ed.). New York: McGraw-Hill.

Fellin, P. (2001a). *The community and the social worker* (3rd ed.). Belmont, CA: Brooks/Cole.

Fellin, P. (2001b). Understanding American communities. In J. Rothman, J. L. Erlich, & J. E. Tropman (Eds.), *Strategies of*

community organization (3rd ed., pp. 118–132).

Fellin, P. & Litwak, E. (1968). The neighborhood in urban American society. *Social Work, 13*(3), 72–80.

Finn, J. L., & Jacobson, M. (2003). *Just practice: A social justice approach to social work.* Peosta, IA: Eddie Bowers.

Finn, J. L., & Jacobson, M. (2008). *Just practice: A social justice approach to social work* (2nd ed.). Chicago: Lyceum.

Finnegan, D. G., & McNally, E. B. (1996). Chemical dependency and depression in lesbians and gay men: What helps? *Journal of Gay and Lesbian Social Services, 4*(2), 115–129.

Fisher, R. (1984, Summer). Community organization in historical perspective: A typology. *The Huston Review, 8.*

Fisher, R. (2001). Social action community organization: Proliferation, persistence, roots, and prospects. In J. Rothman, J. L. Erlich, & J. E. Tropman (Eds.), *Strategies of community intervention* (6th ed., pp. 350–363). Itasca, IL: Peacock.

Fisher, R., & Burghardt, S. (2008). Social advocacy: The persistence and prospects of social action. In J. Rothman, J. L. Erlich, & J. E. Tropman (Eds.), *Strategies of community intervention* (7th ed., pp. 315–332). Peosta, IA: Eddie Bowers.

Fong, R. (2008). Asian Americans: Practice interventions. In T. Mizrahi & L. E. Davis (Editors-in-Chief), *Encyclopedia of Social Work* (Vol. 1, pp. 161–163). Washington, DC: NASW Press.

Frame, M. W. (2003). *Integrating religion and spirituality into counseling: A comprehensive approach.* Belmont, CA: Brooks/Cole.

Freedman, R. I. (1995). Developmental disabilities: Direct practice. In *Encyclopedia of social work* (Vol. 1, pp. 721–729). Washington, DC: NASW Press.

French, J. R., & Raven, B. (1968). The bases of social power. In D. Cartwright & A. Zander (Eds.), *Group dynamics: Research and theory* (pp. 259–269). New York: Harper & Row.

Friend, M. (2008). *Special education: Contemporary perspectives for school professionals* (2nd ed.). Boston: Allyn & Bacon.

Fukuyama, M. A., & Sevig, T. D. (1999). *Integrating spirituality into multicultural counseling*. Thousand Oaks, CA: Sage.

Furman, R., Negi, N. J., Iwamoto, D. K., Rowan, D., Shukraft, A., & Gragg, J. (2009). Social work practice with Latinos: Key issues for social workers. *Social Work, 54*(2), 167–174.

Galambros, C. (2008). Health care: Overview. In T. Mizrahi & L. E. Davis (Editors-in-Chief), *Encyclopedia of Social Work*, Vol. 2 (pp. 316–328). Washington, DC: NASW Press.

Gamble, D. N., & Hoff, M. D. (2005). Sustainable community development. In M. Weil (Ed.), *The handbook of community practice* (pp. 169–188). Thousand Oaks, CA: Sage.

Gambrill, E. (2000). The role of critical thinking in evidence-based social work. In P. Allen-Meares & C. Garvin (Eds.), *The handbook of social work direct practice* (pp. 43–64). Thousand Oaks, CA: Sage.

Gardella, L. G., & Haynes, K. S. (2004). *A dream and a plan: A women's path to leadership in human services*. Washington, DC: NASW Press.

Garvin, C. D. (1987). Group theory and research. In *Encyclopedia of social work* (Vol. 1, pp. 683–696). Washington, DC: NASW Press.

Garvin, C. D., & Cox, F. M. (1995). A history of community organizing since the Civil War with special reference to oppressed communities. In J. Rothman, J. L. Erlich, & J. E. Tropman (Eds.), *Strategies of community intervention* (pp. 64–99). Itasca, IL: Peacock.

Garvin, C. D., & Galinsky, M. J. (2008). Groups. In T. Mizrahi & L. E. Davis (Editors-in-Chief), *Encyclopedia of Social Work* (Vol. 2, pp. 287–298). Washington, DC: NASW Press.

Gay Demographics. (2006). Percent of households with children under 18 years. Retrieved June 17, 2006, from http://www.gaydemographics.org/USA/PUMS/nationalintro.htm.

Germain, C. B., & Gitterman, A. (1995). Ecological perspective. In *Encyclopedia of social work* (Vol. 1, pp. 816–824). Washington, DC: NASW Press.

Gibbs, L., & Gambrill, E. (1999). *Critical thinking for social workers: Exercises for the helping profession* (Revised ed.). Thousand Oaks, CA: Pine Forge.

Gibelman, M. (1998, Summer). Women's perceptions of the glass ceiling in human service organizations and what to do about it. *Affilia, 13*(2), 147–165.

Gibelman, M., & Furman, R. (2008). *Navigating human service organizations* (2nd ed.). Chicago: Lyceum.

Gibson, P. A. (2004, Fall). Religious expressions of African American Grandmother caregivers: Social work's role with church communities. *Arete, 28*(1), 21–37.

Gilbert, M. J. (2008). Transgender people. In T. Mizrahi & L. E. Davis (Editors-in-Chief), *Encyclopedia of Social Work* (Vol. 4, pp. 238–241). Washington, DC: NASW Press.

Gilbert, N., & Terrell, P. (2010). *Dimensions of social welfare policy* (7th ed.). Boston: Allyn & Bacon.

Ginsberg, L. (1995). Concepts of new management. In L. Ginsberg & P. R. Keys (Eds.), *New management in human services* (2nd ed., pp. 1–37). Washington, DC: NASW Press.

Ginsberg, L. H. (2005). Introduction: The overall context of rural practice. In L. H. Ginsberg (Ed.), *Social work in rural communities* (4th ed., pp. 1–14). Alexandria, VA: Council on *Social work* Education.

Gitterman, A., & Germain, C. B. (2008a). Ecological framework. In T. Mizrahi & L. E. Davis (Editors-in-Chief), *Encyclopedia of Social Work* (Vol. 2, pp. 97–102). Washington, DC: NASW Press.

Gitterman, A., & Germain, C. B. (2008b). *The life model of social work practice* (3rd ed.). New York: Columbia.

GlenMaye, L. (1998). Empowerment of women. In L. M. Gutierrez, R. J. Parsons, & E.O. Cox (Eds.), *Empowerment in social work practice: A sourcebook* (pp. 2–51). Belmont, CA: Brooks/Cole.

Goldberg Wood, G., & Middleman, R. R. (1989). *The structural approach to direct practice in social work*. New York: Columbia.

Goldenring, J. (2004, January 4). Mental retardation. Retrieved May 22, 2005, from http://nlm.nih.gov/medlineplus/ency/article/001523.htm.

Goldenberg, H., & Goldenberg, I. (2002). *Counseling today's families* (4th ed.). Belmont, CA: Brooks/Cole.

Gotterer, R. (2001). The spiritual dimension in clinical social work practice: A client perspective. *Families in Society, 82*(2), 187–193.

Graham, J. W. (1991). Servant-leadership in organizations: Inspirational and moral. *Leadership Quarterly, 2*(2), 105–119.

Green, J. W. (1999). *Cultural awareness in the human services: A multiethnic approach* (3rd ed.). Boston: Allyn & Bacon.

Greene, R. R. (2007). A risk and resilience perspective. In R. R. Greene (Ed.), *Social work practice: A risk and resilience perspective*. Belmont, CA: Brooks/Cole.

Greene, R. R., Cohen, H. L., Galambos, C. M., & Kropf, N. P. (2007). *Foundations of social work practice in the field of aging: A competency-based approach*. Washington, DC: NASW Press.

Greenleaf, R. K. (1970). *The servant as leader*. Newton Centre, MA: Robert K. Greenleaf Center.

Greenleaf, R. K. (1977). *Servant leadership: A journey into the nature of legitimate power and greatness*. New York: Paulist.

Griffin, R. W., & Moorhead, G. (2010). *Organizational behavior: Managing people and organizations* (9th ed.). Mason, OH: South-Western.

Gruskin, E. P. (1999). *Treating lesbians and bisexual women: Challenges and strategies for health professionals*. Thousand Oaks, CA: Sage.

Gushue, G. V., & Sciarra, D. T. (1995). Culture and families: A multidimensional approach. In J. G. Ponterotto, J. M. Casas, L. A. Suzuke, & C.M. Alexander (Eds.), *Handbook of multicultural counseling* (2nd ed., pp. 586–606). Thousand Oaks, CA: Sage.

Gutheil, I. A., & Congress, E. (2002). Resiliency in older people: A paradigm for practice.

In R. R. Green (Ed.), *Resiliency: An integrated approach to practice, policy, and research* (pp. 40–52). Washington, DC: NASW Press.

Gutierrez, L. M. (2001). Working with women of color: An empowerment perspective. In J. Rothman, J. L. Erlich, & J. E. Tropman (Eds.), *Strategies of community intervention* (6th ed., pp. 209–217). Itasca, IL: Peacock.

Gutierrez, L. M., GlenMaye, L., & Delois, K. (1995). The organizational context of empowerment practice: Implications for social work administration. *Social Work*, 40, 249–257.

Gutierrez, L. M., & Lewis, E. A. (1999). *Empowering women of color.* New York: Columbia.

Gwynne, S. C. (1998, March 9). Miracle in New Orleans. *Time*, 74.

Habitat for Humanity. (2005). 2005 annual report: Respecting our past, building for the future. Retrieved July 21, 2006, from http://www.habitat.org/giving/report/2005/annual_report_2005.pdf.

Hagen, J. L., & Lawrence, C. K. (2008). Temporary Assistance for Needy Families. In T. Mizrahi & L. E. Davis (Editors-in-Chief), *Encyclopedia of Social Work* (Vol. 4, pp. 225–229). Washington, DC: NASW Press.

Haight, W. L. (1999). "Gathering the spirit" at First Baptist Church: Spirituality as a protective factor in the lives of African American children. In P. L. Ewalt, E. M. Freeman, A. E. Fortune, D. L. Poole, & S. L. Witkin (eds.). *Multicultural issues in social work: Practice and research* (pp. 245–255). Washington, DC: NASW Press.

Halley, A. A., Kopp, J., & Austin, M. J. (1998). *Delivering human services: A learning approach to practice* (4th ed.). New York: Longman.

Hallahan, D. P., & Kauffman, J. M. (2006). *Exceptional learners: An introduction to special education* (10th ed.). Boston: Allyn & Bacon.

Hardcastle, D. A., & Powers, P. R. (2004). *Community practice: Theories and skills for social workers* (2nd ed.). New York: Oxford.

Hardina, D. (2004). Guidelines for ethical practice in community organization. *Social Work*, 29(4), pp. 595–604.

Harris, M. B. (2008). Family life education. In T. Mizrahi & L. E. Davis (Editors-in-Chief), *Encyclopedia of Social Work* (Vol. 2, pp. 197–200). Washington, DC: NASW Press.

Harrison, R. J., & Weinberg, D. H. (1992, April). *Racial and ethnic segregation in 1990.* Washington, DC: U.S. Bureau of the Census.

Harrison, W. D. (1995). Community development. In R. L. Edwards (Ed.), *Encyclopedia of social work* (19th ed., Vol. 1, pp. 555–562). Washington, DC: NASW Press.

Hartfort Institute for Religion Research. (2006). A quick question: How does faith exist in social services? Retrieved April 18, 2009, from http://hirr.hartsem.edu/research/quick_question16.html.

Harvey, A. R. (2005). Group work with African-American youth in the criminal justice system: A culturally competent model. In G. L. Grief & P.H. Ephross (Eds.), *Group work with populations at risk* (2nd ed., pp. 238–252). New York: Oxford.

Hasenfeld, Y. (1983). *Human service organizations.* Englewood Cliffs, NJ: Prentice-Hall.

Hasenfeld, Y. (1984). Analyzing the human service agency. In F. M. Cos, J. L. Erlich, J. Rothman, & E. Tropman (Eds.), *Tactics and techniques of community practice.* Itasca, IL: Peacock, 14–26.

Hasenfeld, Y. (2009). Human services administration and organizational theory. In R. J. Patti (Ed.), *The handbook of human services management* (2nd ed., pp. 53–80). Thousand Oaks, CA: Sage.

Hayashi, R. (2005). The environment of disability today: A nursing home is not a home. In G. E. May & M. B. Raske, M. B. (Eds.), *Ending disability discrimination: Strategies for social workers* (pp. 45–70). Boston: Allyn & Bacon.

Haynes, K. S., & Mickelson, J. S. (2003). *Affecting change: Social workers in the political arena* (5th ed.). Boston: Allyn & Bacon.

Healy, K. (2005). *Social work theories in context: Creating frameworks for practice.* New York: Palgrave.

Healy, L. M. (2008). *International social work: Professional action in an interdependent world* (2nd ed.). New York: Oxford.

Hellriegel, D., Jackson, S. E., & Slocum, Jr., J. W. (2002). *Management: A competency-based approach* (9th ed.). Cincinnati, OH: South-Western.

Hellriegel, D., & Slocum, J. W., Jr. (2007). *Organizational behavior* (11th ed.). Mason, OH: South-Western.

Hellriegel, D., & Slocum, J. W., Jr. (2009). *Organizational behavior* (12th ed.). Mason, OH: South-Western.

Hepworth, D. H., Rooney, R. H., Rooney, G. D., Strom-Gottfried, & Larsen, J. (2010). *Direct social work practice: Theory and Skills* (8th ed.). Belmont, CA: Brooks/Cole.

Herek, G. M., Gillis, R. J., & Cogan, J. (1997, May). Study offers "snapshot" of Sacramento area lesbian, gay and bisexual community. Available online at http://psychology.ucdavis.edu/rainbow/default.html.

Herrell, R. K. (1992). The symbolic strategies of Chicago's gay and lesbian pride parade. In G. Herdt (Ed.), *Gay culture in America: Essays from the field* (pp. 225–252). Boston: Beacon Press.

Hesse, H. (1956). *The journey to the East.* London: P. Owen.

Hiroto, J. M., Brown, P., & Martin, N. (1997). *Building community: The tradition and promise of settlement houses.* New York: United Neighborhood Houses of New York.

Ho, M. K., & Rasheed, J. M., & Rasheed, M. N. (2004). *Family therapy with ethnic minorities* (2nd ed.). Thousand Oaks, CA: Sage.

Hodge, B. J., Anthony, W. P., & Gales, L. M. (2003). *Organization theory: A strategic approach* (6th ed.). Upper Saddle River, NJ: Prentice-Hall.

Hodge, J. L., Struckmann, D. K., & Trost, L. D. (1975). *Cultural bases of racism and group oppression.* Berkely, CA: Two Riders Press.

Hoefer, R. (2006). *Advocacy practice for social justice.* Chicago: Lyceum.

Hofstede, G. (1980). *Culture's consequences: International differences in work-related values.* Thousand Oaks, CA: Sage.

Hofstede, G. (1993, Spring). A conversation with Geert Hofstede. *Organizational Dynamics*, 50–54.

Hokenstad, M. C., & Midgley, J. (1997). Realities of global interdependence: Challenges for social work in a new century. In M. C. Hokenstad & J. Midgley (Eds.), *Issues in international social work: Global challenges for a new century* (pp. 1–10). Washington, DC: NASW Press.

Holland, T. P., & Petchers, M. K. (1987). Organizations: Context for social service delivery. In *Encyclopedia of social work* (18th ed., Vol. 2, pp. 729–736). Silver Spring, MD: National Association of Social workers.

Homan, M. S. (2008). *Promoting community change: Making it happen in the real world* (4th ed.). Belmont, CA: Brooks/Cole.

Homans, G. C. (1950). *The human group*. New York: Harcourt Brace Jovanovich.

Hopkins, K. M. (2009). Supervision, development, and training for staff and volunteers. In R. J. Patti (Ed.), *The handbook of human services management* (2nd ed., pp. 283–294). Thousand Oaks, CA: Sage.

House, R. J., & Mitchell, R. R. (1974). Path-goal theory of leadership. *Journal of Contemporary Business*, 3, 81–97.

Hugen, B. (2001). Spirituality and religion in social work practice: A conceptual model. In M. Van Hook, B. Hugen, & M. Aguilar (Eds.), *Spirituality within religious traditions in social work practice* (pp. 1–17). Belmont, CA: Brooks-Cole.

Human Rights Campaign (HRC). (2009). Employment non-discrimination laws on sexual orientation and gender identity. Retrieved April 15, 2009, from http://www.hrc.org/issues/4844.htm.

Hyde, C. A. (2008). Feminist social work practice. In T. Mizrahi & L.E. Davis (Editors-in-Chief), *Encyclopedia of Social Work* (Vol. 2, pp. 216–221). Washington, DC: NASW Press.

Hynes, H. P. (1995). *A patch of Eden: America's inner-city gardeners*. White River Junction, VT: Chelsea Green.

International Association of Schools of Social Work (IASSW). (2009a). Overview. Retrieved May 25, 2009, from http://www.iassw-aiets.org/.

International Association of Schools of Social Work (IASSW). (2009b). Welcome to IASSW. Retrieved May 25, 2009, from http://www.iassw-aiets.org/.

International Consortium for Social Development (ICSD). (2009). About ICSD. Retrieved May 26, 2009, from http://www.iucisd.org/about.htm.

International Council on Social Welfare (ICSW). (2009a). Our members. Retrieved May 25, 2009, from http://www.icsw.org/intro/ourmembe.htm.

International Council on Social Welfare (ICSW). (2009b). What is our mission? Retrieved May 25, 2009, from http://www.icsw.org/intro/missione.htm.

International Federation of Social Workers (IFSW). (2004). Ethics in social work: Statements of principles. Retrieved May 26, 2009, from http://www.ifsw.org/cm_data/Ethics_in_Social_Work_Statement_of_Priniciples_to_be_publ_205.pdf.

International Federation of Social Workers (IFSW). (2009a). IFSW human rights. Retrieved May 26, 2009, from http://www.ifsw.org/f38000026.html.

International Federation of Social Workers (IFSW). (2009b). Introduction. Retrieved May 26, 2009, from http://www.ifsw.org/f38000057.html.

International Federation of Social Workers (IFSW). (2009c). Welcome to IFSW. Retrieved May 26, 2009, from http://www.ifsw.org.

Intersex Society of North America (ISNA). (2006). How common is intersex? Retrieved May 14, 2008, from http://www.isna.org/book/print/91.

Ivey, A. E., Ivey, M. B., & Zalaquett, C. P. (2010). *International interviewing and counseling: Facilitating client development in a multicultural society* (7th ed.). Belmont, CA: Brooks/Cole.

Jacobs, E. E., Masson, R. L., & Harvill, R. L. (2009). *Group counseling strategies and skills*. Belmont, CA: Brooks/Cole.

Jansson, B. S. (2005). *The reluctant welfare state: American social welfare policies: past, present, and future* (5th ed.). Belmont, CA: Brooks/Cole.

Jansson, B. S. (2008). *Becoming an effective policy advocate: From policy practice to social justice* (5th ed.). Belmont, CA: Brooks/Cole.

Jansson, B. S. (2009). *The reluctant welfare state: American social welfare policies: Past, present, and future* (6th ed.). Belmont, CA: Brooks/Cole.

Jaskyte, K. (2008). Management: Practice interventions. In T. Mizrahi & L. E. Davis (Editors-in-Chief), *Encyclopedia of Social Work* (Vol. 3, pp. 158–163). Washington, DC: NASW Press.

Johnson, D. W., & Johnson, F.P. (2009). *Joining together: Group theory and group skills* (10th ed.). Upper Saddle River, NJ: Pearson.

Johnson, L. C., & Yanca, S. J. (2004). *Social work practice: A generalist approach* (8th ed.). Boston: Allyn & Bacon.

Jouzaitis, C. (1993, February 19). Working poor benefit from tax credit plan. *Chicago Tribune*, p. 17. Retrieved September 30, 2004, from proquest.umi.com.

Juran, J. (1989). *Juran on leadership for quality: An executive handbook* (4th ed.). New York: McGraw-Hill.

Kamya, H. G. (1999). African immigrants in the United States: The challenge for research and practice. In P. L. Ewalt, E. M. Freeman, A. E. Fortune, D. L. Poole, & S. L. Witkin (Eds.), *Multicultural issues in social work: Practice and research* (pp. 605–621). Washington, DC: NASW Press.

Kantner, R. M. (1979, July-August). Power failure in management circuits. *Harvard Business Review*, 31–54.

Karenga, M. (1965). *Kwanzaa: Origin, concepts and practice*. Los Angeles: Kawaida Publications.

Karenga, M. (1997). *Kwanzaa: A celebration of family, community and culture*. Los Angeles: University of Sankore Press.

Karenga, M. (2000). Making the past meaningful: Kwanzaa and the concept of sankofa. In S. L. Abels (Ed.), *Spirituality in social work practice: Narratives for professional helping* (pp. 51–67). Denver, CO: Love.

Karger, H. J., & Stoesz, D. (2010). *American social welfare policy: A pluralist approach* (6th ed.). Boston: Allyn & Bacon.

Katzenbach, J., & Smith, D. (2003). *The wisdom of teams.* Cambridge, MA: Harvard Business School Press.

Kaye, L. W. (2005). A social work practice perspective on productive aging. In L. W. Kaye (Ed.), *Perspectives on productive aging: Social work with the new aged.* Washington, DC: NASW Press.

Kaye, L. W. (2008). Aging: Practice interventions. In T. Mizrahi & L. E. Davis (Editors-in-Chief), *Encyclopedia of Social Work* (Vol. 1, pp. 96–100). Washington, DC: NASW Press.

Kazdin, A. E. (2001). *Behavior modification in applied settings* (6th ed.). Belmont, CA: Wadsworth.

Keene, J. (2006, February 3). The House narrowly passes the Deficit Reduction Act of 2005. Retrieved June 27, 2006, from http://www.imakenews.com/eletra/mod_print_view.cfm?this_id=526167&u=csac&issue.

Kendall, D. (2007). *Social problems in a diverse society* (4th ed.). Boston: Pearson.

Kennedy, J., & Everest, A. (1991, September). Put diversity in context. *Personnel Journal,* 50–54.

Kenyon, P. (1999). *What would you do? An ethical case workbook for human service professionals.* Belmont, CA: Brooks/Cole.

Kettner, P. M., Moroney, R. M., & Martin, L. L. (2008). *Designing and managing programs: An effectiveness-based approach* (3rd ed.). Thousand Oaks, CA: Sage.

Kirk, G., & Okazawa-Rey, M. (2007). *Women's lives: Multicultural perspectives* (4th ed.). Boston: McGraw-Hill.

Kirst-Ashman, K. K. (2010). *Introduction to social work and social welfare: Critical thinking perspectives* (3rd ed.). Belmont, CA: Brooks/Cole.

Kirst-Ashman, K. K., & Hull, G. H., Jr. (2006a). *Generalist practice with organizations and communities* (3rd ed.). Belmont, CA: Brooks/Cole.

Kirst-Ashman, K. K., & Hull, G. H., Jr. (2006b). *Understanding generalist*

practice (4th ed.). Belmont, CA: Brooks/Cole.

Kirst-Ashman, K. K., & Hull, G. H., Jr. (2009a). *Generalist practice with organizations and communities* (4th ed.). Belmont, CA: Brooks/Cole.

Kirst-Ashman, K. K., & Hull, G. H., Jr. (2009b). *Understanding generalist practice* (5th ed.). Belmont, CA: Brooks/Cole.

Knopf, R. (1979). *Suviving the BS (bureaucratic system).* Wilmington, NC: Mandala Press.

Kondrat, M. E. (2008). Person-in-environment. In T. Mizrahi & L. E. Davis (Editors-in-Chief), *Encyclopedia of Social Work* (Vol. 3, pp. 348–354). Washington, DC: NASW Press.

Kongstvedt, P. R. (2009). *Managed care: What it is and how it works* (3rd ed.). Sudbury, MA: Jones & Bartlett.

Kopels, S. (1995). The Americans with Disabilities Act: A tool to combat poverty. *Journal of Social work Education, 31*(3), 337–346.

Kornblum, W., & Julian, J. (2007). *Social problems* (12th ed.). Upper Saddle River, NJ: Prentice Hall.

Kramer, R. M., & Specht, H. (1983). *Readings in community organization practice* (3rd ed.). Englewood Cliffs, NJ: Prentice-Hall.

Kretzmann, J. P., & McKnight, J. L. (1993). *Building communites from the inside out: A path toward finding and mobilizing a community's assets.* Chicago, IL: ACTA Publications.

Kronenberg, P., & Loeffler, R. (1991). Quality management theory: Historical context and future prospect. *Journal of Management Science & Policy Analysis, 8,* 203–221.

Krout, J. (1994). Community size differences in senior center resources, programming, and participation. *Research on Aging, 16,* 440–462.

Lad Lake, Inc. (2005). *Small steps: 2005 annual report.* Dousman, WI: Author.

Laird, J. (1995). Lesbians: Parenting. In *Encyclopedia of social work* (Vol. 2, pp. 1604–1616). Washington, DC: NASW Press.

Lane, H., Hoffmeister, R., & Bahan, B. (1996). *A journey into the Deaf-world.* San Diego: Dawn Sign Press.

Lasky, G. B., & Riva, M. T. (2006). Confidentiality and privileged communication in group psychotherapy. *International Journal of Group Psychotherapy, 56*(4), 455–476.

Lawrence, J. (2008). "Community organizer" slams attract support for Obama. Retrieved April 24, 2007, from http://www.usatoday.com/news/politics/election2008/2008-09-04-community_N.htm.

Lazzari, M. M., Ford, H. R., & Haughey, K. J. (1996). Making a difference: Women of action in the community. *Social work, 41*(2), 197–205.

Leashore, B. R. (1995). African Americans overview. In R. L. Edwards (Ed.), *Encyclopedia of social work* (19th ed., Vol. 1, pp. 101–115). Washington, DC: NASW Press.

Lee, C. C., & Armstrong, K. L. (1995). Indigenous models of mental health intervention: Lessons from traditional healers. In J. G. Ponterotto, J. M. Cases, L. A. Suzuki, & C. M. Alexander (Eds.), *Handbook of multicultural counseling* (pp. 441–456). Thousand Oaks, CA: Sage.

Lee, J. A. B. (1994). *The empowerment approach to social work practice: Building the beloved community.* New York: Columbia.

Lee, J. A. B. (2001). *The empowerment approach to social work practice: Building the beloved community* (2nd ed.). New York: Columbia.

Lee, J. B. (1996). The empowerment approach to social work practice. In F. Turner (Ed.), *Social work treatment: Interlocking theoretical approaches.* New York: Free Press.

Leigh, J. W., & Green, J. W. (1982). The structure of the Black community: The knowledge base for social services. In J. W. Green (Ed.), *Cultural awareness in the human services* (pp. 106–107). Englewood Cliffs, NJ: Prentice Hall.

Leininger, M. M. (1990). Historic and epistemologic dimensions of care and caring with future directions. In J. Stevenson (Ed.), *American Academy of nursing* (pp. 19–31). Kansas City, MO: American Nurses Association Press.

Leininger, M. M. (1992). *Cultural care diversity and universality: A theory of nursing* (Publication No.

15-2401). New York: National League for Nursing Press.

Leong, F. T. L., Lee, S. H., & Chang, D. (2008). Counseling Asian Americans. In P. B. Pedersen, J. G. Draguns, W. J. Lonner, & J. E. Trimble (Eds.), *Counseling across cultures* (6th ed., pp. 113–128). Thousand Oaks, CA: Sage.

Leon-Guerrero, A. (2005). *Social problems: Community, policy, and social action.* Thousand Oaks, CA: Pine Forge.

Leon-Guerrero, A. (2009). *Social problems: Community, policy, and social action* (2nd ed.). Los Angeles: Pine Forge.

Lewin, K. (1951). *Field theory in social science.* New York: Harper & Row.

Lewin, K., Lippitt, R., & White, R. K. (1939). Patterns of aggressive behavior in experimentally created social climates. *Journal of Social Psychology 10,* 271–299.

Lewis, E. A., & Suarez, Z. E. (1995). Natural helping networks. In *Encyclopedia of social work* (Vol. 2, pp. 1765–1772). Washington, DC: NASW Press.

Lewis, J. A., Lewis, M. D., Packard, T., & Souflee, Jr., F. (2001). *Management of human service programs.* Belmont, CA: Brooks/Cole.

Lewis, J. A., Packard, T. R., & Lewis, M. D. (2007). *Management of human service programs* (4th ed.). Belmont, CA: Brooks/Cole.

Lindberg, C. A. (2007). *The Oxford college dictionary* (2nd ed.). New York: Spark.

Line, C. M. (2005). Social work in a rural school district. In L. M. Grobman (Ed.), *Days in the lives of social workers: 54 professionals tell "real-life" stories from social work practice* (3rd ed., pp. 105–109). Harrisburg, PA: White Hat Communications.

Link, R. J., Ramanathan, C. S., & Asamoah, Y. (1999). Understanding the human condition and human behavior in a global era. In C. S. Ramanathan & R. J. Link (Eds.), *All our futures: Principles and resources for social work practice in a global era* (pp. 30–51). Belmont, CA: Brooks/Cole.

Lohmann, R. A. (1997). Managed care: A review of recent research. In R. L. Edwards (Ed.), *Encyclopedia of social work: Supplement 1997* (19th ed., pp. 200–213). Washington, DC: NASW Press.

Lohmann, R. A., & Lohmann, N. (2005). Introduction. In N. Lohmann & R. A. Lohmann (Eds.), *Rural social work practice* (pp. xi–xxvii). New York: Columbia.

Long, C. R., & Curry, M. A. (1998). Living in two worlds: Native American women and prenatal care. *Health Care for Women International, 19*(3), 205–215.

Longres, J. F. (1995). Hispanics overview. In *Encyclopedia of social work* (Vol. 2, pp. 1214–1222). Washington, DC: NASW Press.

Longres, J. F. (2008). Diversity in community life. In J. Rothman, J. L. Erlich, & J. E. Tropman (Eds.), *Strategies of community intervention* (7th ed., pp. 77–106). Peosta, IA: Eddie Bowers.

Longres, J. F., & Aisenberg, E. (2008). Latinos and Latinas: Overview. In T. Mizrahi & L. E. Davis (Editors-in-Chief), *Encyclopedia of Social Work* (Vol. 3, pp. 31–41). Washington, DC: NASW Press.

Loprest, P. J. (2003). Fewer welfare leavers employed in weak economy. Retrieved January 12, 2005, from http://www.urban.org/urlprint.cfm?ID=8550.

Lorber, J. (2005). *Gender inequality: Feminist theories and politics* (3rd ed.). Los Angeles: Roxbury.

Loue, W. (1998). Defining the immigrant. In S. Loue (Ed.), *Handbook of immigrant health* (pp. 19–36). New York: Plenum Press.

Lum, D. (1995). Asian Americans: Chinese. In *Encyclopedia of social work* (Vol. 1, pp. 238–241). Washington, DC: NASW Press.

Lum, D. (2004). *Social work practice and people of color: A process-stage approach* (5th ed.). Belmont, CA: Brooks/Cole.

Lum, D. (2005). *Cultural competence, practice stages, and client systems: A case study approach.* Belmont, CA: Brooks/Cole.

Lum, D. (2007). *Culturally competent practice: A framework for understanding diverse groups and justice issues* (3rd ed.). Belmont, CA: Brooks/Cole.

Lupu, I. C., & Tuttle, R. W. (2008). The state of the law 2008: A cumulative report on legal developments affecting government partnerships with faith-based organizations. Retrieved April 18, 2009, from http://www.religionandsocialpolicy.org.

Lussier, R. N. (2009). *Management fundamentals* (4th ed.). Mason, OH: South-Western.

Macionis, J. J. (2008). *Social problems* (3rd ed.). Upper Saddle River, NJ: Pearson Prentice-Hall.

Mackelprang, R. W., & Salsgiver, R. O. (2009). *Disability: A diversity model approach in human service practice* (2nd ed.). Chicago: Lyceum.

Madden, J. (1996, November 14). Offending art: Graffiti on Beverly walls attracts attention, criticism. *Salem Evening News,* pp. A1, A10.

Mallon, G. P. (2008). Gay families and parenting. In T. Mizrahi & L. E. Davis (Editors-in-Chief), *Encyclopedia of Social Work* (Vol. 2, pp. 241–247). Washington, DC: NASW Press.

Mapp, S. (2008). *Human rights and social justice in a global perspective: An introduction to international social work.* New York: Oxford.

Managed care. (1998, January). *NASW News,* p. 1.

Mann, W. M. (1997). Portraits of social services programs for rural sexual minorities. *Journal of Gay and Lesbian Social Services, 7*(3), 95–103.

Marsella, A. J. (1998, June). Urbanization, mental health, and social deviancy. *American Psychologist, 53*(6) 624–634.

Martin, J. I. (2008). Gay men: Overview. In T. Mizrahi & L. E. Davis (Editors-in-Chief), *Encyclopedia of Social Work* (Vol. 2, pp. 247–256). Washington, DC: NASW Press.

Martin, J. L. (2003, July). What is field theory? *The American Journal of Sociology, 109,* i1 p. 1 (50). Retrieved May 17, 2007, http://infotrac.thomsonlearning.com.

Martin, K. S. (2000). Home health care, outcomes management, and the land of Oz. *Outcomes Management for Nursing Practice, 3,* 610–618.

Martin, L. L. (1993). *Total quality management in human service organizations.* Newbury Park, CA: Sage.

Martinez-Brawley, E. E. (1990). *Perspectives on the small community: Humanistic views for practitioners.* Silver Spring, MD: NASW Press.

Martinez-Brawley, E. E. (1990). *Perspectives on the small community: Humanistic views for practitioners.* Silver Spring, MD: NASW Press.

Martinez-Brawley, E. E. (1995). Community. In *Encyclopedia of social work* (Vol. 1, pp. 539–548). Washington, DC: NASW Press.

Martinez-Brawley, E. E. (2000). *Close to home: Human services and the small community.* Washington, DC: NASW Press.

Mary, N. L. (1998). Social work and the support model of services for people with developmental disabilities. *Journal of Social Work Education, 34*(2), 247–260.

Maryland Development Disabilities Council. (2006). Developmental Disabilities Assistance and Bill of Right Amendments of 2000. Retrieved August 10, 2006, from http://www.md-council.org/about/add_act.html.

Massat, C. R., Constable, R., McDonald, S., & Flynn, J. P. (2009). *School social work: Practice, policy and research* (7th ed.). Chicago: Lyceum.

Mathie, A., & Cunninghan, G. (2008). From clients to citizens: Asset-based community development as a strategy for community-driven development. In J. Rothman, J. L. Erlich, & J. E. Tropman (Eds.), *Strategies of community intervention* (7th ed., pp. 282–298). Peosta, IA: Eddie Bowers.

Matza, B. R. (1990). Empowerment: The key management skill of the 90s. *Retail Control, 58*(11), 20–23.

May, G. E. (2005). Changing the future of disability: The disability discrimination model. In G. E. May & M. B. Raske, M. B. (Eds.), *Ending disability discrimination: Strategies for social workers* (pp. 82–98). Boston: Allyn & Bacon.

McCammon, S., & Knox, D. (2007). *Choices in sexuality* (3rd ed.). Mason, OH: Thompson.

McDonald, M. (1998, January 5). How to reduce teen pregnancy:

Voluntary community service. *U. S. News & World Report,* 48–49.

McGregor, D. (1960). *The human side of enterprise.* New York: McGraw-Hill.

McInnis-Dittrich, K. (2009). *Social work with elders: A biopsychosocial approach to assessment and intervention* (3rd ed.). Boston: Allyn & Bacon.

McLaughlin, L. A., & Braun, K. L. (1999). Asian and Pacific Islander cultural values: Considerations for health care decision-making. In P. L. Ewalt, E. M. Freeman, A. E. Fortune, D. L. Poole, & S. L. Witkin (eds.). *Multicultural issues in social work: Practice and research* (pp. 321–336). Washington, DC: NASW Press.

Melville, M. B. (1980). *Twice a minority: Mexican American women.* St. Louis: C. V. Mosby.

Mercer, S. O. (1996, March). Navajo elderly people in a reservation nursing home: Admission predictors and culture care practices. *Social Work, 41*(2), 181–189.

Mercy Corps. (2009). *Our history.* Retrieved on October 24, 2009 from http://www.mercycorps.org/10638.

Mercy Corps. (n.d.). Restoring lives in Indonesia. Retrieved August 27, 2005, from http://www.mercycorps.org.

Merritt, C. D., & Collins, T. (2008). The place of rural community development in urban society. In J. DeFilippis & S. Saegert (Eds.), *The community development reader* (pp. 148–156). New York: Routledge.

Merton, R. K. (1968). *Social theory and social structure* (enlarged ed.). New York: Free Press.

Messinger. L. (2004). Comprehensive community initiatives: A rural perspective. *Social Work, 49*(4), 535–546.

Messinger, L. (2006). Social welfare policy and advocacy. In D. F. Morrow & L. Messinger (Eds.), *Sexual orientation & gender expression in social work practice: Working with gay, lesbian, bisexual, & transgender people* (pp. 427–459). New York: Columbia University Press.

Messinger, L., & Brooks, J. W. (2008). Lesbians: Overview. In T. Mizrahi

& L. E. Davis (Editors-in-Chief), *Encyclopedia of Social Work* (Vol. 3, pp. 71–79). Washington, DC: NASW Press.

Meyer, D. R. (1995). Supplemental Security Income. In *Encyclopedia of social work* (Vol. 3, pp. 2379–2385). Washington, DC: NASW Press.

Meyerson, D. E., & Scully, M. (1999). *Tempered radicalism: Changing the workplace from within* (CGO Insights No. 6). Boston: Simmons Graduate School of Management, Center for Gender in Organizations.

Miah, M. R. (2008). Social development. In T. Mizrahi & L. E. Davis (Editors-in-Chief), *Encyclopedia of Social Work* (Vol. 4, pp. 38–41). Washington, DC: NASW Press.

Midgley, J. (1997a). Social work and international social development: Promoting a developmental perspective in the profession. In M. C. Hokenstad & J. Midgley (Eds.), *Issues in international social work: Global challenges for a new century* (pp. 11–26). Washington, DC: NASW Press.

Midgley, J. (1997b). *Social welfare in global context.* Thousand Oaks, CA: Sage.

Midgley, J., & Livermore, M. (2004). Social development: Lessons from the global south. In M. C. Hokenstad & J. Midgley (Eds.), *Lessons from abroad: Adapting international social welfare innovations* (pp. 117–135). Washington, DC: NASW Press.

Midgley, J. & Sherraden, M. (2009). The social development perspective in social policy. In J. Midgley & M. Livermore (Eds.), *The handbook of social policy* (2nd ed., pp. 279–294. Thousand Oaks, CA: Sage.

Miller, D. (1991, November). The "grandparents who care" support project. Paper presented at the 44th Annual Meeting of the Gerontological Society of America, San Francisco.

Miller, J., & Garran, A. M. (2008). *Racism in the United States: Implications for the helping professions.* Belmont, CA: Brooks/Cole.

Miller, R. L., Jr. (2008). Gay men: Practice interventions. In T. Mizrahi & L. E. Davis (Editors-in-Chief),

Encyclopedia of Social Work (Vol. 2, pp. 256–260). Washington, DC: NASW Press.

Milligan, S.E. (2008). Community building. In T. Mizrahi & L. E. Davis (Editors-in-Chief), *Encyclopedia of Social Work* (Vol. 1, pp. 371–375). Washington, DC: NASW Press.

Miltenberger, R. G. (2008). *Behavior modification: Principles and procedures* (4th ed.). Belmont, CA: Brooks/Cole.

Minkler, M., & Roe, K. M. (1993). *Grandmothers are caregivers: Raising children of the crack cocaine epidemic*. Newbury Park, CA: Sage.

Mish, F. C. (Editor-in-Chief). (1995). *Merriam Webster's Collegiate Dictionary* (10th ed.). Springfield, MA: Merriam-Webster, Inc.

Mish, F. C. (2008). *Merriam-Webster's collegiate dictionary* (11th ed.). Springfield, MA: Merriam-Webster, Incorporated.

Mizrahi, T., & Gorin, S. H. (2008). Health care reform. In T. Mizrahi & L. E. Davis (Editors-in-Chief), *Encyclopedia of Social Work* (Vol. 2, pp. 340–348). Washington, DC: NASW Press.

Moberg, D. (2007, April 27). Obama's community roots. Retrieved April 24, 2009, from http://www.thenation.com/doc/20070416/moberg/.

Mokuau, N. (1995). Pacific Islanders. In *Encyclopedia of social work* (Vol. 3, pp. 1795–1801). Washington, DC: NASW Press.

Mokuau, N. (2008). Native Hawaiians and Pacific Islanders. In T. Mizrahi & L. E. Davis (Editors-in-Chief), *Encyclopedia of Social Work* (Vol. 3, pp. 308–310). Washington, DC: NASW Press.

Mooney, L. A., Knox, D., & Schacht, C. (2009). *Understanding social problems* (6th ed.). Belmont, CA: Wadsworth.

Moore, S. E. (2008). African Americans: Practice interventions. In T. Mizrahi & L. E. Davis (Editors-in-Chief), *Encyclopedia of Social Work* (Vol. 1, pp. 81–85). Washington, DC: NASW Press.

Morales, E. (1996). Gender roles among Latino gay and bisexual men. In J. Laird & R-J. Green (Eds.), *Lesbians and gays in couples and families: A handbook for therapists*

(pp. 273–297). San Francisco: Jossey-Bass.

Morrow, D. F. (2006). Sexual orientation and gender identity expression. In D. F. Morrow & L. Messinger (Eds.), *Sexual orientation & gender expression in social work practice: Working with gay, lesbian, bisexual, & transgender people* (pp. 3–17). New York: Columbia University Press.

Morrow, D. F. (2008). Lesbians: Practice interventions. In T. Mizrahi & L. E. Davis (Editors-in-Chief), *Encyclopedia of Social Work* (Vol. 3, pp. 79–87). Washington, DC: NASW Press.

Morrow-Howell, N., & Hasche, L. (2008). Aging: Services. In T. Mizrahi & L. E. Davis (Editors-in-Chief), *Encyclopedia of Social Work* (Vol. 1, pp. 110–119). Washington, DC: NASW Press.

Moxley, D. P. (1989). *The practice of case management*. Newbury Park, CA: Sage.

Muckian, M. (1994, June). TQM bumps and bruises. *Business*, 20–35, 39.

Murase, K. (1995). Asian Americans: Japanese. In *Encyclopedia of Social work* (Vol. 1, pp. 241–249). Washington, DC: NASW Press.

Murphy, Y., Hunt, V., Zajicek, A. M. Norris, A. N., & Hamilton, L. (2009). *Incorporating intersectionality in social work practice, research, policy, and education*. Washington, DC: NASW Press.

Murray, S. (1992). Components of gay community in San Francisco. In G. Herdt (Ed.), *Gay culture in America* (pp. 107–146). Boston: Beacon Press.

Naleppa, M. J., & Reid, W. J. (2003). *Gerontological social work: A task-centered approach*. New York: Columbia.

Naparstek, R. J., & Dooley, D. (1997). Community building. In *Encyclopedia of social work supplement* (19th ed., pp. 77–89). Washington, DC: NASW Press.

Naparstek, R. J., & Dooley, D. (1998). Countering urban disinvestment through community building initiatives. In P. L. Ewalt, E. M. Freeman, & D. L. Poole (Eds.), *Community building: Renewal, well-being, and shared*

responsibility (pp. 6–16). Washington, DC: NASW Press.

Napholz, L. (2000). Balancing multiple roles among a group of urban midlife American Indian working women. *Health Care for Women International, 21*(4), 255–266.

National Association of Social workers. (2005, February). Association joins global coalition. *NASW News*, 1.

National Association of Social workers. (2008). *NASW code of ethics*. Washington, DC: Author.

National Association of Social Workers (NASW). (2009). *Social work speaks: National Association of Social Workers policy statements 2009–2012*. Washington, DC: Author.

NCSET (National Center on Secondary Education and Transition). (2005). Part III: What works in dropout prevention. Retrieved May 16, 2009, from http://www.ncset.org/publications/essentialtools/dropout/part3.3.11.asp.

National Institute of Child Health and Human Development (NICHHD). (2008). *Autism spectrum disorders*. Retrieved May 20, 2009, from http://www.nichd.nih.gov/health/topics/asd.cfm.

Negroni-Rodriguez, L., K., & Morales, J. (2001). Individual and family assessment skills with Latino/Hispanic Americans. In R. Fong & S. Furuto (Eds.), *Culturally competent practice: Skills, interventions, and evaluations* (pp. 132–146). Boston: Allyn & Bacon.

Neighborhood House of Milwaukee, Inc. (2006a). Mission and vision statements. Retrieved August 2, 2006, from http://www.nh-milw.org/about_nh/mission/mission.html.

Neighborhood House of Milwaukee, Inc. (2006b). Outdoor/environmental education. Retrieved August 2, 2006, from http://www.nh-milw.org/programs/naturecenter/naturecenter.html.

Netting, F. E., Kettner, P. M., & McMurtry, S. L. (2008). *Social work macro practice* (4th ed.). Boston: Allyn & Bacon.

Netting, F. E., & O'Connor, M. K. (2003). *Organization practice: A social worker's guide to understanding human services*. Boston: Allyn & Bacon.

Noble, D. N. (2008). Children: Overview. In T. Mizrahi & L. E. Davis (Editors-in-Chief), *Encyclopedia of Social Work*, (Vol. 1, pp. 243–251). Washington, DC: NASW Press.

Nobles, W. W. (1976). African consciousness and black research: The consciousness of self. In L. M. King, V. Dixon, & W. Nobles (Eds.), *African philosophy: Assumption and paradigms fore research on black persons* (pp. 163–174). Los Angeles: Fanon Center.

Norman, E (2000). Introduction: The strengths perspective and resilience enhancement—a natural partnership. In E. Normal (Ed.), *Resiliency enhancement: Putting the strengths perspective into social work practice* (pp. 1–16). New York: Columbia.

Northouse, P. G. (2007). Leadership: *Theory and practice* (4th ed.). Thousand Oaks, CA: Sage.

Obama, B. (1990). Why organize? Problems and promise in the inner city. *Illinois Issues*. Retrieved April 24, 2009, from http://www.edwoj.com/Alinsky/AlinskyObamaChapter1990.htm.

Okazawa-Rey, M. (1998). Empowering poor communities of color: A self-help model. In L. M. Gutierrez, R. J. Parsons, & E. O. Cox (Eds.), *Empowerment in social work practice: A sourcebook*. Pacific Grove, CA: Brooks/Cole.

Olaveson, J., Conway, P., Shaver, C. (2004). Defining *rural* for social work practice and research. In T. L. Scales & C. L. Streeter (Eds.), *Rural social work: Building and sustaining community assets* (pp. 9–20). Belmont, CA: Brooks/Cole.

Orren, D., Smith, R., Norlin, J. M., & Chess, W. A. (2006). *Human behavior and the social environment: Social systems theory* (5th ed.). Boston: Allyn & Bacon.

Ouchi, W. G. (1981). *Theory Z*. New York: Avon Books.

Outsama, K. (1977). *Laotian themes*. New York: Center for Bilingual Education.

Oxfam. (2006). Oxfam. Retrieved September 10, 2006, from http://www.oxfam.org.uk.

Packard, T. (2008). Organizational development and change. In T. Mizrahi & L. E. Davis (Editors-in-Chief), *Encyclopedia of Social Work* (Vol. 3, pp. 324–327). Washington, DC: NASW Press.

Padden, C., & Humphries, T. (1988). *Deaf in America: Voices from a culture*. Cambridge, MA: Harvard University Press.

Paniagua, F. A. (1998). *Assessing and treating culturally diverse clients: A practical guide* (2nd ed.). Thousand Oaks, CA: Sage.

Paniagua, F. A. (2005). *Assessing and treating culturally diverse clients: A practical guide* (3rd ed.). Thousand Oaks, CA: Sage.

Papalia, D. E., Olds, S. W., & Feldman, R. D. (2007). *Human development* (10th ed.). Boston: McGraw-Hill.

Parsons, R. J. (2008). Empowerment practice. In T. Mizrahi & L. E. Davis (Editors-in-Chief), *Encyclopedia of Social Work* (Vol. 2, pp. 123–126). Washington, DC: NASW Press.

Parsons, R. J., Gutierrez, L. M., & Cox, E. O. (1998). *Empowerment in social work practice: A sourcebook*. Belmont, CA: Brooks/Cole.

Parsons, T., Bales, R. F., & Shils, E. A. (Eds.). (1953). *Working papers in the theory of action*. New York: Free Press.

Patti, R. J. (2008). Management: Overview. In T. Mizrahi & L. E. Davis (Editors-in-Chief), *Encyclopedia of Social Work* (Vol. 3, pp. 148–158). Washington, DC: NASW Press.

Payne, M. (2005). *Modern social work theory* (3rd ed.). Chicago: Lyceum.

Perez-Koenig, R. (2000). The Unitas extended family circle: Developing resiliency in Hispanic youngsters. In E. Norman (Ed.), *Resiliency enhancement: Putting the strengths perspective into social work practice* (pp. 143–153). New York: Columbia.

Perrow, C. A. (1961). The analysis of goals in complex organizations. *American Sociological Review*, 26(6), 856–866.

Pew Hispanic Center. (2006). A statistical portrait of Hispanics at mid-decade. Retrieved May 18, 2009, from http://pewhispanic.org/reports/middledace.

Pfeiffer, D. (2005). The conceptualization of disability. In G. E. May & M. B. Raske, M. B. (Eds.), *Ending disability discrimination: Strategies for social workers* (pp. 25–44). Boston: Allyn & Bacon.

Phillips, N. K., & Straussner, S. L. A. (2002). *Urban social work: An introduction to policy and practice in the cities*. Boston: Allyn & Bacon.

Poertner, J. (2008). Management: Quality assurance. In T. Mizrahi & L. E. Davis (Editors-in-Chief), *Encyclopedia of Social Work* (Vol. 3, pp. 180–183). Washington, DC: NASW Press.

PollingReport.com. (2009). Same-sex marriage, gay rights. Retrieved May 19, 2009, from http://www.pollingreport.com/civil.htm.

Poole, D. L., & More, S. (2004). The use of asset-based community development to increase rural youth participation in higher education. In T. L. Scales & C. L. Streeter (Eds.), *Rural social work: Building and sustaining community assets* (pp. 147–159). Belmont, CA: Brooks/Cole.

Popple, P. R. (2008). Social services. In T. Mizrahi & L. E. Davis (Editors-in-Chief), *Encyclopedia of Social Work* (Vol. 4, pp. 98–101). Washington, DC: NASW Press.

Potocky-Tripodi. M. (2002). *Best practices for social work with refugees & immigrants*. New York: Columbia.

Poulin, J. (2005). *Strengths-based generalist practice* (2nd ed.). Belmont, CA: Brooks/Cole.

Powell, G. N., & Graves, L. M. (2003). *Women and men in management* (3rd ed.). Thousand Oaks, CA: Sage.

Powell, T. J. (1995). Self-help groups. In *Encyclopedia of social work* (Vol. 3, pp. 2116–2123). Washington, DC: NASW Press.

Proehl, R. A. (2001). *Organizational change in the human services*. Thousand Oaks, CA: Sage.

Puglia, B., & House, R. M. (2006). Group work: Gay, lesbian, and bisexual clients. In D. Capuzi, D. R. Gross, & M. D. Stauffer, M. D. (Eds.), *Introduction to group work* (4th ed., pp. 515–547). Denver: Love.

Race, P. R. (2008, January), Evidence-based practice moves ahead. *NASW News*, 4.

Rapp, C. A. (1998). *The strengths model: Case management with people suffering from severe and persistent mental illness.* Oxford University Press: New York.

Raske, M. (2005). The disability discrimination model in social work practice. In G. E. May & M. B. Raske, M. B. (Eds.), *Ending disability discrimination: Strategies for social workers* (pp. 99–112). Boston: Allyn & Bacon.

Redmond, H. (2002, March 18). A social worker's outlook on the managed care crisis. *Social work Today,* 22–23.

Reichert, E, (2006). *Understanding human rights: An exercise book.* Thousand Oaks, CA: Sage.

Reiman, J. (2007). *The rich get richer and the poor get prison* (8th ed.). Boston, MA: Allyn & Bacon.

Renz-Beaulaurier, R. (1998). Empowering people with disabilities: The role of choice. In L. M. Gutierrez, R. J. Parsons, & E. O. Cox (Eds.), *Empowerment in social work practice: A sourcebook* (pp. 73–84). Pacific Grove, CA: Brooks/Cole.

Rivera, F. G., & Erlich, J. L. (1995). Organizing with people of color: A perspective. In J. E. Tropman, J. L. Erlich, & J. Rothman (Eds.), *Tactics and techniques of community intervention* (3rd ed.). Itasca, IL: F. E. Peacock, 198–213.

Rivera, F. G., & Erlich, J. L. (2001). Organizing with people of color. In J. Rothman, J. L. Erlich, & J. E. Tropman (Eds.), *Strategies of community intervention* (pp. 254–269). Itasca, IL: Peacock.

Robbins, S. P., Chatterjee, P., Canda, E. R. (2006). *Contemporary human behavior theory* (2nd ed.). Boston: Allyn & Bacon.

Robert, H. M. (1971). *Robert's rules of order revised.* New York: William Morrow.

Rose, S. D. (1986). Group methods. In F. H. Kanfer & A. P. Goldstein (Eds.), *Helping people change: A textbook of methods* (3rd ed., pp. 437–469). New York: Pergamon Press.

Rose, S. D. (1998). *Group therapy with troubled youth: A cognitive-behavioral interactive approach.* Thousand Oaks, CA: Sage.

Rosenberg, D. (2006, June 12). Politics of the altar: GOP leaders are putting gay marriage back on the agenda. Will voters respond? Retrieved June 17, 2006, from http://www.msnbc. msn.com/id/13121953/site/newsweek.

Rosenberg, T. (2000, October 26). Looking at poverty, seeing untapped riches. *New York Times,* p. A34.

Ross, M. G. (1967). *Community organization: Theory, principles, and practice* (2nd ed.). New York: Harper & Row.

Rothman, J. (1987). Community theory and research. In *Encyclopedia of social work* (Vol. 1, pp. 308–316). Silver Spring, MD: National Association of Social workers.

Rothman, J. (2001). Approaches to community intervention. In J. Rothman, J. L. Erlich, & J. E. Tropman (Eds.), *Strategies of community intervention* (pp. 27–64). Itasca, IL: Peacock.

Rothman, J. C. (2003). *Social work practice across disability.* Boston: Allyn & Bacon.

Rothman, J. (2007). Multi modes of intervention at the macro level. *Journal of Community Practice,* 15(4), 11–40.

Rothman, J. (2008). Multi modes of community intervention. In J. Rothman, J. L. Erlich, & J. E. Tropman (Eds.), *Strategies of community intervention* (7th ed., pp. 141–170). Peosta, IA: Eddie Bowers.

Rowe, W., Hanley, J., Moreno, E. R., & Mould, J. (2000). Voices of social work practice: International reflections on the effects of globalization. *Canadian Social Work,* 2(1), 65–87.

Rubin, A. (2008). *Practitioner's guide to using research for evidence-based practice.* Hoboken, NJ: Wiley.

Rubin, H. J., & Rubin, I. S. (1992). *Community organizing and development* (2nd ed.). Boston: Allyn & Bacon.

Rubin, H. R., & Rubin, I. S. (2001). *Community organizing and development* (3rd ed.). Boston: Allyn & Bacon.

Rubin, H. J., & Rubin, I. S. (2008). *Community organizing and development* (4th ed.). Boston: Allyn & Bacon.

Ruscio, J. (2006). *Critical thinking in psychology* (2nd ed.). Belmont, CA: Wadsworth.

Rynecki, D., Smith, T., Shanley, M., & Wheat, A. (2003, August 11). Field guide to power. *Fortune,* 126–127.

Sacco, T. (1996). Towards an inclusive paradigm for social work. In M. Doel & S. Shardlow (Eds.), *Social work in a changing world: An international perspective on practice learning.* Brookfield, VT: Arena Ashgate.

Saleebey, D. (2002a). Community development, neighborhood empowerment, and individual resilience. In D. Saleebey (Ed.), *The strengths perspective in social work practice* (3rd ed., pp. 228–246). Boston: Allyn & Bacon.

Saleebey, D. (2002b). Introduction: Power in the people. In D. Saleebey (Ed.), *The strengths perspective in social work practice* (3rd ed., pp. 1–22). Boston: Allyn & Bacon.

Saleebey, D. (2006). *The strengths perspective in social work practice* (3rd ed.). Boston: Allyn & Bacon.

Saleebey, D. (2009). *The strengths perspective in social work practice* (4th ed.). Boston: Allyn & Bacon.

Santiago-Rivera, A. L., Arredondo, P., & Gallardo-Cooper, M. (2002). *Counseling Latinos and la familia: A practical guide.* Thousand Oaks, CA: Sage.

Sashkin, M., & Kiser, K. J. (1993). *Putting total quality management to work: What TQM means, how to use it and how to sustain it over the long run.* San Francisco: Berrett-Koehler.

Saulnier, C. F. (1997). Alcohol problems and marginalization: Social group work with lesbians. *Social Work with Groups,* 20, 37–59.

Schmid, H. (2009). Agency-environment relations. In R. J. Patti (Ed.), *The handbook of human services management* (2nd ed., pp. 411–433). Thousand Oaks, CA: Sage.

Schopler, J. H., & Galinsky, M. J. (1995). Group practice overview. In *Encyclopedia of social work* (Vol. 2, pp. 1129–1142). Washington, DC: NASW Press.

Segal, E. A. (2007). *Social welfare policy and social programs: A values perspective.* Belmont, CA: Brooks/Cole.

Segal, E. A. (2010). *Social welfare policy and social programs: A values perspective* (2nd ed.). Belmont, CA: Brooks/Cole.

Senghor, L. S. (1966). Negritude. *Optima,* 16, 1–8.

Shapiro, J. P. (1995, September 11). *U.S. News & World Report*, 59.

Shaw, S. M., & Lee, J. (2004). *Women's voices, feminist visions: Classic and contemporary readings* (2nd ed.). Boston: McGraw-Hill.

Sheafor, B. W., & Horejsi, C. R. (2003). *Techniques and guidelines for social work practice* (6th ed.). Boston: Allyn & Bacon.

Sheafor, B. W., & Horejsi, C. R. (2009). *Techniques and guidelines for social work practice* (8th ed.). Boston: Allyn & Bacon.

Siegel, L. M., Attkisson, C. C., & Carson, L. G. (2001). Need identification and program planning in the community context. In J. E. Tropman, J. L. Erlich, & J. Rothman Eds.), *Tactics & techniques of community intervention* (4th ed., pp. 105–129). Itasca, IL: F. E. Peacock.

Sigelman, C. K., & Rider, E. A. (2009). *Life-span development* (6th ed.). Belmont, CA: Brooks/Cole.

Slattery, J. M. (2004). *Counseling diverse clients: Bringing context into therapy*. Belmont, CA: Brooks/Cole.

Sluyter, G. V. (1998). *Improving organizational performance: A practical guidebook for the human services field*. Thousand Oaks, CA: Sage.

Smith, D. D. (2007). *Introduction to special education: Making a difference* (6th ed.). Boston: Allyn & Bacon.

Smith, D. P. (2005). The sweat lodge as psychotherapy. In R. Moodley & W. West (Eds.), *Integrating traditional healing practices into counseling and psychotherapy* (pp. 196–209). Thousand Oaks, CA: Sage.

Smith, R. F. (1995). Settlements and neighborhood centers. In *Encyclopedia of social work* (Vol. 3, pp. 2129–2135). Washington, DC: NASW Press.

Smolowe, J. (1995, July 31). Noble aims, mixed results. *Time*, pp. 54–55.

Soifer, S. (2002). Principles and practices of community economic development. In A. R. Roberts & G. J. Greene (Eds.), *Social workers' desk reference* (pp. 557–562).

Solomon, B. B. (2002). Social work practice with African Americans. In A. R. Morales & B. W. Sheafor

(Eds.), *The many faces of social work clients* (pp. 295–315). Boston: Allyn & Bacon.

Sowers, K. M., & Rowe, W. S. (2007). *Social work practice & social justice: From local to global perspectives*. Belmont, CA: Brooks/Cole.

Staples, L. H. (2004). Social action groups. In C. D. Garvin, L. M. Gutierrez, & M. J. Galinsky (Eds.), *Handbook of social work with groups* (pp. 344–359). New York: Guilford.

Stauffer, M. D., Pehrsson, D. E., & Briggs, C. A. (2006). Groups in mental health settings. In D. Capuzi, D. R. Gross, & M. D. Stauffer, M. D. (Eds.), *Introduction to group work* (4th ed., pp. 355–383). Denver: Love.

Strong, B., DeVault, C., Sayad, B. W., & Yarber, W. L. (2005). *Human sexuality: Diversity in contemporary America* (5th ed.). Boston: McGraw-Hill.

Strong, B., Yarber, W. L., Sayad, B. W., & DeVault, C. (2008). *Human sexuality: Diversity in contemporary America* (6th ed.). Boston: McGraw-Hill.

Streeter, C. L. (2008). Community: Overview. In T. Mizrahi & L. E. Davis (Editors-in-Chief), *Encyclopedia of Social Work* (Vol. 1, pp. 347–355). Washington, DC: NASW Press.

Sue, D. W. (2006). *Multicultural social work practice*. Hoboken, NJ: Wiley.

Sue, D. W., & Sue, D. (2008). *Counseling the culturally diverse: Theory and practice* (5th ed.). Hoboken, NJ: Wiley.

Summers, N. (2009). *Fundamentals of case management practice: Skills for the human services* (3rd ed.). Belmont, CA: Brooks/Cole.

Sundel, M., & Sundel, S. S. (2005). *Behavior change in the human services: Behavioral and cognitive principles and applications* (5th ed.). Thousand Oaks, CA: Sage.

Swinomish Tribal Mental Health Project. (1991). *A gathering of wisdoms, tribal mental health: A cultural perspective*. LaConner, WA: Swinomish Tribal Community.

Tangenberg, K. M. (2005). Faith-based human services initiatives: Considerations for social work

practice and theory. *Social Work, 50*(3), 197–206.

Taylor, R. (1979). Black ethnicity and the persistence of ethnogenesis. *American Journal of Sociology, 84*, 6.

Texas Workforce Commission. (2004, May 10). Charitable choice bulletin board: Frequently asked questions. Retrieved April 18, 2009, from http://www.twc.state.tx.us/svcs/charchoice/ccfaq.html.

Texeira, E. (2005, April 10). Great gap in wealth remains between races in America. *Milwaukee Journal Sentinel*, 23A.

Toseland, R. W., & Horton, H. (2008). Group work. In T. Mizrahi & L. E. Davis (Editors-in-Chief), *Encyclopedia of Social Work* (Vol. 3, pp. 298–308). Washington, DC: NASW Press.

Toseland, R. W., & Rivas, R. F. (2005). *An introduction to group work practice* (5th ed.). Boston: Allyn & Bacon.

Toseland, R. W., & Rivas, R. F. (2009). *An introduction to group work practice* (6th ed.). Boston: Allyn & Bacon.

Tracy, E. M. (2002). Working with and strengthening social networks. In A. R. Roberts & G. J. Greene (Eds.), *Social workers' desk reference* (pp. 402–405). New York: Oxford.

Treguer, A. (1992). The Chicanos—muralists with a message. *UNESCO Courier, 45*, 22–24.

Tripodi, T., Lalayants, M. (2008). Research: Overview. In T. Mizrahi & L. E. Davis (Editors-in-Chief), *Encyclopedia of Social Work* (Vol. 3, pp. 512–520). Washington, DC: NASW Press.

Tropman, J. (2008). Phases of helping. In J. Rothman, J. L. Erlich, & J. E. Tropman (Eds.), *Strategies of community intervention* (7th ed., pp. 127–140). Peosta, IA: Eddie Bowers.

Tully, C. T. (2001). *Lesbians, gays, and the empowerment perspective*. New York: Columbia University Press.

Turner, G. (2001, Winter). The puzzling world of international social work careers. *The New Social Worker*, 4–7.

United Nations (UN). (1948). *Universal declaration of human rights*. Adopted December 10, 1948. GA Res. 217 AIII (Un Doc. A/810). Retrieved May 26, 2009, from http://www.un.org/Overview/rights.html.

United States Agency for International Development (USAID). (2009). About us. Retrieved May 25, 2009, from http://www.usaid.gov/about_usaid/.

U.S. Census Bureau. (2003). *Statistical abstract of the United States: 2005.* Washington, DC: U. S. Department of Commerce.

U.S. Census Bureau. (2004). *Statistical abstract of the United States: 2005.* Washington, DC: U. S. Department of Commerce.

U.S. Census Bureau. (2005). *Statistical abstract of the United States: 2006.* Washington, DC: U. S. Department of Commerce.

U.S. Census Bureau. (2008). *Statistical abstract of the United States: 2009* (128th ed.). Washington, DC: U.S. Department of Commerce.

U.S. Department of Justice. (2002, May). Americans with Disabilities Act questions and answers. Retrieved August 10, 2006, from http://www.usdoj.gov/crt/ada/q%26aeng02.htm.

van Soest, D., & Garcia, B. (2003). *Diversity education for social justice: Mastering teaching skills.* Alexandria, VA: Council on Social Work Education.

van Wormer, K. (2006). *Introduction to social welfare and social work: The U.S. in global perspective.* Belmont, CA: Brooks/Cole.

van Wormer, K. (2004). *Confronting oppression, restoring justice: From policy analysis to social action.* Alexandria, VA: Council on Social Work Education.

van Wormer, K., Well, J., & Boes, M. (2000). *Social work with lesbians, gays, and bisexuals: A strengths perspective.* Boston: Allyn & Bacon.

Vandiver, V. L., (2008). Managed care. In T. Mizrahi & L. E. Davis (Editors-in-Chief), *Encyclopedia of Social Work* (Vol. 3, pp. 144–148). Washington, DC: NASW Press.

Vecchio, R. P. (2006). *Organizational behavior* (6th ed.). Mason, OH: South-Western.

Vietnam-culture.com. (2009). Vietnamese culture values. Retrieved May 1, 2009, from http://www.vietnam-culture.com/zones-6-1/Vietnamese-Culture-Values.aspx.

Verschelden, C. (1993). Social work values and pacifism: Opposition to war as a professional responsibility. *Social Work, 38*(6), 765–769.

Vourlekis, B. S. (1999). Cognitive theory for social work practice. In R. R. Green (Ed.), *Human behavior theory and social work practice* (2nd ed., pp. 173–205). New York: Aldine de Gruyter.

Walsh, J. (2006). *Theories of direct social work practice.* Belmont, CA: Brooks/Cole.

Walsh, K. T. (2007, August 26). On the streets of Chicago, a candidate comes of age. Retrieved May 11, 2009, from http://www.usnews.com/usnews/news/articles/070826/3obama_print.htm.

Wamseley, G. L., & Zald, M. N. (1976). *The political economy of public organizations.* Lexington, MA: Heath.

Warren, E. (1977). The functional diversity of urban neighborhood. *Urban Affairs Quarterly, 13*(2), 151–179.

Warren, R. (1983). A community model. In R. M. Kramer & H. Specht (Eds.), *Readings in community organization practice* (pp. 28–36). Englewood Cliffs, NJ: Prentice-Hall.

Warren, R., & Warren, D. I. (1977). *The neighborhood organizers handbook.* South Bend: University of Notre Dame Press.

Watkins, T. R. (2004). Natural helping networks: Assets for rural communities. In T. L. Scales & C. L. Streeter (Eds.), *Rural social work: Building and sustaining community assets* (pp. 65–76). Belmont, CA: Brooks/Cole.

Weaver, H. N. (2005). *Explorations in cultural competence: Journeys to the four directions.* Belmont, CA: Brooks/Cole.

Weaver, H. N. (2008). Native Americans: Overview. In T. Mizrahi & L. E. Davis (Editors-in-Chief), *Encyclopedia of Social Work* (Vol. 3, pp. 295–299). Washington, DC: NASW Press.

Wetzel, J. W. (1995). Global feminist zeitgeist practice. In N. Van Den Bergh (Ed.), *Feminist practice in the 21st century* (pp. 175–192). Washington, DC: NASW Press.

Wetzel, J. W. (2004). Mental health lessons from abroad. In M. C. Hokenstad & J. Midgley

(Eds.), *Lessons from abroad: Adapting international social welfare innovations* (pp. 93–116). Washington, DC: NASW Press.

Wheelan, S.A. (1999). *Creating effective teams: A guide for members and leaders.* Thousand Oaks, CA: Sage.

White, G. W., Gutierrez, R. T., & Seekins, T. (1996). Preventing and managing secondary conditions: A proposed role for independent living centers. *Journal of Rehabilitation, 62*(3), 14–22.

Williams, C. (2005). *Management* (3rd ed.). Mason, OH: South-Western.

Williams, C. (2009). *Management* (5th ed.). Mason, OH: South-Western.

Williams, C. (2010a). *Effective management* (4th ed.). Mason, OH: South-Western.

Williams, C. (2010b). *MGMT* (2nd ed.). Mason, OH: South-Western.

Wilson, W. J. (1996). *When work disappears: The world of the new urban poor.* New York: Knopf.

Wireman, P. (1984). *Urban neighborhoods, networks, and families: New forms for old values.* Lexington, MA: Lexington Books.

Women Work! (2006, May 24). TANF reauthorization that works. Retrieved June 27, 2006, from http://www.womenwork.org.

Wong, J. (2005). Asian Pacific Islanders. In K. L. Guadalupe & D. Lum (Eds.), *Multidimensional contextual practice: Diversity and transcendence* (pp. 388–429). Belmont, CA: Brooks/Cole.

Wong, J. (2005). Asian Pacific Islanders: Ethnic-specific communities of people. In K. L. Guadalupe & D. Lum (Eds.), *Multidimensional contextual practice: Diversity and transcendence* (pp. 388–429). Belmont, CA: Brooks/Cole.

Wood, G. G., & Middleman, R. R. (1989). *The structural approach to direct practice in social work.* New York: Columbia.

Woodside, M., & McClam, T. (2006). *Generalist case management: A method of human service delivery* (3rd ed.). Belmont, CA: Brooks/Cole.

Woodword, K. L., & Johnson, P. (1995, December 11). The advent of Kwanzaa: Will success spoil an African-American fest? *Newsweek,* 88.

Yalom, I. D. (1985). *The theory and practice of group psychotherapy* (3rd ed.). New York: Basic Books.

Yamashiro, G., & Matsuoka, J. K. (1997). Help-seeking among Asian and Pacific Americans: A Multiperspective Analysis. *Social work*, 42(2), 176–186.

Yan, M. C. (2004). Bridging the fragmented community: Revitalizing settlement houses in the global era. *Journal of Community Practice*, 12(1/2), 51–69.

Yessian, M. R., & Broskowski, A. (1983). Generalists in human service systems: Their problems and prospects. In R. M. Kramer & H. Specht (Eds.), *Readings in community organization practice* (pp. 180–198). Englewood Cliffs, NJ: Prentice-Hall.

YMCA. (2006a). Welcome to the YMCA. Retrieved July 20, 2006, from http://www.ymca.net.

YWCA. (2006b). Eliminating racism, Empowering women. Retrieved July 20, 2006, from http://www.ywca.org.

Zald, M. N. (1970). Political economy: A framework of comparative analysis. In M. N. Zald (Ed.), *Power in organizations* (pp. 221–261). Nashville, TN: The Vanderbilt University Press.

Zastrow, C. H. (2006). *Social work with groups: A comprehensive workbook* (6th ed.). Belmont, CA: Brooks/Cole.

Zastrow, C. H. (2009). *Social work with groups: A comprehensive workbook* (7th ed.). Belmont, CA: Brooks/Cole.

Zastrow, C. H., & Kirst-Ashman, K. K. (2010). *Understanding human behavior and the social environment* (8th ed.). Belmont, CA: Brooks/Cole.

Zhang, W. (2010). National and international perspectives on counseling skills: Use with care—Culturally incorrect attending can be rude. In A. E. Ivey & M. B. Ivey (Eds.), *Intentional interviewing and counseling: Facilitating client development in a multicultural society* (7th ed., p. 76). Belmont, CA: Brooks/Cole.

Name Index

Flynn, J. P., 317
Fong, R., 234, 236
Ford, H. R., 379
Frame, M. W., 88, 167, 284, 299, 393
Freedman, R. I., 404, 405, 415
French, J. R., 97
Friend, M., 399, 400, 401, 402
Fukuyama, M. A., 395
Furman, R., 115, 228, 373

Galambros, C., 189, 190, 391
Galaway, B., 15, 110, 111, 112, 130
Gales, L. M., 139, 198
Galinsky, M. J., 68, 78, 101, 102, 104
Gallardo-Cooper, M., 58, 374, 375, 376, 377, 378
Gamble, D. N., 315, 336, 441
Gambrill, E., 33, 35, 37
Garcia, B., 61, 62
Gardella, L. G., 248, 249, 262
Garran, A. M., 378
Garvin, C. D., 68, 70, 71, 76, 77, 78, 79, 101, 357
Germain, C. B., 20, 23, 24, 25, 26, 27, 155
Gibbs, L., 33, 35
Gibelman, A., 115
Gibelman, M., 228, 249
Gibson, P. A., 371
Gilbert, M. J., 49, 50
Gilbert, N., 184, 185, 187, 188
Gilson, S. F., 411
Ginsberg, L., 170, 171, 196, 257, 288, 289, 292, 295
Gitterman, A., 20, 23, 24, 25, 26, 27, 155
GlenMaye, L., 87, 250, 252, 372
Goldenberg, H., 374
Goldenberg, I., 374
Goldenring, J., 400
Gordon, E., 303, 311
Gorin, S. H., 190, 191
Gotterer, R., 285

Gragg, J., 373
Graham, J. W., 259
Graves, L. M., 144, 146, 147, 249
Green, J. W., 285, 374
Greene, R. R., 281, 391
Greenleaf, R., 259
Griffin, R. W., 139, 141, 143, 152, 198, 199, 200, 204, 218, 222
Grobman, L. M., 328
Gross, D. R., 97
Gruskin, E. P., 287
Gushue, G. V., 435
Gutheil, I. A., 57
Gutierrez, L. M., 55, 65, 81, 82, 83, 84, 85, 88, 89, 104, 146, 250, 252, 312, 372
Gutierrez, R. T., 406
Gwynne, S. C., 334

Hackney, H., 91
Hagen, J. L., 184
Haight, W. L., 394, 395
Hallahan, D. P., 400, 401, 402, 403, 407, 415
Halley, A. A., 311
Hamilton, L., 48
Hanley, J., 452
Hardcastle, D. A., 121, 306, 307, 438
Hardina, D., 308
Harrington, D., 43, 308
Harris, M. B., 136
Harrison, W. D., 266, 272, 436, 438
Harvey, A. R., 118, 119, 120
Harvill, R. L., 98, 102, 105
Hasche, L., 391, 392
Hasenfeld, Y., 148, 149, 150, 167, 171, 175
Haughey, K. J., 379
Hayashi, R., 413
Haynes, K. S., 248, 249, 262, 385
Healy, K., 271

Healy, L. M., 436, 438, 442, 446, 454
Hellriegel, D., 113, 130, 197, 208, 209, 210, 211, 212, 213, 214, 228, 243
Hepworth, D. W., 410
Herrell, R. K., 288
Hesse, H., 259
Hickerson, J. C., 287, 288
Hiroto, J. M., 358
Hitchcock, D. E., 258
Ho, M. K., 377
Hodge, J. L., 53
Hodge, B. J., 139, 198
Hoefer, R., 429
Hoff, M. D., 315, 336, 441
Hoffmeister, R., 401
Hofstede, G., 451
Hokenstad, M. C., 428, 447
Holland, T. P., 175, 177
Homan, M. S., 6, 11, 38, 61, 63, 70, 96, 204, 261, 266, 298, 304, 305, 306, 307, 312, 332, 341, 342, 343, 354, 355, 361, 436, 438, 439
Homans, G. C., 79
Hopkins, K. M., 121
Horejsi, C. R., 56, 65, 121, 316, 317, 318, 319, 336, 452
Horton, H., 110, 115, 116
House, R. J., 245
House, R. M., 51, 117
Hugen, B., 285
Hull Jr., G. H., 7, 14, 31, 102, 123, 200, 201, 215, 219, 233, 260, 289, 319, 355, 387, 404
Hunt, V., 48
Hunter, S., 287, 288
Hyde, C. A., 85, 87, 88, 144, 146, 147
Hynes, H. P., 352

Ivey, A. E., 91
Ivey, M. B., 91
Iwamoto, D. K., 373

Subject Index

484   Subject Index

Output, 17, 20, 154, 155, 268
and goal displacement, 172,
174
Ovariectomy, 382
Overt victimization, 52

PACE. *See* Political Action for
Candidate Endorsement
Paraphrasing, 215
Paraprofessional, 8, 111, 137
Parliamentary procedure, 102
Parents Without Partners, 120
Parkinson's disease, 164
Parochial neighborhoods,
345–346
Participation, citizen, 307–308,
310
Participative leadership, 245
Participatory decision-making,
248
Path-goal theory, 245
Patriarchal perspective, 87
Patriarchy, end of, 389
Pattern maintenance, 79, 80
Peace House, 170
Peer review, 35
People of color, 50
Perception, 207–208
critical thinking about, 212
individual errors in,
210–213
of U.S. in world, 433
Performing phase, 104
Personal empowerment, 313,
314
Personalismo, 58, 377
Personal is political concept, 87,
89, 146, 389
Personality
agency's, 197–198
critical thinking about, 210
factors, 204, 209
Personal Responsibility and
Work Opportunity
Reconciliation Act
(PRWORA), 167, 180
Personal social services, 137

Person-in-environment fit,
23, 27
Personnel resources, 176
Persuasion, 260
Pervasive developmental
disorder (PDD), 402
Planned change process, 13–14
Planned Parenthood, 3
Planning and policy practice, 32
Planning step, 14
Playgrounds, community, 353
Policy advocate, 32
Policy practice, 32
Political action committee
(PAC), 385
Political Action for Candidate
Endorsement (PACE), 385
Political action organizations
definition of, 382
empowerment for GLBT
people, 381–388
Political capacity model,
355–356
Political diagnosis, 219
Political-economy theory, 139,
148–149, 156
Political forces, 10, 11
Political ideology, 50
Political network, 219
Politics
in communities, 307
in organizations, 217–221
Popularity fallacy, 36
Population, trends in rural
areas, 290–291
Populations-at-risk, 61, 63, 389
Positive feedback, 18, 20, 154,
155, 219
Positive forces, 70
Positive functions, 273
Positive reinforcement, 73, 74,
75, 76
Positive social functions, 275
Positive verbal communication,
90
Postmodern feminism, 84
Poverty, 61, 63, 429–433

absolute/relative, 430
complexity of defining,
430–431
critical thinking about, 181,
307
definition of, 429–430
global, 428, 432, 433
and Hurricane Katrina, 370
problems related to, 432
widening gap in the U.S.,
431
Poverty line, 181, 430–431
Power
base, 215
concept of, 216
critical thinking about, 217
definition of, 61, 63, 96, 275,
278, 304–305, 312
dimension of empowerment
theory, 82, 84
in formal structure, 204
gender-based, 145
in groups, 70, 71, 96–97, 100
and informal structure,
204–207
in organizations, 215–217,
250
and people in communities,
304–307, 310
political, 10
sources of, 97
versus service provision, 149
types of, 216
who has it, 305–307
of youth, 309–310
Power-oriented managers, 218
Power structure, 271, 305
Practice-based research, 37
Practice setting, ethical responsibilities to, 46
Pratt-Smoot Act, 414
Preferred provider organization
(PPO), 187
Prenatal care, 389
Primary settings, 163
Private social agencies, 138
Privilege, 61, 63

Seizure disorder, 400, 402
Self-determination
  definition of, 45, 84
  managed care issues, 189
Self-direction, 26, 27
Self-disclosure, 92, 100
Self-esteem, 26, 27
Self-fulfilling prophecy, 279
Self-oriented roles, 96
Self-promotion, 214
Self-worth, 55, 86
Senior centers, 391
Sentiments, group, 78, 80
Servant leadership, 244,
  259–261
Service
  NASW core value, 44, 151,
    324
  objectives, 168
  seven sins of, 255–256
Service directories, 332
Service provision, power versus,
  149
Settlement houses, 353,
  357–358
Seven sins of service, 255–256
Sex, definition of, 49, 50
Sexual orientation, 51, 381
  communities based on,
    287–288
  definition of, 50, 83
  homophobia, 52
  NASW Code of Ethics
    regarding, 382
  versus sexual preference, 385
  terms, 51
Shared Beginnings, 389–390
Sheltered employment, 177, 414
Silent communication, 233
Similarity error, 211
Skills, leadership, 98–100
Small cities, 289
Small towns, 289
Social action, 31, 32
  and structural theories and,
    271
Social action groups, 125–126

critical thinking about, 128
and empowerment, 126–129
social advocacy, 32
Social agencies, 8, 137–138.
  See also Social agencies;
  Social services
  types of, 137–138
Social class, 50, 276, 278, 350
  and ethnicity in neighbor-
    hoods, 349–354
Social connectedness, 344–347
Social context, group's, 102
Social control, 437
Social development, 440–442
Social disorganization, 274, 275
Social dysfunctions, 274
Social empowerment, 313–314
Social environment, 6, 27, 30,
  251
  ecological perspective term,
    22
  involvement with multiple
    systems, 25–30
  and personal characteristics,
    26
Social exchange theory, 70–72
Social forces, 9–10, 11,
  178–191
  managed care reflects,
    187–191
  settlement houses, 357
Social functions, 273
Social institutions, 10, 11, 149,
  267, 388
Social interaction, 348
Socialist feminism, 84
Socialization, 83, 437
  multicultural, 83, 84
Socialization groups, 120–121
Social justice, 60–61, 63, 351,
  429, 447
  concepts related to, 63
  dimension of empowerment
    theory, 81, 84
  global, 448–449, 452–453
  NASW core value, 44, 151,
    324, 429

for people with developmental
  disabilities, 410–413
social legislation, 179
Social networks, 308, 310
Social participation, 437
Social planning, 31, 32
Social problems, 274, 275
Social-psychological theories,
  270, 283
Social reinforcement, 75, 76
Social responsibility, 248
Social Security Act, 180
Social services, 8, 11, 136
  empowerment of GLBT
    people through, 387
  faith-based, 167–170
  institutional, 137
  organizations providing,
    136–138
  personal, 137
  terms, 137
Social services agency/
  organizations, 11. See also
  Organizations
  applying ecosystems concepts
    to, 154–155
  enhancing ethical communi-
    cation, 215
  environmental context of,
    174–178
  impact of social and economic
    forces on, 178–191
  interpersonal communication
    in, 207–215
  policy and worker discretion,
    239–240
  politics in, 217–221
  power in, 215–217
  primary and secondary
    settings, 163–165
  problems frequently
    encountered by, 236–241
  unethical behavior in,
    220–221
  value discrepancies, 228–230
  women management in,
    248–250